CAMBRIDGE LIBRA

Books of enduring

History

The books reissued in this series include accounts of historical events and movements by eye-witnesses and contemporaries, as well as landmark studies that assembled significant source materials or developed new historiographical methods. The series includes work in social, political and military history on a wide range of periods and regions, giving modern scholars ready access to influential publications of the past.

Biographia Navalis

John Charnock (1756–1807) was a professional naval biographer and historian. After completing his studies at Trinity College, Oxford, he joined the Navy as a volunteer and began to research historical and contemporary naval affairs. This six-volume work, first published between 1794 and 1798, contains biographies of over two thousand post-captains and admirals who served in the Navy between 1660 and 1793. Charnock researched this monumental project using collections of historical naval biographies made available by his friend Captain William Locker, lieutenant-governor of Greenwich Hospital. He also drew on his own experiences and his contacts among serving officers to provide valuable insights into contemporary events. However, his sometimes uncritical approach to sources means his work is best consulted together with other evidence. The biographies are arranged by year of first appointment, and alphabetically within each year. Volume 5 contains biographies of officers appointed between 1740 and 1746.

Cambridge University Press has long been a pioneer in the reissuing of out-of-print titles from its own backlist, producing digital reprints of books that are still sought after by scholars and students but could not be reprinted economically using traditional technology. The Cambridge Library Collection extends this activity to a wider range of books which are still of importance to researchers and professionals, either for the source material they contain, or as landmarks in the history of their academic discipline.

Drawing from the world-renowned collections in the Cambridge University Library, and guided by the advice of experts in each subject area, Cambridge University Press is using state-of-the-art scanning machines in its own Printing House to capture the content of each book selected for inclusion. The files are processed to give a consistently clear, crisp image, and the books finished to the high quality standard for which the Press is recognised around the world. The latest print-on-demand technology ensures that the books will remain available indefinitely, and that orders for single or multiple copies can quickly be supplied.

The Cambridge Library Collection will bring back to life books of enduring scholarly value (including out-of-copyright works originally issued by other publishers) across a wide range of disciplines in the humanities and social sciences and in science and technology.

Biographia Navalis

Or, Impartial Memoirs of
the Lives and Characters of Officers
of the Navy of Great Britain,
from the Year 1660 to the Present Time

VOLUME 5

JOHN CHARNOCK

CAMBRIDGE UNIVERSITY PRESS

Cambridge, New York, Melbourne, Madrid, Cape Town, Singapore,
São Paolo, Delhi, Dubai, Tokyo, Mexico City

Published in the United States of America by Cambridge University Press, New York

www.cambridge.org
Information on this title: www.cambridge.org/9781108026352

© in this compilation Cambridge University Press 2011

This edition first published 1797
This digitally printed version 2011

ISBN 978-1-108-02635-2 Paperback

This book reproduces the text of the original edition. The content and language reflect the beliefs, practices and terminology of their time, and have not been updated.

Cambridge University Press wishes to make clear that the book, unless originally published by Cambridge, is not being republished by, in association or collaboration with, or with the endorsement or approval of, the original publisher or its successors in title.

SIR CHARLES SAUNDERS K.B.

Admiral of the Blue Squadron, First Lord Commissioner of the Admiralty, Member of his Majesty's most Honorable Privy Council, and Treasurer of Greenwich Hospital.

From an Original Picture in Greenwich Hospital.

Published as the Act directs, July 1st 1799 by R. Faulder Bond Street.

BIOGRAPHIA NAVALIS;

IMPARTIAL MEMOIRS

LIVES AND CHARACTERS

OFFICERS OF THE NAVY OF GREAT BRITAIN,

FROM THE YEAR 1660 TO THE PRESENT TIME;

DRAWN FROM THE MOST AUTHENTIC SOURCES, AND DISPOSED IN A CHRONOLOGICAL ARRANGEMENT.

By JOHN CHARNOCK, ESQ.

WITH PORTRAITS, AND OTHER ENGRAVINGS,
BY BARTOLOZZI, &c.

Nautæque, per omne
Audaces mare qui currunt, hac mente laborem
Sese ferre, senes ut in otia tuta recedant.
HORACE, Sat. 1. Lib. 1.

VOL. V.
BEING THE FIRST VOLUME OF THE CONTINUATION.

LONDON:

PRINTED FOR R. FAULDER, BOND-STREET.

1797.

BIOGRAPHIA NAVALIS, &c.

1740.

ALLEN, ROBERT, was the second son of captain William Allen, unhappily killed, in 1696, on board the Bonadventure, and of whose gallantry on that occasion we have already given a short account, (vol. ii. p. 406.) This gentleman was born in 1689, and was on board his father's ship at the time of the encounter which proved fatal to him, leaving this gentleman, his son, then scarcely eight years old. Pursuing the same profession with much eagerness, and nothing intimidated at the disaster which had befallen his parent, he was very deservedly patronized, early in life, by admiral Hopson, and promoted, through that gentleman's recommendation, aided by his own deserts, to be second lieutenant of the Reserve. No other mention is made of him till the year 1711, when he was appointed first lieutenant of the Norfolk, a large third rate. Without friends, and, consequently, without interest, he continued a lieutenant for nearly thirty years after this time, but during this very mortifying period held various appointments, as first lieutenant of different ships. Those particularly mentioned were, the Sterling Castle, his commission for which he received in 1726: in the following year he was removed into the Lion: and, in 1728, into the Bredah. In 1733, he was made lieutenant of the Berwick: and, lastly, in 1737, of the Gloucester. Having at length sufficiently attracted the notice of his superiors by his long and very meritorious service, he was, on May 8, 1740, promoted to be captain of the Biddeford frigate, though in some accounts he is erroneously stated as captain of the Lyme a short time before the above date. In the Biddeford he continued only till July following, and was then promoted to the Rochester, a fourth rate of fifty guns; in which ship he remained till the ensuing year; he was then made captain of the Royal Sovereign, a first rate, fitted as a flag-ship: but, in 1742, was removed into the Charlotte yacht. In the month of September 1745, he was appointed to the Somerset; in which command he remained only till the month of November following, and then honourably retired from the line of active service, on being made captain of the Mary yacht. We have no other intelligence concerning him, except that he died in the course of the year 1752, to that time retaining his last appointment.

BALCHEN, George,—was the only son of the brave and unfortunate sir John Balchen, knight*, born sometime in the year 1717. Having, according both to report and every probable conjecture, been brought up and properly instructed in the several necessary duties of an officer under the immediate eye of his worthy parent, he was, on the 12th of September 1740, promoted to be captain of the Greyhound. In 1742 he was captain of the Folkstone, of 44 guns, on the Mediterranean station, and bore a distinguished share, under the command of commodore Barnet †, in the encounter with the chevalier de Caylus. After his return to England he was promoted to the Pembroke, and ordered to the West Indies, where unhappily in the prime of life, being only twenty-eight years old, he died, universally regretted, on the 18th of December 1745, having not long survived the unhappy fate of his gallant father ‡.

BERTIE, Lord Montague §, was the second son of
Robert,

---

* See Vol. iii. p. 155.
† See vol. iv. p. 212. Commodore Barnet is there erroneously stated to have had with him another ship of the line; but we now find this ship to have been the Folkstone.
‡ Ibid. p. 162.
§ This family originally came into England, from Bertiland in Prussia, when the Saxons first invaded this nation; and by the gift of
one

Robert, first duke of Ancaster, &c. and Albinia his second wife, daughter to major-general William Farrington, of Chiselhurst, in the county of Kent. He was, on the 18th of July 1740, appointed captain of the Lyme frigate; in which ship he continued during all or the greater part of the following year: but no other mention is any where made of him as a naval officer. He married Elizabeth, daughter of William Piers, esq. member of parliament for Wells, in the county of Somerset, by whom he had two daughters. He died of a dropsy on the 12th of December 1753, and was buried at Chiselhurst aforesaid.

BOLTON, Harry Powlet, Duke of,—was the second son of Harry, the fourth personage who was invested with that high title. On the 15th of July 1740, he was promoted from the rank of lieutenant to the command of the Port Mahon, of 24 guns. He was employed in the month of November ensuing in escorting the Oporto trade, as he also was, in the month of February 1741, in convoying that to Lisbon. From the Folkstone he was soon advanced to the Oxford, of fifty guns, a ship on the Mediterranean station. In the month of August 1742, we find him serving under commodore Martin, with the squadron sent into Naples by admiral Mathews; the cause and event of which expedition have been already related at length*. After this time he was employed with several small detachments, and was present afterwards at the action off Toulon, but not engaged, the Oxford, with several other fifty-gun ships, being stationed as a reserve in case any of the enemy's fleet should be fortunate enough to force their way through the British line. After the conclusion of that unfortunate encounter,

---

one of the Saxon kings had a castle, and also a town, which was denominated from them Bertiested, near Maidstone in Kent, sted and stad denoting, in the Saxon language, a town.

It appears from an ancient manuscript in the Cotton library, that Leopald de Bertie was constable of Dover-castle in the reign of king Ethelred, from whom descended Hieronymus de Bertie, founder, or at least a great benefactor to one of the monasteries in Kent, the north part of which he built at his own expence, and himself was buried in a chapel there, where these arms were put up against a pillar, viz. Three Battering Rams in Pale.

* See the life of Mr. Martin, vol. iv. p. 72.

captain Powlet was ordered to attend the difabled fhip Marlborough into Port Mahon. No other remarkable notice is taken of him during the time he continued on the above-mentioned ftation. We hear nothing more of him till the month of June 1745, when, having in the interim returned to England, he was promoted to the command of the Sandwich, a fecond rate of 90 guns: but we have no farther particulars concerning him during the time he retained that ftation, except his having been one of the members of the court-martial held, on board the Sandwich, at Spithead, in the month of June 1745, for the trial of captain Green of the Lizard. In 1746, he was examined as one of the witneffes on the trial of vice-admiral Leftock, touching his conduct in the engagement off Toulon.

His next command was the Ruby, a fourth rate of fifty guns. In April 1746, we find him to have been, by order, captain of the Defiance, of fixty guns, a fhip at that time employed as a cruifer. On the 21ft he fell in with and captured, after a very fmart engagement, which continued two hours, a very large French frigate carrying forty guns and three hundred and fixty-five men, called the Ambufcade, new from the ftocks. As a proof of the judicious manner in which the Defiance was conducted during the action, captain Powlet had only one man killed and three wounded, while the enemy had on the fame occafion twenty-fix. He returned afterwards, for a fhort time, into the Ruby, but was foon removed into the Exeter, of 60 guns, and ordered to the Eaft Indies, where he continued to ferve during the remainder of the war; but is not, far as we have been able to difcover, mentioned in any other way than has been already related in the life of Mr. Bofcawen*. After his return to England † admiral

---

* See vol. iv. p. 318. Mr. Bofcawen, after the lofs of the Namur, hoifted his flag on board the Exeter, and returned to England with captain Powlet. That gallant admiral is faid to have declared, on all occafions, that the Exeter was one of the beft regulated and conducted fhips he had ever been on board of.

† On the 13th of May 1752, he married Mary, daughter of —— Nunn, of Eltham in the county of Kent, efq. By this lady, who died May 31, 1764, and is buried at Eltham, he had one daughter, Mary-Henrietta, born October 1753, married April the 24th, 1772, John, now earl of Sandwich, and died March the 30th, 1779, in the twenty-fixth year of her age.

Griffin,

Griffin, who was himself tried and difmiffed the fervice for his mifconduct in the Eaft Indies, had publicly mentioned fome exceptions which he thought proper to take againft captain Powlet's conduct. A court-martial was accordingly ordered to enquire into the matter: it affembled on board the Devonfhire, in the river Medway, on the 1ft of September 1752, admiral Townfhend being the prefident. No perfon, however, appearing to fubftantiate the charge, it was unanimoufly pronounced, in the ftricteft fenfe of the word, groundlefs.

In the month of February 1753, he was appointed captain of the Somerfet, a third rate of feventy guns, commiffioned as a guard-fhip at Chatham.

By the fucceffion of his father, the lord Harry Powlet, to the dukedom of Bolton, on the 26th of Auguft 1754, he himfelf became, as his fecond fon, invefted with the fame honorary title. In the fame year he was elected reprefentative in parliament for the borough of Lymington, as he was, in that which fucceeded, for the city of Winchefter. In 1755 he was captain of the Barfleur, a fecond rate, one of the fleet ordered to cruife, in foundings, under the command of fir Edw. Hawke, to watch the motions of the French, whofe treacherous and hoftile intentions had been for fome time fufpected. An occurrence took place while he was thus employed which made confiderable noife, and caufed him to be much, and, as it appears, very undefervedly cenfured; a whimfical miftake in the terms ufed by him in his plea of defence, was humouroufly and *ingenioufly*, though, we muft own, not very fairly held out as an incontrovertible proof of the guilt of this noble perfon, popular opinion difdains ever to confefs its error, and rather prefers calumniating the moft innocent and fpotlefs character, than foregoing a prejudice haftily, and, perhaps, very wantonly taken up.

The whole of the tranfaction alluded to having undergone a ferious and legal inveftigation, we cannot, perhaps, act more fairly, than briefly to ftate the proceedings which took place, and the facts as given in evidence.

He was tried by a court-martial held on board the Prince George, at Portfmouth, on the 20th, 21ft, and 22d of October 1755, before Henry Ofborne, efq. vice-admiral of the red, on a charge of quitting his ftation without leave from admiral Hawke, of whofe fquadron the Barfleur,

fleur, as has been already stated, was one. Upon this trial it was proved that, on the morning of the 22d of August lord Powlett, by verbal order from sir E. Hawke, gave chase to a sail that appeared to the south-east, and continued the pursuit to leeward of the fleet from ten o'clock till twelve, when he came up and spoke with the vessel, which proved to be a friend : he then stretched away to the westward till two; and at two tacked and stood towards the fleet till seven. Some of the fleet were seen standing on one tack and some on another, so that it was doubtful whether the fleet stood east or west. Lord Powlett therefore ordered the master to set the admiral, who bore N. E. by N. about four leagues distant, but about eight o'clock, night coming on, and the Barfleur being still at a distance, he entirely lost sight of the fleet.

As the ships had been seen standing on different tacks, lord Powlett was now in doubt what was really the track of the fleet; upon which he advised with the master, and it was concluded that the most likely method to join it was to stand eastward till midnight; and then, if no part of it should be seen, to put about to the westward.

Having, in consequence of this determination, steered east till twelve at night, crowding all the sail he could, and having discovered no lights during that time, he tacked to the westward, and kept on that course till between five and six in the morning of the next day; at that time a midshipman at the mast-head called out that he saw three sail bearing about E. by N. The lieutenant of the watch concluding that these three ships were part of the fleet, immediately prepared to put about in order to join them: but while this was doing another sail was discovered from the masthead in the south-west quarter. The lieutenant being then in doubt what course to take, went down to lord Powlett and acquainted him with what the midshipman had seen in both quarters. Lord Powlett immediately gave orders to chase the sail to the south-west, for the following reasons :

1st. He supposed her a French man of war homeward bound.

2dly. By the direction he judged her to be in with respect to the fleet, he knew there was no probability

lity that she would be spoken with by any other vessel.

3dly. Admiral Hawke had then more than double the force of any squadron the French had at sea, and therefore lord Powlett's absence could not probably produce any ill consequence.

4thly. He imagined it to be a general rule with all commanders of a cruizing squadron to chase every vessel that appeared; and if no ship belonging to such squadron was, when out of sight of the admiral, to give chase, many of the enemy's ships would escape that might be easily taken. And,

5thly, He had great probability of joining the fleet next day, if the wind had shifted; and if not, of joining it at the rendezvous.

After chasing this vessel to the S. W. about three hours, another appeared to the S. E. upon which lord Powlett shaped his course between both. About six o'clock in the evening, after a chase of twelve hours the vessel first pursued made sir Edw. Hawke's distinguishing signal, and proved to be an English man of war: lord Powlett, however, still continued to stand on for some time, that if she was one of sir Edward's squadron he might acquaint her, that on the 23d the admiral had changed his rendezvous: but the vessel still standing from him, he left her and gave chase to the other vessel which had appeared to the S. E. and about seven o'clock he found that this also was a friend: he then tacked once more, and stood to the northward to join the fleet, which he supposed to be about twenty leagues to windward of him, at the rendezvous. Early the next morning, that is to say on the 25th, the ship having steered very hard for three or four days before, the *tiller* was unshipped and the *goose-neck* shifted an inch and an half farther forward, it having born so hard upon the sweep as almost to have worn it through; and a few hours afterwards the carpenter made a report to the officer of the watch, that the *stern-post* was loose and worked very much; that the second and third *pintles of the rudder*, which had been before complained of, worked much more than they had ever yet done; and that the upper *brace* upon the *stern-post* was loose.

Upon

Upon this report lord Powlett sent the first lieutenant and master, with the carpenter, to examine whether it was well-grounded, who finding that it was, he caused the *stern-post* and standard to be *frapped* together, and both of them to be frapped to the mizen-mast. Lord Powlett also ordered the two aftermost-guns in the gun-room to be removed into the hold, to ease the weakened part of the ship. When these precautions had been taken, the ship still continued to stand to the northward till the morning of the 26th, and then tacked and stood to the eastward.

The carpenter however continued to urge the dangerous condition of the ship, so that on the 27th lord Powlett sent his two mates to examine the condition of the ship a second time. They reported, under their hands, the defects mentioned by the carpenter, and declared, that though, by the precautions that had been taken these defects were in some measure remedied: yet, if a hard gale should happen, or a rough sea, they could not answer for the consequence. Lord Powlett neverthelefs still continued to stand eastward till the 28th, at noon, hoping to make sir Edward's rendezvous, having got into the latitude the evening before. But seeing nothing of the fleet after beating about several hours, and considering the report of the carpenter, the lieutenants and the master, he at length gave orders that they should steer for Spithead.

Upon hearing the evidence on both sides, by which these facts were established, the court unanimously agreed to the following resolutions:

That he did not judge and act right in giving chace, on the 24th of August, to a sail seen in the south-west, when three sail were seen in the north-east, which might probably be part of the fleet. But it having clearly appeared to them that his intentions were upright towards the service, as he had before used his utmost endeavours to rejoin the fleet, on the station it was, when he separated from it; and did afterwards use the like endeavours to join it on the rendezvous; they do not think this error deserving of reprehension, and do therefore unanimously only judge it proper to admonish him, as he is hereby admonished, to be more cautious in his future conduct.

As

As to his returning into port, the court are of opinion that, considering the defects of the ship's rudder, his proceeding therein was very justifiable; and therefore they do unanimously acquit him of all blame upon that account, and he is hereby acquitted accordingly.

But the report given by the carpenter of the Barfleur of the condition of the ship, upon which lord Powlett acted, being contradicted by the builder at Chatham, the admiralty-board thought fit to break him.

The fact, as related to us on the best and most impartial authority, appears to have been, that the gudgeons of the stern-post and rudder-pins, which worked in them above and below, became loose, one or two in the center remaining firm, this caused the cambering of the sternpost, insomuch that the ship would not steer till the gooseneck was taken off, and brought farther forward upon the sweep. The ill-judged report of the carpenter, founded on his ignorance of the real cause, gave birth to those repeated and illiberal jests which were perpetually vented by those who, on all public occasions, take upon them to decide on questions they little understand, and always prejudge according to the bias of what is called popular opinion. His lordship, completely restored both to the service, and good opinion of all unprejudiced men, was, on the 4th of June 1756, raised to the rank of rear-admiral of the blue. In 1757 he was advanced to be rear-admiral of the white, and for a short time commanded first in the Downs and afterwards at the Nore. On February 7, 1758, he was made rear-admiral of the red, but does not appear to have been invested with any command after those last-mentioned*. He afterwards passed through the different ranks of a flag officer till he attained that of admiral of the white †. He succeeded to the title of Bolton on the death

of

---

* Admiral Boscawen, when appointed to the Mediterranean command, in 1759, desired his lordship might serve under his command. This was refused, being, as it was pretended, disagreeable to his majesty: such are the intrigues of party, and baneful effects of prejudice.

† On the 14th of February 1759, he was appointed vice-admiral of the blue, as he was of the white on the 9th of December 1760. On the 18th of October 1770, he was made admiral of the Blue. His civil offices were those of vice-admiral of the counties of Southampton and Dorset, and governor of the Isle of Wight and Carisbrooke castle, which last appointment he received in the month of December 1766,

and

of his only brother, Charles, the fifth duke. His grace married, April the 8th, 1765, Catherine, daughter of Robert Lowther, efq. and fifter to the prefent earl of Lonfdale.— By this lady he left two daughters, the lady Catherine, now countefs of Darlington, and the lady Amelia. Having long enjoyed an uninterrupted tranquillity, and as much retirement as was compatible with fo high a rank, he died, univerfally regretted and lamented by all who knew his benevolence and virtues, on the 25th day of December 1794, having attained the 75th year of his age.

COTES, Thomas,—was promoted to be captain of the York * on the 12th of May 1740: this was one of the fhips which, in the month of November following, compofed the reinforcement, commanded by fir Chaloner Ogle, fent to Mr. Vernon in the Weft Indies, previous to the attack of Carthagena, which took place immediately fubfequent to the arrival of the fleet. We find him particularly mentioned as having been one of the captains appointed to command, under Mr. Bofcawen, the feamen which attacked and carried the Barradera battery. He ferved in the fame ftation on a fecond affault, under the orders of captain Watfon, the Spaniards having, by exertions almoft incredible, partially reftored their works. He was afterwards concerned, under Mr. Knowles, in the bold and fuccefsful affault on fort St. Jofeph, of which poft he was left commanding officer, while his feniors in command, the captains Knowles and Watfon, pufhed on with the boats to board the Gallicia, the Spanifh admiral's flag-fhip, which lay at no great diftance. No material mention is made of him during the remainder of the expedition.

---

and did not then retain it longer than three or four years. On the 6th of April 1782, he was reftored to this office, and in addition to it, was appointed lord-lieutenant and cuftos rotulorum of the county of Southampton: the former he refigned fome years previous to his deceafe; the latter he held till the time of his death.

* Other accounts ftate him to have been firft appointed to the Lively frigate, and quickly afterwards promoted to the York: but this we believe to be a miftake, occafioned by captain Jolley being appointed to that frigate on the fame day.

Captain

Captain Cotes was one of the officers ordered to remain on the Weſt Indian ſtation with Mr. Vernon, after the unfortunate failure of the enterprize juſt alluded to, and the conſequent detachment of that part of the fleet ordered back to England under Mr. Leſtock. Not however being in a condition for ſervice when Mr. Vernon and ſir Chaloner Ogle ſailed on the expedition againſt St. Jago de la Vega, the York, with two other ſhips, the Auguſta and Deptford, were left behind at Jamaica, with commodore Davers, but under orders to follow the fleet as ſoon as they ſhould be equipped. The general events of war which afterwards took place in the Weſt Indies were, with ſome very few exceptions, extremely unintereſting; and captain Cotes paſſed ſome years of his ſervice in the undiſtinguiſhed crowd of brave men, his cotemporaries, who were employed on the ſame ſtation. He continued captain of the York till the year 1745, and indeed did not return from the Weſt Indies long before that time. After his arrival he was advanced to the Edinburgh, of ſeventy guns, a ſhip employed, during the greater part if not the whole of the following year, as a cruiſer in the Channel. He met with conſiderable ſucceſs in this occupation, having made ſeveral valuable and conſequential prizes, one of which was a very large private ſhip of war, new from the ſtocks, called the Duc de Chartres, mounting thirty-two guns. He continued in the Edinburgh during the remainder of the war, always actively employed, and exerting himſelf on every occaſion where the ſmalleſt opportunity offered of diſtinguiſhing himſelf. In 1746 he was commodore, or rather captain of a ſmall ſquadron ſent before the fleet under Mr. Leſtock, to reconnoitre Port L'Orient, and inform himſelf of the foundings, and every other neceſſary particular preparatory to a deſcent. This appointed ſervice he executed with ſuch great diligence and exactneſs, that the ſubſequent failure of the expedition could not be, in the ſmalleſt degree, imputed to the omiſſion, or want of exertion and preciſion on his part. In 1747 he ſerved in the ſquadron under rear-admiral Hawke, and had the good fortune to be the firſt diſcoverer of L'Etendiere's ſquadron, which was totally defeated and nearly the whole taken.

In

In 1748 he was appointed commodore of a small squadron ordered out, in the month of April, to join his former admiral. When proceeding on that service in pursuance of his orders, the following occurrence took place which being certainly too honourable to his reputation and character to be omitted or slightly passed over, we have inserted the following official account of it.

" Admiralty-office, April 4.

" Captain Cotes, commander of his majesty's ship the Edinburgh, of seventy guns, having been sent to sea with the said ship, together with the Eagle, Windsor, and Princess Louisa, of sixty guns each, and the Inverness, of twenty-four guns, in order to join sir Edward Hawke, has sent the Inverness to England with the following advices, viz. That on the 7th of last month, being in his station off Cape Cantin, looking out for sir Edward Hawke, he fell in with a fleet of Spanish ships consisting of nine men of war of the line,

	Guns.		Guns.
El Sobervio	74	La Pastora	64
Leon	74	El Rosario	60
Colorado	70	Xavier	54
Oriento	64	La Galgo	54
Brillante	64		

having under their convoy about twenty-seven merchant-ships, with which they sailed from Cadiz four days before. That the men of war drew into a line to receive him, but not being strong enough to attack them, he endeavoured to cut off as many of the ships under their convoy as he could, and accordingly five of them were taken, three being register-ships bound to Vera Cruz, and the other two bound to Carthagena. That the Spanish men of war continued to lay-to in a line, and did not endeavour to retake the said ships: and captain Cotes observing that the said ships under their convoy steered away to the westward, scattered, and in confusion; as soon as it was dark detached the Eagle and Windsor, both very good sailers, to pursue them, and endeavour to cut off any which separated from the men of war."

Peace

NAVAL OFFICERS OF GREAT BRITAIN. 15

Peace being concluded very foon after the foregoing very fpirited enterprize, may well account for our finding no mention made of this very brave and deferving officer till the re-commencement of war with France in 1756. On the 4th of June he was promoted to be rear-admiral of the white; and before the conclufion of the year was nominated commander-in-chief on the Jamaica ftation. He did not however fail with his fquadron, and the fleet of merchant-fhips which he was inftructed to take under his convoy, till the 9th of February. After his arrival on the ftation he difplayed the greateft activity and diligence in the diftribution of his cruizers, as well as every other particular of fervice in which he was connected, or had the management of. He had the peculiar fatisfaction of reflecting that, in all probability, under no preceding commander in the fame quarter, had the pecuniary loffes of the enemy been greater from the interruption given to their commerce, or their character as a warlike nation, fuffered more from the many gallant enterprizes executed by the private captains under his immediate command. Thefe however will be with more propriety related hereafter in the accounts or memoirs of the different perfons more particularly concerned in executing them.

On the 31ft of January 1758, Mr. Cotes appears to have been, while then abfent on the ftation already mentioned, advanced to the rank of vice-admiral of the blue. He retained the fame command for fome time afterwards; and though no opportunity was afforded him of being particularly concerned as commander-in-chief of the fquadron employed in that part of the world, in any remarkable or confequential enterprize againft any of the enemy's fettlements, yet muft we juftly beftow on him all the praife poffible to be gained by the ftricteft attention to the milder and lefs dazzling duties of his ftation. On the 14th of February 1759, he was advanced to be vice-admiral of the white, as he was again, on the 21ft of October 1762, to be vice of the red. After his return from the Weft Indies he was elected, in the twelfth parliament of Great Britain, which met on the 3d of November 1761, reprefentative for Great Bedwin, in Wiltfhire; and in the courfe of the year laft-mentioned, was chofen chosen one of the elder brethren of the Trinity-house; but was no otherwise connected with public affairs. He henceforth passed a life totally abstracted from the naval service; and died at last regretted by every person who had heard his public character, and lamented by all who were acquainted with his private virtues, in the month of October 1767.

EDWARDS, Richard,—was, on the 4th of November 1740, appointed captain of the Fox frigate. He remained in that ship till after the year 1742, but is only mentioned as having captured a small Spanish privateer, of ten guns, called the Justa Refina. We know nothing relative to him subsequent to this time till the month of February 1744-5, except that, during a part of the intermediate period, he was captain of the Torrington. He commanded the Princess Mary early in 1746, and was appointed governor of Newfoundland: he was ordered, however, to put himself under the command of commodore Warren, who was then occupied in the siege of Louisburg: with him he was to continue till the reduction of that fortress. He arrived there on the 11th of June, four days only before its surrender, with the Princess Mary, the Hector, and the Lark. That expedition being completed, he proceeded from thence according to his original appointment and destination: but little other mention is made of him after his return to England, except that he commanded a yacht, which having afterwards quitted, he was refused the rank of a flag officer unless he returned to the service as a captain previous to his obtaining it. He accordingly procured, through the interest of his friends, the command of the Princess Amelia, a station he did not long retain. On June 3, 1757, he was put on the superannuated list with the rank and half-pay of a rear-admiral, and died in England on the 16th of June 1773.

FORRESTER, Right Hon. George, Lord,—was the eldest son of George, fifth lord Forrester, who was a military officer, and signalized himself in a very remarkable manner, under the generals, Wills and Carpenter, at Preston, in Lancashire, during the rebellion, which broke out an. 1715. As a reward for his very great bravery, he was advanced to be colonel of the 4th troop of horse-guards. George, his son, the sixth lord Forrester, having

entered

entered into the navy, was, on the 24th of November 1741, promoted to be captain of the Biddeford frigate. He was foon afterwards ordered to Gibraltar and the Mediterranean, on which ftation he continued during the following year; during this time no mention is made of him except his having been concerned with captain Norris, of the Kingfton, in the capture of two Spanifh prizes, the St. Anthonio and Senora Rofaria, which they carried into Gibraltar. Early in the year 1742 we find him captain of the Leopard, of fifty guns, and ftill continuing on the fame ftation, where, in the month of Auguft, he captured a valuable prize, as he before had one on the 11th of March preceding. Of this circumftance he gave the following report, in a letter written to the fecretary of the admiralty, which we have inferted as well on account of the fact itfelf, as of the fingular ftile in which the memory of it is preferved.

"On the 9th inftant, between cape St. Mary's and Cadiz, I faw a fhip ftemming right in for the latter place; and, as fhe lay immediately in my route, I fired two fhot at her and brought her to. On examination I found her to be a Spaniard, of about two hundred and odd tons, laden with logwood, cochineal, and cocoa, and feveral other forts of dyes, the names I do not know, canary wines, four camels, and a great prefent, yet unknown, for the king of Naples, as alfo a bifhop, a prieft, a Spanifh general, and other officers, with great fums of piafters."

We believe him to have continued captain of the Leopard till the beginning of the year 1745, when he was promoted to the Defiance, of fixty guns. He had unhappily contracted an habit of intemperance which occafionally rendered him very unfit for command, and betrayed him into feveral breaches of duty. His mifconduct at laft became fo apparent and glaring, that he was brought before a court-martial, of which Mr. Griffin was prefident, held on board the Tilbury, at Portfmouth. The charge againft him being incontrovertibly proved, he was fentenced to be difmiffed the fervice on the 28th of March 1746. He did not long furvive this difgrace, the caufe of which while we condemn we muft at the fame time compaffionate. He died, according to Mr. Hardy, on the 26th of July 1748.

FRANKLAND,

FRANKLAND, Sir Thomas, — was the nephew of a baronet of the fame name, who was for many years one of the commiffioners for executing the office of lord high admiral. He was, on the 15th of July 1740, promoted to the command of the Rofe frigate; and at the conclufion of the year was ordered out to the Bahama Iflands, to convey thither Mr. Tinker, who had been appointed governor two years before. After he had landed his paffenger he continued on the fame ftation, being inftructed to remain there and cruize for the protection of thofe iflands and the adjacent coaft from the depredations of the guarda-coftas. In the month of June 1742, he diftinguifhed himfelf, by his activity, in capturing a Spanifh veffel of that defcription, together with three veffels which fhe herfelf had made prizes of a fhort time before.

The guarda-cofta, which carried ten carriage and as many fwivel guns, fupported by two of the prizes, which were armed veffels, engaged the Rofe for nearly three hours: but finding her too powerful and too well conducted to afford them any hope of ultimate fuccefs, the two prizes ftood away, one keeping to windward, the other large, with all the fail they could croud. The guarda-cofta maintained a running fight for an hour longer through the defperation of her captain: and even at laft, the crew, in oppofition to him, hauled down their colours and called for quarter. Captain Frankland fhifted the prifoners with all poffible expedition, and having put fome of his own men, under proper officers, on board the prize, difpatched her after the veffel which had hauled her wind, he himfelf following the other two. So fuccefsful was his activity on this occafion that the three veffels were all, without difficulty, captured and carried fafely into Carolina. The caufe of the obftinate defence made by the Spanifh veffel was, on enquiry, difcovered to be owing to her captain being Fandino, the fellow who fome years before had cut off the ears of captain Jenkins, and thereby caufed fo great, fo juft and general an indignation through the whole Britifh nation. Captain Frankland judging a monfter of fo cruel a defcription, who had manifefted a conduct that would have difgraced a pirate, unfit to be releafed as a prifoner on parole, or even exchanged, sent him home to be treated as administration should think proper.

Captain Frankland continued in the same command, and remained on the same station some years; but is not again particularly mentioned till the year 1744*, when he signalized himself remarkably in an action with a very large, and, as it afterwards proved, valuable Spanish ship: the particulars we shall insert at length from the account officially given of this very spirited encounter.

"Being on his passage to his station as a cruiser between the Roques, Cape Florida, and the Pan of Matanzas, on the north side of Cuba, about thirty-five leagues to the westward of Havannah, on December 21, just before day-light, he found himself almost on board a large ship, of which he was to windward, and astern withall. Captain Frankland, who kept his wind till day-break, then found his antagonist had but one tier of guns, but was by her working full of men, for before the captain shewed his colours she had run her courses up, bunted her main-sail, and had every thing ready to engage, her decks being crowded with people. About seven in the morning they began an engagement which lasted until half an hour past twelve. There was a fresh gale and a great sea; notwithstanding which they were alongside each other three or four times before the enemy struck. She had near 100 men killed outright, and four of her guns on one side disabled. She is called the Conception, of St. Malo, Adrian Mercan master, bound from Carthagena to Cadiz, but was to touch at Havannah to land upwards of 200 seamen, besides officers. The Rose had only five men killed, and about ten or twelve dangerously wounded, including the master, and several slightly. The cargo of the prize consisted of hides, and cocoa, with seventy chests of gold and silver, containing about three hundred and ten thousand pieces of eight. She had several passengers on board, from whom they got about 5000 ounces of gold in doubloons, pistoles, bars, &c. The crew of the Rose consisted of no more than one hundred and seventy-seven men, officers and boys included. The prize was safely carried into South Carolina."

---

* In the preceding year he married Miss Rhett, daughter of the chief-justice of Carolina, by whom he had six sons and eight daughters.

Captain Frankland retained the command of the Rose till the month of October 1746, and was then promoted to the Dragon, of sixty guns, in which ship he continued till the conclusion of the war, being, in 1748, on the West India station with Mr. Pocock. We do not find any subsequent mention made of him till the month of July 1755, when he was appointed commodore on the Antigua station. He hoisted his broad pendant on board the Winchester, of fifty guns, at Spithead, on the 10th of August, and sailed very soon afterwards for the West Indies. On his arrival there his first operation was to quarrel with commodore Pye, whom he was sent out to succeed. The first pretence was frivolous in the extreme, consisting merely in an exception, or affront Mr. Frankland thought proper to take, because the former had not struck his broad pendant on the instant he was informed of the latter's arrival.

A second, and, as it proved afterwards equally futile and, indeed unjust cause was, a more serious charge of misconduct against his predecessor, in having condemned the Advice, his own ship. Mr. Frankland asserted this measure to have been improper; and made a regular representation against it to the board of admiralty. In farther proof of the propriety of his opinion, as if he supposed his own hardiesse sufficient to establish it, he ordered the Advice to be fitted for himself, and absolutely went so far as to make a short cruize in her. The final event, however, did not reflect any very great honour on Mr. Frankland's judgement: the ship, on its return to England, proved so very defective, and unfit to keep the sea, that it was with the utmost difficulty the crew could, by frapping her round with hawsers and every other precaution, prevent her from almost literally falling to pieces during her passage. Mr. Frankland after his return to England appears no more in the character of a naval commander. In the month of June 1756, he was advanced to be rear-admiral of the blue, as he was progressively afterwards, through the different gradations and ranks of flag-officers, till he at last arrived at that of admiral of the white, the highest in the service, the admiral of the fleet or senior admiral on the list excepted. On the death of his brother, sir Charles Frankland, at Bath, in the year 1768, he succeeded to the title, and continued during his life totally
abstracted

abstracted from all public business, farther than his occasional attendance in the house of commons, as representative for the borough of Thirsk, in Yorkshire, for which place he had been member ever since the year 1749. Sir Thomas died at Bath on the 21st of November 1784.

FROGMORE, Rowland, — was, in the month of January 1740, made commander of the Swift sloop; from which he was, on the 18th of July, promoted to be captain of the Ruby, a fourth rate of fifty guns, then stationed in the Bristol Channel. He served during the following year as captain of the same ship in the Channel fleet, then under the orders of sir John Norris: but we do not meet with any other mention made of him till we find him commanding the Boyne, of eighty guns, one of the fleet employed in the Mediterranean with Mr. Mathews. His conduct during the encounter with the combined fleets off Toulon, was deemed so reprehensible that he was one of the officers supposed most culpable, and named in the address of the house of commons, to his majesty, beseeching him to order their behaviour to be investigated before a court-martial. Fate, however, prevented this request from being complied with, captain Frogmore dying in the Mediterranean on the 8th of November 1744, retaining till that time the command of the Boyne.

GIDEON, Solomon,—was, on the 6th of September 1740, appointed captain of the Panther. He was soon afterwards ordered to the Mediterranean, where he continued to serve, first under Mr. Haddock *, as long as he

remained

---

* He was a man of a singular turn of mind, possessing a natural bravery which could not have been too much admired, had it not on some few occasions appeared rather too extravagant for that proper degree of prudence which ought always to attend the most distinguished courage. He conceived the Panther, which was a ship mounting only fifty guns, and of very small dimensions, capable almost of contending with the most powerful vessel in the Spanish navy. Once on returning from a cruise to Gibraltar he had nearly drifted under the Spanish batteries at Algeziras. Admiral Haddock, who was then lying at Gibraltar with the fleet, immediately dispatched all the boats to his assistance for the purpose of towing him into safety. Captain Gideon with some little emotion enquired what they wanted? and when answered that they had been dispatched for the purpose of enabling him to get out of reach of the enemy's battery, under which he was so near drifting, that they would soon be enabled to reach and injure him materially, if not disable him by its fire: he replied, perfectly

uncon-

remained on that station, and afterwards under Mr. Mathews who succeeded him. In the month of August 1742, he was one of the captains sent, under commodore Martin*, to demand satisfaction of the king of Naples. He was promoted, we believe in the early part of the year 1745, from the Panther to the Shrewsbury, of eighty guns, one of the ships which appear to have been then employed in the Channel. This is the last mention we find made of him, except that, in the year 1755, he was put on the superannuated list with the rank and half-pay of a rear-admiral. He in all probability received many subsequent appointments, though so inconsiderable as to be unnoticed either by historians or collectors of anecdotes relative to the naval service. He did not long survive his last advancement, dying in England on the 3d of September 1756.

GRAHAM, Right Hon. Lord George,†— was the fourth son of James, the fourth marquis and first duke of Montrose, by the lady Christian Carnegie, daughter to David, earl of Northesk. Impelled by his natural spirit, inherited as it were from his brave and truly noble, though unfortunate ancestor, James, the first marquis, he entered

---

unconcerned, " Well then, I will cast loose my lower-deck guns and fire at them." A multitude of pleasant anecdotes are related of him, which prove him to have been, though in some innocent respects, a man of some eccentricities, to have at the same time possessed the most consummate good humour.

* He was the only officer on shore, captain De Langle excepted, who went in an official character. As to captain Gideon, he scorned to be trammelled by common rules; and the singularity and oddity of this character caused his conduct to be overlooked.

† No sirname in Scotland claims a higher origin than Graham. The traditional account thereof, handed down to us by our historians, is, that they are descended of the renowned Græme, who, in the year 404, was general of king Fergus the Second's army, and was governor of Scotland in the minority of his grandchild, king Eugene II. He fought with the Romans, and defeated the Britons. In the year 420, he made a breach in, and forced that mighty wall which the emperor Severus had reared up between the rivers Forth and Clyde, as the utmost limits of the Roman empire, to keep out the Scots from molesting them in their possessions; which wall has ever since retained, and to this day goes under the name of Græme's Dyke.

The

entered at an early age into the navy, and was advanced, more in confequence of his own merit and worth than any advantage he derived from his noble birth, through the different fubordinate ftations, till the 15th of March 1740, when he was appointed captain of the Adventure*; and in the enfuing month governor of Newfoundland. He held that ftation only for the current feafon, for he was fometime in the following year removed into the Lark, of forty guns, and fent to convoy the outward bound Turkey trade. We have no fubfequent account of him till the beginning of the year 1745, when he was appointed to the command of the Cumberland, of fixty guns, which he foon declined, and chofe rather, as better fuited to his active turn of mind, to accept that of the Bridgewater, fome accounts erroneoufly fay, the Sheernefs, a frigate of twenty-four guns, ftationed in the Channel. In June following he diftinguifhed himfelf exceedingly in the attack and capture of feveral privateers and their prizes, of which brilliant action we have the following account in an official letter from Oftend.

" Yefterday afternoon lord George Graham, in his majefty's fhip the Bridgewater, of twenty-four guns; captain Gordon, in the Sheernefs, of twenty-four guns; and lieutenant Ferguffon, in the Urfula armed veffel of fixteen guns, anchored in fight of this town. This morning, about half paft one, the town was alarmed with firing, which arofe from the three above-mentioned fhips being engaged with three Dunkirk privateers, the Royal of twenty-eight guns; the Dutchefs de Penthievre, of twenty-fix guns; a dogger of twelve guns, and feven prizes which they had taken and were carrying to Dunkirk.

The foundation of this great rampart has been of late traced from one river to the other, and is fully marked by feveral ftones found therein, which have Roman infcriptions cut out upon them, denoting the limits where, and by whom they were fet, &c. A good many of thefe ftones are at prefent to be feen in the college of Glafgow, and are well defcribed in Mr. Gordon's Itinerarium Septentrionale.

This great man is faid to have married a lady of the royal houfe of Denmark, and was progenitor of all the Grahams in the kingdom of Scotland.

* He was, previous to this, commander of the Mercury firefhip.

"The fight was obstinate till about four o'clock, when the four large prizes, three of them Virginia ships, struck to the Sheerness; the two large privateers to the Bridgewater; two Bremeners and a Scotch brig to the Ursula; but the dogger privateer made her escape. The Bridgewater, Sheerness, two large privateers, and four large prizes struck the ground, but were all got off the following tide, except one of the privateers."

He was immediately after this promoted to the Nottingham, of sixty guns; and in the course of a short cruise, on which he immediately proceeded, sunk a large French privateer, called the Bacchus: all the crew were, however, saved, except the first lieutenant. His lordship was taken ill on his return into port, and unhappily did not long survive this exploit, dying *January 2, 1746-7.

From a multitude of concurrent testimonies he appears to have been an officer who attained a great share of popularity, and was indeed, very deservedly, the idol of all seamen who knew him, as well on account of the high opinion entertained of his gallantry, as an invincible fund of good humour, which latter quality conciliated the affections of men in the same degree that the first related excited their admiration and esteem.

HARRISON, Henry.—This gentleman entered into the navy during the war with France in the reign of king William, and served progressively, as a volunteer, on board the London and Dunkirk. In 1700 he acted in the station of a midship-man on board the Pendennis, a ship at that time commanded by captain Charles Strickland, with whom he afterwards removed into the Romney, and served in that ship, as master's mate, from the month of June 1701, till April 1703. During this time he had the singular happiness of preserving that ship, together with the lives of her whole crew, though at the utmost hazard of his own.

This circumstance, which does him so much honour, is thus related by himself in a MS. and authentic memorandum, which has been transmitted to us.

"The preservation of his majesty's ship, the Romney, was effected in the following manner. We were then in the white sea, on our passage from Archangel; and

---

* He was, at the time of his death, representative in parliament for the county of Stirling.

being,

being, by a ſtrong unknown current, driven near to the iſland of Candenoze in a dark and ſtormy night, were obliged to come to an anchor. The next morning, we found ourſelves on a lee ſhore and ſo near a ledge of rocks that, without caſting the ſhip to ſtarboard, ſhe muſt inevitably have been on ſhore, not having room to wear the ſhip; the wind at the ſame time ſhifted two points more to the ſtarboard bow, and blew ſo hard that, added to the current and a great ſea, there was no poſſibility of either lowering a boat or ſtanding in the head to put a ſpring on the cable. The viol and meſſenger were both broke in heaving, and the hitches jammed in the hawſe hole, ſo that the ſhip rode entirely by the hawſe piece with a rope reeved in a block at the bow-ſprit end. I ſwung myſelf from the head of the lion as far as the buoy, and ſwam to it with a deep ſea-line in my hand, which being faſtened to the end of a hawſer, I reeved in the ſtrap of the buoy, and was hauled on board with it. I was above twelve minutes in the water, the ſea making a free paſſage over me, and at the ſame time there were above fifty tons of ice hanging about the ſhip. The hawſer was brought on the larboard quarter of the main capſtan, and hove up with it to bring the wind on the larboard bow, when, cutting the cable with ſome chiſels in the hawſe, we caſt the ſhip the right way."

In the month of April 1703, he was promoted to be lieutenant of the Dartmouth, and in the following year was at Elſinore, ſtill continuing to ſerve in the ſame ſtation on board the ſame ſhip. Being ordered on ſhore with the long boat to Elſingburgh, he diſtinguiſhed himſelf in a very ſingular and ſpirited manner, terminating at once a diſpute which, had leſs peremptory meaſures been uſed, might not improbably have been productive of ſerious conſequences. The Swediſh commandant ſeized on ten of his boats crew under the frivolous pretence of a treſpaſs, committed by ſome of them, in cutting broom. Two or three were wounded in the ſcuffle, and all of them immediately put into cloſe confinement. Not content with this flagrant breach of that amity which ſubſiſted between his court, and that of England, the Swede inſiſted on the ſum of four hundred rix dollars to be paid as a compenſation for the pretended injury. The captains, Watkins, Strickland, and Tudor Trevor, who were then on ſhore,

were

were unable to prevail on him to relax in his arbitray demand. What the mild and conciliating attempt of perfuasion was unable to produce, the spirit of Mr. Harrison almost instantaneously effected. Taking with him a proper number of resolute and chosen men, and watching his opportunity cautiously, he seized the person of the governor himself when passing over the bridge of the town. He executed this spirited and truly daring act notwithstanding a guard of soldiers was kept close to the place where it was performed; and though, moreover, there were upwards of twenty Swedish officers and persons who saw the seizure carried into execution, but were too timid, or prudent to attempt its prevention.

The commandant being carried on board the ship, was immediately compelled to give an order for the release of the people, which was punctually, though, as we may suppose, not very willingly complied with. In 1705 he, Mr. Harrison, was appointed lieutenant of the Dunwich, and in this station much distinguished himself by his ingenuity on a different line to the foregoing. The ship which he served on board of was at that time employed as a cruiser for the protection of commerce against privateers. Experience soon taught both himself and his comrades, that the prudence of their antagonists, who most cautiously avoided them, precluded any hope of success, except such as should be the result of some sudden and uncommon accident. Mr. Harrison proposed to disguise the ship and make her resemble, as nearly as possible, a Dutch fly boat. This scheme so wonderfully answered the end proposed, that, in the course of their different cruises, they captured five privateers, besides driving six on shore near Calais, and a French frigate of twenty-four guns on the beach at Dieppe. He continued lieutenant of the Dunwich, we believe, during the whole war; and someti・e before its conclusion distinguished himself in a very remarkable manner by attacking and boarding a French privateer, of six guns and thirty-four men, with the crews of the pinnace and yawl belonging to the frigate, though it was then above a league distance and their numbers amounted to no more than nineteen persons. The privateer was under sail when taken, and even had the advantag of a very fresh breeze of wind, two circumstances
which

which added confiderably to the hazard, and, confequently, to the heroifm of the foregoing act. It was, and very defervedly, thought fo highly of by captain Graves, who commanded the Dunwich, that, with the unanimous confent of the whole crew, he beftowed the whole of the prize on Mr. Harrifon and his brave affociates.

In 1711 he was appointed, by admiral fir John Leake, to act as captain of the Dunwich and in preference to any of his own lieutenants, a circumftance that reflected on him the higheft honour: but, however well he might have deferved this promotion, the board of admiralty, either from his want of friends or fome unknown caufe, refufed to ratify his promotion. In the year 1714 he, by order of the board of admiralty, took upon him the command of the Mary fmack. Being fent to reconnoitre the port of Breft and others adjacent, on the coaft of France, where it was faid preparations were making for fome fudden and unexpected attempt, as well by the equipment of a fleet as the collection of a formidable land force, he executed this fervice in the completeft manner, and fo expeditioufly withal that he was only eleven days abfent.

Notwithftanding his very long and meritorious fervice, he was ftill, though on no other apparent ground whatever than that of being deftitute of intereft, thought unworthy of promotion, or if not unworthy, at leaft as not yet poffeffing a fufficient right peremptorily to claim it. The patience with which he bore his difappointment was at laft exhaufted, and he ventured to tranfmit to lord Onflow, who appears in fome meafure to have taken him under his protection, a plain and modeft memorial, ftating, in the moft moderate terms the hardfhips he conceived he laboured under. Thefe were of a two-fold nature, having relation not only to the neglect with which he was treated, but what was a ftill more ferious confideration, the narrownefs of his circumftances, being left for a length of years, to fupport a wife and nine children on the fcanty pittance of a lieutenant's half pay. "Lord Torrington* (fays he) was of opinion my commiffion, as captain of the Dunwich, ought to have been confirmed, and three years fince, promifed to be my advocate, and procure me a fhip; but I ftill remain on the lift of lieutenants." There could

---

* Sir George Byng.

not

not, perhaps, have been framed a more pathetic appeal to the paſſions than ſuch a plain and artleſs lamentation.

Paſſing over all diſplay of his ſervices, either on account of their length or particular merit, he reſts his claim to promotion with hoping the admiralty-board would promote him from the rank of lieutenant, that he might, with the greater decency, be able to maintain his wife and family. This application to the feelings of miniſters appears to have had but little effect either on their juſtice or their generoſity, for he did not receive any promotion till ſome years afterwards. At length, having attained an age when many brave men are, alas! obliged, through infirmities, to retire totally from all command, he was, on the 28th of February 1740, appointed captain of the Mary galley. He did not continue in this veſſel longer than the end of the current year; nor does he appear to have received any other commiſſion till the month of April or May following, when he was promoted to the Argyle, of fifty guns, as ſucceſſor to captain Richard Norris. This ſhip was one of the fleet ſtationed in Soundings during the enſuing ſummer, under ſir John Norris; and being ſent out to cruiſe a ſhort time before the fleet itſelf ſailed, captured a Spaniſh ſtore-ſhip, laden with cannon and ammunition, called the Rehoboam. In the month of July he was detached to cruiſe off Cape Prior for the purpoſe of intercepting any veſſels that might be paſſing from any of the Spaniſh ports to Ferrol or Corunna.

He did not meet with any very extraordinary ſucceſs during the time he was thus employed, having only captured a ſmall brigantine, from Rebadrus, laden with lime for the garriſon of Corunna, and driven on ſhore four Spaniſh barks, with a ſimilar lading, under Cape Prior. After ſounding the different bays, and reconnoitering the ports of Corunna and Ferrol, he was on his way to rejoin ſir John Norris, when, on the 15th of July, he fell in with a Portugueſe veſſel, which came the day before out of the harbour of Camaria, near Cape Finiſterre, having left there an Engliſh brigantine which had been captured and ſent in a few days before by a Spaniſh frigate of war, from the Havannah. Captain Harriſon immediately formed the ſpirited reſolution of attempting to cut the prize out of the harbour, with his boats manned and armed; but ere he he could carry this project into execution, he fell in with fir John Norris and the fleet. Having communicated his intentions to the admiral, he was ordered to purfue them; and, the better to enfure his fuccefs, was reinforced by the Gibraltar, a fmall frigate, which, from her fhallow draught of water, was peculiarly adapted to fupport fuch a kind of fervice. About ten o'clock the fame evening the boats went in, and boarded the floop, which being nearly dry, could not be brought off, and was therefore fet on fire. This fervice being accomplifhed, captain Harrifon proceeded, according to the admiral's inftructions, for the ifles of Bayonne, in the double hope of difcovering a convenient place to water at, and deftroying fome privateers which were faid to have taken fhelter there with feveral prizes they had taken. On the 18th he anchored within the iflands, and having accidentally met with the Grampus floop of war ordered that veffel to accompany him. Finding the intelligence he had received relative to the privateers to be erroneous, he came to a refolution, with the captains Cockburn and Parry, to proceed up to the town of Vigo, at break of day on the enfuing morning, in order to poffefs themfelves of, or deftroy fuch veffels as they might find there: but before the time arrived when this refolution was to have been executed, he received intelligence from a Portuguefe fchooner, out of which he obtained a pilot, that there were no fhips at Vigo itfelf, but at Redondella, which was very near it, there were five prizes. Captain Harrifon, in confequence of this intelligence, altered his fyftem of operations; and proceeding the next morning with the Gibraltar and Grampus to the place juft-mentioned, carried his plan of attack into execution with the greateft fuccefs, having brought off all the veffels he went up in queft of, and fent them to Oporto under convoy of the frigate and floop of war.

Captain Harrifon's fuccefs did not end with this very fpirited enterprife; continuing his cruife, he captured, in the month of Auguft, two other valuable prizes, which he fent to England under the protection of captain Martin, in the Affiftance. We do not find any farther particular mention made of him till the month of March

1743, when he was made captain of the Superbe, a sixty-gun ship. He did not long retain this station, from which he experienced a farther advancement, to the Monmouth, a third rate. In this ship he continued till the conclusion of the war. During the year 1745 we do not meet with any occurrence concerning this gentleman worth recording, but his having, in the month of May, been stationed as a cruiser in the Channel, in company with the Captain. While employed in the above service he captured a stout French privateer, carrying twenty guns and one hundred and sixty men, which had done considerable mischief to the British commerce. In 1747 he served under the admirals Anson and Warren, at the time they were sent out for the purpose of intercepting Jonquiere's squadron. The Monmouth was one of the vessels * detached after the convoy, when the action with the ships of war was ended by their capture. In this pursuit two merchant frigates, the Vigilant and Modeste, mounting twenty-two guns each, were taken.

From this time, till the conclusion of the war, captain Harrison appears to have been principally employed as a cruiser, for he was not one of the commanders under rear-admiral Hawke, when, towards the conclusion of the year, he defeated the second French squadron, under Mr. L'Etendiere, nor do we find any subsequent mention made of him till the month of February 1747-8. On the 2d of March he arrived at Plymouth with a large French privateer, called the Count de Maurepas, carrying twenty-eight carriage and swivel guns, with one hundred and thirty-six men, which he captured on the 19th of the preceding month, after a very long chace of three days continuance. In less than three weeks afterwards he captured another large French private ship of war, called the Rostan. This vessel belonged to Bourdeaux, and though carrying only twenty-two guns, had a crew amounting to no less than two hundred and seventy men; but having received much injury by the cannon-shot fired at her in the pursuit, she sunk before the prisoners were completely

---

* The others were the Yarmouth, captain Piercy Brett, and the Nottingham, captain Saumarez, both of whom had been Mr. Anson's lieutenants.

shifted, having, unfortunately, nine English seamen, together with one hundred of her own people on board, all of whom appear, unhappily, to have been drowned.

After the conclusion of the war Mr. Harrison appears to have lived totally in retirement, from the service, till the year 1755: he had then attained an advanced age, and the board of admiralty had it for that reason actually in contemplation, as it is said, to put this brave veteran on the superannuated list, as an officer past service: but when it became tolerably apparent to every person that a rupture with France must inevitably take place, he applied particularly for the command of his old ship, the Monmouth, quaintly observing, that he entertained no doubt of being able to patch that vessel, old and shattered as she was, so that she should last a year or two, which, he supposed would be at least as long as he himself should live. The admiralty changed their intention and appointed him to the ship he requested. He sailed under the command of sir Edw. Hawke, in the course of the current summer, on a cruise in the Bay of Biscay. He distinguished himself by his activity during the period of his being thus employed, more especially in the pursuit of some very valuable French ships from Martinico. Nothing, however, very particular appears to have taken place during the time he continued in the station of a private captain.

In the month of June 1756, he was advanced to be rear-admiral of the blue, and appointed to command at the port of Plymouth, he having hoisted his flag on board the Monmouth, still continuing in his old ship. In such a situation no very material or interesting occurrence could be expected, nor any other means of adding to that degree of reputation he had already so justly acquired, except by his diligence and careful attention to what may, with some propriety, be called the civil duties of his situation; these were always as conspicuous, as when a younger man, and in active service, his gallantry and spirit constantly had been. In 1758 he was advanced to vice-admiral of the blue, as he was, moreover, early in the ensuing year, to be vice of the red. This promotion he did not long enjoy, dying, in an advanced age, on the 13th of March in the same year. From his having for so long a space of time continued in the Monmouth, he was
face-

facetioufly diftinguifhed, by the wits in the]fervice, under the jocular and honourable name of Harry of Monmouth. As well by his exemplary conduct as by the intrinfic merit of his fervices, he acquired the efteem and refpect of all his cotemporaries, dying univerfally regretted by them as a warm friend, an able commander, and, what is a ftill greater character, an honeft man.

HEWET, Sir William *,—was the fon of William Hewet of St. Neots, efq. which William laft-mentioned

---

* The family of Hewet is of ancient extraction. There was a fir Walter Hewet, who made a confiderable figure in Edward the IIId's wars, in France. Vide Barne's Edw. IIId. p. 652. and other places. Of this family was fir William Hewet, lord mayor of London, 1559, but whether brother to this Robert is not certain. Of this fir William we find the following remarkable hiftory in Stow's Survey of London, vol. ii. b. 5. p. 133.

" Sir William Hewet, cloth-worker, mayor 1559, fon to Edmond Hewet, of Wales, in Yorkfhire; he died the 6th of February 1566. His wife was the daughter of Levefon, of Kent.

" This mayor was a merchant poffeft of a great eftate, valued at 6000 l. *per* annum, and was faid to have had three fons and one daughter, to which daughter this mifchance happened (the father then living upon London bridge) the maid playing with her out of a window over the river Thames, by chance dropt her in. Almoft beyond expectation of being faved, a young gentleman, named Ofborne, the apprentice to fir William, the father, (which Ofborne was one of the anceftors of the duke of Leeds, in a direct line) at this calamitous accident, immediately leaped in bravely, and faved the child. In memory of this deliverance, as well as in gratitude, her father afterwards beftowed her in marriage on the faid Mr. Ofborne, with a very great dowry, whereof the late eftate of fir Thomas Fanfhaw, in the parifh of Barkin, in Effex, was a part, as the late duke of Leeds himfelf told the reverend Mr. John Hewet, from whom I have this relation, and, together with that eftate in Effex, feveral other lands in the parifhes of Harthil and Wales, in Yorkfhire, now in the poffeffion of the faid moft noble family. All this from the old duke's own mouth, to the faid Mr. Hewet.

" Alfo, that feveral perfons of quality courted the faid young lady, and particularly the earl of Shrewfbury; but fir William was pleafed to fay, Ofborne faved her, and Ofborne fhould enjoy her. The late duke of Leeds, and the prefent family, preferve the picture of the faid fir William, in his habit of lord mayor, at Kiveton-houfe, in Yorkfhire, to this day, valuing it at 200 l.

" Of the fame family was Robert Hewet, efq. who poffeffed a confiderable eftate at Killamarch, in Derbyfhire, in the reign of Henry VIII. He left two fons; Robert, who died without iffue, and William, who fucceeded his father: the latter died 1599, aged feventy-feven, and is buried in St. Paul's cathedral, London."

was the great-grandson of sir John Hewet, of Headley Hall, in the county of York, baronet, so created October 11, an. 1621, temp. Jac. Ist. On the death of his uncle, sir John, on the 3d of February 1737, without issue, he succeeded to the title. This gentleman had entered into the navy before the time of queen Anne's death, and had been promoted to the rank of lieutenant about the year 1716, without experiencing for many years any farther advancement. In the month of July 1740, not long after the commencement of the war with Spain, he was promoted to be commander of the Basilisk bomb-ketch, from which vessel he was still farther advanced, on the 29th of November, to be captain of the Colchester, a fourth rate of forty guns; rear-admiral Hardy, through mistake, gives us the Sandwich as the ship in which he first took rank as a post captain. He was not long afterwards ordered to convoy the outward-bound fleet to Virginia*, and on his return was promoted to the Winchester, of fifty guns, in the month of May 1744. From this ship, on the 26th of July, he was advanced to the command of the Princess Louisa. No mention is made of any particular occurrence having taken place during the time he held either of the two foregoing commands; nor have we any other particulars concerning him, except that he was one of the masters of the court-martial convened for the trial of Mr. Lestock. He died, in England, on the 22d of May 1749, having been, as we believe, for some time unemployed.

He married Elizabeth, daughter of Mr. Levermore, of Gosport, in the county of Southampton. By her we know him to have had three sons, William, Levermore, and Herbert.

HOLBURNE, Francis, — was the descendant of a respectable family in Scotland, the representative of which had been advanced to the rank of baronet, by queen Anne, in the year 1706. Having entered into the navy and served for some time as a lieutenant, particularly on

---

*. He is said to have been appointed captain of the Sandwich, a second rate, in the month of July 1742. If this information is true, as we believe it to be, he could only have retained that command a short time.

board the Namur, to which ship he was appointed in the month of August 1732, he was, in August 1739, advanced to be commander of the Swift sloop of war. He was from thence, in the month of January 1740, removed into the Trial, a vessel of the same description; and was quickly afterwards, on the 15th of February ensuing, promoted to be captain of the Dolphin frigate. During a part of the time Mr. Holburne held this command he was employed to cruise in the Channel, where he had no other good fortune than that of capturing two small Spanish privateers, one, called the Nuestra Senora del Carmin, mounting six carriage and four swivel guns, with a crew of forty men; the other, of six guns, and forty-four men. In 1741 he was sent on the Leith station, which being farther removed from the track of the enemy he appears to have had still less success, no mention being made of him during the above time.

In 1742, having returned back to the Channel service, he, in the month of June, captured and carried into Plymouth a stout privateer, called the St. Juan Baptiste, of eighteen carriage and fourteen swivel guns, with a crew of upwards of one hundred men. On his quitting the Dolphin we believe him to have been promoted, first to the Argyle, a fourth rate of fifty, and quickly afterwards to the Rippon, of sixty guns; but no mention is made either of the station or service on which he was employed during the time he held those commands. In the month of December 1747, he was advanced from the Rippon to the Kent, as successor to captain Fox. In the beginning of the month of January 1748, he sailed under admiral Hawke for the Bay, and continued to be employed on the same station and service till the conclusion of the war: but, as has been already remarked in the memoirs of the commander-in-chief, nothing in any degree worthy relating took place during that period, except the capture of the Magnanime, in which Mr. Holburne was not personally concerned.

Soon after the ratification of the articles of peace, Mr. Holburne was made commodore, as it is said, of a small squadron ordered to the West Indies: we do not, however, believe this appointment to have been more than titular, and what is commonly bestowed on all senior captains

captains commanding detachments. We find him sent to the West Indies about the month of January 1750, having under him the Rose frigate and Jamaica sloop, being dispatched thither with the orders of the king of France, transmitted through the British ambassador at Paris, to M. Caylus, governor of Martinico, commanding him immediately to evacuate the islands of St. Lucia, Dominica, St. Vincents, and Tobago. On Mr. Holburne's arrival at the place of his destination, he was not a little surprised at being forbid landing, but he nevertheless insisted on delivering his dispatches, which he immediately sent by his secretary, accompanied by captain Bladwell of the Rose frigate. The officer who received them declared he acted only in conformity to the orders of M. Caylus, the governor, whom he represented to be in the country at a considerable distance from his usual place of residence, but that a final answer should be returned in twelve hours.

This was merely a finesse to gain time, for the governor was then actually on the spot; and, after some consultation, sent very impertinent peremptory orders for Mr. Holburne to withdraw immediately with his ships, as he had no instructions from his own court to comply with the requisition. Not having a sufficient force, or, indeed, authority to make any attempt at compelling this shuffling opponent to an act of bare national justice, he reluctantly complied. During the time he continued to be employed on that station he could only remonstrate and represent, instead of employing the more powerful arguments which would, in all probability, have been much more productive of success. We hear nothing of him after his return from this station * till the beginning of the year 1755. He at that time is said to have commanded the Ramillies, of ninety guns, one of the ships fitted out and collected at Portsmouth, in consequence of the behaviour of the French court, which became insufferable from the daily insults offered to the British flag. On February 5, he was advanced to the rank of rear-admiral of the blue, and

---

* He was succeeded by commodore Pye, who was appointed February 1752.

immediately afterwards hoifted his flag on board the fhip he had before commanded as a private captain.

He not long afterwards removed into the Terrible, on being appointed to command a fquadron ordered to America for the purpofe of reinforcing Mr. Bofcawen. He accordingly failed on the 11th of May, with the Terrible, Grafton, Yarmouth, Chichefter, Edinburgh, Augufta, and Arundel. Nothing material took place during the voyage to Halifax, where he arrived, after a very profperous and fpeedy paffage, on the 28th. Having watered his fquadron, and completed fome requifite points of refitment, he proceeded to join Mr. Bofcawen, whom he met off Louifburgh on the 21ft of June. The fubfequent events of this unintereſting naval campaign comprife nothing confequential enough to require particular mention, except that Mr. Holburne returning to England, with vice-admiral Bofcawen, and the fleet arrived fafe at Spithead on the 15th of November. We do not find any mention made of him, during the year 1756, except that he was, for a time, fecond in command of the fleet, ftationed off Breft, under Mr. Bofcawen, to watch the French fhips in that port, and was one of the members of the court-martial affembled for the trial of admiral Byng. In the beginning of the enfuing fummer, having been in the interim promoted, through the intermediate ranks, to be viceadmiral of the blue, he was appointed commander-inchief of the fleet ordered on the expedition againft Louifburg.

He failed from St. Helen's on the 16th of April; and after calling at Cork for fome tranfports which were lying there in order to join him, took his final departure from thence, with thirteen fhips of the line and the convoy on the 7th of May. Owing to the common impediments to the paffage of fo numerous a fleet, occafioned by contrary winds, and their natural confequences, he did not reach Halifax, in Nova Scotia, the appointed place of rendezvous, till the 9th of July. This deftructive, though, perhaps, unavoidable delay, following that which had taken place at home in fending out the fleet, rendered its arrival at the fcene of intended operations

tions * too late to hope for much fuccefs: but it has been farcaftically remarked, that the feafon was not yet fufficiently

---

* The following anonymous defence both of the admiral and general appears too temperate and fair to be omitted here.

The refentment expreffed by fome great perfons againft lord Loudoun and admiral Holburne, for not attempting a defcent on Cape Breton, feems to be very ill-grounded, becaufe our naval force was not only too fmall but difpatched too late in the year. Our operations againft Cape Breton fhould commence there with the fpring, not later than the end of March or the beginning of April; that is, they fhould begin as foon as the navigation to it is open and fafe; till that time, the fea is covered with thick fogs, and the harbours of Cape Breton are choaked with ice. The moment that thefe begin to clear away is the proper time for making a defcent; and it was wholly owing to our obferving and feizing it, that the New England men fucceeded in their gallant attempt; and whoever hopes for the fame fuccefs muft take the fame meafures, for the following reafons:

1ft. Becaufe a French army or fleet cannot winter in that inhofpitable part of the world; and, therefore, by attacking it earlier in the fpring before any reinforcements or fupplies can be received from Europe, we fhall take the French at a total difadvantage; whereas, if we delay but a little later than April, the enemy may be fo well provided againft our defign by reinforcement and fupplies, both from Europe and Quebec, as will make all our efforts ineffectual.

2d. The fleet and army therefore which fhall be deftined to conquer Louifbourg muft winter in North America, part at Bofton, part at Annapolis Royal, and part at Halifax; there the men will be comfortably lodged, and fupplied with all the neceffaries, and even the conveniencies of life, at a much cheaper rate than they can at home. Thus they will turn out healthy and vigorous in the fpring, ready to enter on brifk action before any fhips can ftir from France or England. The king's fhips and tranfports can lie fafe, and be as well cleaned, repaired, careened, or even docked in America, efpecially at Halifax, as in England, provided 1000 or 1500l. be laid out in re-building the docks and wharfs. Many naval ftores can be purchafed there for two-thirds of the money they coft here, and the price of all thefe things paid to Britifh fubjects. Thus, and not otherwife, will the fleet, with the army, be ready and in good order to proceed on the attack early in the fpring, before the French from Europe, or from Quebec, can have reinforced the place.

It appears, therefore, that lord Loudoun ought to have been enabled to begin his operations againft Louifbourg in April, whereas admiral Holburne, without whofe affiftance he could not proceed, did not arrive till July 9. He ought to have landed on Cape Breton before any fhips of war from France or Quebec could get there to annoy his troops in their debarkation: inftead of that, the annexed lift will fhew that there were eighteen capital fhips in Louifbourg harbour, ten days before admiral Holburne arrived at Halifax. He ought to have been affifted

sufficiently advanced to preclude all hope of a fortunate issue to the expedition, and a considerable time was, unne-

---

assisted by a naval force superior, at least equal, to the French fleet; whereas, it appears by the list, the French were very superior to him in the number of their capital ships, carrying a greater number of guns, all of much heavier metal, and larger calibres, than those of the British fleet. His first intelligence was, indeed, that there were only seven capital ships of war in the harbour of Louisbourg; upon which, tho' such a force was capable of gauling his troops most terribly in their landing, yet he embarked them in order to dispute the point; but captain Edwards, on the Newfoundland station, taking an advice boat about the same time, sent him a true account of the French strength: whereupon a council of war being called, consisting of both land and sea officers, it was agreed unanimously, excepting only one dissenting vote, that the attempt was impracticable at that time; and, in such circumstances, what other resolution could the bravest man, endued with common prudence, come to; suppose, that on being informed of the French naval force, and that there were 3500 regulars in garrison at Louisbourg, (which was the case) they had nevertheless ventured to make the intended descent, what could they in reason expect, but that the French fleet would come out, defeat admiral Holburne, and then sink or destroy all our transports, with 11,000 land-forces on board? The consequence would have been the immediate and utter loss of the whole colony of New York first, and then of all North America: this would have been a decisive blow to the whole British interest in that part of the world. If this was what any man of cool thought would and must expect to be the event, lord Loudoun, and every officer who voted for deferring the attack of Cape Breton, in such circumstances, deserves, instead of censure, the same encomiums that were bestowed by the Romans, on Quintus Fabius Maximus, *qui cunctando restituit rem*, instead of desperately attacking Hannibal when he had no chance of victory.

He is indeed blamed for wasting time in frequent councils of war, instead of going upon action immediately: but is there a man who will say, it would have been prudent in him to put every thing to the risque without endeavouring to get any intelligence? It is also said, that the French fleet was so greatly weakened by sickness that it could have made very little opposition: but supposing this to be true, how could lord Loudoun, or admiral Holburne, know it? They were indeed informed, by a fisherman, that the French crews were sickly, yet not so sickly as to render them despicable enemies. Besides, we see how little the intelligence of fishermen was to be depended upon, for they said there were but seven sail of French ships in the harbour, when there were eighteen of the line, and six frigates from twenty-six to 40 guns. Some think it extraordinary that admiral Holburne should venture up to Louisbourg, and cruize off the port with only five or six ships of the line, and yet think it imprudent to go up with his whole force and the transports; but they do not rightly consider the difference,

had

unneceffarily confumed, at Halifax, in exercifing the troops, in order to accuftom them to the different

had the French come out with a fuperior force. In one cafe he might have made at worft a running fight of it; but, in the other, what would have become of the tranfports and land forces? he muft either have left them to perifh by themfelves, or have perifhed with them.

To conclude, the conduct of lord Loudoun and admiral Holburne feems not only juftifiable, but commendable; and, inftead of being recalled, they ought to be ordered to winter in North America, that they may be ready to act early in the fpring.

The comparative force of the different fleets will be clearly feen by the following fubjoined lifts.

ENGLISH.

Ships.	Guns.	Ships.	Guns.
Newark	80	Defiance	60
Invincible	74	Tilbury	60
Terrible	74	Windfor	60
Northumberland	70	Centurion	54
Grafton	68	Sutherland	50
Orford	68		
Bedford	64		1090
Captain	64	Five twenty-gun fhips	100
Naffau	64	Six floops	72
Nottingham	60		
Kingfton	60	In all	1262
Sunderland	60		

N. B. July 9, admiral Holburne arrived with fourteen fail of the above fhips, together with the twenty-gun fhips and floops. The Windfor arrived Auguft 4, in the afternoon of that day the refolution of abandoning the enterprize was taken.

FRENCH.

Ships.	Guns.	Ships.	Guns.
June 4, arrived M. Reveft with		Le Superbe	74
Le Hector	72	Le Glorieux	74
L'Achille	64	Le Heros	74
Le Vaillant	64	Le Dauphin Royal	70
Le Sage	64	Le Belliqueux	64
		Le Celebre	64
June 5, arrived M. Beaufremont with		Le Bizarre	64
L'Etonnant	80		1270
Le Defenfeur	74	FRIGATES.	
Le Diademe	74	La Brune	36
L'Inflexible	64	Le Bien Acquis	40
L'Eveille	64	La Comete	30
		La Hermione	26
June 29, arrived de la Mothe with		La Coquine Flute	36
		La Fortune de Lis	36
Le Duc de Bourgogne	80		
Le Formidable	84	In all	1474

manœuvres

manoeuvres and modes of attack they might probably be required to execute when called into actual service.

The troops were at last embarked, and ready to proceed by the 1st of August; but while the fleet was on its passage, a French packet was, as it is presumed, thrown purposely in its way, and captured. By the dispatches which were found on board her, the commanders-in-chief were informed there was a naval force, amounting to seventeen ships of the line and three frigates in the harbour of Louisburg; that the town was defended by a formidable land force, consisting of six thousand Europeans, three thousand colonial troops, together with three hundred Indians; that the magazines were plentifully stored with provisions and ammunition of all kinds. The receipt of this intelligence necessarily produced a council of war, in which it was almost unanimously resolved to abandon the expedition. The troops were immediately sent back, but admiral Holburne continued cruizing with the fleet off Cape Breton. On the 20th he was off Louisburg, and within two miles of the entrance of the harbour, so that he could distinctly see the French admiral make the signal to unmoor: but being far inferior in force, he immediately retired to Halifax, where, being reinforced by four ships of the line, he returned to his former station in hopes of enticing the French to stand out to sea and engage him.

The admiral was not fortunate enough to succeed; and, continuing in the same occupation, was, on the 25th of September, overtaken by a most tremendous storm or hurricane, which continued upwards of fourteen hours. When the gale commenced the fleet were at an offing of nearly forty leagues from the shore, and when it abated was driven within two miles of the breakers: even then, had not the wind suddenly and providentially shifted, the whole fleet would in all probability have been driven on shore and totally lost. As it was the ships were dispersed and exceedingly shattered; the Tilbury was driven on shore and wrecked; the Grafton totally disabled, her rudder beaten off, and the ship otherwise so much damaged that her preservation was considered as almost miraculous: several other ships were nearly wrecked, and the whole squadron so much damaged that the admiral, with such ships as he could collect, was obliged to make for England as expeditiously as possible.

Mr. Holburne arrived at Spithead on the 7th of December, and was quickly afterwards appointed port admiral at Portsmouth. On the 7th of February following he was promoted to be vice-admiral of the white, and continued employed in the above uninteresting manner during the usual term for which such appointments are generally held; but is no otherwise mentioned than as having been, in the month of February 1759, advanced to be vice-admiral of the red. He struck his flag, and quitted his command on the 1st of November 1761, and does not appear to have held any naval appointment after that time. In the first parliament assembled after the accession of his present majesty, he was chosen representative for the united burghs of Sterling, Innerskeithen, &c. and in the ensuing parliament was chosen member for the town of Plymouth, a station he continued to retain till his death. About the year 1766, he was advanced to be admiral of the blue. Honours and appointments began not long after that time to flow rapidly in upon him. On the 24th of February 1770, he was nominated one of the commissioners for executing the office of lord high admiral; and on the 28th of October following was promoted to the rank of admiral of the white; about the same time he received the civil appointment of rear-admiral of Great Britain, as successor to sir Charles Knowles, who had resigned a little time before, on accepting a command in the Russian service. Early in the year 1771 he was made governor of Greenwich-hospital, an honour he did not long live to enjoy, dying, on the 15th of July following, at the age of sixty-seven. He married ———, widow of Edward Lascelles, esq. collector of the island of Barbadoes, and father to the present lord Harewood. By this lady he left one son, the present sir Francis Holburne, who succeeded to the title of baronet, in Scotland, on the death of sir Alexander Holburne, his cousin.

The character of this gentleman has been as variously represented by his friends and enemies as that of any of his predecessors or cotemporaries. An elevated station rarely fails to give birth to controversies of this nature, and few instances occur where public opinion is not oppositely,

and,

and, generally speaking, unwarrantably divided. An anecdote of him, which has been related to us from the best authority, is, however, too honourable to his character to be omitted in this place. During his passage to England, from America, we believe from Louisburg, in which, as it is well known, he encountered a most violent and tremendous tempest, he had observed a young officer particularly diligent, active, and useful on so trying an occasion; but at the same time had taken notice of his striking several of the common men whom he thought slow or remiss in their duty. When the tempest had in some measure subsided, he sent for the young gentleman into his cabin, and addressed him in the following manner: "Sir, I have observed, with the greatest pleasure, your diligence and exertions; I shall, in consequence of them, use my utmost endeavours to procure your promotion, but if I ever know that you again strike a seaman, from that moment I renounce you—you will lose all pretensions to my favour and friendship."

HOLCOMBE, Essex*,—was, on the 12th of October 1740, appointed captain of the Winchelsea frigate, one of the vessels employed, immediately afterwards, in cruising at the entrance of the Channel, off Cape Finisterre. These services and stations were unhappily so unimportant, so little calculated to raise his fame and renown, that we do not find any other mention made of him, except that he was, after 1743-4, stationed in the Mediterranean as capt. of the Winchelsea. He continued there nearly the whole of the war; and, in April 1748, commanded the Nassau, of 70 guns. He was then employed in convoying to Corsica a small number of transports, having on board two battallions of Sardinian and one of Austrian troops; but peace being concluded soon afterwards, the interference of a foreign power became improper, so that we have nothing farther to relate, except the foregoing occurrence, the Corsicans and Genoese being, as it is elsewhere remarked, left to themselves. The Nassau was, in all probability, put out of commission, soon after its return to England, in

---

* He is said, in one account we have seen, to have commanded the Blast bomb-ketch in 1741; but we know not whether this circumstance is to be depended upon.

conse-

consequence of the cessation of hostilities; and captain Holcombe is not known to have had any subsequent appointment. He retired indeed from the service altogether about the year 1755, with the rank and half-pay of a rear-admiral on the superannuated list. He enjoyed this honourable proof of the estimation in which he had been held, as a good officer and worthy man, till the time of his death, which happened on the 29th of January 1770.

HUGHES, Sir Richard,—in the beginning of the year 1740, commanded the Anne Galley fireship, one of the small vessels attached to the fleet on the Mediterranean station, commanded by admiral Haddock. He was, on the 24th of October 1740, promoted to be captain of the Dursley Galley frigate, and continued on the same station many years, as will be presently seen. While he was captain of the Dursley Galley we find no other mention made of him than what is common to all officers employed in a similar unenviable manner during a war; he was totally occupied in attending on the fleet, and in short cruises, which afforded him no opportunity of acquiring either emolument or fame, as the presence of the British naval force confined to the harbours of the enemy all their smaller vessels, whether intended for the purposes of war or commerce.

About the beginning of the year 1742, we find him to have been promoted to the Feversham, of forty guns, one of the ships sent, in the month of August following, under commodore Martin, to remonstrate with the king of Naples; the particulars of which expedition have been already given at length in the account of the commodore *. We find no subsequent mention made of him till 1745, and he is then only noticed as having been captain of the Chatham, and one of the members composing the court-martial convened at Mahon, in the month of January, to enquire into the conduct of captain Richard Norris. In 1746 he was commodore of a small squadron, stationed off the coast of Italy by the commander-in-chief, and employed totally in cruising for the protection of commerce, or that of transports, with stores, for the use of the Imperial army. We find no farther account of him,

---

* Vol. iv. p. 72.

in the line of active service, except that he was sometime afterwards appointed captain of the Essex; and, in the month of February 1753, was commissioned to the Fougueux, of sixty-four guns, a guardship at Portsmouth.

In 1754 he retired totally from this line of service, being appointed commissioner-resident at Portsmouth, as successor to his father. This station he continued to fill with high reputation, and the approbation of all men, till the year 1773; when, in the month of June, he was created a baronet by his majesty, who made an excursion to Portsmouth at that time. He soon afterwards retired from all public functions on a pension of 500l. *per annum.* He died, as we believe, some time in the course of the year 1782.

JOLLY, Thomas,—was, on the 12th of May 1740, appointed captain of the Lively frigate: he was very soon afterwards, that is to say in the following month, promoted* to the Rippon, of sixty guns, one of the ships equipped, in the ensuing autumn, for the intended expedition against Carthagena. He was one of those unhappy commanders who fell victims to the unwholesomeness of that climate, dying there in the month of May 1741.

LIMEBURNER, Thomas,—was, on the 11th of July 1740, promoted, from being commander of a sloop of war, to be captain of the Seahorse frigate, at the special instance of Mr. Pultney afterwards earl of Bath, who, on his sailing almost immediately afterwards to the West Indies, recommended him to Mr. Vernon in the following warm terms. " This will be delivered to you by captain Limeburner, one whom sir Charles Wager preferred at my recommendation; you will find him, I dare say, a very sensible honest man; and if he be such, I am confident he will meet with your farther encouragement and protection." After his return to Europe he was promoted to the Hampshire, of fifty guns; but in some accounts he is erroneously stated to have been appointed to the Plymouth. The Hampshire was principally, if not entirely employed as a cruiser, a service in which captain Lime-

---

* He is said, but we believe erroneously, to have progressively commanded, for a short time, during the course of the summer, the Assistance, of fifty, and the Montague of sixty guns.

burner

burner appears to have been very alert. On the 9th of April he captured a stout Spanish privateer, called Le Galgo, mounting twenty-four carriage guns, and ten large patararoes, with a crew of one hundred and forty men; and on the 22d of January ensuing, two others, one of nearly the same force with the Galgo, the other of sixteen carriage and swivel guns, with one hundred and twenty-four men. No other mention is made of this gentleman except that he was afterwards appointed captain of the Fubbs yacht; in which station he died on the 5th of November 1750.

LISLE, William,—was the descendant of a very ancient and respectable family long settled in the county of Southampton, where they had very large possessions. The name is supposed to have been derived from that very circumstance, L'Isle-vel De L'Isle, the greater part of the Isle of Wight having, as it is said, formerly belonged to them. This gentleman was, on the 28th of May 1740, appointed captain of the Scarborough, a bomb-ketch; in which vessel he continued till the year 1743, if not till a later period*, he having been, at the time just mentioned, one of the commanders employed, under Mr. Knowles, at the different attacks of La Guira and Porto Cavallo. The appointments of this truly worthy and brave man were, for some time, so little consequential, that no mention whatever is made of him till the month of September 1746, when we find him to have commanded the Severn, of fifty guns, one of the ships which had been, previous to that time, on the West India station, where we believe captain Lisle to have commanded her. He was on his return to England, in company with the Woolwich, a ship of the same force, and a fleet of merchant ships under their convoy, when they unhappily fell in with a small French squadron of four ships, commanded by the well-known marquis de Conflans. Capt. Lisle defended himself with the greatest gallantry for two hours, when the very superior

---

* Previous to this time he was employed as a cruiser, and in the year 1742 drove on shore a privateer sloop, and sunk one of much more considerable consequence, mounting twenty-four guns, and manned with a very formidable crew, after a very smart action, off the island of Porto Rico.

force of the enemy compelled him to furrender. In the month of October 1747, being not long after he was exchanged, he was advanced to the command of the Vigilant, of fixty-four guns, one of the fquadron ordered for the Eaft Indies under the command of rear-admiral Bofcawen. The leading events of that expedition, even thofe in which captain Lifle was immediately concerned, have been already related in the life of the commander-in-chief*, fo that it is needlefs to attempt any repetition of them, or, to fay more than that he was appointed, during the courfe of it, an eftablifhed commodore with a broad pendant.

It was at one time determined he fhould continue in India as commander-in-chief after the return of Mr. Bofcawen to England, as appears from the following extract of a letter from Gombroon, dated Feb. 11, 1750. " Captain Lifle is ordered to hoift a broad pendant in India, where he is to ftay three years, and to difpofe the fhips under his command to fuch parts of India as may be thought beft for the company's intereft." He did not, however, continue on his ftation during fo long a period; but died at the Cape of Good Hope, when on his return to England, on the 26th of January 1752. He had been long and moft grievoufly afflicted with the gout, which we believe to have been an hereditary diforder, and was attacked on his paffage by a moft violent fit, which feized him both in his head, and feet. When he arrived at the Cape it was recommended to him to ufe a hot bath. He declared himfelf perfectly ready to comply with the advice, becaufe, if he rejected it, he might probably incur the charge of obftinacy; but he at the fame time expreffed a firm perfuafion, that he fhould not furvive the acquiefcence many minutes. The event fully and moft unfortunately proved the truth of the prediction. Soon as he was immerfed in the hot water his pains were inftantaneoufly affuaged, but, in a few moments after being taken out, he fell back and expired.

There is a traditional report that this gentleman, immediately after the commencement of hoftilities with Spain, being then captain of a bomb-veffel, unluckily fell

---

* See vol. iv. p. 316 et feq.

in with a Spanish ship of war, mounting forty guns or upwards. The enemy bore down to him as to a certain prize: Mr. Lisle was, however, too gallant and spirited an officer to surrender without making some effort to escape. By the dexterous management of his small vessel, and occasionally returning the fire of the enemy with the few guns he had, this purpose was happily effected: what also afforded an additional satisfaction, both to himself and his countrymen, was, that during the whole of this very difficult attempt, few, or none of his crew were either killed or wounded. Such is the outline with which we have been furnished of this highly honourable transaction; and we can only lament not being able to relate it more particularly and minutely.

MARTIN, Roger,—was, on the 24th of September 1740, appointed captain of the Litchfield, of fifty guns. In this ship he did not continue longer than the month of November, being then succeeded by captain Cleland. He was next appointed to the Assistance, and ordered out on a cruise; during which, in the month of August 1741, we find him to have captured, and brought into Spithead, two valuable Spanish prizes, one called the Conception, the other the St. Dominic.

Extraordinary as it may appear, we have no other particulars concerning him, except that, in the month of December 1747, he was one of the members of the court-martial, convened at Portsmouth, for the trial of captain Fox, of the Kent; so that it is very evident he was at that time in actual service. In the month of February 1753, he was commissioned to the Monarch, a guardship of seventy-four guns, at Portsmouth. In March 1755, he was appointed captain of the Royal George, a command he retained till the month of May 1756, when he retired on the rank and half-pay of a rear-admiral. He died about the year 1779.

MAYNARD, Robert,—was, on the 22d of September 1740, promoted, by admiral Vernon, to be captain of the Sheerness frigate; but we find no other mention made of him. In the month of March 1742, he was advanced to th command of the Antelope, of fifty guns, and not improbably ordered soon afterwards for the Mediterranean, where we find him, in the month of January 1745, one
of

of the members of the court-martial convened for the trial of captain Richard Norris; and it appears he at that time continued to command the Antelope. No other particulars concerning this gentleman have come to our knowlege, except that he died in England fometime in the courfe of the year 1750.

MITCHELL, Matthew,—was, on the 3eth of June 1740, appointed to command the Pearl, of forty guns, one of the fhips compofing the fmall fquadron then under orders for the South Seas. When the fhips arrived at Madeira, captain Norris, at that time commander of the Gloucefter, applied for leave to return to England in confequence of ill health, which he alledged prevented him from proceeding on fo long a voyage. This requeft was immediately complied with by commodore Anfon, who appointed captain Mitchell to command the Gloucefter in his room. The fubfequent events of this alternately difaftrous and fortunate expedition having been already given at fome length in our account of Mr. Anfon, fo that it is needlefs to add much more, than that captain Mitchell and his unfortunate fhip, having narrowly efcaped being burnt, having afterwards encountered a feries of difficulties and hardfhips almoft incredible in the paffage round Cape Horn, at laft got fight of the ifland of Juan Fernandez on the 21ft of June. The crew was by this time fo much reduced by the fcurvy, that had not the commodore, who had reached that hofpitable fpot fome days before, difpatched his long boat with water and vegetables, the miferable remnant that ftill remained alive muft have perifhed of abfolute thirft. They had been for fome time at an allowance of a pint a day to each man; and even that fcanty fupply would have been exhaufted in the next twenty-four hours.

Though they had fo nearly reached the point, where not only the ravages of difeafe were likely to be put an end to, but where they alfo might be certain of procuring relief to their other wants and neceffities, the meafure of their diftrefs was not yet full, that wretched crew were tantalized for upwards a month with an occafional fight of the ifland without being able to reach it, fome days driven to fuch a diftance as almoft to reduce them to the extremity of defpair, that they fhould never be able to re-meafure

back

back their courſe, attacked as they were at different times, in their diſabled crippled veſſel, by ſuch violent guſts of wind, that they were under momentary apprehenſions of foundering. At length, on the 23d of July, they ſucceeded in getting round the north-weſt point of the bay; and having received a reinforcement of recovered men from the commodore, were fortunate enough to bring their crazy veſſel to an anchor, in little more than an hour from the time their more fortunate comrades on ſhore conſidered their arrival as certain. This ill-fated crew was reduced to eighty-two perſons; but happily, though the diſtreſs they had experienced previous to their arrival had been infinitely greater than that which their comrades, on board the commodore's ſhip, had encountered, their mortality ceaſed almoſt immediately on their landing, a circumſtance ſuppoſed to be attributable to the violence of the diſeaſe being mitigated by the vegetables and freſh water ſent to them, by Mr. Anſon, when the ſhip was firſt diſcovered. The Anna Pink victualler being condemned as unfit for ſervice, her crew, conſiſting of eleven perſons, including the maſter, were turned over to the Glouceſter as a reinforcement, as were alſo twenty-three ſailers and ſix paſſengers, from on board the Carmelo, a Spaniſh prize captured by the Centurion.

The commodore ſailed, as has been already related in our account of him, on the 19th of September, leaving inſtructions for captain Mitchel to follow him, when his ſhip ſhould be as well re-equipped as circumſtances would admit of, and cruiſe off the iſland of Paita till the Centurion ſhould join him. The Glouceſter, during this interval, captured only two ſmall veſſels, one of them a ſnow, the other a Spaniſh launch, or large boat; their cargoes were, conſequently, inconſiderable; but, as is frequently the caſe in thoſe ſeas with prizes, that might on their firſt ſeizure be deemed too inſignificant to anſwer the trouble of taking poſſeſſion, they were found, on examination, to have ſpecie on board to the amount of nearly 20,000l*. Mr. Anſon, who in the interim had burnt the town of Paita, joined captain Mitchel on the 18th of November: and nothing material took place, in addition

---

* The ſnow 7,000l; the launch 10,000l.

to what has been already related, till the beginning of the month of August following (1742). At this time the Gloucester, unfortunate almost from the hour of quitting St. Hellen's, after having considerably retarded the Centurion, on their passage from South America to the Ladrone islands, had the additional misfortune to lose both her fore and main-top-masts in a gale of wind: she was, moreover, so leaky as to have seven feet water in her hold. The wind at this time rose almost to an hurricane; and the Centurion herself sprung a leak. Though under such circumstances the administration of any relief was next to an impossibility, yet Mr. Anson sent his boat on board, by which captain Mitchell returned an instrument, signed by himself and the rest of his officers, stating, " that the leaks were irreparable at sea; that he needed spare top-masts to get up in the place of those which had been carried away; that many of the knees and clamps were loose, and the quarter-deck ready to drop down; that the crew, notwithstanding several trivial reinforcements, was reduced to ninety-seven men, officers and prisoners included, with eighteen boys, out of which number, which had they been all in health, was in itself extremely inconsiderable for the bare purpose of navigating so large a ship, there were only sixteen men and eleven boys able to keep the deck, many of which were very infirm; that provisions and fresh water could not be got at without extreme difficulty, the ship having then in her hold seven feet water, which was hourly encreasing." This deplorable statement being immediately authenticated by a regular survey, captain Mitchel was directed to remove his people, together with such valuables and stores as he could get at, on board the Centurion, and then destroy his ship.

Two days were unavoidably consumed in this operation, which, under more favourable circumstances, might almost have been accomplished in as many hours. It was not without much difficulty that the specie was saved; but nearly the whole of the prize-goods which were on board her, and were of very considerable value, were abandoned to the same unfortunate fate as the vessel which contained them. Even of the provisions, five casks of flour could only be preserved, and three of them were damaged by the salt water. Of the sick, amounting in number

number to upwards of seventy persons, three or four expired in the act of being conveyed on board the Centurion, notwithstanding all possible tenderness was used in their removal. The ship was set on fire, and, after burning all night, blew up with a very inconsiderable report, the Centurion being at that time about four leagues distant.

Captain Mitchel continued on board the Centurion till after the arrival of that ship at China: he from thence took his passage in a Swedish ship, bound from Macao for Europe. On his arrival, about the month of June 1743, he was received with much attention by administration, and was not long afterwards appointed captain of the Worcester. In 1746 he was commodore of a small squadron, stationed off the coast of Flanders for the purpose of preventing any supplies passing from Dunkirk, and other ports in that neighbourhood, for the support of the rebel army in Scotland*. He was singularly active † and successful in this employment, and remained on the same station nearly till the conclusion of the war. A short time after the general election, in 1747, he was elected representative in parliament for the borough of Westbury, but did not long continue to fill the station of a senator, dying, in the prime of life, on the 29th of April 1752.

He married, on the 4th of March 1749, Frances, daughter of —— Ashfordby, esq. of Norfolk-street, London, with whom, it is said, he received a fortune of 20,000l.

MURRAY, Honourable George,—was the second son of George, fourth lord Elibank, and Elizabeth, daughter of Mr. George Stirling, of Edinburgh. The first mention we find made of him in the naval service, to which he betook himself early in life, is in the month of July 1740,

---

* The Hazard sloop, afterwards captured on the coast of Scotland, is particularly mentioned as having been obliged, by the commodore's vigilance, with his cruisers, to put back six different times; but at last, and then too unfortunately for herself, succeeded in consequence of a very thick fog, which completely shrouded her from his sight.

† At the latter end of May 1746, he drove on shore a French frigate, mounting twenty-four guns; and, in a very few days afterwards, a large armed cutter belonging to the same nation.

at which time he commanded the Trial sloop of war, a small vessel attached to the squadron sent to the South Seas, under the orders of Mr. Anson. On the arrival of this force at Madeira, and the return of Mr. Norris, captain of the Gloucester, to England, Mr. Murray was advanced to be captain of the Wager, on the 3d of November 1740, as successor to captain Kidd, who was promoted to the Pearl. On the death of this gentleman, on the 31st of January 1740-1, he again followed him as successor into the Pearl. The subsequent distresses of this unfortunate squadron are well known: the Pearl and Severn, after having for a considerable time combated against difficulties, daily encreasing and growing more formidable, were at length compelled to put back, having lost sight of the squadron on the 10th of March, about a month after they had passed the Streights Le Maire.

After combating, for the space of nearly forty days, with a storm almost continual, they were fortunate enough to get into Rio Janeiro on the 6th of June, their ships much disabled, and the crews considerably diminished by sickness and death, induced by the scurvy and excessive fatigue: they were afterwards, however, fortunate enough to reach England * without experiencing any sinister accident. The first particular mention we find made of this gentleman, after his fortunate return, is his appointment, in the month of October 1743, to be captain of the Hampshire, a fourth rate of fifty guns. He was soon afterwards ordered to the Mediterranean, where we find him, in the month of January 1745, one of the court martial assembled on board the Torbay, at Mahon, for the purpose of examining the conduct of captain Richard Norris. We do not discover any other notice taken of him till the month of May 1755, when he was appointed captain of the Trident, as he was soon afterwards of the Revenge. He did not long retain this command, and retired from the service early in the following year. In the month of May he was advanced to the rank of rear-admiral on the superannuated list. By the death of his elder brother, sometime in the year 1781,

---

* They sailed from Rio Janeiro for Barbadoes, where they arrived February the 5th, 1742.

he succeeded to the title of lord Elibank. He himself died, at Ballinerig in Scotland, on the 11th of November 1785.

NORRIS, Harry, — was the youngest son of admiral sir John Norris. He was promoted, on the 26th of September 1740, to be captain of the Ruffel: other accounts however assert, that his first appointment was to a frigate, of twenty guns. We find no other mention made of him till the month of March 1743, when he was made captain of the Jersey, a fourth rate of sixty guns. No particular or interesting circumstance is recorded of him during the time he held this command, in which he indeed, at farthest, continued only till the end of the year 1744. He was then advanced to the Prince Frederic, a third rate of seventy guns, employed, during the ensuing year, on the home station, where, notwithstanding the rebellion had, at the instigation of the French court, taken place in Scotland, very few occurrences of note took place in the department of naval war, so that we find no notice taken of him, except his having been a member of the court-martial held for the trial of commodore Griffin and the captains under his command, on the 31st of January. In the month of February 1746, he was ordered, with some other ships, to cruise at the entrance of the Channel, where he had the good fortune to capture, after a long chace, a large French privateer belonging to St. Maloe's, mounting twenty-two guns. He retained the same command till the conclusion of the war, and being at that time in the Prince Frederic, was one of the commanders, under the orders of the admirals Anson and Warren, at the defeat of the French fleet off Cape Finisterre.

Nothing farther is said of this gentleman till the month of March 1755, when he commanded the Yarmouth, of seventy guns, one of the ships fitted at Chatham in consequence of the expected rupture with France. This ship was one of those which were sent, under the command of Mr. Holburne, to North America, for the purpose of reinforcing Mr. Boscawen, in the month of May. Captain Norris accompanied him, continuing in me Yarmouth till he was promoted to a flag. This advancement took place in June 1756, to be rear-admiral of the white, as moreover, on the 31st of January 1758, to be rear of the red; and, on the 14th of February 1759, to be vice-admiral of the white: this appears to have been the higheſt rank he ever attained. Though very highly and deſervedly eſteemed by men of all ranks, he was not, we believe, ever employed, as a flag officer, in active ſervice, except during a part of the year 1756, when he was one of the admirals commanding the fleet ſtationed off Breſt*. He did not long ſurvive the concluſion of the peace in 1763, dying, much regretted, on the 13th of June 1764.

OSBORNE, Peter, — was the brother of admiral Henry Oſborne, of whom we have already given ſome account. At the end of the year 1739 this gentleman was lieutenant of the Affiſtance; from thence he was, on the 28th of July 1740, promoted to be captain of the ſame ſhip. He was, in the enſuing month removed into the Diamond frigate as ſucceſſor to captain Knowles, and out of that ſhip was, in the month of September, made captain of the Saliſbury. He was very ſoon afterwards ordered to Cork, and from thence to the Mediterranean, where he continued ſeveral years ſerving progreſſively under the admirals Haddock and Mathews. We find, however, no other particular mention made of him, except his having been left, by commodore Martin, in the month of September 1742, together with the captains Weſt and Balchen, for the protection of the port of Leghorn. After his return to England, and the concluſion of the war, he was, in the year 1750, appointed one of the captains in the Greenwich-hoſpital, a ſtation he conſequently retained till his death, an event that happened on the 24th of February 1754.

PETT, Robert,—a deſcendant of ſir Phineas Pett, was, on the 15th of July, promoted from the ſtation of lieutenant, to be captain of the Bridgewater, of twenty-guns. During the remainder of the current, and a part of the enſuing year, this ſhip was ſtationed as a cruiſer in the German Ocean: from the above ſhip he was promoted to the Diamond, of forty guns. We hear nothing farther

---

* He was, in the month of December following, one of the members of the court-martial convened for the trial of Mr. Byng.

concerning

concerning him till the beginning of the year 1744, when we find him captain of the Princeſſa, of ſeventy guns, and ordered to the Mediterranean, with one or two other ſhips, as a reinforcement to the fleet under Mr. Mathews. He behaved with great gallantry and good conduct in the encounter with the French and Spaniſh fleets off Toulon; but no other mention, except his having been one of the members of the court-martial, aſſembled at Port Mahon, for the trial of captain Richard Norris, is made of him in the ſervice, except that, in the month of February 1753, he commanded the Invincible of ſeventy-four guns, a guard-ſhip at Portſmouth: he retired from it altogether in the year 1755, being appointed one of the commiſſioners of the victualling-office. He retained this ſtation till the year 1776; and then, being far advanced in years, retired from all public employment on a penſion of ſuperannuation. He ſurvived but a very ſhort time, dying on the 19th of October in the year laſt-mentioned.

PEYTON, Edward,—was, on the 4th of April 1740, appointed captain of the Greyhound frigate*. He was not long afterwards removed into the Kennington, a ſhip of the ſame force as the preceding. During the early part of his time of ſervice in that command he was principally employed in convoying the trade to and from Liſbon. He was afterwards ordered to the Mediterranean, where he continued ſome time; and on his return to England was promoted to the Medway, of ſixty guns, one of the ſmall ſquadron ſent to the Eaſt Indies, in the month of May 1744, under commodore Barnet. In a few days after the ſhips ſailed from the iſland of Madagaſcar, where they had put in for a ſupply of water and proviſions, captain Peyton in the Medway, together with captain Moore in the Diamond frigate, of twenty guns, parted company from the commodore, and proceeded to the ſtreights of Malacca. In their way thither they put into the port of Achin, where they captured a ſtout French privateer, fitted out purpoſely to cruiſe in the Chineſe

---

* During the time he held this command he was principally employed as a cruiſer; in which employment we do not find him particularly mentioned, except as the captor of the Potencia, a Spaniſh privateer, of twelve guns and eighty-eight men, which he carried into Gibraltar.

feas ; and fortune ftill favouring them in their paffage thro'
the Streights, made prize of a French merchant fhip
from Manilla, of confiderable value. Mr. Peyton proceeded foon after this fuccefs to Batavia, which was the
appointed place of rendezvous for the whole force.

On the death of commodore Barnet, a melancholy
event which took place on the 29th of April 1746, the
chief command devolved on Mr. Peyton, as the fenior
captain on that ftation; an honour which he had not long
enjoyed, when, on the 25th of June following he fell in
with the French fquadron, under the command of Mr.
Bourdonnais. This tranfaction having made confiderable
noife, we fhall be fomewhat particular in our account of
it, and the more fo becaufe the Eaft India company appear to have propagated, with no fmall degree of induftry,
a report highly injurious to the reputation of a brave and
worthy man. The official account, publifhed by government, is plain, fair, and concife. It ftates fimply, that
the Englifh fquadron, confifting of the Medway, of fixty
guns, captain Peyton; the Prefton, of fifty guns, lord
Northefk; the Harwich, of fifty guns, captain
Carteret; the Winchefter, of fifty guns, lord Thomas
Bertie; the Medway's Prize, of forty guns, captain
Griffith; and the Lively, of twenty guns, commanded by
captain Stevens, fell in with the French commodore, who
had his diftinguifhing pendant on board the Achilles, of
feventy-four guns; the Duke of Orleans and the Bourbon,
of fifty-fix; the Phœnix, Neptune, and St. Louis, of
forty-four; the Lys, of forty; the Infulaire, and another
fhip, name unknown, of twenty guns each. The
French, fays the account, put back to Pondicherry, having
fuffered much in men and rigging : *the Englifh men of war
alfo were much damaged, and the Medway got into Crankanella
to refit, being very leaky.*

It is evident from this ftatement, which is taken from
the beft authorities we have been able to procure, that
the French were, at leaft, one-fourth fuperior in point of
force, the number of guns in their fquadron amounting
to three hundred and ninety-eight; while that under Mr.
Peyton carried only two hundred and feventy; fo
that the complete defeat of the latter could not fairly have
reflected any difgrace on him. Neverthelefs, if any credit
is to be given to that account which, publifhed by thofe
who

who have the best opportunity of ascertaining, and becoming masters of the truth, is consequently deemed the most authentic of any existing, Mr. Bourdonnais was actually discomfited in the engagement and retired. The directors of the East India company were much dissatisfied with this transaction in the first paroxysms of their disappointment at not having so superior a force completely annihilated, they were driven almost to desperation by the fear of having their property and possessions plundered by a merciless enemy. At the same time not daring, or not honest enough to blame the true authors of the misfortune, had it really befallen them; transferring from administration at home all the blame of not having sent from Europe a sufficient force to protect their wealth, and unjustly sinking the delinquency, or miserable œconomy of their own servants, in not having equipped all the force in their power and put it under the command of Mr. Peyton, the better to have enabled him to counteract that of the *French East India company*, which had joined the French kings commodore; they vented at once their spleen and their fears in the following illiberal and sarcastic account of the transaction alluded to. Frequent instances of the same kind of unjust treatment, shewn by corporate bodies, to the bravest and most worthy men, occur in the English history.

" July the 25th, at day break, his majesty's squadron in Negapatam road, made signal for several ships in the offing, to which they went out, and found them to be nine French ships: the wind being light they could not get up with each other till half past four in the evening, at which time the engagement began, and lasted till about seven, when it grew dark. The two squadrons continued near one another all the next day. At four in the afternoon captain Peyton summoned a council of war, where it was agreed not to engage the enemy, but to proceed to Trincomalè bay, as the French did for Pondicherry, and arrived there on the 27th: fourteen were killed and forty-six wounded in the English squadron. The French squadron consisted of the Achilles, a seventy-gun ship; six company's ships, and two country ships.

" Captain Peyton kept the squadron at Trincomalè till the beginning of August, when he came on the coast,

and

and on the 6th appeared off Negapatam. The French fquadron, confifting of eight fhips (one being gone to Bengal, and fince loft in that river with two hundred and eighty Europeans) weighed from Pondicherry, July 24, for the fouthward, and ftood out to meet the Englifh fquadron, which ftood to the fouthward from them, and the French then returned. The 7th of Auguft both fquadrons did the fame; as likewife on the 8th and 9th. The 10th the Englifh difappeared; on which the French returned, and on the 13th anchored in Pondicherry road.

" The 17th the eight fhips weighed for Madrafs road, where they arrived the 18th, and fired on the fhip Princefs Mary, which was returned from the fhip and from the fort. Each fhip gave a broadfide as fhe ftood to the northward, and another as fhe returned, and then ftood to the fouthward again. We are fince informed the French had two motives for this expedition; one was to make a plea with the country government that the Englifh committed the firft hoftilities afhore; the other to fee if captain Peyton would come to our affiftance or not.

" The 25th captain Peyton, with the fquadron, ftood into Pullicat road, where he fent his lieutenant, Mr. Weymefs, on board a veffel in the road. He was there told of all the circumftances of their attacking the fhip Princefs Mary, and of their then being between Madrafs and Pondicherry. On this captain Peyton difappeared and has never been heard of, or from, by any of the Englifh, though there has been no coft, or pains, fpared for that purpofe, as may eafily be imagined from the fince melancholy fituation of affairs on the coaft. The laft letter received from any one belonging to the fquadron, was from captain Peyton, to governor Morfe, dated Auguft 4, when he was juft come out refitted.

" This unhappy conduct of his fo animated the French that they determined on attacking Fort St. George. We call it unhappy, becaufe it has truly proved fo in its confequence; though what reafons captain Peyton may have had for this proceeding we know not."

Mr. Campbell is ungenerous and prejudiced enough to join in the outcry, and remarks, " that although Mr. Peyton called a council of war, and that determined as councils generally do, not to fight; yet, when a commander-mander-in-chief, invested with full power to act by his sole authority, calls a council of war, it creates a strong suspicion that he wants to divide the blame of an unjustifiable action." He is afterwards particularly, and rather indecently sarcastic on the man who presumes to take such measures, in collecting the general opinion of those under his command: but however productive such counsels may, on some few occasions, have been, of events sinking below the public hope, yet, considering their general utility, we cannot but most pointedly dissent from the idea of any impropriety in convening them, on all occasions, like that now before us, where there exists even a doubt of success.

No particular occurrence took place after the above time till the arrival of Mr. Griffin, who superceded commodore Peyton and treated him with that asperity and cruelty which frequently attends the workings of a narrow and imbecile mind. He confined Mr. Peyton in the most degrading and insulting manner, sending him home immediately afterwards loaded with every restraint, and ignominious treatment, that could have been bestowed on a real delinquent of the blackest kind. Mr. Peyton on his arrival in England, dispelled, by his presence, the invidious clouds of envy, malice, and prejudice, which had been raised against him during his absence: the loudest of his enemies became silent; and the East India company, hardened as they were, even at that day, in the oppression of all who, they thought, had not courage, or power, sufficient to resist them, dared not to erect their former passionate and violent obloquy into any thing like a charge of misconduct: in short, he was accused by a shadow only, no one venturing to stand forth and prefer any thing like a specific charge. Mr. Peyton, not improbably oppressed with grief and indignation at the treatment he had experienced, did not long survive his return, dying on the 4th of April 1749.

Those who do not encourage the smallest shadow of superstition; those who are the greatest disbelievers of providential retribution, can scarcely reflect on the foregoing transaction, and the sequel of Mr. Griffin's life, without admitting that something more interesting than the common course of events, marks the conduct and fate of the latter. In all the authoritative pride and inso-
lence

lence of superior command, he was base enough to tyrannize over an innocent man, with whose guilt, suppoſing that really to have been the caſe, humanity ought to have ſympathiſed as an undone and unfortunate fellow creature. It is certainly the part of a noble mind to ſhed a tear of pity at the time it brandiſhes the ſword of juſtice; but the power even of legal puniſhment becomes tyranny in its moſt depraved and horrid form, when that puniſhment is aggravated by wanton inſult. It is not effaced from our recollection that Mr. Griffin, after an inglorious command on the ſame ſtation, fell under a charge of a ſimilar nature to that which had been haſtily and injuriouſly advanced againſt Mr. Peyton. There is this difference, however, in their fates; the charge againſt the latter was never ſubſtantiated, and the baſe imputation of impropriety might not a little contribute to ſhorten that life which it had rendered miſerable; while Mr. Griffin, againſt whom the ſame was fairly purſued, both to conviction and puniſhment, bore up againſt the cenſure of his countrymen and braved their indignation with the ſteadieſt and moſt ſtern effrontery: he ſought not even in retirement to render his diſgrace leſs remembered, by removing himſelf from the public ſight; but choſe rather to ſubmit to any conditions that could be impoſed on him, and enter into the meaſures of any cabal, for the purpoſe of procuring a diſhonourable reſtoration to that rank he had, in the opinion of his judges, forfeited, by his conduct, a rank which, however honourable in moſt inſtances, cannot confer honour on the poſſeſſor when obtained by any other means than the ſteady and invariable purſuit of honour and public virtue.

PURVIS, Charles Wager,—was a commander in the navy previous to the year 1738. In the month of May 1739, he was appointed to the Charlotte yacht; but ſtill continued, contrary to the preſent regulations of the naval ſervice, to have only the rank of a commander till the 18th of July 1740; he was then promoted to be captain of the Gibraltar, a ſmall frigate of twenty guns. He was employed for ſome little time after this as a cruiſer, in which ſervice he does not appear to have met with any extraordinary ſucceſs; and though he continued not in the ſame command longer than the enſuing ſpring, we do
not

not hear any thing farther of him till the beginning of the year 1744, when he commanded the Diamond, a fifth rate, attached to the fleet stationed in the Mediterranean under the chief command of admiral Mathews. He was soon afterwards promoted to the Dunkirk, of sixty guns, which he commanded in the encounter with the French and Spanish fleets off Toulon. He was stationed to lead Mr. Lestock's division, and *unfortunately* incurred the censure of that gentleman, who was so *strict an observer of discipline*, that, in his answer to the queries sent him by admiral Mathews relative to his own conduct, he makes the following harsh mention of captain Purvis.

" Those ships of my division which were ahead of me were the Dunkirk and Cambridge, both which ships could have made more sail, but they kept to windward of their station, particularly the Dunkirk. Though there was but little wind, with a swell, yet as they sailed well it was my opinion they might have stopped those four ships of the enemy until I and my division got up; therefore I fired a shot to windward of them, and at the same time made the captain of the Dunkirk's signal, but to no purpose."

How far this charge was just we cannot take upon us to decide, but we believe it may well be admitted, without the smallest partiality to either side of the question, that this charge was at least exaggerated. One of the points objected against Mr. Lestock, by admiral Mathews, was, " that he had been guilty of a most scandalous breach of trust, by sending his own captain to captain Purvis, at that time under confinement in order to be tried by a court-martial for misbehaviour, *with instructions to captain Purvis how to conduct himself at the court-martial, and that he would do him no harm.*"

As to the actual conduct of captain Purvis, it does not appear to have been deemed very reprehensible by his judges, for though we have not been able to collect the absolute terms of the decision given by the court-martial, we may very well presume it to have been extremely favourable to captain Purvis, who was continued in his command, and remained on the * same station, at least till after the

---

* The charge, far as it related to captain Drummond, of the Cambridge, was thought so nugatory or impertinent, that no farther investigation of it appears to have been ever deemed necessary.

commencement of the enfuing year, he having been at that time one of the members of the court-martial convened for the trial of captain Richard Norris.

No other mention is made of this gentleman, except that he was, in the year 1756, put on the fuperannuated lift with the rank and half-pay of a rear-admiral, and died on the 15th of January 1772.

RENTONE, James.— Our information relative to this gentleman commences with his having ferved as lieutenant, under vice-admiral Vernon, when he proceeded, in 1739, on the expedition againft Porto Bello. On account of the knowledge he had obtained of that coaft, he was particularly employed, in piloting and directing the courfe of the fquadron, as well during the voyage as the attack itfelf. The ability he difplayed on this occafion, and the fervices he rendered to the expedition in general, were thought fo highly of by Mr. Vernon, that immediately on the reduction of the place, he was promoted to be commander of the Triumph, a Spanifh fnow found in the harbour. He was, as an additional honour, chofen, by the admiral, to be the bearer of his difpatches to England, which announced his fuccefs.

Captain Rentone arrived in London on the 13th of March; and being prefented to the king, received not only a prefent of two hundred guineas, but a promife of farther and immediate promotion. He was accordingly, on the 17th of April following, advanced to be captain of the Experiment frigate; in which fhip he was immediately afterwards ordered for Jamaica to join his former admiral and patron, Mr. Vernon*. Not having the command of a fhip of the line, he could not be fuppofed to be very particularly engaged in fuch parts of the attack as depended merely on the fhips. In thofe independant and fupplementary fervices, however, where his genius and particular fpecies of knowledge and judgement could be ferviceable, he was employed, and moft effentially promoted the fuccefs of the naval operations, by the information he furnifhed relative to the coaft, and

---

* Carrying to him information of the armament that was preparing for the Weft Indies under fir C. Ogle.

its different foundings. After the return of the squadron to Jamaica captain Rentone was promoted, by the vice-admiral, to command the Rippon, of sixty guns, which had arrived at Jamaica during his absence.

The first service on which this gentleman was ordered, after he was invested with his new command, was a cruise to windward of St. Jago, to which station he was sent, by Mr. Vernon, for the purpose of reconnoitring the coast, and intercepting the Spanish trade, just before he himself sailed on the expedition against the island of Cuba. No other particular mention is made of him during his continuance in the West Indies, where he remained still captain of the Rippon, till his return to England with sir C. Ogle, with whom he arrived on the 2d of June 1745. We find him, on the 17th of the same month, one of the members of the court-martial held on board the Sandwich, at Portsmouth, for the trial of captain Green, of the Lizard sloop: and also, in 1746, one of the court-martial, convened at Deptford, for the purpose of trying the admirals, Mathews and Lestock. He was, not long after this time, appointed captain of the Stafford, a fourth rate of sixty guns; in which ship we find him, under Mr. Knowles, at the attack of Port Louis, on the 8th of March 1748. This enterprize unhappily proved fatal to captain Rentone, who was killed even before his ship came to an anchor, a cannon shot having taken off his thigh. This is the information given * in a private letter, written in a day or two after the action, by an officer present, and we believe it to be strictly authentic, though some have asserted he did not die of his wounds till three days after the action.

THOMPSON, Bradshaw, — in 1739, as well as the preceding year, was third lieutenant to admiral Nicholas Haddock, by whom he was sent home master of the Joseph Prize. On the 15th of July 1740, he was appointed captain of the Success frigate. We have not been able to collect any other particulars relative to this gentleman, except that he died in England on the 15th of February 1756.

---

* It is confirmed by that given in the official account.

YOUNG, Benjamin, — is in the fame predicament the only information we have concerning him being, that he was appointed captain of the Briſtol, on the 27th of September 1740, and died ſometime in the courſe of the year 1754.

1741.

ALLEN, Edward.—This gentleman at the time hoſtilities commenced with Spain, in 1739, was, as we believe, lieutenant of one of the ſhips employed in the Weſt Indies, under vice-admiral Vernon, who promoted him, about the end of the year 1740, to be commander of the Terrible bomb-ketch. On the 19th of May 1741, he advanced him ſtill farther, to be captain of the Seahorſe frigate. He remained in the Weſt Indies after the return of Mr. Leſtock and a conſiderable part of the fleet to England, but is not particularly mentioned till the year 1743, when he commanded the Greenwich, a ſhip employed as a cruiſer on the Jamaica ſtation, where he was extremely active, and met with ſome ſucceſs. He remained on the ſame ſtation till 1744, and unfortunately periſhed in a dreadful hurricane, which happened on the 20th of October in that year. The Greenwich was at that time preparing to heave down along-ſide of the Lark hulk, and being, together with that veſſel *, overſet by the violence of the wind, immediately ſunk: captain Allen, his firſt lieutenant Mr. Betteſworth, and eighty-four of the crew, were drowned.

AYLMER, Henry Lord, — was the ſecond ſon of Henry lord Aylmer, and grandſon to that brave and worthy admiral Matthew, firſt lord Aylmer, of Balrath†. Having entered early in life into the navy, he, after a regular progreſſion through the different ſubordinate ‡ ranks, was

---

* She tore away a part of the hulk's broadſide with her laſhings, and then overſet.

† See Vol. ii. p. 35.

‡ In 1733 we believe him to have been lieutenant of one of the ſhips on the African ſtation, and afterwards of the Warwick, in 1735, at Liſbon.

promoted

promoted, on Sept. 18, 1741, to the command of the Port Mahon frigate, as succeffor to capt. Barnfley. He continued in the fame veffel a confiderable time, employed entirely as a cruifer. The firft fubfequent mention we find made of him is in May 1742, when he was concerned with captain Warren, of the Launcefton, in capturing a Spanifh privateer, of eighteen carriage and fwivel guns with one hundred and forty men, which they brought into Portfmouth. In the month of May 1743, he fell in with and captured, after a running fight of five hours, another Spanifh privateer, with fixteen carriage guns, and an hundred and forty-feven men, called the Santa Therefa de Jefus, belonging to Saint Sebaftian's. The excellence of failing which the enemy's fhip poffeffed, prevented captain Aylmer from getting up till after the chace and diftant conteft already ftated: but though the Spaniard had ten of his people killed and fourteen defperately wounded, the injury fuftained on board the Port Mahon amounted only to one man flightly wounded in the arm.

In the month of February 1744, he had the good fortune to preferve the Duke of Lorrain, a very valuable fhip belonging to the Englifh Eaft India company, from being captured by a Spanifh privateer, mounting forty guns, which fhe had engaged for feven hours. The enemy, when the Port Mahon made her appearance, immediately defifting, fled, and, by throwing his guns overboard, added to the affiftance derived from his oars, was fortunate enough to effect his efcape. In the month of May enfuing he had the additional good fortune to capture a very valuable French fhip, bound from Miffifippi to Rochelle, laden with bale goods and a confiderable quantity of fpecie, which, though mounting eighteen carriage guns, a force nearly equal to that of the Port Mahon, which was only a twenty gun fhip, does not appear to have made any refiftance. He quitted the Port Mahon in the enfuing month, June the 4th, 1744, and we do not find any mention made of his having held a fubfequent command.

He married Anne, daughter of William Pierce, of the province of Virginia, efquire, and had iffue by her one daughter, Anne, and a fon, Henry, who was his fucceffor in eftate and title. He himfelf became lord Aylmer, on the death of his father, on the 26th of June 1754, and died on the 7th of October 1766.

BAMFF, Alexander Ogilvie, Lord,—the fixth who enjoyed that title, was the fecond fon of George, fourth lord Bamff, and Helen, daughter of fir John Lauder, of Fountain-hall, one of the fenators of the college of juftice in Scotland. Having entered into the navy, we find him, in 1740, firft lieutenant of the Ludlow Caftle. He was, on February 19, 1741, promoted to be captain of the Haftings, or, according to other accounts, which we believe to be erroneous, of the Liverpool: this is a miftake, probably occafioned by the Haftings being a frigate then fitting for fea at the port of Liverpool. This veffel we believe to have been principally employed as a cruifer in the Channel and Bay of Bifcay; but we find no particular mention made of his lordfhip's fuccefs in this fervice till the month of January 1742, when he captured, off the ifland of Madeira, after a fpirited refiftance of two hours, a large Spanifh regifter fhip, mounting twenty guns, bound from Cadiz to the Havannah*; and in about ten days afterwards, as he was employed in convoying the prize into port, he captured a privateer of a force little inferior.

He was afterwards ordered to Virginia in the fame fhip, but is not known to have met with any very remarkable occurrence, except the capture of a ftout Spanifh privateer, carrying thirty carriage and fwivel guns, on the July 23, 1743, may be faid to deferve that name. On his return from the above ftation, the Haftings was ordered to be fold, as unfit for fervice, and his lordfhip was, in Auguft 1745, promoted to the command of the Tilbury, a fourth rate of fixty guns. In this fhip he was fent to Louifburg, in the month of April 1746, with the Mermaid and Lynn, of forty guns each, to convoy thither a fleet of tranfports with a reinforcement of troops for that newly captured port, and a neceffary fupply of ftores and ammunition. We do not meet with any other mention made of this nobleman in the line of fervice, which we

---

* This veffel is reported to have had on board treafure to the amount of 1,300,000 dollars.

believe

believe him to have quitted not long after his return, and to have repaired to Portugal for the recovery of his health, which was in a declining ſtate. This meaſure was not, however, attended with the hoped-for ſucceſs, his lordſhip dying, at Liſbon, on the 27th of September, 1748.

BARGRAVE, Charles,— was appointed a lieutenant as far back as 1707, his firſt commiſſion bearing date on the 26th of February in that year. Having continued in the ſame ſtation till the year 1741, he was promoted out of the Royal Sovereign, to be captain of the Advice, of fifty guns, without appearing to have paſſed through the intermediate rank of commander of a ſloop of war. This veſſel is ſtated, in ſome private papers, to have been employed on the Mediterranean ſtation during the courſe of the current year; but we conceive this information to be extremely doubtful. Nothing more is known of this officer, except a circumſtance extremely painful to be related, eſpecially of a man who had ſerved for ſuch a number of years, previous to the time of its taking place, with irreproachable character. He was diſmiſſed not only from the above ſhip, but from the ſervice alſo, by the ſentence of a court-martial, on the 24th of February 1741-2. The nature of his offence is not known.

BRETT, John,— was, ſoon after the rupture had taken place with Spain, appointed commander of the Grampus ſloop of war. From this veſſel he was, on the 25th of March 1741, promoted to be captain of the Roebuck, a fifth rate of forty guns. In this ſhip he was, almoſt immediately afterwards, ordered to the Mediterranean. He returned from that ſtation in the month of May 1742, bringing home, as a paſſenger, admiral Haddock, whoſe ill-ſtate of health had compelled him to quit his command: in the month of November following he was removed into the Angleſea, a ſhip of the ſame rate as the former. In this veſſel he remained till the month of April 1744, when he was advanced to the command of the Sunderland, of ſixty guns. No particular mention is made of the manner in which he was employed during the remainder of the year; but early in the enſuing he was ordered, with captain Griffin of the Captain, and the captains Moſtyn and Fowke, of the Hampton Court and Dreadnought, on a cruiſe off the French coaſt. This service was marked with that event which has been already related at length in the lives of the admirals Griffin and Moſtyn *. As to captain Brett, he was totally exempt from participating, in the ſlighteſt degree, of that obloquy attached by many, though perhaps undeſervedly, to the characters of thoſe gentlemen, having been prevented from joining in the purſuit, by the loſs of his main-top-maſt, ſoon after it had commenced. Honourably acquitted by the court-martial convened for the purpoſe of inveſtigating the conduct of all the captains preſent, he was ordered immediately afterwards, together with capt. Geary, of the Cheſter, to cruiſe in ſoundings; and in February, captured, after a chace of eight hours, a ſmall French frigate, bound from Miſſiſſippi to Rochfort, having on board ſeveral paſſengers of rank, a valuable cargo of indigo and other commodities, with 24,000 pieces of eight in ſpecie.

Captain Brett was, ſoon after his return into port, ordered to Louiſburg, with ſome other ſhips of war, for the purpoſe of reinforcing commodore Warren, who was then actually engaged in the attack of that important place. He arrived ſometime before the place ſurrendered, and early enough to diſtinguiſh himſelf exceedingly, both by his ſpirit and activity in the ſervice. From the time of his quitting the Sunderland no mention is made of him till the year 1755, when he commanded the Chicheſter, one of the fleet ordered to America, under the command of Mr. Holburne, for the purpoſe of reinforcing Mr. Boſcawen. After his return he commanded the St. George, of ninety guns, for a ſhort time; but having been very unwarrantably omitted in the promotion of flag-officers, which took place in 1756, he very ſpiritedly reſolved to quit the ſervice for ever, though on his remonſtrance, previous to his actual declaration of this reſolution, the admiralty board, aſhamed of its conduct in having, even for a moment, ſet aſide a brave and deſerving man, offered him the rank of rear-admiral of the white, the ſame which he would have been entitled to in the ordinary courſe of ſervice if the partiality exerted in the favour of others had not happened.

---

* Vide Vol. iv. pages

His anſwer to this palliating propoſal reflects on him too much honour to be ſuppreſſed. "No rank or ſtation (ſaid he) can be, with honour, received by a perſon who has been once thought undeſerving or unintitled to it." It is neceſſary to ſtate briefly the cauſe why a brave and worthy man ſhould have been ſo injuriouſly treated; the lord Anſon, at that time firſt commiſſioner of the admiralty, was, in one particular point, perfectly unfit for that high ſtation. He might poſſeſs a ſpirit of enterprize, a perfect knowledge of all particulars relative to the marine department, and, in ſhort, every other *Public* virtue and requiſite that could grace the character of a miniſter: in private life, however, he wanted that impartiality which, we had nearly ſaid, is indiſpenſibly neceſſary to conſtitute an upright man. Perſonal friendſhip and attachment frequently interfered with his public duties, and betrayed him into acts ſtrongly reſembling thoſe of injuſtice. Theſe were, perhaps, the leſs excuſeable in him, conſidered in his abſtract character of a private friend, becauſe thoſe whom he patronized were men too high in the opinion of all men to need his aſſiſtance, and far too honourable to deſire it: but the moſt exalted perſonages are not exempt from trivial failings, as perfection is abſolutely incompatible with the frailty of human nature.

As to Mr. Brett, he continued ever afterwards to paſs his life in retirement, rendered moſt truly honourable by the cauſe of it, dying univerſally revered, and regretted in the month of April 1785.

BRODERICK, Thomas.—The firſt mention we find made of this gentleman is in the year 1739, at which time he was third lieutenant of the Burford, under Mr. Vernon. He diſtinguiſhed himſelf exceedingly at the attack of Porto Bello, having been the commander of the party which ſtormed the lower battery of the Iron Fort, an action ſo ſpirited that the defenders imagining no reſiſtance they could make would be ſufficient to ſtem the torrent of the aſſailants, fled from what they conceived a certain deſtruction, leaving their governor and a few others who eſcaped into the upper part of the fort, and immediately afterwards ſurrendered at diſcretion.

Mr. Vernon, highly pleaſed at ſo conſpicuous and ſerviceable a diſplay of gallantry, conceived no inconſiderable degree

degree of attachment to this gentleman, and advanced him to be commander of the Cumberland firefhip. He attended the fleet on the well-known expedition againſt Carthagena, and was there promoted, on the 25th of March 1741, to be captain of the Shoreham frigate, as fucceſſor to Mr. Boſcawen, who was promoted to the Prince Frederic. In a few days afterwards he was one of the officers ordered to command the boats on a repetition of the attack of the Barradera battery, which the Spaniards had in part re-eſtabliſhed. Mr. Broderick behaved on the occaſion we have juſt been relating, in a manner by no means derogatory to that reputation he had before ſo deſervedly acquired in a ſervice nearly ſimilar at Porto Bello. He afterwards accompanied Mr. Vernon on his ſtill leſs fucceſsful expedition againſt Cuba, and was detached from thence to cruiſe off Carthagena; in which ſervice he had the good fortune to capture a Spaniſh veſſel, laden with bale goods of conſiderable value, and ſpecie to the amount, it is ſaid, of ſeventy thouſand dollars. He was, after this fucceſs, ſent to cruiſe off Cape Francois for the protection of the Britiſh commerce, at that time much incommoded by the multitude of Spaniſh privateers which infeſted thoſe ſeas. He continued employed in ſimilar ſervices till the month of October 1742, when he was appointed to command the convoy ſent, with a ſmall body of troops, to the provinces of Carolina and Georgia, for their better protection againſt any defultory expeditions that might be undertaken by the Spaniards.

No other particular mention is made of this gentleman while he continued in the Weſt Indies. After his return to England he was, in the month of March 1744, advanced to the command of the Exeter, a fourth rate of ſixty guns, at that time fitting for ſea at Plymouth, where that ſhip had been juſt before rebuilt. As ſoon as equipped it was ſent to Liſbon as one of the fleet commanded by the brave and unfortunate admiral Balchen; and, on its return from thence, very narrowly eſcaped being involved in the ſame unhappy fate which befel the much lamented commander-in-chief. The Exeter, during that dreadful ſtorm which overtook the fleet, was in the greateſt extremity of diſtreſs, having loſt both her main and mizen maſts, and

being

being thrown on her beam ends, so that twelve of the lee-guns were obliged to be thrown overboard, with the greatest dispatch, to preserve her from sinking. In the month of February 1745, he was one of the members composing the court-martial for the trial of commodore Griffin, and the different captains with him, a circumstance we have before related and referred to. In the ensuing month he was removed into the Dreadnought, a ship of equal force with the Exeter, which probably had received so much damage in the preceding storm as to be unfit for immediate service.

We do not find any other memorable mention made of this gentleman till the year 1756*, when he commanded the Prince George, a second rate. In the month of May he was appointed commodore of a small squadron, consisting of four or five ships†, ordered to the Mediterranean as a reinforcement to Mr. Byng. He left Plymouth on the 30th of May, with some transports full of troops and stores for Gibraltar, and arrived there, after a speedy passage, on the 15th of June. He was promoted at home to be rear-admiral of the blue in four or five days after he left port, and continued to serve on the same station during a part of the ensuing season, under sir Edward Hawke, who superceded Mr. Byng in less than three weeks after Mr. Broderick's arrival. He returned to England before the conclusion of the year, in the St. George, the ship on board which the court-martial was afterwards held for the trial of admiral Byng, one of whose judges he was consequently appointed. In 1757 he was appointed third in command of the fleet fitted out for the purpose of attacking Rochfort, the particulars of which expedition have been already given at some length in the memoirs of his superior officers, sir Edward Hawke and sir Charles Knowles. He hoisted his flag on board the Namur, a second rate; but is in no other way mentioned even in that torrent of obloquy which burst forth on the failure of the expedition, than as having been

---

* We believe him, in 1749, to have commanded the Sunderland.
† A letter from Plymouth states this little squadron to have consisted of the St. George, the Nassau, Hampton-court, and Ipswich: but Mr. Byng, in his dispatch informing of his arrival, states Mr. Broderick to have brought out five ships of the line.

employed in reconnoitering and founding the coast. To have been little engaged in an unsuccessful enterprize is certainly the least disadvantageous to the reputation of a commander, and therefore on such occasions only, want of employment is to be particularly coveted.

In 1758 Mr. Broderick, who was on the last day of January advanced to the rank of rear-admiral of the white, was appointed to succeed Mr. Osborne as commander-in-chief in the Mediterranean. A fleet of transports and merchant-ships bound thither being put under his convoy, he hoisted his flag on board the Prince George, and sailed the beginning of April. The melancholy misfortune which befel this ship and the greater part of her crew, on the 13th of April, while on their passage to Gibraltar, is still recent enough to leave the most afflicting impression on the minds of those who read the dreadful narrative*. Mr. Broderick with the remnant of his people,

---

* We have inserted several letters, relative to this event, notwithstanding they have made their appearance already in many publications; but we are induced to it because they form a very authentic account of this highly lamentable disaster.

" From the Rev. Mr. Sharp, chaplain.

" Glasgow, off Lisbon, April 20.

" On Thursday the 13th instant, at half an hour past one in the afternoon, word was passed into the ward-room, by the sentry, that the fore part of the ship, the Prince George, was on fire: the lieutenants ran immediately forward; and myself, with many others, went directly on the quarter-deck, when we found the whole ship's crew was alarmed: the pumps were handed out, the engine and buckets carried forward, and every immediate remedy applied. The admiral, with the lieutenants on watch, kept the quarter-deck, from whence he sent such orders as he thought most expedient for the preservation of the ship, and the souls in her. Captain Peyton and the lieutenants, on search, found that the fire broke out first in the boatswain's storeroom, to which place large quantities of water were applied, but in vain, for the smoke was so very great and hot, that the poor creatures could not get near enough to the flames for their labour to have any effect. On this captain Peyton ordered scuttles to be made, that the water might be poured in by that means; but there he was defeated likewise, for only two carpenters could be found, and they had nothing to work with for a long time but a hammer and a chissel each. The lower gun-deck ports were then opened; but the water that flowed in was not sufficient to stop the violence of the flames. He ordered,

people, purſued his voyage, on board the Glaſgow, as ſtated beneath, to Gibraltar. On his arrival there he hoiſted

ordered, likewiſe, the powder-room to be wetted, left the ſhip ſhould immediately be blown up and every ſoul periſh in an inſtant. This had the deſired effect, and for ſome minutes we had glimmering hopes. I mention the above particulars as I was below myſelf, worked with the men as long as I could ſtand it, went up for air and returned again inſtantly, conſequently an eye witneſs, I can declare them as facts. The fire ſoon increaſed, and raged violently aft on the larboard ſide; and as the deſtruction of the ſhip was now found inevitable, the preſervation of the admiral was firſt conſulted. Captain Peyton came on the quarter deck and ordered the barge to be manned, into which the admiral entered with near forty more, for now there was no diſtinction, every man's life was equally precious. The admiral finding the barge would over-ſet, ſtripped himſelf naked and committed himſelf to the mercy of the waves; and after toiling an hour, he was at length taken up by a merchant-man's boat. Captain Peyton kept the quarter-deck an hour after the admiral left it, when he happily got into a boat from the ſtern ladder, and was put ſafe on board the Alderney ſloop. I muſt be deficient even to attempt a deſcription of the melancholy ſcene that was before me; ſhrieking, cries, lamentations, bemoanings, raving deſpair, and even madneſs itſelf preſented themſelves. It was now high time to think of taking care of myſelf: I looked from every part of the ſhip for my preſervation, and ſoon ſaw three boats off the ſtern. I went immediately to my cabbin and offered up my prayers to God, particularly thanking him for giving me ſuch reſolution and compoſure of mind. I then jumped into the ſea from one of the gun-room ports, and ſwam to a boat, which put me ſafe on board the Alderney ſloop. There are near three hundred people ſaved; and more might have been ſaved had the merchant-men behaved like human creatures; but they kept a long way to windward the whole time, and, if poſſible, to their greater ſhame be it ſpoken, inſtead of ſaving the men that ſwam to their boats, they were employed in taking up geeſe, fowls, tables, chairs, and whatever elſe of the kind came near them."

" From Mr. Parry, an officer, dated as above.

" About half paſt one, at noon, being in the office adjoining to the cabbin, I ſaw the admiral run out with two or three officers. On enquiring the cauſe I was alarmed with a report of the ſhip's being on fire forward, and it was believed in the boatſwain's fore ſtore-room. Every method was taken to extinguiſh it, but the ſmoke was ſo violent no perſon could get near enough to find where the fire was. About half paſt two we made the ſignal of diſtreſs; but to render our ſituation more wretched the fog came on very thick, and the wind freſhened; ſo that it was near four before the Glaſgow and Alderney got intelligence of our condition. They then repeated the ſignal, hoiſted out

hoisted his flag on board the St. George, of ninety guns, and served under Mr. Osborne till that gentleman quitted the station, and returned to England in the month of July.

He

out their boats, and stood towards us: but not knowing we had taken care to float our powder, were under sad apprehensions we might blow up, and therefore could not, consistent with their own safety, give us the assistance our deplorable condition rendered us so much in need of. We attempted to scuttle the decks to let the water on the fire, but the people could not stand a minute without being nearly suffocated. About half past four the smoke increased, and the flames began to break out. The admiral then ordered the boats to be hoisted out, got the barge out, and went off, promising to bring a ship along-side of us. I observed her so full that her gun-wale was almost even with the water; and in a few minutes after saw her sink at some distance a stern. Not above three or four were saved out of nearly forty, among whom it pleased God to preserve the admiral. The weather was now become clear, but none of the merchantmen would come near us. Our officers behaved well, and endeavoured to keep the people to the pumps and drawing water; but they were now become quite ungovernable. About a quarter before five captain Peyton left the ship, and promised as the admiral, but was not able to accomplish it. About five the long boat was endeavoured to be got out, in which were near one hundred people; but as they were hoisting her out one of the tackles gave way, by which she overset, and almost every soul perished. We were now reduced to the greatest distress. You may have some idea of our miserable condition, when I tell you the ship began be in flames fore and aft, spreading like flax; people distracted, not knowing what they did, and jumping overboard from all parts, I was reduced to the melancholy choice of either burning with the ship, or going overboard. Very few that could swim were taken up, and I that could not swim must have little hopes indeed. About a quarter past five I went into the admiral's stern gallery, where two young gentlemen were lashing two tables together for a raft. I assisted them. One of them proposed to make fast the lashing to the gallery, and lower ourselves down to the tables, then cutting the lashing to commit ourselves to the mercy of Providence. We hoisted over the tables, but being badly lashed one of them we lost; as soon as the other was down, I proposed to venture first, which they readily consented to. There were about three boats astern; this was the time or never: down I went by the rope; but as there was a great swell of sea it was impossible for any one to follow me, and I was turned a drift. By the cries of the people from the ship to the boats, in about five minutes I was taken up, very near drowned."

715 compliment	260 saved
30 passengers to Gibraltar	485 lost
745	745

" From

He then removed into the Prince, which had been his predeceſſor's flag-ſhip, and commanded-in-chief in the Mediter-

---

"From a midſhipman, dated as above.

"On Thurſday the 13th, about half an hour paſt one in the afternoon, we were alarmed with a cry of fire in the boatſwain's fore ſtoreroom, which put us all into great diſorder; and, it being a very thick fog, we could not ſee one ſhip in the fleet. We kept firing guns of diſtreſs, and no ſhip appearing in ſight for an hour we were all in the greateſt conſternation; but the fog then difpelling, the Glaſgow hailed us, to whom we told our condition, and earneſtly begged of them to ſave our lives.

"The fire ſtill increaſing we were obliged to hoiſt out our boats, which, from our confuſion, were near three hours fixing to the tackles, &c. every body being engaged in preparing to ſave himſelf. The poop, ſtern, and quarter galleries, with the ſides, were lined with men and boys, crying out in a moſt moving manner to be aſſiſted. During this time, out of twenty-three ſail of ſhips we had but three boats to our aſſiſtance, and thoſe would not come near the ſhip for fear of being ſunk; the poor fellows continually jumping overboard, great numbers of whom were drowned in our ſight.

"We got our boats out, which never returned after going once. By this time the fire had communicated itſelf to the middle gun-deck, and nobody could go down below, every one expecting his death every minute, either by fire or water, and were taking leave of each other. Soon after going out of the admiral's cabin I ſaw the flames coming out in the hatchway of the upper gun-deck. I returned immediately and taking my leave of the petty officers that were there, went over the ſtarboard ſtern ladder to ſave myſelf by ſwimming, when, thanks to almighty God, I reached a boat, and was taken up.

"I had juſt got clear of the ſhip when the flames became general, and thoſe poor unhappy wretches, that could not ſwim, were obliged to remain upon the wreck with the fire falling down upon them. Shortly after the maſts went away and killed numbers; and thoſe that were not killed by the maſts thought themſelves happy to get upon them; but the ſhip rolling by reaſon of the great ſea, the fire had communicated itſelf to the guns, which ſwept them off the deck in great numbers, they being all loaded and ſhotted.

"Such a terrible ſight the oldeſt men in the fleet ſay they never ſaw. Thus ended our unhappy ſhip, after burning ſix hours and a half, who had as complete a crew, and was as well manned as any ſhip that ever ſailed from England."

"Letter from the maſter of a merchantman under convoy of admiral Broderick.

"Thurſday April 13th, Uſhant bearing Eaſt 60 leagues diſtance, at noon, I ſaw admiral Broderick hoiſt a ſignal of diſtreſs, upon which I made what ſail I could and went down to him. At one in the after-

Mediterranean, till the arrival of Mr. Boscawen in the ensuing spring. In the month of February 1759, he was advanced to be vice-admiral of the blue, and continued as second in command of the fleet during the summer. The naval operations in that part of the world were rendered extremely brilliant by the total discomfiture and defeat of M. De la Clue in the month of August. Mr. Broderick was not able, we believe, to get up time enough to have much share in the action itself; but he is particularly mentioned, by Mr. Boscawen, as having, with his division, burnt the Redoubtable, of seventy-four guns, and captured the Modeste on the following day. We do not find any mention made of him in the line of service after his return to England; nor, indeed, is he otherwise

---

afternoon I could discern the Prince George on fire: at two we drew pretty near her and thought they might have quenched the fire: at three o'clock I saw plainly it was impossible. I was within a hundred yards of her stern, but durst not venture alongside, the sea running high, besides the going off of her guns, and danger of blowing up. At four in the afternoon the admiral was taken up, swimming, by a merchantship's boat, as by this time the ships that had boats sent them all out, and a good many of them were lost, the weather proving bad. Towards night I was within pistol-shot, and remained there some time picking up four of her crew. Had not two of my men run away with my boat the night before we sailed from St. Helen's, I am confident I could have saved sixty or eighty of them at least as I was all the time nearer to them than any ship in the fleet. What made me venture so near was, that I knew my ship went well, and was under good command. At six what a dismal sight, the masts and sails all in a blaze; hundreds of souls hanging by the ropes alongside; I could count fifty of them hanging over in the stern-ladder, others in the sea on oars and pieces of wood, a melancholy spectacle; besides the dismal cries from the ship, which still ring in my ears! At half an hour past six the flames broke out at her broadside, and in less than five minutes every part of her was in flames, and so continued till seven, when she overset but did not sink: I then ran within twenty yards of her, but my people compelled me to go farther off for fear of striking on the wreck. All I can say of it in addition is, there never was a more shocking sight; pray God I may never see the like again: it was very grievous to me that I could not save more of her men without running the risk of sharing her fate. The 18th of April the Glasgow, a twenty gun ship, hoisted the signal for all masters of merchant-ships to come on board, where the admiral had his flag hoisted, to know how many of his people we had saved amongst us and to deliver them up. By the then list it appeared that the admiral, captain Peyton, and about two hundred and fifty-three men, were saved."

noticed

noticed than as having been, on the 22d of October 1762, advanced to be vice-admiral of the white. He died, on the 1st of January 1769, of one of the most grievous maladies that afflicts the human race, a cancer in his face.

CAMPBELL, William, — was, at the latter end of the year 1740, commander of the Scipio fireship. He was advanced from thence, on the 26th of April 1741, to be captain of the Sapphire frigate, of forty guns. He was immediately afterwards ordered on the Irish station. In the following year a charge was preferred against him for misconduct in leaving his station without orders, and ill-treatment to his officers. He was in consequence brought to a court-martial, and sentenced to be dismissed the service, to which he was never again restored. He retired to Scotland, his native country, and died there on the 27th of October 1755.

CHEAP, David, — was promoted, by commodore Anson, from the rank of lieutenant to be commander of the Trial sloop of war, on the 3d of November 1740. He was advanced by the same gentleman to be captain of the Wager on the 19th of February 1740, as successor to captain Murray, who was promoted to the Pearl. The distresses encountered by the squadron in its passage round Cape Horn, have been already related at some length in the memoirs of Mr. Anson: these were not felt by any ship more severely than by the Wager. Captain Cheap, who, whatever trivial failings may be advanced against him by the virulence and injustice of his enemies, must certainly be admitted, by the most violent of them, to have possessed the greatest activity and zeal for the service of his country. He was exposed in the ship least capable of any in the squadron to resist the violence of such a continued and tremendous tempest; nevertheless, perfectly aware of the consequence the Wager was of to the expedition, having on board all the stores, cannon and ammunition, necessary to any land operation, he exerted himself to the utmost to keep company with the squadron, though, during the greater part of the time, he was so ill as to be almost incapable of quitting his cabin.

On the 8th of April the Wager lost her mizen-mast. In about ten days afterwards she parted company with the

the commodore, and every ship in the squadron. The tempestuous weather still continued with unabated violence: the ship was reduced to a mere wreck, and the crew so debilitated by sickness and the scurvy, that by the beginning of May there were scarcely twenty persons capable of duty. To add, if possible, to their distress, captain Cheap, on the ship's ralling in with the land on the 13th of May, exerting himself to work the ship off the shore, had the misfortune to fall and dislocate his shoulder, an accident which rendered him incapable of keeping the deck, or any longer encouraging the people by his presence and example. At this time all the crew capable of service amounted only to twelve persons, officers included: and, as it might have been thought, to conclude at once their sufferings, at half past four o'clock on the morning of the 14th of May, the ship struck upon a sunken rock: from this she luckily beat off, but in a very short time afterwards struck and grounded between two small islands, a spot to which, as it is elsewhere with much truth remarked, they were providentially driven, for the safety of their lives, as few other situations could have been found in which the people could have been preserved from instant destruction.

Soon as day-light appeared, which was quickly after the above fatal accident took place, the boats were launched over the ship's side, and the barge sent on shore for the purpose of discovering whether the place was inhabited, which was quickly found not to be the case. Happily for captain Cheap, and the miserable remains of his unfortunate though meritorious crew, the ship did not go to pieces for a very considerable time after her being stranded, so that a great quantity of provisions and other necessaries were preserved, without which they must all have inevitably perished. Immediately on the loss of the ship, notwithstanding the very distressed situation of the people, a scene of anarchy and confusion took place among the crew, owing to an idea at that time prevalent, that in cases of wreck all command ceased; nor could regularity and order have been restored except by the most spirited exertions of captain Cheap and some few of the principal officers, who remained faithful and true to him. Among the chief and principal exciters of this mutiny and difturbance, was a fellow of the name of Cozens, who, though of a very mean family in the county of Somerfet, had, through the intereft of fome friends, been introduced into the naval fervice as a midfhipman. This perfon had, on many occafions, behaved not only with the moft intolerable infolence to the captain, for which he was at one time very defervedly put in confinement, but had actually endeavoured to render the fituation of his unhappy fellow-fufferers ftill more defperate than it naturally was, by embezzling fome of the ftores which were faved, and deftroying others. On the 10th of June, nearly a month after the lofs of the fhip, one of the men, on what account is not particularly mentioned, had his allowance of wine ftopped: this coming to the knowledge of Cozens, who had for fome days very impudently taken upon himfelf the office of a reformer, he immediately went to the purfer and demanded the reafon. That gentleman conceiving the behaviour of Cozens as the prelude to a mutiny, difcharged a piftol at him, which was prevented from taking effect by the cooper having canted the purfer's elbow at the inftant it went off. Captain Cheap hearing the difturbance, ran out of his tent with a cocked piftol, and, when in the act of coming out, being informed, by the lieutenant of marines, that Cozens was endeavouring to raife a mutiny, he, perhaps with rather too much precipitation, difcharging his piftol at the offender, the ball from which lodged in his cheek. This act, for we know not how to call it accident, proved the caufe of much fubfequent mifery to the fcarcely more happy furvivors.

Cozens died on the 14th day: and as perfons of his character fcarcely fail of being what is called popular among thofe of the loweft rank, fo did the mifcreant's death rather encreafe than allay the turbulent diffatisfaction of his adherents, who were bafe enough, without the fmalleft regard to truth, to infift that the neglect fhewn to him after being wounded, in confequence of the captain's interference and influence, was as much the caufe of his death as the wound itfelf. Captain Cheap was a man of confiderable ability as a feaman, and to his maritime knowlege added a zeal for the fervice of his country, which it is not, perhaps, paffing too great an encomium

on,

on, to fay, it has never been exceeded. The fhip he commanded was the ftorefhip of the fquadron; the artillery, ammunition, and other articles neceffary for the intended enterprize againft Baldivia were on board her: this confideration induced the captain to combat every difficulty and diftrefs previous to the lofs of the fhip, knowing well that, without his junction with the commodore, the principal intention of the expedition muft be fruftrated. The fame degree of fpirit induced him afterwards to ftrain every nerve, by his influence over the people, and by a moft exemplary difplay of his own perfonal intrepidity, in hopes of inducing them to attempt joining the commodore at the ifland of Juan Fernandes, the fecond rendezvous, well knowing that a reinforcement of fo many men in tolerable health, which they had wonderfully recovered after being put on fhore, even in that inhofpitable climate, muft be a confiderable acquifition to a force originally weak, and now much, as he truly fuppofed, diminifhed by ficknefs.

The preliminary meafure to fo bold and enterprifing an undertaking was lengthening the fhip's long boat, fo that it might be able to convey thither the people, amounting in number to upwards of one hundred, with the provifions neceffary for their fupport during the paffage: but the fatal accident we have juft had occafion to recount, encreafed the difturbances among the people to fuch an height, that they at length peremptorily refufed to obey their commander; and in diametrical oppofition to his propofal, determined on attempting, as foon as the boat fhould be completed, to return back through the ftreights of Magellan.

A formal refolution to this effect was entered into on the 2d of Auguft, and figned by the gunner, carpenter, mafter, boatfwain, many of the petty officers, and the greater part of the crew, fome engaging through affection to, and fome through fear of the malcontents. The long boat being completed in the beft manner circumftances would admit of, was launched on the 12th of October, at day light, and called the Speedwell. Three or four days before this time, captain Cheap, together with lieutenant Hamilton of the land-forces, his brave his faithful friend and adherent, were put under an arreft by captain Pemberton of the marines, fupported by Mr. Beans, who had

been

been the lieutenant of the ſhip. This very extraordinary and unwarrantable conduct towards the former was juſtified on the frivolous paltry charge of his having been guilty of murder in ſhooting Cozens; and againſt the latter on no other pretext than his having, on all occaſions, firmly eſpouſed the cauſe of his commanding officer. Nevertheleſs, when the long boat was about to depart, it was agreed to leave him behind, with Mr. Hamilton, the ſurgeon, and eight deſerters who had quitted their companions ſoon after the loſs of the ſhip, and to give them the pinnace, with fourteen pieces of beef, as many of pork, and one hundred and ninety pounds of flour for their ſupport. This party was afterwards joined by ſeveral other ſeceders from the main body, among which were the honourable Mr. Byron, and Mr. Campbell, midſhipmen. By theſe means their number was at laſt encreaſed to twenty; and the barge alſo was left with them for their conveyance.

The long boat put to ſea and left them about the middle of October; but captain Cheap and his companions did not ſet out for Chiloe, the moſt ſouthern of the Spaniſh ſettlements on that coaſt, and conſequently the neareſt where they could expect any effectual relief, till the 15th of December. After having in vain combated all the dangers of that tempeſtuous ſea for nearly two months, they were obliged to put back to the deſolate ſpot from whence they had ſet out: but a party of Indians coming in there about a fortnight after their arrival, their chief, or cacique, was prevailed on to undertake conducting them northward in their barge, on condition of being rewarded with it for his trouble.

Their number, now reduced to thirteen, accordingly embarked, attended by the Indians in two canoes: but after they had proceeded ſome way on their voyage, captain Cheap, with the reſt of the officers, having gone on ſhore in the hope of procuring a ſupply of proviſions, the men left in the barge took that opportunity of abandoning them, and ſailing away. The Indian chief was at this time abſent, having got out to kill ſeal; and on his return, though the barge, which was to have been his reward, was gone, he was nevertheleſs prevailed on to fulfil his engagement to the miſerable remnant left behind, conſiſting only of captain Cheap, lieutenant Hamilton, Mr. Campbell, and Mr. Byron This compliance,

Vol. V. F

ance, however, was not the mere refult of compaffion, a fowling-piece, belonging to Mr. Byron, and fome trifles contributed by the captain, induced their guide to proceed with them to the ifland of Chiloe, where, Mr. Hamilton, unable to proceed, having been left under the beft Indian care that country afforded, the remainder arrived in fafety after experiencing almoft every difficulty and fpecies of fuffering that the human body was capable of undergoing, without an abfolute extinction of life.

It was the month of June, thirteen months after the lofs of the fhip, ere they reached Chiloe. The weather was uncommonly fevere, the ground covered to a great depth with fnow : it netherthelefs appeared to the diftreffed travellers a paradife, compared to the defart coaft which they had been fo long accuftomed to; and the poor inhabitants received them with all the hofpitality their own wretched ftate would permit them to difplay. Captain Cheap and his companions were very foon afterwards conveyed to Caftro, a large Spanifh town at fome diftance, and from thence to Chacao. Here they were again joined by Mr. Hamilton, who was brought forward by a party of men fent to the fouthward, by the governor, for that purpofe. On the 2d of January 1742-3, they all embarked on board a fhip which annually fails from Chiloe to Lima, and, after a paffage of fix days, arrived fafe at Valparaifo, a port in Chili, where they were again landed. After a ftay of fome days, captain Cheap and Mr. Hamilton, having preferved their commiffions, were known to be officers, and were conducted to St. Jago, the capital of the province. They continued at this place fome time, during which they were treated with the utmoft hofpitality and attention; and the captain, Mr. Hamilton, together with Mr. Byron, by whom they had been joined fome time before, embarked, on the 20th of December 1744, in a French fhip bound from Lima to Spain; and, without experiencing any remarkable accident or occurrence, came to an anchor, in Breft road, on the 27th of October 1745. They afterwards got on board a Dutch dogger, the captain of which engaged to land them at Dover; but, as if inconvenience and difappointment were deftined to attend them to the laft moment of this perilous and difaftrous voyage, they would have been, as

is

is reported in Mr. Byron's narrative, treacherously set on shore in France, had they not been fortunate enough to fall in with the Squirrel frigate, which taking them on board put a period to this scene of misery by landing them in England.

Captain Cheap arrived in London on the 24th of March 1746, and was soon afterwards appointed captain of the Lark; in which vessel, being ordered out on a cruise, he had the good fortune to capture a large and valuable Spanish prize off the island of Madeira, being then in company with captain Charles Saunders. After his return from this successful expedition we do not believe him to have gone to sea, or held any command, at least, we do not find any mention made of him in the service. On the 14th of September 1748, he married a widow lady, named Brown, belonging to York. He had not, however, the happiness of long enjoying this peaceable repose, from those singular and trying fatigues he had encountered in the service, dying on the 21st of July 1752.

COCKBURN, George,—was promoted from the rank of lieutenant, to be commander of the Drake sloop of war in March 1741. He was appointed captain of the Gibraltar on the 11th of June 1741: this frigate was one of those attached to the fleet under the command of sir John Norris, who ordered him, in the month of July, to accompany captain Harrison, in the Argyle, on the little expedition he had planned, and with so much gallantry executed against the Spaniards, the particulars of which have been already given at some length in his memoirs *. In what particular services he was employed, from this time till the month of June 1742, when he was promoted to the Medway of sixty guns, does not appear. In this ship he very gallantly supported captain Windham in attacking the town of Santa Cruz, as already related in the life of that gentleman †; but owing to some disagreement with captain Windham respecting the cruise, he thought proper, on his return to England, to resign his command, and was not appointed to any other ship during the war; after the conclusion of which he was made captain of the Glory, on the African station. Being a person of great interest, the Yarmouth, a third rate of sixty-

---

* Vide vol. v. p. 29. † See vol. iv. p. 251.

four guns, and at that time a guardſhip at Chatham, was reſerved for him againſt his return, captain Palliſer being appointed to command her in the interim. Captain Cockburn had long been in the habit of frequently requeſting eave of abſence; and the board of admiralty, wearied at length with ſolicitations which it was extremely injurious to the diſcipline of the ſervice to comply with, ſignified to him at laſt that he was not to expect any farther indulgence: he, in conſequence, immediately reſigned his command. This happened early in 1755, juſt after which time the guardſhips were ordered to complete their complements for ſervice. He immediately applied for a ſhip, and was appointed to the Naſſau, a third rate alſo, but very inferior to the Yarmouth in ſize, weight of guns, &c. In this veſſel he made only one cruiſe, and another officer was appointed to command the ſhip *pro tempore*; but on its being ordered on foreign ſervice he again thought proper to reſign. On the 22d of June, 1755, he was appointed extra-commiſſioner of the navy; and in December following was promoted to the office of comptroller. He continued in this ſtation till the time of his death, an event which happened, on the 20th of July 1770, at Brighthelmſtone. Mr. Hardy imagines him to have retired on a penſion in 1769, but in this circumſtance he is evidently miſtaken.

COLEBY, Charles,—was a lieutenant belonging, in the year 1740, to one of the ſhips on the Jamaica ſtation, under the command of vice-admiral Vernon; who promoted him, previous to his ſailing on the expedition againſt Carthagena, to be commander of the Eleanor fireſhip. He was advanced, by the ſame admiral, on the 12th of January 1740-1, to be captain of the Boyne, under commodore Leſtock, who hoiſted his broad pendant on board as commander of one of the diviſions of the fleet. He in all probability returned to Europe with Mr. Leſtock, as we do not find any other mention made of him till June 1742, when he was appointed to the Falmouth. In this ſhip he continued a conſiderable time being ordered for the Weſt Indies, where he ſerved with the greateſt reputation under ſir Chaloner Ogle. In June 1744, he was ſent, with captain Knight of the St. Alban's, to demand reſtitution from the governor of Porto Bello, of a Britiſh veſſel which had been ſeized and carried in there, though trading under a Spaniſh paſs. The particulars of this tranſtranfaction, as well as of the fpirited behaviour of thefe two gentlemen, have been already given at fome length in the memoirs of captain Knight*. He returned to England in the month of May 1745, having, previous to his departure from the Weft Indies, been removed into the Experiment frigate, and fent home exprefs by fir Chaloner Ogle, whofe arrival he only preceded two or three days. He fat immediately afterwards as one of the members of the court-martial, held on board the Sandwich, at Portfmouth, on the 17th of June, for the trial of captain Green, commander of the Lizard floop.

In 1746 he was one of the members of the court-martial held for the trials of the admirals Leftock and Mathews; but, ftrange as it may appear, we do not find any mention made of him as a captain in actual fervice, after his quitting the Experiment, till the year 1755; when he was made captain of the Torbay, a fhip of feventy-four guns, equipped at Chatham in confequence of the rupture which was daily expected to take place with France. The Torbay was very foon afterwards fent, under Mr. Bofcawen, to North America, and was taken by that admiral for his flag-fhip, Mr. Coleby ferving as his captain. In the following year he quitted the fervice as a naval commander, being appointed, on June 22, commiffioner refident at Gibraltar, with a falary of 1000l. *per annum.* He retained this office till the conclufion of the war, and the confequent recal to England of nearly all the fhips on that ftation, rendered its continuance unneceffary. He retired, in the year 1763, on a penfion of 400l. a year, as a fuperannuated commiffioner, and enjoyed that honourable teftimony of his paft fervices till his death, which took place on the 9th of February 1772.

DANDRIDGE, William.—The firft information we have relative to this gentleman is, that, in 1740, he was commander of the Wolf, a fmall floop of war on the American ftation, and was prefent in the early part of the war at the fruitlefs attack made on the town of St. Auguftine, by general Oglethorpe. Not long after its failure he was fent to the Weft Indies with orders to join Mr. Vernon. He attended that admiral on his expedition againft

---

* See vol. iv. p. 293. Some accounts make the name of the largeft prize to have been the Couillandeau, inftead of the Tamerlane, as afferted in the life of captain Knight.

Carthagena, but was detached ahead of the fleet for the purpofe of reconnoitering Port Louis. He rejoined the admiral with an account of his having difcovered nineteen fail of large fhips in that harbour, one of them with a flag at the main-top-maft head, and a fecond with a broad pendant flying. An immediate fignal was accordingly made for the flag-officers and generals to affemble; and the information received being communicated to them, it was unanimoufly agreed to fteer for the ifle of Vache, as well for the purpofe of obferving the motions of the French, as of procuring more perfect intelligence of their force and particular deftination. On the 12th of February the greater part of the fleet came to an anchor under the ifland abovementioned, two leagues to the weftward of Port Louis; and it was foon found that captain Dandridge had been deceived by the thick haze, through the medium, of which he had made his obfervations.

Erroneous as his report was, he was not in any degree deemed reprehenfible for the miftake, but on the 19th of the fame month was promoted, by Mr. Vernon, to be captain of the South Sea Caftle. He does not, neverthelefs, appear to have been confirmed in that command, by the board of admiralty, till the month of November following. No mention is made of his fervices during the time he continued in this fhip, except that he was, about the month of May, ordered to America; and in the month of July was fent from Virginia * to Savannah, in Georgia, where general Oglethorpe was then vigoroufly attacked by the Spaniards. We do not find any other mention whatever made of him till the year 1744, when, in the month of July, having previoufly returned to England, he was appointed captain of the Mary galley, a fifth rate of forty guns. We are totally ignorant of any other particular concerning him, except that he died in England on the 17th of October 1747.

DENNIS, Henry,—was, in the early part of the year 1740, commander of one of the fmall veffels attached to the fleet

---

* There is fome, but not pofitive, reafon to fuppofe this gentleman commanded the Tilbury, of fixty guns, at the time that fhip was unfortunately burnt, at Navaffa, in the month of September 1742; if fo, he had, in all probability, received this appointment a fhort time before, on the indifpofition of captain Dent, who had previoufly commanded that veffel.

under

under vice-admiral Vernon *, by whom he was promoted, on the 6th of June 1741, to be captain of the Experiment, at least that date is assigned to his first commission as a captain in all the lists of the navy we have seen: nevertheless, his name is given as commander of the Strombolo fireship, in the beginning of the year 1745, a station which, according to the regulations of the navy at that time, did not give rank as a post captain. We have not been able, after the strictest search, to collect any other particulars concerning him, except that he was put on the superannuated list with the rank and half-pay of a rear-admiral on the 29th of September 1757, and died in the course of the year 1767.

DILKE, William.—The first intelligence we have of this gentleman commences in the year 1737; he was then lieutenant of the Berwick under captain Solguard, but did not proceed to the Mediterranean, being left behind for the purpose of being promoted, as he was immediately afterwards, to be commander of the Hound sloop. He was appointed captain of the St. George, a second rate, then equipping at Portsmouth, on the 16th of January 1740-1. He soon afterwards removed into the Nassau, one of the ships that went out with Mr. Lestock to reinforce admiral Haddock. He afterwards changed to go home in the Winchester. No other mention is made of him till the beginning of the year 1743-4, when he commanded the Chichester, and was ordered out, in company with the Boyne, of eighty guns, to join the Mediterranean fleet under admiral Mathews, whom he fell in with the day before the action took place with the French and Spanish fleets †. His conduct on that occasion was deemed so reprehensible, that, although no apparent notice was taken of it ‡ for some time, and he was not complained of by the

---

* He was one of the commanders sent, during the siege of Carthagena, to attack the Barradera battery, under the orders of captain Watson.

† On the death of Mr. Russel he was appointed, by the admiral, to command the Namur as his captain; and when Mr. Mathews resigned the command, he removed into the Revenge, of sixty-four guns.

‡ He was himself one of the members of the court-martial assembled on board the Torbay, at Port Mahon, for the trial of captain Richard Norris, who had commanded the Essex in the Toulon engagement, and was heavily charged with misconduct.

commander-in-chief, he was one of the officers named, in the house of commons, in their addrefs to his majefty, requefting him to caufe a legal enquiry to be inftituted relative to their behaviour.

He was accordingly brought to trial, at Deptford, and fentenced, on the 5th of December 1745, to be cafhiered, being at the fame time declared incapable of holding any fubfequent naval commiffion. The punifhment was, however, afterwards remitted fo far, that he was reftored to his half-pay. It is almoft needlefs to obferve, we have nothing farther to record of him, except that he died on the 30th of May 1756.

DRAPER, John,—was, about the year 1740, commander of a floop of war, called the Wolf, at that time employed on the Weft India ftation. In this veffel he was caft away when on his paffage from thence to England; but he himfelf with the greater part of his crew being taken up by the marquis d'Antin, he was, not long after his return from France, re-appointed to a fecond floop of the fame name. He is otherwife only noticed as having been appointed captain of the Adventure on the 8th of September 1741. Being foon afterwards ordered to the Weft Indies, he died there on the 17th of July 1743 *.

ELLIS, William.—This gentleman is nearly in the fame predicament with the officers before-mentioned. He was appointed commander of the Drake floop of war early in the year 1741: from this veffel he was, on the 19th of February following, promoted to be captain of the Gofport, a fourth rate of forty guns, newly re-built; and being foon afterwards ordered to New York, died there on the 13th of June 1742.

ELTON, Jacob,—was, on the 28th of December 1741, appointed captain of the Deal Caftle frigate. This veffel we find to have been employed, during the enfuing fummer, as a cruifer off the coaft of Spain. He particularly diftinguifhed himfelf in a little defultory

---

* In fome accounts he is faid to have commanded the Revenge about the end of the year 1742, and to have captured a very valuable Dutch veffel which he detected in trading with the Spaniards in the Weft Indies. It appears, however, very doubtful whether he really was captain of the veffel above-mentioned.

enterprife he was concerned in, with the earl of Northefk, againſt the town of Vigo, the particulars of which will be found in his lordſhip's life, he having been the fenior or commanding officer. He was afterwards promoted to the Anglefea, of forty guns: in which ſhip he was, early in the year 1745, ſtationed as a cruifer in the Channel. On the 29th of March he unhappily fell in with a French privateer, called the Apollo, commanded by a captain Belleiſle. Its force is, in many accounts, ſtated as much fuperior to that of the Anglefea, being called a ſhip of fifty-four guns and five hundred men. Several unlucky coinciding circumſtances contributed to encreafe the advantage the enemy naturally poſſeſſed in point of force: the Apollo fo nearly refembled a Britiſh ſhip of war which was known to be cruifing, that the miſtake was not difcovered till ſhe began to fire on the Anglefea. The ſhip was not cleared for action; the crew weak, and far from well-difciplined; the confuſion into which every perfon on board was thrown by an occurrence unforefeen and totally unexpected, all tended to facilitate the enemy's conqueſt. This appears to have been principally owing to a fatal fecurity into which captain Elton had fuffered himfelf to be betrayed by a total want of information; but though that fecurity is certainly extremely reprehenſible, as militating moſt ſtrongly againſt thoſe principles of prudence and caution, which ſhould induce every commander to confider every ſhip he fees as an enemy, till he is pofitively convinced of the contrary, it certainly claims our pity in fome little degree, and ſhould blunt the edge of our cenfure.

As to captain Elton, finding too late his fatal error, he exerted himfelf with all the activity that can render the character of a man of gallantry moſt truly refpectable, by endeavouring to animate his crew to a recovery from the confuſion into which they had fallen. His attempts were ineffectual, and he himfelf, together with his firſt lieutenant, paid, with their lives, in the early part of the action, the forfeit of their unhappy neglect. The ſhip itſelf was furrendered by the fecond lieutenant, though not till, as it is faid, fixty of the crew, which at the beginning of the action, confiſted of only two hundred, were killed or wounded. The lieutenant was afterwards tried by a court-martial on the 25th of June, and condemned to be ſhot; a fentence

tence which was carried into execution on the 19th of July*.

FENWICK, Benjamin, — was promoted from the rank of lieutenant to be commander of the Ætna firefhip, about the month of March 1740. In the month of October following he was fent to the Weft Indies with the fleet under fir C. Ogle. No particular mention is made of him during the fiege of Carthagena; but after the unfortunate termination of that expedition, and the return of the fleet to Jamaica, he was, on the 8th of June, promoted to be captain of the Briftol, of fifty guns, one of the fhips which had arrived from England during the abfence of the fleet; and was left behind at Port Royal, with other fhips, in the month of July, under the orders of commodore Davers, when Mr. Vernon failed on his expedition againft Cuba. No other mention is made of him, except that he died in England on the 14th of March 1757.

GODSALVE, Henry, — was, in the year 1738, lieutenant of the Berwick, to which he was promoted, by admiral Haddock, as fucceffor to Mr. Dilke. He was promoted, early in 1741, to be commander of the Salamander bomb-ketch: he was farther advanced, on the 17th of May, to be captain of the Guardland frigate. He continued in this veffel till about the year 1744, when he was made captain of the Romney. He returned to England at the clofe of the year laft-mentioned; when the Romney being ordered to be difmantled, and put out of commiffion, captain Godfalve is believed never to have held any fubfequent command. In 1748 he was intended for the Ipfwich, of feventy guns; but peace being concluded before that fhip was ready for fervice, no commiffion was ever made out. He retired altogether from the line of active fervice, being put on the fuperannuated lift, with

---

* The court-martial are faid to have been induced to pafs fo fevere a fentence on Mr Phillips, from the circumftance of his having quitted the deck, from a miftaken notion of duty and propriety, in the hope of being able to induce, by his perfuafions, the furviving part of the crew to return to their quarters. Mr. Hardy's lift, as well as many others we have feen, erroneoufly ftate the Anglefea to have been captured on the 25th of June, which was the day fentence was paffed, as above ftated, on Mr. Phillips.

rank and half-pay of a rear-admiral, in the year 1756. He died in England on the 1ſt of December 1765.

GREGORY, Thomas,—was, in the month of September 1740, promoted from the rank of lieutenant to be commander of the Thunder bomb-ketch. Being ordered quickly afterwards to the Weſt Indies, he was promoted there by Mr. Vernon, on the 7th of September following, to be captain of the Norwich. He continued in the Weſt Indies till the beginning of the year 1743, when he appears to have been one of the commanders under the orders of Mr. Knowles, at the expedition againſt La Guira. His conduct on that occaſion was deemed ſo reprehenſible by the commodore, who was at particular times rather captious in his obſervations on the behaviour of thoſe under his command, that he not only ſuperceded him during the action, but complained of and ſent him to England under arreſt. He was tried on the charge of miſbehaviour before a court martial, held at Spithead, on the 17th of September 1743, admiral Stewart being the preſident, and ſentenced to be diſmiſſed the ſervice.

In 1745 Mr. Vernon, under whom he had before ſerved, and probably was no ſtranger to his gallantry and good qualities, ſtood forth as his patron. He ſerved under that admiral for a ſhort time as a volunteer, and diſtinguiſhed himſelf exceedingly, by his activity and adroitneſs, in reconnoitering the French ports of Dunkirk and Calais, as well as in procuring much collateral information, relative to their embarkations on the coaſt for the ſupport of the pretender. Theſe ſervices, particularly at ſo critical a time, were ſo acceptable, that, ſupported by this ſtrong claim to favour, and the recommendation of Mr. Vernon, he was once more reſtored to the ſervice, and appointed captain of the Folkſtone frigate, being admitted, by order of council, to take rank from the 12th of November 1745. Some accounts make him to have been appointed, in the month of April following, captain of the Duke William, a large ſhip mounting fifty guns: but this circumſtance we totally diſbelieve. He afterwards ſerved under commodore Mitchel, who was ſtationed with a ſmall cruiſing ſquadron off the coaſt of Holland. While thus employed he unhappily fell into ſome diſpute with the commodore's secretary *, which terminating in a duel, captain Gregory was unfortunately killed. This event is said, by Mr. Hardy, to have taken place in 1747; but other accounts state it to have happened in the preceding year.

HAMAR, Joseph.—Our information relative to this gentleman commences with his having been, about the latter end of the year 1740, commander of the Royal Escape, a small yacht mounting four guns, then stationed at the Nore for the purpose of receiving men. On the 22d of October 1741, he was promoted to be captain of the Flamborough frigate. Of such little importance were the different services † in which it was his misfortune to be employed, that we do not find the smallest mention made of him ‡, notwithstanding we believe him to have been continually in commission, till the year 1755, when he was captain of the Eagle, of sixty guns, a guard-ship. He is said to have been superseded in that command for misconduct; but no mention is made of the particulars. He was notwithstanding retained on the list as a captain, and in the month of October 1758, was put on the superannuated list with the rank and half-pay of a rear-admiral. He died at Manchester, where he had for some time resided, on the 14th of January 1773.

HAMILTON, Honourable John,—was the second son of James seventh earl of Abercorn, and Anne, daughter of colonel John Plummer, of Blakesware, in the county of Hertford. Having betaken himself to a naval life, he was, very early in the year 1741, promoted to be commander of the Seaford fireship; and on the 19th of February following was advanced to be captain of the Deal Castle. No particular mention is made of him during the time he continued in this vessel, which appears to have been only for a short space, as, in 1742, we find him

---

* Mr. George Tymewell, who was afterwards tried by a court-martial at Deptford for the murder, of which he was acquitted; but being found guilty of a misdemeanour, was sentenced to two years imprisonment in the marshalsea, and rendered incapable of ever serving again in the navy.

† We do not find any particular notice taken of them, except that, in 1742, he was employed on the American station.

‡ Except his having been one of the members of the court-martial convened for the trial of the admirals, Mathews and Lestock, in 1746.

captain of the Kinfale, a cruifing frigate. In this fervice, however, the moft material notice that is taken of him appears to be that fubjoined in a note beneath *. In 1744 he was promoted to the Augufta, and in the month of March 1745, we find him ftationed as a cruifer on the Irifh ftation. In this employment he was rather fuccefful, having captured and carried into Kinfale a large French privateer, belonging to St. Maloes, called the Compteffe de la Riviere, carrying twenty-two guns and one hundred and fixty men. In the preceding part of the fame cruife he is faid to have fallen in with a privateer of thirty-fix guns, during the night, which he engaged for a fhort time; but as, after exchanging a few broadfides, the enemy fuddenly difappeared, and as feveral concurring circumftances occurred to ftrengthen fuch an opinion, it was concluded it had funk. In this trivial encounter two men were killed and three wounded on board the Augufta.

No notice of confequence is taken of captain Hamilton in the line of fervice during the remainder of the war. It is not improbable but, during that period, he continued in the Augufta, and employed in the fame manner we have already feen him generally occupied. In 1746 he was one of the members of the court-martial affembled, for the trials of the admirals, Leftock and Mathews. A circumftance occurred on that occafion which made no little noife, and which Mr. Hamilton is faid to have been one of the principal inftigators and promoters of. Rear-admiral Mayne, the prefident, and captain Renton, one of

---

" * Whitehall, September 18.

" On the 7th inftant his majefty's fhip the Kinfale, commanded by the honourable captain Hamilton, being on a cruize off Dieppe, and ftanding in fhore, he faw a veffel lying-to, which, as foon as fhe faw the man of war, made fail towards her and hoifted French colours. The Kinfale ftanding for her they foon came within half gun-fhot; when the privateer hawled down her colours, and intended to board the Kinfale, which fhe took for a collier. Captain Hamilton has brought her into Spithead: fhe is a new veffel and well found: has a lute ftern and a horfe head; and is rigged fometimes as a fchooner and fometimes as a brig: had fifty-eight men when taken, twenty-four of whom were French; is mounted with two carriage guns and thirteen fwivels. This privateer is the fame that engaged the Grampus and killed captain Gordon."

the members composing the court-martial, had been arrested by a writ, at the suit of a lieutenant Frye, for a sentence passed on him at a court martial, of which they were members, held in the West Indies. Captain Hamilton, after the writ had been read, moved the resolutions inserted beneath*, which produced the correspondence

---

* " Resolved, That it appears the highest indignity offered to the court, and through this court to every other court of judicature that is or may hereafter be formed in this kingdom, and the highest infraction of the prerogative of the lord high admiral, and of the statute law of this realm, to arrest or serve any writ of capias upon the president, or any member of this court now sitting, or of any other court-martial, and therefore the court unanimously resolve to desist farther proceeding on this trial till satisfaction be made for this high insult.

" Resolved, That this court make representation, by letter, to the lord high admiral, of the infringement made on his prerogative by arresting the president of the court, duly assembled by virtue of his authority; and that the court do adjourn till Thursday morning nine o'clock, to give time for every member to deliberate upon proper methods for obtaining satisfaction for the high insult on their president, from all persons, *how high soever in rank or office*, who have *set on foot* this arrest, or in *any degree promoted* or *advised* it."

These resolutions being signed by the president, and the several members of the court, the president directed it to be enclosed in a letter, and delivered by the judge advocate to the lords of the admiralty.

Then the court adjourned till Monday morning nine o'clock, and from thence to Thursday the 22d.

On the 22d, the followig letter from Mr. Corbett, secretary to the lords commissioners of the admiralty, enclosing one from the duke of Newcastle to their lordships, was read before the court.

" Mr. Corbett's letter to the president.

" Having laid the letter of the 16th instant, and also the resolutions of the court-martial of the same date, brought hither by the judge advocate, before the lords commissioners of the admiralty, their lordships thought the said resolutions to be a matter of such importance that they laid the same before his majesty; in consequence of which their lordships received a letter from his grace the duke of Newcastle, principal secretary of state : I am commanded to send you enclosed an attested copy thereof, in order to your laying the same before the court-martial at their meeting to morrow: their lordships make no doubt but that every gentleman, who is a member of the court, will be greatly satisfied with his majesty's most gracious expressions contained in the said letter; and as they are assured of his majesty's

dence annexed to them, between the duke of Newcaftle, Mr. Corbet, fecretary to the admiralty, and the members of

jefty's protection, and of having full fatisfaction for the late indignity offered them, and that methods will be taken to prevent any thing of the like nature for the future, their lordfhips hope they will be unanimous in agreeing to go on immediately in hearing and adjufting the trials that are depending, and to continue fo till they are finifhed.

"I am yours, &c.

"Admiralty-office, May 21, 1746.   "T. CORBETT."

Duke of Newcaftle's letter.

"To my lords commiffioners of the admiralty,

"I received your lordfhip's letter of the 16th inftant, with the papers enclofed relating to the writ ferved on rear-admiral Mayne, who prefides at the court-martial at Deptford, for enquiring into the conduct, &c. of Mr. Leftock and others, and the refolutions of the court thereupon, which I have laid before his majefty. His majefty expreffed great difpleafure at the infult offered to the court-martial, by which the military difcipline of the navy is fo much affected; and the king highly difapproves the behaviour of lieutenant Frye on this occafion. His majefty has it under confideration what fteps may be advifeable to be taken on this incident; and in the mean time his majefty would have your lordfhip's acquaint the members of the court-martial, that they may depend on his majefty's moft gracious protection, for procuring them a fufficient fatisfaction for the late indignity offered them; and that proper methods will be taken for preventing any thing of the like nature for the future.

"I am, &c.

Received May 22, 1746.   "H. N."

The anfwer of the court martial to the letter fent by Mr. Corbett, by order of the lords of the admiralty, May 21ft.

"Sir,

"We defire you will be pleafed to inform their lordfhips, that having heard their lordfhip's letter read to us, as well as the inclofed authentick copy of the letter to their lordfhips, from his majefty's principal fecretary of ftate, the duke of Newcaftle, fignifying his majefty's royal affurance of his moft gracious protection, for procuring to us a fufficient fatisfaction for the late indignity offered to us; and that proper methods will be taken for preventing any thing of the like nature for the future:

"According to their lordfhip's defire we are unanimoufly agreed to proceed upon the bufinefs of thefe trials, but think it incumbent upon us to give their lordfhips our reafons for the fteps we have already taken, fubmitting them to their lordfhip's further confideration,

of the court-martial, in their judicial capacity. This matter appears, however, to have been very unwisely and

---

tion, as this attack appears to us of the most dangerous consequence, to the security of the nation, the authority of the lord high admiral, the privilege of the honourable the house of commons in parliament assembled, and the prerogative of the crown:

" First, it appears that sir John Willes, knight, lord chief justice of the court of common pleas, having no regard to the honour and safety of his majesty, the security of the liberties and properties of his subjects, the support of the constitution and defence of his dominions, in time of actual war with two powerful nations, favoured, aided, and abetted, by rebellion at home, contrary to his duty and trust, in violation of the statute laws of the realm, as well as those established by use and custom, time immemorial, by which his majesty's arms by sea have been prudently, wisely, and effectually governed to the great glory of his majesty and protection of his subjects, as well as in open defiance of his majesty's commands, in consequence of an address of the honourable house of commons in parliament assembled, he, the said sir J. W. knt. did issue his writ on the 12th day of May, in the nineteenth year of the reign of his present majesty, to arrest, seize, and secure the persons of P. Mayne, esq. and J. Renton, esq. members constituant and judges of a court martial then sitting, by order of the lords commissioners for executing the office of lord high admiral of Great Britain, by virtue of the power to them given by the statute of the 13th of king C. the Second, the said judges being duly qualified as the act requires, and did cause the said writ to be served on P. M. esq. by which crafty and subtile device, as far as in him lieth, he did let, respit, and disannul the laws of the land, and, by forcibly taking away the judges, prevent the execution of justice, and delude the commands of his majesty, grounded upon the address of the honourable house of commons in parliament assembled; and though in a clause subjoined to the same writ, it is artfully added that the president is served with this process to the intent that he may, by his attorney, appear in his majesty's court of common pleas, it appears to us that this evasion is only provided to the intent that we might possibly, through oversight, proceed in our judicial capacity, and that by some reserved device as well as our general proceedings, as our final determination, and sentence might be interrupted and declared void and of none effect, to the entire defeating of this solemn, grand, and national enquiry.

" 2d. That the grounds of this writ were an action recommended, by the said L. C. J. in open court, for damages against the said P. M. esq. and J. R. esq. for the sentence of a court-martial legally held, by virtue of the statute laws of the realm, at Jamaica, of which court the said P. M. esq. and J. R. esq. where members, constituents, or judges, properly qualified as such by the known laws of the realm, as well statutes as use and custom.

" 3d

and rashly entered upon. The chief justice of the common pleas not only proved the propriety and legality of the measures taken, under the authority of the court where he presided, but also that he himself was personally unacquainted with all matters and particulars concerning them, farther than having directed the procedure as a matter of course, founded on the strictest principles of justice. This being explained, a public apology was made by the members of the court collectively, and this very disagreeable affair ended *.

In

" 3d. That in consequence of this breach and violation of the laws of the kingdom, as well as insult to a supreme court of judicature sitting to determine in the dernier resort, which by its constitution never can acknowledge any superior court, nor any appeal from its sentence but to his majesty's prerogative, as far as in him lieth; the whole order, discipline, and government of his majesty's armies by sea is entirely and absolutely dissolved, the statute of the 13th of king Charles the Second is made null and void, by which most wicked device the honour of his majesty is betrayed, the security of his subjects is exposed, and the fundamental laws of the constitution subverted.

" We are, &c."

" Court-martial on board the Prince
of Orange, at Deptford, 22d May,
1746."

* Soon as the court-martial discovered the erroneous principles on which they had founded their too hasty censure, they passed the following resolution, which they formally sent to the chief justice.

" As nothing is more becoming a gentleman than to acknowledge himself to be in the wrong, as soon as he is sensible that he is so, and to be ready to make satisfaction to any person he has injured; we therefore, whose names are underwritten, being thoroughly convinced that we were entirely mistaken in the opinion we had conceived of the lord chief justice Willes, think ourselves obliged, in honour as well as justice, to make him satisfaction, as far as it is in our power; and as the injury we did him was of a public nature, we do in this public manner declare, that we are now satisfied the reflections cast upon him in our resolutions of the 16th and 21st of May last, were unjust, unwarrantable and without any foundation whatsoever; and we do ask pardon of his lordship, and the court of common pleas, for the indignity offered both to him and the court.

VOL. V. G " Perry

In 1748 captain Hamilton was appointed to the Vanguard, of fixty guns, a guardſhip at Plymouth, at which port he was, in the month of July, commanding officer, with the temporary rank of commodore. On the 14th of

" Perry Mayne,   C. Molloy,
J. Byng,   Smith Callis,
E. Legge,   R. Erſkine,
Ja. Rentone,   J. Pittman,
Th. Frankland,   Cha. Catford,
Cha. Colby,   Tho. Hanway,
J. Hamilton,   E. Spragge,
Sheldrake Laton,   John Orme."
Joſ. Hamer,

On the receipt of this apology ſir John Willes made the following ſhort ſpeech in open court, and this very diſagreeable altercation cloſed.

" Although the injury I received might have required a private ſatisfaction, yet as the offence was of a public nature, and offered to the whole court of common pleas, as well as myſelf, I thought it more conſiſtent with my character, and the dignity of the poſt which I have the honour to fill, to have ſatisfaction in this public manner; and deſire, with the concurrence of my brothers, that it may be regiſtered in the remembrance office, as a memorial to the preſent and future ages, that whoſoever ſet themſelves up in oppoſition to the laws, or think themſelves above the law, will in the end find themſelves miſtaken, for we may with great propriety ſay of the law, as of truth, *magna eſt et prævalebit.*"

The following paragraph, taken from one of the periodical publications of the time, will beſt prove the ſtate of the fact, and ſhew very perfectly the true ſhare ſir John had in countenancing, as was ſuppoſed perſonally, an act which cauſed ſo much diſturbance.

" Friday, February 21, 1746, was tried, at the common pleas, an action of falſe impriſonment, brought by lieutenant Geo Fry, againſt ſir Chaloner Ogle, when a verdict was given for the plaintiff with 1000 l. damages; and he has the ſame cauſe of action againſt all the court-martial. His caſe is briefly thus: in 1740 he went volunteer to Carthagena, and for his gallant behaviour general Wentworth made him firſt lieutenant of marines; but for refuſing to apprehend another lieutenant, without a written order, he was confined fourteen months, debarred pen, ink and paper, and was ſo cruelly treated that it threw him into an epileptic diſorder and convulſions. After this he was tried by a court-martial for refuſing to obey orders; and was, on the evidence of illiterate people whom he had never ſeen, (nor was ſuffered to croſs examine) ſentenced to fifteen years impriſonment, and to be incapable of his majeſty's ſervice: he was accordingly brought to the marſhalſea; but, on his petition to the king, was, with the advice of the privy council, reſtored to his commiſſion."

September

September 1749, he married the widow of Richard Elliot, of Port Elliot, Cornwall, efq. by whom he left a fon, who is now marquis of Abercorn. In 1755 he commanded the Lancafter, of fixty-fix guns, a fhip equipped in the early part of that year at Chatham. This veffel having afterwards gone round to Spithead as part of the naval armament collected there in confequence of the expected rupture with France, captain Hamilton was unhappily drowned, on the 18th of December in the fame year, the boat having overfet on its paffage from Spithead to the fhore. He fwam for the fpace of near twenty minutes; and while his ftrength of fpeech furvived to him, continually exhorted his men to refignation, at the fame time encouraging them to all poffible exertion of their ftrength to fave their lives.

HARDY, Sir Charles,—was the fon of the admiral of the fame name, of whom we have before given fome account *. Having purfued the fteps of his worthy parent, and betaken himfelf to the naval fervice, he was, on the 10th of Auguft 1741, promoted to be captain of the Rye, of 24 guns, as fucceffor to captain Lufhington. In this veffel he was quickly afterwards ordered to Carolina, where we find him, in the month of July 1742; and immediately fubfequent to that time occupied in cruifing off the coaft of Georgia, on which colony the Spaniards had effected a formidable defcent. In 1744 he commanded the Jerfey, of fixty guns; he was, by commiffion bearing date June the 9th, in that year, appointed governor and commander-in-chief of the ifland of Newfoundland, with the port of Placentia and all its dependencies. Some of the fhips under his convoy having been captured by the enemy on his return from his government, at the conclufion of the year, this matter was ordered to be inveftigated by a court-martial, which was held on the 2d of February enfuing, and ended in his honourable acquittal.

In the month of July following, he ftill continuing captain of the Jerfey, we find him to have been concerned in the following very gallant exploit, which is thus re-

---

* See vol. iv. p. 9. et feq.

lated in a letter from Lisbon, officially publifhed in the Gazette, No. 8457.

"Lifbon, July 28, N. S.

"His Britannick majefty's fhip, which fell in with the French man of war, called the St. Efprit, of feventy-four guns, near the Streight's mouth, was the Jerfey, of fixty guns, captain Hardy. The engagement lafted from half an hour paft fix in the evening till nine, when the French man of war bore away on her return to Cadiz to refit. We hear that the St. Efprit had loft her fore-maft, bolt-fprit, and twenty men in the action."

We have no fubfequent information concerning him during the continuance of the war. In the month of July 1749, we find him to have married ——, daughter of Bartholomew Tate, of Delapree, in the county of Northampton, efq. During a confiderable part of the enfuing peace he is erroneoufly faid to have commanded a yacht; but we have no certain information concerning him till 1755, when he was advanced to the very honourable appointment of governor of New York. On the 12th of April in this year, that being moft probably the time when he received the commiffion laft mentioned, the honour of knighthood was annexed to it. In 1756, being then abfent at his government, he was raifed to the rank of rear-admiral of the blue. His commiffion being fent out to him thither, he hoifted his flag on board the Nightingale, in that harbour, on the 6th of May; and having afterwards removed into the Sutherland, of fifty guns, prepared to put to fea with all the fhips of war he could collect, as convoy to the fleet of victuallers and tranfports intended to convey lord Loudon and his troops to Halifax, preparatory to the intended attack on Louifburg. The admiral was kept in a ftate of uncertainty for fome time, both as to the arrival of Mr. Holburne, who was daily expected from England with a formidable fleet, and alfo the fituation as well as force in which the enemy were, at the threatened place of attack: but two veffels which had been difpatched to reconnoitre the neighbouring coaft having returned without feeing any thing of the enemy, fir Charles hefitated no longer in putting to fea from Sandy Hook, which he did on June 20. He arrived fafe at Halifax on the

30th

30th with his whole charge, amounting (the ſhips of war, which were very few in number, included) to one hundred and one ſail.

Mr. Holburne himſelf arriving at Halifax on the 9th of July, ſir Charles hoiſted his flag, as ſecond in command, on board the Invincible: but the leading events of the expedition we are now treating of, having been already noticed in the account of the commander-in-chief, it is needleſs to enter into any farther detail of them. Having reſigned his ſtation as governor at the concluſion of the year, he returned to England, where, on February 7, 1758, he was farther advanced to be rear-admiral of the white. Having hoiſted his flag on board the Captain, of ſixty-eight guns, he was ordered again to New York for the purpoſe of forwarding the neceſſary arrangements previous to the meditated renewal of an attack on the enemy in the ſame quarter where it had the preceding year proved unſucceſsful. Mr. Boſcawen having followed not long afterwards, ſir Charles joined him off Louiſburg on the 14th of June; but in the courſe of the enſuing night was blown off to ſea by a violent gale of wind: he returned, however, without having experienced any diſaſter. He was occupied during the remainder of the ſiege, having removed his flag into the Royal William, in blocking up the harbour, as well for the purpoſe of ſhutting up five ſhips of the line then in the port, as preventing the enemy from receiving any ſupplies. Sir Charles was extremely vigilant; and, what does not invariably prove the conſequence of ſuch meritorious activity, was very ſucceſsful, all the ſhips of the line being deſtroyed*, except the Bienfaiſant, which, as we ſhall hereafter ſhew in our account of captain Balfour, fell into the hands of the aſſailants.

---

* The Apollo, of fifty; the Fidelle, of thirty-ſix; the Chevre and the Biche, of ſixteen guns each, were ſunk at the entrance of the harbour: the Echo, of thirty-two guns, attempting to get out, was captured by ſir Charles: ſo that of the whole naval force in the harbour at the time of the inveſtiture, mounting to five ſhips of the line, one of fifty guns, four frigates, and two corvettes, the Comette and Bizarre frigates only got off: the latter too made her eſcape on the very day the troops were landed, conſequently before the ſiege could be ſaid to be formed.

After the well-known reduction of this important place, sir Charles was detached, with seven ships of the line and three frigates, to convoy some troops sent to Gaspe, on the river St. Lawrence; and having rejoined Mr. Boscawen not long afterwards, returned to England with him in the month of October. He arrived safe at St. Helen's on the 1st of November, having had a partial and inconsiderable skirmish * with seven of the enemy's ships from Quebec, which took the advantage of the approaching night to decline any farther contest. In 1759 he served as second in command of the Channel fleet, under sir Edward Hawke, and was promoted to be vice-admiral of the blue. He retained this station in that very memorable and glorious encounter with the French fleet under Conflans; and is noticed in the following terms by a person of intelligence, a chaplain of one of the ships who was there also. " Sir Charles Hardy (he reports) in the Union, with the Mars, Hero, and several other ships, were crowding to the admiral's assistance, when the retreat of the French, covered by the obscurity of the evening, put an end to the engagement."

In the following year he was employed on the same station, having, during a considerable part of it, his flag on board the Mars: but the recent defeat having completely prevented the French fleet from putting to sea, nothing more remarkable is said of him, than his having been obliged to put into port in the middle of the month of September, having sprung all his masts in a heavy gale of wind Having proceeded to sea in the month of October to join his commander-in-chief in the Bay of Biscay, he shifted his flag, on their junction, into his old ship, the Union. The year 1761, during which he retained the same appointment, was, owing to the cause already stated, consumed in a manner equally uninteresting with the preceding. In 1762 he remained on the same station commanding alternately, with sir Edward Hawke, the squadrons stationed off Brest, which relieved each other successively, for the purpose of watching the shattered

---

* The British force consisted of the Namure, Royal William, and another ship of the line, with the Bienfaisant prize.

remnant

LIGNE DE BATAILLE

De l'armée combinée sous les ordres de monsieur le compte D'Orvilliers, lieutenant-general des armées navalles de sa majesté tres chretienne, grand croix de lordre royal militaires de St. Louis, 1779.

* Son excellence M. de Cordova, commandant l'escadre Espagnole, a dit que son intention et de marcher en echiquier, sur la ligne opposée a l'ordre de bataille de la grande armée au vent de celle en observant pour point de relevement le vaisseau le Citoyen placé a l'extremeté de la ligne de bataille Francaise.

Division	Vaisseau	Canons
Premiere division	Le Citoyen	74
	Saint Miguel, Espagnol	70
	L'Auguste, chef	80
	Le Prothé	64
	Saint Pablo Espagnol	70
	Le Veillé	64
	Arrogante, Espagnol	70
	La Ville de Paris, chef	100
	Le Glorieux	74
	Serio, Espagnol	70
Seconde division	Saint Pedro, Espagnol	64
	L Indien	70
	Saint Joseph, chef	74
	Le Palmier	74
Escadre Blanche et Blue	La Victoire	74
Troisieme div.	Le Zodiaque	74
	Guerrero, Espagnol	74
	Saint Vincente, chef	80
	Le Scipion	70
4me division	Le Bien Aime	74
	L'Actif	74
	Saint Carlos, Espagnol	80
	La Bretagne, chef	110

CORVETTES, FREGATTES, LOUGRES, ET COTTERS.

L'Aigrette
La Favorite
La Surveillante
Le Pilaute
La Bellone
Assumption
La Grana
La Curieuse
Le Chasseur
L'Atalante
L'Espiegle
La Junon
La Concorde
L'Etourdie
La Diane
Le Senegal
Le Mutin
Santa des Carmen
Santa Catarina
La Magiciéne

FREGATES.

Sainte Rosalia
Sainte Gertrudis

† ESCADRE LEGERE.

Le Saint Michel	60
Espagne	64
La Couronne	80
Migno	60
Le Triton	64

BOMBARDES.

Le Pluvier
Le Saumon

Brulots.

Le Menagere — Francais
Le Dashwood — et
Le Boudeuse — Espagnol.
Santa Rafa
Jupiter

Division	Ship	Guns
Escadre Blanche 5me division	Le Neptune	80
	Vincidor, Espagnol	70
	Le Deflin	74
	Le Saint Joaquin, Espagnole	70
	Saint Isabel, chef	70
	La Bourgogne	74
	Le Solitaire	64
6me division	L'Hercule	74
	Septentrion, Espagnol	64
	Le Saint Esprit, chef	80
	L'Intrepide	74
7me division	Saint Angel Garde, Espagnol	70
	La Bizarre	64
	Le Conquerant	74
8me division	El Rayo, chef, Espagnol	80
	Saint Damas,	70
	L'Actionnaire	64
Escadre Blue	L'Alexander	64
	Le Brillant, chef, Espagnol	70
	Saint Louis, chef, Espagnol	80
9me division	Le Caton	64
	Le Pluton	74

† Monsieur de la Touche Treville commandant l'Escadre legére marchera dans l'ordre de l'echiquier sur la ligne opposée à l'ordre de bataille de la grand armée en observant de retenir au vent autant que la circonstance le permétra et ayant pour point de relief de vaisseau le Pluton placé à l'extremité de la ligne de bataille. F.

* Escadre d'Observation, Espagnole.		
Trinidade Espagnol chef	-	116
Monarca	-	70
Saint Paschal	-	80
Saint Nicholas	-	70
Saint Rafael	-	70
Saint Eugenio	-	70
Princessa	-	70
Atlante	-	70
Velasco	-	70
Saint Francis de Paule	-	74
Saint Francis D'Assise	-	80
Galicia	-	70
Diligente	-	64
Saint Isidore	-	70
Asato	-	70
Ferdinando	-	64
Saint Isidro	-	64

Autre Refonnaiment.

	Flutes.
Emeralda	
Regla	
Annontiation	

Hopiteaux Espagnol
Santa Rita

Recapitulation.

Escadre d'Observation	-	1244
Escadre Blanche et blue	-	1088
Escadre Blanche	-	1138
Escadre Blue	-	1066
Escadre Legere	-	318
	Total	4854

Les fregattes, se tendront à une portée de canon des vaisseaux, pavillon du cotte opposé aux ennemis, les corvettes se tiendront trés près du commandant de leur escadres et les lougrés et cotters se tiendront entres les vaisseaux et corvettes qui douivent avoir lieux également lors que l'armée marcherat sur trois collonnes en observant que les trois chargées de repetée doivent se tenir au contre de leur escadre quand même le geneteaux marcherait a la tetto.

To face Page 103, Vol. V.

remnant of the French naval force. Indeed, the hiftory of fir Charles is fo clofely implicated during this period with that of fir Edward, his fuperior in command, that the hiftory of the former might in great meafure fuffice for that of the latter with a mere change of name.

In the month of October 1762, he was promoted to be vice-admiral of the white, and, during the fhort remainder of the war, was occupied as already ftated. After the conclufion of the peace he enjoyed a relaxation from the fatigues of public fervice : neither is he particularly mentioned even in private life, except that, in the month of November 1767, he was one of the fupporters of the canopy at the funeral of his royal highnefs the duke of York. On the 28th of October 1770, he was farther advanced to be admiral of the blue; as he was on the death of admiral Holburne, in the following year, to be mafter and governor of Greenwich-hofpital. In 1774 he was elected reprefentative in parliament for the borough of Plymouth; but appeared in no other light as a public character till 1779*: he was then, on the refignation of admiral Keppel, appointed admiral and commander-in-chief of the main or Channel fleet. Its force may be thought formidable when ftated at forty-four fhips, of two and three decks: in this number, however, were many included which were extremely deficient in men, as well as in other refpects unfit for fervice, from their being juft returned from a foreign ftation, and confequently much out of condition. Thus was he fituated, when the Spanifh fleet from Cadiz, having formed a junction with that of France, from Breft, entered the Britifh Channel. Such was their fuperiority of force when united †, that fir Charles, reflecting the fate of his country was, in great meafure, fuppofed to be connected with that of the fleet under his command, prudently refolved to act merely on the defenfive inftead of rifking an encounter, which, if unfuccefsful, would have been productive, at leaft of the

---

* In 1778 he was advanced to be admiral of the white.
† The following is a very exact and correct lift of the enemy's force at this period, which never having been publicly afcertained with any degree of precifion, cannot be thought otherwife than extremely curious.—See annexed table.

greateſt national alarm, if not actual misfortune. The event, if not glorious was not unfortunate. The combined fleets, after having enjoyed the uſeleſs and paltry parade of traverſing the Channel for a very ſhort period, without daring to undertake the ſmalleſt enterprize worthy of commemoration, returned back to their own ports with no greater advantage than the inſignificant triumph of not having been themſelves defeated.

The fleet returned towards the concluſion of the year into port; and being refitted on the approach of the enſuing ſpring, ſir Charles prepared to reſume the command: this, however, his unfortunate, and we may alſo add, from the general, the univerſal opinion entertained of him as a truly brave and worthy man, his premature death, prevented him from executing. He died ſuddenly, in an apoplectic fit, at Portſmouth, on the 18th of May 1780.

An obſervation we have more than once before had occaſion to make, and particularly in the caſe of Matthew lord Aylmer, is in no caſe more ſtrongly applicable than the preſent—brave, prudent, gallant, and enterprizing, without the ſmalleſt oſtentatious diſplay of his noble qualities — generous, mild, affable, and intelligent — his virtues commanded the moſt profound reſpect, enabling him to paſs through days, when the rage and prejudice of party blazed with a fury nearly unquenchable, without exciting envy or diſlike, without ever furniſhing to the moſt captious man of party the ſmalleſt ground of reprehenſion or complaint.

HERBERT, Edward,—was a collateral deſcendant of the noble family of Herbert, earl of Pembroke. He is ſaid, in rear-admiral Hardy's naval liſt, to have been appointed commander of the Torrington frigate, as ſucceſſor to captain Knight, on the 5th of March, 1741. We believe this information to be correct, notwithſtanding almoſt all other accounts ſtate him to have taken poſt on that day in the Tyger, a fourth rate. He was, however, certainly removed into that ſhip in a very ſhort time afterwards, and accompanied Mr. Vernon on his unſucceſsful expedition againſt the iſland of Cuba. The Tyger being wrecked not long after the return of the armament, captain Herbert was tried by a court-martial, aſſembled at Jamaica, on the 10th of July, 1742, and mulcted, for neglect

neglect of duty, all the pay then due to him; but was as at the same time recommended for farther employment by his judges. We believe him to have been a short time afterwards appointed to the Woolwich; and, in April 1744, to have captured a very valuable Spanish ship, called the Ascension, bound from Cadiz to Vera Cruz, carrying twenty-four guns, and one hundred and twenty men. On the 11th of August following he was brought to a court-martial, at Antigua, for disobedience of the orders given him by the commander-in-chief, for which offence he was not only sharply reprimanded by the president, but was also fined twelve months pay. We have no proof of his having received any subsequent commission, but believe him to have lived in retirement after the time above stated. He died in Wales on the 19th of November 1752.

HORE, Daniel, — was, at the end of the year 1740, commander of the Succefs fireship, one of the small vessels attached to the fleet commanded by admiral Vernon. Having, consequently, been concerned in the expedition, undertaken early in the ensuing year against Carthagena, he was, after the assault made on Fort St. Lazar had unfortunately failed, ordered to command the Gallicia, of sixty guns, which had been just captured from the Spaniards, in whose service she had been the flag-ship of Don Blafs, their admiral. This vessel was fitted up as a floating battery by Mr. Vernon's orders, and warped as close to the walls of Carthagena as possible on the night of the 15th of April; being intended as an experiment for the purpose of convincing the general, that any diversion attempted by the fleet would have been productive of no real advantage.

Although the conclusions drawn from the little succefs attending this project, are deemed by many persons far from being positive evidence of the truth of what the admiral insisted on, all accounts uniformly bestow the greatest praise on the conduct and gallantry of captain Hore. No ship, say the historians who have recorded this transaction, could be brought nearer, nor could any fire be more regularly and closely kept up, than by the officers and seamen on board this ship, which sustained the cannonade from three bastions an half moon, and a ravelin, from five in the morning till near twelve at noon, without

out the smallest intermission or diminution. The ship had, by the time just mentioned, received so much damage as to render it extremely dangerous for her to continue the attack ; and the admiral, supposing the most incredulous would be satisfied with the experiment already made, sent orders to captain Hore to cut his cables and suffer the vessel to drive off from the town with the sea breeze. He accordingly obeyed, but kept his broadside to the town, on which he continued to fire till the vessel grounded on a shoal*; a circumstance, if report says true, that was rather fortunate for the crew, for it was generally believed, if that had not been the case, that the ship must otherwise, in consequence of the number of shot received in her hull, have quickly foundered at her anchors.

Captain Hore, in consequence of the great spirit he displayed on the foregoing very trying occasion, was promoted, on the 21st of April, N. S. to be captain of the Ludlow Castle, of forty guns; other accounts say the Defiance, a fourth rate, of sixty guns : but this ship we believe him not to have been appointed to in the first instance, but to have been removed into not long afterwards. He remained on the West India station for some time; but is not particularly noticed, except as having been, in the month of September 1742, the happy means of preserving near an hundred and fifty of the crew belonging to the Tilbury, of sixty guns, which accidentally took fire off Navassa. He did not long remain in the Defiance, and afterwards commanded the Canterbury; in which ship he arrived at Louisburg on the 11th of September : and immediately afterwards obtained leave from rear-admiral Knowles to quit that ship and return to England on account of his ill health. It is stated, but without any truth, by an anonymous publisher of naval anecdotes, that captain Hore was appointed to the Lark, by Mr. Knowles, in 1748, he being at that time commander-in-chief at Louisburg, Mr. Crookshanks, her former captain, being under suspension.

No other information relative to captain Hore has come to our knowledge, except that he was put, in 1756, on the superannuated list, with the rank and half-pay of a

---

* Where she immediately afterwards filled, and was destroyed.

rear-

rear-admiral, in which station and honourable retirement, he died in England on the 25th of June 1762.

LAKE, Thomas,—was, on the 2d of December 1741, appointed captain of the Tartar pink. He afterwards, though for a short time only, commanded the Exeter, of sixty guns; but quitted that ship when ordered soon afterwards to the East Indies. In 1747 he himself proceeded thither under the orders of admiral Boscawen, being at that time captain of the Deptford, a fourth rate. No particular mention is made of him during this expedition, which he did not long survive, dying, very soon after his return to England, on the 15th of April 1750.

LATON, Sheldrake.—We find no mention made of this gentleman till the 25th of August 1741, when he was promoted to be captain of the Flamborough frigate : we neverthelefs believe him to have been, for a confiderable time previous to that appointment, commander of a sloop of war. He did not long continue in the Flamborough, being succeeded in that command by captain Hamar, on the 22d of October following. We have not been able to collect any other information relative to him in the line of service *, from which he altogether retired in 1756, being put on the superannuated list with the rank and half-pay of a rear-admiral. He lived afterwards in Norfolk, where he died, much lamented by all who had ever enjoyed the fatisfaction of his acquaintance, and knew consequently his general worth, on the 22d of April 1776.

LONG, Charles,—was, on the 13th of May 1741, appointed captain of the Chester, a ship of fifty guns. He was afterwards ordered to the Mediterranean, where he served under Mr. Mathews † during the memorable encounter

---

* Except that we believe him to have been in commiffion during nearly the whole war; and find him, in 1746, one of tne members of the court-martial affembled for the trial of the admirals, Mathews and Leftock.

† We find the following erroneous memorandum concerning captain Long : " The laft letters from admiral Mathews mention, that *commodore* Long, with a fmall fquadron, had anchored at the mouth of the Tyber, where he had not only affifted prince Lobkowitz with four

pieces

counter with the French and Spanish fleets off Toulon, but having been stationed as captain of the Ruffel, of eighty guns, second astern of Mr. Lestock, was not actually engaged. The Namure, in which Mr. Mathews had hoisted his flag, being much disabled, he shifted it, when the firing ceased, into the Ruffel, which i the only material circumstance we can collect relative to Mr. Long on that memorable occasion. He continued on the same station while he remained in service, being afterwards removed into the Royal Oak, as successor to captain Williams, who was sent to England for trial. Mr. Long unhappily possessed a, most strange and ungovernable temper, a violent and truly unwarrantable display of which banished him the service. The circumstances related to us are, that having been detached by admiral Medley, the commander-in-chief, on some service of no great consequence, he made a signal for one of the ships under his orders to send a boat on board him with a lieutenant, others say with the captain himself. There was a fresh breeze of wind which carried the ships ahead very fast; and captain Long having never brought-to for the boat, it was not without the most laboured and difficult exertions that the officer could get on board.

The officer accordingly expostulated, but in very decent and proper terms. It however irritated captain Long to so great a degree, that, not content with using language very unbecoming any gentleman, particularly in his station, he drew his sword upon his visitor; and, but that his opponent possessed more prudence and propriety of conduct than himself, would have provoked him to a duel. Mr. Long was brought to a court-martial, by Mr. Medley, for his notorious breach of order and discipline, and was, certainly not undeservedly, dismissed the service on the 16th of September 1746. He resided for a considerable part of th remainder of his life in the island of Barbadoes, and died in England on the 4th of August 1761, retaining to the latest moment of his life the same violence of

---

pieces of cannon for a battery, but was also to take some of his troops on board the ships under his command."

N. B. He certainly did not command the Ruffel at the above time, captain Robert Long being then in that ship, and the commodore mentioned by Mr. Mathews.

temper, and exclaiming in the moſt vehement terms againſt thoſe, whoſe cool deliberate judgement decided on his diſmiſſion.

LOVET, John,—was appointed captain of the Neptune, a ſecond rate of 90 guns, under commodore Leſtock, on November 16, 1741. He ſailed immediately afterwards for the Mediterranean, where he retained the ſame ſtation ſome time; and is erroneouſly ſtated, in ſome few accounts, to have acted as Mr. Leſtock's captain in the well-known encounter with the French and Spaniſh fleets. But this is a very manifeſt miſtake, he having, on that occaſion, commanded the Kingſton of ſixty guns, the rear-ſhip of Mr. Rowley's diviſion, and is mentioned as one of the officers who carried his ſhip into action with the moſt becoming ſpirit. He remained on the Mediterranean ſtation ſome conſiderable time afterwards, as we find him one of the officers compoſing the court-martial aſſembled, for the trial of captain R. Norris, at Port Mahon, on the 1ſt of January, 1745. His name, however, does not otherwiſe occur in the ſervice; nor, indeed, do we find any proof of his having held any commiſſion after his return to England. He died on the 20th of February 1758.

NORTHESK, George Carnegie, Earl of, — was the ſecond ſon of David, fourth earl of Northeſk, and the lady Margaret, daughter of James, lord Burntiſland, and Margaret, counteſs of Wemyſs. George, of whom we are ſpeaking, ſucceeded to the title on the death of his elder brother, David, June the 23d, 1741 : he was at that time a lieutenant in the navy, a ſtation he had filled, with the higheſt credit to himſelf, for ſeveral years. We find him particularly mentioned as lieutenant of the Dragon, under Mr. Barnet, who appears to have entertained for him an high degree of friendſhip and attachment, which ended not but with the death of ſo able an inſtructor and adviſer. His lordſhip was promoted to be captain of the Biddeford frigate on the 25th of Auguſt, 1741. In the month of March 1742, he was promoted to the Loo, of forty guns. This ſhip appears to have been one of the cruiſers ſtationed off Cape Finiſterre, in which ſervice he was employed in the month of June ; and having received intelligence of a ſmall privateer having put into Porta Nova,

Nova, he refolved to purfue her thither; but the enemy, on difcovering him, ran higher up the river than his lordfhip could venture to purfue. It becoming calm he was obliged to anchor near the town, where he landed fome men, and difmounted four guns that were on a battery there. Putting to fea from thence he had the good fortune to meet the Deal Caftle frigate on the 7th of July; and having information that feveral veffels were then in the harbour of Vigo, which was not far diftant, they both ftood in to the river and anchored before the town, where they made prizes of four veffels, two of which they burnt, being light, and not having their fails on board.

This little enterprize reflected the greateft honour both on his lordfhip and captain Elton who fupported him, as a very fpirited refiftance was made by the enemy, who kept up an exceeding brifk fire from the fhore, as well on the fhips themfelves, as the boats which were employed in cutting the veffels out. All that was poffible for gallantry and good conduct to effect being carried into execution, his lordfhip again put to fea; and learning on the 19th that the privateer he had before purfued into Porta Nova ftill remained there, he ran in and came to an anchor under the ifland of Blydones, where, having put one of his lieutenants with fixty men, and two of the fhip's fix-pounders, on board one of the veffels captured at Vigo, he difpatched her up the river in fearch of the enemy. He unhappily did not experience that fuccefs moft truly due to his diligence and perfevering fpirit; fo that no other injury was done to the foe, than by chacing on fhore and burning a fmall veffel of inconfiderable value, together with deftroying a fmall town, from whence a number of petty privateers had been equipped, and had been accuftomed occafionally to take refuge.

His lordfhip was, immediately after his return to England, promoted to the Prefton, of fifty guns: but in this command we find no particular mention made of him till the year 1744, when, in the month of May, he failed for the Eaft Indies under the orders of his former friend and inftructor, if we may be allowed the application of fuch a term, commodore Barnet! The leading naval tranfactions, even thofe where his lordfhip was more particularly concerned, which took place as well during the short time that gentleman lived to enjoy the command, as under his immediate successor, Mr. Peyton, have been already stated at length in their different memoirs *. Suffice it therefore to say, his behaviour on all occasions was productive of every advantage to his country that could be effected by his situation and the force of the ship he commanded, as well as of all possible honour to himself. We have thought it necessary to make this short remark, merely on account of the clamour very unjustly raised by many against Mr. Peyton, and the officers under his command, of whom, as we have just stated, his lordship was one, though he appears to have been happily exempt, even from the undeserved obloquy under which the commodore himself fell.

His lordship returned to Europe about the year 1748, and is not particularly mentioned for some years, except as having, in 1755, commanded the Orford, of seventy guns, then fittting out in the Medway, but resigned the command on account of ill health. In the following year he was advanced to be rear-admiral of the blue, as he was, in the year 1758, to be rear of the white: but having never accepted of any command after his promotion from the list of private captains, we can only lament having nothing more to record of a nobleman, possessing his lordship's acknowledged abilities and worth, than the mere date of his different advancements, through the rank of a flag officer, till he at last attained to that of admiral of the white. In 1759 he was made vice-admiral of the blue; in 1762 of the white; on the 28th of October, 1770, admiral of the blue; and admiral of the white in 1778. This noble person, not more illustrious for his noble birth than for his manifold virtues, died in an advanced age, at his seat in the county of Forfar, on the 22d of January, 1792. He married Anne, daughter to the earl of Leven, by whom he left a son, William, now earl of Northesk, a captain in the navy, of whom hereafter.

PEERS, James.—The first, and nearly sole information we have of this gentleman is, that, on the 2d of February, 1741, he was promoted to be captain of the Fowey, of forty-guns; on what particular stations or ser-

---

* Vol. iv. p. 219. Vol. v. p.

vices he was employed we know not, nor have we been able to collect any other particulars concerning him, except that he died in England on the 26th of November, 1746.

PHILPOT, Thomas,—was, towards the end of the year 1740, promoted from the rank of lieutenant to be commander of the Furnace bomb-ketch, a veffel we find to have been ftationed at Yarmouth in the month of February 1741, on what particular fervice or occafion does not appear. On the 5th of March in the fame year he was promoted to be captain of the Lynn; but did not long enjoy this advancement, dying on the 13th of May following.

PYE, Sir Thomas,—is an officer who, with fome few others, affords, as we have before remarked, an example of the poffibility of paffing through life, and attaining the higheft rank in the fervice, without the happinefs of experiencing a fingle opportunity of diftinguifhing himfelf, except by thofe qualities which are little valued by the million, though highly to be regarded and honoured by the difcerning. The firft mention we find made of this gentleman is, his promotion to the rank of poft captain, and appointment to the Seaford, a new frigate of twenty-four guns, newly launched at Shoreham, on April 13, 1741. He continued in this fhip, having in the interim ferved for a fhort time on the Mediterranean ftation, where he removed into the Norfolk on the refignation of the honourable John Forbes, late admiral of the fleet. We find him continuing there on the 1ft of January, 1745, and at that time one of the members of the court-martial convened, at Port Mahon, for the trial of captain Richard Norris. No other mention is made of this gentleman till the year 1748, when he was appointed to the Norwich; and in the following year was removed into the Humber, a fhip of forty guns*, in which, or the Gofport, a veffel of the fame force to which

---

* But before he failed we find him, in the month of July, one of the members of the court-martial, held for the purpofe of trying the mutineers on board the Chefterfield.

he was appointed in 1751, he was ordered to the coaſt of Guinea. Soon after his return from thence he was, in the month of February 1752, promoted to the Advice, of fifty guns, and ſent out to the Weſt Indies, as commodore on that ſtation, and ſucceſſor to Mr. Holburne. He continued there till ſuperceded by commodore Frankland in 1756. He was extremely ill-treated by that gentleman, who very capriciouſly, and, indeed, ridiculouſly reprimanded him for not hawling down his broad diſtinguiſhing pendant as ſoon as ever he had heard of the arrival of a ſenior officer as his ſucceſſor.

Not contented with this extravagant and oſtentatious diſplay of his ſuperior authority, he charged Mr. Pye with having very improperly condemned the Advice as unfit for ſervice. To prove the truth of this allegation, he himſelf went to ſea in that ſhip for a ſhort cruize; but the diſtreſs it underwent, and the narrow eſcape the crew had ſoon afterwards, when on their return to England, ſtrongly contributed, as we have already obſerved, to prove the propriety of Mr. Pye's conduct, and the want not only of candour, but of judgement alſo in Mr. Frankland. Mr. Pye however came home under a cloud, and was brought to a court-martial, which was held at Portſ- mouth about the end of February 1758; the deciſion of which, as well as the particulars of the charge, are thus related in a letter from thence, dated March the 4th.

" The court-martial on commodore Pye ended this day. He was charged with mal-practices in the ma- nagement of his command abroad: but the court acquitted him of that part of the accuſation preferred againſt him, and only reprimanded him for neglect, through which the naval officer had, by miſtake, charged 200l. ſterling for a ſchooner, which he purchaſed there for 200l. currency. He was alſo reprimanded for having interfered in the purchaſe of naval ſtores, a proper officer in that depart ment being then on the ſpot."

This diſagreeable affair occaſioned Mr. Pye to loſe his regular turn of promotion to the rank of flag officer; nor was he, after the deciſion of the court-martial, advanced to the ſtation he would regularly have held had it not been for his ſuſpenſion. There appears to have been a good deal of management in this buſineſs, management to be attributed

attributed to lord Anson, and intended for the purpose of keeping sir C. Saunders his senior on the list of admirals, though junior to him as a private captain. This end being notably accomplished, and the business arranged accordingly, Mr. Pye was, on the 8th of July, 1758, advanced to be rear-admiral of the blue, but never, we believe, had any command during the war. He was, nevertheless, advanced in the following year to be rear admiral of the white; and, in 1760, to be rear of the red. In 1762 he was farther promoted to be vice-admiral of the blue, and appointed to command, in 1764, as port-admiral at Plymouth. After some continuance there he was once more sent to the Leeward Island station. He continued there during the time usually allotted for the duration of such commands*; and soon after his return, that is to say on the 28th of October, 1770, was promoted to the rank of vice-admiral of the red, and sent out commander-in-chief early in the following year, of the small squadron then stationed in the Mediterranean. On his return to England he was appointed commander-in-chief at Portsmouth; and holding that station in the month of June 1773, at the time his present majesty made his first excursion thither, had the honour of entertaining him on board the Barfleur. On the 25th of that month he received the honour of knighthood under the royal standard, and was advanced to be admiral of the blue. He was succeeded in his command by sir James Douglas, after having retained it the time usually allotted to it; and again resumed it as successor to sir James, after the expiration of a period of the same duration.

In 1778 he was raised to be admiral of the white, and acted as president of the court-martial, held at Portsmouth for the trial of admiral Keppel. It is certainly no small matter of praise, or slender proof of his worth, that at a time when parties ran to such an extravagant height in their censures, and different modes of expressing their dislike, his conduct was so truly impartial and honourable in that delicate situation, as not to afford the smallest ground or opportunity of disapprobation from either party. He retained his command, which rather resembles a civil than a warlike appointment, during the continuance of hostilities, and is universally reported to have been a man most

---

* Having his flag, in 1769, on board the Lark frigate.

eminently

eminently qualified to fill the duties of that station, which, though it may not require those more brilliant and shining points which are necessary to constitute the character of the warrior and the hero, certainly demands the most solid abilities and sedulous attention. After the conclusion of the war he passed the short remainder of his days in retirement, but did not long enjoy that relaxation from the fatigues of public service, dying in London during the course of the year 1785.

ROGERS, Sir Frederic, — was the son of sir John Rogers, baronet, representative in parliament, during three successive sessions, and also recorder for the town of Plymouth, by Mary his lady, daughter of sir Robert Henly, of the Grange, in the county of Southampton, knight. The first information we have of this gentleman, as a naval officer, is, that on the 2d of December, 1741, he was promoted to be captain of the Bridgewater frigate. He was employed in this ship as a cruiser; but we do not find any particular mention made concerning him till twelve months afterwards, when the following relation is inserted in the Gazette, No. 8182. Dated Whitehall, December 25.

" On the 7th instant, in latitude 49. 50. Scilly bearing E. half N. distant 63 leagues, his majesty's ship the Bridgewater, commanded by captain Rogers, fell in with a Spanish privateer at half past nine o'clock in the forenoon, the enemy being to windward bore down upon the Bridgewater: captain Rogers kept close upon a wind under double-reefed top-sails and courses. At eleven o'clock the privateer hoisted an English ensign, and fired a shot at the Bridgewater; whereupon captain Rogers hoisted a Dutch ensign, hauled up his main-sail, and backed his main-top-sail: but finding soon afterwards that the privateer made sail from him, he hauled down the Dutch ensign, hoisted English colours and gave her a broadside. Upon this, the privateer struck her English ensign, and hoisting Spanish colours made all possible sail from the Bridgewater, at the same time firing her stern-chace guns. Captain Rogers made sail after her, and plyed her with his bow-chace guns till three in the afternoon, when he came up with her and gave her another broadside, which she returned; but captain Rogers then finding that she shot from him, deferred firing any more till he got close up with her. About nine, being clofe under her lee-quarter, he gave her another broadfide, and a difcharge of fmall arms, which compelled her to call for quarter. She is called the Santa la Rita, alias El Neptuno; carries one hundred and forty men, with eighteen carriage and eight fwivel guns.—N. B. The Bridgewater was, in point of force, in no degree fuperior to the enemy."

Very little other interefting mention is made of this gentleman. The circumftances which have come to our knowledge are, that, during the fummer of the year 1744, he commanded the Dover, of forty guns, and was principally employed in convoying to and fro the Baltic fleet. Before the end of the feafon he was promoted to be captain of the Maidftone, of fifty guns: he is faid by fome to have afterwards commanded the Prince Frederic, but of this circumftance we are not certain; and if really a fact, he could not have obtained that commiffion till after the conclufion of the war. In the month of February 1753, he was appointed to the Vanguard, of feventy guns, a guardfhip at Plymouth, but did not long retain that ftation, having quitted the link of active fervice in November following, on being appointed commiffioner of the navy, refident at the port laft-mentioned*. He continued to fill this office with the higheft credit till the year 1775, and then retired with the ufual penfion granted on fuperannuation. He did not long furvive, dying at his feat in Devonfhire on the 9th of June 1777.

SAUNDERS, Sir Charles —This brave and excellent officer, to whom fortune was particularly munificent in affording him numerous opportunities of acquiring renown by difplaying that gallantry he naturally poffeffed, entered at a very early age into the naval fervice. After pafling through the more fubordinate ftation and attaining the rank of lieutenant, he was, at the particular recommendation of Mr. Anfon, appointed to ferve on board the Centurion in that capacity, when that fhip was ordered to be equipped for the well-known expedition to the South Seas. Captain Kidd, of the Pearl frigate,

---

* By the death of his elder brother, fir John Rogers, on the 20th of December 1773, he fucceeded to the title of baronet.

dying at sea, on the last day of January, when the squadron was on its passage to port St. Julian, captain Cheap, of the Trial sloop, was promoted to the Wager storeship, as successor to captain Murray, advanced to the Pearl, and Mr. Saunders was appointed, his successor by the commodore. He was at that time dangerously ill of a fever on board the Centurion; and, in consequence of the opinion of the surgeons that it would be extremely hazardous to remove him in the condition he then was, Mr. Anson gave an order to Mr. Saumarez, who had become his first lieutenant on the promotion just stated, to act as temporary commander of the sloop till the recovery of Mr. Saunders should enable him to undertake the charge himself.

This was not long afterwards the case: and captain Saunders had immediately to encounter a series of dangers and distresses in his passage round Cape Horn, the melancholy detail of which has been already given at some length in our account of lord Anson, and may completely save us from the disagreeable task of again recounting them.

We shall content ourselves therefore with briefly noticing, that ere the Trial reached the island of Juan Fernandez, she had buried nearly one-half her crew; those who still remained alive were in the most infirm and deplorable state; so that captain Saunders, his lieutenant and three men, were the only persons that could be said to be capable of enduring the fatigues necessarily attendant on navigating and working the vessel. Such was their condition when they reached this hospitable though uninhabited spot, where they found the commodore had arrived two days before.

The crew having in great measure recovered from the baneful influence of the scurvy, captain Saunders was dispatched to Masa Fuero, a small island not far distant from Juan Fernandez, hopes being entertained that some of the missing ships of the squadron had put in there, mistaking it for the appointed place of rendezvous. The Trial having circumnavigated the whole island, and carefully examined every creek and harbour without success, returned to Juan Fernandez, where a Spanish prize, captured by the Centurion, was not long afterwards brought in.

in. The prisoners on board this ship on seeing the Trial, knew not how sufficiently to praise and commend the indefatigable diligence, and almost incredible exertions of the English, in having, under the then existing circumstances, fatigued, dispirited, and reduced as they were in numbers, built and completely equipped so suddenly, a vessel of her description; they, the Spaniards, not believing it possible that, figuratively speaking, such a cockboat should have been capable of effecting a passage round Cape Horn, when the finest and best equipped ships in the Spanish navy had been compelled to put back.

All things being nearly ready for the final departure of the few remaining ships of this ill-fated squadron, and it being generally believed that the Spaniards, still ignorant of any of the British ships having reached the South Seas in safety, had several valuable vessels at sea, the Trial was dispatched on a cruise in the month of September; and on the 18th, a very few days afterwards, took, after a long chace, a valuable merchant-ship, of six hundred tons burthen, bound from Callao to Valparaiso. As a counterbalance, however, to this good fortune, captain Saunders had sprung one of his masts during the chace: his disasters did not end here; being soon afterwards joined by the commodore, with the Spanish prize he had himself taken previous to his quitting Juan Fernandez, the Trial sprung her remaining mast in a squall, and became so leaky as to be scarcely kept free, except by continued exertions at the pumps: it was determined, therefore, that captain Saunders should scuttle the Trial and remove on board his prize, which was to be commissioned as a frigate, having been not long before employed as one in the Spanish service, by the viceroy.

The guns of the Trial, together with those which had belonged to the Anna Pink victualler, amounting together to twenty, were accordingly put on board; and captain Saunders having removed his crew, together with such stores as could be got out, took rank as a post captain by commission from the commodore, dated the 26th of September, 1741, to command this vessel, which was called, in honour to his diligence and exertions, the Trial's Prize. The commodore had parted company with captain Saunders before these matters were completely adjufted, in fearch of fome more of the enemy's fhips, leaving the Centurion's prize to affift him, with orders, that, after thefe preliminary duties were fulfilled, they fhould proceed in company to cruize for a month off the ifland of Valparaifo, from whence they were to proceed down the coaft to an appointed rendezvous off Nafca, where, without having met with any fuccefs, they joined the commodore on the 2d of November. The well-known affault on the town of Paita took place in a few days afterwards, but captain Saunders does not appear to have been otherwife concerned than being prefent at it. He continued in company with the commodore and the reft of the fquadron till the fpring following without meeting with any remarkable occurrence; the crews, then fo much reduced in numbers, and divided as they were into five veffels, three of which were large, being totally inadequate to the purpofe of navigating them acrofs that immenfe fouthern ocean which lay before them, it was determined to deftroy captain Saunders's frigate, together with the two other prizes. This refolution was, after removing on board the Centurion and Gloucefter the moft valuable part of what they contained, accordingly carried into execution, in the harbour of Chequetan, on the 27th of April.

The greater number both of officers and men were fent on board the Gloucefter, that fhip being by far the worft manned of the two. Her untimely fate, as well as all the principal circumftances and events which took place on board the Centurion herfelf, previous to her arrival at Macao, when captain Saunders quitted her, have been already given in our account of Mr. Anfon*. In the month of November 1742, which was immediately after the Centurion reached China, captain Saunders, being charged with difpatches from the commodore, took his paffage to England on board a Swedifh fhip, in which he arrived in the Downs, after a profperous paffage, in the month of May 1743. He was not long afterwards appointed captain of the Sapphire, of forty-four guns, one of the veffels employed, during the enfuing fpring, in cruifing off the coaft of Flanders, and in watching the port of Dunkirk. The only fuccefs he appears to have met with while thus

---

* See vol. iv. p. 112, et feq.

employed was the capture of a galliot hoy, from Dantzick, on the 7th of April, having on board nearly two hundred officers and foldiers, belonging to connt Lowendahls regiment at Dunkirk, which had been raifed at the former place for the fervice of the French king. He continued in the Sapphire, we believe, till his promotion to the Sandwich, of ninety guns, which took place in the month of March 1745. He remained in this fhip, which we believe to have been employed as a guard-fhip but a very fhort time, being, in the month of April enfuing, removed into the more active ftation of captain of the Gloucefter, of fifty guns, a new fhip juft launched, fupplying the place of that before loft with Mr. Anfon.

In 1746, being then engaged on a cruife in company with, and under the orders of captain Cheap, in the Lark, they captured Le Fort de Nants, a regifter fhip from New Spain, valued at upwards of one hundred thoufand pounds. We have no fubfequent information concerning him till October 1747 *, when he commanded the Yarmouth, of 64 guns, one of the fhips under the command of rear-admiral Hawke, which totally defeated and captured nearly the whole of the French fquadron, under monf. L'Etendiere. To this very brilliant victory captain Saunders very eminently contributed ; two of the enemy's fhips, of feventy-four guns each, the Neptune and Monarque, having, as is confidently reported, ftruck to the Yarmouth. Though his lofs in the preceding action was very confiderable, amounting to nearly one hundred of his crew killed and wounded, he is faid to have propofed to the captains Saumarez and Rodney, of the Nottingham and Eagle, the former of which gentlemen had ferved with him in the Centurion, that they fhould purfue the Tonnant, of eighty guns, and Intrepide, of feventy-four, which were then endeavouring to make their efcape. This meafure appears to have been carried into execution, but its fuccefs was fatally prevented by the unfortunate death of captain Saumarez of the Nottingham †.

He

---

* In the abfence of fir Piercy Brett, the proper captain, he himfelf having been appointed to the Tyger, a new fourth rate of fixty guns.

† The following account of his gallantry on this occafion is given in a letter, written by an officer belonging to the Yarmouth. It bears teftimony too honourable to the character of captain Saunders to be here omitted.

" Though

He was one of the witnesses examined on the trial of captain Fox, of the Kent, in the month of November; but is not otherwise mentioned, as connected with the service, during the continuance of the war. In the month of April 1750, he was elected representative in parliament for the borough of Plymouth as successor to the lord Vere Beauclerck, then created a peer of Great Britain by the title of lord Vere, of Hanworth. On the 26th of September in the following year, he married ———, only daughter to James Buck, esq. a banker in London. In January following he was nominated commodore of the squadron ordered for the Streights for the purpose of relieving Mr. Keppel, who then held the chief command there; but his destination was afterwards changed, for, in May following, he was appointed commodore and commander-in-chief on the Newfoundland station, for the purpose of protecting the fishery in that quarter. Having hoisted his

---

" Though the Yarmouth without dispute had as great a share as any single ship in the fleet, if not a greater, in the engagement with the French, October 14th, yet, in all the accounts I have seen, she is not so much as mentioned, as though no such ship had been there. It is something surprizing that admiral Hawke should see and notice, in his long account, the behaviour of the Lion, Louisa, Tilbury, and Eagle, and yet could discover nothing of the extraordinary courage and conduct of captain Saunders, of the Yarmouth, who lay two hours and a half close engaged with the Neptune, a seventy-gun ship, with seven hundred men, which he never quitted till she struck, although the Monarch, a seventy-four gun ship, who struck to us likewise, lay upon our bow for some time, and another of the enemy's ships upon our stern. When the Neptune struck, after killing them one hundred men and wounding one hundred and forty, she was so close to us that our men jumped into her; and, notwithstanding such long warm work, the ship much disabled in masts and rigging, and twenty two men killed and seventy wounded, his courage did not cool here. He could not with patience see the French admiral and the Intrepide, a seventy-four gun ship getting away, and none of our ships after them; nor could he think of preferring his own security to the glory and interest of his country, but ardently wished to pursue them, he proposed it therefore to captain Saumarez in the Nottingham, and captain Rodney in the Eagle, who were within hail of us; but captain Saumarez being unfortunately killed by the first fire of the enemy, the Nottingham hauled their wind and did no more service; and the Eagle never came near enough to do any; so that the Yarmouth had to deal with both of the enemy's ships for some time, till at length they got out of the reach of our guns. I think so much bravery and noble spirit ought not to lie in oblivion."

pendant

pendant on board the Penzance, of forty guns, he failed quickly afterwards, having additional inftructions to fearch for a pretended ifland, which it was fuppofed had been difcovered in latitude 49' 40", longitude 24° 30", from the Lizard, in hopes of difcovering which Mr. Rodney had juft before, cruifed for ten days without fuccefs.

Captain Saunders was not in any degree more fortunate than his predeceffor. In the month of April 1754, he was appointed treafurer of Greenwich-hofpital, an office he held twelve years, and then refigned on being promoted to the very elevated ftation of firft commiffioner of the admiralty. In the parliament which met at Weftminfter, May the 31ft, 1754, he was elected reprefentative for the borough of Heydon, in Yorkfhire, a truft repofed in him, through the intereft of his fteady, conftant friend lord Anfon. In the month of March 1755, a rupture with France being then almoft daily apprehended, he was appointed commander of the Prince, a new fhip of ninety guns, launched a fhort time before, and, in the month of June, gave a moft fplendid entertainment to a moft numerous affemblage of the firft nobility in the kingdom, who repaired to Portfmouth on the anniverfary of the king's acceffion, for the purpofe of feeing the formidable fleet then collected at Spithead, dreffed in the colours of different nations, as is cuftomary on fuch occafions.

Mr. Saunders refigned the command of the Prince, in the month of December following, on being appointed comptroller of the navy. Immediately after this promotion he was, in teftimony of that univerfal refpect in which he was held, elected one of the elder brethren of the trinity-houfe. His feat in parliament having become vacated by his appointment of comptroller, he was re-elected for the fame borough he had before reprefented. In the month of June 1756, advice being received of the mifcarriage of the fleet, under Mr. Byng, in the Mediterranean, a fpecial promotion of flag-officers was made, and extended purpofely to Mr. Saunders, who failed immediately afterwards, with fir Edward Hawke, as a paffenger on board the Antelope, for Gibraltar, where he was to hoift his flag as rear-admiral of the blue. On the return of fir Edward to England, in the month of

January

January 1757, he was left commander-in-chief on the Mediterranean ſtation; but no occurrence very worthy notice* appears to have taken place during the time he held this very honourable appointment. No mention is made of this gentleman after his return from this ſtation till the month of February 1759, except that, in 1758, he was advanced to be rear-admiral of the white. Early in 1759, having been previouſly promoted to be vice-admiral of the blue, he was appointed commander-in-chief of the fleet deſtined for the attack of Quebec. He ſailed for Louiſburg, from Spithead, on the 17th of February, having the following ſhips under his orders: the Neptune, ninety guns, (flag ſhip); the Royal William, eighty-four; the Dublin, Shrewſbury, and Warſpite, ſeventy-four; Orford, ſeventy; Alcide, and Sterling Caſtle, ſixty-four; the Lizard, of twenty; the Scorpion ſloop, the Baltimore, Pelican and Racehorſe bomb veſſels; the Cormorant, Strombolo and Veſuvius fireſhips. Admiral Holmes, who ſerved under him, had ſailed from Spithead with a diviſion three days before him. Mr. Saunders was in ſight of Louiſburg on the 21ſt of

---

* The moſt remarkable appears to have been the following ſkirmiſh, which took place early in the year, with a ſmall French ſquadron, bound to Louiſburg, under monſieur Reveſt. The Phœnix, captain Wharfe, arrived at Plymouth on the 26th of April, in eighteen days from Malaga, and reports, that on the 2d inſtant admiral Saunders, at Gibraltar, had received an expreſs from Malaga, with advice, that there were, off that port, four French men of war of ſeventy four guns each: on which he went out with the Culloden, Berwick, Princeſs Louiſa, Guernſey, and Portland, to cruiſe in the gut; and on the 5th, about four o'clock in the afternoon, ſaw the French. He being to leeward formed a line; and about ſun-ſet the enemy did the ſame, about two miles to windward of our admiral, and began to fire, but did not reach our ſhips. The Guernſey and Louiſa got within ſhot and began to engage; but before the reſt got up it was night, and the two ſquadrons loſt ſight of each other. About nine o'clock, the moon getting up, the Guernſey and Louiſa ſaw the French again. The admiral made a ſignal to chaſe, but could not come up with them. On the 8th the Phœnix ſpoke with one of the admiral's ſhips, who ſaid they had loſt ſight of the French the day before. Theſe French men of war have a good number of land forces on board, and are ſuppoſed to be bound to America; having, by favour of a levant wind, eſcaped and proceeded on their voyage. The names of the ſhips were, the Hector, Achilles, and Valiant, of ſeventy-four guns each; the Soubize, of ſixty-ſix, and a polacca, of twenty-ſix.

April;

April; but that harbour being blocked up with ice, he was obliged to bear away for Halifax in Nova Scotia. Having received intelligence before he left England that a fmall French fquadron, with fome victuallers and tranfports, had failed before him for the deftined object of his attack, he immediately detached admiral Durel with a divifion of the fleet, to cruife off the ifle of Coudres, in the river St. Lawrence, in hopes he might be able to intercept the enemy; but, notwithftanding this diligent exertion, the Englifh fquadron arrived not in time to effect that purpofe. As foon as the navigation was deemed fufficiently open, which was not the cafe till the end of May, the vice-admiral failed with the remainder of his force, and on the 6th of June was off Scatari, ftanding in for the river St. Lawrence, from whence he fent intelligence to England of the progrefs he had then made.

The fleet which, when united, confifted of twenty-one fhips of the line, befides frigates, fmaller veffels of war and tranfports, did not reach the deftined point of difembarkation, on the ifland of Orleans, till the 26th; and on the following day the troops were landed. On the 28th the enemy made an attempt to burn the Britifh fhips, by fending down from Quebec feven fire rafts, or veffels; but fuch expeditious exertions were made, that, although the fleet, together with the tranfports, which were numerous and fpread acrofs the greater part of the channel, the fireveffels were all towed clear, by the boats, without doing the fmalleft injury. On the 28th of July a fecond attempt of a fimilar nature was made by the enemy, who fent down a raft of fire-ftages, confifting of nearly one hundred radeaux, a meafure which fucceeded no better than the former had done. The fubfequent events of this very memorable fiege have nothing to diftinguifh them from thofe occurrences which ufually take place on fuch occafions; and it is only neceffary to add, that the prudence, the diligence, the general ability of the vice-admiral, proved completely competent, far as his department was concerned, to the removal of thofe numerous obftacles which fo long impeded the day of victory and fuccefs, and the provifion for thofe unforefeen exigencies which, for a confiderable fpace of time, appeared as it were daily to multiply.

Immedi-

Immediately on the surrender of Quebec, Mr. Saunders having supplied that place with provisions from the ships as well as circumstances would permit, sailed, on his return to England, with such part of the fleet as it was necessary for him to bring home. He had nearly reached the Channel when he is said to have been informed that the Brest squadron was at sea, and instantly took the spirited resolution of proceeding to join sir Edward Hawke, dispatching a vessel to England with intelligence to the admiralty of the step he had taken, and the hopes he entertained of their approval. Receiving, however, while pursuing his route, intelligence that the contest had been gloriously decided by the total defeat of the French admiral, he changed his course once more and went ashore at Cork. He travelled by land to Dublin, where he arrived on the 15th of December; and going accidentally to the play, he was received with that unanimous applause, by the whole audience, which being most truly and honestly merited, could not be otherwise than highly gratifying, even to a character perfectly unassailed by vanity and proof against the most subtle flattery.

On the 26th of the same month he arrived in London, where his reception, both by his sovereign and the people, was equally honourable to him. Some days previous to his arrival * he was appointed lieutenant-general of marines. On taking his seat in the house of commons on the 23d of January 1760, the thanks of the house were given him by the speaker. In the ensuing spring he was appointed commander-in-chief in the Mediterranean, and sailed from Spithead on the 21st of May, having his flag still on board the Neptune, with the Somerset, of seventy guns; the Firme, of sixty; and the Preston, of fifty. He arrived at Gibraltar on the 9th of June. No material occurrence took place during the remainder of the year, for the naval power of France was annihilated in the Mediterranean. In the new parliament, which was chosen in the beginning of 1761, but did not meet till the month of November, he was re-elected member for

---

* See Gazette, Dec. 8, 1759.

Heydon;

Heydon; and, on the 26th of May*, was inftalled, by proxy, knight companion of the moft honourable order of the Bath. Sir Charles continued at Gibraltar till the conclufion of the war; and was, during his abfence, in the month of October 1762, advanced to be vice-admiral of the white. On the 30th of Auguft 1765, he was appointed one of the commiffioners for executing the office of lord high admiral; and, on the 16th of September 1766, being advanced to be firft commiffioner, was fworn in one of the members of his majefty's moft honourable privy council.

A fhort anecdote, and of the moft honourable kind to fir Charles, relative to this appointment, we have already had occafion to relate, as connected with our account of admiral fir George Pocock†. He retained his high office only till the 13th of December following, and then refigning, never, fubfequent to this time, returned to any public ftation. In the funeral proceffion of the duke of York, on the 3d of November 1767, he was one of the admirals who fupported the canopy. In the new parliament, which met in the month of May 1768, he was again rechofen reprefentative for the borough of Heydon. In the month of October 1770, he was advanced to be admiral of the blue. In the new parliament convened in 1774, he was a candidate for the borough of Yarmouth, where he was unfuccefsful; but was, for the fourth time, re-elected for Heydon. He did not long furvive this event, dying, at his houfe in Spring-gardens, of the gout in his ftomach, on the 7th of December 1775.

To fay he died lamented and regretted by all who knew him, would be beftowing only that faint praife which contracts the extent of that high eftimation, even to veneration, in which he was univerfally held by men of all parties, defcriptions, and opinions. In a very few hours after his deceafe fir George Saville, and Mr. Edmund Burke, who had been his intimates, announced his death with all the affectionate honefty, impaffioned warmth and

---

* His cruifers were more fuccefsful in the courfe of this year than they had been in the preceding, having taken many prizes, one of them the Oriflamme, of which we fhall hereafter fpeak.

† See vol. iv. p. 405.

effufion

effufion of private friendfhip, exalted, if poffible, beyond itfelf by the bitter reflection on what might be deemed a public lofs. The juftice of the eulogium they feverally pronounced on that melancholy occafion was unanimoufly confeffed by all who heard it, and caufed an encreafe of forrow, by painting in its proper colours the extent of a national lofs. His corpfe was privately interred in Weft-minfter-abbey, on the 12th of the fame month, near the monument of general Wolfe, who had been his noble affociate in war, his compeer in gallantry, but, from the untimely fate of the general, not in fortune. Sir Charles died poffeffed of a very confiderable property, the bulk of which he bequeathed to his niece; but, independant of that, left feveral very handfome legacies; one in particular to the late lord vifcount Keppel, with whom he had ferved on board the Centurion.

SWANTON, Thomas,—was, on the 19th of January 1741, promoted, from the rank of lieutenant to be captain of the Liverpool, a fifth rate of forty guns. Very few particulars are related concerning his fervice, which appears to have been totally confined to cruifing off the coaft of Spain; in which employment we muft, however, obferve, he met with fome fuccefs. He was early in the year 1744, ordered to the Mediterranean, on which ftation he died, in the employment of convoying an outward-bound fleet to Turkey, on the 12th of Auguft enfuing.

SWAYSLAND, Henry, — was, in 1740, advanced from the rank of lieutenant to be commander of the Shark floop; from which veffel he was promoted, on the 22d of January 1740, to be captain of the Lively frigate, a veffel employed at that time, with one or two others of the fame force, in protecting the iflands of Guernfey and Jerfey. Extraordinary as it may appear, we do not find the leaft fubfequent mention made of this gentleman, except that, in 1756, he was put on the fuperannuated lift, with the rank and half pay of a rear-admiral, a circumftance he did not long furvive, dying on the 19th of October in the following year.

TUCKER, Thomas.—The firft information we have of this gentleman is, that he was, at the end of the year 1740,

1740, appointed commander of the Princeſs Royal*, an hoſpital ſhip attached to the fleet ſent out to the Weſt Indies under rear-admiral ſir Chaloner Ogle. It cannot be ſuppoſed any thing very intereſting ſhould occur while he retained ſuch a command: after his return from that unhappy expedition he was promoted, on the 17th of July 1741, to be captain of the Fowey; in which ſhip, being ſtationed in the Weſt Indies, in 1743 he had the good fortune to capture a Spaniſh regiſter ſhip, called the St. Joſeph Le Deſiderio, ſaid to have been worth upwards of one hundred thouſand pounds; otherwiſe he is unhappily in the ſame predicament with the gentleman laſt-mentioned on the ſcore of incelebrity, being no otherwiſe noticed than as having been, as well as captain Swayſland, put on the ſuperannuated liſt, in 1756, with the rank and half-pay of a rear-admiral. He died in Wales on the 8th of Auguſt 1766.

UTTING, Aſhby,—was, on the 25th of March 1741, promoted to be captain of the Mary galley, and was ſent to the Mediterranean, from whence he ſoon returned back to England. Being ordered in the ſame ſhip to America, he died at South Carolina, in the prime of life, on the 26th of July 1742, as we are informed, of a total decay, induced merely by intemperance. May his untimely end deter others from purſuing the ſame unhappy courſe †.

WARD, Henry,—was, on the 25th of May 1741, promoted to be captain of the Sheerneſs frigate by Mr. Vernon, under whom he had previouſly ſerved as lieutenant. Very ſoon after he received this appointment he captured and carried to Jamaica a very rich Spaniſh ſhip, called the Nueſtra Senora Del Roſario. We have not been able to procure any ſubſequent information relative to this gentleman till the month of January 1753, when

---

* Other accounts make this ſhip to have been commanded by a captain Nathaniel Tucker, who never had any other appointment: this we doubt.

† Such is the date given by Mr. Hardy of this gentleman's death as well as of the ſhip he commanded. Another account ſtates him to have died at the ſame time, but captain of the Aldborough frigate. A third account, which we moſt credit, ſtates him to have died on the Carolina ſtation in 1746, being at that time captain of the Goſport, of forty-four guns. He is likewiſe ſaid to have commanded the Loo, a ſhip of the ſame force, about the year 1744.

he was appointed to command the Culloden, of seventy-four guns, then newly equipped and commissioned as a guard ship in the Medway. In 1755, when a rupture with France was apprehended, he was ordered to the Nore, as is customary on the expectation of such an event. In the following year he was sent out in the same ship with Mr. Byng, but does not appear to have been engaged, or at most very trivially so, in the encounter with the French fleet off Mahon. His inaction was, we must in justice to him observe, unavoidable, he having been stationed in the line as the admiral's second astern, and, owing to circumstances that have been already explained*, consequently prevented from closing with the enemy. Not long after his return from the Mediterranean†, that is to say on the 1st of July 1757, he was put on the superannuated list with the rank and half pay of a rear-admiral. He died on the 4th of December 1766.

WATSON, Nathaniel,—was, on the 16th of January 1741, promoted to the Feversham, a fifth rate of forty-four guns, then newly rebuilt. He was soon ordered to the Mediterranean, and some time after the arrival of Mr. Mathews resigned that command. No subsequent mention, far as we have been able to discover, is made of him in the service, which we have been, indeed, informed he quitted soon afterwards. He died in England on February 17, 1766.

WARING, Rupert,—was, on the 16th of September 1741, promoted to be captain of the Greyhound frigate‡. After his return to England he was ordered to Jamaica, where the Lark was to serve as an hulk. Whether he commanded

---

* See the memoirs of Mr. Byng, vol. iv. p. 151. Captain Ward was one of the witnesses examined on that admiral's trial, and bore exceedingly hard upon him. He deposed that the enemy's shot fell short of him though to leeward of the Ramillies; and declared, as his sentiments, that if Mr. Byng had borne down, the greater part of the French fleet might have been taken. This, however, is a mere matter of private opinion.

† From whence he was ordered home as an evidence against Mr. Byng.

‡ This should be the Lark. A private memorandum, with which we have been obligingly furnished, informs us he did not take post in the Greyhound, being only appointed, by order of admiralty, to proceed to Lisbon in this ship, carrying with him a commission to captain Francis Parry, of the Grampus sloop upon that station, to command the Greyhound; and for which sloop captain Waring had a commission, with orders to swear captain Parry into the command of the ship first mentioned.

Vol. V. I that

that veſſel at the time it overſet in the harbour of Port Royal, on the 20th of October 1744, does not appear. He is not otherwiſe mentioned, except as having died in England on the 13th of February 1753.

YOUNG, Robert.—We find this gentleman mentioned as lieutenant of the Mary Galley ſoon after the commencement of the war with Spain. About May 1741, he was advanced to be commander of the Scipio fireſhip, and from thence promoted, on the 1ſt of October following, to be captain either of the Biddeford or Blandford frigate. No mention is made of him while he continued in this veſſel, nor, indeed, afterwards till the year 1744, at which time he commanded the Kinſale on the Newfoundland ſtation. He diſtinguiſhed himſelf exceedingly, in the month of September, by an enterprize he projected and cauſed to be carried into execution, with much ſucceſs, againſt ſome French ſhips in the harbour of Fiſhotte, a particular account of which may not, perhaps, be thought unintereſting.—He had made prize of a large ſhip a ſhort time before, having manned that veſſel with eighty of his own crew, and as many ſtout volunteers from the ſhore; arming her alſo with twenty guns, he ſent her with three ſtout privateers, carrying three hundred men, to attempt the enemy. The prize led into the harbour, but unfortunately grounded thrice: the laſt time in ſwinging off, ſhe fell athwart the bow of the Moderate, one of the French ſhips, carrying twelve guns and ſeventy-five men; and having quickly carried her by boarding, her force was immediately employed againſt four other French ſhips, all armed, which were then lying in the harbour. A deſperate action immediately commenced, and after a moſt ſpirited conteſt, which continued five hours and an half, ended in the ſurrender of all the enemy's ſhips. Theſe were, the St. Denis, of fourteen guns and fifty-three men; the Marquis De Se, of fourteen guns and eighty-ſix men; the Duc De Penthievre, of twelve guns and eighty-four men; and the Jaſon, of fourteen guns and eighty men. This conqueſt was not, however, atchieved without ſome loſs; ten of the Engliſh were killed and thirty wounded: but a much greater ſlaughter was made on board the enemy's ſhips: the number of priſoners taken, not much exceeding two hundred, leaving ninety perſons unaccounted for in any other way

way than by suppoſing them ſlain. This action was rendered the more honourable to the aſſailants from the circumſtance of the privateers having been unable to join in the attack, or get into the harbour till the victory was atchieved.—Captain Young proceeded to Liſbon, with the fleet accuſtomed to proceed thither from Newfoundland, in the month of November; but we have not been able to procure any other information concerning him, except that we believe him to have retained the command of the Kinſale till nearly the time of his death, which happened, according to the beſt accounts we have been able to procure, on the 19th of November 1750; but, according to Mr. Hardy's, which in this inſtance we believe to be erroneous, on the 4th of December 1754.

1742.

BURNABY, Sir William,—was the deſcendant of a very reſpectable Oxfordſhire family; and having attached himſelf to a naval life, was, about the month of Auguſt 1741, promoted from the rank of lieutenant to be commander of the Thunder bomb-ketch, and ſoon afterwards ſent out to Mr. Vernon on the Weſt India ſtation *: he was there promoted by that admiral to be captain

---

* A whimſical anecdote has been related to us, from good authority, relative to the firſt interview which took place between Mr. Vernon and himſelf, on his arrival on the Weſt India ſtation. Mr. Burnaby was a man extremely attached to exterior appearance, and aimed, on all occaſions, at being the beſt dreſſed man in whatever company he mixed: he even carried this deſire, on ſome occaſions, to an height which expoſed him to ridicule and the imputation of abſurdity. Mr. Vernon, it is well known, was of a very different turn of mind: he, on the oppoſite direction, ſunk his ideas of dreſs into a ſlovenly appearance, highly improper in an officer of any rank, and truly reprehenſible in a commander-in-chief like himſelf, as well as derogatory to the decency of a gentleman. A meeting between two ſuch oppoſite characters muſt have been not a little amuſing, ſuppoſing them both to have had an opportunity of diſplaying their different inclinations. This abſolutely took place, and in the following manner: Mr. Burnaby, immediately after his arrival at Jamaica, proceeded, as is cuſtomary, to pay a viſit of ceremony to the commander-in-chief. On this

ſolemn

captain of the Litchfield, of fifty guns, on the 9th of December 1742, though many accounts erroneously state him to have taken post in the Lark. He distinguished himself exceedingly in the month of October 1743, till which time we find no mention made of him. He had been ordered out on a cruise off Porto Rico, and the following account is given of the transaction above alluded to in a letter, dated on board the Cumberland, November the 8th.

" This day arrived here, from off Porto Rico, his Britannic majesty's ship, the Litchfield, captain Burnaby commander, with two privateer sloops taken in her cruise, one called the St. Raphael, whose men all left her and went ashore, having first scuttled her, endeavouring to sink her; she has ports for fourteen guns: the other, called the St. Antonio de las Animas, has eight carriage, fourteen swivel guns and forty-two men: besides which captain Burnaby sunk and destroyed two more privateers; one off the east end of Hispaniola, and the other off the west end of Porto Rico; he burnt also another sloop in Aguada Bay, and destroyed a battery ashore, which she had got under, of four guns. Landing some men, with an officer, he dismounted the said guns, knocked off the trunnions, spiked them up, burnt the carriages and guard-house, and brought off the colours in the presence of a multitude of Spaniards, of whom the assailants are supposed to have killed near two hundred, and with the loss of only one man."

---

solemn occasion he equipped himself gorgeously in a suit of silk, or, as some say, velvet, very splendidly laced. The admiral was, as was not uncommon with him, coarsly dressed in a very ordinary manner. When Mr. Burnaby was announced, Mr. Vernon rose from his escrutore with much apparent and pretended confusion, and hurrying into an inner apartment put on a wig of ceremony, which having adjusted with pretended haste and embarrassment, he advanced towards Mr. Burnaby with great gravity, and desired to know his commands? when the latter informed him, with much precision and attention to form, " that he had the honour to command the bomb vessel which had just arrived from England." Mr. Vernon, with a ludicrous and grotesque alteration of countenance, replied, " Gad so, sir, I really took you for a dancing master." Certainly the coarse rudeness and reprehension of the admiral was, to the full, as ridiculous as the finical attention to dress was in the other.

We

We do not find any other particular mention of him during the time he continued in the West Indies, except that he was afterwards appointed to the Cumberland, by sir Chaloner Ogle, who had his flag on board that ship, and with whom he returned to England in 1744. This particular affords us a singular proof how fallible many of the articles of biographical information are, which are extracted from what might be deemed the most authentic sources, as they certainly are next to positive, living testimony, namely private letters written at the very time. From one of these we collect that the Litchfield, then commanded by captain Burnaby, arrived in the Downs, from Jamaica, on the 4th of March 1744, having on board a very considerable quantity of specie, collected from the Spanish prizes taken in the West Indies. This intelligence we should certainly have implicitly relied on as most strictly to be depended upon, had we not been accidentally furnished with positive proof of the promotion already stated. In a few days after his arrival we find him one of the members of the court-martial held upon captain Green, of the Lizard sloop, on board the Sandwich, at Spithead: but no other particular mention is made of him during the continuance of the war.

On the 9th of April 1754, he received the honour of knighthood, but on what particular account or occasion does not appear. In the following year he served the office of sheriff for the county of Oxford; and, before its conclusion, we believe in the month of October, was appointed captain of the Jersey, one of the ships then ordered to be equipped in consequence of the expected rupture with France. He continued in this ship without meeting with any occurrence remarkable, or worthy notice, till the month of June or July 1757*, when he was promoted to the command of the Royal Anne, a first rate. This ship, being extremely old, was principally, if not entirely employed as a guardship; so that, as may be naturally expected, we do not again find any particular

---

* Just before he quitted the Jersey he was married to Miss Ottley, by whom he left several children, the eldest of whom having pursued his father's profession, died, not long since, a captain in the navy, as will be hereafter seen.

mention made of him during the time he retained the above command, nor indeed subsequent to that, till his promotion, in 1762, to be rear-admiral of the red. In the month of June, or July 1763, he was appointed commander-in-chief of a squadron ordered to the West Indies, where, though he continued the usual time allotted to such commands, having his flag on board the Dreadnought, nothing in any degree remarkable enough to merit particular notice took place, a circumstance more to be expected than wondered at during a period of peace, immediately consequent to so long a war. On the 31st of October 1767, not long, as it is presumed, after his return from the West Indies, he was advanced to the rank of a baronet of Great Britain, but does not appear to have received any promotion in the line of his profession till 1770, when we find him to have been advanced to the rank of vice-admiral of the white, as he was, on the 24th of October in the same year, to be vice-admiral of the red. At the end of the year 1771, he was made commander-in-chief on the Jamaica station; and, after his return from thence, appears to have received no subsequent appointment. He died some time in the year 1776.

BURY, Thomas. —We know nothing of this gentleman till his promotion, on the 3d of July 1742, to be captain of the Solebay, a new twenty-gun ship. In this vessel we believe him to have been principally employed as a cruiser, but without meeting with any success or occurrence deserving particular notice, till the month of February 1744, at which time he was on the Gibraltar station. His first piece of good fortune was trivial, compared to that which almost immediately followed it. Being off Cape Spartel on the 23d of the month just mentioned, he gave chace to a Spanish privateer, which, in the hope of avoiding him, ran in for the shore. Captain Bury pursued with the greatest alacrity, firing at intervals as he could bring his guns to bear: at length the night compelled him to abandon his prize, which, though it escaped falling into his hands, fled only as it were to meet a more disastrous fate: having received considerable damage from the fire of the Solebay, the Spaniard is supposed to have sunk, during the night, off Point Pedro.

Two days afterwards captain Bury, with better fortune both as to the event itself, and the value of the object he pursued, gave chace to a large ship, with which he closed about nine o'clock in the morning. The enemy, when first discovered, displayed French colours; but on approaching within gun-shot hawled them down, and hoisting those of Spain, which properly belonged to her, resolutely commenced action by firing a shot acrofs the Solebay Captain Bury was in no degree dilatory, but striking the Dutch colours, which he had then flying, and hoisting English, began to engage. The encounter was maintained with much spirit on both sides till one o'clock, when the enemy, on her surrender, proved to be the Concordia, a Spanish register ship, from Vera Cruz, bound to Cadiz, mounting twenty-six guns, and carrying a crew of one hundred and forty men, seven of whom were killed and upwards of twenty wounded, several of them so dangerously as to be past recovery; while the Solebay had on her part only seven persons immaterially wounded. The great value of the prize*, though it may be thought by most persons an object well worthy so serious and spirited a contest, unfortunately proved, in the end, of little advantage to captain Bury himself. There were several of his brother commanders who, though not personally concerned in the capture already mentioned, had, nevertheless, according to the rules and regulations of the service, a legal right to share with him in his good fortune. Estimating his prize at a much higher rate than, great as it was, it really merited, in the first paroxyms of his joy he rashly and inconsiderately agreed to farm of his fortunate copartners their respective shares, and pay them for each the specific sum of ten thousand pounds; this engagement being complied with, he not only found himself abridged of all emolument from his prize, but is even said to have had his own private fortune very materially injured by the extra distribution.

He continued on the same station during the summer, and on the 28th of June fell in with and captured, after

---

* The cargo consisted of 190,000 heavy dollars, 1095 serons of cochineal, 556 of indigo, 424 hides, and some other valuable commodities.

an inconfiderable refiftance, a Spanifh privateer, called the Grand Carlo Magno, mounting twenty-four carriage and fwivel guns: thefe fucceffes were, however, fhortly afterwards interrupted by the capture of the Solebay. In a return of prizes for the month of October, that fhip is ftated, in general terms, to have been captured by the Breft fquadron, no particulars being added. Neverthelefs he was fentenced, by the court-martial held to enquire into his conduct, after his return from captivity, on the 15th of January 1744-5, to forfeit twelve months pay, as a punifhment for his mifconduct on that occafion. Mr. Hardy ftates the judgement to have been more fevere, extending to his difmiffion from the fervice " for not having made any defence, or attempting to difable the chace." A private MS. memorandum we have obtained relative to this bufinefs, ftates him to have been difmiffed the fervice, but to have been afterwards reftored. The fentence firft ftated is that which we are perfuaded was actually paffed, nor fhould we have mentioned the others, but for the purpofe of pointing them out as erroneous. Captain Bury, if ever afterwards employed, is not fufficiently particularifed to enable us to mention even the fhip he commanded, or any other anecdotes or circumftances concerning him, except that he died during the year 1748.

CALLIS, Smith,—was promoted, about the end of the year 1741, from the rank of lieutenant of one of the fhips on the Mediterranean ftation, to be commander of the Duke firefhip. In this ftation he diftinguifhed himfelf exceedingly, under the orders of captain Norris, in the deftruction of five Spanifh gallies in the neutral port of St. Tropez, the particulars of which have been already given in the life of cap. Norris*, together with a proper tribute to the high and diftinguifhed merit of Mr. Callis. So highly, indeed, and moft juftly, was his conduct approved by his majefty George the Second, that he honoured him with a gold chain and medal, as a public token of his efteem and favour. On the 9th of Auguft, which was very foon after his arrival in England with the difpatch from admiral Mathews, containing an account of the above

---

* See vol. iv. p. 300.

event, he was promoted to the command of the Affiftance, of fifty guns, in which fhip he was almoft immediately ordered to the Weft Indies, where he diftinguifhed himfelf exceedingly, in the month of February 1743, under commodore Knowles, in the unfortunate attack on La Guira, where he had eighty-four of his crew killed and wounded. His behaviour was fcarcely lefs confpicuous in the equally unfuccefsful affault of Porto Cavallo which fucceeded it, in the month of April following: a more particular and enlarged detail of both which enterprifes will be found at large in the life of admiral fir Charles Knowles*. We do not find him concerned in any other remarkable undertaking during his continuance in the Weft Indies, from whence he returned in the month of June 1745.

Immediately on his arrival he had a new opportunity of difplaying at leaft his diligence and zeal, and there certainly can fcarcely exift two more valuable qualities in a naval commander. Soon after he came up to Spithead from Jamaica, he received information that the Mediator floop of war, which had been difpatched exprefs for the Weft Indies, had been taken in going through the Needles by a French Privateer. Without waiting for the formality of an order, Captain Callis immediately flipped his cable, and retook the floop of war with fifty of the privateer's crew on board. Trivial as the above circumftance may be thought by fome, we ourfelves certainly conceive it worth infertion, as being highly conducive to his honour, in having been fo decidedly active at a time when the fmalleft delay might have rendered every fubfequent exertion ineffectual †.

We hear nothing of captain Callis after the above event till the beginning of the year 1747, when he was appointed to the Oxford, of fifty guns; in which fhip, being on a cruife off the coaft of Spain, in the month of October following, he fell in with the Gloriofo, a Spanifh fhip of

---

* Vol. iv. p. 350, et feq.
† In 1746 he was one of the members of the court-martial held for the trial of the admirals, Leftock and Mathews. See page 98.

war*, mounting seventy guns, which was soon afterwards captured by captain Buckle, in the Ruffel: but after having unsuccessfully engaged her for some time, was obliged to abandon the contest in consequence of her very superior force. So jealous was captain Callis of his own honour, that he demanded and obtained a court-martial to enquire into the cause of his failure; it is almost needless to add he was most honourably acquitted. Peace quickly succeeding to the above event, we hear nothing farther of him till the month of July, or August, 1756, when he was appointed to the Culloden, of seventy-four guns, as successor to captain Ward, who was ordered home to England as one of the evidences on Mr. Byng's trial. He, captain Callis, having, as we believe, been sent out for the express purpose of taking that command, he retained the same station till the year 1759, when he distinguished himself highly, under the orders of admiral Boscawen, in an attempt, though an unsuccessful one, to cut out, or destroy two French ships which were at anchor within the entrance of Toulon harbour; the particulars of which very spirited enterprize have been already given†. He was at this very time actually a flag officer; and as soon as intelligence of his promotion arrived in the Mediterranean, which was not till after the defeat of monsieur De la Clue‡, to which by his gallantry he very eminently contributed, he returned to Europe, but did not long enjoy his retirement from the fatigues of public service, dying at Bath on the 22d of October 1761. He was buried in the abbey church, where a small but neat monument is erected to his memory.

---

* This ship was rendered exceedingly remarkable by having been engaged, in the first instance, by the Lark and Warwick, of which hereafter; secondly, by captain Callis, as just stated; thirdly, by a squadron of stout privateers, the King George, the Prince Frederic, the Duke, and Princess Amelia, commanded by commodore Walker; immediately after by the Dartmouth, which was blown up in the action; and, lastly, by the Ruffel, which captured her.

† See vol. iv. p. 331.

‡ Owing, as was supposed, to some official manœuvre, Mr. Callis's commission was omitted to be sent out to him; in consequence of which he continued to serve as a captain for some considerable time after his actual promotion to a flag. A proper apology was afterwards made to him for this apparent neglect.

CARTERET,

CARTERET, Philip,—was, on the 10th of May 1742, appointed captain of the Greyhound frigate, which is the earlieſt information we have been able to procure concerning him. He afterwards ſerved in the Eaſt Indies as captain of the Harwich, a fourth rate of fifty guns, one of the ſquadron commanded in ſucceſſion, by Mr. Barnet, Mr. Peyton and Mr. Griffin. He did not long ſurvive his return from that ſtation to England, where he is ſaid to have died on the 28th of September 1748.

CORNISH, Sir Samuel.—This gentleman owed his promotion in the line of his profeſſion, as well as that honourable title beſtowed on him, towards the cloſe of his life, merely to his own intrinſic merit. We have been informed, and we ſtrictly believe with truth, that he ſerved a regular apprenticeſhip to the maſter of a collier; and afterwards entered himſelf as a private ſeaman on board * one of his majeſty's ſhips. In this inferior capacity he did not long remain, his diligence and activity having ſo far recommended him to his commander, that, ſingular as ſuch an advancement may be deemed by ſome, he ſoon was appointed boatſwain † of the ſhip. He ſoon roſe from that ſtation into the line of a commiſſioned officer; but we have not any particulars, or memoranda of his ſervices previous to his appointment, about the end of the year 1741, to the command of a bomb-ketch; not long after which, that is to ſay, on the 12th of March 1742, he was taken, by Mr. Mathews, to be captain of the Namure, a ſecond rate, the ſhip on board which he hoiſted his flag; but he did not long continue in that ſtation, to which he was in all probability preferred merely to give him the rank of poſt captain. His next appointment was to the Guernſey, of fifty guns, one of the reſerve ſquadron on the ſame ſtation. In this ſhip he was preſent at the encounter

---

* Other accounts, and probably with more truth, aſſert that he was originally in the India ſervice, from which he was brought forward into the royal navy, at the inſtance of captain Samuel Mead, who was his very warm patron.

† This circumſtance is confidently ſaid to have been related by the admiral himſelf, to a young gentleman introduced to him on his firſt entrance into the navy, and was meant as an incentive to future exertions, from which at leaſt an equal degree of promotion might be expected as a natural conſequence.

with

with the French and Spanish fleets off Toulon; but not having from the nature of his command found any opportunity of signalizing himself in that action*, if he was so unfortunate on one hand as to be incapable of manifesting his natural gallantry and turn for enterprize, he was, on the other, totally preserved from that vortex of censure which attempted indiscriminately to destroy the characters and fame, both of the innocent and the guilty.

We must not omit that, on the 19th of January preceding the above inglorious event, captain Cornish had, in company with captain Ambrose in the Rupert †, captured the Maria Fortune, a Spanish register ship, of three hundred and fifty tons, mounting sixteen guns, and having on board the governor of Paraguay and his suite. This vessel was bound from Cadiz to Buenos Ayres, and was valued at upwards of one hundred thousand pounds. We do not find any particular account or memorandum relative to this very brave and worthy man, either as to his private life or his public services, till the year 1755, when he commanded the Stirling Castle, a ship employed in the Channel, and on trivial services where no memorable occurrence took place.

In 1758 he was appointed to the Union, a 2nd rate, one of the Channel fleet, during that season, under the orders of Lord Anson, which covered the desultory attacks made by the flying squadron, under commodore Howe, on the smaller French ports. There is a private anecdote relative to the conduct of Mr. Cornish soon after he became invested with this command, which we think too descriptive of his character and natural spirit to pass unnoticed. Lord Anson had appointed him to the ship merely as a temporary commander, and what is technically termed in the service, by order, intending it for the flag ship of sir Charles Saunders, and that Mr. Cornish should be then removed into one of lower rate. Mr. Cornish, when informed of this circumstance, and fully sensible of the

---

* He was dispatched immediately after its conclusion to Nice, and having given a verbal account of it to Mr. Villettes, the British resident there, became the means through which the intelligence of the foregoing event was conveyed to England a considerable time sooner than it otherwise would have been.

† As we have already related in his life. See vol. iv. p. 255.

indig-

indignity as well as infult offered him, fir Charles being a very few months his fenior, wrote to the commander-in-chief in the livelieft terms, and requefted that, as he heard the Union was intended for a flag, he might have the honour of being permitted to continue in that fhip as captain to the admiral, a more elegant or jufter reproof could not, perhaps, have been framed by the ableft politician or the fhrewdeft courtier. Lord Anfon affected not to confider it in that light, or probably had not penetration enough to perceive the force of Mr. Cornifh's well turned reprimand. Charmed with his apparent condefcenfion he continued him in the fame fhip, and promoted him to the rank of commodore.

On May 19, 1759, he was appointed a commodore to go to the Eaft Indies * with a fmall fquadron, confifting of the Lenox, of 74 guns, his own fhip; the Duc d'Aquitaine, of fixty-four; the York, of fixty; and the Falmouth, of fifty guns; intended as a reinforcement to Mr. Pocock, with whom he formed a junction on the 18th of October, off Madrafs. In the month of February 1760, he was detached with part of the fquadron, by Mr. Stevens, who had fucceeded admiral Pocock as commander-in-chief, to Fort St. George, where he arrived on the 28th of February. In the month of March he affifted in the attack of the very important port of Karical, which furrendered, on the 5th of April, to himfelf and major Monfon. By this, in addition to thofe fucceffes which had preceded it, the French, who a fhort time before had been fo powerful and even threatened the deftruction or capture of all the Britifh poffeffions in that part of the world, were themfelves nearly extirpated from the fame quarter, being now confined to the fingle port of Pondicherry, which itfelf was not long afterwards reduced by rear-admiral Stevens, Mr. Cornifh, and colonel Coote.

Mr. Stevens and himfelf having, according to the ufual practice, gone into port with fuch fhips as needed repair. to refit, about the end of October, were in the month of December following on their return to their ftation off Pondicherry, when, on the 16th, he parted company with the commander-in-chief in a gale of wind, which he was

---

* He was to have hoifted a broad pendant on board the Lenox, a third rate of feventy-four guns; however it was afterwards determined he fhould be appointed a flag-officer, as he was before he failed from England.

fortunate

fortunate enough to weather, as well as that more tremendous one, almost immediately subsequent to it, which did so much injury to such part of the British squadron as was employed at that time in the blockade of this last remnant of the French East Indian power. Mr. Cornish got in, with little or no injury, on the 5th of January, with the Lenox, York and Weymouth, and the place surrendered in ten days afterwards. Warlike operations now from necessity ceased, there being no enemy to contend with till the dæmon of discord raised up a very impotent one in the court of Spain; previous, however, to this, Mr. Cornish was advanced to be rear-admiral of the white in 1760, and in the ensuing year, to be rear of the red. On the 17th of May 1761, he succeeded, on the death of Mr. Stevens, to the supreme command in that part of the world; and the rupture with Spain having once more furnished Mr. Cornish with an opportunity of displaying his talents and gallantry, we shall now proceed to a short detail of those operations which reflected on him so much honour, and brought the most valuable of the Spanish possessions under the same dominion with those of her ally.

The principal settlement in that quarter of the world, belonging to Spain, is, as it is well known, called Manilla, situate in Luconia, one of the Philippine islands, where, to render the chain of commerce complete, a large galleon annually arrives from Acapulco, laden with specie and the most valuable commodities produced in Spanish South America, which are exchanged for the produce of China and the East Indies. The interruption of so grand a source of national wealth was in itself an object of no small magnitude; and the reduction of the place, together with that of a strong fortress, the capital of an extensive dominion, contributed to enhance, in the highest degree, the consequence of the expedition.

The force destined to attempt this great enterprize consisted of seven ships of the line, including fourth rates; three frigates, two storeships, and the Osterly East India ship, on board which were embarked colonel Draper's regiment, the seventy-ninth, a company of artillery, six hundred sepoys, thirty artillery-men furnished by the government of Madrass, a company of caffres, one of
topazes,

topazes, and one of pioneers; two small corps of French refugees and deserters, and some hundred lascars for the use of the train. This motly army was reinforced by Mr. Cornish, on its arrival at Luconia, with a battalion of volunteer seamen, consisting of five hundred and fifty, with their proper officers, and the marines of the squadron, amounting to nearly three hundred rank and file.

The admiral had, the instant the expedition was resolved on, with the most prudent and laudable precaution, dispatched the Seahorse frigate to cruise at the entrance of the Chinese Seas, for the purpose of intercepting all vessels bound for the Manillas, and preventing the enemy from receiving any intelligence of the storm of war which was ready to burst over them. The greatest expedition was necessary as well on account of its being conducive to the surprize of the enemy, as that it would be impossible for the fleet to prosecute their voyage, if the north-west monsoon set in with any violence before it was ready for sea. Energy and dispatch was consequently most conspicuously apparent in every department; in the short space of three weeks, the troops were collected, formed and embarked, together with all their stores and camp equipage, added to a proportionate quantity of artillery: a business which could not be effected without the most difficult exertions, in consequence of a perpetual and raging surf which considerably impeded and embarrassed every measure. The subsequent operations of this glorious and successful expedition will be best explained by the plain narrative and account given by Mr. Cornish himself, in his letter to Mr. Cleveland, dated in the bay of Manilla, 1762.

" It is with the greatest pleasure I have the honour to acquaint their lordships with the success of his majesty's arms in the reduction of the city of Manilla, which was taken by storm on the morning of the 26th instant. In my letters of the 23d and 31st of July, I acquainted their lordships with my proceedings to that time; after which I used every possible means at Madrass for dispatch, the decline of the south-west monsoon making it of the utmost importance: to promote this end, I put on board the Elizabeth,

zabeth, Grafton, Lenox, Weymouth and Argo, such of the troops and military stores as they were allotted to carry, and on the 29th sent them away, under the command of commodore Tiddeman, to proceed to Mallaca, with a view that they might compleat their water there by the time I should arrive with the remainder of the squadron.

"Having accomplished the embarkation of every thing designed for the expedition, I sailed, on the 1st of August, with the ships under-mentioned, viz. Norfolk, Panther, America, Seaford, South Sea Castle storeship, Admiral Stevens storeship, Osterly company's ship, leaving the Falmouth, at the request of the president and council, to convoy the Essex India ship, who was not ready to sail, having the treasure to take on board for the China cargoes, and to bring to Manilla such of the company's servants as were to be put in possession of that government, if the expedition succeeded.

"On the 19th I arrived at Mallacca and was disappointed in not finding Mr. Tiddeman there, who did not join till the 21st, having met with long calms. The difficulty of watering the squadron at that place made it the 27th before I could leave the road.

"On the 2d of September I arrived off Pulo Timean, and was joined by captain Grant, in the Seahorse, whom I had detached, upon my first arrival at Madrass, to cruise between this island and the Streights of Sincapore, to stop any vessels he might suspect going to Manilla.

"On the 19th I made the coast of Luconia, but was drove off again by a strong north-west wind, which separated some of the squadron. The 22d the gale broke up; and the wind shifting to the south-west, on the 23d we recovered the land again. The next day we entered the bay of Manilla; and, in the close of the evening, anchored off the fort of Cavita with the whole squadron, except the South Sea Castle and Admiral Stevens, the Falmouth and Essex having joined me off the coast. In the night I sent the masters to sound near the fortifications of Cavite, and, by their report, found it might be attacked by ships.

"On the 25th, in the morning, the wind not being favourable to attack the Cavite, I took two of the frigates, and, with general Draper and some other officers, reconnoitred

noitred the fhore about Manilla, and obferved fome churches and other buildings to ftand near the works on the fouth fide of the town, particularly towards the fouth-weft baftion. We had fome defign of attacking the Cavite firft, in order to have the conveniency of that port for the fhipping; but confidered, though the attack fhould be attended with all the fuccefs we could hope, yet it would caufe a delay, at leaft, of two days before we could land at Manilla. This time would have afforded opportunity to the enemy to demolifh the buildings near their works, as well as to prepare many obftacles to our landing, and perhaps recover from confternation our unexpected arrival had thrown them in; moreover, Manilla being the capital, if that fell, Cavite would in confequence capitulate alfo.

"From thofe confiderations I joined in opinion with the general, to take advantage of circumftances fo favourable for a defcent, and land the troops with all difpatch, endeavouring at the fame time to get poffeffion of fome pofts near their works, which, if effected, would greatly facilitate the reduction of the city.

"In confequence of thefe refolutions I immediately made the fignal, on board the Seahorfe, for the fquadron to join me, and for the troops to prepare to land. About feven in the evening, the twenty-ninth regiment with the marines, in boats, under the direction of the captains Parker, Kempenfelt and Brereton, pufhed for the fhore, under the fire of the three frigates, they effected their landing at a church, called the Moratta, about a mile and a half from the walls.

"On the next morning the general took an advanced poft about two hundred yards from the glacis, and there, under cover of a blind, erected his battery againft the face of the fouth-weft baftion. The number of troops being fmall, I landed about feven hundred feamen.

"On the 25th I difpatched three armed boats after a galley coming up the bay to Manilla. They came up with her, refolutely boarded her, and took her notwithftanding fhe kept up a fmart fire with pattararoes and mufkets. She mounted two carriage and feventeen brafs fwivel guns, having a crew of eighty men. By letters found in her we difcovered fhe was difpatched by the galleon St. Phillipina, from Acapulco, and whom fhe had left, the 1ft of September, at Cajoyagan, between the Embocadaro and Cape Spiritu Santo. Upon this difcovery I came to a refolution of fending the Panther and Argo in queft of her; but it was the 4th of October before the weather permitted their failing..

" On the 28th of September the general acquainted me he was beginning to work on the battery, and that if fome fhips could get near enough to throw fhot into the works of the town oppofed to it, by taking off fome of the enemy's fire and attention, it might thereby facilitate it's deftruction. In confequence of this, I ordered commodore Tiddeman, with the Elizabeth and Falmouth towards the town, as near as the depth of water would permit, with inftructions to place the fhips in fuch a pofition as would beft anfwer the purpofe intended ; this was accordingly done the next day, and their fire had a good effect.

" On the 30th the South Sea Caftle arrived with ftores, which were much wanted, particularly the intrenching tools, for which the army had been fo greatly diftreffed that I was obliged to employ all the forges in making fpades, pickaxes, &c. for them. The firft of October it began to blow frefh, and in the night increafed to a hard gale, which drove the South Sea Caftle afhore near the Pulverifta, a little to the fouthward of the camp. This accident, however, had fome confiderable advantages attending it, as the fituation fhe lay in rendered her cannon a protection for the rear of the camp : it was likewife the means of all her military ftores being got on fhore with fafety and difpatch, as well as the army fupplied with the provifions fhe had on board; both which were articles they ftood in immediate need of, and could not have been put on fhore by boats, as it continued blowing weather for feveral days after, with a furf breaking very high on the beach. This gale being from the W. S. W. directly on the fhore, gave me much concern for the fafety of the fquadron, particularly the Elizabeth and Falmouth, which were only in four fathom water; and, as I have fince been informed, with the furge of the fea ftruck ; but the bottom being mud, and foft to a confiderable depth, they received no damage. On the 4th, in the morning, the general opened the battery, which was fo well managed, and feconded by the fhips before the town,

expected from Cadiz, Ferrol and Carthagena, with the French ships that were fit for sea in the ports of Brest, Rochfort and L'Orient, Mr. Geary immediately proceeded off Brest. Nothing material occurred till the 3d of July, when the Monarch, being a head of the fleet on the look-out, made a signal at ten o'clock in the morning for discovering a fleet consisting of twenty sail: these were immediately concluded to be the enemy of whom they were in search, and the utmost alacrity was used in endeavouring to get up with them. The chace continued the whole day, and at five o'clock in the afternoon the headmost ships came up * with the sternmost of the fugitives,

---

sake, if you should be so lucky as to get sight of the enemy, get as close to them as possible. Do not let them shuffle with you by engaging at a distance, but get within musket shot if you can; that will be the way to gain great honour, and will be the means to make the action decisive. By doing this you will put it out of the power of any of the brawlers to find fault. I am fully persuaded you will faithfully do your part, therefore hope you will forgive my saying so much on the subject. I find the Russians are gone from the Downs so that you will have no trouble about them. My good friend, God bless you; may the hand of Providence go with you and protect you in the day of battle, and grant you victory over our perfidious enemies: and may you return with honour to your country and family again; these are the sincere and hearty wishes of him who is most truly and faithfully,

" My dear Sir,
" Your most obedient and most humble servant,

" Sir F. Geary. " HAWKE."

* A whimsical and entertaining anecdote is related of him on this occasion. Rear-admiral Kempenfelt, who at that time acted as his first captain, was universally and most deservedly esteemed one of the bravest and best informed officers in the service, as to the management, and requisite mode of manœuvring a large fleet previous to the commencement of, and during the continuance of an action itself. Lord Hawke, than whom no man was a sounder judge of nautical abilities, adds, in a postscript to one of his letters to admiral Geary, " I am glad you have got so excellent an officer with you as I am convinced Kempenfelt is: he will be of great service to you." But in the attainment of this universally acknowledged and valuable qualification, he had contracted a habit of using more signals than men less practised in that particular branch of service deemed necessary: of this latter class of commanders was admiral Geary. As soon as the enemy were discovered and the signal made for a general chace,

Kempen-

morning after the reduction of Manilla, was drowned with five of his people.

"Captain Kempenfelt, by whom I fend this, has been of the greateſt aſſiſtance to me during the courſe of this enterprize; his great merit makes it my duty to recommend him as a very able and good officer."

On the 21ſt of October 1762, as though in ſympathetic gratitude and honourable reward for the gallant ſervice he had rendered, he was promoted at home, to be vice-admiral of the blue. A ludicrous anecdote is related of him, which we think merits inſertion as ſtrongly marking the character of an honeſt blunt ſeaman, and as having reference to the foregoing expedition. The form of the capitulation and agreement for the ranſom, which it is well known was never paid, was ſettled between the Spaniſh archbiſhop and general Draper: the latter valued himſelf extremely on being, as he certainly was, a very elegant ſcholar; ſo that the whole of the converſation and ſubſequent arrangement paſſed in Latin. When the demur, and the conſequent refuſal of the Spaniſh court to pay the ſtipulated ſum took place, on an alledged and paltry ground of miſunderſtanding between the negociating parties: Mr. Corniſh exclaimed humourouſly and with an affectation of much paſſion, " that he never would again accept of a command where his colleague ſpoke Latin."

Peace not only having been concluded ſoon after his laſt-mentioned very brilliant ſucceſs, but there being literally no enemy any longer to contend with, the vice-admiral returned to Europe with the greater part of his force, and does not appear to have held any command during the reſt of his life. Indeed ſuch an appointment was little to be expected, none offering during a time of profound peace, unleſs he had accepted of that of a port admiral, or a three year's ſtation in North America, or the Weſt Indies. On the 9th of January 1766, he was, in conſideration of his many honourable ſervices, advanced to the rank of a baronet of Great Britain; and was in a few days afterwards, elected repreſentative in parliament for the borough of Shoreham, a ſtation he retained till the time of his death. He received no addition to his naval rank till the 28th of October 1770, when he was advanced to be vice-admiral of the red; but did not long ſurvive

vive this promotion, dying two days afterwards univerſally eſteemed, as a brave commander, a valuable friend, and a truly honeſt man.

CROOKSHANKS, John.—Our acquaintance with this gentleman commences with his appointment, on the 3d of July 1742, to be captain of the Loeſtoffe, a twenty-gun ſhip, ordered not long afterwards to the Mediterranean, where he continued during the years 1743 and 4. The only material articles of intelligence we find concerning him during that period are, that, in the month of June 1744, he captured, and carried into Gibraltar, a very valuable French merchant-ſhip, bound from Cadiz to Martinico, worth, as it is ſaid, upwards of twenty thouſand pounds. On the 18th December following, he had the additional good fortune to make prize of a French ſhip, mounting ſixteen carriage and twenty ſwivel guns, called the Firme. In a manuſcript liſt we have ſeen of the ſhips under the command of Mr. Mathews, in the encounter with the combined force of France and Spain, off Toulon, the name of captain Crookſhanks is inſerted as commander of the Diamond, of forty guns: but this appointment, if true, could only have been temporary, and ſhort. He returned to England in the Deptford ſtoreſhip not long after his latter ſuccefs, and was quickly promoted to the Lark, a fifth rate of forty guns. Nothing very obſervable appears to have marked his life or ſervice till the month of June 1747, when he was ordered to take the Warwick, of ſixty guns, commanded by captain Erſkine, with him to Newfoundland, as convoy to the merchant-ſhips bound thither. This ſervice being performed, captain Crookſhanks was inſtructed to proceed to Louiſburgh, where he was to join the ſquadron already there under Mr. Knowles. Mr. Crookſhanks ſailed on this ſervice, from Spithead, about the 15th of June; and, after a ſhort ſtay at Plymouth, finally quitted port on the 20th with twenty-four merchant-ſhips under his convoy, together with a tranſport, and the Beaufort packet, a ſmall armed veſſel in the ſervice of the ordnance.

No material occurrence took place till the 14th of July, when being in latitude 40. 38. longitude 21. 22. from the Lizard, captain Crookſhanks and his fleet about ſeven in the morning, it being then almoſt a dead calm, diſcovered a fail to the weftward, which, after a little obfervation, was found to be a large fhip of force, and judged a cruifer. The chace was continued during the whole day with indifferent fuccefs; but though the Lark, and her confort the Warwick, gained confiderably on the chace, they were not able to clofe, and bring her to action, though nothing impeded the purfuit. By four o'clock on the morning of the 15th, Mr. Crookfhanks was near enough to afcertain that his antagonift was a very large Spanifh fhip of war of two decks, mounting feventy guns. This difcovery does not appear to have intimidated or diverted the purfuers from their object, notwithftanding it led them, as captain Crookfhanks himfelf expreffes it in his narrative of the tranfaction, " Directly out of the courfe of the voyage."

The chace was continued with flow but gradual advantage during the whole day, and about eleven at night the Lark, being abreaft of the enemy's fhip, which was afterwards found to be the Gloriofo, and about 350 yards from her, began to fire; almoft at the fame inftant the Warwick, which till then had kept in the wake of the Lark, tacked, and ftood to the northward. The probable reafons which induced captain Erfkine to take that meafure will hereafter be ftated in the life of that gentleman. Suffice it to fay in this place, that a difference of opinion, for fuch at leaft there certainly was between the two captains, caufed the total failure of this attempt. The Lark and the Warwick becoming, in confequence of the manœuvre juft mentioned, widely feparated, the Spaniard feized the opportunity of attacking the latter, and totally difabled her before the Lark could get up to her fupport.

This appears to be the fair ftate of the fimple matter of fact. This affair afterwards became a fubject of no fmall controverfy; and captain Crookfhanks, on his arrival at Louifburg being put under an arreft, in confequence of a charge preferred againft him by captain Erfkine, to commodore Knowles, was fentenced, by a court-martial, to be difmiffed the fervice. The beft, and at the fame time the moft concife account we can give of the foregoing fingular tranfaction, is by inferting the following letter, written by captain Crookfhanks to the

honourable

honourable Mr. Legge, and dated at sea on the 20th of July, a few days after the action.

"Sir, I have just time to give you an account, by a ship we met at sea, of an engagement with a Spanish man of war, which, far as we could judge, was of seventy-four guns. As we had the misfortune to lose her, you may, perhaps, have the Spanish account before ours, and it may, in some measure, satisfy your curiosity to have one from us as soon as possible.

"About eleven at night I ran along side of her, as near as the wind would permit, and, in passing, fired, hoping thereby, though not in close engaging distance, to embarrass her, and give the Warwick the surer chance of securing a station on her lee quarter, designing to stretch ahead, tack, and on gaining the wind, secure our station on her opposite bow: but the Warwick tacked on her quarter, being then a small distance astern of us, which measure I think was the only means of destroying my plan. The Spaniard wore, hawled the wind for a very short time, edged away toward the Warwick and engaged, by which she enlarged her distance from us. We stood after them immediately; but having little wind, and they going nearly before it, we were not able to get up, to sustain the Warwick, till we saw them draw off from each other, and the Warwick's main-top-mast gone. We then stood towards the enemy proposing to have engaged her at daylight; but, on the Warwick's lying with her head from us, and firing a gun, which I was to conclude a signal of distress, I thought it indispensably my duty to quit that design, making the best of my way to her assistance, and to collect the convoy.

"I am, &c.
"Signed, J. CROOKSHANKS*."

To this letter we shall beg to subjoin the defence made by the above gentleman to the charge which was preferred against him.

---

* Captain Crookshanks, who has published this letter in a defence written by himself, adds in a note, " By this method it would have been next to impossible for the enemy to have escaped, or have dragged the British ships farther out of their way, but he must probably have fought them in the morning in the manner that captain Crookshanks should then have found it expedient to attack him."

" To the introductory part of captain Erſkine's charge againſt me, I take the liberty to ſay, in anſwer, that it would have been as juſt, and equally as good ſenſe, to have written the Warwick in company with the Lark, as her captain was the commanding officer. I make this ſmall remark, inſignificant as it may appear, upon obſerving that ſome of the very few people, whom I have had occaſion to ſpeak to on this ſubject, have thought otherwiſe, in places where my accuſer, or ſome perſon for him, has wickedly appeared to have had hopes of cruſhing me, in the opinion of the world, by invectives, inſinuations, and relating ſtories much to my diſadvantage, as well as foreign to the caſe in queſtion, all which can be made very apparent: but I find myſelf relieved, and happy, in being now brought before a court, to whoſe candour and equity I chearfully ſubmit the determination of my cauſe, being perſuaded that each member is guarded againſt prepoſſeſſions, and will take the facts only as they ſhall hereafter be made to appear.

" We diſcovered and began the chace of the enemy ſometime after ſeven o'clock on the morning of the 14th of July, bearing between the north and the weſt from us, appearing, at different times, a large ſail, with her top-ſails only out of water, from the Lark's fore-caſtle, where I went to look at her with my glaſs, and could diſcover her head laid different ways, but whether by tacking or wearing I could not judge. About ten I made a ſignal for the Montague Bilander, in the ordnance ſervice, to chace to the north-weſt, which Mr. Conolly, her maſter, very alertly obſerved between twelve and one. In the afternoon of the 15th I made the Warwick's ſignal to chace and open to the north-eaſt, which I well remember was not obeyed. We continued following the chace, the Montague and Warwick with us, till near nine at night, having before the cloſe of day, ſuppoſed the Montague nearly up with the chace, as it afterwards appeared ſhe was, and rather on our weather bow. About ten they paſſed us to the eaſtward, and, being convinced of it, by the Montague's ſignals of falſe fires, and muſkets, obſerving alſo the difference of the ſound of the guns ſhe and the enemy fired at each other, I made the general ſignal to tack, hoping that the Warwick would have been inſtantly prepared to obey it, for ſhe was ſo near on our

weather

weather quarter as to lay in our track. This obliged me, in tacking firſt, to pay round off, and paſs to leeward of her, thereby loſing the better chance of gaining the enemy's wake, while the Warwick might have endeavoured to gain the reach of him, provided the enemy had attempted to ſail large, capt. Erſkine knowing that to be the favourite way of his ſhip's going beſt.

" We chaſed cloſe, hawled up till daylight, and then again ſaw the enemy, a very tall ſhip, and the Montague on her larboard or weather quarter. About ſeven I could diſtinctly count fifteen lower-deck ports regularly hawled up, and was ſo near as plainly to diſcover, in my glaſs, men on her poop and gang boards, ſo that I was then at no loſs to form a judgment of the ſize of the ſhip and the force ſhe was capable of carrying. The queſtion that aroſe for my better government was, whether or not ſhe was well appointed? In the common prudence of an officer I certainly ought to think ſhe was, and hope for the beſt.

" Thus I did then, and always, determine, vigorouſly and reſolutely, with the proper aſſiſtance of the Warwick, to engage the enemy. I do ſolemnly, before God and and this court, aver, ſtill reſerving to myſelf an undoubted right of judging, when to begin, and in what manner, that from daylight in the morning till eleven at night (I ſpeak now of the 16th of July) the greateſt care and pains were taken, to trim the hull and ſails of the Lark to the beſt advantage, to ſteer and bring the ſhip up with the enemy, as, I flatter myſelf, will appear, from the evidence of every officer and man in the Lark, who was capable of making obſervations. In this manner I led up to the Glorioſo, the Warwick following in our wake on one quarter or other, as ſmall ſhifts of wind and common unavoidable accidents might occaſion. Some little time before we reached up with the enemy, when there was a ſtrong appearance of our doing it, I ſent for the firſt lieutenant and gave him orders to ſtand by the foremoſt gun, to keep it pointing, and to call to me when he found it almoſt growing uſeleſs, giving him alſo ſome few, as I thought neceſſary, cautions, in regard to managing the men and battery under his more immediate care and direction. I alſo ſent for the ſecond lieutenant from his

quarters,

quarters between decks, intimated the orders I had given to the firſt, and directed him to be in immediate readineſs, that if he heard a gun fired upon the upper deck, it ſhould be a ſignal to haul all the ports up, run the guns out, and make the beſt uſe of them he could, recommending particularly that he ſhould endeavour to keep the men cool, to fire ſlow, having his guns ſo pointed as to be in a manner ſure of doing execution. I was then rather determined not to engage till I got cloſe on the enemy's weather bow, reſpecting the poſition of ſailing he was then in; but I fired, upon obſerving the Warwick, which I thought was unluckily and accidentally caught in ſtays. The lines of fight are frequently known to deceive the ſkilful; but, to the beſt of my judgment, the Warwick was, at the time of putting helm alee, aſtern in a parallel to the windward of the Lark, very nearly the ſame diſtance from the Lark as the Lark was from the enemy a-breaſt.

"The Lark then only got abreaſt of the enemy, which the Warwick might have done, and conſiderable nearer, but ſhe tacked, and fired in tacking; though, I conceive, ſhe could not fire with any ſort of good view till after the wind was a-head, or rather that ſhe paid two or more points off, unleſs for reaſons I cannot enter into, and ſhould imagine captain Erſkine, as late commander of the Warwick, will not chuſe to avow.

"A mile, ſtandard meaſure, is 1760 yards: 350 to 400 yards, is the moſt extreme diſtance that any body on board the Lark (I have heard of) has judged her to have been from the enemy, when firing at each other, abreaſt, beam and beam.

"Diſtances at ſea, eſpecially at night, are ſomewhat difficult to determine in a very nice degree; ſo is point-blank ſhot, which is commonly called a quarter of a mile, or 440 yards: therefore I can only aſk leave to offer arguments from certain facts, admitting probabilities amounting very near to poſitive truth. The Lark paſſed the enemy, as tall a ſhip as the Princeſſa, to leeward of her with all the ſail that could be ſet by the wind, which was then moderate, and, what is often termed by ſeamen, juſt a pleaſant working gale, and the water ſmooth: by this I mean to ſhew the Lark heeled two or three ſtreaks. The enemy had only her top-ſails and top-gallant-ſails:

I am

I am not pofitive whether the latter were hoifted, or on the caps; but, with her fuperiority of length and breadth, I prefume fhe was nearly upright; and it has been judged that moft, if not all of the guns fhe fired at us were from her upper decks. Now it is certain we received a fhot through the lower part of the fore-ftay-fail; one through the main-fail a little above the collar of the mizen-ftay; a fhot went through the mizen-ftay-fail, a large deep fail, a little above the foot rope; another through the fecond cloth from the maft, of the mizen, about eight feet above the quarter deck; many others too paffed and dropt in a particular and obferved manner. I conceive, from all thefe circumftances, the Lark was within point-blank-fhot (tho' not in a very clofe engaging diftance) and fhe was conded and fteered, fometimes by myfelf, as near as the wind would let us pafs.

"The Warwick tacked when it is wifhed fhe had not; but how they reconcile coming to a clofe engagement, in ten minutes, after being a mile to leeward (the words of the charge) is what I cannot pretend to account for: yet I think I am not miftaken when I fay it muft have been full fifty minutes, or more.

"I ufed my beft endeavours to return and fupport the Warwick; I did return fo near, as to have properly renewed my part of the engagement in ten, at the moft fifteen minutes, if the Warwick had not hawled off to the fouthward. The enemy, on the Warwick's going off, fired ten or twelve guns very fmartly at her, and hawled to the northward. Upon obferving the Warwick's main-top-maft gone, and not able to guefs what farther damage fhe might have fuftained, I concluded it was beft to hawl to the northward to be near the enemy at day-break, for the better opportunity of difcerning her condition, as well as that of the Warwick: the latter, ftill lying in the fame pofition, fired a gun, which I could not but confider as a fignal of diftrefs; and very foon after I was confirmed in this opinion, by Mr. Conolly, in the Montague bilander, who told me he had been hailed by the Warwick, and defired to acquaint me with the condition of that fhip, which was quite difabled.

"We wore and joined the Warwick. And now, fir, ftanding heavily accufed of running away from the enemy, which

which I take to imply, and mean cowardice, the moſt ſhocking and ignominious character that can poſſibly be given to a military man, I cannot, in duty and juſtice to myſelf, omit declaring ar opinion, and with confidence too, that if captain Erſkine had managed, or even miſmanaged in any other manner than preciſely what he did, the enemy could not have taken, I ſay ſnatched, ſuch advantages as he did of the Warwick, in addition to his ſuperior force; I venture then to think my conduct in ſuch caſe would ſcarcely now have been called in queſtion; I am, in the higheſt degree, poſitive my perſonal reſolution could not have ſuffered ſuſpicion.

"Conſidering that part of what I have now ſaid may, in ſome degree, prepare the court to hear and canvas the evidence, as well in ſupport of the charge as in my defence: and in confideration that my greateſt and only comfort, while I exiſt, depends on my clearing ſo baſe and villainous an aſperſion as has been ſpread about, I have depended, and am to hope for excuſe in having treſpaſſed on your time."

Notwithſtanding the court thought proper to paſs a ſentence of diſmiſſion of this gentleman during his majeſty's pleaſure, it was declared to him by the preſident, that it did, by an unanimous reſolve, acquit him even of the ſuſpicion of cowardice, diſaffection, or want of zeal. Mr. Crookſlanks bore his ſituation with extreme impatience: he reprobated the conduct of admiral Knowles and the judge advocate, whom he loudly charged with oppreſſion and injuſtice. He aſked the admirals permiſſion to ſerve as a volunteer in a private capacity; but this requeſt, though not peremptorily denied, was not complied with. He repeatedly applied to Mr. Knowles for a court-marrial on captain Erſkine; but this was alſo refuſed, under pretence that ſuch application was prompted only by a vindictive ſpirit of recrimination: ſo that at length wearied out with fruitleſs ſolicitations, for what he deemed a mere act of juſtice to himſelf and his character, and provoked as he himſelf reports by repeated and ſtudied affronts, he took his paſſage from Jamaica on board the Plymouth, with captain Digby Dent, who had been preſident of the court-martial which tried him, and
who

who appears to have entertained an high esteem for him. He arrived at Portsmouth after a passage of nearly seven weeks, and immediately began a fresh application to the board of admiralty for a court-martial on captain Erskine. Still was his request negatived, but not for the same reasons which had been given by Mr. Knowles. Mr. Corbet, the secretary to the admiralty, wrote him in very plain terms, that " he ought to have applied abroad, in proper time, to the commander-in-chief, but not then after his condemnation, which proceeded only from a recriminating temper." Mr. Knowles had before told him in the West Indies, he did not think it legal for him to order a court-martial without particular orders from the lords of the admiralty: so that, to speak candidly, we cannot help thinking Mr. Crookshanks was unwarrantably, and shamefully bandied about from one jurisdiction to another, without any intention to afford him a satisfaction he appears to have had a very legal right to demand. To sum up the business, captain Erskine was not tried, nor captain Crookshanks employed.

Matters continued pretty quiet till about 1758, when Mr. Crookshanks having published an account of his conduct and treatment, a short and insignificant paper war took place between him and admiral Knowles, in which captain Erskine was also involved. Soon after this time, having repeatedly petitioned his majesty that he might be restored to his rank as a captain in the navy, the king was pleased to refer his case to the consideration of the admiralty-board; and their report we may naturally conclude to have been favourable, as he was immediately reinstated in his former station on the list of captains, with the usual allowance of half-pay, which he continued to enjoy during life. This in some degree appears wonderful, as Mr. Crookshanks informs us that lord Anson, at that time first lord of the admiralty, had the indecent effrontery to tell him, when applied to for the purpose of reinstatement some years before, " that he laboured under a suspension which he believed would continue for ever; that it was very happy for him he had been tried abroad, as he (*his lordship*) was convinced, had the court-martial been held in England he would have met with another sort of fate." This appears the more extraordinary, as it is certain, without

any

any wish of deteriorating his lordship's character, that as brave and as able men as himself have been of a very different opinion.

We cannot reconcile to ourselves this seeming contradiction and alteration of opinion, or account, for the softened asperity of his lordship's sentiments, except supposing it occasioned by a publication from Mr. Crookshanks, of what had passed between himself and his lordship on that occasion, and a discovery on the part of the latter, that neither his rank nor supposed popularity prevented the world from considering that assertion as an ungenerous and unfounded insult. Mr. Crookshanks continued to live ever afterwards in retirement, having unsuccessfully made repeated applications for employment, as will appear from the following petition to his majesty and the letter annexed to the earl of Sandwich, first lord of the admiralty at the time it was written.

" To the KING.

" Captain John Crookshanks, late commander of your majesty's ship the Lark, humbly begs leave to represent—

" That on his petition to your royal grandfather, his late majesty was graciously pleased to order that the said petition should be read and considered by his board of admiralty: that, in consequence of a report from the lords commissioners of the said board made to his majesty in council, he was farther graciously pleased to order, that your petitioner should be restored to his rank, which is now done, and his name stands on the naval books, in the list of captains, according to his rank of seniority.

" But as the service of his king and country was then, is still, and ever will be uppermost in his thoughts, and the first object both of his former and present application, your petitioner most humbly takes leave to beg that he may be again actually employed in your majesty's service according to his rank in the navy; and this he presumes to entreat with the greatest earnestness, as this is a time of war when no man, able to serve his sovereign and the public, would wish to be unemployed."

My

" My Lord,

" My prefent and future tranquility are fo deeply concerned that I muft venture to unburthen my mind; I find it irrefiftible; yet hope to avoid the fufpicion of not poffeffing every refpect due to your lordfhip.

" You obferved, when I had the honour of feeing you, that mine was a very old and an almoft obfolete ftory, and you chofe to avoid entering upon the matter. This I was not quite unprepared to expect: but when you faid you was mafter of the affair, that you had formed your opinion, and a pretty ftrong one too, I was more hurt than I can defcribe; and by fo much the more fo as I do not believe England produces a man who has held, and does hold, your fkill and abilities, for governing the naval department, in higher eftimation than myfelf. You conveyed to my idea that your opinion was unfavourable, and left it fhould be fo I rifque to fay, that your lordfhip is not mafter of the affair: you have taken falfe information, and therefore only could have drawn a wrong conclufion. I hazarded chaftifement from the admiralty, and a pecuniary mulct in Weftminfter-hall, for having broke my convoy orders, and inftructions: but I had formed a plan of doing a gallant action, which I knew I fhould have executed, far as it could have depended on the refolution of one brave man, and I have no fcruple to fay, an able feaman; but my defigns were fruftrated by a felf-fufficient junior officer, to fay no worfe of him, whom I ought to have treated with rigour; I fhould then have prevented, and might have defyed all the fcandalous, wicked, and mean machinations that were afterwards wantonly played off againft me, by one I had then never offended. Thefe are points, my lord, I know the truth of, and that will prove themfelves when and wherefoever they are clofely and candidly examined into, by the unprejudiced men of fkill and penetration.

" I hope your lordfhip will generoufly pardon me, if I have differed in opinion in one fingle inftance, that is fo nearly connected with my own credit and happinefs; and allow me to declare, that I wifh every honour and advantage to the Britifh navy under a long continuation of your lordfhip's aufpices: although time has not divefted me of very quick feelings, yet it can never enter

into

into my plan to offend your lordſhip, for I am with un-feigned reſpect,

"My lord, &c.

To the oarl of Sandwich, 1771.

"J. CROOKSHANKS."

Theſe repeated applications did not, however, produce his re-employment; nor could it reaſonably have been expected by himſelf that they ſhould: he had attained a very advanced age; and, added to that, was ſo extremely infirm, that, however his own ſpirit might prompt him to ſollicit a command, reaſon and common ſenſe muſt have united in diſſuading him from entering on ſuch an engagement with thoſe diſadvantages which, as we have already ſtated, he laboured under. That he was in many points an ill-uſed man we believe few officers, of candour and ability, have ever attempted to deny; that if in ſome degree reprehenſible, and, by way of parentheſis, we muſt beg to remark, the only point in which blame appears to attach to him is, his having ſtood to the eaſtward five or ſix minutes longer than was neceſſary, after he paſſed the Glorioſo; he certainly could not merit ſo ſevere a ſentence, while his junior officer, who had manifeſtly con-tributed, by his conduct, to prevent ſucceſs, and had, as was fairly proved to the underſtanding of all unbiaſſed men, been abſolutely guilty of diſobedience of orders, was ſuffered to paſs through life untried, and, far as related to the ſervice itſelf, uncenſured.

Capt. Crookſhanks appears to have been, in his younger days, a man poſſeſſed of too much warmth of temper; at the ſame time his greateſt enemies could not but allow him to have poſſeſſed conſiderable ability as a ſeaman, while the court-martial which tried him bore the hand-ſomeſt teſtimony of his perſonal ſpirit and gallantry. He died in retirement, at Pimlico, on the 20th of February, 1795, in the 87th year of his age.

DAWNEY, Honourable George,—was the fifth ſon of ſir Henry, ſecond lord Viſcount Down, and his lady, Mildred, daughter of William Godfrey, of Thunich, in
the

the county of Lincoln, efq.* Having betaken himfelf to a naval life, he was, on the 8th of January, 1742, promoted to be captain of the Biddeford frigate. This veffel was principally, if not entirely employed, during the current year, as a cruifer, in which occupation we do not find any other mention made of captain Dawney's fuccefs, than his having captured, on the 26th of June, a Spanifh privateer, called the St. Anthonio, belonging to Bilboa, carrying fourteen carriage ten fwivel guns, and ninety-nine men. Early in the enfuing year this gentleman removed into the Lyme, a fhip of the fame force with that he before commanded. This is the laft mention we find made of him in the naval line, for unhappily falling under a derangement of mind, from which he did not, we believe, ever recover, he of confequence retired altogether from the fervice many years before his death. This happened, according to Mr. Hardy's lift, on the 16th of November, 1766.

De L'Angle, Merrick, — was, during the earlier part of his fervice both as a commander and a poft captain, employed on the Mediterranean ftation. He is faid in fome accounts, which we muft confefs we are rather doubtful as to the authenticity of, to have commanded the Anne Galley firefhip early in the year 1741; but we can fpeak with much greater confidence of his appointment, in the month of Auguft 1742, to the Durfley Galley, a frigate of twenty guns†, a command which, contrary to the

---

* " This family is of very great antiquity in this county. Sir Paine Dawney, of Dawney Caftle in Normandy, from whom this family is defcended, came into England with king William the Conqueror."—
See Archdale's Peerage.

† We muft not omit the following very honourable ancedote concerning this brave and worthy man, in the very words in which it is related.

" A year or two fince, his majefty's fhip the Durfley Galley, of twenty guns, captain De L'Angle commander, cruizing the eaftward of Alicant bay, made a fmall fail, to which fhe gave chace. Coming up with it towards evening, and firing a gun, the bark ftruck; and the boat going off to take poffeffion of her, found her a fmall xebeque, bound from Malaga to Yvica, with provifions and fome paffengers of both fexes, whom our failors, without much ceremony, plundered of what money or things of value they had on board.

the usual customs and regulations of the service, we do not find to have conferred upon Mr. De L'Angle the rank of a post captain*. In this vessel we find him employed immediately afterwards under commodore Martin, in the memorable expedition to Naples; on which occasion the whole discussion of the complaint, which had caused the appearance of a British squadron off that port, appears to have been completely confided to him. A very particular account has been already given of this

---

"The surgeon of the man of war (from whom I have this narrative) soon after going on board the prize, it being almost dark, could just perceive a Romish clergyman (for such he appeared by his dress) leaning in a disconsolate manner over the side of the vessel, with a young girl by him all in tears. On seeing this, he took occasion to speak to him in Latin, which brought on a conversation in that language, by which he understood this prelate was bishop of Yvica, on his passage from Spain to that island, and that the young girl was a relation left under his care. The surgeon, after a few compliments of condolement, returned to his ship, and gave captain De L'Angle an account of what had passed. This worthy commander immediately sent his pinnace for the bishop and his fair kinswoman, for whom he had provided an elegant supper, during which, being placed at the head of the table, they were treated by him and his officers with all the politeness and respect due to their rank and quality: in the mean while the captain had taken such proper measures, that, as soon as supper was ended, he caused to be restored to these distressed prisoners all the little money, jewels, plate, cloaths, &c. which they had lost, excepting a silver chalice, which could not be recovered. Imagine, sir, to yourself, the sentiments of this honest prelate, at such unexpected treatment from those, whom no doubt he had been taught to regard as cruel hereticks, and from whom he probably apprehended the worst usage, both for himself and his young relation. The simplicity, the goodness of his heart discovered itself by a flood of tears, more expressive than the rhetoric of a jesuit, or the wit of a cardinal. Captain De L'Angle, pleased with the sincerity of his joy, assured him of his being safe as well as free, and that next morning he should be at full liberty to pursue his voyage without any fears of future danger. Accordingly, after an agreeable breakfast, he was reconducted on board his own bark, with some kind presents, and arrived soon after safe at Yvica.

"I am well informed that this bishop has so lasting a sense of this obligation, that, whenever (though the war yet subsists) an English man of war appears off the port of Yvica, he never fails to send out a boat, with such refreshments as the island affords, and his compliments to the captain, in acknowledgments for the favours shown him on board the Dursley Galley. This, therefore, ought to recommend a generous behaviour even to our enemies."

* So that it is most probable he only commanded by order.

business,

bufinefs, fee vol. iv. p. 72, to which we refer; contenting ourfelves with faying, what it would be an act of the higheft injuftice to captain De L'Angle's merit to omit, that he executed this very delicate commiffion with all the fpirit and addrefs of an able politician, and experienced negociator. It is rather to be wondered at that, after having difplayed fo much fuccefsful ability, he fhould not have been advanced to the rank of poft captain till the 13th of November following, when he was removed into the Winchelfea, a veffel of no greater force than the Durfley Galley. In this fhip he was employed the following year on a variety of fervices, during the greateft part of which nothing occurred fo remarkable as to demand our notice. The moft interefting of all his occupations, during the period juft ftated, is beft defcribed in the annexed letter, written by himfelf; and which, though rather too long for our purpofe, we think, as containing a genuine account of Turkifh manners, curious enough to warrant its infertion *.

Soon

" * Winchelfea, Oct. 22, 1743.
" Dear brother,
" I begin this letter at fea, in the Channel of Malta, Mount Etna on the ifland of Sicily bearing N. E. and the ifland of Malta S. by E. diftance ten leagues, being on my return from a very unfuccefsful cruife in the Archipelago, which I am fure you will fay was a very unfortunate one ere you have read to the end of this epiftle.

" On the 31ft of July I joined the admiral in Villa Franca harbour, from Genoa; he told me he was going to fend me into the Archipelago in purfuit of a Spanifh privateer (or rather pirate, for he plunders all nations) which he had been informed had done great mifchief to our trade in thofe feas; that he was very rich, infomuch that, if I fhould have the good fortune to take him, I need never trouble myfelf about the fea again as long as I lived; that he was a fhip of twenty-four guns and one hundred and fixty men, which was juft my match; from whence I imagined we muft fight hard for it fhould we meet.

" I failed from Villa Franca on the 3d of Auguft; on the 14th we arrived at Malta, where I was to have taken on board a pilot, but could not get one, which you will find was a great misfortune. We did not come to an anchor there, but made fail again in the evening. On the 25th we came to an anchor at Caria, in the ifle of Candia, which was once in poffeffion of the Venetians, but now belongs to the Turks: here we ftopped to fill our water cafks and get intelligence.—I believe I muft now detain you a little to tell you in what manner we were

received,

Soon after captain De L'Angle's return from the expedition juſt mentioned, he was promoted to the Barfleur,

received, as it may poſſibly divert you, and ſhew you in what eſteem an Engliſhman is held by thoſe people. As ſoon as the ſhip was moored I ſent an officer to make my compliments to the governor, who is a baſhaw of three tails (a poſt of great rank in their ſervice) and an admiral of the Turkiſh fleet. He returned me a very obliging anſwer, and ſaid I was not only welcome to every thing the place afforded, but that he ſhould take a pleaſure in aſſiſting me with any thing I might be in want of. The next morning he ſent an officer on board to enquire after my health and to invite me aſhore, he attended his compliment with a preſent of four bullocks, ſeven dozen of fowls, two hundred weight of ruſk, a great number of water-melons, muſk-melons, and a large quantity of fruit of all ſorts. I had like to have forgot ſeveral very large cheeſes, which you know I am extremely fond of. In the afternoon I went on ſhore to wait on him, attended by the Engliſh conſul and ſeveral officers belonging to the ſhip. He received me with great marks of ceremony and reſpect, expreſſed the great regard he had to the Engliſh nation in general, and how much pleaſure it gave him in particular to have an opportunity of converſing with a gentleman bred in his own way, having himſelf been brought up to the ſea from his cradle. I told him I was come into thoſe ſeas in queſt of a Spaniſh privateer, commanded by one Andrea Scirenſi, and ſhould be glad if he could give me any intelligence of him; that I apprehended, if I ſhould have the good fortune to deſtroy him, it would be doing a public good, as I was very well aſſured he was little better than a pirate, for that he ſhewed no regard to the colours of any nation, but plundered all alike. He told me my information was true, and that the grand ſignior had ſome time ago ſent a ſhip of fifty guns to look for him, which had ſight of him, but could not come up with him: that he had very lately cleaned at Serigatto, an uninhabited iſland in that neighbourhood: that he mounted twenty-four guns, and had two hundred men, having lately increaſed his complement by entertaining a parcel of Greeks and other fellows of deſperate fortunes. I told him I had in my paſſage ſpoke with ſeveral French veſſels, but their accounts were ſo different I could give but little credit to them; upon which he ſhook his head, and ſaid the Engliſh were upright and juſt, that their ways were as ſtraight as the flight of an arrow; but the French twiſted and winded like a ſerpent.

"He then called for a chart, ſhewed me where he had been ſeen within ten days, and where, he then ſaid, he was now cruizing. You may be ſure this haſtened my departure, it being not more than forty leagues from where we were; and you will find his intelligence was good, as I after met him at the very place: but before I go from hence you or my ſiſter may expect to hear in what manner I was entertained.

"When I came in, the Baſhaw was ſitting upon a ſofa, from which he aroſe and bid me welcome to Candia. He then ſeated himſelf

fleur, of ninety guns, as captain under rear-admiral Rowley. In this station he distinguished himself exceedingly

himself again; after which I was placed on a brocade stool just before him, and the gentlemen who came with me on a bench just by. We had first, sweetmeats, then coffee; after that sherbet, and then more sweetmeats. Afterwards, we were all perfumed, I being informed this would be the last piece of ceremony, got up; two men then put a caftan, or vest, upon me, which the bashaw told me he did not present me with on account of the value of it, but as the greatest honour the grand signior could do me. Every gentleman was presented with a brocade handkerchief, and so we retired: I was then conducted into a large gallery facing a square, where all the music were drawn up, to the number of twenty or more, consisting of drums, trumpets and hautboys, and two fellows with instruments, different from what I ever met with in all my travels, nor can I tell what they were like, unless it be to the top of a warming-pan, for they were much of the size and made of brass (I wish you and my sister had been there, doctor); they held one in each hand, which they struck together. They entertained me with a point of war, or, that you may better understand me, a march they play when they lead on their troops to battle. This lasted near half an hour, and I then went on board.

" But I should have told you, that I made the bashaw a present of a perspective glass, that cost me about two guineas at Genoa, with which he was much delighted, and said I could not have given him any thing that was so acceptable.

" We compleated our water the next day and sailed in the evening, making the best of our way for the place where the bashaw told me the privateer cruised; this was between the east end of the isle of Candia, and Searpante another island, where we remained for three days without seeing any thing of him; we then apprehended the ship had sprung a leak, for we made sometimes more than four feet water in a wa c'h, which obliged us to think of some place to put into, that we might examine our bows, the leak being forward. Accordingly, the next morning, September 2, we bore away, the wind being then N W. and at ten o'clock came to an anchor in the bay of Castra Paulis, on the east end of the island of Candia. Here we lay in a storm of wind from the time we came in until the 7th. The leak was occasioned by the rats, who had eaten several holes in our hause piece. We sailed again the 7th, in the evening, to our former station, this we cruised until the 12th, when, in the break of the morning, we discovered a large ship about four leagues to windward, which, by her appearance and the posture she lay in, gave us great room to believe it was the vessel we were looking for. He had no sails set but the top-sails upon the cap, a certain token of his being a cruiser; but the day coming on put it past all dispute; for with our glasses we could make his hull, which, together with the size of his masts and yards, answered exactly to the description we had received of him. Our next business was to consider how we could get nearer to him: he not being

ingly in the encounter, with the united flags of France and Spain, off Toulon. He continued to retain the same

being three weeks foul, and the Winchelsea above ten months; so that we had but little hopes to come up with him should we begin the chase. It being our constant custom to disguise the ship as much as possible before day-light, and being then in that posture, upon a wind, though on a different tack, we held on our course imagining he might take us for a merchant-ship and bear down upon us. In this manner we remained near-half an hour; but when I found that bait would not take, and saw that he began by little and little to make sail, I flung off the cloak and put the ship about, making all the sail we could in chase: when he perceived this, he did the like and stood from us. We had as much wind as we could carry, to all our sails, and in a very little time perceived we wronged him; which, as soon as he saw, he endeavoured to get before the wind, which, by the wind's shifting, he soon had an opportunity of doing: that however availed him nothing, for we still came up with him, and by twelve o'clock were within random shot of him, when it fell calm. We then got our boats ahead and our oars out, and he did the same, but had the better of us from having two large launches which rowed with sixteen oars each, and pulled him from us; but whenever there came any wind we came up with him. In this manner we pursued him till twelve at night, when we lost sight of him under the shade of land, where he, being well acquainted, ran among some rocks, where we could not follow him for the want of a pilot.

"We stood in so far that we had almost put the ship ashore before we tacked. Many times in the day I would not have given any man forty shillings to have insured him, for a quarter of an hour would have carried us alongside; but it is now past, and there is an end of it.

"I believe he lived the next day on the joy of having escaped, for he flung all his sheep, fowls, hen-coops, bulkheads, and a great many other articles overboard during the chase, which came swimming along our side.

"I fired several shot at him just before it was dark, one of which I believe went on board him, but it was at too great a distance to do much mischief. I kept off the place until the next morning to see whether he might not have anchored, or possibly been on shore among the rocks, but he was gone. The wind being then northerly, I concluded he must have stood to the southward; I therefore made all the sail I could and ran down all along the island of Rhodes, and from thence to the coast of Carimania, but saw nothing of him. I then hauled to the northward again and went round the north side of the island of Candia; visited the islands of Sarigo and Serigatta; but getting no tidings of him at either of those places, I bore up for Zuder, a good port on the south side of Candia, to fill our water in order to our return. I stayed there three days, and in sailing from thence put the people to short allowance that I might stay some little time longer

fame ftation for a confiderable time, according to fome reports till 1745, or even a later period. After his return to England we do not find any particular mention made of him till the month of December 1747, when he commanded a fhip of the line a Portfmouth, and was one of the members of the court-martial convened for the trial of captain Fox, of the Kent. In the month of December 1748, he was captain of the Devonfhire, a guardfhip, mounting eighty guns: but peace having taken place, the only fubfequent notice we find taken of him is, that, in the month of February 1750, he again was employed, on a court-martial held for the purpofe of trying fome of the captains, who had ferved under rear-admiral Knowles in the Weft Indies, as he moreover was, in the month of December following, in the fame very unenviable line of occupation, for the trial of Mr. Griffin. Nothing elfe has come to our knowledge relative to this very able and good man, except that he died in England on the 18th of May 1753.

DURELL, Philip.—Our information relative to this gentleman commences with his appointment, on February 6, 1742, according to that of Mr. Hardy and fome other accounts, to be captain of the Gibraltar Frigate: but others, whofe authenticity we have a greater opinion of, fay the Seahorfe. No fmall degree of perplexity attends the attempt to inveftigate fuch particulars as properly belong to the life of this worthy officer. This difficulty, which we have already frequently complained of on former occafions, arifes from the too frequent omiffion of the Chriftian name, a circumftance which renders it nearly impoffible to appropriate to each commander the ftations and particular fervices on which he was employed, when two perfons of the fame furname are cotemporaries. We have before ftated, vol. iv. p. 262, captain John Durell * to have commanded the Eltham. This, however, is a

---

in thofe feas. I afterwards cruifed a few days among the iflands of the Archipelago, and ran down on the coaft of the Morea as far as Cape Matapan, from whence we took our departure for Mahon, where we are now going to perform quarantine.

* We cannot help remarking as rather a fingular circumftance, that the firft appointment of captain Thomas Durell, fee vol. iv. p. 82, was to the Seahorfe, and of captain John Durell to the Gibraltar.

circumſtance rendered rather doubtful by the cauſe juſt given. To ſay the truth it is of little conſequence, as will be ſeen by reference to that account; nor ſhould we, perhaps, have mentioned it, but for the purpoſe of parrying a probable charge of negligent inaccuracy.

In 1747, we believe we may venture to ſtate with confidence, that this gentleman commanded the Glouceſter, of fifty guns, one of the ſhips belonging to the ſquadron under the orders of rear-admiral Hawke, which, in the month of October, totally defeated that of France commanded by monſieur L'Etendiere. Till the concluſion of the war we believe him to have continued under the ſame commander; and not long after the peace, that is to ſay, early in the year 1749, was appointed to the Rocheſter, of fifty guns, juſt before launched and fitted as a ſtationed ſhip. We have no account of him after this time till the month of March 1755, when we find him to have been captain of the Terrible, a third rate of seventy-four guns, ordered to be fitted for ſea at Portſmouth. In the month of May he ſailed, under the command of Mr. Holburne, for America, with the ſquadron ordered thither as a reinforcement to admiral Boſcawen; of which expedition a particular account has been already given. In 1757 he is ſaid to have had a command in America, with the rank of commodore, and again, early in 1758, he was nominated commander-in-chief of the ſhips and veſſels left to winter at Halifax. Having hoiſted his broad pendant on board the Diana frigate, on the 12th of January, he ſailed for his appointed ſtation. In the month of May following he was made third in command, though with the rank only of commodore, of the fleet ſent againſt Louiſbourg, under admiral Boſcawen. He hoiſted his broad pendant on board the Princeſs Amelia; but, as we have before remarked in our account of Mr. Boſcawen, it is needleſs, and almoſt extraneous to enter into the operations of the ſiege, in which the fleet was not particularly concerned otherwiſe than by the protection it afforded the army. We muſt, however, make a ſmall and honourable exception with regard to Mr. Durell, who appears to have been the perſon particularly ſent, by the commander-in-chief, to reconnoitre the coaſt and point out the moſt convenient and eligible ſpot for the

debark-

debarkation of the troops. This, however, appears to have been a task of no small or common difficulty; and it will be readily admitted to us on referring to the report of the various artificial impediments carefully and most scientifically contrived by the French to prevent an attack, or at least to render it abortive. On such an occasion success is the most concise as well as convincing proof of merit; and though much applause cannot but be bestowed on those brave and distinguished leaders who forced their way at the head of their troops, in spite of accumulated obstacles, yet still no small portion of praise is due to the man who is daring enough to hazard his own reputation, by giving the first advice, as he is said to have done, for the prosecution of so bold a measure.

Mr. Durell, during his absence on the above service, was promoted to be rear-admiral of the blue; and about the same time had the misfortune to lose his lady, who died at Bristol of a decline. After the fortunate conclusion of the expedition just mentioned, Mr. Durell was left at Halifax to command in chief during the winter; in the course of which, we believe on the 14th of February, 1759, he was advanced to be rear-admiral of the red. Early in the ensuing spring he was joined by vice-admiral Saunders and rear-admiral Holmes, with a very strong fleet from England destined for the attack of Quebec, the capital of French America. Soon after the junction, Mr. Saunders, who was the commander-in-chief, detached rear-admiral Durell with a small squadron to the isle of Courdres, in the river St. Lawrence, hoping he might be in time to intercept a numerous fleet of transports, victuallers, and storeships, which were said to be on their passage thither from France. His success was not, however, equal either to his expectations or his deserts. He, indeed, captured two storeships, but seventeen others had got up the river before his arrival. Little or no mention is made of his having been particularly concerned in any of the operations of the siege: but sir Charles Saunders, the commander-in-chief, pays him the highest compliments for the assistance he derived from his advice and exertions through the whole of that interesting, that perplexing period: and the house of commons very justly included him in their vote of thanks.

After

After his return from America he does not appear to have held any commiffion till the beginning of the year 1761, when he was appointed port admiral at Plymouth on the 14th of June following. While he held this command he married the widow of the unfortunate capt. Wittewronge Taylor, who commanded the Ramillies when wrecked. In 1762 he was promoted to be vice-admiral of the blue; and, after the conclufion of the peace, was appointed commander-in-chief on the American ftation, where he had his flag flying on board the Launcefton, of forty-four guns. He died at Halifax, holding this ftation, about the month of Auguft, 1766. Mr. Hardy erroneoufly ftates this event to have happened on the 6th of December.

ERSKINE, Robert.—Our information relative to this gentleman commences with his appointment, on the 13th of November, 1742, to be captain of the Fox frigate. We do not find any fubfequent mention * made of him till the year 1747, when he commanded the Warwick, of fixty guns; and, in the month of July, was ordered out to America with captain Crookfhanks of the Lark, as convoy to fome merchant-fhips bound thither. On their paffage they fell in with the Gloriofo, a Spanifh fhip of war mounting feventy guns, which having efcaped from them occafioned no fmall degree of reprehenfion to fall on both thefe captains; and, as we have already fhown, actually caufed the difmiffion of the former from the fervice, under the fentence of a court-martial †. We cannot, however, in

---

* Except that, in 1746, he was one of the members of the court-martial affembled for the trials of the admirals Leftock and Mathews.

† The following account, though an extreme partial one, is extracted from the journal of an officer ferving at the time on board the Warwick, and we have inferted it merely to fhew how prejediced perfons can glofs over, and explain away facts which militate againft them.

" July 14, 1747, being off the Weftern Ifles, in company with his majefty's fhip the Lark, of forty guns, captain Crookfhanks, and thirteen fail of merchantmen under convoy for North America, in the morning we faw a fail, and the Lark having the command made the fignal to chafe. Being both but indifferent failers, though we gained upon the chafe we fhould probably have loft her in the night if it had not been for captain Conolly, who being in a fmall veffel in the ordnance fervice, and a prime failer, kept her in fight all night, and

by

in juſtice to that gentleman, help cenſuring, in the ſtrongeſt manner, the conduct of captain Erſkine: he certainly acted

by firing guns and ſhewing falſe fires directed us how to purſue. Next morning we got ſight again of the enemy: ſhe appeared a very large ſhip at four or five miles diſtance, and all things were prepared to engage accordingly. Mean time captain Conolly gave us no ſmall diverſion, though he durſt not venture very near her, for two or three of her guns would have torn him all to pieces: but he kept to windward, and every now and then popped his four pounders at her, under Engliſh colours, hoping to make her ſhew hers, cut ſome of her rigging, or provoke her to bear towards him, and ſo retard her courſe. The enemy neverthelefs (for then we were ſure ſhe was one) would not hoiſt a colour, but now and then returned the fire and ſtood on. About eleven at night, being nearly abreaſt of the enemy to leeward, and the Lark a little way ahead of us, at about half a mile diſtance, we gave the enemy a broadſide, which ſhe briſkly returned under Spaniſh colours: the Lark then ſtood on and we loſt ſight of her. In ten minutes captain Erſkine, being nearer, gave her his ſtarboard broadſide, raked her fore and aft, and clapping about again ſtood within piſtol-ſhot, when he diſcharged his ſtarboard broadſide into her, with a volley of ſmall arms, as we paſſed; all which the enemy ſmartly returned and ſtood on. During the whole actions he ſeemed to be upon the defenſive, and to want rather to get away than fight. As ſoon as poſſible the Warwick tacked after her, ran alongſide of her within piſtol-ſhot and began to engage large, ſometimes before the wind, and all the time after that within piſtol-ſhot, ſo that the wadding of the enemy's guns fell thick upon our decks, and threatened to ſet fire to our ſails and rigging.

" Our people ſeeing the enemy a much larger ſhip than the Warwick, with a great number of guns, which ſhe plyed well, the Lark, keeping at a great diſtance, and giving them no manner of aſſiſtance, were ſomewhat diſcouraged; but then again reflecting that, if they could make the enemy ſtrike without the aſſiſtance of the Lark the greater would be their glory, they expreſſed the higheſt reſolution and bravery, continuing a dreadful fire till three in the morning, firing in the whole between twenty-five and thirty broadſides: the Warwick at that time torn and ſhattered to pieces in her maſts, yards, ſails and rigging, and the ſhip lying like a wreck, not in a condition to make a farther attack, nor to retreat, fell off to the ſouthward; which the enemy no ſooner obſerved than he hawled to the northward. The number of our men killed and wounded was not very great, which is imputed partly to the enemy's firing chiefly at our rigging and ſails, and partly to their overſhotting their guns, for we found a vaſt many of their ſhot ſticking in the ſides of our ſhip, having few come through. We wanted between forty and fifty men of our complement; many were raw and inexperienced, and ten of them were boys. When the engagement was over we found in our ſhip the enemy's ſhot, double-headed fifty-eight pounders, round

acted in a manner tending to defeat the plan of his commanding officer, the propriety or probable effect of which he had no right to queſtion. Had captain Crookſhanks been properly ſupported and the attempt failed, the blame would then have very properly reſted ſolely on himſelf: but inſtead of that captain Erſkine aſſumed to himſelf an extravagant and unjuſtifiable right of cenſuring the manœuvres of his ſenior officer, and acting in a manner that would have totally deranged the beſt digeſted ſyſtem of attack.

His immediately ſubſequent conduct appears ſtill leſs defenſible. He in a very underhand manner took an opportunity of preferring his charge, and was certainly guilty of a poſitive breach of orders; which breach, though of no material conſequence to the ſervice, is, neverthelefs, highly to be reprehended, as eſtabliſhing a precedent of the moſt dangerous kind. Commodore Knowles, however, who was at that time commander-in-chief at Louiſburg, whither the Lark and Warwick were bound, thought differently of captain Erſkine's conduct, for about the middle of September, having hoiſted his broad pendant on board the Canterbury, he appointed that gentleman her commander as ſucceſſor to captain Hoare, who had obtained leave to return to England. He did not, however, long remain in the Canterbury, Mr. Knowles having, immediately on his arrival at Jamaica,

---

round twenty-five, twenty and ſixteen: whereas the Warwick's guns are only twenty-four pounders on the lower deck, nine pounders on the main-deck, and ſix on the quarter.

" The Lark joined us about ſix in the morning, but did not think fit to purſue the enemy, who was ſtill in ſight, as we were incapable of going along with him. About noon we were informed by one of the convoy, who had run cloſe to the enemy after the engagement, that ſhe was likewiſe in a very ſhattered condition, with her foremaſt gone and her ſails and rigging cut to pieces. This ſeemed to give the captain of the Lark ſome courage, and he propoſed to captain Erſkine to go after her again, which that brave and prudent commander did as ſoon as he could clear ſhip and put her into ſome ſort of order; but the favourable opportunity was loſt, and we could not get ſight of her again. Thus, by the unaccountable bad behaviour of the Lark, both her company and the Warwick's have loſt immenſe riches; for had not the Lark left the Warwick in the beginning of the action, or had ſhe joined her any time when ſhe was engaged, the enemy muſt certainly have fallen into our hands."

on the 28th of January, 1748, found his commiffion there advancing him to be rear-admiral of the white. He hoifted his flag on board the Cornwall, and Mr. Erfkine was, about the month of May, removed into the Milford frigate, in which fhip he returned to Europe in the courfe of the fummer*.

Refle&ion, and a reconfideration of his cafe, probably induced the admiralty board to confider this gentleman in fome degree more culpable than he was at firft thought to be. We are led to this belief by not finding any mention made of his having been appointed to any command after his return to England. He was for fome years the fenior captain on the lift of thofe capable of ferving; the promotion of admirals in 1759, having ftopped with captain Rodney who took rank immediately before him. In 1762 he was put, at a promotion which then took place, on the lift of fuperannuated rear-admirals, in confequence of which he became entitled to an encreafe of half-pay during life. This he did not however long enjoy, dying on the 7th of November, 1766.

FOWKE, Thorpe.—This gentleman had ferved with much reputation a confiderable number of years, in the ftation of lieutenant, before he was advanced to the rank of captain, he having been on board the Terrible floop, in that capacity, in the month of Auguft 1732. We have no fubfequent account of him till his promotion, on the 24th of May 1742, to be captain of the Gibraltar frigate. He was ordered, quickly after his appointment, to Jamaica, with inftru&ions to vice-admiral Vernon and general Wentworth to return to England. No mention is made of him while employed on that ftation, nor fubfequent to his return till the month of November 1744†, when he was appointed captain of the Torrington, a fifth rate of forty-four guns. He remained but a very fhort time in that fhip, having, in the month

---

* Mr. Knowles, though repeatedly applied to by captain Crookfhanks, refufed to order a court-martial on Mr. Erfkine, notwithftanding Mr. Crookfhanks fays, in his own account of his condu&, that the admiral had, as it was publickly known, the moft ftrong and juft reafons to be angry with Erfkine, for his *unfaithful* and unofficer-like behaviour on a certain occafion.

† Except that he is faid to have commanded, for a fhort time, the Seahorfe.

of

of January 1745, commanded the Dreadnought, of sixty guns. This vessel was one of the ships under the orders of commodore Griffin*; but the want of success appears to have been by no means owing to any misconduct in captain Fowke, as is evident from the following extract of a letter written by an officer belonging to the Hampton Court.

" At dusk the Dreadnought was about seven miles astern of the Sunderland, almost out of sight, we were then abreast of our chace, which we found to be two French ships of war. We made false fires for the Dreadnought, the only ship that could come to our assistance; neither could she, except the French shortened sail, which they did soon after; and the Dreadnought, by a great pressure of sail came up with us about nine at night. Captain Mostyn hailed the Dreadnought, and told captain Fowkes he supposed the chace to be two French men of war, the one of seventy-four and the other sixty-four guns; and that he would go along-side of the larger ship at daylight. Captain Fowkes told him he would be along-side of the other. The Dreadnought kept pretty close astern of us all night. At break of day we found the French had made sail, and were then nearly two miles ahead. We then crowded, and by half past nine got abreast of them, and within musket-shot. The Dreadnought had now fallen astern, about a league. The French ships opened their lower tier, hoisted their colours, and hawled up their main-sails. We instantly did the same, except opening our lower tier, which was not possible, our ship lying along so much that our ports were under water, even the aftermost, which was the only one we could shew; we shipped prodigious large and frequent seas, their ships at the same time being almost upright. The French seeing we waited for the Dreadnought, in a few minutes struck their colours, and let fall their main-sails. Captain Mostyn then held a consultation with his officers, who all gave it as their opinion that we ought not to engage before the Dreadnought came up: the reason was obvious to the meanest capacity; for when the main-sail was up, even the quarter-deck guns

---

* See vol. iv. p. 225. et seq.

would not carry above thirty yards from the ſhip. The French then rightly judged of the advantage they would have of engaging us under ſail, when our decks were expoſed to them, we at the ſame time not being able to uſe our great guns nor have a man of theirs open to our ſmall arms: we fell aſtern, and the Dreadnought came up with us about half paſt ten. It was then agreed, if the weather moderated, to follow and engage the enemy; but the Dreadnought loſt ground though ſhe made all poſſible fail."

The deciſion of the court martial was, conſequently, in the higheſt degree honourable to captain Fowke, he having been declared to have done his duty in every reſpect. He was afterwards, in the courſe of that year, appointed to the Sapphire; as he was, we believe in the courſe of the ſame war, to the Superbe. No particular occurrence however appears to have taken place with reſpect to him. We find him appointed to the Tilbury in 1755, it being then the eve of the rupture between Great Britain and France. In this ſhip he continued, tho' but unintereſtingly employed, till 1757, when he was advanced to be captain of the Bedford, of ſixty-four guns, one of the fleet ſent, under admiral Boſcawen, on the expedition againſt Louiſburg in the year 1758. No other particulars are known concerning this gentleman relative to the ſervice, from which he altogether retired, in the year enſuing, on the rank and halfpay of a rear-admiral.

He repaired to Southampton, where he continued to live the remainder of his days, and is ſaid to have at laſt put a period to his exiſtence at that place, where he at any rate died, on the 14th of March, 1784. All farther particulars relative to the death of this gentleman, or its immediate cauſe, are at preſent unknown to us.

GEARY, Sir Francis, — was the deſcendant of an ancient family long ſettled near Aberyſtwyth, in the county of Cardigan. Having made choice of a naval life, he was, in 1727, entered, by an admiralty order, which, according to the earlier uſage of the navy, was termed the king's letter, a volunteer on board the Revenge, a ſeventy-gun ſhip, at that time commanded by captain Conningſby Norbury, and one of the fleet under the orders of ſir John Norris, ſent to Copenhagen for the purpoſe of preventing a rupture between the courts of Denmark

Denmark and Sweden. The end for which this force was sent, being effected, the squadron returned to England, and the Revenge was ordered immediately to Gibraltar as a reinforcement to sir Charles Wager, who commanded there to cover the place which was then besieged by the Spaniards. Mr. Geary continued after the above time in service, employed as a midshipman, and afterwards as a lieutenant, till the 30th of June, 1742, when he was promoted from that rank to be captain of the Squirrel, of twenty guns. He was, not long afterwards, ordered out on a cruise off the island of Madeira, and on the 10th of February, 1743, was fortunate enough to fall in with a French ship, called the Pierre Joseph, a ship chartered by the Spanish merchants at Cadiz, and bound thither from the ports of Vera Cruz and the Havannah.

The enemy had used consummate art in endeavouring to conceal, from any ship that might casually meet them, the knowledge of the persons to whom the cargo in reality belonged. The papers were all thrown overboard, and the supercargo concealed himself. The master was a Frenchman, untrue to his trust, and dishonest to his employers, for he confessed the whole cargo was totally Spanish property. It consisted of sixty-five chests of silver, each containing three thousand pieces of eight, five bales of cochineal, fifty-seven of indigo, and one case of vanilla, a quantity of sugar, and three thousand five hundred hides. Captain Geary had the good fortune, previous to this time, to capture a Spanish privateer, which he manned and employed as an armed tender; in company with which vessel, on the 29th of the month preceding his last-mentioned success, he had the additional happiness to burn a second Spanish armed ship off the island of Madeira *.

---

* There is an anecdote which we have heard well authenticated of this gentleman while he held this command, which is far too honourable to him to be suppressed. Previous to his sailing on a cruise he had entered into an engagement with captain ———, to share with him whatever prizes they might take during a given period. The Pierre Joseph was not captured till after the expiration of the term of partnership; but captain Geary, nevertheless, divided with him equally the whole of his part, declaring at the same time, that he was sure Mr. ——— would have acted in the same manner towards him had he been equally successful.

Early

Early in 1744 this gentleman commanded, for a very short time, the Dolphin; but, on the 17th of February, was promoted to the Chester, of fifty guns: and being sent out to cruise, in company with captain Brett, of the Sunderland, captured, on the 20th of February, a French frigate of twenty guns and one hundred and thirty-four men, besides many passengers of consequence, having on board twenty-four thousand dollars, and a very valuable cargo * He continued in the Chester a considerable length of time †, as will be presently seen. In the month of February 1745, he was one of the members of the court-martial, held on board the Lenox, in Portsmouth harbour, for the trials of the captains Griffin, Mostyn, Brett, and Fowke. He was almost immediately afterwards ordered for Louisburg, to reinforce the small squadron at that time employed under commodore Warren in the reduction of that place; but being sent home with an express to England soon after its surrender, was deprived of sharing in the immense property subsequently captured there, and thence sustained a negative loss, as it is said, of nearly 12,000l‡.

Soon after the arrival of Mr. Geary in England he was appointed, by the special interest of the duke of Bedford, at that time first lord commissioner of the admiralty, who knew well the value of his services and abilities, to be captain of the Culloden, of seventy-four guns. In this ship he was, in 1747, ordered into the Bay of Biscay,

---

* We have the following private account of a very successful capture in which Mr. Geary was about that time concerned, but of which we do not find any official notice taken.

"July the 1st, 1744.—Yesterday morning an express arrived at the admiralty office with an account, that his majesty's ships the Hampton Court and Chester, with the Grampus sloop, have taken eight French West Indiamen from Hispaniola and Martinico, carrying one hundred and thirty-eight guns and five hundred and eighteen men. The Chester and Grampus are since arrived in the Downs with the prizes."

† In a memorandum made by himself, sir Francis states, that while he commanded the Chester he captured, after a trifling skirmish, as he terms it, but in which he had an officer killed, and several men killed and wounded, a French frigate, called the Elephant. Whether this circumstance took place in Europe, or during the time he was at Louisburg, he is silent.

‡ We can readily credit this from the account given of the valuable prizes made by the Chester, and other ships, after Mr. Geary had quitted his command and sailed for Europe. See vol. iv. p. 187.

with the squadron under the command of rear-admiral Hawke, with whom he continued on constant service till the conclusion of the war*. He was then appointed commander-in-chief of the ships in the Medway with the rank of commodore. We do not exactly know how long he continued to retain that station, but believe only for a short time, as we find him to have quitted the Culloden in September following; on the 20th of which month he was married to Miss Bartholomew, a Kentish lady of fortune†.

During the remainder of the ensuing peace capt. Geary lived in a temporary retirement from active service, not having, as we believe, received any subsequent appointment till the beginning of the year 1755. The restless conduct of the French court having then created a daily apprehension of the commencement of hostilities, he was commissioned to the Somerset, of seventy guns, one of the ships equipped by way of precaution in case those suspicions should be suddenly realised. In the month of April he sailed for North America under the command of admiral Boscawen, the particulars of which expedition, and the capture of the two French ships of war, the Alcide and Lys, have been already treated of in that officer's life.

On the return of Mr. Geary to England at the close of the year, he was ordered to join the Channel squadron then under the orders of sir Edward Hawke; but, as we have already observed in our account of that gentleman, no occurrence took place in any degree interesting enough to require particular mention, speaking even collectively of the operations of the whole armament. Mr. Geary ‡ continued to be uninterruptedly employed in the Channel service,

---

* While in this ship he had the misfortune to encounter a violent storm, in which he lost one of his masts.

† In consequence of which union the estate of Oxenhoath is now in possession of his son, the present sir W. Geary.

‡ In 1756 he was one of the members of the court-martial assembled on board the Prince George, in Portsmouth harbour, for the trial of admiral Byng; and in the month of April following met with the following success, which was certainly far from trivial.

" At dawn of day the Somerset and Rochester men of war discovered five sail about two leagues distance; they consisted of three ships, one snow and a schooner: upon which the Somerset and Rochester immediately chased the two largest, who bore away to the northward, and the other three hawled to the north-west. Before noon the Somerset and Rochester took them, one named the Renommee, burthen three

service, and as commander-in-chief, or port-admiral at Portsmouth and Spithead during the war, with the exception only that for the space of ten months he commanded in-chief at the Nore, with the rank of an established commodore, having hoisted a broad pendant, by an admiralty order, and being allowed a captain under him. In 1758, we believe during the month of February, he was appointed captain of the Lenox, a new third rate of seventy-four guns, but quitted that ship in the following year for the Resolution, a ship of the same force. He sailed with the fleet commanded by sir Edward Hawke, on the 18th of May 1759, having then only the rank of a private captain in the Resolution, as we have just stated; but in three days afterwards he was ordered, by the commander-in-chief, to hoist a red broad pendant on board the said ship as commander of a division, or squadron, consisting of ten ships of the line, two frigates, and a fireship. Having been, on the 5th of June*, promoted to be rear-admiral of the white squadron, his commission for that purpose was forwarded to him while at sea, with instructions to put himself under the command of sir Edward Hawke. On receiving these orders he accordingly hoisted his flag on board the Resolution, on the 11th of June; but removed it into the Sandwich on the 7th of the ensuing month, as he afterwards did into the Royal George on the 29th of August, the Sandwich being ordered into Plymouth to refit.

The re-equipment alluded to being completed, the Sandwich rejoined the fleet off Ushant; and Mr. Geary removed his flag into that ship on the 29th of September. He continued under sir E. Hawke watching Conflans fleet, then lying in Brest harbour, till the strong westerly winds drove the British ships from their station, and compelled them, after repeated and fruitless efforts to regain it, to put into Torbay in the beginning of November. The Sandwich having sprung her main-mast was prevented from getting

---

three hundred and fifty tons, laden chiefly with pork, flour, and two hundred muskets; the other the Superb, burthen seven hundred and fifty tons, laden with some provisions, bale goods, and several cases of small arms, both letter of marque ships from Bourdeaux to Quebec, having on board two hundred and forty-two officers and soldiers of the royal regiment of foreign volunteers, which, with the seamen and passengers, amounted to three hundred and ninety-one prisoners."

* The admiralty list says, on the 19th of May.

in till after the fleet. Sir Edward having, on the 14th, put to sea in quest of the enemy, he ordered Mr. Geary into Plymouth to land his sick, which amounted to eighty-seven in number, and to get up a new top-mast. After this he was to proceed off Ushant, which was appointed as the place of rendezvous, bringing with him out of the sound every ship that was ready for sea.

The accident just mentioned, added to the necessity of landing his sick men, unfortunately prevented Mr. Geary from rejoining the commander-in-chief time enough to share in the well known glorious encounter and total defeat of the French armament under the marquis de Conflans. Having, however, used all the dispatch possible, he sailed from Plymouth on the 19th of November, carrying with him the Foudroyant and Bienfaisant: but on his passage to the appointed rendezvous, he received a letter and order from sir Edward Hawke, instructing him to continue cruising off Brest, with all the ships of his squadron, till farther orders. On the 22d of November the Acteon joined him with a duplicate of the order last-mentioned, enclosed to him by commodore Hanway, from Plymouth. When off Ushant he unfortunately encountered a most tremendous gale, which drove him near two hundred leagues to the westward: he then made sail and regained his station, where he continued though without being fortunate enough to meet with any success till towards the end of December, and returned into port on the 27th, having been seven months and nine days at sea, with the trivial interval of putting into Plymouth Sound for three days, by order of sir Edward Hawke, to put his sick men on shore, to procure water and get up his top-mast.

Mr. Geary continued in port till the 30th of April, when he received an order, from admiral Boscawen, to proceed with the following ships under his command, the Sandwich, Warspite, Orford, Torbay, Chichester, Princess Amelia, and Unicorn frigate, to cruise off Rochfort for the purpose of intercepting a squadron of French ships of war fitting for the East Indies in that port. He continued cruising on that station and occasionally anchoring in Basque Road, in sight of the enemy's squadron, till the 6th of September, his ships being occasionally revictualled by vessels purposely sent from Ireland,

such

such being the consequence attached to the service on which he was then employed; for it was well known that if the French squadron had got out to sea, and arrived safely in India, their naval force in that quarter would have become evidently superior to that of the English. Administration, therefore, appear to have very properly adopted the prudent method of preventing their putting to sea at all, instead of the more expensive and less decisive measure of sending out a reinforcement to counteract them.

On the day already stated, Mr. Geary received orders to join sir Edward Hawke in Quiberon Bay, it being well established, on the most accurate information, that the French had totally abandoned the intended expedition, and actually unrigged their ships. He effected this junction on the 7th, and continued on that station, with sir Edward, till the 3d of October, when he received orders from the commander-in-chief to proceed to Spithead, where he arrived on the 25th of the same month. On the following day he struck his flag, having obtained leave of absence from the admiralty-board, but soon afterwards was invested with the command as port-admiral of the ships and vessels at Spithead, being successor to vice-admiral Holburne: he accordingly hoisted his flag on board the Royal Sovereign.

His first consequential charge, after entering on this office, was the equipment of the squadron intended for the expedition against Belleisle, and the embarkation of the troops destined for that service. The same occupation, though not on so extensive a scale, notwithstanding the object itself was more important, was repeated in 1762. This was the superintendance of the equipment of that part of the armament which sailed from England, under the command of sir George Pocock, destined for the attack of the Havannah and the island of Cuba. The great diligence and attention to the service, as well as the indefatigable exertions displayed by Mr. Geary, in forwarding every thing that related to it, were so conspicuous that the earl of Albemarle, the general-in-chief, made a very particular representation of his conduct to his majesty, who signified his highest and most gracious approbation of his behaviour*.

---

* On the 21st of October, 1762, Mr. Geary was advanced to the rank of vice-admiral of the blue.

Mr. Geary retained his command, which, from the circumstances we have related, was of much more than ordinary truſt, till the preliminary articles of peace were ſigned; ſoon after this event he received orders to ſtrike his flag, the ſervice on which he had been there employed being fully complete, and ended. In the ſame packet which conveyed to him thoſe inſtructions, were encloſed the thanks of the houſe of commons, both to himſelf, and the officers under his command, for his diligence and conduct, more particularly on thoſe occaſions which had already eſtabliſhed him in the higheſt reputation both with his ſovereign and his countrymen.

After this time he appears to have lived in retirement, far as related to the naval ſervice, till the year 1770 *, when

---

* Soon after he entered on this command a very diſagreeable diſpute aroſe between him and Mr Elphinſtone, of the Engliſh ſervice, who was alſo a rear-admiral in that of Ruſſia. This, however, ended highly to the credit of Mr. Geary, as will plainly appear by the letters annexed.

" Achilles in Portſmouth harbour, half paſt eleven P.M. the 24th February, 1770.

" Sir,

" Be pleaſed to acquaint their lordſhips that I was in hopes, from your letters of the 1ſt and 7th inſtant, which captain Hughes ſhewed me concerning the Netromena, a Ruſſian ſhip of ſixty-ſix guns, ſetting and diſcharging the watch in this harbour, that ſhe would not preſume to commit the like irregularities in future; but being acquainted this day that the ſaid ſhip fired a gun laſt night and this morning upon the like occaſion, I ordered captain Fielding to go to captain Elphinſtone, who is ſaid to be a rear-admiral in the Ruſſian ſervice on board that ſhip, to know on what occaſion he fired the ſaid guns. His anſwer was, that it was for the relief and ſetting of the watch, and that he had a right to do ſo. On this I ſent captain Fielding to him again, ordering him to deſiſt from firing the watch guns for the future at his peril, for I conſidered him neither as an admiral's ſhip nor even as a ſhip of war, ſhe having neither flag nor pendant flying. His reply was ‡, that I had nothing to do with him or his ſquadron, and that he would continue to fire it, which he has accordingly done this evening. I therefore think it my duty to ſend captain Fielding expreſs with this letter for their lordſhips information, and farther directions thereon, which I hope will meet with their approbation.

" I am, ſir, your moſt obedient ſervant,

" Philip Stephens, Eſq. " FRANCIS GEARY."

" Rear-

when the well known difpute between the Britifh and Spanifh courts, relative to Falkland's ifland, rendering a rupture

"‡ Rear-admiral Elphinftone prefents his compliments to vice-admiral Geary, and does himfelf the honour of acquainting him, in regard to the meſſage fent by him through captain Fielding, to know whether "he ſhould fire the morning and evening gun when he got to Spithead," that, to prevent miſtakes in verbal meſſages, the anſwer was to ſuch a queſtion, He ſhould do as he pleaſed when he got there: but as the matter in queſtion does not at all concern the honour of the Ruſſian flag, and as he looks upon Spithead in the fame light as Portfmouth harbour, he ſhall do *then* as he does *at preſent*, from the ſame motives."

" Dear fir,

" I arrived at fir Edward Hawke's, with your exprefs, about eleven yefterday morning. He did not open it, as I told him the contents from my memorandums. He was exceedingly angry with captain Elphinftone, and approved very much of every ftep you had taken. I carried the letter to Mr. Stephens, who was to do what was thought proper about it. I have not heard this day any thing concerning it. Sir Edward ordered me not to go out of town till I had heard from him.

" I am, fir,

" London, Feb. 26, 1770. " Your moft obedient humble fervant, Vice-adm. Geary, Portfmouth. " C. FIELDING."

" Admiralty-office, 26th Februrary, 1770.

" Sir,

" I yefterday received by captain Fielding, and loft no time in communicating to my lords commiſſioners of the admiralty, your letter of the 24th inftant, repreſenting to them, that, notwithftanding the directions which it is apprehended the Ruſſian miniſter had given to rear admiral Elphinftone, the Netromena, a Ruſſian ſhip of war, had again fired guns in Portfmouth harbour, at the ſetting and diſcharging the watch, and acquainting their lordſhips with the ſteps you had taken upon that occaſion. In return, I am commanded by their lordſhips to inform you, that a copy of your letter was immediately ſent to the earl of Rochford, and I ſend you incloſed a copy of the letter, which I have received from Mr. Sutton, in anſwer thereto, by which you will ſee that the Ruſſian miniſter is extremely ſenſible of the impropriety of rear-admiral Elphinftone's conduct, and that he has promiſed to write to him thereupon, without lofs of time, in the ftrongeft manner. Their lordſhips do therefore take it for granted, that Mr. Elphinftone will immediately defift from ſuch irregular and abfurd proceedings, and that there will not be any ground for a complaint of this nature for the future. Their lordſhips commanded me to add, that they entirely approve of the ſteps you have taken in this matter; and I have the honour to be,

" Sir,

" Your moft obedient humble fervant,

" Vice-adm. Geary, Portfmouth. " PH. STEPHENS."

" White-

rupture highly probable, Mr. Geary was re-appointed to the Portſmouth command; and about the ſame time was advanced to be vice-admiral of the red ſquadron. Diſpatch was particularly required of him in his inſtructions, and though he had but one flag officer, Mr. Buckle, to aſſiſt in a caſe of ſuch emergency, as to demand the moſt energetic and laboured exertions, the activity of Mr. Geary appears to have been perfectly equal to the public exigencies.

The diſpute having been terminated by the conceſſions of the court of Spain, conceſſions not improbably produced merely by the rapidity with which an armament ſufficiently formidable to awe them into compliance was equipped, Mr. Geary once more paſſed into retirement and private life, a ſtation to which no man could do more honour, either as a friend, a relative, or a gentleman; perfectly independent in his principles, ſtrictly honourable in all tranſactions with which he was connected, and

---

" Sir,   " Whitehall, 26th February, 1770.

" Having laid your letter of the 25th, with the incloſure, before the earl of Rochford, his lordſhip appointed monſieur De Mouſſin Pouſchkin, the Ruſſian miniſter, to be with him this morning, and acquainted him he had taken it for granted, that, in conſequence of his writing, as he had promiſed to do ſome time ago, rear-admiral Elphinſtone would immediately have deſiſted from the abſurd pretenſion of firing a gun at the ſetting and diſcharging the watch in Portſmouth harbour: but finding by vice-admiral Geary's Letter, communicated to him from the lords of the admiralty, that he had reſumed that practice, and declared his intention of continuing it, he was obliged to aſſure him, monſieur Mouſſin Pouſchkin, that if admiral Elphinſtone perſiſted in it, orders muſt neceſſarily be immediately given for him to quit the port; which, as it was the king's wiſh to give every accommodation poſſible to the empreſs's ſquadron, muſt naturally be very diſagreeable to his majeſty to order, as it would be to himſelf to convey. The Ruſſian miniſter ſeemed extremely ſenſible of the impropriety of admiral Elphinſtone's conduct, and promiſed to write to him, without loſs of time, in the ſtrongeſt manner, hoping that the orders might be ſuſpended till his letter was received.

" I am, &c.

" RICHARD SUTTON."

exhibiting

exhibiting on every occasion the character of a man possessing every moral and social virtue*.

The death of sir Charles Hardy, in the month of May, 1780, caused this gentleman, though at that time in a very indifferent state of health, to return once more to the service: his majesty having been pleased to signify to him, through the earl of Sandwich, at that time first lord commissioner of the admiralty, his intention to appoint him to the chief command of the Channel fleet, in case he thought his health would permit him to undertake such a trust. Mr. Geary immediately repaired to town and declared his readiness to accept of the honourable station his majesty was so gracious as to offer him. Having received his necessary instructions he repaired to Portsmouth, and hoisting his flag on board the Victory, a first rate, on the 24th of May, took upon him the command. The fleet consisted of twenty-four ships of the line, with a proportionate number of frigates, fireships, and smaller vessels, commanded, under Mr. Geary, by the admirals Barrington, Darby, Digby, and sir John Lockart Ross†.

The

---

* On the 31st of March, 1775, he was advanced to be admiral of the blue; and, on the 29th of January, 1778, to be admiral of the white.—Mrs. Geary died on the 20th of August following.

† The following are copies of letters written to Mr. Geary by that great and ever to be revered character lord Hawke; one prior to his first putting to sea, the other immediately after his return into port. We doubt not these will be considered extremely interesting, as displaying the private thoughts of so brave and great a commander, even at the latest period of his life, and showing that, however age and disease might have enervated his body, they had nothing impaired the vigour of his mind. Added to this consideration, the terms used by his lordship, certainly displaying the high estimation in which he held admiral Geary, it would be an injustice to that gentleman's character to suppress any thing that reflects on him so much honour.

" My dear Sir,

" This is principally to thank you for the favour of your letter of the 3d instant, and for all the kind acts you have been so kind as to do for my Parson, which was doing every thing in your power. I have this day dispatched him away for town in order to take up his warrant, so that he will be ready at a moment's warning to obey the commands of his captain.

" I find

The principal and firſt objeƈt this armament was intended to effeƈt being the junƈtion of the fleet of Spain, expeƈted

"I find by the papers that you are getting ready for ſea with all the diſpatch that is poſſible, and that you will ſail the inſtant that it is in your power; and though I could wiſh this could get to your hands firſt, yet the times are ſo very preſſing from many unfortunate events, that I think the ſooner you can get to my old ſtation off Breſt the better it will be for my country. When you are there watch thoſe fellows as cloſe as a cat watches a mouſe; and if once you can have the good fortune to get up to them make much of them, and don't part with them eaſily.

"Forgive my being ſo free: I love you. We have ſerved long together, and I have your intereſt and happineſs ſincerely at heart. My dear friend, may God Almighty bleſs you; and may that all-powerful hand guide and proteƈt you in the day of battle; and that you may return with honour and glory to your country and family, is the ſincere and faithful wiſh of him who is moſt truly,

"My dear Sir,
"Your moſt obedient and moſt humble ſervant,
"Hawke."

"P. S. Pray remember me to my friend Barrington, and hope he approves of young Baron.

"F. Geary, eſq. admiral and commander-in-chief at Spithead."

"Sunbury, 26th Auguſt, 1760.
"My dear Sir,
"I am greatly obliged to you for the favour of your letter of the 20th on your arrival at Spithead; indeed it was more than I expeƈted, well knowing the hurry and buſtle you muſt be in on your firſt coming into port. I do not wonder at the men being ſickly upon ſo long a cruiſe: ſix weeks is long enough in all conſcience; any time after that muſt be very hurtful to the men, and will occaſion their falling down very faſt. I hope in God they will ſoon recover, that you may be enabled to proceed to ſea immediately, for by all accounts the enemy is out, ſo that nothing can well ſtir from home with ſafety. I wiſh the admiralty would ſee what was done in former times, it would be the means of making them aƈt with more propriety, both for the good of officers and men. I take it for granted that the great ones will let you have no reſt till they get you out to ſea again.

"Although I am in a good deal of pain, and much in the invalid order, yet I cannot refuſe myſelf the pleaſure of wiſhing you all imaginable good fortune when you go out again; and I truſt in God your next cruiſe will prove a happy and glorious one, both for your country and yourſelf. My good friend, I have always wiſhed you well, and have ever talked freely and openly to you upon every ſubjeƈt relative to the ſervice. Recolleƈt ſome of theſe paſſages; and, for God's ſake,

expected from Cadiz, Ferrol and Carthagena, with the French ſhips that were fit for ſea in the ports of Breſt, Rochfort and L'Orient, Mr. Geary immediately proceeded off Breſt. Nothing material occurred till the 3d of July, when the Monarch, being a head of the fleet on the look-out, made a ſignal at ten o'clock in the morning for diſcovering a fleet confiſting of twenty ſail: theſe were immediately concluded to be the enemy of whom they were in ſearch, and the utmoſt alacrity was uſed in endeavouring to get up with them. The chace continued the whole day, and at five o'clock in the afternoon the headmoſt ſhips came up * with the ſternmoſt of the fugitives,

---

ſake, if you ſhould be ſo lucky as to get ſight of the enemy, get as cloſe to them as poſſible. Do not let them ſhuffle with you by engaging at a diſtance, but get within muſket ſhot if you can; that will be the way to gain great honour, and will be the means to make the action deciſive. By doing this you will put it out of the power of any of the brawlers to find fault. I am fully perſuaded you will faithfully do your part, therefore hope you will forgive my ſaying ſo much on the ſubject. I find the Ruſſians are gone from the Downs ſo that you will have no trouble about them. My good friend, God bleſs you; may the hand of Providence go with you and protect you in the day of battle, and grant you victory over our perfidious enemies: and may you return with honour to your country and family again; theſe are the ſincere and hearty wiſhes of him who is moſt truly and faithfully,
"My dear Sir,
"Your moſt obedient and moſt humble ſervant,

"Sir F. Geary.   "HAWKE."

* A whimſical and entertaining anecdote is related of him on this occaſion. Rear-admiral Kempenfelt, who at that time acted as his firſt captain, was univerſally and moſt deſervedly eſteemed one of the braveſt and beſt informed officers in the ſervice, as to the management, and requiſite mode of manœuvring a large fleet previous to the commencement of, and during the continuance of an action itſelf. Lord Hawke, than whom no man was a ſounder judge of nautical abilities, adds, in a poſtſcript to one of his letters to admiral Geary, "I am glad you have got ſo excellent an officer with you as I am convinced Kempenfelt is: he will be of great ſervice to you." But in the attainment of this univerſally acknowledged and valuable qualification, he had contracted a habit of uſing more ſignals than men leſs practiſed in that particular branch of ſervice deemed neceſſary: of this latter claſs of commanders was admiral Geary. As ſoon as the enemy were diſcovered and the ſignal made for a general chace,

Kempen-

tives, which were now discovered to be nothing more than a convoy from Port-au-Prince, under the protection of a single ship of fifty guns. The chace was continued by the pursuers, who did not bring to for the purpose of securing the ships they passed, leaving that duty to some others of the fleet who were still astern. Unfortunately a very thick fog came on about seven o'clock and proved the preservation of nearly half the enemy's convoy: twelve sail, however, were captured; and nothing but the accident just related could have preserved the whole of them from falling into the hands of the British fleet *.

Mr. Geary having continued at sea for upwards of two months, and, having two thousand five hundred sick men on board the fleet, thought it proper as well as prudent to return to Spithead, where he arrived on the 18th of August. Very soon after his arrival he was unfortunately taken ill, and was obliged to sollicit permission from the admiralty

---

Kempenfelt, burning with as much impatience as his commander-in-chief to get up with the enemy, though differing in a trivial degree in his idea as to the best mode of effecting it, brought up the signal book, which he opened and laid on the binnacle with the greatest form and precision; admiral Geary, eagerly supposing the chace to be the Brest fleet, went up to him with the greatest good humour, and squeezing him by the hand in a manner better to be conceived than expressed, said quaintly, "Now my dear, dear friend, do pray let the signals alone to day, to-morrow you shall order as many as ever you please."

* Those taken were the

Voyageur, valued at	£.15,900
Compte D'Argout	14,500
L'Hazard	10,500
Compte D'Estaing	9,000
Cosmopolite	5,700
Courier	5,500
L'Aurore	5,500
Solitaire	5,000
Marie Therese	5,000
St. Bartholomew	6,900
Eleonore	4,700
Jeune Francois	2,800
Which, with the Compte de Halwied	17,000
And La Marguerite,	18,000
Made in the whole	£.126,000

board

board to go on shore, to his own house at Polesden, in Surry, in hopes, by that means, of facilitating and hastening his recovery. This, however, he was not able to effect by the time the fleet was ready for sea; and very properly thinking such a trust too consequential to be undertaken by any man, however zealous in the cause of his sovereign and the country, whose imbecillity of body prevented, as it certainly in some degree must, the utmost exertion of the vigour of his mind, which on some, and those too indispensible occasions, must be absolutely necessary: he sollicited leave to resign his command, a request which the board of admiralty could not, with propriety, refuse their assent to, however contrary it might be to their wishes.

This gentleman continued to live ever afterwards in retirement, spending the remainder of a life with a character rendered truly exalted by a long and most meritorious service: the grateful remembrance of which procured him the honourable advancement to the rank of a baronet of Great Britain on the 3d of August, 1782. Having attained the advanced age of eighty-six years, he died on the 7th day of February, 1796, most highly revered as a naval commander, and not less sincerely lamented as a friend, a gentleman, and a Briton. In this, therefore, among many other instances, we have the satisfaction of saying, without the imputation of flattery, that honour, benevolence, public spirit, and general worth formed the leading traits of his character, and that mankind have not been so ungrateful as to forget them *.

---

* We cannot conclude this account without adding an anecdote, the authenticity of which has been confidently reported to us by persons totally disinterested: it is, perhaps, a more just and proper eulogium on the character of this worthy man than the most laboured or highly-finished detail of his services and conduct would have been.

" At the late contested election for the county of K. a sailor was carried down to vote by a gentleman in the interest of Mr. H. but on his arrival at the booth, after enquiring who the other candidates were, of whom sir W. Geary's son was one, immediately declared, with a tremendous oath, that it should never be said he voted against his worthy old admiral's son, for him alone he would poll, and in that instance, at least, kept his word."

GRENVILLE,

GRENVILLE, Thomas,—was the seventh son of Hester, sister to sir Richard Temple, afterwards created baron and viscount Cobham*, and Richard Grenville, of Wotton, in the county of Buckingham, esq. He was born on the 4th of April, 1719; and being brought up to the sea, arrived, at an early age, though not till after regularly passing through the different subordinate ranks with much reputation to himself, at the rank of captain. Suffice it to say, that on the 6th of April, 1742, he was promoted to the command of the Romney, a fourth rate of fifty guns. While in this ship he is not otherwise particularly mentioned than as having been employed as a cruiser; in which occupation he had the good fortune to capture, on the 2d of March, 1743, a very valuable Spanish register ship, mounting twenty guns, called the Santa Rosa. Captain Grenville continued in the Romney till the beginning of the year 1744, when he was appointed to the Falkland, a ship of equal force, just launched. His occupation continued the same; but though his activity was not diminished, his success, at least, when considered in a pecuniary light, was considerably so; the most interesting mention we find made of him while he held this command being the capture of a French privateer, of fourteen guns, which he carried into Kinsale in the month of March 1745.

---

* Titles to which this lady succeeded, by limitation, after the death of her brother, on the 13th of September, 1749, and by letters patent bearing date the 18th of the following month, was created countess Temple, " The branch (says Collins) of the family of Grenville, Grenville Greinville, or Grenevyle, as the name in very ancient times was variously written, has been incontestably seated at Wotton under Barnwood, in Buckinghamshire, at least from Henry the First's reign, which is apparent, as well from the charter of Walter Giffard, earl of Buckingham, hereafter-mentioned, and the register of the abbey of Nutley (within four miles of Wotton) as from 140 deeds, sans date, concerning this family at Wotton, and a regular succession of a great number of dated deeds, which prove the family in every king's reign from king John, to have been possessed of the following manors in Buckinghamshire, viz. Wotton, Chilton cum Easington, Ashington, Ham, Grenville's manor in Hadenham, Nether Winchenden, Policott, Widmere and Foscott; and also divers estates in Dorton, Crendon, Adingrave, Grendon, Brill, Borestall, Kingsey, Oakeley, Buckingham, and Wicomb in the said county; besides manors, lands, &c. in other counties."

Towards

Towards the end of the year 1746, he was promoted to the Defiance, of sixty guns; and, in the month of December, was elected representative in parliament for the borough of Bridport. In the ensuing spring, the Defiance was one of the squadron sent out, under the admirals Anson and Warren, to intercept the French squadron under orders for the East Indies, and North America. The particulars of the successful encounter which took place on their meeting have been already given at some length in the lives of the commander-in-chief and sir P. Warren *, so that we shall content ourselves with saying, as we in justice are compelled to do, that the name of Grenville stands remarkably prominent, even among those heroes who most particularly distinguished themselves. " The Namur, DEFIANCE and Windsor (says the Gazette) being the next headmost ships, soon entered into action; and after having disabled those French ships, with which they were engaged, in such a manner that the British ships astern must soon come up with them, they made sail ahead to prevent the van of the enemy from escaping." His conduct on this brilliant occasion, when he met with his unhappy and untimely death, needs neither the aid of the historian nor the panegyrist. The concise account given by his commander-in-chief speaks of him in more forcible terms than would the best adorned and most polished eulogium. " The loss on our side (says Mr. Anson) was not very considerable, except that of captain Grenville, of the Defiance, who was an excellent officer, and whose death cannot be sufficiently lamented †."

The

---

* See vol. iv. p. 125 and 188.

† His remains were interred at Wotton. The following account is extracted from a letter, dated Gosport, May the 26th.

" On the 22d, about two o'clock in the afternoon, the corpse of that truly British commander, captain Grenville, was landed in Stoke's bay, where a hearse waited to receive it, to carry it to be buried in the vault belonging to the family. The corpse was attended by all the boats of the squadron at Spithead, to which he belonged. His sword was drawn and laid across his coffin; and from the time of the boats putting off from the ship's side to their landing, minute guns were fired by the whole squadron, who likewise hoisted their colours half-mast high on the melancholy occasion. He was a gentleman of true
courage

The above much-to-be-lamented event took place on the 3d of May, 1747.

HODSELL, James,—we find to have been employed as commander of the Anne Galley firefhip, a veffel attached to the fquadron, under the orders of Mr. Leftock on the Mediterranean ftation, in the month of April 1742. He

---

courage and conduct; a humane and generous commander, never failing to reward merit where he found it. He was as eafy of accefs to the meaneft failor as to any of his officers, and never failed to reward or punifh according to the merit of the cafe. His officers refpected him, his failors loved and efteemed him as their father: in fhort,

"He was, but words are wanting to fay what;
Say all that's good and brave, and he was that."

A fuperb monument is erected to his memory in Stow Gardens, with the following infcriptions in Latin and Englifh.

Sororis fuæ filio
THOMÆ GRENVILLE,
Qui navis Præfectus regiæ
Ducente claffem Britannicam Georgio Anfon,
Dum contra gallos fortiffimè pugnaret
Dilaceratæ navis ingenti fragmine
Femore graviter percuffo
"Perire," dixit moribundus, "omnino fatius eft
Quam inertiæ in judicio fifti."
Columnam hanc roftratam.
Laudans at mærens pofuit
Cobham,
Infigne virtutis, cheu! rariffimæ
Exemplum habes
Ex quo difcas
Quid virum præfecturâ militari ornatum
Deceat
MDCCXLVII.

Tranflation.

As a monument to teftify his applaufe and grief, Richard, lord vifcount Cobham, erected this naval pillar to the memory of his nephew, captain Grenville, who, commanding a fhip of war in the Britifh fleet, under admiral Anfon, in an engagement with the French, was mortally wounded in the thigh by a fragment of his fhattered fhip. Dying, he cried out, "*How much more defirable is it thus to meet death, than, fufpected of cowardice, to fear juftice!*" May this noble inftance of virtue prove inftructive to an abandoned age, and teach Britons how to act in their country's caufe.

is particularly mentioned in the difpute between that gentleman and captain Barnet, but only as the official bearer of the different letters and meffages which paffed between them on that occafion *. From the veffel juft mentioned, he was, on the 24th of July, 1742, promoted to be captain of the Durfley Galley, a twenty gun fhip. This appointment appears to have been made merely for the purpofe of giving him rank, for in a few days afterwards, that is to fay on the 9th of the enfuing month, the Durfley Galley was commanded by captain De L'Angle, who had not at that time the rank of captain. Mr. Hodfell's next command was that of the Diamond frigate, which alfo was of fhort duration, and in which we do not find any interefting mention made of him. His third fhip was the Feverfham, of forty guns, into which he removed previous to the encounter with the French and Spanifh fleets off Toulon; but on which occafion nothing farther is related of him, than that he was ftationed to attend the divifion of Mr. Leftock. He was one of the members of the court-martial convened at Mahon, on the 28th of January, 1745, for the trial of captain Richard Norris, which is the only notice we obferve taken of him till the month of May 1746, at which time he was captain of the Nonfuch on the fame ftation. It is not improbable he continued there during the remainder of the war, as we have no account of his having been employed in any other quarter. He is faid to have commanded a third rate after the Nonfuch ; but have no farther authentic particulars concerning him except the mere memorandum of his death, which happened on the 6th of April, 1754.

HOLMES, Charles,—was a defcendant from the fame honourable family with fir Robert Holmes, of whom an account has been already given. Of the earlier part of this gentleman's fervice, however meritorious it might be, no mention is made: our information concerning him, that of his family only excepted, commencing with his appoin'tment, on the 20th of February, 1742, to be captain of the Sapphire, of forty guns, a cruifing fhip. On the 25th of December following he diftinguifhed himfelf

---

* See vol. iv. p. 213, et feq.

in a very remarkable manner by the attack of a number of privateers in the harbour of Vigo. We cannot, perhaps, do greater and more material juftice to his bravery than by giving the account in the precife terms of that officially publifhed *.

Except that, about the commencement of the rebellion, he was captain of the Enterprize, we have no intelligence of this brave and worthy gentleman till the end of the year 1746, when we find him in the Lenox, a feventy gun fhip, on the Jamaica ftation. He was one of the members of the court-martial held at Port Royal for the trial of captain Crookfhanks, and in the month of September 1748, was ordered home as convoy to the fleet of merchantfhips bound from thence. The Lenox was fo weak a fhip, and in fo bad a condition,

---

* " February 8th.—His majefty's fhip the Sapphire, captain Holmes, being on a cruize off the coaft of Portugal, Dec. 25th, faw two fail and gave chace. About two o'clock in the afternoon the two fail parted, one keeping her wind, the other bearing away. He continued chafing the former, and about five took her, fhe being a Spanifh privateer of about fifty tons, with eight carriage fix fwivel guns, and fifty-two men. It being then calm, captain Holmes immediately fhifted her men into his fhip, and put a lieutenant and thirty men on board her to row after the other veffel, which they came up with the next evening and retook, when they found her to be a floop from Limerick, bound to Lifbon with butter.

" On January 11th, captain Holmes was informed by the mafter of a Dutch fhip, who had been ill-treated by a privateer at Vigo, which place he left the 8th, that there were five privateers in that harbour, two of them cleaning on the fand, and the other three near them at the quay : that in the town, by the church, they had mounted fix fix pounders on a new battery ; and on a plain, to the fouthward of the quay, fix or eight guns, from three to four pounders. Upon this intelligence captain Holmes failed for Vigo, and on the 15th came off that town. When his fhip was about half a mile from it, the Spaniards fired from their twenty-four pound battery on the quay. One of the fhot difmounted one of the Sapphire's lower-deck guns, killed one man, fhot off another's leg, and the arm of a third, wounding with the fplinters five or fix more. Another fhot went through the center of her fore-maft, about feven feet above the forecaftle ; a third took her between wind and water, and lodged in the carpenter's ftore-room. Captain Holmes ran a little farther in and came to an anchor ; having brought his broadfide to bear on the batteries and privateers, he began firing about twelve o'clock, and between two and three the two privateers, which were afloat, funk ; the other privateers, which were on the fand, received many fhot in them, by which they are rendered unferviceable, at leaft for fome time."

that

that twenty-four of her guns were taken out in order to enable her to make the paſſage home with greater ſafety. Captain Holmes not being able to get through the windward paſſage bore away through the gulph, and on the 29th of September fell in with admiral Reggio's ſquadron, conſiſting of ſix large ſhips of the line and a frigate. The proper precautions were immediately, and, as it proved, ſucceſsfully taken for the ſecurity of the convoy: as ſoon as this objeƈt was attained, though reaſons exiſted which, to a man not thoroughly animated with the love of his country and zeal for the ſervice of his ſovereign, would have been more than ſufficient to induce him to purſue his voyage, captain Holmes, with the moſt laudable deciſion as well as ſpirited reſolution, changed his courſe and proceeded to the Tortuda bank, off which he knew Mr. Knowles, the commander-in-chief, was then cruiſing, in the double hope of giving him information of the enemy, and aſſiſting in their defeat.

He was fortunate enough to fall in with the Britiſh ſquadron on the 1ſt of Oƈtober; but though he behaved, during the ſubſequent aƈtion, with that bravery and gallant ſpirit, which it is notorious he diſplayed on all poſſible occaſions, yet was he not fortunate enough to eſcape the cenſure of Mr. Knowles, a cenſure, as it is ſaid, ſecretly, and therefore improperly ſpread. This, propagated by the induſtrious calumny and envy of men leſs honourable than himſelf, at laſt reached the ears of Mr. Holmes, and induced him to demand a court-martial; but it did not take place till January 1750, the ſubſequent month to that in which Mr. Knowles himſelf had been tried and gently reprimanded.

We cannot aƈt more candidly than by ſimply inſerting the reſolution of the court, than which none, perhaps, was ever more honourable to the party accuſed.

"The court, in purſuance of an order from the honourable the lords of the admiralty, to William Rowley, eſq. (dated the 1ſt of laſt month) proceeded to enquire into the conduƈt and behaviour of capt. C. Holmes, upon a charge exhibited againſt him, by rear-admiral Knowles, for bad conduƈt, breach of orders, diſobedience of ſignals, and not doing his utmoſt to take and endamage a Spaniſh ſquadron, in an aƈtion off the Havannah in 1748.

Having heard the witnesses produced both by Mr. Knowles and the prisoner, and thoroughly considered their evidence, the court unanimously agree, that it hath appeared captain Holmes behaved like a good and gallant officer during the whole action: that he likewise shewed very good conduct, for the preservation of his convoy when he fell in with the Spanish squadron, a day or two before the action, and also great zeal for his king and country in quitting his homeward course to go in quest of rear-admiral Knowles, in order to inform him of that squadron, and to strengthen him with the addition of his ship, the better to enable him to engage them, when he had at the same time not only a large part of his own fortune on board the ship, but was pressed by the passengers to proceed directly home. The court do therefore unanimously agree to acquit captain Holmes, with honour, of every part of the charge exhibited against him; and he is accordingly hereby honourably acquitted."

In the month of January 1753, he was appointed captain of the Anson, of sixty guns, a guardship at Portsmouth. We believe him to have, not long afterwards, removed into the Lenox, of seventy guns, other accounts say the Somerset, a ship employed as the former. In the month of March 1755, he was captain of the Grafton, also a third rate, one of the squadron dispatched in May following, under Mr. Holburne, as a reinforcement to Mr. Boscawen, who had previously sailed for North America. During the ensuing year he was again employed on the same station, with the rank of commodore, still continuing on board the Grafton. This summer's service was rendered remarkable by a very spirited encounter he had with a small French squadron, though of force infinitely superior to that of the English. It took place off Louisburg, and his conduct on this occasion we shall probably best describe by inserting the following plain and modest account of the transaction, given by the commodore himself in his letter to the admiralty board.

" Grafton, off Louisburg, Aug. 25, 1756.
" On the 26th of July I was cruizing in his majesty's ship Grafton, with the Nottingham, the Hornet and Jamaica sloops, off Louisburg, about three leagues south by east. At

At eight A. M. the man at the top-maſt head diſcovered four ſail to the north-eaſt, directly to windward: we gave chace, and made our firſt board to the ſouthward, they ſteering directly for us till within two leagues. We tacked in hopes to have cut them off from their port, as they hawled in for it. At half paſt one P. M. they came to an anchor in their harbour; a little afterwards we brought to about a league from it and hoiſted our colours, the lighthouſe bearing north as we lay. At four we made ſail to the eaſtward: ſoon as it was dark I diſpatched the Hornet for Halifax, with orders for captain Spry to ſend out ſome of the ſhips under his command to come and join me; we then ſtood on as before, till three o'clock, when we tacked and ſtood in for the land. At ſeven in the morning of the 27th, the man at the maſt head called out he ſaw ſix ſail under the land: about eight o'clock I could ſee four ſhips in chaſe of us; I could, with my glaſs, make them to be men of war, and ſee the French commodore's white pendant very plain. On this I ſtood from them to the ſouth-eaſt, about a point from the wind, which drew them from their harbour, and thought it the beſt of our ſailing, for I judged them above our match or they would not have come out of their port again in ſo few hours: 1 believe they had only put their ſick and lumber on ſhore and taken troops off, for they were very full of men. At half paſt one, P. M. the headmoſt of the French ſquadron, a frigate of about thirty-ſix guns, fired on the Jamaica ſloop, which ſhe returned, and rowed at the ſame time up to the Nottingham. On our firing at the frigate ſhe hawled her wind, and the Jamaica bore away to the ſouth-weſt, which the French commandant obſerving, made a ſignal for the two frigates to chaſe the ſloop, which they immediately obeyed. About two the Nottingham fired her ſtern chaſe at the French commandant, which he returned with his bow; and ſoon after I fired mine. Finding our ſhot reached each other, hauled up my courſes, bunted my main-ſail, and bore down on the French commodore, being about a quarter of a mile from him: it fell calm and we began to engage, he being on our ſtarboard ſide, the other large French ſhip aſtern of him, and the Nottingham on our larboard bow; the two frigates a mile from us, and the Jamaica ſomething more. Though the French commandant held us fo cheap at firſt as to fend his frigates away, he was foon fo fenfible of his miſtake, that, the inſtant there was any wind, he made the frigate's ſignals to rejoin him; and, fearing they did not come faſt enough to his affiſtance, bore down to them and was followed. At feven they were all clofe together; at duſk the action ceaſed; they ſtanding to the fouthward and we to the S. S. E. Our men lay at their quarters all night expecting to renew the action in the morning. At daylight the French ſhips bore N. W. by W. diſtance four or five miles, going away with little wind, at E.S.E. right before it, for Louiſburg. We wore and ſtood to the weſtward, but they never offered to look at us. The wind freſhening, they failed much better than our ſhips, and the weather growing hazy we loſt fight of them about noon. Their chief fire was directed at our maſts, which they wounded, as well as cut our ſtays and rigging confiderably. I had one lower-deck gun difmounted and one upper; fix men killed and twenty wounded, which is all the damage the Grafton received."

On the return of this gentleman to England he was appointed one of the members of the court-martial held for the trial of the unfortunate admiral Byng. In 1757 he returned to the American ſtation under the command of Mr. Holburne, the few particulars of which uninterſting expedition have been already given in our account of that gentleman: to thefe we have only to add, that the Grafton was feparated from the body of the fquadron; and having loſt, not only her maſts but her rudder, was, with the greateſt difficulty, navigated to England; nor could ſhe have been preferved but by the moſt extraordinary exertions and the invention of a fubſtitute rudder, contrived by rigging out a fpare top-maſt from the ſtern. In ſhort, the prefervation of his ſhip may be confidered as one of the moſt extraordinary interventions of Providence, in fupport of human efforts almoſt unparalleled.

In 1758 Mr. Holmes was employed at home, and was fent commodore of a fmall, but very fuccefsful expedition, to Embden in Germany. It deferves particular relation, more on account of his activity, than the confequence attending it. The force appears to have confiſted only of the Seahorfe, on board which ſhip Mr. Holmes himſelf was,

was, and the Strombolo; but from the tenor of the account, and the particularly benevolent expreſſions uſed in it, we ſhall, as in the preceding inſtance, give it in his own words.

" It is with the greateſt pleaſure that I acquaint my lords commiſſioners of the admiralty of the ſucceſs of his majeſty's ſhip in this river*.

" The enemy had not ſuffered the buoys to be laid this year, thinking by that means to obſtruct any attempts for the recovery of Embden by ſea: it was therefore with equal ſurprize and concern, that they obſerved the arrival of his majeſty's ſhips Seahorſe and Strombolo. After having doubled the number of their workmen upon the batteries they had begun, they ſet about raiſing three more towards the ſea with all expedition, expecting to be attacked from that quarter.

" On the 17th the Seahorſe and Strombolo anchored between Delfziel and Knock, and on the 18th they came to their ſtation between Knock and Embden, by which the enemy ſaw themſelves cut off from all communication down the river.

" They continued working on their batteries towards the ſea, but at the ſame time made all the neceſſary preparations for evacuating the place.

" The garriſon conſiſted of one thouſand three hundred French foot, one thouſand two hundred horſe, one thouſand one hundred Auſtrian foot, and two companies of artillery of ſixty men each, in all three thouſand ſeven hundred and twenty.

" On the 19th, at ſix in the morning, the French troops were under arms, and marched out of the town before night. On the 20th the Auſtrians began their march at nine in the morning.

" About noon, and not before, I had intelligence of theſe operations, and that they had been tranſporting their baggage and cannon up the river in ſmall veſſels over night, that one of them was lying round a point of land at ſome diſtance from us to go up by next tide. As ſoon as we could ſtem the tide I diſpatched an armed cutter and two of my boats, who came up with the veſſel we had intelligence of, and took her. I reinforced them

---

* The Elbe.

by another boat; and the whole detachment, commanded by captain Taylor, continued the chace up the river. The enemy at this time lined both fides of it, and gave the firſt fire on the boats, who were then nearly up with three of their armed veſſels. The fire was briſkly returned on our ſide, in ſight of their army, and under their fire; captain Taylor came up with one of them, attacked her, drove her on ſhore and carried her, after a ſhort ſkirmiſh. The officers and men left the veſſel to recover the ſhore; in attempting which, ſome of them were killed by the fire from our boats. The other two veſſels, which had the cannon on board, got clear, under favour of the night and cover of their army.

"The firſt veſſel taken had the ſon of lieutenant-colonel Schollheens, of prince Charles of Lorrain's regiment, one corporal and one pioneer on board, with ſome baggage belonging to the lieut.-colonel. There was ſome money found, which, partly from the ſpecie, and partly from the manner of its being made up, was concluded to be pay for the troops, and therefore detained, together with the corporal, the pioneer, and all the little implements of war they had with them. As for the ſon he is but a boy, and not of an age to be regarded as an enemy, for which reaſon I have ſent him on ſhore to be returned to his father, with all his and his father's effects; and have written to lieut.-colonel Schollheens, ſaying, that upon his giving me his honour the money is truly his private property, it ſhall be returned.

"Another veſſel was taken which had on board major de Bertrand; M. Van Longer, commiſſary of war; M. Trajane, adjutant de la place; M. le Bouffe, lieutenant of artillery, and a guard of private men, with three hoſtages which they had carried off from Embden. From them I had the account I have already given to their lordſhips, of the happy effect the preſence of his majeſty's two ſhips have produced, by occaſioning the ſudden evacuation of the enemy out of the town of Embden. This ſervice is the more eſſential, as advice was received at the Hague, on the 18th, that the French, in Eaſt Frieſland, had received counter orders, and were conveying all their magazines to Embden."

This

This gentleman was, not long after this time, advanced to be rear-admiral of the blue, but is not otherwise particularly mentioned during the course of the current year than as having been employed in the squadron, commanded by lord Anson, in the blockade of Brest, and in covering the desultory expeditions made on the French coast in the course of that year. Early in 1759 he was fixed upon to be third in command of the fleet destined for the expedition against Quebec; but, previous to the actual commencement of the undertaking, was ordered, with a convoy of sixty transports, for New York. He accordingly hoisted his flag on board the Somerset, of seventy guns, and sailed from Spithead on the 14th of February with the Northumberland and Terrible, of seventy-four guns each; the Trident and Intrepid, of sixty-four; the Medway, of sixty; the Maidstone, Adventure, Diana, Trent, Europa, Vestal, Eurus, Boreas, and Crescent frigates. Having, after his arrival at New York, taken the necessary measures to expedite those particular branches of service, for the accomplishment of which he had been dispatched, he joined, off Louisburg, vice-admiral Saunders who had sailed from Spithead three days after his departure. In the different operations previous to the actual siege, which we have already said was the immediate object of this armament, he was engaged in supporting brigadier-general Murray in an attack of several of the magazines, belonging to the enemy, collected above the town. Mr. Holmes went ten or twelves leagues up the river, and then found it impracticable to proceed farther. In the month of September he was particularly employed in dividing and distracting the attention of the enemy at the time general Wolfe meditated and effected that landing which was productive of his own fame and death, together with the ever-to-be-remembered victory on the heights of Abraham. His services on this occasion were so highly esteemed that he received the thanks of the house of commons, of which he had been for some time a member, as representative for the borough of Newport, in the Isle of Wight, a station he retained in the succeeding parliament till the time of his death. He returned at the conclusion of the year to England, where

he

he remained during the enfuing winter, in which time he was promoted to be rear-admiral of the white.

Early in the fpring he was appointed commander-in-chief on the Jamaica ftation, as fucceffor to Mr. Cotes; and having hoifted his flag on board the Cambridge, failed from St. Helen's on the 16th of March, 1760. He arrived at Jamaica on the 13th of May following. So active was he in the difpofition of his cruifers, that, in the month of October, four out of five * French frigates were either taken or deftroyed; and, not long afterwards, eight privateers, and a frigate called the Bien Aime, fhared a fimilar fate. In the month of June enfuing he had the additional good fortune of caufing the capture of the St. Anne, of fixty four guns, which is thus officially related by the Gazette.

"Admiralty-office, July 28, 1761.

"Rear-admiral Holmes, having intelligence that feveral fhips of war of the enemy had failed from Port Louis on the 5th of June, as alfo that the St. Anne French fhip of war had failed from Port-au-Prince on the fame day, he difpofed feveral fhips of his fquadron in the manner he thought moft likely to meet with thofe of the enemy. In the morning of the 13th the Hampfhire fell in with the St. Anne to windward, and chafed her right down upon the Centaur to leeward. Upon difcovering the Centaur, the St. Anne hauled up, and was kept between the two fhips till fhe was run quite in fhore, and becalmed about a league to the northward of Donna Maria Bay, when fhe began to fire her ftern chace. Soon after one o'clock the Centaur got clofe alongfide the St. Anne, and fhe ftruck her enfign. She is a very fine fhip conftructed for fixty-four guns, and had on board fix twenty-four pounders, twenty-fix twelve pounders, and eight eight pounders, with three hundred and eighty-nine perfons; was commanded by M. Aquillon, and was carrying home a cargo of indigo, coffee and fugar, to the value of nine million of French livres."

This is the laft memorable mention we find made of this brave and truly worthy man, who died at Jamaica

---

* Three of them belonged to the king, the other two to the merchants.

on the 21ſt of November enſuing, leaving behind him a reputation moſt truly unſullied, and a character highly revered, whether conſidered in the light of a private citizen, or a public commander.

MOLLOY, Sir Charles.—We have very little to add, in our account given of this gentleman, to that afforded us in the inſcription on his monument. The only particulars not recorded there are, that he took poſt on being appointed to the command of the Royal Caroline yacht on the 6th of April, 1742; and, in 1746, was one of the members of the court-martial aſſembled at Deptford, for the trials of the admirals Mathews and Leſtock. He was buried in the chancel of Shadoxhurſt church, in the county of Kent, where a marble monument is erected to his memory. The upper part ccnſiſts of angels heads in the clouds; under which is written, "Bleſſed are the dead which die in the Lord." In a marble medallion is the head of the deceaſed, ſupported by an infant weeping, ſurrounded by military and naval ornaments. Beneath this inſcription.

> Sir CHARLES MOLLOY, knight, lord of this manor, late captain of his majeſty's ſhip Royal Caroline, ſometime a director of Greenwich-hoſpital, an elder brother of the Trinity-houſe, and one of his majeſty's juſtices of the peace for the county of Kent, &c. After a long and faithful ſervice of near ſixty years in the royal navy, where he went very young with king William's letter, in the latter part of his war with France, and ſerved in that and all queen Anne's wars, he gradually roſe to the rank of lieutenant, after the hard fought battle ff Malaga, in the Mediterranean, with the French fleet, in the year 1704, being then in the Royal Oak, who had a large ſhare in that day's action. In this poſt he continued till the year 1710, when he was by the earl of Berkeley, who then commanded the fleet, appointed captain of his majeſty's yacht the William and Mary, in which, and afterwards in the Mary yacht, he ſerved until the 7th day of April, 1743; his majeſty being then on board at Graveſend, and the royal ſtandard hoiſted, he was pleaſed of his royal favour,

favour, to confer on him the honour of knighthood, in all which employs he ever difcharged his duty as became an officer and a feaman. He was twice married. His firft wife was Ann, relict of Ifaac Elton, efq. fon of fir Ab^m. Elton, bart. of the city of Briftol. He afterwards married Ellen, eldeft daughter of Jn°. Cork, efq. of Swifts, near Cranbrook in the county of Kent. She left no iffue, and departed this life Auguft 24, 1760, ætatis fuæ 60.

Ens entium miferere mihi.

PARRY, Francis,—in the earlier part of his fervice as a naval officer, was lieutenant of the Monmouth, and afterwards of the Berwick. In 1741 he was commander of the Grampus floop of war, and diftinguifhed himfelf very much under the command of captain Harrifon, of the Argyle, in cutting five prizes out of the harbour of Redondella. On the 10th of February, 1742, he was promoted to be captain of the Greyhound frigate, and being almoft immediately afterwards ordered to Lifbon, died there on the 17th of April following. In Mr. Hardy's lift he is erroneoufly faid to have died in the Weft Indies on the 19th of May, 1761.

PRITCHARD, John,—was, on the 5th of February, 1742, appointed captain of the Lyme. In the month of September following he was ordered to Elfinore in order to convoy from thence the homeward-bound Baltic trade. Immediately after his return he was removed into a fhip of twenty guns, which, in all the accounts we have feen, is called the Revenge. But we apprehend this to be a miftake, as no fhip fo named, and of that force, appears to have been in the navy. This gentleman, in 1744, commanded the Severn, of fifty guns; in which fhip he continued alfo but a fhort time. He afterwards was fucceffively commiffioned to the Devonfhire and the Duke, but in what year or years we do not precifely know. In 1758 he was put on the fuperannuated lift with the rank and halfpay of a rear-admiral. Having thus honourably retired from the fervice he continued to refide at Plymouth, where he died about the year 1779.

RODNEY, Lord.—We have but few particulars relative to this nobleman, in addition to that account publifhed of his life family by Collins: neverthelefs, this

this circumſtance we hope will not be conſidered as a want of induſtry in us, but as a proof of the general care and correctneſs of that heraldic author.

GEORGE BRIDGES RODNEY was the ſecond ſon of Henry Rodney, of Walton-upon-Thames, in the county of Surry, eſq. and Mary, eldeſt daughter and co-heir to ſir Henry Newton, knight, envoy-extraordinary to Genoa, Tuſcany, &c. LL.D. judge of the high court of admiralty, and chancellor of the dioceſe of London. He was born in the month of December 1717, and was baptized in the pariſh of St. George in the Fields, in the county of Middleſex, on the 13th of February following. Having entered at a very early age into the navy, he gained much reputation and eſteem, while in the more ſubordinate ranks, of thoſe who were his ſuperiors in command. He was taken, early in the year 1742, by Mr. Mathews, to be one of his lieutenants when that gentleman proceeded to the Mediterranean as commander-in-chief on that ſtation, having his flag on board the Namur. He was promoted by that admiral to be captain of the Plymouth, of ſixty guns, on the 9th of November 1742. This commiſſion was-confirmed by the admiralty board, but he removed, not long after his return to England, into the Sheerneſs, a frigate of twenty guns. This commiſſion was dated in the month of Auguſt 1743; and about the ſame time in the enſuing year he was promoted to the Ludlow Caſtle*, of forty-four guns. He does not appear, during this period, to have met with any opportunity of acquiring either fame, popularity, or fortune.

How long he continued in the Ludlow Caſtle is not preciſely known, but could not have been for any great length of time, for, in the month of May 1746, he was captain of the Eagle, a new ſhip of ſixty guns, then employed as a cruiſer on the Iriſh ſtation. In this occupation he had the good fortune to capture two very ſtout privateers, one of them a Spaniard, called the Eſperance, of ſixteen guns with one hundred and thirty-ſix men, which he carried into Kinſale; and the other a French ſhip, formerly the Shoreham frigate, and when captured retaining the ſame name, carrying twenty-two guns and two hundred and ſixty men. He came up with the latter after a chace of ſixteen

---

* Some accounts have, though we believe erroneouſly, ſtated his ſecond appointment to have been to the Phœnix.

hours.

hours, and carried it into Crookhaven in the month of October. He continued in the Eagle during the remainder of the war, and was one of the commanders under the orders of rear-admiral Hawke, in the month of October 1747, at the time he attacked, and defeated L'Etendiere's fquadron. On this occafion he behaved with much fpirit, and may be faid to have then laid the foundation of that popularity he afterwards in fo high a degree poffeffed.

The Eagle was, at one time in the action, engaged with two fhips at once; and, in confequence of having been fo warmly concerned, had her wheel fhot away, as well as her braces and bowlings, fo that the fhip was abfolutely ungovernable. In this very fhattered condition fhe fell on board the Devonfhire at the very time the admiral was crouding into action to her fupport. Captain Rodney was, in the month of November following, one of the principal evidences againft captain Fox, of the Kent; and declared, that while he was engaged between two fires, as already defcribed, captain Fox had it in his power to have come up to his fupport, but did not. It is, however, the opinion of fome, that captain Rodney was, on this occafion, rather too harfh and fevere, owing, probably, to that degree of irritation which fome men feel, when they conceive themfelves neglected or abandoned.

The peace had not been long concluded when captain Rodney was, in the month of March 1749, appointed to the Rainbow, a fourth rate; and, on the 9th of May following, was nominated governor and commander-in-chief in and over the ifland of Newfoundland. Immediately afterwards he proceeded thither with the fmall fquadron annually fent there, in time of peace, for the protection of the fifhery. In the enfuing year he was fimilarly occupied with the additional employment of fearching for an ifland, faid to have been difcovered in latitude 50° N. about three hundred leagues to the weftward of Scilly. He was not, however, fortunate enough to difcover this Utopian country. In the Reading Mercury of April 10, 1752, and not improbably in many other newfpapers of the fame date, is the following article of intelligence.

" Commodore Rodney arrived this day at Woolwich: he cruifed ten days in queft of the ifland faid to have been difcovered by captain Acton. The men at the maft head were

were more than once deceived with those appearances which the sailors call fog banks, *which we may suppose to have been the best solution of the supposed discovery.*"

In the month of May 1751, a day or two only after he had sailed on the expedition (if it deserves that name) last-mentioned, he was chosen representative in parliament for the borough of Saltash. Some time after his return he married, on the 2d of February, 1753, Miss Jane Compton, daughter of Charles Compton, esq. and sister to Spencer, then earl of Northampton. He was about the same time appointed captain of the Kent, of seventy guns, commissioned as a guardship at Portsmouth*. He retained the above command till the year 1755, when he was promoted to the Prince George, of ninety guns, at Portsmouth. This ship not being employed on any memorable or distinguished service, we do not find any particular mention made of captain Rodney till the year 1757, when he commanded the Dublin, of seventy-four guns, to which ship he was appointed in the month of April. He served this year, under the command of sir Edward Hawke, in the memorable but too successless expedition against Rochfort; and, as being the oldest captain in the fleet, was one of the members of the council of war. In the following spring he was ordered to Louisburg with admiral Boscawen; but his having been a party concerned in this expedition was merely accidental, he having been ordered out to supply the place of captain Bentley, whose ship, the Invincible, was unfortunately lost by running on a shoal in going out.

Nothing material occurred to him while thus employed, except that the Dublin being very sickly he was obliged to bear away for Halifax. This was the last service in which he was engaged as a private captain, for, on the 14th of February, 1759, he was advanced to be rear-admiral of the blue. The first occupation in which he was employed as a flag officer, was the command of a small squadron of ships of war and bomb vessels, equipped

---

* During this period, that is to say some little time after the meeting of the new parliament, he was returned as member for the borough of Oakhampton.

for

for an expedition againſt Havre de Grace, where, as it was ſaid, a large quantity of flat boats were built or collected, and a variety of other preparations ſtill more formidable and expenſive were making, in aid of the armament equipping, by order of the French government, for the invaſion of Great Britain or Ireland.

This ſervice he executed, having hoiſted his flag on board the Deptford with the greateſt adroitneſs, diſpatch and ſucceſs, for, having on the 3d of July, anchored in the great road of Havre, he immediately made the neceſſary diſpoſitions to carry his orders into execution. The bomb-ketches were placed in the narrow channel of the river leading up to Harfleur, that being the moſt proper, and, indeed, only ſpot from whence the expected deſtruction could be effected, the ſhips of war being at the ſame time judiciouſly ſtationed to ſupport and protect them. All theſe neceſſary and preliminary arrangements being made early in the morning of the 4th, the bombardment immediately commenced and continued, without intermiſſion, for fifty-two hours. So ſucceſsfully was this ſervice executed that the town was repeatedly in flames in different parts: the grand magazine of ſtores for their flat boats burnt with the greateſt fury for ſix hours, in ſpite of every poſſible effort made by the enemy to extinguiſh it. A conſiderable number of the boats themſelves were overſet, ſunk, or ſo much damaged as to be of no farther ſervice. To complete the good fortune which attended the operations of this little armament, this ſucceſs was atchieved with very inconſiderable loſs to the bold aſſailants, though many of the enemy's ſhot and ſhells fell and burſt among the boats and bomb-ketches. "Thus had Mr. Rodney the happineſs (as Collins remarks) of totally fruſtrating the deſigns of the French court, and ſo completely ruined not only the preparations, but the port itſelf, as a naval arſenal, ſo that it was no longer in a ſtate to annoy Great Britain during the continuance of the war."

In the month of Auguſt he again repaired to his ſtation, but no farther injury to the enemy remained to be effected. On the 24th of September he returned into port to victual, and ſo expeditious was he, that in two days afterwards he once more failed for Havre; ſo that, by keeping the enemy in a perpetual ſtate of alarm and anxiety, he

rendered

rendered them incapable of making the smallest effort to restore or repair those shattered remains which the preceding conflagration had left undestroyed. He continued occupied precisely in the same line of service during the year 1760, but the only remarkable occurrence which took place was the destruction of some of the enemy's boats in the month of July, a service more remarkable and useful from the consequences it produced than for what immediately appeared on the face of the encounter itself.

He drove five flat-bottomed boats ashore that were laden with cannon and shot, and totally destroyed them, together with a fort, under which they ran for protection, at Port Baffin; at the same time ten others which were in company, escaped, with the greatest difficulty, up the river Orne, leading to Caen. The enemy had sailed in the middle of the day, with the greatest confidence, from Harfleur, having their colours flying, and making all the extravagant parade frequently attendant on presumptive security. The hills on each side of the river, and the walls of Havre de Grace, were covered with spectators, who were astonished that the English squadron made no motion whatever. The admiral knew it would be to no purpose to attempt any thing till the vessels had passed the river Orne, as, till then, they had it in their power to take shelter in several small ports: however he kept his eye constantly on them, and had given directions to his squadron to be ready the moment he made the signal to chace. When the enemy got the length of Caen river they kept standing backward and forward upon the shoals, and the admiral plainly perceived they intended to push for it after dark; upon which he gave directions to his small vessels, the moment the day closed, to make all the sail possible for the mouth of the river Orne, to cut off the enemy's retreat, and with his other ships made the utmost dispatch, without signal, for the steep coast of Port Baffin. This had the desired effect; the enemy were met by two of his squadron, disguised like Dutchmen, who turned them, off Point Percee: when perceiving their retreat cut off, they ran ashore and met the fate just described. They were remarkable fine vessels upwards of one hundred feet long, and capable of containing from three to five hundred men for a night's run. This success had the desired effect, the enemy having unloaded one hundred other boats that were ready to fail, and sent them all up again to Rouen.

He continued on the same station during the remainder of the year, and for a considerable part of the ensuing, displaying much diligence and obtaining many advantages, which, though of a trivial nature, were all which the caution of the enemy would permit him to obtain. In the new parliament convened in 1761, he was elected member for Penryhn, in Cornwall, and in the following autumn was appointed commander-in-chief of the expedition then fitting out for the reduction of the French island of Martinico. He sailed from Spithead, on the 18th of October, in the Marlborough, with the Modeste, Vanguard, Nottingham and Syren; the Grenada, Thunder and Basilisk bomb-ketches, with the Fly sloop of war. He arrived in the beginning of November at Barbadoes, where he was joined by commodore Barton and a convoy from Belleisle, with a part of the army that had been just before employed in the conquest of that island; as he was soon afterwards by a second corps from North America, under the command of general Monckton. All the troops, and ships destined for this expedition, being collected, the rear-admiral proceeded to Martinico, off which island he arrived on the 7th of January.

The neighbouring batteries of the enemy, which defended the coast in St. Anne's bay, being silenced, the troops were landed, without farther opposition, on the 16th, at Cas Navire. Such vigorous measures were pursued that the citadel of Fort Royal surrendered on the 4th of February; and the Pigeon Island, which formed the principal defence of the harbour, in three days afterwards. These successes were preliminary not only to the surrender of the whole colony, which capitulated on the 13th of the same month, but to that of the islands of Grenada, St. Vincent's, St. Lucia, and, in short, all the French possessions in the West Indies, which passed under the Dominion of Great Britain immediately afterwards.

Towards the conclusion of the * year Mr. Rodney was advanced to be vice-admiral of the blue, and was raised to the dignity of a baronet of Great Britain, by letters patent bearing date January 21, 1764. In the month of No-

---

* On the 21st of October.

vember * 1765, he was appointed mafter of Greenwich-hofpital. In the month of November 1767, he was one of the vice-admirals who fupported the canopy at the funeral of his royal highnefs the duke of York. In the year 1768, on the diffolution of the parliament, he offered himfelf as a candidate for the town of Northampton. His election for that place he carried againft Mr. Howe by a poll of 611 to 538, after a ftrong and very expenfive conteft, by which he very confiderably impaired his fortune. In the month of October 1770, he was progreffively advanced to be vice-admiral of the white and red fquadrons; and, in the month of Auguft 1771, to be rear-admiral of Great Britain. In the very early part of this year he refigned the mafterfhip of Greenwich-hofpital, and was immediately afterwards appointed commander-in-chief on the Jamaica ftation, whither he repaired, having his flag on board the Princefs Amelia, of eighty guns. The appointment of this fhip to that fervice was intended as a particular and pointed compliment, it being extremely unufual to fend a three-decked fhip on that ftation, except in time of actual war. It is faid the command in India was offered to him, which he declined, entertaining hopes of being appointed governor of Jamaica in cafe of the death of fir William Trelawney, who then held that poft, and was faid to be in an ill ftate of health.

In this hope fir George was difappointed, and on his return to England at the expiration of the time allotted for the continuance of his command, retired to France, where he lived fome years in obfcurity, and, as it is confidently afferted, in rather diftreffed circumftances. On January 29, 1778, he was advanced, being then abfent in France, to be admiral of the white. The war breaking out foon after this time, fir George was enabled, by the liberal loan of a French nobleman, which he afterwards very honourably repaid, to revifit his native country and follicit a command. He did not, however, receive any appointment till the end of the year 1779, when he was nominated commander-in-chief on the Leeward Ifland ftation; he accordingly hoifted his flag at Portfmouth,

Erroneoufly ftated, by Collins, December the 3d.

on board the Sandwich, a second rate. Intelligence was about that time received by the admiralty-board, that the Spaniards had a force of twelve or thirteen ships off Cape St. Vincent, having procured information that sir George was under orders, in his way to the Leeward Islands, to protect a convoy into Gibraltar for the relief of that garrison, then heavily threatened with a siege, which soon afterwards in reality commenced. The force intended to proceed with him to his ultimate destination was to consist, exclusive of the flag-ship, only of three third rates of 74 guns each, namely, the Ajax, Terrible and Montague; and the treacherous intelligence afforded to the Spaniards of this circumstance recoiling on themselves, proved their own destruction; the force under the rear-admirals Digby and Ross, consisting of fifteen or sixteen ships of the line, was ordered to proceed through to Gibraltar, instead of quitting sir George off Cape Finisterre as first intended; the event is too recent to have been forgotten.

Previous, however, to this happy and glorious circumstance, sir George, who may certainly be ranked among the most fortunate men that ever appeared in the naval service, fell in, on the 8th of January, about fourscore leagues to the N. E. of Cape Finisterre, with a Spanish convoy from St. Sebastian's, bound for Cadiz under protection of the Guipuscoana, of sixty-four guns, four frigates and two corvettes, belonging to the royal company of the Caraccas. The merchant ships amounted to sixteen sail, laden principally with flour, provisions and naval stores; these, together with the ships of war, were all captured, without the smallest difficulty or resistance, which, indeed, would have been fruitless and extravagant in the extreme, considering the very formidable force which surrounded them. Pursuing his course towards Gibraltar, sir George, on the 16th of the same month, fell in with Don Langara's squndron, on their station off Cape St. Vincent, the particulars of which encounter will, perhaps, be best given in his own words.

" At one, P. M. the Cape then bearing north four leagues, the Bedford made the signal for seeing a fleet in the S. E. quarter; I immediately made a signal for the line of battle abreast and bore down upon them; but before that could be well effected, I perceived the enemy were endeavouring

vouring to form a line of battle ahead upon the starboard tack; and as the day was far advanced, being unwilling to delay the action, at two P. M. I hawled down the signal for the line of battle abreast, and made that for a general chace; the ships to engage as they came up by rotation, and to take the lee-gage in order to prevent the enemy's retreat into their own ports.

" At four, P. M. perceiving the headmost ships very near the enemy, I made the general signal to engage and close. In a few minutes the four headmost ships began the action, which was returned with great briskness by the enemy. At forty minutes past four one of the enemy's line of battle-ships blew up with a dreadful explosion, and every person perished. At six, P. M. one of the Spanish ships struck. The action and pursuit continued with a constant fire till two o'clock in the morning; at which time the Monarca, the headmost of all the enemy's ships, having struck to the Sandwich, after receiving one broadside, and all firing having ceased, I made the signal to bring-to*."

On

---

* The fruits of this victory were, the Phœnix, of eighty guns, the flag-ship of admiral Juan de Langara; the Monarca, Princessa and Diligente, of seventy guns each, captured; and the St. Domingo, of the same force, blown up in the action. The St. Julien and St. Eugenio, of seventy guns, also surrendered; an officer, with some men, were put on board one of them; but these ships were afterwards driven on shore by the violence of the wind, and the latter, if not both, totally lost.

On the 29th of February the thanks of the house of commons were unanimously voted to sir George Rodney for this great and important service; and the same testimony of gratitude was, on the next day, offered by the house of lords also. On the 6th of March, the freedom of the city of London was voted in common council, to be presented to him, in a gold box of an hundred guineas value: a similar compliment of the freedom of the city of Edinburgh having been previously paid to him.

Sir George had now acquired the very zenith of popularity: the praises universally lavished on him amounted almost to idolatry. At the general election which took place in the month of September in the current year, he was, though absent, elected member for the city of Westminster without his sollicitation, and merely on the ground of that high estimation in which he was then held, particularly by that which called itself the patriotic party. How strangely and rapidly he quickly afterwards fell in their esteem, will be presently shewn.

On the 18th the fleet and convoy entered the gut, but the violence of the wind, added to the strength of the current, prevented the Sandwich, and many other ships, from getting to an anchor in Gibraltar Bay till the 27th. The relief of that fortress, which was, as we have already stated, the first object of this expedition, being happily, and, indeed, easily accomplished, sir George quitted the bay on the 13th of February, and parted company five days afterwards with the rear-admirals Digby and Ross. He arrived in the West Indies, without meeting with the smallest sinister accident, in the month of March, and immediately took upon himself the command of the armament on that station, amounting, after the junction above-mentioned, to twenty ships of the line besides frigates. As soon as he had refreshed the crews of his ships, and made some necessary arrangements, sir George repaired to St. Lucia, where he arrived on the 27th of March, and found that the enemy, who had for some days previous to his arrival made a ridiculous parade off St. Lucia, with a fleet consisting of twenty-five ships of the line, had thought proper, on the news of his approach, to retire into Fort Royal Bay a few hours only before he reached Gros Islet. As soon as his fleet could be put in a proper condition for immediate service, which was effected by the 2d of April, he proceeded off Fort Royal, where for two days he continued offering the enemy battle, who did not think proper to accept so fair and open a challenge: he therefore left a squadron of his best-sailing copper-sheathed ships to watch the motions of the enemy, and with the remainder returned to Gros Islet Bay, where he lay at single anchor, holding himself in constant readiness to pursue the enemy on the first notice he should receive of their having put to sea.

In this situation affairs continued till the 15th, when the enemy slipped out, with their whole force, in the

---

On the 14th of November his majesty, as a very distinguished mark of his royal favour, though there was at that time no vacant stall belonging to the order of the Bath, nominated sir George a supernumerary knight companion thereof, a very convincing proof that he at that time held a place equally high in the opinions and estimation of all men.

middle

middle of the night. This being made known to fir George, by his fquadron of obfervation, he immediately followed; and, after looking into Fort Royal Bay, and the road of St. Pierre, got fight of them on the 16th, about eight leagues to leeward of the Pearl Rock. By five o'clock in the evening he had neared the enemy fufficiently to difcover that their force confifted of twenty-three fhips of the line, one of fifty guns, three frigates, a lugger and a cutter, a force evidently fuperior to his own, which amounted to no more than twenty fhips of the line and one of fifty guns, fome of which were in a very crazy ineffective condition. The manœuvres of the enemy manifefted an evident inclination to avoid an action, and it needed every poffible exertion, on the part of the Britifh admiral, to prevent their effecting that purpofe, which implicated with it their efcape. It was the intention of fir George, as he himfelf declares in his difpatches, to have attacked only the rear of the enemy's line with his whole force, and thereby compelled them to abandon the fhips, with which he clofed, to his mercy, or engage him upon his own terms. Some of the officers under his orders are faid to have mifunderftood his fignals, and by that means to have brought on a more general encounter, fhip to fhip, than the commander-in-chief intended. It is neither our bufinefs nor inclination to do more on the prefent occafion than to ftate the mere matter of fact, without pretending to enter into any, even the fmalleft difcuffion of the matter, or prefuming to hazard the fhadow of an opinion. We fhall therefore content ourfelves with ftating, in the precife words of fir George, that, " at the conclufion of the battle, the enemy might be faid to be completely beat." But fuch was the diftance of the van and rear from the centre, and the crippled condition of feveral fhips, particularly the Sandwich, which for twenty-four hours was, with difficulty, kept above water, that it was impoffible to purfue them that night without the greateft difadvantage: every endeavour however was ufed to put the fleet in order, and on the 29th he again got fight of the enemy. He purfued them for three fucceffive days but without effect, they ufing every endeavour poffible to avoid a fecond action, and attempting to pufh for Martinique.

The British fleet cut them off; and, to avoid a second encounter, they took shelter under the island of Guadaloupe.

The condition of many of the ships, and the lee currents, compelled the British admiral to anchor in Choque Bay, St. Lucia, in order to refit, as well as to land his sick and wounded men. He first, however, took the precaution of dispatching frigates to windward and leeward of every island, that he might have the earliest notice of the enemy's approach towards Martinique, which was the only place in those seas where they could be properly refitted. On the 6th of May intelligence was received of their approach, and sir George put to sea in nearly the same force as before. On the 10th he again got sight of the enemy, who persevered in their disinclination to hazard a contest. The French ships had a very evident superiority in point of sailing, and this advantage encouraged them frequently to approach very near the British fleet with much seeming resolution; but as soon as they came within little more than random shot they always brought to the wind, and retreated. A lucky change of the wind, on the 15th, would have enabled the British admiral to weather, and force them to an action, had it not unfortunately, when he had nearly got up with the enemy, again changed six points, and once more reinstated them in their original advantageous position to windward.

A partial action, however, took place between the rear of the French and the van of the British fleet, which was productive of nothing decisive. A second skirmish of the same kind, and brought on nearly by the same means, again happened on the 19th; and the condition of many of the ships not permitting sir George to persevere any longer in an hopeless pursuit, which had already drawn him forty leagues to windward of Martinico, he sent three of his most disabled ships to St. Lucia, and with the remainder put into Carlisle Bay, in the island of Barbadoes, on the 22d.

Here he made every possible expedition in refitting, revictualling and watering his fleet. He was the more induced to this by intelligence he had received from captain Mann, of the Cerberus, of the approach of a Spanish squadron, consisting of twelve ships of the line, which sailed from Cadiz on the 28th of April, and which he consequently hoped to intercept and capture, or destroy, before the French ships, which had put into Martinico in a very shattered condition, should be again fit for sea. In this hope he was unfortunately disappointed, for the Spanish admiral altered his original rendezvous, which was known to sir George, and proceeded no farther than Guadaloupe, from whence he detached a frigate to Martinico, desiring monsieur de Guichen would put to sea and join him, as he accordingly did with eighteen ships of the line.

The superiority of the combined squadrons compelled the British admiral to continue inactive, and merely on the defensive, till some reinforcements, daily expected from England, should reach him. These were so late in their arrival, that the approach of that season, when hurricanes are generally expected, made it necessary for the ships to separate, as well for their own safety as in order to carry into execution a variety of services which were indispensibly necessary to be provided for. Sir George having made up his different detachments repaired to America, with eleven ships of the line and four frigates. No occurrence, in the smallest degree interesting, took place during the time he continued on the American station, from whence he returned to the West Indies as soon as the dangerous season, just alluded to, was over. It was, as may be well remembered, attended this year with circumstances of unusual horror, which were reported to the admiral, and general Vaughan, the commander-in-chief of the land forces, to have been particularly destructive to the fortifications erected by the enemy, on the island of St. Vincent's, which they had made themselves masters of on the first commencement of hostilities with Great Britain. The probability of recovering, on easy terms, so valuable a possession, induced the joint commanders to undertake an expedition against it, on which service they sailed from Gros Islet Bay on December 14. On their arrival off the island, on the following day, they found the distress, to which the enemy was reported as reduced, together with the supposed ruinous state of their works, was extremely misrepresented and exaggerated: the troops, which were not very numerous, were, however, landed; but the impregnability of the enemy's position to so inadequate

dequate a force being fully difcovered, the men were immediately taken off without the fmalleft moleftation; fo that though fuccefs was wanting, that want was not attended with the fmalleft lofs, or fuperadded misfortune.

A reinforcement, confifting of feven fhips of the line, arrived from England, early in the year, under the command of rear-admiral Hood; and intelligence of the rupture, which had taken place between Great Britain and the States General, quickly followed it. This was accompanied by inftructions for the immediate attack of the different Dutch poffeffions in the Weft Indies, and particularly the ifland of St. Euftatia, which had long become the grand depot of naval and military ftores. From hence the wants of the enemies of Great Britain were abundantly fupplied, in defiance of all treaties, and violation of every thing like national faith. The orders and information juft alluded to arrived at Barbadoes, in the Childers, on the 17th of January. On the 3d of February the fleet, with a fufficient detachment of foldiers on board, to fecure conqueft, appeared before the ifland. Refiftance was not even attempted, and the rock (for St. Euftatia is really no more) together with the whole property it contained, to the amount, as it was faid, of nearly three millions fterling, fell under the dominion of Great Britain.

All the effects found were immediately put, by the commanders-in-chief, fir George and general Vaughan, in a ftate of confifcation, as a punifhment for the conduct of the inhabitants, who had, in conjunction with the Dutch Weft India company, and the merchants of Amfterdam, been, as we have before ftated, in a conftant habit, during the whole preceding part of the war, of fupplying the united opponents of Britain—the Americans, the French, and the Spaniards, with naval and warlike ftores. With this perfidious affiftance, fo contrary to the good faith of a neutral power, they were enabled to fuftain an offenfive war, which they muft otherwife have been compelled totally to abandon, and have been content with acting on the defenfive only, perhaps not very fuccefsfully. Sir George in his difpatches makes ufe of the following very ftrong expreffions relative to the foregoing tranfactions. "I moft fincerely congratulate their lordfhips on the fevere blow the Dutch Weft India company, and the

perfidi

perfidious merchants of Amsterdam have sustained by the capture of this island." Generally speaking, his censure, and perhaps the very vigorous measures he took, were by no means improper*. Nevertheless, as in all cases of a similar nature to the present, persons less criminal must be involved in an equal distress with culprits of the worst and most infamous description, so in this instance did those who boasted themselves of the former class, excite so tremendous a clamour, that Britain, almost with an appearance of turning traitor to itself, appeared, with an unanimity conformable only to the strictest patriotism, acquiescing in the complaints of those who affected popularity, eminence, and the vain honour of becoming public characters, and joined the cause of the guilty, by condemning, unheard, the measures of the British commanders.

The subsequent events of the naval campaign in this part of the world contributed, perhaps in no small degree, to strengthen and give spirit to this censure. Sir George, with two or three ships only, remained at St. Eustatia, as was sarcastically, and, perhaps, untruly remarked, merely to superintend the sale of his prizes. But this calumny he afterwards very fairly refuted, on his return to England at the close of the year, by explaining in his place, as a member of the British parliament, the springs which actuated

---

* The private and patriotic opinion of sir George and his colleague, are well explained by a sentence in a subsequent dispatch, dated St. Eustatia, March 17th.

" Give me leave to congratulate your lordship on the acquisition of the two Dutch colonies of Demarary and Issequibo, upon the Spanish Main; and although more colonies have surrendered upon the supposed terms granted to St. Eustatia, yet general Vaughan and myself thought they ought to be put quite on a different footing, and not treated as an island whose inhabitants, though belonging to a state who, by public treaty, was bound to assist Great Britain against her avowed enemies, had, nevertheless, openly assisted her public enemy, and the rebels to her state, with every necessary implement of war, and provisions, perfidiously breaking those treaties they had sworn to maintain."

N. B. With the island of St. Eustatia were captured one hundred and fifty merchant-ships richly laden, one frigate of thirty-eight guns, and five other ships and vessels of war of inferior consequence, carrying from fourteen to twenty-six guns. To render the success complete, a convoy, which had sailed for Europe under protection of the Mars, a sixty four gun ship, about thirty-six hours before the arrival of

actuated his conduct. Having received advice from England that a French squadron of considerable force had sailed from France, for the West Indies, under the orders of the count De Graffe, he detached rear-admirals Hood and Drake, with eighteen ships of the line, to intercept him. The intelligence conveyed to him from Europe unfortunately was erroneous, for the force of the enemy proved to be far superior to the British fleet sent to oppose them, as it consisted of twenty-one ships of the line in the best condition. The event was negatively unfortunate, as the French admiral, by sustaining a distant and defensive action, was enabled to make good his passage into Port Royal. Sir George instantly, on receiving intelligence of the enemy having parried his attack, put to sea with his two remaining ships, the Sandwich and Triumph, sending orders to the Panther to join him at sea, which when effected, he proceeded off Port Royal with his squadron, to offer battle to the enemy with a force of twenty-one ships of the line.

The count, notwithstanding he out-numbered sir George, by several ships, used every possible manoeuvre to avoid an action, and by a feint attacked the island of St. Lucia in the beginning of the month of May. After a failure in that attempt, which was represented by the court of Versailles as by no means intended in a serious light, the enemy, after a desultory previous assault, fell, with their whole force, on the island of Tobago, which surrendered to them, without much resistance, on the 2d of June. Sir George, with a fleet inferior in number by three ships, pursued them on the first notice of their attack. Their success, as just related, had already taken place; and, notwithstanding their superiority in numbers, the enemy continued to manifest every disposition, every intention of avoiding an action. Sir George considering the manoeuvres of the French admiral as merely intended to

---

of sir George, was pursued by a small detachment under captain Reynolds, now lord Ducie, and the whole of them captured. In the month of May, soon after intelligence of the foregoing success was received in England, his majesty was pleased to settle an annuity of 2000l. *per annum* on sir George, 500l. on lady Rodney, 1000l. on his eldest son, and 100l. on each of the younger children.

decoy

decoy him into the Channel between Grenada and the Spanish main, where the British fleet would, in all probability, been driven far to leeward by the rapidity of the current, acted with proper caution to avoid falling into a snare, which might have endangered the safety of the other colonies in that quarter of the world still appertaining to Britain.

The enemy on their part persevering in the line of conduct they had before displayed of avoiding all contest, where success was in the smallest degree doubtful, the short remainder of the season passed on without affording any occurrence worthy our remembrance. When the approach of the hurricane months, and the departure of the French admiral for America, made it again necessary for the British naval force to proceed thither, sir George resigned the command of the fleet to sir Samuel Hood, and shifting his flag to the Gibraltar, which ship needed some considerable repairs, sailed for England, where he arrived at the close of the year, though in a very indifferent state of health, for the recovery of which he had returned. His conduct during the preceding unsuccessful, and in some degree disastrous campaign, became the immediate subject of enquiry in the house of commons; but he appears to have very honourably acquitted himself, by completely refuting every particular of the charge adduced against him *.

---

* After a short preface he said, that when he appeared before St. Eustatia it was for the purpose of cutting off supplies from the enemy, and with the fixed resolution not to grant any terms to the inhabitants. The Dutch, though nominally the friends of this country, had, during the course of his command in the West Indies, been the friends of our enemies. To punish and check both, nothing had appeared more effectual than the reduction of an island, the inhabitants of which were animated with a rooted aversion to us, and the most cordial regard for our enemies. Among those inhabitants there were many, who, while they called themselves Englishmen, were not ashamed to disgrace themselves and their country, by assisting her enemies with the means to wound her: such people deserved no favour, and to them he had resolved to shew none. But when he seized all the property on the island it was not for his own use, at the time and ever since he thought it would all belong to the king, and that it was his duty to see the most made of it to carry into the public treasure: he wished not for a shilling of it: he had no other idea at that

On the 6th of November he was advanced, on the death of the late lord Hawke, to be vice-admiral of Great Britain,

time but that the whole belonged of right to his country, and therefore in all he had done for the prefervation of that property, it was for his country, and not for himfelf, that he had been acting. The *honourable* member* charged him with having fuffered the ftores, provifions, &c. to be carried into the enemy's ports, directly or circuitoufly, through the neutral iflands; but this was THE VERY REVERSE OF TRUTH, for he had given orders that none of the ftores or provifions fhould be fold, but fent to his majefty's yard at Antigua. So ftrict had he been in this refpect, that he was not fatisfied with examining the clearance of every fhip that went out, but caufed her to anchor under his ftern, that fhe might be examined by commiffioned officers, and if fhe had more provifions on board than were neceffary for the voyage they were always taken out. So much for the manner of fale and confifcation of property belonging to people who had fupplied the Americans with every article neceffary for fitting out a fhip, they themfelves being barely able to build the hull and put in the mafts. He had been charged with remaining inactive for three months at St. Euftatia: his anfwer was, that he had in that time planned two expeditions which he was juft on the point of carrying into execution, the one againft Curacoa, the other againft Surinam, when he received advice from the commander of a convoy, by a quick failing veffel, that he had feen ten or twelve French fail of the line, with about feventy tranfports, fteering for Martinique, and that he had kept them in fight for two days. This intelligence made him renounce his defigns againft the Dutch fettlements, and he difpatched fir Samuel Hood, with fifteen fail of the line, to cruife in the track of Martinique. Sir Samuel Hood was as good an officer, if not a better, than himfelf, and therefore there was no crime in difpatching him on that fervice, and he thought fifteen fhips were quite able to fight ten or twelve. Unfortunately the intelligence had not been true with refpect to the real number of the enemy; and fir Samuel had been driven fo far to leeward, that he could not prevent the fhips in Fort Royal from getting out to join De Graffe. This, however, was not a fault, it was unavoidable. His inftructions had been good. He had ordered the ifland to be blocked up, and that frigates fhould be ftationed ten, fifteen, twenty, thirty, forty, fifty leagues from the fhore in the track of the enemy.

As to the fhips he had detained at St. Euftatia, the Sandwich and the Triumph, were at the time in fo bad a condition that he intended to fend them home with the firft convoy.

As foon as he heard of the affair between fir Samuel Hood and the comte De Graffe, he joined the fleet with a determined refolution to renew the action, if the enemy would give him a fair opportunity of doing it. When the French landed at St. Lucia he undoubtedly would have had the defired opportunity to come to action, if intelligence had not been conveyed to the enemy that he was approaching. A letter had been fent to monfieur De Graffe with that advice, and a dupli-

* Burke.

Britain, and lieutenant of the navies and seas thereof; and was, in a few days afterwards, reappointed to the

a duplicate of it soon followed: the first reached its address, the second was intercepted; the contents were, that the English were doubling Guadaloupe, and in twenty-four hours would be upon the French admiral with their whole force. This put an end to, what comte De Grasse called his feint against St. Lucia, for before day-break he embarked the troops, and sailed away.

With regard to Tobago, as soon as he heard it had been attacked he immediately sent rear-admiral Drake with six sail of- the line to relieve it. This he thought a sufficient force, as he understood that the descent had been covered only by two or three ships of the line; the six he sent against them were the best sailers, in the best condition of any in his fleet, and all copper-bottomed. When he found the whole of the enemy's fleet was at sea he was obliged to watch their motions: they endeavoured to allure him to leeward, but if he had attempted to follow them Barbadoes would have fallen; he therefore was obliged to keep to windward, still determined to succour the island. He dispatched to Tobago three officers in three different vessels; two of them fell into the hands of the enemy, the third got to the house of a planter, and there, to his great surprize, learned that the island had surrendered two days before. It was further told by him that 10,000 men could not retake it: at this time the two fleets were in sight of the island. As to the charge brought by the governor of Tobago, all he would add to what he had already said, was, that the guns he had sent the year before, for the defence of the island, had never been mounted. As to the disaster in America, he would tell the house what steps he had taken to prevent it. He had sent to the commander-in-chief at Jamaica, ordering him to detach the Prince William and Torbay to America with the greatest dispatch; and he had sent also to the commander-in-chief in America, desiring he would collect his whole force and meet him with it off the Capes of Virginia; requesting him, that if he could not meet him he would let him know it by one of his frigates. No answer, however, had been sent to him or to sir S. Hood, for he himself was so ill that he was coming home. He had sent twice to the admiral at Jamaica, and three times to the admiral at New York. One of his three dispatches miscarried, the vessel that conveyed it being forced on shore by some privateers: and from that circumstance he had learned, always in future, to keep copies of every dispatch, for of that he had none. If the admiral in America had been fortunate enough to meet sir Samuel Hood near the Chesapeak, the probability was, that De Grasse would have been defeated, and the surrender of lord Cornwallis prevented.

The last charge was, that he had brought home the Gibraltar. The fact was, she was in a very bad condition, and he had not been without his fears he should not have been able to have got her home, for by some error at Plymouth, before she went out last, a part of the iron of the rudder had been wasted from the size of his arm to that of his finger; and though perhaps the finest two decker in the world, it was with difficulty she was preserved.

West

West India command. He in consequence hoisted his flag on board the Arrogant; from which ship he soon afterwards removed into the Formidable, a second rate. He proceeded for the West Indies with a squadron of twelve ships of the line, and, after uniting with sir Samuel Hood, being joined by some other ships dispatched after him from England, found himself at the head of a fleet consisting of thirty-six ships of the line. The ships from Europe having recruited their water, sir George put to sea with his whole force, in hopes of intercepting some reinforcements for the French fleet, which were then daily expected from Europe. In this he was disappointed, and on receiving information of those getting into Port Royal, he returned to Gross Islet Bay, in the island of St. Lucia, from whence he might be better able to keep a watchful eye on the French fleet, than he could by continuing to cruise. The count De Grasse put to sea on the 8th of April, and sir George pursuing him with the utmost speed, came up with his fleet under the island of Dominica. The French acting with that caution and attention to avoiding a general action which uniformly marked their conduct, a partial action only took place for that time; but the British fleet continuing to pursue one of the enemy's ships disabled in the former skirmish, it was left so far astern that it was very evident, without speedy and effectual succour, it must have fallen into the hands of sir George. The count De Grasse, in hopes of rescuing it, and still preserving his defensive system of action, bore down with much apparent resolution. He approached, however, so near, that sir George found himself enabled, after an heavy cannonade between the two fleets in passing each other on contrary tacks, to weather the enemy and force them to an action, which ended not till, as the admiral expressed himself, the setting sun put an end to the contest. The victory was complete and decisive; the French commander-in-chief himself in the Ville de Paris, of one hundred and ten guns, together with the Glorieux, the Cæsar, the Hector, of seventy-four guns each; and the Ardent of sixty-four, were captured; besides one ship of seventy-four guns sunk in the encounter. This signal success is said to have been principally owing to the skilful manœuvre, till that time

nearly

nearly new in practice, of breaking through the enemies line, which was executed about the middle of the action. As foon as the principal and moft urgent damages fuftained by the fleet were repaired, fir Samuel Hood was detached, with twelve fhips of the line, round the ifland of Porto Rico, through the Mona Paffage, in purfuit of fuch fugitives as might have taken that route. He was fo fuccefsful when proceeding to Cape Tiberoon, which was the appointed place of rendezvous, that he captured two fhips of fixty-four guns, a frigate of thirty-two, and a corvette*. This fuperadded fuccefs, joined to the lofs of one or two fhips of the line, which foundered or were wrecked in attempting their efcape, under Vandrueil, to St. Domingo, diminifhed the French fleet to nine or ten fhips of the line, and two veffels of fmaller rate. Sir George purfuing his courfe with fuch part of his force as had fuftained the greateft damage in the preceding action, joined rear-admiral Hood on the 26th of April off Cape Tiberoon; and having left that gentleman with a very ftrong force to cruife, proceeded with the remainder to Port Royal, where he arrived in fafety on the 29th of the fame month.

The intelligence of this important defeat was received in England with an unanimous and almoft frantic joy, for the people, difpirited by the conquefts of the enemy in former years, could fcarcely difpoffefs themfelves of a fear that they would be repeated, and that their fleet would continue, in effect, to ride triumphant in thofe feas, by their extreme and too fuccefsful caution in preventing the Britifh admiral from fully clofing with, and bringing them to a decifive action. Previous to its arrival the recal of fir George had been determined on by the new adminiftration, the greater part of whofe members had been his opponents and accufers on the St. Euftatia controverfy. His fucceffor, admiral Pigot, was not only appointed, but had actually embarked and failed on board the Jupiter to take upon him his command; fo that,

---

* Thefe fhips were not prefent in the preceding action, having been detached, a day or two before it took place, to Cape François, but were becalmed on their paffage, and overtaken as we have fhewn above.

though an exprefs ordering him to return was immediately difpatched to Plymouth, it came too late to effect its purpofe. Succefs, as is almoft invariably the cafe, raifed fir George from that indifferent rank in the public opinion in which he had been held for fome time, through the clamour of thofe who condemned his chaftifement of the Dutch, and he became raifed on an inftant to the higheft pinnacle of popularity. The people adored him *, minifters careffed him, and the fovereign ennobled him, for he was advanced, by patent bearing date June the 19th, 1782, to the rank of a peer of Great Britain by the title of baron Rodney, of Rodney Stoke, in the county of Somerfet. For the better fupport of this dignity, and as a more fubftantial remuneration for the services juft ftated, the houfe of commons, on the 1ft of July following, voted a penfion of 2000 l. *per annum*, fettling it not only on his lordfhip but on fuch as fhould afterwards fucceed to and enjoy the title.

Nothing occurred material enough to demand our particular notice during the time of his lordfhip's continuance in the Weft Indies, from whence he returned foon after Mr. Pigot's arrival. Having fhifted his flag into the Montague, of feventy-four guns, he failed from Port Royal on the 23d of July, and arrived, without meeting with any extraordinary occurrence, at the Cove of Cork, on the 7th of September. After this time his lordfhip never took upon him any command, or interfered in public bufinefs farther than by his occafional attendance to his duty as a peer in parliament. He died in London on the 24th of May, 1792†. It is almoft needlefs to add any obferva-

---

* A column, and other monuments were erected at the expence of private individuals, and fums were collected alfo, by public fubfcriptions, to perpetuate the memory of his victory. At Spanifh town, in Jamaica, a temple was built, at a very great expence, for the exprefs purpofe of receiving his ftatue. In fhort, honours fo great were never before that time paid to any commander whatever.

† We derive from Collins the following heraldic information refpecting his lordfhip.

"On February 2, 1753, he was married to his firft wife, Jane, daughter of Charles Compton, efq. and fifter to Spencer, earl of Northampton. She died in January 1757, and was buried at Old Alresford,

observation on the character of this noble lord: his memoirs, which we trust we have very impartially given, will furnish the reader with very sufficient opportunity of arranging it in his own mind. Thus far we shall beg briefly to remark, that though he was condemned by some he experienced no harder fate than has befallen many of his very brave cotemporaries. Applauded, as we have seen him, by a much greater number, his merit must be in some degree admitted, as it enabled him to stem completely a torrent of censure, which though probably not entirely undeserved, was at least unwarrantably exaggerated, and industriously propagated by every art, some of them of the meanest kind, which the malignity of his enemies could invent.

One of his most powerful opponents, on a motion made by one of the friends of the ex-ministry to censure those who advised the recal of the admiral, declared, in the house of commons, in an extraordinary and peculiar stile of insulting panegyric, " That he would advise his friends to leave matters as they then stood; his late glorious victory had hushed the murmurs which had so much prevailed against him for his conduct at St. Eustatia; but that if ministers were pressed on the score of their ill-usuage of the admiral, they must of necessity expose that which they wished to bury in oblivion." In the former part of his speech the same gentleman was indecent enough to make the following allusions which, in bare justice to his lordship's character, we think it our duty to animadvert on and condemn in the most decided manner. " There *are cases* (said he) in which it would be neither wise nor

---

Alresford, Hampshire: having had issue one daughter, Jane, who died an infant, and was buried at Old Alresford; and two sons, 1st. George, who succeeded to the title; and, 2d. James, who commanded the Ferret sloop of war, and was lost at sea in August 1776, unmarried.

" His lordship married, secondly, Henrietta, daughter of John Clies, of Lisbon, merchant. Their issue are, two sons and four daughters, viz. John, born May 10, 1765, now a captain in the royal navy; Jane, born December 24, 1766; Henrietta, born January 27, and baptized February 18, 1769; Margaret Ann, born, at Paris, in May 1776; Sarah, born May —, 1780; and Edward, born June 17, and baptised July 1, 1783."

prudent,

prudent, in adminiftration, to declare the caufes of any meafure like that at prefent under difcuffion, for though a commander might have the hearts of the people, yet, poffibly, fuch a man might prove a traitor and render his recal neceffary, when it might be imprudent to give the caufe of it to the world." The infinuation here intended is too dark, too defpicable, to require any refutation or anfwer; nor fhould we have mentioned it but for the purpofe of fhowing to what bafe lengths the influence of party and political prejudice will force the human mind. His lordfhip, however, had the fatisfaction of feeing his popularity rife fuperior to the malignant malice of his enemies, on which alone was grounded the whole of his perfecution. We may conclude our account with briefly obferving, that though in private life he poffeffed a contempt of money, which led him into extravagancies and difficulties fcarcely juftifiable, or pitiable, yet thofe very diftreffes appear to have carried with them a fufficient punifhment to render all pofthumous cenfure unneceffary. Even his moft violent opponents muft admit, that no commander ever yet lived who had the good fortune to atchieve fo many notable fervices, or reduce and deftroy, by the fleet under his immediate command, fo great a number of the enemy's fhips*.

SMITH, Elliot,—was, in the year 1741, commander of the Fly floop of war, a veffel on the Lifbon ftation. In the month of November he captured and carried into the Tagus a large Spanifh tranfport, with ordnance ftores and fome foldiers, which is the only mention we find made of him while thus employed. On the 25th of February, 1741-2, he was promoted to be captain of the Advice, a fifty-gun fhip. He was not long afterwards ordered to the Weft Indies, and returned from thence in the month of January, 1744. He retained that command beyond even that time, if we may credit a lift of the navy made out about the end of 1745, in which his name is inferted as then continuing to hold it. We do not, however, find

---

* Three admirals. One Spanifh, the don Juan de Langara; one Dutch, rear-admiral van Binkes; one French, the comte de Graffe, together with eighteen fhips of the line, and nearly as many frigates and veffels of inferior confequence.

any

any other mention made of him; nor, indeed, do we know whether he ever obtained any fubfequent command. In 1758 he retired altogether from the fervice, on being appointed one of the captains in Greenwich-hofpital. He died there on the 31ft of March 1769.

STEVENS, Charles.—This gentleman was, in 1737, lieutenant of the Falmouth, a fhip of fifty guns, ordered for the coaft of Africa, with a fmall fquadron fent thither under Mr. Anfon. When they arrived at Madeira the route of this fhip was changed, in confequence of private inftructions to the commodore, and failed for Jamaica. In the paffage his captain, whofe name we have not been able to afcertain with precifion, having acted improperly, was confined by Mr. Stevens, who carried the fhip to her place of deftination. It is not improbable he remained on that ftation, as we find him promoted there, by Mr. Vernon, in 1741, from the rank of lieutenant to be commander of the Cumberland firefhip*. On the 11th of January, 1741-2, he was advanced to be captain of the Ludlow Caftle, a fhip of forty-four guns, on the fame ftation. He was ordered from thence, with a fleet of merchant-fhips under his convoy, in the autumn following; but having met with a violent gale of wind on the 8th of October, was obliged to put back to Antigua for the purpofe of refitting, and afterwards repaired to England.

He continued in the Ludlow Caftle, or out of commiffion for fome time after his return to England; but in September 1744, was promoted to the Portland, of fifty guns. He appears to have been principally employed as a cruifer; and, in the month of February, 1745-6, had the good fortune to fall in with and capture a French fhip of war, mounting fifty guns: the circumftances of which action are thus related by himfelf.

"On the 9th inftant, at four in the afternoon, Scilly bearing N. by W. diftance twenty-feven leagues, in the latitude of 49. 00. N. with his majefty's fhip Portland under my command, I engaged the Auguft, a French fhip of war of fifty guns, and four hundred and feventy men.

---

* Some accounts make this to have been a captain Richard Stevens, who never rofe to an higher rank than that of a commander, and we believe them to be true.

After two hours and a half clofe action fhe ftruck, having fifty men killed and ninety-four wounded, all her mafts fo fhattered that they went by the board, and fo many fhot in the hull, that, with the late hard eafterly wind, I was obliged to put away with her before it one hundred leagues to the weftward, and am now towing her for Plymouth, Scilly bearing E. N. E. ninety-five leagues. My officers and men behaved with the braveft gallantry, and were greatly rejoiced to have met fo equal a force, to try the ftrength of his majefty's arms. We have loft three feamen and two marines killed, with feven feamen and fix marines wounded; my ftanding and running rigging almoft fhot away; ftanding-maft and fore-top-maft wounded, but not difabled; main-yard quite deftroyed: I am now making another, and as the wind is now fetting in wefterly, I hope foon to add to his majefty's fleet a new fhip which fails very well *.

" I am, &c.
" CHARLES STEVENS."

He arrived at Plymouth in fafety, with his prize, a few days afterwards; but we do not find him any more particularly noticed till the year 1747. In June 1745, he was one of the members of the court-martial, held at Portfmouth, on capt. Green of the Lizard floop: when, ftill continuing in the fame fhip, we find him one of the captains under the orders of rear-admiral Hawke, concerned in the glorious defeat and capture of the French fquadron under L'Etendicre. He continued under the fame flag during the enfuing winter, the fquadron having kept out at fea as much as poffible to diftrefs the French trade, which was deprived of fupport by the almoft total annihilation of the marine of that country. On the laft day of January the Portland, together with the Nottingham, commanded by captain Harland, gave chace, by a fignal from the admiral,

---

* The following extraordinary anecdote is related concerning this action.

" A we an on board the Auguft behaved moft heroically, for though the men in feveral inftances ran from their guns, fhe, difplaying the contrary fpirit, continued to fight, and actually difcharged her mufket fix times after fhe was wounded."
Letter from on board the Portland.

to a fail feen in the north-weft quarter. The Portland, being the fternmoft fhip, could not get up to fupport her confort till fhe had been engaged near an hour with the chace, which was now found to be a French fhip of war, mounting feventy-four guns. The fea ran fo high as to render it impracticable for either party to open their lower ports, and poftponed the furrender of the French fhip till four o'clock in the afternoon. Notwithftanding the length of the foregoing encounter the Portland, partly owing to the circumftance juft ftated, and in a greater degree, perhaps, to the judgment of captain Stevens, in keeping conftantly on the quarter of the enemy, the Portland had only four men wounded. Mr. Stevens continued in the Portland during the remainder of the war, and is faid to have been reappointed to that fhip in the month of January, 1748.

In the month of July, 1749, we find him one of the members of the court-martial affembled for the trial of captain Obrien Dudley, of the Chefterfield; lieutenant Couchman, and others. He was at that time captain of the Tyger. The next fhip he commanded was the Litchfield; but, till the early part of the year 1755, we find no particular mention made of him. It was intended he fhould have hoifted a broad pendant, but without a captain under him, and proceeded commander-in-chief to the Leeward Iflands; the appearance of a rupture with France, caufed, however, a new arrangement. He was in a very fhort time after this promoted to the Orford, in which he captured, towards the end of the year, the Efperance, of feventy-four guns, of which encounter we do not believe any official account was ever given.

In 1757, having hoifted a broad pendant on board the Elizabeth, he was appointed commodore of a fmall fquadron ordered to the Eaft Indies as a reinforcement to the Britifh armament there. He proceeded to Bombay, where, having waited for the change of the monfoon and refitted his fhips, he failed for Madrafs, where he did not arrive till the 22d of March, 1758, having been much retarded by contrary winds off Ceylon. The leading particulars of his fervice, while fecond in command, have been already unavoidably related in the life of fir George Pocock,

Pocock, to which we beg to refer*, ſtating only, that no man could have more bravely, diligently, and actively ſeconded the views and efforts of his principal commander than Mr. Stevens.

In the action which took place with the French ſquadron on the 4th of Auguſt, 1758†, the commodore was wounded in the ſhoulder by a muſket ball. He had been ſometime before advanced to be rear-admiral of the blue, but did not receive the information of his promotion till towards the end of the year. In the beginning of the enſuing he received a ſecond advancement, to be rear-admiral of the red. About this time he removed his flag into the Grafton, and in the month of September was a ſecond time engaged with the French fleet, under count D'Ache, off Pondicherry. On the return of Mr. Pocock to Europe in the enſuing ſpring, he became commander-in-chief on that ſtation. Soon as the ſeaſon would permit after the departure of Mr. Pocock, the preparations which had for ſome time been making for the ſiege of Pondicherry being ſufficiently advanced, Mr. Stephens undertook the blockade by ſea with the ſquadron, while colonel Coote undertook a ſimilar operation on the land ſide with the army. Thus matters proceeded till the 23d of October, when the admiral ſailed from Trincomale to refit, leaving captain Haldene with a detachment of five ſhips of the line, that were in the beſt condition for ſervice, to continue the blockade.

Mr. Stevens reſumed his ſtation off Pondicherry on the 25th of December. On the 1ſt of January, 1761, one of thoſe tremendous hurricanes, not uncommon in that part of the world, aroſe and drove the admiral, together with the whole of his ſquadron to ſea: all the ſhips ſeparated from each other, and ſome of them were loſt. Mr. Stevens, who had his flag on board the Norfolk, was fortunate enough to weather the gale without experiencing any difaſtrous occurrence. Some other ſhips of the ſquadron being equally fortunate, the blockade was reſumed

---

* See vol. iv. p. 387. et ſeq.
† He was very deſervedly included in the vote of thanks given by the Eaſt India company to vice-admiral Pocock, for the great gallantry and conduct diſplayed on theſe occaſions.

on the 4th, when Mr. Stevens returned into Pondicherry road, and pressing the siege with reiterated vigour, the place surrendered on the 15th. The short remainder of this gentleman's life were principally confined to the civil and other arrangements, which became immediately necessary on so important a conquest, and now became his principal, or indeed only care. The settlement of these weighty concerns, extending to the complete demolition of the fortifications, and the annihilation of the French power in India, he scarcely could be said to survive, inasmuch as he died on the 17th of May following.

WICKHAM, John,—was, in the early part of the Spanish war, appointed commander of a xebeck. On the 1st of November, 1742, he was promoted to be captain of the Succefs frigate. In this vessel we believe him to have been employed on the Lisbon station, from whence he returned about the month of March 1744. He was soon afterwards appointed to the Lark, a command he did not long retain, being promoted to the Panther, in which ship we find him on the Newfoundland station in the month of August 1747. This is the last mention we have been able to find that is made of him in the line of active service. In 1759 he was put on the superannuated list with the rank and half-pay of a rear-admiral; but did not long enjoy this honourable proof of his former meritorious services, which age, misfortune and infirmities contributed to render little conspicuous. He died in England on the 21st of October, 1763.

1743.

BOYS, or BOYCE, William.—This gentleman was originally brought up in the service of the merchants; and, as far back as the year 1727, was second mate of the Luxborough galley, a vessel in the employment of the South Sea company. In that year the most lamentable of all

all difasters befel the unfortunate ship above-mentioned, of which, as well as the subsequent distresses of the major part of the unfortunate crew, we have the following highly interesting though lamentable account *.

Having

* " On the 23d day of May, 1727, we sailed from Jamaica; and on Sunday, the 25th day of June, were in the latitude of 41. 45. N. and in the longitude of 20. E. from Crooked Island, when the galley was perceived to be on fire in the lazaretto. It was occasioned by the fatal curiosity of two black boys, who, willing to know whether some liquor spilt on the deck was rum, or water, put the candle to it, which rose into a flame, and immediately communicated itself to the barrel from whence the liquor had leaked. It had burned some time before it was perceived, as the boys were too much intimidated to discover it themselves, having tried all possible means to extinguish the fire in vain. We hoisted out the yaul, which was soon filled with twenty-three men and boys, who had jumped into her with the greatest eagerness. The wind now blowing very fresh, and she running seven knots and a half by the log, we expected every moment to perish, as she was loaded within a streak and a half of her gunnel. We had not a morsel of victuals nor a drop of liquor, no mast, no sail, no compass to direct our course, and above a hundred leagues from any land. We left sixteen men in the ship who all perished in her. They endeavoured to hoist out the long-boat; but, before they could effect it, the flames reaching the powder-room she blew up, and we saw her no more. A little before this we could distinguish the first mate and the captain's cook in the mizen top, every moment expecting the fate that awaited them. Having thus been eye-witnesses of the miserable fate of our companions, we expected every moment to perish by the waves, or, if not by them, by hunger and thirst. On the two first days it blew and rained much; but the weather coming fair on the third day, viz. the 28th, as kind Providence had hitherto wonderfully preserved us, we began to contrive means how to make a sail, which we did in the following manner. We took to pieces three men's frocks and a shirt, and with a sail-needle and twine, which we found in one of the black boy's pockets, we made shift to sew them together, which answered tolerably well. Finding in the sea a small stick, we woulded it to a piece of a broken blade of an oar, that we had in the boat, and made a yard of it, which we hoisted on an oar with our garters, for halyards and sheets, &c. A thimble, which the fore-sheet of the boat used to be reeved through, served, at the end of the oar or mast, to reeve the halyards. Knowing, from our observations, that Newfoundland bore about north, we steered as well as we could to the northward. We judged of our course by taking notice of the sun, and of the time of the day by the captain's watch In the night when we could see the north star, or any of the great bear, we formed the knowledge of our course by them. We were in great hopes of seeing some ship or other to take us up. The fourth or fifth night a

man,

Having afterwards entered into the king's service, we find him, in the month of October 1741, to have commanded

---

man, Thomas Croniford, and the boy that unhappily set the ship on fire, died, and, in the afternoon of the next day, three more men, all raving mad, crying out miserably for water. The weather now proved so foggy that it deprived us almost all day of the sight of the sun, and of the moon and stars by night. We used frequently to halloo as loud as we could, in hopes of being heard by some ship. In the day time our deluded fancies often imagined ships so plain to us, that we have hallooed out to them a long time before we have been undeceived; and, in the night, by the same delusion, we thought we heard men talk, bells ringing, dogs bark, cocks crow, &c. and have condemned the phantoms of our imagination (believing all to be real ships, men, &c.) for not answering and taking us up. The seventh day we were reduced to twelve in number, by death. The next night the wind, being about E. N. E. blew very hard, and the sea running high, we scudded right before it with our small sail about half down, expecting every moment to be swallowed up by the waves. July the 5th, Mr. Guishnet died; and, on the 6th, died Mr. Steward (son of Dr. Steward, of Spanish Town, in Jamaica) and his servant, both passengers. In the afternoon we found a dead duck, which looked green, and not sweet. We eat it, however, very heartily (not without thanks to the Almighty): and it is impossible for any body, except in the like unhappy circumstances, to imagine how pleasant it was to our taste at that time, which, at another, would have been offensive both to our taste and smell. On the 7th day of July, at one in the afternoon, we saw land about six leagues off. At four o'clock another man died, whom we threw overboard to lighten the boat: our number was then reduced to seven. We had often taken thick fog-banks for land, which as often had given us great joy and hopes, that vanished with them at the same time: but when we really saw the land, it appeared so different from what we had so often taken for it, that we wondered how we could be so mistaken: and it is absolutely impossible for any man, not in our circumstances, to form an idea of the joy and pleasure it gave us, when we were convinced of it's reality. It gave us strength to row, which we had not for four days before; and must infallibly, most of us, if not all, have perished that very night if we had not got on shore. Our souls exulted with joy and praises to our Almighty Preserver. About six o'clock we saw several Shallops fishing, which we steered for, having a fine gale of wind right on shore. We went with sails and oars about three or four knots, when we came so near that we thought one of the Shallops could hear us (being just under sail and going in with their fish). We hallooed as loud as we could; at length they heard us and lowered their sail. When we approached pretty near them they hoisted it in again, and were going away from us; but we made so dismal and melancholy a noise, that they brought to and took us in tow. They told us our aspects were so dreadful that they were frightened at us. They gave
us

manded the Ætna firefhip; into which veffel we believe him to have been promoted from the rank of lieutenant, by

---

us fome bread and water. We chewed the bread fmall with our teeth, and then, by mixing water with it, got it down with difficulty.

" During our voyage in the boat, our mouths had been fo dry, for want of moifture for feveral days, that we were obliged to wafh them with falt water every two or three hours, to prevent our lips glewing faft together. We always drank our own water; and all the people drank falt water, except the captain, furgeon, and myfelf. In foggy weather the fail having imbibed fome moifture, we ufed to wring it into a pewter bafon, which we found in the boat. Having wrung it as dry as we could we fucked it all over; and ufed to lick one another's clothes with our tongues. At length we were obliged, by inexpreffible hunger and thirft, to eat part of the bodies of fix men, and drink the blood of four, for we had not, fince we came from the fhip, faved, only one time, about half a pint, and, at another, about a wine glafs full of water, each man, in our hats. A little food fufficing us, and finding the flefh very difagreeable, we confined ourfelves to the hearts only. Finding ourfelves now perifhing with thirft, we were reduced to the melancholy, diftrefsful, horrid act of cutting the throats of our companions an hour or two after they were dead, to procure their blood, which we caught in a pewter bafon; each man producing about a quart. But let it be remembered in our defence, that without the affiftance this blood afforded to nature, it was not poffible that we could have furvived to this time. At about eight o'clock at night we got on fhore at Old St. Lawrence harbour, in Newfoundland, where we were kindly received by captain Lecrafs, of Guernfey, or Jerfey, then admiral of the harbour. We were cautioned to eat and drink but little at firft, which we obferved, as well as the infirmity of human nature, fo nearly ftarving, would allow. We could fleep but little, the tranfports of our joy being too great to admit of it. Our captain, who had been fpeechlefs thirty-fix hours, died about five o'clock the next morning, and was buried, with all the honours that could be conferred upon him, at that place.

" The names of thofe perfons who were burnt in the fhip, who were ftarved in the boat, and who lived to get on fhore, are as follows: viz.

" Burnt in the fhip.

Ralph Kellaway, 1ft mate.
Ifaac Holroide, 3d mate.
Jerald Hedge, gunner.
James Crook, cooper.
  Seamen.
John Johnfon,
William Coats,
William Day,
James Ambrofe,

Charles James,
Francis Mitto,
Edward Thicker,
Evander M'Avy.
Thomas Hind, quarter-mafter.
Sharper,
Jemmy,   } black boys.
Coffea,

" Starved

by admiral Vernon, who difpatched him home, in the month of October, with intelligence of his having taken poffeffion of Walthenham harbour, in the ifland of Cuba. He afterwards was removed into the Baltimore floop. We hear nothing more of him till the 25th of June, 1743, when he was advanced to the rank of captain in the navy, and appointed to the Greyhound frigate. We believe him to have been, not long afterwards, ordered to the Weft Indies*, as he returned from thence in the month of April 1745, with a convoy, being then captain of the Princefs Louifa, of fixty guns. His fhip being immediately refitted and victualled, captain Boys was immediately ordered out on a cruife off the coaft of France, in company with the captains Griffin and Harrifon. The particulars of their joint fuccefs, which was far from in-

"Starved in the boat.

Thomas Steward, paffenger.	William Walker,
Mr. Steward's fervant.	John Simenton,
William Piggs, paffenger.	William James,
Seamen.	Thomas Nicholfon.
John Horn,	Henry Guifhnett, clerk.
John Eaft,	Canfor, ⎫
Henry White,	Hamofe, ⎬ black boys.
Thomas Croniford,	Merry Winkle, ⎭
Simon Emer,	

"Lived to get on fhore.

William Kellaway, captain.	William Gibbs, carpenter.
William Boys, fecond mate.	Robert Kellaway, a boy.
Thomas Scrimfour, furgeon.	George Mould, feaman.
William Batten, boatfwain.	

"The boat in which we got to Newfoundland, diftance 100 leagues, was only fixteen feet long, five feet three inches broad, and two feet three inches deep. It was built for the Luxburgh galley, by Mr. Bradley, of Deal."

"N.B. Lieutenant-governor Boys was accuftomed to pafs annually, in prayer and fafting, the number of days the fhip's crew were in diftrefs, as above-mentioned, in commemoration of his wonderful deliverance."

* We rather believe he was only fent out to meet the homeward-bound fleet in a certain latitude, for, on the 31ft of January preceding, he was one of the members of the court-martial, held on board the Lenox, in Portfmouth harbour, for the trial of the captains Griffin, Moftyn, Fowke and Brett, for the particulars of which fee their refpective lives.

considerable, we have already related*. At the perfuafion of Mr. Griffin, he quitted the Princefs Louifa foon after this time, and took the command of the Pearl frigate, one of the fquadron ordered for the Eaſt Indies with that gentleman, who had the appointment of commodore and commander-in-chief on that ſtation. Nothing, however, material or beneficial to his fame or fortune took place while he continued in that part of the world. No mention is made of him fubfequent to his return to England till after the recommencement of hoſtilities with France. He then for a ſhort time commanded the Royal Sovereign, a firſt rate; and was removed from thence, about the year 1759, into the Preſton. Towards the cloſe of the fummer we find him promoted to be commodore of a fmall fquadron, ſtationed off Dunkirk, to watch the ſhips fitted for fea at that port, and deſtined for a defultory attack on Ireland, under the command of that very active, gallant, and indefatigable naval partizan, monfieur Thurot.

The enemy had the good fortune to elude the vigilance of the Britiſh commodore, who, on hearing the former had efcaped, purfued him with the utmoſt expedition, but without fuccefs, Thurot taking refuge in the Swediſh port of Gottenburgh, where he continued in no fmall diſtreſs till the commencement of the year enfuing; but of this hereafter. Mr. Boys was after his return appointed to command as commodore at the nore; and in the enfuing year retired from the line of active fervice on being made lieutenant-governor of Greenwich-hofpital. He retained this very honourable ſtation till his death, which happened on the 4th of March, 1774.

It is related of him, and we ſtrictly believe it to be true, that this gentleman, from the year 1727 to his death, annually obferved a ſtrict and folemn faſt, on the 7th of July, being the day of his arrival at Newfoundland, after the melancholy lofs of the Luxborough Galley. So rigid was he in this act of humiliation and thankfgiving, that, when in the decline of life he became fettled at Greenwich, and could in that particular inſtance indulge his own inclination to the fulleſt extent, he not only abſtained from food, but even from the light of the fun, not even

---

* See the life of Mr. Griffin vol. iv. p. 228.

NAVAL OFFICERS OF GREAT BRITAIN. 239

suffering converse with any person whatever during the time he was thus occupied in commemorating and returning fervent thanks to the Supreme Being, for his extraordinary, and, indeed, almost miraculous escape.

BRETT, Sir Piercey. — The first account we have of this gentleman is, his having served as a midshipman in the Gloucester*, of fifty guns, one of the small squadron ordered into the South Seas under Mr. Anson. On the promotion of Mr. Cheap to be captain of the Wager storeship, Mr. Brett was appointed by the commodore into his own ship, the Centurion, to be his second lieutenant. He appears, indeed, to have soon conceived an extraordinary and well-deserved attachment to this worthy gentleman, insomuch that he confided to him the attack on the town of Paita, a service he executed with the greatest skill, promptitude and exactness†. After the capture of the Manilla galleon, and the arrival of the Centurion at Macao, Mr. Brett was promoted, by the commodore, to command that ship, under him, as captain, he being, as he supposed, authorised, by his instructions, to issue such a commission. This point was, nevertheless, strongly contested on the arrival of the Centurion in England, and the lords of the admiralty peremptorily refused to confirm Mr. Brett's rank, insomuch that Mr. Anson retired, for a short time, from the service in much disgust; nor did he return till a subsequent change in the members of the board last-mentioned, with a compliance in the first lord and his colleagues who succeeded, in the demands of Mr. Anson, together with the allowance of Mr. Brett's rank‡, according to the date of his first commission, restored perfect peace and harmony on all sides.

Mr. Brett therefore ranks as a captain in the navy from the 30th of September, 1743, being the date of his commission to the Centurion, then lying in Macao river. Not long after the matter was adjusted, as already related, that is to say, about the month of April 1745, he was appointed captain of the Lion, of sixty guns, a ship

---

* Some accounts say he was a lieutenant of that ship.
† See vol. iv. p. 108.
‡ He was, nevertheless, immediately on his arrival in England, officially promoted to the rank of captain, and appointed to the Mary Galley.

stationed to cruise in the Channel. His first success was the capture of a privateer, mounting ten carriage and seven swivel guns, with a crew of one hundred and fifteen men, which had long infested the Channel; and had a short time before captured the Mediator sloop of war. This first success, which he met with on the 29th of June, 1745,' when on his passage from Portsmouth to Plymouth, appeared but as the prelude to that high renown he gained, on the 9th of the ensuing month, in an encounter with a French ship of the line; the particulars are officially related in the following manner.

"On Tuesday, the 9th of this month, his majesty's ship the Lion, of fifty-eight guns, being in the latitude of 47. 57. N. and W. from the meridian of the Lizard 39 leagues, captain Brett, her commander, saw two sail to leeward, to which he immediately bore down, and by three in the afternoon made them to be two of the enemy's ships. By four o'clock he was within two miles of them: they then hoisted French colours and shortened sail. One of them was a man of war, of sixty-four guns; and the other a ship of sixteen guns. At five the Lion ran alongside the large ship and began to engage within pistol-shot. The ships continued in that situation until ten, during which time they kept a continual fire at each other; when the Lion's rigging being cut to pieces, her mizen-mast, mizen-top-mast, main-yard, fore-top-sail-yard, and main-top-sail-yard shot away; all her lower-masts and topmasts shot through in many places, so that she lay muzzled in the sea, and could do nothing with her sails: the French ship sheered off, and in less than an hour was out of sight, the Lion not being able to follow her. The small ship in the beginning of the engagement made two attempts to rake the Lion, but was soon beat off by her stern chace, and after that lay off at a great distance. Forty-five of the Lion's men were killed outright, and one hundred and seven wounded, seven of whom died of their wounds soon after.

Captain Brett was wounded and very much bruised in the arm; and his master had his right arm shot off in the beginning of the engagement. His lieutenants were all wounded two hours before the action was over; nevertheless they would not leave the deck, but continued

encou-

encouraging the men to the laſt, excepting the firſt lieutenant who was ſo much hurt that he was obliged to be carried off at nine o'clock, not being able to ſtand any longer.

The bravery * manifeſted by this gentleman on the foregoing occaſion was rendered more conſequential to his country, from the circumſtance of the ſhip which he had engaged being convoy to the frigate in which the ſon of the Pretender, then on his paſſage to Scotland, had embarked. Some judgement may be formed, of the intrinſic ſervice rendered to Britain, by the foregoing encounter, from the following extract of a private letter from the Hague, dated July the 30th.

" The frigate, on board which the eldeſt ſon of the Pretender had embarked, was joined off Belleiſle by the Elizabeth, of ſixty-ſix guns. They intended to go round Ireland, and land in Scotland, but were met on the 20th by ſome Engliſh merchant-ſhips, convoyed by three ſhips of war; one of which, the Lion, bore down on the Elizabeth and attacked her; upon which the Pretender ſailed away in the frigate. The fight laſted nine hours, but night coming on, the Elizabeth, quite diſabled, got away to Breſt; the captain and ſixty-four men killed, one hundred and thirty-ſix dangerouſly wounded, and a great number ſlightly. She had on board 400,000l. ſterling, and arms for ſeveral thouſand men."

---

* Admiral Vernon, in a ſpeech made by him in the houſe of commons, in the year 1747, in oppoſition to a motion of lord Baltimore's, for bringing in a bill to reſerve a portion of the captures of merchant-ſhips, and thereby encourage that of ſhips of war, makes the following highly honourable mention of captain Brett.

" I have been too long engaged in naval affairs not to know ſeveral of the ſea officers. I have, by thoſe opportunities of knowing them, found them to be men who would omit no occaſion of being ſerviceable to their country; and to appeal from imagination to certain facts, ſeveral of them have ſhewn as much alacrity in attacking ſhips of war as they have in taking merchant ſhips; nor do I doubt but the reſt are ready to do it, whenever occaſion ſhall offer. That this is the character which, at leaſt, ſome of our officers deſerve, is proved by the gallant behaviour of ſeveral, and particularly captain Brett. Did that gentleman behave as if he wanted farther encouragement to perform his duty? Did he not attack a ſhip of ſuperior force to his own, and with ſuch courage and ſkill as brought honour to himſelf, his country, and the Britiſh flag?"

The force of the blow given, in this inſtance, to the embryo of rebellion, may be eaſily admitted. The blood of thouſands was, not improbably ſaved, by the foregoing event; and humanity muſt ever rejoice more at the prevention, than the cure of an evil.

We have no farther account of this gentleman, or the particular ſervices on which he was employed, till the year 1747, when he commanded the Yarmouth, of ſixty-four guns, one of the ſquadron, under Mr. Anſon, which, in the month of May, defeated and captured that of France, commanded by monſieur De la Jonquiere. He was one of the captains ſent, after the concluſion of the action, in purſuit of the convoy, of which Mr. Campbell, and other hiſtorians, aſſert, two only were captured, the Vigilante and Modeſte, of twenty-two guns each, the reſt of the ſhips having made their eſcape. We find, however, it is aſſerted, peremptorily, in the periodical publications of the time, that five more French ſhips were brought into Portſmouth, and three into Plymouth. Mr. Brett quitted the commend of the Yarmouth almoſt immediately on his return into port; and we do not know to what ſhip he was afterwards appointed, as we do not find any mention made of him during the war, except his having been one of the members of the court-martial, aſſembled at Portſmouth in the month of November following, for the trial of captain Fox, of the Kent.

On the 3d of January, 1753*, he received the honour of knighthood from his majeſty, in conſequence of his having carried him to Holland inſtead of ſir C. Molloy; and towards the end of the year was appointed captain of the Caroline yacht, as ſucceſſor to that gentleman. In this veſſel we believe him to have continued till the month of September 1755, when, on the daily expectation of a rupture with France, ſir Piercy was appointed to the Cambridge. In the month of November, or December 1756, he removed back into the Caroline yacht. How long he continued in that veſſel is not exactly known; but, in the beginning of the year 1758, we find him commo-

---

* About this time we believe him to have been elected repreſentative in parliament for the burough of Queenborough, and not long afterwards choſen one of the elder brethren of the Trinity-houſe.

dore in the Downs, having his pendant on board the Norfolk. He was in the same year appointed first captain to lord Anson in the Royal George, who commanded, in the Channel, the covering fleet to the squadron employed, under lord Howe, on the coast of France. On the conclusion of this expedition he returned to his command in the Downs; and while thus occupied it is not to be wondered at if we have no material occurrence to record concerning him. On the 22d of March, 1760, he was appointed colonel of the Portsmouth division of marines. In 1761, still continuing to hold the Downs command, we find him frequently, and actively employed in reconnoitering the opposite coast and ports of France. Towards the conclusion of the year he returned to Portsmouth for refitment; which being completed, he re-hoisted his pendant on board the Newark, at Portsmouth, on the 15th of December. He was immediately afterwards ordered for the Mediterranean with seven ships of war, as second in command to sir C. Saunders, and had soon afterwards the good fortune to share there, as a flag, in the rich Spanish prize, the Hermione. He remained on the same station during the continuance of the war, but peace soon afterwards taking place, nothing in any degree memorable seems to have occurred, except that, in the course of this year, he was advanced to the rank of rear-admiral of the red. From this time he never appears to have accepted any command, but, on the 13th of December, 1766, was appointed one of the commissioners for executing the office of lord high admiral, an office which he continued to hold till the 24th of February, 1770.

On the 24th of October, 1770, he was promoted to be vice-admiral of the blue; and, on the 28th of the same month, to be vice-admiral of the white; as he was, on the 31st of March, 1775, to be vice-admiral of the red. On the 29th of January, 1778, he was, moreover, advanced to be admiral of the blue. He died in the month of May 1781, and was buried at Beckenham*, in the county of

---

* The following epitaph is inscribed on a plain monument, erected to his memory, in Beckenham church.

Sacred to the memory of sir PIERCEY BRETT, knight, admiral of the blue, who departed this life the XII day of October, MDCCLXXXI, in the LXXII year of his age.

Kent. "De mortuis nil nifi bonum," is an old adage; but if ever it fhould be ufed in relation to this gentleman, we have to add, that whether living or dead, the voice of flander and malevolence was abafhed at his manifold virtues, ever filent not only at his approach, but even at the bare mention of his name.

CALMADY, Warwick,—was, on the 30th of September, 1743, appointed captain of the Lively frigate, and foon afterwards ordered to Jamaica. On his paffage from thence to England, in the month of May 1744, he fell in with three French privateers, mounting thirty guns each, which he engaged for an hour and an half; when having all his running rigging fhot away, and finding the enemy were making attempts to board him, he put before the wind and left them. The gallantry difplayed on this occafion by Mr. Calmady, was certainly very highly confpicuous; and his good fortune, in having preferved his fhip from the attacks of a force treble his own, was rendered the more remarkable from the circumftance of his having been totally unacquainted that a rupture had taken place between Great Britain and France, till the fire of his antagonifts informed him of it. His fhip was, neverthelefs, completely ready for action; and this anecdote, if leffons and examples were neceffary on fuch an occafion, might prove an ufeful hint to commanders at fea, even in the time of profound peace, to be always prepared for defence, or the chaftifement even of the flighteft infult.

Captain Calmady having, on the enfuing day, fallen in with a French fchooner, bound from Martinico to Havre de Grace, thought himfelf juftified, as he undoubtedly was, in detaining, and bringing her into port. Soon after his return he was appointed to the Weymouth, of fixty guns, and ordered out to the Weft Indies to join Mr. Knowles, who was then commodore on that ftation. On the 16th of February, 1745, this fhip unfortunately ftruck on a reef near Sandy Ifland, at the entrance of St. John's road. The accident, with its preceding caufes, being enquired into by a court-martial, Mr. Calmady himfelf was moft unequivocally and honourably acquitted; but the lieutenant on duty was fined fix months pay, the mafter declared incapable of ever ferving again in the navy, and
the

the pilot fentenced to be fent to England and imprifoned two years in the Marfhalfea.

Captain Calmady, immediately after his acquittal, is faid to have been appointed to the Launcefton, of forty-four guns, one of the fhips prefently afterwards employed, under commodore Warren, in the fiege of Louifburg. We do not find any mention made of his having a fubfequent command, or being again engaged in fervice, from which he retired altogether, according to Mr. Hardy's account, on the 2d of February, 1757.

CATFORD, Charles,—was, on the 14th of October, 1743, promoted to be captain of the Lyme frigate. The commands and fervices on which he was employed during the remainder of the war, were, unhappily for him, of fo little confequence, that the only mention we find made of him during that period is, his having been one of the members of the court-martial convened for the trial of vice-admiral Leftock. He appears, neverthelefs, to have been in high eftimation as a worthy and a brave man. In the month of January 1749, we find him captain of the Monmouth, and in February 1753, he was appointed to the Berwick, a fhip of feventy guns; ftationed as a guard-fhip at Portfmouth. In the month of March 1755, he removed into the Captain, a fhip of the fame force and rate, commiffioned alfo at the fame port. Early in the year 1756, he was ordered to the Mediterranean with the unfortunate Mr. Byng. He behaved with all the fpirit due to his character and ftation, in the fhort and indecifive fkirmifh with the French fleet off Minorca, having had fix men killed and thirty wounded. He was one of the officers ordered home as an evidence on the trial of his unfortunate admiral, but unhappily died, when on his paffage, on the 24th of September 1756, the fhip he was on board of not having then reached Gibraltar.

DODD, Edward,—was, in the earlier part of his fervice, lieutenant of the Dragon*, at that time commanded by Mr. Barnet, and on the 25th of January 1743, was pro-

---

* From his advanced age, confidering his rank, he was generally known in the fervice by the name of Old Dodd. He was feverely wounded in the fhoulder at the attack of a xebeck, which he was fent in purfuit of, as commanding officer of the Dragon's boats. The enemy was, however, captured. Being afterwards commiffioned, was given to Mr. Dodd, and called the Dragon's Prize.

moted to be captain of the Blandford, a twenty-gun ſhip. We have the following account of an affair in which he was concerned, from a MS. memorandum, dated in the month of June 1745.

" His majeſty's ſhip the Blandford, of twenty guns, captain Dodd commander, has had the misfortune to fall in with a French ſquadron of ſeven ſail, between Liſbon and Gibraltar, and was ſent to Breſt. The captain was threatened with being hanged if he did not diſcover to the commodore whether there was any Engliſh ſpuadron at ſea. . This he very bravely refuſed to comply with,"

No notice is taken of the foregoing event in any hiſtory or printed account, far as we have been able to diſcover; nor is even the capture of the above veſſel ever named. Captain Dodd does not appear to have had any ſubſequent appointment; nor have we been able to aſcertain, with any preciſion, the time of his death, but believe it to have happened about the year 1763.

FIELDING, William,—was the ſecond ſon of John Fielding, D. D. canon of Saliſbury, and his firſt wife, Suſannah, daughter of ſir Robert Booth, chief juſtice of the court of common pleas in Ireland. This gentleman having, as is remarked by Collins, paſſed through the ſeveral ſubordinate ſtations, was, from being commander of the Fly ſloop on the Iriſh ſtation, promoted, on the 11th of January, 1742-3, to the rank of captain in the navy, and appointed to the command of the Bridgewater, a ſhip of twenty guns. This ſhip was unfortunately loſt, at Newfoundland, on the 18th of September following; but captain Fielding being very honourably acquitted of all blame on that occaſion, was, in the month of May 1744, appointed to the Pearl, of forty-four guns; in which ſhip he continued till it was ordered to the Eaſt Indies with commodore Griffin. We have no farther account of the commiſſions he held, or the ſervices on which he was employed, except that, at ſome intervening period, he is ſaid to have commanded the St. George, a guardſhip at Spithead. In 1755 he commanded the Fly ſloop, but with the rank of poſt captain; and in 1762 was put on the ſuperannuated liſt with the rank and half-pay of a rear-admiral. He continued to live ever afterwards in retirement, at Biſhops Waltham, in the county of Hants, where he died on the 23d of September, 1773.

GAGE,

GAGE, John.—The name of this gentleman is very improperly omitted in Mr. Hardy's and many other lifts of naval captains, an omiſſion moſt probably owing to the ſhort time he unhappily held that rank. As a commander, we find him in the Lightning fireſhip, and afterwards, in 1740, in the Carcaſe bomb-ketch: he was from thence removed into the Otter ſloop of war, in which veſſel he behaved with much gallantry in the Weſt Indies, under commodore Knowles. Being ordered from the ſquadron to chace a Spaniſh ſhip, mounting twenty two guns, and full of men, he came up with and attacked her with the utmoſt gallantry, though more than double his force. The action continued nearly two hours till the enemy was driven cloſe under the forts of Porto Cavallo, and a large Spaniſh galley with three hundred men in her, coming out to their countrymen's reſcue, conſequently deprived captain Gage of the well-earned fruits of his bravery. He was on the 24th of February, 1743, immediately ſubſequent to the unſucceſsful attack on La Guira, promoted, by the commodore, to be captain of the Lively frigate; in which command he died, in the Weſt Indies, on the 2d of Auguſt following.

GODDARD, Samuel,—was, on the 1ſt of February, 1743, promoted to be captain of the Deal Caſtle. He was afterwards appointed to the Lynn, of forty guns, one of the Weſt India ſquadron under Mr. Knowles. He was brought to a court-martial, by that gentleman, in the month of February 1745, on a charge of having ſuffered a Spaniſh ſhip, belonging to admiral De Torres's ſquadron, to eſcape from him off Porto Rico, though the enemy was in a very diſabled ſtate, being under jury main, and mizen maſts. It was proved on the trial that he was in ſome degree deranged in his mind; in conſequence of which he was diſmiſſed from his command, and does not appear to have ever recovered in a ſufficient degree to enable him to hold any ſubſequent commiſſion. He died in England on the 5th of November, 1762.

MARSH, William,—in 1742, was commander of the Terrible bomb-ketch. He was promoted, on the 25th of May, 1743, to be captain of the Sterling Caſtle*, one of the ſhips belonging to the Mediterranean fleet. He

---

* Mr. Hardy and many others ſay the Elizabeth.

was quickly removed into the Royal Oak; but this, however, was quite a temporary command, by order only. He returned back for a few days into his original veffel, the Terrible, and was from thence removed into the Winchelfea, of which fhip he was captain at the memorable encounter with the French and Spanifh fleets off Toulon, being ordered by the admiral to watch the entrance of the port juft mentioned, and the movements of the combined fleets. He acquitted himfelf with the greateft diligence and addrefs in this fervice, as well as that of a fimilar nature in which he was employed after the enemy came out. He returned to England in the Winchelfea about the end of the fame year; and whatever fervices or commands he might be employed in fubfequent to this time, were fo unconfequential[*], that we find no mention whatever made of him till the year 1758, when he commanded the Naffau, of fixty-four guns. He was in this year appointed commodore of a fmall fquadron deftined for the attack of the French fettlement in the river Senegal. Its force confifted of the Naffau before mentioned; the Harwich, of fifty; and the Rye, of twenty guns: the Swan floop of war, and two buffes. The land-forces amounted to two hundred marines, commanded by major Mafon; a fmall detachment of artillery men, under captain Walker, with a train of ten pieces of cannon and eight mortars.

Captain Marfh, attended by Mr. Cumming, a quaker, who was the original projector of the expedition, failed from Plymouth on the 9th of March; and after touching at the ifland of Teneriffe, where the fhips took in a fupply of water and other neceffaries, came to an anchor at the entrance of the river Senegal, on the 24th of April. Fort Louis, by which the fettlement is defended, is fituated on the ifland of Senegal, about four leagues within the bar. The governor, foon as the Britifh force was difcovered, fent down an armed brig and fix floops to difpute the paffage. In the interim the boats of the fleet were employed in putting the ammunition and ftores, neceffary for the attack, on board the fmall craft belonging to the fquadron; and a fkirmifh, productive of no confequence, took place between them and the veffels above-mentioned. Captain Millar, however, who commanded the London

---

[*] He is faid to have commanded the Durfley galley in 1745, but this circumftance we very much doubt.

bufs,

bufs, having difcovered the proper channel, feized the opportunity of a change of the wind, and paffing the bar, came to an anchor within, where he lay unfupported, though expofed till night to all the fire the enemy could make. He was the next morning joined by the remainder of the flotilla, and a fmart engagement enfued, which was warmly maintained on both fides till the buffes and another of the fmaller veffels ran aground. The troops immediately took to their boats, and pufhed for the fhore, where they made the neceffary difpofitions to defend themfelves, till the landing of the corps of volunteer feamen, amounting in number to three hundred and fifty, on the following day, rendered their force fufficiently formidable for them to undertake offenfive operations.

Thefe the enemy did not allow them time to commence, for the corps laft-mentioned had fcarcely landed, when deputies* came out of the fort, from the French commandant, with offers to capitulate. The terms were arranged and agreed to in the courfe of the day by the commodore and major Mafon: fo that this far from inconfiderable conqueft was achieved not only without difficulty, but happily alfo without a fingle perfon being killed or wounded on either fide. This fuccefs encouraged the commodore to make an attempt on Goree, a much more confiderable and better fortified fettlement, belonging to France, on the fame coaft, at the diftance of about thirty leagues. The force, however, being totally inadequate to fuch an undertaking, its failure was little to be wondered at; though we muft not omit inferting, that, to the honour of the commodore and the principal officers who directed the attack, the meafures taken by them to cover and fecure the retreat of the affailants, were fo prudent and judicious, that the lofs they fuftained was almoft too trivial to be called a repulfe.

Captain Marfh paffed over from the coaft of Guinea to the Weft Indies, which is the ufual route of the fhips of war annually fent on the African ftation. He does not appear to have had any opportunity of particularly diftinguifhing himfelf while in this part of the world. He removed into the Harwich fometime after the reduction of Senegal, and was unfortunately loft on the ifland of Pieras, commonly called Pines, in the year 1760. Captain

---

* On the 30th of April.

Marſh and his crew were happily ſaved. He returned to England ſome ſhort time afterwards, and retired from the ſervice, in 1762, with the rank and half-pay of a ſuperannuated rear-admiral. He died in England on the 15th of October, 1765.

MOORE, Sir John.—We believe the firſt, or if not, among the earlieſt of the naval appointments held by this gentleman, was that of midſhipman on board the Shoreham: he afterwards ſerved in the ſame ſtation in the Torrington. He was afterwards a lieutenant in the Lancaſter, cotemporary with Mr. James Young, who, as well as himſelf, lived, moſt deſervedly, to attain to nearly the higheſt rank, as an admiral, in the ſervice. Mr. Moore was next taken, by Mr. Mathews, to be one of the lieutenants of his own ſhip*. On the 24th of December, 1743, he was promoted to be captain of the Dolphin, other accounts ſay the Squirrel, but in a very ſhort time afterwards removed back into the Dolphin, being perſuaded by Mr. Barnet, who was then going out to the Eaſt Indies, to accompany him. This ſolicitation was owing entirely to the high opinion entertained of him by the commodore, and is too honourable a teſtimony of this gentleman's worth to be omitted, or ſlightly noticed. He returned to England in the Deptford † with a convoy of India ſhips, after the deceaſe of his friend and commander, and was appointed captain of the Devonſhire, a ſhip memorable for having been that which carried ſir Edward Hawke's flag when L Etendiere was defeated: nor need we add any thing to the very honourable encomium beſtowed on his conduct by the admiral, who ſent him as the meſſenger of his victory.

---

* He did not continue with him to wait his turn for promotion, having, as the readieſt mode of obtaining it, returned to England in the Lenox, at the recommendation of the admiral himſelf.

† Into which ſhip he removed after the arrival of the ſquadron in the Eaſt Indies, and the death of captain Philipſon, on the 30th of March, 1745, till which time he continued in the Dolphin. A particular account of the ſeveral occurrences which took place while he held this command have been already given in the life of the earl of Northeſk, with whom he was detached, by the commodore, for the ſtreights of Malacca, ſoon after the ſquadron quitted Madagaſcar.

N. B. Campbell, as well as all other hiſtorians, erroneouſly ſtate this ſhip to have been the Diamond, a miſtake they have fallen into by following the authority of the official accounts with which, ſtrange to ſay, the blunder originates.

" I have

" I have sent (says the rear-admiral) this express by captain Moore, of the Devonshire; and it would be doing great injustice to merit not to say, that he signalised himself greatly in the action."

As the bearer of intelligence so interesting and glorious, he received the customary present from his majesty of five hundred pounds. Early in the year 1749 he was appointed to the Monmouth; but, as is to be expected in time of peace, we hear nothing of him after this time till the year 1756*, when he was, either in the month of March, or April, re-appointed to his old ship the Devonshire †. No particular subsequent mention is made of him till the year 1758, when he was commander-in-chief, with the rank of commodore, on the West India station, having his broad pendant on board the Cambridge. Nothing material took place till the month of January 1759, when, having been joined by a reinforcement from England, consisting of eight ships of two decks, with a frigate and four bomb-ketches, under commodore Hughes, and a considerable body of troops under the command of general Hopson, he sailed on an expedition against Martinico, which island was marked out as the first object of attack. The troops were landed on the 16th; but many unforeseen difficulties, and impediments appearing, which were deemed insuperable by a force no greater than that under the joint commanders, the attack was declined, and the army reimbarked without opposition. After a demur of two or three days as to the expediency of making an attack on any other part of the island than that first assaulted, it was agreed to be most advantageous for the public service, that the squadron and its convoy should, without delay, proceed to Guadaloupe, to the conquest of which the squadron, and troops it escorted, were deemed perfectly competent.

The commodore arrived off the town of Basseterre on the 22d of January, and immediately removed his pendant into the Woolwich, for the purpose of being better able

---

* Except that during a part of the peace he commanded the William and Mary yacht, which he relinquished when the armament took place in 1755.

† At the conclusion of the year he was one of the members of Mr. Byng's court-martial, and was one of those who wished the oath of secrecy might be dispensed with.

to superintend and direct the attack than he could have been had he continued in the Cambridge and been personally engaged in it. The necessary dispositions were made on the following day, and with such vigour and effect was the assault executed, that all the batteries, and the fort itself were so completely silenced by night, as to enable the troops which were landed on the 24th, to take possession of them without loss, or even molestation. The character of the commodore was much traduced by some persons, for his behaviour on the foregoing occasion, and, as it appears, very undeservedly so. The exception taken against him appears to have been principally founded on his quitting his station in the line, as already stated, and going on board a frigate. But however unprecedented such a measure might at that time be, few persons can doubt but that it would, on many accounts, be more advantageous to the service, were it to become a general and unalterable practice. The only ground on which censure could, in the present instance, be founded, is decidedly and completely done away by the very spirited personal carriage of the commodore on all the numerous preceding, as well as some subsequent occasions, and the very conspicuous gallantry he had on all such opportunities uniformly displayed.

To return to the event of the expedition, suffice it to say, it was concluded by the surrender of the whole island, which, from its peculiar strength, the heat of the climate, and the great force of the enemy, was enabled to hold out for three months. The capitulation was signed on the 1st of May. Nothing material took place after this time during the continuance of the commodore on the West India station, from whence, having previously removed into the Berwick, he returned with a convoy, and arrived in the Downs on the 23d of June, 1760. He does not appear to have been again invested with any command till his promotion to be a flag officer. His first advancement, which took place on the 21st of October, 1762, was to the rank of rear-admiral of the red. He was appointed, according to Campbell, to command in the Downs during the short continuance of the war; but during that

---

* Its surrender was critical, for in a few hours afterwards, M. Bompart arrived with a strong squadron to its relief; but hearing of the event immediately returned to Martinico.

period

period no material occurrence or event happened. On the 1st of March, 1766, he was created a baronet, and was, not long afterwards, invested with the Portsmouth command. This station he retained during the usually allotted period, having passed through it with that dull want of incident consequent to a time of profound peace. On Oct. 18, 1770, he was advanced to the rank of vice-admiral of the blue, and on the 24th ensuing of the white, as he was to that of the red on March 31, 1775; and, lastly, on Jan. 29, 1778, to be admiral of the blue. As he had no appointment posterior to that at Portsmouth, which we have already related, our farther account of this gentleman is necessarily confined to a mere memorandum of his several promotions, among which we must not forget to record, that he was, early in the year 1771, invested with the order of the Bath.

He died in the year 1779; and, notwithstanding the no small degree of obloquy raised against him on a particular occasion, which we have already pointed out, and, in justice to him, endeavoured to controvert, he left behind him, in the opinion of the impartial, unprejudiced and intelligent, the honestly earned character of an able, a judicious, a good officer, and of a worthy man.

PITMAN, John.—This gentleman was, on Feb. 8, 1742-3, appointed from the Cruiser sloop to be captain of the Aldborough, as successor to capt. Toms, who then removed into the Alderney. During the ensuing spring he was employed as a cruiser, in which occupation he had the good fortune to capture a valuable French prize from Martinico, bound to Havre de Grace. A gentleman of the same name was in the ensuing year commander of the Saltash sloop of war on the coast of Scotland, and has been improperly confounded with this person; but the former never attained to the rank of captain, the Saltash having overset not long after the time just mentioned; the commander and the major part, if not the whole of the crew, perished on that unfortunate occasion. Little other mention is made of capt. Pitman, except that, in 1745 and 1746, he was one of the members of the court-martials convened for the trials of the officers charged with misconduct in the Mediteranean, and commanded a ship, we believe the Canterbury, at the siege of Cape Breton. He died in England on the 5th of March, 1752.

POWLET,

POWLET, Charles.—The firft mention we find made of this gentleman is his promotion, on Oct. 10, 1743, to be captain of the Biddeford frigate. He continued till the beginning of 1748 in the fame veffel; he was then on the Jamaica ftation under commodore Dent, and is faid to have been afterwards promoted to the Falmouth. At the end of that year he commanded the Tilbury, of fixty guns, one of the fquadron under the orders of Mr. Knowles, who had arrived at Jamaica fome time before to take the command, and promoted him to the fhip he was then captain of. His conduct in the encounter with the Spanifh admiral, Riggio, was, and, as it proved, very undefervedly cenfured by his commander, who did not openly and regularly prefer a fpecific charge againft him, but threw out many infinuations which were at laft productive of a court-martial. The inveftigation of his conduct ended much more honourably for him, than it had done juft before for his commander-in-chief: fuffice it to fay, he was moft honourably acquitted. No other particulars relative to this gentleman have come to our knowledge*, except that, during a confiderable part of the fucceeding war, he was regulating captain at Winchefter. He died April 4, 1762.

PRATTEN, Edward, — we find firft mentioned as lieutenant of the Suffolk, under capt. Knowles, at the well-known and unfortunate attack on La Guira. In confequence of his gallantry difplayed on that occafion, he was promoted to be commander of the Pembroke Prize; and from thence was, by the fame patron, on the 2d of June, 1743, made captain of the Eltham. Out of this fhip he was, not long afterwards, promoted to the command of the Suffolk, a third rate. The only occafion on which we find his name fubfequently mentioned during the then exifting war, is, that in the month of December 1747, he was one of the members of the court-martial affembled for the trial of captain Fox, of the Kent. Soon after the ratification of the treaty of peace, that is to fay, in the

---

* When earl Temple was on the point of quitting the admiralty-board, in 1756, captain Powlet was appointed to the Royal William, and was ordered to repair to town to take up his commiffion; but on his arrival was told there was no commiffion for him. The fact was, the junior lords of the admiralty took upon them to fupercede the commiffion in order to ferve friends of their own, as earl Temple went no more to the board.

month of January 1749, he appears to have commanded the Affurance, of forty-four guns; and in the month of April or May following to have removed into the Blandford frigate. After this time no particular notice is taken of him till about the month of April 1751, when he was made captain of the Prince Edward.

He removed, about the month of July following, into the Charlotte yacht; and we believe him to have retained this honourable, though far from confpicuous ftation, for fome confiderable time, no notice being taken of him till after the commencement of the war with France, in 1756. We believe him to have been one of the officers fent out to the Mediterranean, for the purpofe of fupplying the place of thofe who were ordered to England as evidences on the trial of Mr. Byng, as we find him reported to have been captain of the Buckingham, on that ftation, when the fquadron was, at the conclufion of the year, commanded by fir Edward Hawke. About the month of July 1757, he removed into the Intrepid, and in the following year was commanding-officer of a fmall fquadron, ordered to cruife to the weftward. In this occupation he was extremely diligent and active; qualities which did not pafs unrewarded, many prizes having been made by the fhips under his orders; one of them, the Raifonable, a French man of war, mounting fixty-four guns, which was captured, after a fmart action, by the Dorfetfhire and Achilles. In 1759 he again ferved in the Mediterranean, and as a private captain in the fquadron under the orders of Mr. Bofcawen. He was prefent at the total defeat of Mr. De la Clue's fquadron in the month of Auguft; but having failed to affift captain Kirke in the deftruction of the Ocean, the French commander's fhip, which had ran afhore to preferve herfelf from being captured, he was fuperfeded by the admiral, and not again employed. It does not appear that any court-martial was held for the purpofe of enquiring into his conduct: and the whole of the charge advanced by the admiral, that was made public, is framed in the following flight and apparently indecifive terms. "I fent the Intrepid and America to deftroy the Ocean; captain Pratten having anchored could not get in, but captain Kirke performed that fervice alone." Neverthelefs he remained under total fufpenfion, deprived even of his half-pay, till the year 1762, when he was so far restored as to be put on the list of captains with his former rank. He did not, however, long survive this circumstance, dying on the 22d of October, 1763.

SAUMAREZ, Philip. — This gentleman was the descendant of a very respectable family in Guernsey*. We find him first mentioned in the service as one of the lieutenants of the Centurion †, under Mr. Anson, at the time he proceeded in that ship on his expedition to the South Seas. On the promotion of Mr. Saunders to be commander of the Trial sloop ‡, he became the first lieunant to the commodore: and having already related at some length, in our account of that gentleman, the leading and most prominent occurrences of the voyage, we shall only remark, that at the time that ship was blown from her moorings off the island of Tinian, as already related in the account just mentioned §, Mr. Saumarez was the commanding officer then on board. Nothing short of the most indefatigable exertions, for the space of nineteen days, could have brought back that ship to her former station, considering the weakness of her crew, for, notwithstanding their number little exceeded one hundred persons, officers and all included, many of the people were, as a still farther encrease of their difficulties, in a very weak though convalescent state.

The capture of the Caba-Donga, better or more generally known as the Manilla galleon, is still fresh enough in the memory of all, to render needless any ‖ addition to the account of that event, which has been already given. Mr. Saumarez, who had acted with the greatest activity and spirit during the action, was appointed commander of the prize, by Mr. Anson; from the date of which commission, on the 21st of June, 1743, he took rank as a captain in the navy. The subsequent events are immaterial. The prize having been disposed of by the commodore to the Chinese mer-

---

* He was the son of Mathew De Saumarez, of the island of Guernsey, esq. and Ann Durell, his wife, a lady from Jersey: he was born on the 17th of November, 1710.

† At which time he was thirty years old, and had served in the royal navy upwards of fourteen years.

‡ Which vessel he himself acted as commander of, *pro tempore*, during the illness of captain Saunders.

§ Vol. iv. p. 113.

‖ Vol. iv. p. 117.

chants, Mr. Saumarez returned to England in a private capacity. His firſt appointment after his arrival was to the Sandwich, a ſecond rate; in which ſtation he had no opportunity of diſplaying that gallant ſpirit which was inherent in him, and which at laſt, moſt unfortunately for his country and his friends, produced his very untimely death.

Early in the month of October 1746, he was made captain of the Nottingham, a ſhip of ſixty guns, as ſucceſſor to lord Graham, who was taken ſuddenly ill; and being ordered out on a cruiſe* fell in with, on the 11th, a French ſhip of war, called the Mars, mounting ſixty-four guns, the lower tier of which were braſs. We cannot help remarking, that we do not think ſufficient juſtice was done this brave man, in the account officially publiſhed of this tranſaction, which is related, in the Gazette, in the following ſlight and curſory manner:

"Plymouth, October the 21ſt. His majeſty's ſhip the Nottingham has brought in hither the Mars, a French man of war, of ſixty-four guns and five hundred and fifty men, which ſhe met with off Cape Clear, and took after an engagement of two hours, wherein the Nottingham loſt but three or four men, the Mars forty."

In the early part of the year enſuing, he continued under the command of Mr. Anſon, and was preſent with him at the encounter with the French ſquadron under Jonquiere. Having received very trivial injury in the preceding action, he was one of the three commanders diſpatched in the evening, after the admiral brought to, in purſuit of the convoy, which was then four or five leagues diſtant. Such, however, were the diligence and activity of Mr. Saumarez and his companions, that the Modeſte and Vigilant, mounting twenty-two guns each, and ſix prizes of inferior conſequence, were captured by them on the following day.

We now come to the laſt occurrence which graces the life of this brave and worthy man. The Nottingham was one of the ſhips compoſing the ſquadron ſent out under

---

* Subject to the orders of his former commander and friend, admiral Anſon.

rear-admiral Hawke, in the month of August, to cruise for the French squadron then fitting for sea, to be commanded by monsieur L'Etendiere. After an anxious interval of two months, the enemy, who had for some time delayed their departure, were discovered to the westward of Cape Finisterre. In the action which consequently took place, Mr. Saumarez bore a very conspicuous share; and eager in the pursuit of the Intrepide and Tonnant, which were endeavouring to make their escape under the cover of the night, he came up with those ships about eight o'clock in the evening. After having engaged them some time, he was unfortunately killed, an accident which terminated an unsuccessful though glorious contest.

Captain Saumarez was, at the time of his death, in the 37th year of his age. His body, being brought to England, was interred in the old church at Plymouth, and a plain but neat monument was erected to his memory in Westminster-abbey, by his surviving brothers and sisters.

SCOTT, Arthur*.—The first intelligence we have been able to procure relative to this gentleman is, that he was on the Mediterranean station one of the lieutenants to

---

* A particular though concise account of the private biography of this gentleman is given in his epitaph.

In a side chancel belonging to Brabourn church, Kent, against the wall, is a marble with this inscription.

Near this place lie the remains of
ARTHUR SCOTT,
Son of George Scott, of Scott Hall,
By Cecilia his 2d wife, daughter of sir Edward Deering, bart.
Of Surrenden in this county.
He married Mary, the eldest daughter of the hon. Charles Compton,
And sister to the present earl of Northampton,
But left no issue.
He was commander of one of his majesty's ships of war 1743,
And commissioner of the royal navy 1754.
He died the 27th day of February 1756,
Aged 37 years and 9 months,
Greatly lamented by his family and friends.
In this world respected by his superiors,
Beloved by all.
An ornament to his profession,
An honour to his country,
A friend to mankind.

Erected 1759, at the desire of Wm. Scott, brother to the deceased.

Mr.

Mr. Mathews, who promoted him to be captain of the Rochester, a fifty-gun ship, on the 4th of August, 1743. We find no subsequent mention made of him till the year 1746, when he was ordered to the Baltic with a convoy, in what ship does not appear, for he quitted the Rochester, to say the latest, in the month of July 1744. In 1747 he was captain of the Lion, and distinguished himself exceedingly under rear-admiral Hawke, in the encounter with the French squadron under L'Etendiere. The French chef d'escadre, payed him, and captain Watson of the Princess Louisa, the highest compliments on account of their gallantry, having attributed his defeat as in great measure owing to their exertions, in stopping and bringing to action the rear of his force till the remainder of the British squadron got up. In 1748 he commanded at the Nore with the rank of commodore*. No other particulars occur relative to this gentleman till the year 1754, when, as related in his epitaph, he retired from the line of active service, on being appointed commissioner of the navy resident at Chatham. He held this office only till the year ensuing, when he was made extra-commissioner of the navy, and died in that office, at the time already stated.

SIMCOE, John. — The name of this gentleman is omitted in many of the navy lists we have seen. In some of them he is stated to have been promoted to the rank of captain in the navy, and appointed to the Kent on the 28th of December, 1743; but Mr. Hardy states his first commission to have been to the Falmouth, agreeing, however, with the date just given. We find no other mention made, not even of the commands held by this gentleman, till the latter end of the year 1756, when he was captain of one of the ships then lying at Portsmouth, and was one of the members of the court-martial convened, in the month of December, for the trial of admiral Byng. Nothing farther occurs relative to him, except that, in 1758, he commanded the Pembroke, one of the fleet ordered in the ensuing year on the expedition against Quebec. He died on board that ship, in the river St. Laurence, on the 14th of May, before any operations had taken place.

---

* In the month of July he was president of the court-martial held on Mr. Tymewell, for killing captain Gregory.

STEPNEY, George,—was, in the early part of his fervice, lieutenant of the Garland frigate on the Mediterranean ftation, from whence he was promoted to be commander of a fmall armed veffel captured by that fhip, and from thence denominated the Garland Prize. On the 11th of June, 1743, he was advanced to be captain of the Neptune, the fhip on board which Mr. Leftock carried his flag at the unfortunate encounter with the French and Spaifh fleets off Toulon. He does not appear to have been in any degree implicated in the fubfequent controverfy and difpute which quickly afterwards took place. He continued captain of the Neptune, if we may believe fome accounts*, till after the year 1745, but is not otherwife mentioned during the continuance of the war. Some time after the ratification of the treaty of peace at Aix la-Chapelle, he was appointed to the Affiftance, and ordered to the coaft of Guinea, on which ftation he died on the 24th of May, 1753.

STEWART, Henry, — was, on the 16th of April, 1743, appointed captain of the Succefs frigate, a veffel at that time on the Weft India ftation. We believe this gentleman to have been put into fome fhip as acting captain for upwards of twelve months previous to the date of his commiffion as juft given, for we find no other perfon of the fame name, at that time, a captain in the navy; and the following circumftance is related by too many hiftorians of undoubted veracity to be queftioned even for a moment.

" In May 1742, two Englifh frigates, commanded by captain Smith † and captain Stewart, fell in with three Spanifh fhips of war near the ifland of St. Chriftopher's. They forthwith engaged, and the action continued till night, by the favour of which, the enemy retired to Porto Rico in a fhattered condition."

On the fuppofed mifbehaviour of captain Gregory, of the Norwich, at the unfortunate attack on La Guira,

---

* Thefe are erroneous, captain Stepney having certainly removed into the Torbay when Mr. Rowley fhifted his flag into the Neptune.
† Vide vol. iv. p. 433.

captain Stewart was ordered into that fhip, *pro'tempore*, as acting captain; and the following, we doubt not well-deferved blunt encomium, is paffed on his conduct, in a private letter written from thence. " The commodore ordered captain Henry Stewart to command the Norwich, who, like a man of honour, foon convinced the Spaniards they had not a coward to deal with." We have not been able to collect any thing farther concerning him, except the appointment firft mentioned, and that he died in England on the 7th of April, 1746.

STURTON, Thomas,—was on the 28th of March, 1743*, appointed captain of the Gofport; but we find no mention made of him after this promotion till the month of May 1744, when, having in the interim been removed into the Roebuck, a fhip of the fame force, he was ordered out with the fquadron under fir Charles Hardy. Having been feparated from the reft of his companions, he fell in with and captured, after a fmart action of an hour's continuance, about fifty leagues to the weftward of Cape Finifterre, a Spanifh regifter-fhip, from St. Sebaftian's bound to La Guira, carrying eighteen guns and one hundred and fifty-feven men. This veffel proved a very valuable prize; her cargo, which confifted principally of bale goods, and cordage, having coft, in Spain, 220,000 pieces of eight.

He arrived at Lifbon, with his prize, on the 6th of May; and though it is by no means improbable he was conftantly employed, he is not again mentioned till the month of December 1749, when he was one of the members of the court-martial affembled at Deptford, for the trial of rear-admiral Knowles. No other particular mention is made of him, except that he died on the 12th of May, 1754.

TAYLOR, Polycarpus,—was appointed lieutenant of the Augufta, a fixty-gun fhip, ordered to the Mediterranean in the year 1739. He was promoted, on the 2d of May, 1743, to be captain of the Fowey frigate, and in this fhip we find him in the following year on the Jamaica ftation. Returning from thence in the month of

---

* Previous to this time he is faid, in fome accounts, to have been commander of the Phaeton firefhip.

June, with the homeward-bound trade under his convoy, he captured, when on his paſſage, a very valuable French ſhip from Martinico, called the Mentor. His ſhip being refitted, it was employed, during the ſummer of the year 1745, as a cruiſer in the Channel, a ſervice in which he acquired no inconſiderable ſhare of renown *. He continued in the Fowey till the year 1747, when, ſtill retaining the ſame command, he was ordered out to America. From thence he proceeded to St. Cnriſtopher's and Jamaica, in the month of January 1747-8, with commodore Knowles.

Soon after the arrival of the ſquadron at the laſt-mentioned ſtation, on which it was intended to remain, captain Taylor was promoted to the Elizabeth, of ſixty-four guns, and attended Mr. Knowles, who was by this time promoted to be a flag officer, on his ſucceſsful expedition againſt Port Louis, and the ſubſequent one againſt St. Jago de Cuba, which, as is well known, did not terminate ſo happily. After the return of the ſquadron to Jamaica,

* The following official account is given of a very ſpirited encounter, in which he appears to have eminently diſtinguiſhed himſelf.

"Admiralty-office, June the 18th.

"His majeſty's ſhip the Fowey, captain Taylor commander, on Wedneſday laſt, the 12th inſtant, about noon, Cape Antifer, on the coaſt of Normandy, bearing S.S.W. ſix leagues, ſaw a ſail giving him chaſe; which ſoon perceiving her miſtake, hawled down her colours and made ſail for the French ſhore. She anchored in the bay of Feſchampe, about five leagues to the eaſtward of Cape Antifer, which being clear of rocks and ſhoals, captain Taylor ventured in; and the privateer obſerving it, cut his cable, ran near to a fort of ſix guns, and came to an anchor. At half an hour paſt four the Fowey anchored within half point blank ſhot of her. She was a ſhip of twenty-ſix guns, and diſcharged them at the Fowey, as did alſo the fort; but upon a boat coming on board ſhe cut her cable and made for the pier. One of her pilots having loſt his head, and the other his thigh, the crew were obliged to truſt to their ſailing; and in about an hour after the Fowey forced the veſſel on ſhore on the beach, about two miles to the eaſtward of Feſchampe. Captain Taylor ſent his boats on board her with directions to burn her, as it was the tide of ebb and no place to lie long at; but finding one hundred and fifty men on board, many ſmall rocks about her, which made ſo great a ſea that it was impoſſible to take the men out, was obliged to leave her upon her broadſide, bilged, her fore-maſt gone, her lee gunnel broke, guns ſpiked, ſmall arms toſſed overboard, and in other reſpects completely diſabled. All the men on board are ſuppoſed to be drowned, except the captain, officers and men brought into Spithead by the Fowey, which are in all not above forty. She was called the Griffin, of St. Malo."

Mr.

Mr. Taylor was taken, by the admiral, to be his own captain in the Cornwall. In this capacity he served in the encounter with the Spanish squadron, under Reggio; but peace taking place almost immediately subsequent to that event, and the admiral, together with the greater part of his squadron, returning quickly afterwards to England, no farther mention is made of any command held by this gentleman till the month of April 1756, when he was appointed captain of the Prince George, a second rate. He did not long continue in that ship, being, soon afterwards, removed, we believe, into the Royal William. He is said to have commanded some other ships subsequent to this time[*]; and also to have been, for one or two cruises, captain to sir Edward Hawke. In 1762 he retired from the service with the rank and half-pay of a rear-admiral on the superannuated list, and continued ever afterwards to live totally in retirement, principally residing in the bishoprick of Durham, where he died sometime in the course of the year 1780.

TOMS, Peter[†].—We find this gentleman, at the end of the year 1742, commander of the Saltash sloop of war. From this vessel he was, on the 12th of February, 1742-3, promoted to be captain of the Alderney, a twenty-gun ship. He retained this command upwards of two years, as we find him in the same ship, in the month of February 1744-5, stationed off the coast of Portugal. While thus employed, he is mentioned only as the captor of a French merchant-ship, called the Badine, of one hundred and fifty tons, six guns, and thirty-one men, laden with provisions and stores, from Rochelle for the colony of St. Domingo. In 1745 he removed into the Lizard, also a twenty-gun ship; and from thence quickly afterwards into the Hornet [‡], a vessel of the same force with the two preceding: but no anecdotes, or particulars concerning him have come to our knowledge during the time

---

[*] The Ramillies in particular, in 1758. On this account he has been frequently confounded with captain Wittewrong Taylor, who commanded that unfortunate ship at the time it was lost.

[†] He is said to have previously been first lieutenant of the Norfolk.

[‡] This vessel, as well as the Lizard, were both on the sloop establishment, though captain Toms had the rank of a post captain.

he held thofe commands, or, indeed, while he continued in the fervice.

In 1762 he retired from it altogether, and was put on the fuperannuated lift with the rank and half-pay of a rear-admiral; but did not long enjoy this honourable kind of penfion, dying at his houfe in Marfham-ftreet, Weftminfter, on the 20th of February, 1763.

TYRREL, Richard.—This gentleman we believe to have been introduced into the navy under the patronage and care of that brave and ever-to-be-revered character fir Peter Warren, who was his uncle. His firft appointment in the rank of poft captain was, according to Mr. Hardy, to the Superbe; but, from more authentic information, we find his firft commiffion, which is dated on the 26th of December, 1743, was to the Launcefton*.

No circumftances, whatever, relative to this gentleman are known to us till the year 1755, when he was captain of the Ipfwich, of fixty-four guns, one of the fhips put into commiffion at Plymouth, we believe in confequence of

---

* In 1748 he commanded a frigate in the Weft Indies, where a very difagreeable affair, which might have terminated very ferioufly, occurred; and on which occafion his behaviour is recorded in the following very handfome terms by Smollet.

" In the beginning of the year the governor of Barbadoes having received intelligence that the French had begun to fettle the ifland of Tobago, fent thither captain Tyrrel, in a frigate, to learn the particulars. That officer found above three hundred men already landed, fecured by two batteries and two fhips of war, and in daily expectation of a farther reinforcement from the marquis de Caylus, governor of Martinique, who had publifhed an ordinance, authorizing the fubjects of the French king to fettle the ifland of Tobago, and promifing to defend them from the attempts of all their enemies. This affurance was in anfwer to a proclamation, iffued by Mr. Greenville, governor of Barbadoes, and ftuck up in different parts of the ifland, commanding all the inhabitants to remove, in thirty days, on pain of undergoing military execution.

" Captain Tyrrel, with a fpirit that became a commander in the Britifh navy, gave the French officers to underftand, that his moft chriftian majefty had no right to fettle the ifland, which was declared neutral by treaties; and that if they would not defift, he fhould be obliged to employ force in driving them from their new fettlement. Night coming on, and Mr. Tyrrel's fhip falling to leeward, the French captains feized that opportunity of failing to Martinique; and next day the Englifh commander returned to Barbadoes, having no power to commit hoftilities."

the apprehended rupture with France. Hiſtory, and every other kind or ſpecies of information, are again ſilent concerning him, till his appointment to the Buckingham, which took place not long after the declaration of war. He was ſoon ordered to the Weſt Indies, where we find him, in 1758, in company with the Cambridge, attacking a ſmall fort in Grand Ance Bay, in the iſland of Martinico. It was deſtroyed and levelled with the ground: no material loſs or injury being ſuſtained by the gallant aſſailants: three out of four privateers which lay under its protection were deſtroyed; the fourth being carried to ſea with them, was converted into a tender. An anſwer made by this brave and worthy man, to his men, who, fluſhed with victory, wiſhed to deſtroy a neighbouring village, is too honourable to his humane diſpoſition to be ſuppreſſed.

" Gentlemen (ſaid he) it is beneath us to render a number of poor people miſerable by deſtroying their habitations and little conveniences of life. Brave Engliſhmen ſcorn to diſtreſs even their enemies when not actually in arms againſt them."

In the month of November he diſtinguiſhed himſelf in that very memorable and well-known encounter with the Floriſſant, of ſeventy-four guns, and two large French frigates, the account of which we ſhall give as related in his own letter to commodore Moore, then commander-in-chief on that ſtation.

" Agreeable to your orders I ſailed on Thurſday night from St. John's road; the next morning I got between Guadalupe and Montſerrat, and gave chace to a ſail we eſpied in the N.W. which proved to be his majeſty's ſloop Weazle; upon enquiry, having found that ſhe had not met his majeſty's ſhip Briſtol, 'I ordered captain Boles to come on board for directions as to his farther proceedings.

" While his orders were writing out, we diſcovered a fleet of nineteen ſail W.S.W. ſtanding to the S.S.W. upon which we immediately gave chace with all the ſail we could poſſibly croud. About two o'clock we diſcovered that they were convoyed by a French man of war of ſeventy-four guns and two large frigates. About half an hour after two the Weazle got ſo cloſe as to receive a whole broadside from the seventy-four gun ship, which did her little or no damage. I then made the signal to call the Weazle off, and gave her lieutenant orders not to go near the seventy-four gun ship, or the frigates, as the smallest of the latter was vastly superior to him in force. By following this advice he could not come to fire a shot during the whole action, neither, indeed, could he have been of any service.

"While I made all the sail I could, they were jogging on under their fore-sails and top-sails, and when we came up within half gun-shot, they made a running fight, firing their stern-chace. The frigates, sometimes raking fore and aft, annoyed me very much, but also so retarded their own way, that I got up with my bowsprit almost over the Florissant's stern. Finding I could not bring the enemy to a general action, I gave the Buckingham a yaw under his lee, and threw into him a noble dose of great guns and small arms, at about the distance of half musket-shot, which he soon after returned, and damaged my rigging, masts and sails considerably. The largest frigate being very troublesome, I gave him a few of my lower-deck pills, and sent him running like a lusty fellow, so that he never returned into action again. The Florissant likewise bore away, by which means he got under my lee and exchanged three or four broadsides (endeavouring still to keep at a distance from me) which killed and wounded some of my men. I presume however we did him as much damage, as our men were very cool, took good aim, were under good discipline, and fought with a true English spirit.

"An unlucky broadside from the French made some slaughter on my quarter-deck, at the same time I myself was wounded, losing three fingers of my right hand, and receiving a small wound over my right eye, which, by the effusion of blood, blinded me for a little while: I also had several contusions from splinters; but recovering immediately, I would not go off the deck till the loss of blood began to weaken me. The master and lieutenant of marines were dangerously wounded at the same time.

"I called to my people to stand by, and do their duty, which they promised with the greatest chearfulness. I then went down and got the blood stopped, but returned upon deck

deck again; till finding the ſtrain made my wounds bleed afreſh, I ſent for the firſt lieutenant, and told him to take the command of the deck for a time. He anſwered me that he would run alongſide the Floriſſant yard-arm and yard-arm, and fight to the laſt gaſp. Upon which I made a ſpeech to the men exhorting them to do their utmoſt, which they chearfully promiſed, and gave three cheers.

" I went down a ſecond time much more eaſy than before. Poor Mr. Marſhall was as good as his word; he got board and board with the Floriſſant, and received a broadſide from her, which killed him as he was encouraging the men; thus he died an honour to his country, and to the ſervice. The ſecond lieutenant then came upon deck and fought the ſhip bravely, yard-arm and yard-arm. We ſilenced the Floriſſant for ſome time; and ſhe hawled down her colours, but after that, fired about eleven of her lower tier, and gave us a volley of ſmall arms; which our people returned with great fury, giving her three broadſides, ſhe not returning even a ſingle gun. Captain Troy at the ſame time, at the head of his marines, performed the ſervice of a brave and gallant officer, clearing the Floriſſant's poop and quarter-deck, and driving her men, like ſheep, down their main-deck. Our top men were not idle, they plied their hand-grenades and ſwivels to excellent purpoſe. It is impoſſible to deſcribe the uproar and confuſion the French were in.

" It being now dark, and we having all the rigging in the ſhip ſhot away, the enemy ſeeing our condition, took the opportunity, ſet her fore-ſail and top-gallant-ſails, and ran away. We endeavoured to purſue her with what rags of ſails we had left, but to no purpoſe. Thus we loſt one of the fineſt two-deck ſhips my eyes ever beheld.

" I cannot beſtow encomiums too great on the people and officers behaviour, and I hope you will ſtrenuouſly recommend the latter to the lords of the admiralty, as they richly deſerve their favour. Notwithſtanding the great fatigue the ſhip's company had experienced during the day, they chearfully continued up all night knotting and ſplicing the rigging and bending the ſails.

" I flatter myſelf, when you reflect that one of the ſhips of your ſquadron, with no more than ſixty-five guns

(as

(as you know some of them were disabled last January, and not supplied) and four hundred and seventy-two well men at quarters, should beat three French men of war, one of seventy-four guns, and seven hundred men; another of thirty eight guns, three hundred and fifty men; and one of twenty-eight guns, two hundred and fifty men; you will not think we have been deficient in our duty. If we had had the good luck to join the Bristol it would have crowned all.

"Captain Boles being on board the Buckingham I gave him directions to go down and superintend the lower deck, which he performed with great alacrity.

"As we have been so greatly damaged in our masts, yards, sails and rigging, particularly our masts, I have thought proper to send the carpenter of the Buckingham, as he can better give you an account, by word of mouth, of what sishes we shall want, than I can in many words of writing.

"Before I conclude I cannot help representing to you the inhuman, ungenerous and barbarous behaviour of the French during the action: no rascally piccaroon, or pirate, could have fired worse stuff into us than they did; such as square bits of iron, old rusty nails, and, in short, every thing that could tend to the destruction of men; a specimen of which, please God, I shall produce to you upon my arrival.

"I send you inclosed a list of the slain and wounded.

"Killed; 1 officer, 5 seamen, 1 marine.

"Slightly wounded; 2 midshipmen, 26 seamen, 3 marines.

"Died of their wounds; 1 midshipman, 1 seaman."

"N. B. The officer killed was Mr. George Marshall, first lieutenant; and the officers wounded were, captain Tyrrell; Mr. Matthew Winterborne, master; and Mr. Harris, lieutenant of marines [*]."

---

[*] Smollet adds, on what authority we know not, though we do not disbelieve the truth of it, that the number of slain on board the Florissant did not fall short of one hundred and eighty, and that her wounded are said to have exceeded three hundred. She was so disabled in her hull that she could hardly be kept afloat until she reached Martinique, where she was repaired; and the largest frigate, together with the loss of forty men, received so much damage as to be for some time quite unserviceable.

No farther particular mention is made of Mr. Tyrrell during the time he continued in the Weſt Indies, from whence he returned in the month of March, with the diſpatches from commodore Moore, containing an account of the attack made, in the month of January preceding, on the iſland of Martinico; and that more ſucceſsful one, which ſucceeded it, on Guadaloupe. It is almoſt needleſs to add, he was moſt gracciouſly and affectionately received by his majeſty, to whom he was introduced, immediately on his arrival, by lord Anſon.

In the month of Auguſt following he was appointed captain of the Foudroyant, a ſhip of eighty guns, taken not long before from the French, and eſteemed, at that time, the fineſt of her rate, in the Britiſh ſervice. How long he continued in this command does not appear, nor do we find any other particulars related, concerning him, during the time he remained a private captain. In the month of October 1762, he was advanced to the rank of rear-admiral of the white, which was the firſt flag he ever held; but does not appear to have been actually employed till after the concluſion of the war, when he was appointed commander-in-chief on the Antigua ſtation. By his vigilance and attention, he, in 1765, defeated a ſcheme the French had in agitation, of forming a ſettlement on ſome of the iſlands in the neighbourhood of Cayenne, the particulars of which diſcovery he carefully tranſmitted to government. This is the only material mention we find made of him during the time he held the above command, which he quitted in the follwing year. Unhappily dying on board the Princeſs Louiſa, his flag ſhip, when on his return to England, on the 27th of June, 1766[*], his corpſe was, at his own deſire, thrown into the ſea[†].

WATKINS,

---

[*] His widow married, in 1767, Robert Fulton, eſq. His mother died in 1771, at the very advanced age of 99, in Little Ormond-ſtreet.

[†] A very magnificent monument was erected to his memory in Weſtminſter-abbey, of which the following is a deſcription, with the epitaph ſubjoined.

It was deſigned and executed by that ingenious artiſt Mr. Read, who was pupil to the celebrated Mr. Roubiliac. On the top of the monument is an archangel deſcending with a trumpet, ſummoning the admiral to eternity from the ſea. The clouds moving and ſeparating diſcover the celeſtial light, and choir of cherubs, who appear ſinging praiſes to the Almighty Creator. The back ground repreſenting
darkneſ.

WATKINS, Richard,—from being commander of the Pembroke Prize, was removed into a bomb-ketch, and, on the 24th of February, 1743, promoted to be captain of the Eltham *. We have no information whatever

---

darknefs. The admiral's countenance, with his right hand to his breaft, is expreffive of confcientious hope, while the pofition of his left arm appears fignificant of his feeing fomething awful and impreffive. He appears rifing out of the fea from behind a large rock, whereon are placed his arms, with the emblems of valour, prudence, and juftice. The fea is difcerned over the rock at the extremity of fight, where clouds and water feem to join. On one fide of it an angel has written this infcription, " The fea fhall give up her dead, and every one fhall be rewarded according to their works." In her left hand is a celeftial crown, the reward of virtue; and her right hand is extended towards the admiral with a countenance full of joy and happinefs. Hibernia, leaning on a globe, with her finger on that part of it where his body was committed to the fea, appears lamenting the lofs of her favourite fon, in all the agony of heart felt grief. On one fide the rock is the Buckingham (the admiral's fhip) with the mafts appearing imperfect. On the other fide a large flag with the trophies of war; near which is the following infcription.

> Sacred to the memory of Richard Tyrrel, efq. who was defcended from an ancient family in Ireland, and died rear-admiral of the white on the 26th day of June, 1766, in the 50th year of his age. Devoted from his youth to the naval fervice of his country, and being formed under the difcipline and animated by the example of his renowned uncle, fir Peter Warren, he diftinguifhed himfelf as an able and experienced officer in many gallant actions, particularly on the 3d of November, 1758, when commanding the Buckingham, of fixty-fix guns, and four hundred and feventy-two men, he attacked and defeated three French fhips of war, one of which was the Floriffant, of feventy-four guns, and feven hundred men: but the Buckingham being too much difabled to take poffeffion of her after fhe had ftruck, the enemy, under the cover of the night, efcaped. In this action he received feveral wounds, and loft three fingers of his right hand. Dying on his return to England from the Leeward Iflands, where he had for three years commanded a fquadron of his majefty's fhips, his body, according to his own defire, was committed to the fea, with the proper honours and ceremonies.

* Many accounts fay the Durfley galley; but this is a miftake, occafioned merely by a confufion between this gentleman and captain R. Watkins, his brother, who was appointed to the Durfley galley, and

ever of the commands held by this gentleman, or the stations on which he was employed, till the year 1756, when he commanded the Blandford, of 20 guns, but how long previous to that time we know not; as also whether he was captain of that vessel at the time it was captured, in 1755, on its passage to Carolina, with Mr. Littleton, the newly appointed governor of that settlement, on board as a passenger. It was, as is well known, immediately released by order of the French court. This gentleman was tried by a court-martial at Antigua, in 1757, on a charge of having disobeyed orders; which being proved, he was sentenced to be dismissed the service. He was afterwards restored to his rank, but not employed, being superannuated on the rank and half-pay of a rear-admiral, on the 15th of March, 1763. He died in England in the course of the month of April 1770.

WATKINS, John,—was the brother to the gentleman last-mentioned. He was first, commander of the Carcase bomb, and from thence, on the 4th of August, 1743, was advanced to the rank of post captain, and appointed to the Dursley Galley frigate; from this vessel he was quickly promoted to the Feversham; and from thence to the Newcastle, one of the Mediterranean fleet, under Mr. Mathews; in which ship he afterwards returned to England. His subsequent occupations and services are unknown*, as well as all other particulars con-

---

and of whom we shall presently speak. The fact is, he had been some time before appointed acting captain of the Eltham, as at the attack of La Guira, which took place on the 19th of February, he certainly was in that capacity, and the following return of the damages sustained by the Eltham will very forcibly prove, how considerable and honourable a share that ship, which only carried forty guns, held in the above unsuccessful, and. indeed, disastrous encounter.

" Eltham, captain Watkins, damages received. Forty-four shot through the hull, thirteen between wind and water; the main-mast shot in five places, the mizen-top-mast through and through, the mizen-yard cut in two; one shot in the bowsprit; the booms, spare top-masts and fishes cut to pieces; some guns dismounted, three of which are quite unserviceable; fourteen men killed, fifty-five wounded."

* We must except the following little anecdote concerning his service, which is far too honourable to his character to be omitted.

He

concerning him, except that he died in England on the 24th of February, 1757.

YOUNG, James,—was, in the earlier part of his service, a midshipman on board the Gloucester, at that time commanded by captain Clinton, we believe the ship he had his broad pendant on board of, as commodore and commander-in-chief on the Mediterranean station. In 1739 he was lieutenant of the Lancaster, captain Cayley; in which ship we believe him to have continued till Mr. Mathews was appointed commander-in-chief on the Mediterranean station. Mr. Young was then appointed to the same station under him, and was advanced first to be commander of the Salamander bomb-ketch; and on May 16, 1743, was promoted to be captain of the Kennington, of twenty guns. His first appointment as a post captain is erroneously stated, by Mr. Hardy and others, to have been to the Neptune, a second rate: whatever might have been the subsequent commands or stations on which he was employed, we have not been able to collect any

---

He was one of the commanders under the orders of captain Powlett, afterwards duke of Bolton, when detached by Mr. Mathews to Civita Vecchia, as related vol. iii. p. 260. Two of the Papal gallies were then in the port, having put in there while the British ships lay off, and before they had orders to proceed to extremities. It was, not long afterwards, determined to attempt burning them in the harbour. Two feluccas coming down the Tyber were therefore detained, and fitted up as fireships for that purpose: the boats of the different ships were ordered to attend them; the whole enterprise to be under the command of captain Watkins, who was the junior captain, and to whom, according to the general custom of the service, the direction of such an undertaking, as it were of right, belonged. Captain Hodsell, who was also present, and was a senior officer, insisted that the command should be entrusted to him. Captain Watkins of course yielded up his claim, but insisted on attending as a volunteer. When the boats and feluccas had proceeded to the very entrance of the harbour, the centinels were heard passing the word, and the bells ringing the hour: every thing else was quiet and appeared to bespeak security. Captain Hodsell, however, alarmed at the foregoing circumstance, ordered his people to lay on their oars, and asked the advice of captain Watkins, Whether it would be prudent to proceed? the latter firmly replied, He was not there to give advice, but to obey orders. The same question was afterwards proposed to other officers of less rank, who unanimously returned the same answer. But captain Hodsell thinking the enemy had taken the alarm, ordered the boats, &c. to return.

parti-

particulars concerning him till the month either of March or April 1748; he was then appointed to the Dunkirk, one of the ships which we believe to have been employed in the Mediterranean. In the month of February 1752, he was made captain of the Jason; and after an interval of more than three years, during which time we again remain unacquainted with any particulars concerning him, was, in the month of July or August 1755, appointed to the Newark, of eighty guns. He did not long retain the same command, being, in the month of October following, made captain of the Intrepid. He was one of the commanders ordered out in the ensuing spring, under the unfortunate admiral Byng, to the Mediterranean, and was one of those who were most materially engaged, having had forty-eight men killed and wounded, a loss greater than that sustained by any ship in the squadron, the Defiance excepted. At the very commencement of the action the Intrepid had her fore-topmast shot away, so that it hung in the fore-sail, and backing it, rendered the ship totally unmanageable, the foretack and braces being cut at the same time*. Captain Young being ordered home not long afterwards as an evidence on the trial of admiral Byng, was one of those whose testimony, though given with the greatest candour†, appears to have borne hardest on that gentleman,

in

---

* Mr. Byng states this circumstance, and its consequences, at some length in his dispatches, see vol. iv. p. 150, et seq.
† See vol. iv. p. 177, his evidence was precisely as follows.
"He did not perceive that the loss of his fore-top mast occasioned any impediment to the rear division in going down and engaging, nor that it endangered any ship being on board him, as he was so far to leeward that they might have wore clear of him and gone down to the enemy, as they did about three quarters of an hour afterwards; that if the rear division had bore down as the van did, they might have come up as near the enemy; and if they had bore in a line of battle abreast, there would have been no danger of their being on board each other, as every ship appeared to him to have room to wear. He deposed also, that there was no possibility of bringing on a general engagement without the admiral and rear division had gone down right before the wind upon the enemy, and carried more sail than the van, their distance being greater; he said his ship was in a bad condition, so that all her ground tier of powder was spoiled; that she was also indifferently manned,

in his most assailable point, his want of that proper spirit of enterprize, which is at all times an essential to constitute a good and complete officer. In 1757 he commanded the Burford, one of the fleet sent, under sir E. Hawke, on the expedition against Rochfort.

The next interesting notice we find taken of this gentleman was not till the year 1759, when he was on board the Mars, of seventy-four guns, with the rank of commodore. In this ship he was present at the glorious encounter between the British fleet, under sir Edward Hawke, and that of France, commanded by monsieur Conflans: but being in the rear at the commencement of the action, could not otherwise manifest his spirit and zeal than by crowding all the sail he could to get up* with the commander-in-chief, a point he had 'nearly effected, when darkness put a premature period to the contest. Immediately after the action, he was detached, by sir E. Hawke, to Quiberon Bay, with a squadron of five ships to search for any stragglers, or disabled ships, belonging to the enemy's fleet, which might have escaped out of the battle; but in this employment he was not fortunate enough to meet with that success his diligence and gallantry merited. Captain Young continued in the Mars, we believe, nearly till the conclusion of the war; and in the month of S ptember 1761†, being then on a cruise off Cape Finisterre, is officially mentioned as the captor of a stout French priv teer belonging to St. Maloe's, called the Amarante. Towards the conclusion of the year he was advanced to be rear-admiral of the red; but peace being, as is well known, shortly afterwards concluded, he does not appear to have accepted of any command. On the 28th of October, 1770, he was advanced to be vice-admiral of the white; as he was farther, on the 31st of March, 1775, to be vice-admiral of the red.

---

manned, but that none of these defects were a detriment to him in the engagement. He deposed also, that the French fleet went off, to all appearance, without damage, except the loss of one top-sail-yard; and that our fleet was not in a condition to attack them at any time before the council of war."

* Biog. Nav. vol. iv. p. 285.
† In this year he was commodore of a small squadron of observation stationed off Havre.

On the commencement of the American war Mr. Young was appointed to command at Antigua, whither he immediately repaired, having his flag on board the Portland. He appears to have been fingularly alert, and to have met with a very confiderable fhare of fuccefs in the capture of a multitude of veffels, many of them of no inconfiderable value. In the year 1778 he quitted his command, and returned to England, where he arrived on the 3d of July, on board the Portland: fhortly after which he was advanced to be admiral of the white. From this time he became no more connected with the public fervice, living in perfect retirement, refpected, honoured, and revered by all naval commanders, who, knowing his manifold deferts, were beft qualified to eftimate their worth and confequence. He died in London, at an advanced age, on the 24th of January, 1789, having furvived his brother, William Young, efq. only twelve days.

1744.

AMHERST, John, — was the third fon of Jeffery Amherft, efq. a bencher of Lincoln's Inn, and Elizabeth his wife, daughter of Thomas Kerril, of Hadlow, in the county of Kent, efq. After having acted as midfhipman on board the Somerfet, about the year 1738, under rear-admiral Haddock, he was fometime afterwards promoted by him to the rank of lieutenant, and ferved progreffively, on the Mediterranean ftation, on board the Dragon and Sunderland. He afterwards acquired the patronage and protection of lord Anfon, with whom he is very erroneoufly reported, by fome, to have proceeded on his voyage round the world, and to have been, under the fame aufpices, promoted to the rank of lieutenant. His firft commiffion, as a poft captain, was to the Succefs, bearing date December the 29th, 1744; from thence he is faid to have been removed, about the month of September following, into the South Sea Caftle. At the latter end of the war he ferved in the Eaft Indies under Mr. Griffin, but as captain of what particular fhip is not mentioned. Returning from thence immediately on the arrangement of

peace

peace taking place, if not previous to the actual ceffation of hoftilities in that quarter of the world, we find him afterwards, in 1750, one of the witneffes examined on the trial of Mr. Griffin, at Portfmouth, whofe behaviour his evidence criminated in no flight degree.

After this time we do not find the fmalleft mention made of him, till the beginning of the year 1753, when he was appointed captain of the Mars, of fixty-four guns, commiffioned as a guardfhip at Plymouth. When a rupture was, in 1755, daily expected with France, and it was refolved in confequence, by government, to difpatch a fquadron to North America, under the orders of Mr. Bofcawen, the Mars, of which fhip Mr. Amherft ftill continued captain, was one of the fleet allotted for that fervice: he accordingly failed with the admiral above-mentioned, in the month of April; but in going into Halifax, in the month of June, the Mars was unfortunately loft, through the ignorance of the pilot, who was conducting it into the harbour. The crew, together with the guns, as well as a confiderable part of the ftores, were faved; and Mr. Amherft being, according to the rules and cuftom of the fervice, tried by a court-martial, was moft honourably acquitted of all blame. Immediately after his return to England he was appointed to the Deptford, of fifty guns, one of the fleet difpatched, in the enfuing fpring, for the Mediterranean, under the orders of the unfortunate Mr. Byng. The Deptford was in no degree concerned in the encounter with the French fleet off Toulon, for, being the fmalleft in the Britifh fquadron, and confequently the leaft capable of refifting the attacks of an heavy French fhip of war, Mr. Byng made the fignal for captain Amherft to quit the line, in order, as he himfelf urged, by way of explanation for this conduct, that the number of fhips drawn into each line might be equal.

After the Intrepid, captain Young, was difabled, the Deptford was ordered to take her ftation; but the action had then ceafed, and was not, as is well known, afterwards renewed. Captain Catford, who commanded the Captain, of feventy guns, being ordered home as an evidence on the trial of Mr. Byng, Mr. Amherft was appointed his fucceffor; and returning to England at the

clofe

close of the year, was, in the enfuing spring, ordered on the projected expedition against Louisburg, with the fleet commanded by Mr. Holburne. Here nothing material appears to have occurred. In 1758 he continued to be employed in the same line of service and station, under the better auspices of Mr. Boscawen. After the surrender of the place he convoyed four regiments, and the second battalion of Royal Scots, back to Boston, where they were to be wintered, his brother the general, afterwards lord Amherst, who had commanded at the siege, taking his passage with him. This gentleman is not again mentioned till the beginning of the year 1761, when he was made captain of the Arrogant, a new ship of seventy-four guns, just launched. Little other consequential mention is made of him during the time he continued a private captain; all the information we have been able to collect being merely accounts of him as a member, or sometimes president of some courts-martial of trivial consequence*; an occupation, for which his natural mildness, patience, and inflexible integrity appeared peculiarly to qualify him, though an occupation by no means pleasant.

In 1765 he was very deservedly raised to the rank of a flag-officer, being appointed rear-admiral of the blue; in October 1770, he experienced a second promotion, to be vice-admiral of the same squadron. On the 3d of January, 1776, having before this time been appointed to command at Plymouth, he was made vice-admiral of the white; and, in the ensuing year, vice of the red; and, after a very short interval, admiral of the blue. The latter promotion he did not long enjoy, dying suddenly, as it is said, at Gosport, on the 14th of February, 1778, having, till the time of his death, retained the Plymouth command. Of his character, suffice it to say, that as few men have lived more universally beloved, so have scarcely any died more

---

* To descend to particulars: he was, in July 1761, one of the members of a court-martial held on board his own ship, for the trial of captain James Allen, for the loss of the Speedwell sloop, captured in the harbour of Vigo, by the Achilles French ship of war, of sixty-four guns, when captain Allen was not only most honourably acquitted, but the capture was declared illegal and contrary to the laws of nations. In the month of February 1762, he was president of a court held, on board the Union, for the trial of some deserters.

sincerely lamented*. He married Anne, daughter of Thomas Lindsey, of Portsmouth, esq. but left no issue.

---

* The following description of a monument erected by Jeffery, the late lord Amherst, to the joint memory of this gentleman and his brother, William Amherst, together with the inscriptions, will probably not be unacceptable.

SEVENOAKS Church (Kent).

In the church, on the south side, is an elegant mural monument dedicated to the memory of two distinguished naval and military officers, related to lord Amherst, of Montreal in this county, decorated with naval and military insignia.

On the urn is inscribed as follows,

JOHN AMHERST
Died February 14th, 1778, aged 59.
WILLIAM AMHERST
Died May 13th, 1781, aged 49,
And left two children;
William Pitt,
Born January 14th, 1773;
And Elizabeth Frances,
Born Jan. 23d, 1774.

Beneath, on a beautiful flat marble, is thus inscribed,

Near this place are deposited,
The remains of JOHN AMHERST, esq.
Admiral of the blue squadron of his majesty's fleet,
And of lieutenant general WILLIAM AMHERST,
Colonel of the 32d regiment of foot,
And adjutant-general of his majesty's forces,
Two of the sons
Of Jeffery Amherst, esq. of Brook's-place in this parish,
By Elizabeth his wife.
They entered early into the military line,
And served with ardour in their country's cause.
The rank they obtained by their sovereign's favour
Proved the merit of their public services,
And was equally their honour and reward.
Universally esteemed when living,
Their death is sincerely lamented.
In memory
Of the unvariable and mutual affection of these brothers,
Jeffery, Lord Amherst,
Caused this monument to be erected 1781.

BARRADELL,

BARRADELL, or BORROWDELL, Blumfield,— was, on July 18, 1744*, promoted to be captain of the Phœnix frigate. How long he continued in this veffel is not precifely known, nor do we find any other particular mention made of him till the year 1747, when he commanded the Falkland, of fifty guns, one of the fquadron under the command of vice-admiral Anfon and rear-admiral Warren, which defeated and captured the French fquadron, under De la Jonquiere, in the month of May. We have not been able to procure any other intelligence relative to this gentleman, except that he died on the 25th of November, 1749, having, fome time before, quitted the command of the Falkland. Mr. Hardy, we believe from erroneous information, ftates his death to have taken place on the 29th of April preceding.

BEAVOR, Edmund.—We have no account of this gentleman previous to his appointment, on the 18th of April, 1744, to be captain of the Fox. During the enfuing part of the current year, we do not find any other mention made of him. In the fpring of 1745, he was ftationed as a cruifer in the German Ocean, where he was exceedingly active, and met with fome fuccefs; the moft confequential of which appears to have been, the capture of a very ftout Dunkirk privateer, mounting thirty carriage and fwivel guns, with a crew of one hundred and forty-five men, which he fell in with on the 15th of May; and after purfuing all night, came up with about ten o'clock on the next day. After the commencement of the rebellion in Scotland, which broke out not long after the time above-ftated, captain Beavor was ordered to the northward, where he continued to behave with the fame degree of affiduity, as is apparent from the following official notice taken of him.

" The rebels had formed a fcheme to get into their poffeffion a fhip in Leith road, on board which were fome new pieces of cannon, about twenty-five barrels of powder, and fome firelocks, for the ufe of the king's

---

* Previous to his obtaining the rank of poft captain, he commanded, in 1742, the Shark floop of war, which was at the above time ftationed at Gibraltar as a cruifer.

troops. This veffel, as there was no accefs for her to Leith, was committed to the care of the Fox man of war in the Frith. Four mafters of fhips had undertaken to go off to her with eighteen hands, cut her cable and let her drive till fhe got out of reach of the man of war's guns, when they intended to carry her into Leith harbour. But the night before this was to have been executed, captain Beavor got intelligence of the plot, and immediately putting twenty of his hands on board her, moored her under his own ftern."

The above-mentioned occurrence took place in the middle of October, and captain Beavor was unfortunate enough to furvive it only one month; being out on a cruife, he was unhappily overtaken by a violent gale of wind, in which the Fox foundered, off Dunbar, on the 14th of November, the captain as well as all the crew perifhing with her.

BENTLEY, Sir John.—This gentleman was one of the lieutenants, we believe the fecond, of the Namur, the flag fhip of admiral Mathews, at the time of the encounter off Toulon, in February 1744. He was promoted by that gentleman, on account of his very meritorious conduct on that occafion, after ten years fervice as a lieutenant, to be commander of the Sutherland hofpital fhip, as fucceffor to lord Colville, immediately after the engagement abovementioned. He was, on the 1ft of Auguft, 1744, promoted to the rank of poftcaptain, and appointed to the Burford, of feventy guns. He did not long retain that ftation, being ordered home as an evidence on the different court's-martial which took place in the years 1745 and 6, particularly in that held on captain Burrifh. In 1747 he was taken by admiral Anfon to be his captain, in the Prince George, of ninety guns, and acted in that capacity at the memorable defeat of De la Jonquiere. He continued ever afterwards the favourite of lord Anfon, but quitted the Prince George immediately on the return of the fquadron into port, and was appointed captain of the Defiance, of fixty guns. In this fhip he ferved, during the remainder of the year, under rear-admiral, afterwards lord Hawke, and, confequently, bore his part in the fecond defeat fuftained by the

the enemy, in the month of October, on the difcomfiture of monfieur L'Etendiere.

We find no fubfequent mention made of this gentleman till the month of June 1749, and then only as having been one of the members of the court-martial, held at Portfmouth, on board the Invincible, of which fhip he was then captain, for the trial of lieutenant Couchman and others, who had piratically feized the Chefterfield man of war on the coaft of Africa. In 1755 he commanded the Charlotte yacht, and in the month of June or July 1756, was appointed to the Barfleur, of ninety guns. At the clofe of that year he was one of the members of the court-martial, held at Portfmouth, for the trial of the unfortunate admiral Byng; but is not otherwife particularly noticed till 1758, a circumftance by no means uncommon in the commander of fo capi al a fhip, even in the midft of war, more particularly as the French court always appeared extremely careful of hazarding an action, except in cafes of the laft and higheft emergency. In the year juft mentioned we find him captain of the Invincible, of feventy-four guns, into which fhip he removed from the Barfleur; but how long he had previoufly held that command we do not know. This fhip was one of the fquadron ordered for the expedition againft Louifburg in the month of February; but in turning out, miffed ftays, and unfortunately running afhore on a flat between the Dane and the Horfe of Langfton harbour, to the eaftward of St. Helen's, notwithftanding every poffible affiftance was rendered her, fhe was totally loft*. His next appointment we believe to have been to the Warfpight, of feventy-four guns, which fhip he commanded in 1759, as one of the Mediterranean fquadron under the orders of Mr. Bofcawen. In the action off Cape St. Vincent with the French fquadon under M. De la Clue, which took place on the 19th of Auguft, he had a very fingular opportunity of highly diftinguifhing himfelf, of which he moft gallantly took the greateft advantage. Admiral Bofcawen, in his official account of the action, mentions him in the following very honourable terms. " Captain Bentley, of the Warfpight, was ordered againft the

---

* In confequence of this unhappy accident he was tried by a court-martial, and moft honourably acquitted.

Temeraire,

Temeraire, of seventy-four guns, and brought her off with little damage, the officers and men all on board."

The continuance of the British squadron on that station being no longer necessary after this victory, Mr. Bentley returned to England, and arrived at Spithead, with Mr. Boscawen, on the 15th of September. Being immediately afterwards presented to his majesty, he was most graciously received, and had the honour of knighthood conferred on him, an honour well earned and worthily deserved. The Warspite was, immediately after this, ordered to join the fleet under sir Edward Hawke, with whom he served at the time of the memorable defeat given to the last naval exertion, or, armament of France, during the war; so that he had the fortune which very few, if any, naval commanders, himself excepted, could ever boast of being present at every naval encounter of consequence, or that deserved the name of an action, from his first entrance into the navy to the time of his death. It is almost superfluous to add, he acquitted himself with equal honour to himself, as well as advantage to his country in them all.

Sir John continued in the same ship, and employed, as in the preceding year, under the command of sir Edward Hawke, during the ensuing naval campaign of 1760. But the enemy having, after their late defeat, no naval force of any consequence at sea, nothing material appears to have occurred to him, except his having been overtaken, with other ships, by a violent storm, in the month of September, by which he was obliged to cut away his main and mizen-masts to prevent driving on shore: he, however, got safely into Plymouth, and is not again mentioned as having been at sea as a naval commander. In 1761, or, according to Beatson, in the ensuing year, he was appointed an extra-commissioner of the navy, an office he resigned on being promoted, on the 28th of December, 1763*, to be rear-admiral of the white. No

---

* In consequence of his having, as he may be, in some degree, said to have done, retired from the line of active service, he was not promoted to be a flag officer till upwards of twelve months after others, his juniors in service. as lord Edgcumbe, Mr. Swanton, Mr. Graves, Mr. Parry, and Mr. Keppel, had been raised to that rank.

other

other notice is taken of him, except that, in the month of October 1770, he was progressively promoted to be vice-admiral of the blue and white, and died holding the latter rank on the 14th of December, 1772.

BERTIE, Lord Thomas, — was the fourth son of Robert, first duke of Ancaster, and Albinia his dutchess, daughter to major-general William Farrington, of Chissel-hurst, in the county of Kent. Having, like his noble brother the lord Montague Bertie, of whom we have before shortly spoken*, betaken himself to the naval service, we find him, in 1744, commander of the Drake sloop; from which he was, on March 14, 1743-4, promoted to the rank of post captain in the navy, and appointed to the Phoenix, of twenty guns. In this ship he was immediately afterwards ordered on a cruise in the Channel, where, on the 20th of the ensuing month, he had the good fortune to fall in with and capture, after a smart action of an hours continuance, a French ship mounting twenty-four carriage guns, called the Neptune, bound from Morlaix to Cadiz. Early in the year 1745 he was promoted to the Winchester, of fifty guns, and ordered for the East Indies, where he served under the commodores Barnett and Peyton, as well as subsequent to them, vice-admiral Griffin. The different actions which took place in that part of the world were not only extremely uninteresting, but have been already particularly related in the lives of the commanders-in-chief. His lordship was ordered to England early in the year 1749, but did not live to revisit his native country, dying on board his ship, after having reached the entrance of the Channel, on the 29th of July, 1749†.

BOWDLER,

---

* See vol. v. p. 4, et seq.
† On the 6th of August following his corpse was carried from Portsmouth, in great funeral pomp, to be interred at Chissselhurst, in which church is a beautiful monument, ornamented with an urn, incircled with a festoon of flowers. Between trophies and naval ensigns of war, in statuary marble, a naval engagement is finely expressed in basso relievo, under which is this inscription.

> Sacred to those virtues that adorn a Christian and a sailor, this marble perpetuates the memory of the right honourable lord THOMAS BERTIE, captain in the royal navy. His eminent abilities in his profession, and amiable qualities in private life, rend-

BOWDLER, John,—was a younger fon of Thomas Bowdler, of Queen-fquare, London, efq. by Jane his wife, eldeft daughter of fir Jofeph Martin, knight, a very eminent Turkey merchant. He was born on the 13th of February, 1708-9, and was originally bred to the law. This profeffion he foon quitted, and having entered into the naval fervice, was promoted by Mr. Mathews, at that time commander-in-chief on the Mediterranean ftation, from the rank of lieutenant to be commander of the Carcafe bomb-ketch. This promotion took place in the year 1743. He was, on November 8, 1744, advanced to be captain of the Dartmouth. In this veffel he did not long continue, being probably appointed to it merely for the purpofe of giving him poft, as we find him, early in 1745, captain of the Loweftoffe frigate, on the Mediterranean ftation, and mentioned particularly as the captor of five veffels, four under Genoefe and one under Neapolitan colours, which he carried into Leghorn. He afterwards repaired to the Weft Indies, but in what particular fhip we know not. His health having been greatly impaired during his continuance on that ftation, we believe him not to have accepted any command after his return from thence. He refided during the latter part of his life at Canterbury*. No other particulars whatever are related concerning him, except that he died there on the 19th of April, 1754.

CHADWICK, Richard,—foon after being appointed a commander in the navy was made a regulating captain, and, in the month of Auguft 1743, was appointed to the Drake floop. On the 16th of January following (1744) he was promoted to be captain of the Gibraltar frigate.

---

rendered his death univerfally regretted. Obiit the 29th of July, 1749, ætatis fuæ 29. He was fourth fon of the moft noble Robert, duke of Ancafter and Kefteven, marques and earl of Lindfey, &c. &c. lord great chamberlain of England, by his fecond wife Albinia, daughter of lieutenant-general Farrington.

* He married Caroline, daughter of —— Hicks, efq. by whom he left two children; Caroline, who died, unmarried, Feb. 5, 1770, aged 19; and Anna, who alfo died, unmarried, Sept. 16, 1772, aged 20.

We believe him to have continued in this ſhip till the month of July, when he was removed into the Cornwall, of eighty guns, as captain to vice-admiral Davers, with whom he proceeded out to the Weſt Indies in the month of November. He continued on that ſtation, and alſo captain of the Cornwall, during the remainder of his life; but the naval events during that period, and particularly in that part of the world, were extremely unintereſting. The firſt material mention we find made of him * is in the month of March 1747-8, when the aſſault took place on the town and fort of Port Louis; the Cornwall was ſtationed in the center, and, being the ſtouteſt ſhip, againſt the heavieſt of the enemy's batteries, a private letter, written by an officer on board, dated two days aftei the action, ſtates, " that the crew were ordered not to fire till the ſhip was moored within piſtol ſhot of the fort." This injunction was punctually obeyed, though they, for a confiderable time, had to receive the enemy's fire, which was extremely hot and furious, and did confiderable damage to the maſts and yards of the Cornwall while bearing down. As ſoon as the ſhip was moored, the compliment was returned with ſuch violence and ſucceſs, that the enemy's cannon were ſilenced in a few minutes, ſo that they only fired a ſhot now and then. One ſhot, a thirty-two pounder, from the Cornwall, killed three out of five officers loſt by the enemy on this occaſion; and the execution otherwiſe done by her was equal almoſt to that ſuſtained by the fire of all the other ſhips, for captain Chadwick was ſo near that not only his great guns, but alſo the muſketry from his tops and forecaſtle, did confiderable execution. He did not long ſurvive this event, dying on the 26th of June following. Mr. Hardy, and many manuſcript liſts of naval officers, through miſtake, ſtate this gentleman to have died on the 9th of June, 1746.

COLLINS, Richard,—was, about the month of Auguſt 1743, appointed commander of the Grampus ſloop. On the 7th of July, 1744, he was promoted to be captain

---

* In the month of February 1747-8, he was one of the members of the court-martial, held at Jamaica, for the trial of captain Crookſhanks.

of the Gibraltar, but did not remain in that veffel longer than till the month of September following, when he was advanced to be captain of the Dover, of forty-four guns. Of fo little intereft were his different fubfequent commands and occupations during the remainder of the war, that we find no mention whatever made of him, nor indeed till nearly the recommencement of hoftilities, in 1755, towards the latter end of which year he was appointed captain of the Princefs Royal. About the month of May or June 1756, he was removed into the Terrible, of feventy-four guns, one of the fleet ordered againft Louifburg, under the command of Mr. Holburne, in the year 1757. No other mention is made of him, but that in 1762, he was put on the fuperannuated lift with the rank and half-pay of a rear-admiral. He died in or about the year 1779.

COLVILLE, Alexander, Lord,—the fourth who bore that title, was the eldeft fon of John, the third lord, and Mifs —— Johnfton, daughter of —— Johnfton, efq. of the kingdom of Ireland. Having betaken himfelf to a naval life, we find him, about the year 1743, lieutenant of one of the fhips on the Mediterranean ftation, under the command of Mr. Mathews, who promoted him, firft to be commander of the Sutherland hofpital-fhip, and, on March 6, 1744, to be captain of the Durfley Galley. Before the conclufion of the year he was advanced to the Leopard, of fifty guns, as fucceffor to the lord Forrefter. He remained on the Mediterranean ftation at leaft till 1746, how much longer we are unacquainted; but in April, in the year juft mentioned, we find him to have put into Leghorn, for the purpofe of repairing fome damages he had juft before fuftained in a violent gale of wind. As foon as refitted he was ordered, by vice-admiral Medley, to cruife off the coaft of Genoa, where he captured a French veffel, and deftroyed eight others, three of them under Genoefe, and five under Papal colours. Thefe veffels were principally laden with corn; and their deftruction being highly felt in that country, where a great want of provifions prevailed, the diftrefs occafioned by this circumftance, was a juft punifhment for the perfidy of the inhabitants and their rulers, who, though pretendedly neutral,

neutral, had taken every poffible means to injure the caufe of Britain, and favour the operations of her enemies.

Singular as it may be thought in the life of an officer of his lordfhip's known merit and activity, we find no other mention whatever made of him during the continuance of the war, nor, indeed, after its conclufion, till the year 1753, when he was appointed to the Northumberland, of feventy guns, one of the fhips fitted for a guardfhip at Plymouth. He continued in the fame fhip nearly as long as he remained in active fervice, a period of nine years, and in the progreffive ftations of captain, commodore, and rear-admiral. In 1755 he was one of the commanders difpatched for North America under Mr. Bofcawen; but, the firft information we have of him after the commencement of the war, is in 1757 when he again repaired to North America, on the unfuccefsful expedition fent againft Louifburg, under admiral Holburne; as he did again, in 1758, on that more fortunate one which then took place, commanded by Mr. Bofcawen. After the reduction of that important place, his lordfhip was left with the temporary rank of commodore to command on the American ftation, during the winter, with a force fufficient for the protection of the conqueft and other Britifh poffeffions in that quarter. In the enfuing fpring he joined fir C. Saunders, who was fent out with a ftrong force from England, and ferved under him at the fubfequent expedition againft the capital of Canada. After the reduction of that important fettlement his lordfhip returned to Halifax for the winter, and was extremely vigilant during its continuance, in preventing the introduction of any fupplies from France, for the fupport and fuccour of the ancient inhabitants and party. In particular he captured, about the month of January, a large French fhip, bound up the river St. Laurence, mounting twenty-two guns; and, as foon as the froft broke up, which event took place about the middle of April, he repaired with his fquadron to the river St. Lawrence, for the purpofe of intercepting any fupplies from France, as well as for the relief of Quebec, then befieged by the French. But notwithftanding the great alacrity and activity difplayed by his lordfhip, that important fortrefs was relieved a day or two before his arrival, as will be prefently feen in the life of Mr. Swanton.

He

He continred on the fame ftation, having under him a fquadron of ten or twelve fhips, during the year 1761*, without meeting with any occurrence attractive enough to merit general or particular notice. In the following year he became more diftinguifhed by the total difcomfiture of a defultory attack, made by the French, on the Britifh fettlements at Newfoundland †. He returned from his ftation, and arrived at Spithead on the 25th of October, with his own fhip the Northumberland, the Superbe, the Shrewfbury, and Minerva frigate. In the courfe of the fame month he was advanced to the rank of rear-admiral of the white. He afterwards commanded in chief on the coaft of America the firft fquadron ordered thither after the conclufion of the war, having his flag on board the Romney. At his return from thence he married, on the 1ft of October 1768, the lady Elizabeth Macfarlane, fifter to the earl of Kelly. We have no other particulars concerning him that merit relation, except that he died in Scotland on the 21ft of May, 1770, having been for fome time in a very declining ftate of health, for the recovery of which he had in vain tried Bath, and other remedies of the fame kind.

CORNWALL, Frederic. — This gentleman, coufin to captain James Cornwall, whofe extreme gallantry we have already had occafion to record, was lieutenant of the Marlborough, of ninety guns, at the memorable encounter with the French and Spanifh fleets off Toulon. That fhip was, as it may be well remembered, reduced to a mere wreck, and her brave commander flain. Mr. Frederick Cornwall bore his fhare in defending this devoted veffel with the moft active intrepidity, till he was difabled from farther exertions by the unhappy lofs of his right arm, after having before received feveral contufions, and injuries which were not, at fuch an exigency, of fufficient confequence to impede his farther exertions. As a very proper reward for his fpirited conduct, and recompenfe for the fufferings he underwent in confequence of it, he was immediately promoted to fucceed

---

* In the early part of this year he was fo much indifpofed, that, report having long forerun the difafter, his lordfhip's death was formally announced in many of the periodical publications of the time.

† M. De Ternay, the French commodore, fled the inftant he heard of his lordfhip's approach.

his deceafed relative in the command of the Marlborough, his commiffion for that purpofe bearing date February the 11th, 1744, being the very day on which the action took place. His wounds, however, as may naturally be conceived, prevented him from executing the neceffary duties of fo confequential a command: and the requifite attention to his recovery and future health, demanded his temporary retirement from a fervice, in which he had acquired, at fuch a perfonal expence, fo much honour.

We hear nothing of this gentleman from this time till the month of June 1749, when he commanded the Sunderland, and afforded as ftriking an inftance of benevolence in private life, as he had before of heroifm in his public capacity. That nobly charitable inftitution the Foundling-hofpital was then in its very infancy, and captain Cornwall is to be recorded as having not only handfomely contributed himfelf, but promoted a farther fubfcription among his officers and people to the advancement of the fame philanthropic end. About the end of the year 1755, he was appointed to the Revenge, of feventy guns, which was one of the fhips ordered to the Mediterranean, under Mr. Byng, in the enfuing fpring. Of the occurrences in that expedition we have already had too much reafon to be explicit: that part which capt. Cornwall bore in that encounter will beft appear from a minute of the evidence he gave on the trial of his unfortunate commander-in-chief*. From this time we believe him to have totally

lived

---

* He faid, that he went to his windows abaft to take a view of the fleet when in line of battle: that he was greatly furprized to fee the admiral and his divifion at fo great a diftance as he was upon the weather quarter: that feeing the Intrepid in diftrefs, and no fignal given for removing her out of the line, he went to her affiftance, and after getting her out of the line, fell into her ftation, engaging the Foudroyant, the French admiral, as the fhip, which he imagined, fell to his lot, according to the then line of battle: he faid he knew of no impediment that could prevent the admiral from engaging at a proper diftance, any more than the reft of the fleet: he obferved, that he was upon his oath to fwear the whole truth, and would do fo, though he knew fome things he was going to fay would affect himfelf. He gave his teftimony with great clearnefs, which in fome points affected the admiral much. The admiral, after afking the captain fome queftions, which feemed to impeach him (the captain) of breaking the line, &c. obferved to the
court,

lived in retirement with refpect to fervice*: indeed the misfortune which had in the early part of his life befallen him, though it did not completely incapacitate, muft have rendered the active ftation of a commander extremely inconvenient to him. He lived many years after he had, as we have above ftated, quitted the fervice, not dying till after the year 1786.

DOUGLASS, Sir James, — far as we have been able to difcover, is no where mentioned till his appointment, on the 19th of March, 1744, to be captain of the Mermaid. We have no account of the fervices or commands in which he was employed after this time, till the beginning of the year 1748, when he was appointed to the Berwick, of feventy guns. This fhip was put out of commiffion in the month of July following. Capt. Douglafs is faid to have been afterwards appointed to the Porcupine frigate; but we are uncertain whether it was this gentleman or captain John Douglafs, of whom we fhall have to give fome account hereafter. About the month of June 1755, he was appointed to the Bedford, of feventy-four guns, a fhip ordered, in the month of Auguft, for Gibraltar, with a convoy. He arrived there fafe with his charge on the 4th of September, having captured three French veffels, laden with merchandife, &c. while on his paffage thither. No mention is made of his fervices during the year 1756, or the manner in which he was particularly employed, except that we find him, in the month of December, to have been one of the members of the court-martial held for the trial of admiral Byng. In the month of May 1757, he was appointed captain of the Alcide, one of the fhips employed in the month of September enfuing, under the command of fir Edward Hawke, in the unfuccefsful expedition againft Rochfort. Captain Douglafs is particularly mentioned, as having been ordered

---

court, that his reputation, which was dearer to him than life, nay, his life alfo, were in the power of the court-martial, and in better hands he defired them not; but faid, he believed he fhould prove, that the Revenge, by breaking the line, was a great impediment in his way; and that if he could not prove that, or fomething like it, he added, " The Lord have mercy upon me."

* He is faid by fome to have been appointed to the Cornwall, of feventy-four guns, a new fhip launched in 1761. This, however, is a circumftance we ftrongly difbelieve.

to assist rear-admiral Broderick, in founding the coast from the Point near Rochelle, down to Fort Fouras. The ill success attendant on this expedition is well known. In the ensuing year captain Douglas continued to be employed on Channel service principally as a cruiser, a service in which he was extremely active, and, as will appear by the following account, not unsuccessful. Having received intelligence that a French frigate of thirty-six guns, called the Felicité, having a vessel arme en flute, mounting 24 guns, under her convoy, had just sailed from Bourdeaux, the latter laden with cannon, shells, and other warlike stores, for the use of the forts and ships of war at Hispaniola, he resolved to attempt intercepting them, and was so fortunate, on the 20th of September, as to overtake them about twenty leagues to the westward of Cape Finisterre. The cargo of the prize was more consequential than valuable, consisting of six twenty-four pounders, twelve eighteen pounders, six mortars, three thousand shells of large dimensions, with a considerable quantity of cordage, canvass, and other stores.

In the beginning of the year 1759 the Alcide was ordered to join the squadron then equipping, under the orders of sir Charles Saunders, and destined for the expedition against Quebec. He was chosen by the commander-in-chief to be the messenger of his success; in consequence of which added to his own meritorious services on the foregoing occasion, he received the honour of knighthood, and the customary gratuity of five hundred pounds from his majesty. Early in the year 1760 he was appointed, successor to Mr. Moore, in command as commodore on the Leeward Island station; and having hoisted his broad pendant on board the Dublin, sailed from St. Helen's on the 10th of March, having with him the Bienfaisant and Belliqueux. He arrived at Antigua, after a quick and prosperous passage, totally undiversified by any remarkable event or occurrence. The diligence and attention paid by himself in the distribution of his cruisers, added to the spirit and the vigilance displayed by the different officers under his command, not only afforded the most complete protection to the British commerce in that quarter of the world, but effected the most serious injuries to that of the enemy, by capturing several of their vessels even under the guns of their fortresses*. It is observed, by an historian of no inconsiderable reputation†, " that Mr. Holmes, of whom we have already spoken, stationed his cruisers with the greatest judgement and success; nor was the squadron stationed off the Leeward Islands, during the years 1760 and 61, less alert and effectual in protecting the British traders, and scouring the seas from the Martinico privateers, of which a great number were taken‡."

In the month of June 1761, he, in conjunction with lord Rollo, who commanded the land forces, undertook an expedition § against the French island of Dominica; the complete reduction of which was effected with the trivial loss of eight men killed and wounded. In 1762, still continuing in the same placid uninterrupted line of success, and retaining the command he had held with so much honour to himself and advantage to his country, he proceeded, according to his instructions from England, with a considerable part of the force under his orders, to join sir George Pocock, who was proceeding on the memorable and successful expedition against the Havannah. He effected this junction off Cape Nicholas, the north-west point of Hispaniola, on the 27th of May. He did not long, however, continue with the fleet, but proceeded in a single ship for Jamaica, from whence he quickly afterwards sailed for the Havannah with a considerable number of merchant-ships, bound for England, under his convoy. His arrival at that juncture was particularly fortunate, and contributed, in the highest degree, to the success which crowned the expedition. The face of the country in the neighbourhood of the Moro Fort was ex-

---

* The captains Obrien and Taylor, in the Temple and Griffin, cut out the Virgin, formerly a British sloop of war, and three privateers, from under the batteries at Grenada, and afterwards took nineteen ships bound to Martinico with provisions; eight or nine privateers were also captured about the same time, by different ships belonging to the squadron.

† Smollet.

‡ By the commodore's dispatches, dated December the 13th, 1760, it was stated, that the Emerald had, a short time before, captured four privateers, the Echo two, and the Levant one.

§ The naval force consisted of the Dublin, Belliqueux, Sutherland, and Montague, ships of the line, with some frigates and smaller vessels.

tremely

tremely rocky, and the earth which covered it fo thin, as by no means to afford, when thrown out from the trenches, a fufficient parapet to them; fo that, had it not been for a large quantity of cotton bags procured from the Jamaica convoy, under the protection of fir James, the profecution of the attack would have been at leaft extremely difficult. The wants of the army being fupplied, fir James, who then had his broad pendant on board the Centurion, took his departure, with his convoy, for England. He arrived fafe in the Downs on the 9th of September, and in the enfuing month was very defervedly advanced to the rank of rear-admiral of the white.

The peace was concluded immediately afterwards, and fir James returned to the Weft Indies as commander-in-chief on that ftation, a period which paffed in that uninterefting manner which it was natural to expect. The only occurrence demanding the fmalleft notice, appears to have been the fuppreffion of an infurrection of negroes at the Berbices, to which the prudent meafures taken by him, are acknowledged, by the Dutch, to have been particularly inftrumental. In the month of October 1770, he was advanced progreffively to be vice-admiral of the blue and white. In 1773 he was appointed commander-in-chief at Portfmouth, and having hoifted his flag on board the Barfleur, continued on that ftation during the ufually allotted period of three years. On the 3d of February, 1776, he was advanced to be vice-admiral of the red; but after he quitted the command juft ftated, appears to have been in no way whatever concerned or connected with the public fervice. In 1778 he was advanced to be admiral of the blue, as he was of the white in 1782. Having lived in peaceable and honourable retirement upwards of ten years, he died at laft in Scotland in the year 1787.

EDGCUMBE, George[*], Earl of Mount Edgcumbe,
—was

---

[*] "This family, denominated from the manor of Eggecombe, Eggcombe, and Egecomb, (as it has been varioufly written in former records) in the parifh of Cheriton Fitz-Pain, near Crediton, has been of great antiquity in Devonfhire; and in that church is Edgecomb's aifle, adorned with divers coats of arms belonging to the family: but in the reign of king Edward IIId. William de Eggecomb taking to wife

—was the second son of Richard, first lord Edgcumbe, so created April 20, 1742. Having made choice of a maritime life, he was sent when very young to sea, as midshipman on board one of the ships stationed in the Mediterranean, under the orders of Mr. Haddock. After passing through that, as well as the superior though still subordinate ranks of lieutenant and commander, he was, Aug. 19, 1744, promoted to be captain of the Kennington, a 20 gun ship. No other mention is made of him for some time, except that, towards the end of the year 1745, he was promoted to the command of the Salisbury, of fifty guns, in which ship he continued till the conclusion of the war. On the 1st of March, 1747, he carried into Plymouth a French East India ship of seven hundred tons, called the Jason, which he fell in with on the 30th of January, in the latitude of 47 degrees 47 minutes north, 106 leagues to the westward of Scilly. She mounted thirty guns, had one hundred and eighty men on board, and was bound from Port L'Orient to Pondicherry, laden chiefly with stores and ammunition, together with eight cases of silver. We do not find him again taken any notice of till the year 1751 *: he then commanded the Monmouth, and was sent out to Gibraltar senior captain, or commanding

---

wife Hillaria, daughter and heir of William de Cotehele, of Cotehele in the county of Cornwall, chiefly resided there. It is now wrote Cuttail, and is separated from Devonshire only by the breadth of the river Tamer. In 1378 the said William de Eggecomb, writing himself of Cotehele in Cornwall, granted lands in Middleton to the convent of Tavistock, in Devonshire. He died 1380, and left issue, by her, William Edgecomb, esq. who married the daughter and heir of —— Denset. He had a grant in 6 Hen. V. with Royal Hethe, of the custody of the lead mines, with the silver ore therein, which were in Devonshire. He left issue Peter Edgecombe, esq. who, in 12 Hen. VI. was returned amongst the chief of the county of Devon, who made oath for themselves, and retainers, to observe the laws then existing, from which Peter Edgecombe this family is lineally descended."— Collins.

* He was returned to the parliament which met, for the dispatch of business, on the 12th of November, 1747, as representative for the boroughs of Plympton and Fowey, but took his seat for the latter of those places. He was re-elected for the same borough at the general election in 1754; as he was, a third time, in 1761; but became a peer of Great Britain before the parliament met, in consequence of the death of Richard the second lord, his elder brother.

officer of a small squadron consisting of three ships of the line, including his own, ordered thither for the purpose of shifting a part of the garrison, and bringing from thence the regiments of Wolfe and Skelton, which had been long stationed there. Nothing appears to have occurred to him during his absence on this service more material than his falling in with a French squadron, consisting of four ships of the line and five frigates, under the command of a rear-admiral, between whom and Mr. Edgcumbe, the compliments and civilities, customary on such occasions, mutually passed.

He arrived at Spithead on the 3d of August, after a passage of twenty-two days. He is no otherwise noticed till the following year, when he removed into the Deptford, of sixty guns, a ship newly launched. He was soon afterwards appointed commander with the nominal rank of commodore of the small squadron ordered to the Mediterranean, and which it is customary to keep there in time of peace even though hostilities are not apprehended from any quarter whatever. Here he remained, almost without interruption, till 1756, when France put a sudden period to public tranquillity in that part of the world, by a formidable attack and invasion of the island of Minorca. Mr. Edgcumbe, with the whole of his small squadron, was in the harbour of Mahon at the time the French fleet first made its appearance off that place, and might easily have been blocked up, as well as not improbably compelled to share its fate. Monsf. Gallisoniere, and the duke de Richlieu, general-in-chief, not extending their views beyond the conquest of the island itself, the passage was left open for the British ships, and Mr. Edgcumbe sailed, on April 20th, for Gibraltar on board the Chesterfield, of forty guns, being followed the ensuing day by the Princess Louisa, Portland, and Dolphin. On his junction with Mr. Byng he removed into the Lancaster, of sixty-six guns; in which ship we find him present at the indecisive rencontre which presently afterwards took place; on which occasion he had one man killed and fourteen wounded. He returned to England at the close of the year, and, during the ensuing summer was employed as a cruiser. In this occupation, which was of no long duration, he appears to have been extremely successful, having, in company with the Dunkirk, which was put under his orders, captured two stout private ships of war, one called the Compte de Grammont, carrying thirty-fix guns and three hundred and feventy men; the other Le Nouveau Saxon, of fixteen guns and one hundred and fifty men, together with a fchooner from Bourdeaux, bound to Quebec, laden with wine and brandy.

In 1758, having been put under the orders of Mr. Bofcawen, who was fent out to America for the purpofe of making a third attempt againſt the fortrefs of Louifburg, he was the meſſenger charged by the admiral with his difpatches to England, communicating the important and agreeable intelligence of his fuccefs. On this occafion he received the cuftomary compliment of 500l. prefented to him by his majefty, and was, not long afterwards, appointed captain of the Hero, a fhip of feventy-four guns, one of the Channel fleet commanded by fir Edward Hawke during the year 1759. He confequently fhared in the glory of defeating the laſt remains and exertions of the naval power of France, off Belleiſle, in the month of November. He continued in the Hero till his advancement to be rear-admiral of the blue, a promotion which took place on the 21ſt of October, 1762. By the deceafe of his eldeſt brother, Richard, on the 10th of May in the preceding year, he became a peer of Great Britain, and on the 18th of the enfuing month took the oaths as lord lieutenant of the county of Cornwall. In the month of June 1762, he refigned the office of clerk of the council of the dutchy of Lancafter, which he had held for fome time.

In 1766 he was appointed port admiral at Plymouth, a ftation he filled for a length of time, fomewhat exceeding that ufually allotted to fuch commands, not having quitted it till the latter end of the year 1770. On the 24th of October in the fame year, till (when he experienced no advancement from the rank he firſt received) we find him appointed vice-admiral of the blue, as he was, on the 25th of June, 1773, to be vice-admiral of the white*. His
lordſhip

---

* A fhort time previous to this he was inveſted with the temporary command of a divifion in the fleet reviewed by his majefty at Spithead.

" Portfmouth, June the 25th, 1773.

" About ten o'clock his majefty went, in the ufual ſtate, on board the Barfleur, and then into the Charlotte yacht, when a fignal of one
gun

lordſhip quitted his command immediately afterwards; previous however to this, he received in common with the other flag-officers and the captains of the different fquadrons, his majeſty's thanks for their great attention during his preceding viſit. In the enſuing month (July) we find his lordſhip one of the noblemen attending lord North at the time of his inſtallation as chancellor of the univerſity of Oxford: on this occaſion he received the honorary degree of doctor of laws. He is no otherwiſe mentioned as a naval officer, than as being included, according to his ſtation, in the different promotions which took place in the liſt of flag-officers, his cotemporaries. On the 3d of February, 1776, he was advanced to be vice-admiral of the red; on the 29th of January, 1778, to be admiral of the blue; and, on the 8th of April, 1782, to be admiral of the white.

The honours and civil appointments of this noble lord appear to have kept pace with his promotions as an officer. On the 17th of February, 1781, he was created a viſcount of Great Britain by the titles of viſcount Mount Edgcumbe and Valletort; and, on the 18th of Auguſt, 1789, was raiſed to the dignity of earl of Mount Edgcumbe. The former of theſe titles is ſaid to have been given him as an honorary compenſation for the deſtruction of ſeveral of the plantations at his beautiful ſeat near Plymouth, which, in the opinion of military men, was abſolutely neceſſary to the ſafety and defence of that very important fortreſs, in caſe of any attack from an enemy: the latter was beſtowed on him, by his majeſty, in return for the attention paid him by his lordſhip, when on a viſit and excurſion of ſome continuance in that part of the country. In reſpect to his varied civil appointments, he was, in 1765, named one of his majeſty's moſt honourable privy council, and appointed treaſurer of the

---

gun was given for vice admiral lord Edgcumbe's ſquadron of the blue to get under weigh; which being complied with, the differ nt ſalutes paſſed between the two fleets, and lord Edgcumbe's immediately convoyed the Royal Yacht to St. Helen's, where they all brought to Here his majeſty dined on board the yacht, and promoted vice-admiral lord Edgecumbe, of the blue, to be vice-admiral of the white, who kiſſed hands on the occaſion, and hoiſted the St. George's flag at the foretop."

houſhold,

houſhold, an office in which he continued only till the following year; but, in 1771, was named one of the joint vice-treaſurers of Ireland, which he reſigned in 1773, on being made captain of the band of gentlemen penſioners. This ſtation he retained till the general change of miniſtry in 1782; after which he filled no office till February 1784, when he was again appointed one of the vice-treaſurers of Ireland. This eminent ſituation he held till the time of his death, an event which took place in the month of February 1795.

ELLIOT, Elliot,—is known to us only as having been appointed captain of the Lively, a ſhip of twenty guns, on the 5th of September, 1744; and as having died in the Eaſt Indies, on the 20th of July, 1745, till then holding the ſame command.

ELLIOT, George, — a deſcendant of a very reſpectable Scottiſh family, was, May 12, 1744, appointed, by ſir C. Ogle, commander-in-chief on the Jamaica ſtation, captain of the Conde de Chinchan. The circumſtances of this advancement were peculiarly honourable to captain Elliot: he was lieutenant of the Rippon, a fourth rate, on that ſtation. In the month of March preceding, his captain being indiſpoſed, the Rippon was put under Mr. Elliot's orders, who was ſent to ſea in her, as acting and temporary commander, for a ſhort cruiſe. During this period he fell in with, in the windward paſſage, a Spaniſh frigate, carrying eighteen carriage and eight ſwivel guns, with one hundred and forty men. He drove her cloſe under the iſland of Tortuga, and then manning his boats brought her off without damage. This prize was bound to Vera Cruz, and her capture was the more conſequential, indeed diſtreſſing to the enemy, from her having on board, excluſive of other very valuable articles, 1200 quintals of quickſilver, intended for the uſe of the Spaniſh mines. Mr. Elliot was firſt promoted, immediately on his return, to be commander of the Mortar ſloop; and according to the date given at the beginning of this account, was advanced to be captain of the very veſſel he had ſo gallantly and induſtriouſly exerted himſelf in the capture of, ſhe being found, after a ſurvey, well calculated for a frigate in the Britiſh ſervice, in reſpect to her being both a new ſhip and a prime ſailer. Captain Elliot returned to England at the
cloſe

close of the same year, being succeeded in the command of the Chinchan by Mr. Graves, and in the month of September was one of the members composing the court-martial, held at Chatham, for the trial of the captains who were charged with misbehaviour in the encounter with the French and Spanish fleets off Toulon. We do not find any other particular mention made of him during the continuance of the war, except that, in 1747, he was appointed captain of the Newark, a new ship of eighty guns, then just launched.

After this time he appears to have retired from the line of active service, for his name does not occur as holding any command. In the year 1762 he was put on the superannuated list with the rank and half-pay of a rear-admiral, an honourable pension which he continued to enjoy many years, living principally at his seat at Copford, in Essex, where he died on the 5th of August, 1795. On this occasion the nominal office of general of the mint, in Scotland, a sinecure place, worth three hundred pounds a year, which was kept up by an express article in the treaty of Union, and which this gentleman had long enjoyed, became vacant.

GORDON, William,—like Mr. Elliot, of whom we have just given some account, was of Scottish extraction. We hear nothing particular of him till the month of May 1744; he was then commander of the Hound sloop of war, and is mentioned as having had the good fortune, during his passage home from Virginia at that time, to have met with and captured a very valuable French merchant-ship, homeward-bound from Martinico, called the Happy Mary, laden with sugar, cocoa, coffee, and other valuable commodities, bound for Bourdeaux. Soon after his arrival he was ordered, in company with the Vulture sloop, to convoy the outward-bound trade to Rotterdam, when on his passage he met with no inconsiderable success, which is officially related in the following terms.

" Admiralty-office, August 3, 1744.

" His majesty's sloops the Hound and Vulture, being in sight of Goree on the 29th past, with the trade under their convoy, bound to Rotterdam, the Hound, captain Gordon, stood after a snow, which proved to be a French privateer

privateer of ten carriage guns and nine fwivels, with eighty-one men, which had been three days out of Dunkirk. She engaged the Hound for an hour and an half and then ftruck, having five men killed and feveral mortally wounded: captain Gordon alfo retook a fhip which the priv teer had juft taken."

In confequence of his very fpirited behaviour on this occafion he was promoted, on the 4th of Auguft following, the day after the account of his fuccefs was publifhed, to be captain of the Gofport, a fifth rate. He is erroneoufly ftated in fome accounts to have been about the fame time appointed to the Ludlow Caftle, and not the Gofport: but this is a manifeft miftake, occafioned by his being very quickly afterwards removed into the Sheernefs, as fucceffor to captain Bridges Rodney, who was himfelf appointed to the Ludlow Caftle. No mention is made of him in the Sheernefs till the year enfuing, when he was, at the end of the month of June O. S. engaged, with lord George Graham his countryman, in the very fuccefsful and fpirited attack of fome French privateers and their prizes off Oftend, the particulars of which we have already given*. Immediately after this enterprife he was appointed to the Loo, of forty-four guns; and was, in the courfe of the autumn, removed into the Chefterfield, a fhip of the fame force. No mention is made of him while he retained t is ftation; and the next notice we find taken of him is, his appointment to be captain of the Affiftance, a fhip of fifty guns, at the latter end of the year 1747. In this fhip he was equally as unfortunate as he had been in that he had-quitted, not having any opportunity of adding either to his fortune or fame. On the conclufion of peace, in 1748, he quitted the Affiftance, which was one of the fhips confequently put out of commiffion, and accepted the command of a twenty-gun fhip, preferring a command comparatively fo trivial, to a life of abfolute inactivity.

It is almoft an unneceffary remark, that we cannot, during the continuance of peace, expect any material mention made of thofe who are fortunate enough to obtain

---

* See page 23.

the moſt diſtinguiſhed commands: As to captain Gordon, his name does not again meet our obſervation till the concluſion of the year 1756, ſometime after the actual commencement of hoſtilities with France: he was then appointed to the Cambridge, of eighty guns, as ſucceſſor to ſir Piercy Brett, removed into the Caroline yacht. In the month of April 1757, he removed into the Princeſs Amelia, alſo a three decked ſhip, and of the ſame force; as he ſoon afterwards did into the Devonſhire*. In the month of September 1761, he was made captain of the Blenheim, a new ſecond rate of ninety guns; and in the following ſpring was advanced to be commodore and commander-in-chief of the ſhips in the river Medway and at the Nore. This ſtation he held during the remainder of the war; and on the 21ſt of October in the ſame year was promoted to be rear-admiral of the blue. After the ratification of the articles of peace, which quickly followed his promotion to be a flag-officer, admiral Gordon does not appear to have taken upon him any command, but to have paſſed the remainder of his life in retirement at Bamff, in Scotland, which we believe to have been his native place, and where he died on the 25th of April, 1768.

GRAVES, Samuel,—this gentleman, the nephew of the brave and much-injured capt. Tho. Graves, of whom ſome account has been already given, (ſee vol. iv. p. 43,) ſerved as lieutenant of the Norfolk at the ſiege of Carthagena †. He continued in all probability in ſome other ſhip, on the ſame ſtation, after its failure; but the firſt ſubſequent particular mention we find made of him is, that of his promotion to be captain of the Chinchan or Rippon's Prize, on the 11th of September, 1744. This frigate was at that time employed on the Jamaica ſtation, where it appears to have continued ſome time, and about the end

---

* In 1758 he ſerved under Mr. Boſcawen on the ſucceſsful and memorable expedition againſt Louiſburg. On his return from thence, being overtaken by a violent ſtorm, the Devonſhire was with the greateſt difficulty brought in, and preſerved from foundering.

† It is ſaid that, at the attack of St. Philip's and St. Jago forts, he ſollicited to be landed for the purpoſe of attacking ſome batteries which, being out of the reach of the cannon of the ſhips, impeded the progreſs of the troops. He conſequently bore a very honourable ſhare in the attack of a ſixteen gun battery.

of the year 1745, to have captured a large French ship, bound from Cadiz to La Vera Cruz, carrying thirty guns with a crew of one hundred and sixteen men. This is the only account we have of him during the continuance of the war, nor do we know, to speak with precision, what subsequent commands he held till the year 1756, when he was appointed to the Duke, a second rate of ninety guns. From this ship he removed in the ensuing year into the Princess Amelia, and in a few weeks afterwards into the Barfleur. The size of all these ships prevented their being employed in any armament or expedition except those of the first magnitude; and as they were severally stationed in the home or Channel squadron, where no action or memorable occurrence took place, the dates and few particulars we have related will be a sufficient account of this gentleman's life during the period above stated.

In 1759 he returned to his former ship the Duke, in which he was present at the memorable defeat of the French fleet under the marquis de Conflans. Mr. Graves continued in the Duke till his promotion, on the 21st of October, 1762, to the rank of rear-admiral of the blue, a period of his service, unfortunately for him, equally undistinguished with that in the earlier part of the war, owing to the extreme caution of the French in keeping all their fleets in port, after the heavy discomfiture they had experienced. He neither held a command nor received any promotion * till the 18th of October, 1770, when he was appointed rear-admiral of the red, and in six days afterwards was advanced to be vice-admiral of the blue. Early in the year 1774 he was appointed admiral and commander-in-chief on the American station. Having hoisted his flag on board the Preston, of fifty guns, he was ordered to Boston, in the month of March, with the Royal Oak and Egmont, of seventy four guns each; and the Worcester, of sixty-four, in consequence of the dispute then originating between Great Britain and America, relative to the duty on tea. The progressive encrease of this disturbance is too recent to be forgotten. The mate-

---

* On the 15th of June, 1769, he married Miss Margaret Spinckes, a lady of large fortune, amounting, as it is said, to 30,000 l. She was the daughter of Elmes Spinckes, esq. of Aldwinkle, in the county of Northampton.

rial occurrences which took place while Mr. Graves held the command, were the commencement of hostilities at Lexington, and the more serious encounter at Bunker's Hill; but thefe were in a line with which the admiral was totally unconcerned, and, from their very nature, he was perfectly unconnected with. He was during his abfence, that is to fay, on the 31ft of March, 1775, advanced to be vice-admiral of the white; and on the 3d of February, 1776, being a very few days after his return to England, on board the Prefton, fartner promoted to be vice-admiral of the red.

Towards the conclufion of the year 1777, he was appointed to command at Plymouth; but this ftation he held only for a fhort time, having, as it is elfewhere remarked, nobly relinquifhed it, through a fixed determination, " never to hold any employment in time of war, except of the moft active kind againft the enemies of his country." He never accepted any appointment after this time, but on the 29th of January, 1778, was advanced to be admiral of the blue, as he was moreover, on the 8th of April, 1782, to be admiral of the white. In this ftation he died at his feat at Hembury Fort, in the county of Devon, on the 8th of March, 1787, after a fhort illnefs, in the 74th year of his age. His complaint was an hæmorrhage in his bladder, a diforder which he bore with the utmoft fortitude. An anonymous writer, who has given us a fhort account relative to this gentleman, exprefles himfelf in the following terms relative to his conduct in the American war.

" In the beginning of the late unhappy war he had the naval command at Bofton; and his conduct there, as was natural, became the fubject of fevere animadverfion amongft thofe who could not know the decifive fpirit which he recommended in all the general councils, and the inadequate force which he had to carry on the naval operations. On his recal from that command, being follicited to publifh a vindication of his own conduct from the unjuftifiable afperfions which had been thrown on it, with the fpirit of a true patriot he replied, that " He would not from any perfonal ill ufage, contribute his fhare to injure government, already too much weakened by party animofity." He added with as much forefight, " that the failure of
his

his succeffors would be his beft vindication." It is added, by the fame hand, that " when he thought the difcipline of the fervice was ftruck at, he was one of the twelve admirals who fubmitted their opinions to his majefty, although at that time, and to his lateft hour, he had the greateft perfonal refpect for the noble earl who prefided at the head of the admiralty board. Few men excelled him in the duties of private life; he was a fincere chriftian, his charities were fuch as became the character, and his lofs is univerfally felt by all ranks of people in the neighbourhood where he lived."

HADDOCK, Richard.—We do not know any particulars concerning this gentleman till the commencement of the year 1744, when we find him commander of the Wolf floop of war, in which veffel he captured, on the 20th of May, a French privateer of fourteen guns. He was, on the 7th of November enfuing, promoted to be captain of the Squirrel frigate. We have no particulars relative to him while he continued in this fhip, from which we find him promoted, early in the year 1746, to be captain of the Advice, of fifty guns. We believe to have been principally employed after this in cruifing, a fpecies of fervice in which captain Haddock, at leaft for a confiderable time after his appointment, is not ftated to have met with any very remarkable fuccefs. Some amends appear to have been made him, by Fortune, in the courfe of the months of March and April 1748, the following fucceffes being given officially from the admiralty-office, in an account bearing date April the 27th.

" On the 10th of laft month his majefty's fhip the Advice, commanded by captain Haddock, failed from Plymouth on a cruife; and on the 28th retook an Englifh fhip, called the Bella, from Philadelphia, laden with fugar and indigo, for London, which had been taken on the 19th preceding, by the Juno privateer, belonging to Bayonne. On the 3d inftant, about 14° 39 weft longitude from the Start, captain Haddock bore down towards a fail feen to the leeward, and at nine in the evening came up with her. After exchanging two or three broadfides with his upper-deck guns (it blowing fo frefh that his lower ports could not be opened) as well as feveral vollies of fmall arms, the chace ftruck, and proved to be

the

the Neptune privateer, of Bayonne, carrying twenty guns, eight pounders, with a crew of 210 men. In the action the Advice had three men killed and five wounded.

" On the 9th inftant captain Haddock took a French brigantine, laden with falt for St. Maloe's. The prizes have been carried into Kinfale."

We believe he continued in the fame fhip till the conclufion of the war; but have no particular account of his having met with any fubfequent fuccefs. At the conclufion of the year 1749, he was one of the members of the court-martial, held on board the Charlotte yacht, at Deptford, for the trial of rear-admiral Knowles, and was alfo one of thofe intended to have compofed the fecond court for the trial of captain Holmes; but being feized with the fmall pox, unhappily died of that, then fatal, diforder, at Chatham, on the 6th of January 1749-50, fome days before the trial commenced.

HANWAY, Thomas, — fon to the captain Jonas Hanway, of whom we have already given fome account*, and brother to the well-known traveller, the philanthropic Jonas Hanway, projector and principal fupporter of the marine fociety, as well as other charitable inftitutions. Of the earlier part of this gentleman's fervice we do not find any mention made: our information concerning him commences with his promotion to the mortar-bomb†, but at what particular time we know not. On April 5, 1744, he was made captain of the Shoreham frigate. In the following year he commanded the Milford, one of the veffels ftationed off the coaft of Scotland for the purpofe of preventing the introduction of any fupplies from France for the fuccour of the pretenders army in that kingdom. While thus occupied he had the good fortune to capture, off Montrofe, a large French fhip, having on board a quantity of ftores and ammunition, with a number of experienced officers belonging to the Irifh brigade, and 210 foldiers, a lofs very feverely felt by the infurgents. In 1746 he was one of the members compofing the court-martial, held on board the Prince of Orange, at Deptford, for the trial of

---

* See vol. iii. p. 248.
† N. B. When captain of the Mortar bomb he captured the Aimable Nannette, bound from Martinico to Havre de Grace; captain Hanway was then on his paffage from Briftol to Spithead.

the officers who were charged with misbehaviour in the encounter with the French and Spanish fleets off Toulon. In 1747 he commanded the Windsor, of sixty guns, one of the squadron under Mr. Anson, which defeated and captured the major part of the French armament under M. de la Jonquiere. Captain Hanway had the happiness of distinguishing himself exceedingly on that occasion, the Windsor being among the first ships that got up with and engaged the enemy.

His behaviour was no less gallant and conspicuous in the month of October, under rear-admiral Hawke, when the French armament, under L'Etendiere, sustained a loss and defeat no less remarkable and heavy than the preceding one had been. The Windsor is said, in a private account we have seen, to have engaged, in rotation, every ship of the French squadron, passing from rear to van, except the Intrepide, which tacked purposely to avoid getting into action. It is reported to have expended, within the space of six hours, seventy broadsides, with eight thousand musket cartridges: nevertheless the loss sustained by this ship was, comparatively speaking, trivial, amounting to no more than eight men killed and fifty-nine wounded, the greater part of them slightly. Capt. Hanway is said in some accounts, but the authority of which we dare not depend on, to have commanded the Winchester, of fifty guns, immediately after the conclusion of the war, otherwise no mention is made of him till the year 1755, when he was captain of the Weymouth, of sixty guns, one of the ships ordered to be equipped at Plymouth in consequence of the daily apprehended rupture with France. In the month of April he repaired to America with the fleet under the orders of admiral Boscawen. We need say nothing farther of that expedition, as we have already had frequent occasion to remark on the few occurrences which took place, and were remarkable enough to require particular mention.

In the month of May 1756, he was promoted to the Chichester, of seventy guns. He did not long continue in this ship, which, while under his command, does not appear to have engaged in any memorable or remarkable service. In 1758 he was captain of the Duke, of ninety guns, and was employed in the Channel fleet under lord Anson.

Anson. He afterwards commanded, at Plymouth, with the rank of commodore. In the beginning of the year 1761 he retired from the line of active command, and was appointed commiffioner of the navy refident at Chatham. This office he exchanged with Mr. Proby, in the month of October 1771, for the comptrollerfhip of the victualling accounts. This his new ftation he unhappily did not long continue to fill, dying at the navy-office on the 1ft of October, 1772, univerfally refpected, revered and loved.

HARDY, John, — the younger brother of admiral fir Charles Hardy of whom we have already given fome account in page 99. In 1742 he was firft lieutenant of the Superbe, under captain Hervey; and being involved in the fame charge with his commander, of cruelty exercifed towards the crew, was accordingly brought to a court-martial with him, but experienced a different fate, for he was honourably acquitted. He was raifed from the rank of lieutenant to be commander of the Drake floop of war early in the year 1744, as fucceffor to the lord Thomas Bertie. He very foon removed into the Vulture, a veffel of the fame clafs, from which he was promoted, on the 17th of October, to be captain of the Bridgewater, a twenty-gun fhip. He was afterwards promoted to the Torrington, of forty-four guns; and, in February 1745, was one of the members compofing the court-martial, held on board the Lenox in Portfmouth harbour, for the trials of the captains Moftyn, Griffin, Brett and Fowke, which, trivial as the circumftance is, is the only mention we find made of him during his continuance in that command. In 1746 he was paid off from the Torrington, at Plymouth, and never had any fubfequent appointment. In the month of October 1762, he retired altogether from the fervice, being put on the fuperannuated lift with the rank and half-pay of a rear-admiral.

The remainder of his life he paffed in retirement, and, forry are we to add, the greater part of it in much indigence. He is the author of a Chronological Lift of the Captains of his Majefty's Navy, publifhed in 1779, which meeting with an extenfive fale, became, as we have been well informed, for fome time his principal fupport. He died in obfcurity about the month of May 1796.

HARRISON,

HARRISON, Thomas,—was nephew to that brave and worthy veteran officer admiral Henry Harrifon* In 1739 he was lieutenant of the Greenwich†. He was advanced in the month of October 1743, from that rank to be commander of the Lightening bomb-ketch. On the 5th of June, 1744, he was promoted to be captain of the Port Mahon frigate, a veffel employed as a cruifer. In this line of fervice he had the good fortune to capture, when on his firft cruife to the fouthward of Cape Clear, a valuable French fhip, bound from Petit Guave to Bourdeaux, called the New Alliance. No other particulars are given us of this gentleman, except that he died in England on the 17th of Auguft, 1752.

KEPPEL, Lord Vifcount,—was the fecond fon of William Anne, fecond earl of Albemarle ‡, and the lady Anne Lenox, daughter of Charles Lenox, firft duke of Richmond. He was born on the 2d of April, 1725; and having attached himfelf to the naval fervice was fent at a very early age to fea, under the protection and care of commodore Anfon, when that gentleman was ordered to the South Seas. Of the very few hoftile encounters in which this armament was concerned, the attack of Paita may be remembered as the moft confequential, and Mr. Keppel is recorded as having had in the trifling defence made by the

---

* See p. 24.

† In the month of July, in this year, he married the daughter of Mr. Winter, of the pipe-office, with whom he had a fortune of 5000l.

‡ Of this family Collins gives us the following particulars.

"One of the moft ancient and eminent families among the nobility of Guelderland is this of Keppel, whofe caftle (fituated in a lordfhip of the fame name, in the county of Zutphen, near the Old Yfel) is not more remarkable for its antiquity than the great privileges it enjoys, a particular account whereof may be feen in the defcription of Guelderland.

"Wolter van Keppel was lord of Keppel in 1179, and 1231, and founded a monaftery at Bethlehem, near Doctinchem. By his wife Beatrice, he was father of Dereck, who became lord of Keppel: and Wolter, who held the lordfhip of Verwoelde, under his elder brother, which however contined to his pofterity, for his younger fon, Hendric van Keppel, was feated at Wefterholt, near Lochum; and the elder, Derck van Keppel (who was living 1326) had, among other children, a fon of his own name, who held the lordfhip of Verwoelde, as a fief of his coufin, Sweder van Voerft, lord of Voerft and Keppel, in the year 1362. From this noble was lineally defcended, in eight generations, Arnold Jooft Van Keppel, who attended king William to England, and was created earl of Albemarle, by that prince, Feb. 10, 1695-6."

enemy.

enemy, a very narrow and fingular efcape. He accompanied Mr., afterwards fir Piercy Brett, who commanded, and one of the few random fhot, fired at the ooats, fhaved, as is expreffed in the account of commodore Anfon's voyage, the peak of a jockey's cap, he then wore, clofe to his temple. No other mention is made of him during the courfe of the expedition, except that he was appointed a lieutenant after the capture of the galleon. He was in September 1744, almoft immediately after his return to England, promoted to be commander of a new floop of war, but was not permitted to continue long in that fituation, being advanced, on the 11th of December in the fame year, to be captain of the Sapphire frigate. This veffel was employed as a cruifer, a fervice in which her commander appears to have been extremely active, and very fuccefsful, he having, on the 15th of April, 1745, captured a large French fhip from Martinico, bound to Rochfort, called the Atalanta. Her cargo was very valuable, confifting principally of fugar, with fome coffee and cotton; nor was her force defpicable, fhe having eighteen guns befides fwivels mounted, and being manned with a proportionate crew.

Good fortune continuing to attend him, on the 20th of May following he fell in with, between the Old Head of Kinfale and Cape Clear, a ftout Spanifh privateer belonging to Bilboa, called the Superbe. This veffel mounted no more than fixteen guns, fo that refiftance would have been fiuitlefs; but being a very faft failer, and exerting every manœuvre to efcape, was not captured till after a chace of feveral hours continuance. In 1746 he commanded the Maidftone, of fifty guns, a fhip employed in the fame line of fervice: but during this year no other mention is made of him, than as the captor of a fmall French privateer, called the Ferret, belonging to St. Maloe's, carrying four carriage and ten fwivel guns, with a crew of one hundred and twenty men. A melancholy accident befel him on the 7th of July, 1747, as he was giving chace to a French privateer. Running too near the fhore on the coaft of France, near Nantz, the Maidftone was unfortunately loft; both himfelf and his crew were happily faved: and there is a picture of him painted by fir Jofhua Reynolds, which reprefents him as juft efcaped from fhipwreck,

shipwreck. Being quickly exchanged, and acquitted honourably of all blame attachable to the preceding misfortune, he was, at the conclusion of the year, one of the members of the court-martial assembled at Portsmouth, for the trial of captain Fox. He was at that time captain of the Anson, a new ship of sixty-four guns, one of the cruising fleet kept at sea in the Channel during the debilitated remainder of the war. The return of peace did not, however, cause the retirement of Mr. Keppel; in 1749, having his pendant on board the Centurion, he was sent commodore of the squadron employed on the Mediterranean station, where he very eminently distinguished himself, as well by his spirited activity as his agreeable and accommodating manners, at the same time displaying the greatest firmness, when * either the honour of his country or his own was at the smallest hazard.

Commo-

---

* The following official particulars will sufficiently explain the honourable manner in which he was received, and the great firmness he displayed on a particular and interesting occasion.—He was sent principally to demand satisfaction for the insult, as well as to procure restitution of the treasure taken out of the Prince Frederic packet-boat, in which he at first met with some obstacles; the conclusion was however fortunate, owing to Mr. Keppel's spirit and perseverance.

" Algiers, July 14, 1750.

" On the 24th of June commodore Keppel arrived here, from Mahon, in his majesty's ship the Centurion, with the Assurance, Unicorn, and Seahorse, and was immediately saluted from the ramparts with the usual compliment of twenty-one guns. On the 2d instant the commodore came on shore, and was again saluted with twenty-one guns. Having demanded an audience, the commodore, together with Ambrose Stanyford, esq. his Britannick majesty's consul, who is joined in commission with him, went in the afternoon, attended by a number of officers, and presented their commission, empowering them to adjust all differences between the two nations. To his highness the Dey, on the 7th, they were admitted to another audience, in which they fully explained to his highness the purport of their commission; at both which audiences they were received with great civility."

" Algiers, August 27, 1750.

" On the 22d past, a French vessel, with about seventy passengers on board, came to an anchor in the road from Tetuan; and a report being immediately spread that the plague was on board, the Dey gave orders that no person should come on shore, and agreed with the French consul that the said vessel should perform a quarantine of forty days:

but

Commodore Keppel continued on the fame ftation no inconfiderable length of time, and about the end of the following year concluded a treaty of peace with the Dey of Algiers, for the arrangement of which he failed from For St. Philip's, in the ifland of Minorca, on the 1ft of May. An act of piracy committed by one of the corfairs juft before this time, rendered it neceffary that fome immediate explanation fhould be given, and that the fubfifting treaty fhould be renewed and republifhed. The Dey received him in the mildeft, and making proper allowances for the eccentricities of the Mahometan cuftoms, the moft fubmiffive manner. He acknowledged to him, " That one of his officers had been guilty of a very great fault, which tended to embroil him with his chiefeft and beft friends; wherefore he fhould never more ferve him by land or fea, and hoped the king his mafter, would look on it as the action of a fool or a madman, that he would take care nothing fhould happen again in the like nature, and concluded by defiring they might be better friends than ever." This declaration was tranfmitted to England by the commodore, and publifhed by the admiralty on the 22d of May, 1751. In the courfe of the enfuing fummer he arranged a fimilar treaty with the ftates of Tripoli and Tunis*. The term of three years, which is the period ufually

---

but as Mr. Keppel, the Britifh commodore, took it into confideration, that as thofe people were abfolutely ignorant of the laws of quarantine, and confequently had neither regulations nor officers adapted thereto, that there would be the greateft danger of the infection being introduced by fome rafh attempt or other of the paffengers; he therefore reprefented to the Dey, that the important command his Britannick majefty had intrufted him with, obliged him to remonftrate to his highnefs, that he could by no means think of ftaying one moment in the bay, unlefs that veffel was ordered away immediately: upon which the Dey fent that inftant for the French druggoman, and gave him orders to fend the veffel away directly; which was done accordingly, not only to the fatisfaction of the Britifh commodore, but to that of the whole city."

* " Gazette, No. 9125. Whitehall, Jan. 7, 1752.

" Commodore Keppel, commander of his majefty's fquadron in the Mediterranean, has tranfmitted hither a treaty of peace and commerce between his majefty and the kingdom of Tripoli, concluded and figned the 19th day of September laft paft, by him, the faid commodore

ufually allotted to commands of this kind, expiring foon after the conclufion of the bufinefs juft mentioned, the commodore returned to England, where he arrived with his whole fquadron on the 26th of Auguft, 1753 *.

In the month of September 1754, he was appointed commodore of the fquadron fent to efcort the troops for Virginia, which were commanded by the unfortunate Mr. Braddock. He hoifted his broad pendant on board the Centurion, of fixty guns, and remained on the fame ftation for fome time after he had accomplifhed the firft object of his miffion. During his continuance there he appears to have been very actively † employed in the arrangement of divers points connected with the operations intended to be carried into execution againft the encroachments of the French, who were feconded by the Indian nations, whom they had fpirited up for that purpofe.

A private letter from Virginia, dated April the 16th, 1755, gives us the following information. " All the governors on the Continent, with general Braddock and commodore Keppel, had a meeting at Annapolis a few days before, when it is fuppofed a plan of operations was

---

modore Keppel, and Robert White, efq. his majefty's conful-general at Tripoli, with the Divan, Kiaja, Bey, and Bafhaw of the ftate or kingdom of Tripoli.

" The faid commodore Keppel has alfo tranfmitted hither a treaty of peace and commerce between his majefty and the ftate of Tunis, concluded and figned the 19th of October laft paft, by the faid commodore and Charles Gordon, efq. his majefty's conful-general at Tunis, with the lord Ali Pafcha, Begler Bey, and fupreme commander of the faid ftate of Tunis "

* Collins erroneoufly ftates the commodore to have reached England before the the end of year 1752

† Mr. Braddock, in a letter written bv him to the fecretary of ftate, dated Williamfburg, Virginia, March 18, 1755, pays Mr. Keppel the following compliment.

" I think myfelf very happy in being affociated with an officer of Mr. Keppel's abilities and good difpofitions, which appears by his readinefs to enter into every meafure that may be conducive to the fuccefs of this undertaking. As but four pieces of twelve pounds were given me with the train, and a greater number appeared neceffary, I applied to him to have four more from his fhips, which he granted me, and many other things I ftood in need of." And again, " I have had from commodore Keppel all the affiftance poffible."

con-

concerted. They went afterwards to the camp of Alexandria, and reviewed the troops, which amounted to about fix thoufand men, who immediately after marched to Will's Creek, where they are to wait farther orders."

He returned to Europe * after the defeat of Mr. Braddock, a paffenger on board the Seahorfe, and the fituation of affairs with refpect to France becoming daily more critical, the equipment of a formidable naval force was purfued with unremitted vigour. Mr. Keppel was appointed to the Swiftfure, from which he quickly afterwards removed into the Torbay, and was ordered to the Mediterranean with a fmall fquadron, confifting of four fhips; but was obliged to return to Plymouth, his people being extremely fickly. In the enfuing month, having in the interim repaired to Spithead, he was fent out fenior officer of a fmall fquadron ordered to cruife in foundings, confifting, exclufive of his own fhip, of the Effex, of fixty-four guns, with the Unicorn and Gibraltar frigates. He failed from Spithead at the fame time with the unfortunate Mr. Byng. No other particular mention is made of him during the remainder of the year, except his having been one of the members of Mr. Byng's court-martial, and as having applied, though ineffectually, to the houfe of commons, of which he was then member, to be releafed from his oath of fecrecy taken on that occafion †. In the enfuing year he ferved under fir Edward Hawke on the unfuccefful expedition undertaken againft Rochfort; but is not particularly noticed, otherwife than as having been one of the captains ordered to chafe a French fhip of the line, which was difcovered ftanding in for the fleet when in Bafque Road, but which, notwithftanding all their vigilance, contrived to get off. During the fummer of the enfuing year he occafionally commanded a fmall flying fquadron employed on fhort cruifes in the Channel, and off the French coaft, a fervice in which he was tolerably

---

* Early in 1755 he was chofen reprefentative in parliament for the city of Chichefter, as fuccoffor to his brother, who became at that time earl of Albemarle, in confequence of the death of his father. At the next general election he was returned for Windfor, which place he continued, through every fucceeding parliament, to reprefent till the year 1780, when he was returned for the county of Surry.

† See vol. iv. p. 173. et feq.

fuccefsful

fuccefsful, having made feveral valuable and confequential prizes.

At the conclufion of the year he was appointed commander-in-chief of the expedition fent againſt the French fettlement of Goree, on the coaſt of Africa, and failed on the 19th of October, having his broad pendant on board the Torbay, with the following force under his command, the Naffau, of feventy guns; the Fougueux, of fixty-four; the Dunkirk, of fixty; the Litchfield, of fifty; the Prince Edward, of forty; the Saltafh floop, two bomb-ketches, one firefhip (the Roman Emperor), and a number of tranfports with two regiments of troops on board. Mr. Keppel is on this occafion faid to have received an extraordinary commiffion appointing him commander-in-ehief of the troops as well as the fquadron. He quitted Cork on the 11th of November, and experienced a number of delays and misfortunes while on his paſſage. The Litchfield, of fifty guns, together with the Somerfet tranfport, were wrecked, on the 29th of November, upon the coaſt of Barbary, about nine leagues to the northward of Saffy; and what rendered the misfortune more lamentable, all the people who lived to reach the fhore were made prifoners by the Moors.

Mr. Keppel with the remainder of his force happily got to an anchor off the ifland of Goree, on the the 24th of December*, about three o'clock in the afternoon. The

---

* The following modeſt but too concife account of this fuccefs was given by the commodore in his letter to the fecretary of ſtate.

" Sir,

" I arrived here with the fquadron under my command on the 28th of December paſt, in the evening. The next morning, agreeable to his majeſty's inſtructions, I attacked, with the fhips, the fort and batteries on the ifland of Goree, which were foon reduced to defire permiffion to capitulate. The governor's demands were, to be allowed to march the French troops out of the garrifon with the honours of war. His terms I abfolutely rejected and began a freſh attack: it was, however, but of very fhort duration, when the forts, garrifon, &c. furrendered at difcretion to his majeſty's fquadron.

" Lieutenant-colonel Worge had his troops embarked in the flatbottomed boats, in good order and readinefs, at a proper diſtance, with the tranfports, to attempt a defcent, when it ſhould be found practicable or requifite.

" Two

The Saltash sloop of war was ordered into a bay between point Barnabas and point Goree, to facilitate and cover the landing of the troops whenever it should be deemed expedient. The arrangements for the attack were not completed till the 28th, when, at four in the morning, the flat-bottomed boats were ordered on board the transports to receive the troops, which were all of them ready to be put on shore by nine o'clock. The ships of war were during this time by no means idle or indifferent spectators, preparing themselves to cannonade the fortress, which, from particular circumstances, was enabled to make no contemptible defence. The west front was the strongest; it nevertheless became necessary to make the attack on that quarter, as it was the lee side, and if the cables of any of the ships should be cut by the enemy's shot, they could put to sea without danger or farther accident, and return again to the attack: whereas, if the assault had been made on the eastern or weakest front, the ships might, in case of the misfortune already suggested, have ran on shore before they could have again brought up.

The following judicious arrangement was made by Mr. Keppel for the attack. The Firedrake bomb was ordered to proceed, covered by the Prince Edward from the fire

---

" Two days after the surrender of the island I ordered it to be delivered up, with the cannon, artillery, stores, and provisions, &c. found in it, to the officer and troops lieutenant-colonel Worge thought fit to garrison the place with; and the colonel is taking all imaginable pains to settle and regulate the garrison in the best manner and as fast as circumstances will admit of.

" The inclosed, sir, is the state of the island, with the artillery, ammunition, and provisions, found in the place at the time of its surrender.

" French, made prisoners of war, three hundred.

" Blacks in arms, a great number; but I am not well enough informed, as yet, to say precisely.

" The loss the enemy sustained, as to men, is so very differently stated to me, by those that have been asked, that I must defer saying the number till another opportunity.

" Iron ordnance, of different bores, ninety-three; one brass twelve-pounder; iron swivels, mounted on carriages, eleven; brass mortars, mounted on beds, two of thirteen inches; ditto, one of ten inches; iron, one of ten inches. In the magazine—powder, one hundred barrels; provisions of all species, for four hundred men, for four months."

of the enemy, to anchor abreaſt of a ſmall lunette battery en barbet, a little below the citadel to the northward. The eldeſt captain, Mr. Sayer, in the Naſſau, was ordered to lead the line of battle on the right, and anchor oppoſite to St. Peter's battery, of five guns: the Dunkirk followed to bring up abreaſt of a battery to the northward of the former, which was not finiſhed, nor an embraſure at that time opened: the commodore, in the Torbay, followed him, taking, for his part, the weſt point battery, of five guns, and the weſt corner of St. Francis's fort, mounting four ſmaller guns: capt. Knight, in the Fougueux, ſtationed ſecond on the left, bringing up the rear, (having directions, at the ſame time, to cover the other bomb on his ſtarboard quarter) had allotted to his ſhare the mortar-battery, ſo called from two large mortars covered by that battery.

The moment the firſt ſhip had dropt her anchor from her ſtern, ſhe was ordered to hoiſt a pendant at her mizen-peak, to acquaint the next ſhip that ſhe had brought up, which ſignal was to be repeated by each ſhip as ſhe ſhould take her ſtation, it being a part of the orders that not a gun ſhould be fired till each captain had his ſhip abreaſt of his poſt, and moored both ahead and ſtern. Mr. Keppel concluded theſe inſtructions with his good wiſhes for their ſucceſs, deſiring they would get on board their reſpective veſſels as faſt as poſſible, and lead on.

The bomb-ketch, and the covering ſhip, the Prince Edward, proceeded for their appointed ſtation about nine in the morning. The former commenced the aſſault in about ten minutes after ſhe got under weigh by throwing a ſhell, which was returned by a very briſk fire from the different batteries of the fort. Their retaliation was too ſucceſsful, for, as it is ſaid, the ſecond ſhot which the enemy fired, carried away the Prince Edward's flag-ſtaff, and ſet fire to her arm-cheſt, which blowing up, killed a marine. This accident cauſing ſome confuſion, the enemy profited by it; and finding their fire not returned, pointed their guns with ſo much care and caution, that ſeveral of the crew were killed and wounded, as well as conſiderable damage done to the ſhip before the was in a condition to take her revenge.

Mr.

Mr. Keppel, who anxiously watched every incident, observing that the Firedrake considerably overcharged her mortars, insomuch that the shells flew over the island and fell considerably beyond it to the southward, a circumstance those on board could not perceive, in consequence of the smoke in which they were inveloped, he sent his boat on board the Furnace ketch, with orders, " That as they saw the error of the other in overcharging the mortars, they would avoid that extreme; and that, as the enemy seemed bent upon sinking the Prince Edward and Firedrake, he desired they would, at the distance they then were, begin their bombardment, and endeavour, as much as possible, to draw part of the enemy's attention from their suffering friends." The Furnace, in compliance with this order, bore up close under the Fougueux's stern, and coming to on her larboard quarter, began to bombard with some success. Mr. Keppel paid attention in the next instance to the Prince Edward, and made the signal for the Nassau to bear down to her assistance; but a long time elapsed before the enemy's attention could be so successfully divided as to cause any material diversion, for, owing to a dead calm, that ship was nearly thirty minutes in wearing. The commodore himself in the Torbay, together with the Fougeux, were also considerably retarded, particularly the latter, which ship was much impeded by the Furnace bomb-ketch, which ran athwart his lee bow.

Mr. Keppel, in the Torbay, brought up abreast of the capital of the west point battery, so that the enemy could not bring a single gun to bear on him from thence; they could only annoy him from two guns mounted on St. Pierre's bastion, and three in a small lunette on the hill, the attention of both which posts was very considerably attracted by the other attacking ships. The fire, indeed, from the Torbay was so rapid, and at the same time so steadily supported, that the best provided fortification would scarcely have been able to withstand its fury. It is elsewhere observed, " the ship was in one continued blaze of fire; and that part of the island itself opposite to which the Torbay brought up, was darkened in a wonderful and almost incredible degree by the impenetrable cloud of smoke." The defenders, terrified at this artificial thunder, unanimously ran from their quarters, but were
ordered

ordered to return on pain of inftant death. The flag, however, was ftruck by order of the governor, and the fire of the Britifh fquadron ceafed.

A lieutenant being ordered on fhore, attended by the commodore's fecretary, in order to fettle and arrange the terms of capitulation, was furprized on being afked before they quitted the boat, "on what terms the furrender was expected?" The lieutenant, aftonifhed at the queftion, afked "if they had not ftruck their flag, intimating an unconditional fubmiffion refting merely on the clemency of the victor?" He was anfwered "No: lowering of the flag was intended only as a fignal for a parley." Being told the commodore would not liften to any other terms than a furrender at difcretion, the French commandant anfwered, "I am ftill prepared to defend myfelf, and will continue to do it, if the French troops are not permitted to march out with the honours of war." The officer remonftrated, but in vain, on the folly of the enemy making any farther refiftance, particularly as all the fhips were fafely and moft judicioufly pofted in their feverally allotted ftations. But this reprefentation being ineffectual he departed, after having told him, "that a gun fired over the ifland, by the commodore, fhould be the fignal for the renewal of hoftilities."

When Mr. Keppel was informed of the commandant's ridiculous obftinacy, he inftantly ordered the fignal to be given. It was immediately followed by a difcharge of his own broadfide, and by a fimilar falute from every gun in the fquadron that was ready, and bore on the works of the enemy. Before, however, the fire could be repeated, the governor finding his foldiers abfolutely refufed to ftand any longer to their guns, ordered the regimental colours to be dropt over the walls, as a fignal of furrendering at difcretion. Mr. Keppel immediately fent a party of marines afhore, who taking poffeffion of the fort, hoifted the Britifh colours, and finifhed the ceremony by three loud huzzas from the battlements of the citadel and caftle of St. Michael. In the preceding attack upwards of one hundred of the affailants were killed and wounded; but it is pofitively afferted by Campbell, "that of the French not a fingle man was killed;" fo that the terror alone of what the Britifh arms were able to effect accomplifhed this, which may, without much impropriety, be called a premature conqueſt.

The commodore having taken his priſoners on board and left a ſufficient garriſon to ſecure his conqueſt, repaired, on the 27th of January, to Senegal, for the purpoſe of making ſome ſmall though neceſſary arrangements there, which being accompliſhed, he returned directly to England, where he arrived in ſafety on the 1ſt of March.

During the remainder of the year he ſerved as a private captain in the Channel fleet, commanded by ſir Edward Hawke, and bore a very conſpicuous diſtinguiſhed ſhare in the defeat of the French armament under the marquis de Conflans, the Theſee, of ſeventy-four guns, having, as it is reported, been ſunk by the fire of the Torbay. In the enſuing year he continued to be employed on the home ſtation, principally in the occaſional command of one of the ſmall ſquadrons ſtationed to watch that remnant of the enemy's fleet which had effected its eſcape from the encounter juſt mentioned. He had in the beginning of this year removed into the Valiant, a new ſhip of ſeventy-four guns, in which he ſerved during the ſummer, under ſir Edward Hawke, in Quiberon Bay. Towards its concluſion he was choſen to command-in-chief a ſquadron of ten ſhips of the line*, beſides frigates and ſmaller veſſels, which were to cover an expedition concerted by the Britiſh miniſtry againſt the coaſt of France; ſome, who pretend to be much in the ſecret, ſay the iſland of Martinico. Matters were in ſo forward a ſtate of preparation, that his late majeſty, two days only before his death, ſaw a battalion of the foot guards, part of the army deſtined for this ſervice, paſs in review before him at Kenſington-palace. The death of the king put, however, a temporary ſtop to the expedition. It was reſumed in the enſuing ſpring, and ſent againſt the iſland of Belleiſle. It failed from Spithead on the 29th of March, 1761; and the firſt part of the undertaking bore rather an inauſpicious aſpect. An attempt was made to land the troops at Lomaria Bay on the 8th of April; but, owing to the natural ſtrength of the part attacked, and the very ſuperior force of the enemy

---

* In the month of February 1760, he was appointed colonel of the Plymouth diviſion of marines.

to that of the affailants who were able to effect their landing, the latter were obliged to defift with fome lofs. The commodore himfelf almoft defpaired of fuccefs, as will appear by the following extract from his official letter.

"While the repair and adjuftment of thefe defects * is in hand, I hope fome fpot may be agreed upon, where we may be more fuccefsful in the attempt than we were on the 8th; but if not fo, I hope his majefty will believe I have nothing more at heart than the exertion of the force entrufted to me, in a manner moft conducive to the honour of his arms."

Thefe gloomy appearances were, however, quickly diffipated by the arrival of a fecond letter, dated on the 23d of April, which we fhall here infert.

"Sir,

"I had the honour to write you a letter by the Acteon frigate, in which I gave but little hopes: fince which time the general and myfelf having confidered, that by attempting a place where mounting the rocks was juft poffible, and where, from the impracticable appearance it had to them, the enemy were no otherways prepared, than by a corps of troops pofted to annoy the boats in the attempt, it carried fome degree of hope with it, that by making a difpofition for the attack of their intrenched bays, and at Sauzon at the fame time, which the arrival of the tranfports with the light horfe enabled me to do, we might poffibly gain a footing. I have now the greateft pleafure in acquainting you, that his majefty's troops have made good a landing on the rocks near Point Lomaria, and cannot fufficiently commend the fpirit and good behaviour of the troops in the attempt, and the judgment with which fir Thomas Stanhope, and the reft of the captains of the king's fhips directed the fire upon the hills.

"Captain Barrington having been employed in many of the operations on this fervice, I have fent him home with this letter, and beg, fir, to refer you to him for the particulars.

"I have the honour to be, &c.

"A. KEPPEL."

---

* The damage fuftained by the tranfports and flat boats in the attack and a gale of wind which fucceeded it.

This gleam of fuccefs was the forerunner of conqueft, the citadel of Palais having capitulated on the 7th of June. The commodore remained afterwards on the ftation, as well for the protection of the new acquifition from any defultory attempt that might be made againft it by the remains of the French navy which lay ready for fea in Breft harbour, as for the purpofe of blocking up that fquadron, confifting of eight fhips of the line with four frigates, and confequently preventing their doing mifchief in any vulnerable quarter. A violent ftorm, which happened on January 12, drove the fquadron off the ftation, and compelled it to return to England for refitment. The Valiant, Mr. Keppel's own fhip, had five feet water in her hold when fhe got into Plymouth, accompanied by four fhips only out of the whole armament, the remainder being totally difperfed. He does not appear to have again returned to his ftation, nor indeed was it poffible, for he was, immediately after his arrival, ordered to put himfelf under the command of fir George Pocock, being chofen to command a divifion or fquadron in the fleet deftined for the expedition againft the Havannah.

He failed from Spithead, with the commander-in-chief, on the 5th of March; and nothing material appears to have occurred to him during the paffage. When the fleet arrived off the Havannah on the 6th of June, the commodore was appointed to cover the landing of the army, having a detachment of fix fhips of the line and a proportionate number of frigates, put under his orders for that purpofe. The fervice intrufted to him he executed with great care, attention and fuccefs, as Mr. Pocock, in his difpatches, makes the following honourable mention of him:

"I am glad on this occafion to do juftice to the diftinguifhed merit of commodore Keppel, who executed the fervice under his direction, on the coxemar fide, with the greateft fpirit, activity and diligence."

On the 21ft of October, 1762, he was advanced to be rear-admiral of the blue, the promotion of flag-officers being in fome degree extended beyond its cuftomary limits purpofely to include him, he being the junior on the lift.

He continued at the Havannah* some time after its surrender, and was remarkably successful, having taken several valuable prizes as well from the French as the Spaniards. The conclusion of the peace consequently put a temporary period to the services of Mr. Keppel; nevertheless, he did not in civil life remain inactive†, for on the 31ft of July, 1765, he was appointed one of the commissioners for executing the office of lord high admiral, a station he continued to hold no longer than the 11th of December, 1766. In the interim, however, that is to say, in the month of September, he took command of the yachts and vessels which convoyed and attended the queen of Denmark to Holland. On the 18th of October, 1770, he was advanced to be rear-admiral of the red; as he was, on the 24th of the same month, to be vice-admiral of the blue: being at the same time intended as commander of the squadron expeditiously fitted for sea, in consequence of an apprehended rupture with Spain, relative to the Falkland islands. The matter was, however, compromised early enough to prevent him from even hoisting his flag.

On the 31ft of March, 1775, he was moreover promoted to be vice-admiral of the white; as he was of the red on the 3d of February, 1776. On January 29, 1778, Mr. Keppel was farther advanced to be admiral of the blue, and it being foreseen that a rupture with France was become inevitable, the greatest expedition was used in equipping a formidable fleet, the command of which was given to him. He hoisted his flag at Spithead, in the month of March, on board the Prince George, of ninety guns. When the Victory was equipped and came round from Chatham, he removed his flag on

---

* " In September a fleet of twenty-five sail of French merchant-ships, richly laden with sugar, coffee and indigo, took their departure from Cape Francois for Europe under cover of four frigates. Five of these vessels were surprised and taken in the night by some privateers of New York and Jamaica. Next day it was their misfortune to fall in with commodore Keppel, who made prize of their whole fleet and convoy, which were carried into the harbour of Port Royal, in Jamaica."—Campbell.

† In 1763 he was appointed one of the grooms of the bed-chamber to his majefly, an appointment he held only till 1766.

board

board that ship, and on the 8th of June sailed from St. Helen's with the following fleet: the Victory, of one hundred guns; the Queen, of ninety guns, vice-admiral Harland; the Ocean, of ninety guns, vice-admiral Pallifer; the Sandwich, of ninety guns; the Prince George of ninety; the Foudroyant, of eighty; the Shrewsbury, Egmont, Valiant, Courageux, Ramilies, Hector, Monarque, Elizabeth, Berwick, Robust, and Cumberland, of seventy-four guns each; the America, Exeter, Stirling Castle, and Bienfaisant, of sixty-four guns each; Arethusa frigate, of thirty guns; Fox and Proserpine, of twenty-eight; the Alert and Meredith armed cutters; and the Vulcan fire-ship; in the whole twenty-seven sail.

On the 17th of the same month *, the Lizard being not more than twenty-five miles distant, two French frigates were discovered, attended by two tenders, apparently reconnoitering the fleet. Ships were ordered by Mr. Keppel to chase and bring the vessels down to him. The Milford frigate coming up with one of them, civilly requested her commander to follow him down to the Victory, which he peremptorily refused, till a shot being fired at him induced him to compliance. The other French ship was closely pursued by the Arethusa and Alert, followed, but at a considerable distance astern, by the Valiant and Monarch, of seventy-four guns each. Mr. Keppel ordered the French frigate, which proved to be the Licorne, of thirty-two guns, to be closely guarded during the night, but to be at the same time treated with every possible civility and attention. On the morrow one of the ships stationed to attend her fired a shot athwart her, in consequence of her putting improperly on the contrary tack. This the Licorne returned by firing a whole

---

* It was known as early as the month of May, that the French had ready for sea, in the road of Breast, twenty-two ships of the line and fourteen frigates, commanded by the count D'Orvilliers; and, as the author of the Continuation of Campbell justly observes, the situation of the admiral must have been peculiarly embarrassing. By commencing hostilities without orders the whole blame of the war, should it take place, might have been laid upon him: but considering, nevertheless, that it was indispensibly necessary to stop these frigates, as well to procure information as to prevent its being communicated, he did not hesitate in taking decisive measures.

broadside into the America, though lord Longford, who commanded that ship, was talking to the French captain in the civilest strain at the very time. This circumstance, together with that of the other French frigate which was pursued by the Arethusa, having resisted and killed several men on board the latter ship, caused Mr. Keppel to detain the Licorne, as he did a second frigate of the same force, called the Pallas, which he met with two days afterwards.

The intelligence he acquired of the superior force of the French fleet*, by papers found on board these ships, induced him in prudence to return into port for a reinforcement. He arrived on the 28th of June, and being joined by such ships as were ready, again sailed on the 10th of July. He soon got sight of the French fleet; and after some days † spent in manœuvring, brought them to action ‡ on the 27th of the same month.

The

---

* Which he now found to consist of between thirty and forty sail of the line, and a dozen frigates.

† "At first the French admiral, from his movements, appeared desirous to bring on an engagement, probably supposing the British fleet to be of the same force it was in the preceding month; but on coming nearer he discovered his mistake, and from that moment evidently determined to avoid an action. This plan he adhered to for the three following days, notwithstanding every effort used by the British admiral to bring him to one. All the advantage he could gain in four days was to separate two of the enemy's line of battle ships, which returned to Brest and could not afterwards rejoin their fleet."—Campbell.

‡ The following account is that which was officially transmitted to the admiralty board, containing a plain state of the principal leading facts.

"Victory, at sea, July 30, 1778.

" Sir,

" My letters of the 23d and 24th instant, by the Peggy and Union cutters, acquainted you, for their lordships' information, that I was in pursuit, with the king's fleet under my command, of a numerous fleet of French ships of war.

" From that time, to the 27th, the winds constantly in the N. W. and S.W. quarters, sometimes blowing strong, and the French fleet, always to windward, going off, I made use of every method to close in with them that was possible, keeping the king's ships at the same time collected, as much as the nature of a pursuit would admit of, and which became necessary from the cautious manner the French proceeded in, and the disinclination that appeared in them to allow of my bringing the king's ships close up to a regular engagement. This left but little

other

The political contest, the diversity of opinions, the private as well as public animosities which this remarkable

other chance of getting up with them, than by seizing the opportunity that offered, on the morning of the 27th, by the wind's admitting of the van of the king's fleet under my command leading up with, and closing with their center and rear.

" The French began firing upon the headmost of vice-admiral sir Robert Harland's division, and the ships with him, as they led up, they cannonaded the leading ships; and the vice-admiral soon returned the fire, as did every ship as they could close up. The chace had occasioned their being extended, nevertheless they were all soon in battle.

" The fleets, being upon different tacks, passed each other very close. The object of the French seemed to be the disabling of the king's ships in their masts and sails, in which they so far succeeded as to prevent many of the ships of my fleet being able to follow me, when I wore to stand after the French fleet. This obliged me to wear again, to join those ships, and thereby allow the French to form their fleet again, and range it in a line to leeward of the king's fleet, towards the close of the day, which I did not discourage, but allowed of their doing it without firing upon them, thinking they meant handsomely to try their force with us the next morning; but they had been so beaten in the day, that they took the advantage of the night to go off

" The wind and weather being such that they could reach their own shores before there was any chance of the king's fleet getting up with them, the state the ships were in, in their masts, yards, and sails, left me no choice of what was proper and adviseable to do.

" The spirited conduct of vice-admiral sir Robert Harland, vice-admiral sir Hugh Pallifer, and the captains of the fleet, supported by their officers and men, deserves much commendation.

"A. KEPPEL."

List of the killed and wounded.

Ships.	Killed.	Wound.	Ships.	Killed.	Wound.
Monarch	2	9	Prince George	5	15
Exeter	4	6	Vengeance	4	18
Queen	1	2	Worcester	3	5
Shrewsbury	3	6	Elizabeth	0	7
Berwick	10	11	Defiance	8	17
Stirling Castle	2	11	Robust	5	17
Courageux	6	13	Formidable	16	49
Thunderer	2	5	Ocean	2	18
Vigilant	2	3	America	1	17
Sandwich	2	20	Terrible	9	21
Valiant	6	26	Egmont	12	19
Victory	11	24	Ramillies	12	16
Foudroyant	5	18			

event gave birth to, are still too recent in the minds of all to make it proper or decent for us to enter into any animadversion or remark on the subject, we shall therefore confine ourselves strictly to the relation of mere facts; for when men present at the encounter, and of the highest reputation in the service, have entertained and publicly declared sentiments * the most opposite from each other, we cannot presume to enter either into exculpation or censure. We cannot, however, refrain from inserting a declaration, as made by the count D'Orvilliers himself, given us by a friend, who soon after the action was a prisoner in Brest. The cool dispassionate opinion of an honourable enemy is, perhaps, among the best evidence that can ever be adduced on any occasion whatever. The count said, "that during the action itself the English had, as he conceived, the advantage; but that, after the firing ceased, he had *out manœuvred* Mr. Keppel." On canvassing his declaration rather closer, it appeared the count imagined he had completely missed and deceived the British admiral, by impressing on him an idea, that he, the count, intended to renew the action on the morrow. This Mr. Keppel himself, in great measure, admits to be true, when he says, in his dispatches, " I allowed their doing it, (forming their line without molestation) thinking they meant handsomely to try their force with us next day."

Mr. Keppel returned into port, and having refitted the ships of his division, sailed from Plymouth on the 23d of August to join sir Robert Harland and sir Hugh Pallifer, who went out the day before. Nothing material, however, enough to merit notice, took place during the remainder of this naval campaign†: a variety of anonymous paragraphs were published soon after this time, some of

---

* " Soon after the action (says Dr. Berkenhout, who betrays evident marks of partiality in his Continuation of Campbell) the periodical publications were filled with encomiums or satires on the admiral, according to the various opinions, inclinations, or humours of the different writers, who chose to celebrate or arraign his character, and conduct. Those who approved all the measures of administration were the loudest in condemning his behaviour; while the anti-ministerial party not only justified his proceedings, but held him forth as an object deserving the warmest gratitude and applause of his fellow-citizens."

† Mr. Keppel finally returned from his cruise on the 28th of October.

which were anfwered by his friends. Thefe invectives and recriminations, as it is elfewhere remarked, might have paffed on both fides, as it is thought, without any material confequence, and the cafe of the two contending parties would have been left to the impartiality of the future hiftorian, had not certain remarks, publifhed in fome of the newfpapers, in the month of December, called up Mr. Keppel in his place, as a member of the houfe of commons, to vindicate, as he faid, his own character. On this occafion he declared, "If he was to go over the bufinefs of the 27th of July again, he would conduct himfelf in the fame manner; every thing that could be done had been done, and, he was happy to fay, the Britifh flag had not been tarnifhed in his hands: he felt himfelf perfectly eafy on that head, and fhould never be afhamed of his conduct on the day alluded to. The oldeft and moft experienced officers in his majefty's navy, in every engagement, faw fomething which they were before unacquainted with, and that day alfo prefented what was new. He impeached no man of neglect of duty, becaufe he was fatisfied that the officer alluded to had manifefted no want of courage, the quality moft effential in a Britifh feaman. He faid he was much furprifed, when an officer under his command had made an appeal to the public in a common newfpaper, figned with his name, before any accufation had been made againft him, and which tended to render him (Mr. Keppel) odious and defpicable in the eyes of his countrymen."

Sir Hugh Pallifer in exculpation of himfelf, protefted "He was fo confcious of not having been any hindrance to a renewal of the action with the Breft fleet, on the 27th of July, that he was equally indifferent with the honourable admiral how foon an enquiry were fet on foot. He had difcovered from what the admiral had juft faid, that the principal matter weighed againft him in the admiral's mind was, the publication in the newfpapers, which he had figned with his name, and by which he would abide; if it was imprudent, if it was wrong, the confequence was to himfelf. To fay any thing againft a friend was, to a man of fenfibility, the moft difagreeable thing in nature; but where an officer's reputation was at ftake, the removing an unjuft ftigma was certainly the firft object. If there was any reafon of accufation, why not make it openly

openly and fairly? If not, Why infinuate that he had been wanting in point of conduct, though a teftimony was given in favour of his courage? This, he faid, was a language extremely different from that of the admiral's difpatch, containing an account of the action, in which he informed the admiralty board of the fpirited and gallant conduct of all the officers under his command."

Mr. Keppel on his part admitted, " he had given that approbation, and was ready to repeat it, and point the teftimony particularly as well as generally. The vice-admiral had alluded to fignals, and faid it was no fault of his, that the fleet of France was not re-attacked. As to that, he could fay, that he prefumed every inferior officer was to obey the fignals of his commander: and now, when called upon to fpeak out, he would inform the houfe, and the public, that the fignal for coming into the Victory's wake was flying from three o'clock in the afternoon till eight in the evening unobeyed; at the fame time he did not charge the vice-admiral with actual difobedience: he doubted not but, if an enquiry fhould be thought neceffary, that he would be able to juftify himfelf, becaufe he was fully perfuaded of his perfonal bravery."

This long and difagreeable altercation was productive of a charge, exhibited by fir Hugh, againft the admiral, which was delivered in to the board on the 9th of December, being to the following purport.

' 1. That, on the morning of the 27th of July, 1778, having a fleet of thirty fhips of the line under his command, and being then in the prefence of a French fleet of the like number of fhips of the line, the faid admiral did not make the neceffary preparations for fight; did not put his fleet into a line of battle, or into any order proper either for receiving or attacking an enemy of fuch force; but, on the contrary, although his fleet was already difperfed and in diforder, he, by making the fignal for feveral fhips of the vice-admiral of the blue's divifion to chace to windward, increafed the diforder of that part of his fleet, and the fhips were, in confequence, more fcattered than they had been before, and whilft in this diforder he advanced to the enemy, and made the fignal for battle; that the above conduct was the more unaccountable, as the enemy's fleet was not then in diforder, nor beaten, nor flying,

flying, but formed in a regular line of battle on that tack which approached the Britiſh fleet, all their motions plainly indicating a deſign to give battle, and they edged down and attacked it whilſt in diſorder. By this unofficer-like conduct a general engagement was not brought on, but the other flag officers and captains were left to engage without order or regularity, upon which, great confuſion enſued, ſome of his ſhips were prevented from getting into action at all, others were not near enough to the enemy, and ſome, from the confuſion, fired into others of the king's ſhips and did them conſiderable damage, and the vice-admiral of the blue was left alone to engage ſingle and unſupported: in theſe inſtances the ſaid admiral Keppel negligently performed the duty impoſed on him.

" 2dly. That after the van and centre diviſions of the Britiſh fleet paſſed the rear of the enemy, the admiral did not immediately tack and double upon the enemy with theſe two diviſions and continue the battle, nor did he collect them together at that time, and keep ſo near the enemy as to renew the battle as ſoon as it might be proper; on the contrary, he ſtood away beyond the enemy to a great diſtance before he wore to ſtand towards them again, leaving the vice-admiral of the blue engaged with the enemy and expoſed to be cut off.

" 3. That after the vice-admiral of the blue had paſſed the laſt of the enemy's ſhips, and immediately wore, and laid his own ſhip's head towards the enemy again, being then in their wake and at a little diſtance only, and expecting the admiral to advance with all the ſhips to renew the fight, the admiral did not advance for that purpoſe, but ſhortened ſail, hawled down the ſignal for battle; nor did he at that time, nor at any other time whilſt ſtanding towards the enemy, call the ſhips together in order to renew the attack, as he might have done, particularly the vice-admiral of the red and his diviſion, which had received the leaſt damage, had been the longeſt out of action, were ready and fit to renew it, were then to windward and could have bore down and fetched any part of the French fleet, if the ſignal for battle had not been hawled down, or if the ſaid admiral Keppel had availed himſelf of the ſignal appointed, by the 31ſt article of the fighting inſtructions, by which he might have ordered
thoſe

those to lead, who are to lead with the starboard tack on board, by a wind, which signal was applicable to the occasion for renewing the engagement with advantage, after the French fleet had been beaten, their line broken, and in disorder; in these instances he did not do the utmost in his power to take, sink, burn, or destroy the French fleet that had attacked the British fleet.

" 4th. That instead of advancing to renew the engagement, as in the preceding articles is alledged, and as he might and ought to have done, the admiral wore and made sail directly from the enemy, and thus he led the whole British fleet away from them, which gave them an opportunity to rally unmolested, and to form again into a line of battle and to stand after the British fleet. This was disgraceful to the British flag, for it had the appearance of a flight, and gave the French admiral a pretence to claim the victory, and to publish to the world that the British fleet ran away, and that he pursued it with the fleet of France, and offered it battle.

" 5th. That on the morning of the 28th of July, 1778, when it was perceived that only three of the French fleet remained near the British in the situation the whole had been in the night before, and that the rest were to leeward at a greater distance, not in a line of battle but in a heap, the admiral did not cause the fleet to pursue the flying enemy, not even to chace the three ships that fled after the rest, but, on the contrary, he led the British fleet another way, directly from the enemy: by these instances of misconduct and neglect, a glorious opportunity was lost of doing a most essential service to the state, and the honour of the British navy was tarnished.

" H. PALLISER."

The official communication of the foregoing charge was made to the admiral the same evening, and the necessary measures were taken to bring the matter to a solemn investigation. A variety of reasons contributed to render it extremely unpopular. Mr. Keppel had by his supposed free condescending manners, rendered himself almost the idol of the service, and considerably ingratiated himself with the whole mass of his countrymen, even those who knew him at a distance, and by character only. His antago-

antagonist, on the other hand, was neither so well and generally known, nor, from his more reserved carriage, so much beloved. He was very industriously represented as the tool of administration; the whole of his conduct was interpreted as tending to a wish of sacrificing his commander-in-chief, and the charge violently imputed to malicious rancour. Moderate men at the same time conceived an impropriety in prosecuting a charge after so long an interval; so that a memorial*, signed by several of those who

---

* " To the KING.

"We, the subscribing admirals of your majesty's royal navy, having hitherto on all occasions served your majesty with zeal and fidelity, and being desirous of devoting every action of our lives, and our lives themselves to your majesty's service, and the defence of our country, think ourselves indispensibly bound, by our duty to that service and that country, with all possible humility, to represent to your wisdom and justice,

"That sir Hugh Pallifer, vice-admiral of the blue, lately serving under the command of the honourable Augustus Keppel, did prefer certain articles of accusation, containing several matters of heinous offence against his said commander-in-chief, to the lords commissioners for executing the office of lord high admiral of Great Britain, he, the the said sir Hugh Pallifer, being himself a commissioner in the said commission; this accusation he, the said sir Hugh Pallifer, withheld from the 27th day of July last, the time of the supposed offences committed, until the 9th day of this present December, and then brought forward for the purpose of recrimination against charges conjectured by him, the said sir Hugh Pallifer, but which in fact were never made.

" That the commissioners of the admiralty, near five months after the pretended offences aforesaid, did receive from their said colleague in office, the charge made by him against his said commander; and without taking into consideration the relative situation of the accuser, and the party accused, or attending to the avowed motives of the accusation, or the length of time of withholding, or the occasion of making the same, and without any other deliberation whatever, did, on the very same day on which the charge was preferred, and without previous notice to the party accused of an intention of making a charge against him, give notice of their intending that a court-martial should be held on the said admiral Keppel, after forty years of meritorious service, and a variety of actions in which he had exerted eminent courage and conduct, by which the honour and power of this nation, and the glory of the British flag, had been maintained and increased in various parts of the world.

"We beg leave to express to your majesty our concern at this proceeding, and to represent our apprehensions of the difficulties and discouragements which will inevitably arise to your service therefrom,

and

had been, and were among the leading and moſt diſtinguiſhed characters in the Britiſh navy, was preſented to his majeſty, befeeching him to ſtop all farther proceedings, as they conceived the profecution of the charge would be totally fubverfive of the rules and difcipline of the navy. This and that it will not be eafy for men, attentive to their honour, to ferve your majeſty, particularly in fituations of principal command, if the practice now ſtated to your majeſty be countenanced, or the principles upon which the fame has been fupported fhall prevail with any lord high admiral, or with any commiſſioner for executing that office.

" We are humbly of opinion, that a criminal charge againſt an officer (rifing in importance according to the rank and command of that officer) which fufpends his fervice to your majeſty, perhaps in the moſt critical exigencies of the public affairs, which calls his reputation into doubt and difcuſſion, which puts him on trial for his life, profeſſion and reputation, and which, in its confequences, may caufe a fatal ceſſation in the naval exertions of the kingdom, to be a matter of the moſt ferious nature, and never to be made by authority but on folid ground, and on mature deliberation. The honour of an officer is his moſt precious poſſeſſion and beſt qualification; the public have an intereſt in it: and whilſt thofe under whom we ferve countenance accufation, it is often impoſſible perfectly to reſtore military fame by the mere acquittal of a court-martial. Imputations made by high authority remain long and affect deeply. The fphere of action of commanders-in-chief is large, their bufinefs intricate, and fubject to great variety of opinion; before they are to be put on the judgment of others for acts done upon their difcretion, the greateſt difcretion ought to be employed.

" Whether the board of admiralty hath by law any fuch difcretion, we, who are not of the profeſſion of the law, cannot pofitively affert; but if we had conceived that this board had no legal ufe of their reafon in a point of fuch delicacy and importance, we fhould have known on what terms we ferved; but we never did imagine it poſſible that we were to receive orders from, and be accountable to thofe who, by law, were reduced to become paſſive inſtruments to the poſſible malice, ignorance, or treafon of any individual who might think fit to difarm his majeſty's navy of its beſt and higheſt officers. We conceive it difrefpectful to the laws of our country, to fuppofe them capable of fuch manifeſt injuſtice and abfurdity.

" We therefore humbly reprefent, in behalf of public order, as well as of the difcipline of the navy, to your majeſty, the dangers of long concealed and afterwards precipitately adopted charges, and of all recriminatory accufations of fubordinate officers againſt their commanders-in-chief, and particularly the mifchief and fcandal of permitting men, who are at once in high civil office and in fubordinate military command, previous to their making fuch accufations, to attempt to corrupt the public judgment, by the publication of libels on their

This application produced no effect, an order having been issued to sir Thomas Pye, admiral of the white, to hold a court-martial, for the trial of Mr. Keppel, on the 7th of January, it accordingly met on that day on board the Britannia. After going through the usual and necessary forms of swearing in the members, &c. it adjourned to the governor's house, a particular act of parliament having, for the accommodation of Mr. Keppel, who was extremely indisposed, been passed for the purpose of authorising a measure, till then unprecedented. It is not within our limits to give even an abridged detail of the trial, which continued, with several short intervening adjournments, till the 11th of February. Suffice it that we briefly state Mr. Keppel was acquitted. Were we even competent to so arduous an undertaking, delicacy to both persons forbids our making the smallest comment on an event so recent. The dæmon of party appears in many instances, on both sides of the question, to have taken full possession of many, who, both as officers and men, stood very deservedly in the highest rank of public opinion. Mr. Keppel having, through reasons already given, possessed considerably the greatest share of what is called popularity, was congratulated on his acquittal by his private friends and his public partizans, with a warmth certainly never yet exceeded, and we believe scarcely equalled.

Though, for the reasons just given, we forbear entering into any account of the trial itself, yet that we may act, as we profess, with the utmost impartiality, we shall subjoin the leading points insisted on by Mr. Keppel in his defence, which will certainly afford no inconsiderable

---

their officers in a common newspaper, thereby exciting mutiny in your majesty's navy, as well as prejudicing the minds of those who are to try the merits of the accusation against the said superior officer.

" Hawke, Bristol,
John Moore, James Young,
Bolton, Matthew Barton,
Samuel Graves, Francis Geary,
Hugh Pigot, Shuldham,
Robert Harland, Clark Gayton."

account of the nature of evidence adduced in support of the different charges exhibited against him*.

His

---

* To the first charge he anfwered,

" I have never underftood preparations for fight to have any other meaning, in the language and underftanding of feamen, than that each particular fhip under the direction and difcipline of her own officers when in purfuit of an enemy, be in every refpect cleared and in readinefs for action; the contrary of which, no admiral of a fleet without reafonable caufe will prefume: and as from the morning of the 24th, when the French fleet had got to windward, to the time of the action, the Britifh fleet was in unremitting purfuit of them, it is ftill more difficult to conceive that any thing more is meant by this charge, than what is immediately after conveyed by the charge that follows it, namely,

" That on the fame morning of the 27th, I did not put my fleet Into a line of battle, or into any order, proper either for receiving or attacking an enemy of fuch force.

" By this fecond part of the charge, I feel myfelf attacked in the exercife of that great and broad line of difcretion, which every officer commanding either fleets or armies is often obliged, both in duty and confcience, to exer ife to the beft of his judgement, and which depending on circumftances and fituations infinitely various, cannot be reduced to any pofitive rule of difcipline or practice; a diicretion which I will fubmit to the court, I was peculiarly called upon by the ftrongeft and beft motives to exercife, and which in my public letter to the board of admiralty I openly avowed to have exercifed. I admit that on the morning of the 27th of July I did not put my fleet into a line of battle, becaufe I had it not in my choice to do fo, confiftent with the certainty, or even the probability of either giving or being given battle; and becaufe, if I had fcrupuloufly adhered to that order, in which, if the election had been mine, I fhould have chofen to have received or attacked a willing enemy, I fhould have had no enemy either to receive or attack.

" I fhall therefore, in anfwer to this charge, fubmit to the court my reafons for determining to bring the French fleet to battle at all events; and fhall fhew that any other order than that in which my fleet was conducted, from my firft feeing them to the moment of the action, was incompatible with fuch determination.

" In order to this, I muft call the attention of the court, to a retrofpective view of the motions of the two fleets, from their firft coming in fight of each other.

" On my firft difcovering the French fleet at one o'clock in the afternoon of the 23d of July, I made the neceffary fignals for forming my fleet in the order of battle, which I effected towards the evening, when I brought to, by fignal, and lay till the morning, when perceiving that the French fleet had gained the wind during the night, and carried a preffed fail to preferve it, I difcontinued the fignal for the

line,

His acquittal, and the almost frantic joy which convulsed his friends and the populace on that occasion, are also too recent

line, and made the general signal to chace to windward, in hopes that they would join battle with me, rather than suffer two of their capital ships to be entirely separated from them, and give me a chance of cutting off a third, which had carried away a top-mast in the night, and which, but for a shift of wind, I must have taken: in this, however, I was disappointed, for they suffered two of them to go off altogether, and continued to make every use of the advantage of the wind.

" This assiduous endeavour of the French admiral to avoid coming to action, which from his thus having the wind was always in his option, led me to believe he expected a reinforcement, a reflection which would alone have been a sufficient reason to determine me to urge my pursuit in as collected a body as the nature of such a pursuit would admit of, without the delay of the line, and to seize the first opportunity of bringing on an engagement.

" But I had other reasons no less urgent.

" If by obstinately adhering to the line of battle, I had suffered, as I inevitably must, the French fleet to have separated from me; and if by such separation the English convoys from the East and West Indies, which I have already stated in the introduction to my defence to have been then expected home, had been cut off, or the coast of England had been insulted, what would have been my situation? Sheltered under the forms of discipline, I, perhaps, might have escaped punishment, but I could not have escaped censure. I should neither have escaped the contempt of my fellow-citizens, nor the reproaches of my own conscience.

" Moved by these important considerations, supported by the examples of of admiral Russel, and other great naval commanders, who, in similar situation, had ever made strict order give way to reasonable enterprize, and particularly encouraged by the remembrance of having myself served under that truly great officer lord Hawke, when rejecting all rules and forms, he grasped at victory by an irregular attack, I determined not to lose sight of the French fleet by being out-sailed, from preserving the line of battle: but to keep my fleet as well collected as I could, and near enough to assist and act with each other, in case of a change of wind, or other favourable circumstances, should enable me to force the enemy to action.

" Such were my feelings and resolutions when the day broke on the morning of the 27th of July, at which time the fleet under my command was in the following position:—Vice-admiral sir Robert Harland was about four miles distant on the Victory's weather quarter, with most of the ships of his own division and some of those belonging to the center—and vice-admiral sir Hugh Pallifer at about three miles distance, a point before the lee-beam of the Victory, with his main-sail up, which obliged the ships of his division to continue under an easy sail.

" The

recent to render a minute detail neceſſary. The admiral
neverthelefs ceafed to be employed, a circumftance to be
expected,

"The French fleet was as much to windward, and at as great a
diftance as it had been the preceding morning, ſtanding with a freſh
wind cloſe hauled on the larboard tack, to all appearance avoiding me
with the ſame induſtry as ever.

" At this time, therefore, I had no greater inducement to form the
line than I had on the morning of the former day, and I could not
have formed it without greatly increaſing my diſtance from the French
fleet, contrary to that plan of operation which I have already ſubmitted
to the judgement of the court.

" The vice-admiral of the blue next charges,

" That although my fleet was already diſperſed, and in diſorder, I,
by making the ſignal for ſeveral ſhips of his diviſion to chace to windward, encreaſed the diſorder of that part of my fleet, and that the ſhips
were in conſequence more ſcattered than they had been before, and
that whilſt in this diſorder I advanced to the enemy, and made the
ſignal for battle.

" In this part of the charge there is a ſtudious deſign to miſlead
the underſtanding, and by leaving out times, and intermediate events,
to make the tranſactions of half a day appear but as one moment.

" It is indeed impoſſible to read it without being poſſeſſed with the
idea, that at half paſt five in the morning, when I made the ſignal for
ſix of the ſhips of the vice-admiral of the blue's diviſion to chace to
windward, I was in the immediate proſpect of cloſing with an enemy
approaching me in a regular line, and all their motions plainly indicating a deſign to give battle; inſtead of which both the fleets were
then on the larboard tack, the enemy's fleet near three leagues to
windward, going off cloſe by the wind with a preſſed ſail. My reaſon,
therefore, for making that ſignal at half paſt five, was to collect as
many of the ſhips to windward as I could in order to ſtrengthen the
main body of the fleet, in caſe I ſhould be able to get to action, and to
fill up the interval between the Victory and the vice-admiral, which
was occaſioned by his being far to leeward; and it is plain that the
vice-admiral muſt have himſelf underſtood the object of the ſignal,
ſince it has appeared in the courſe of the evidence, that on its being
made, the Formidable ſet her main-ſail and let the reefs out of her
top-ſails; and indeed the only reaſon why it was not originally made
for the whole diviſion was, that they muſt have then chaced as a diviſion, which would have retarded the beſt going ſhips, by an attendance
on the vice-admiral.

" Things were in this ſituation, when about nine o'clock the French
fleet wore and ſtood to the ſouthward on the ſtarboard tack; but the
wind immediately after they were about, coming more ſoutherly, I
continued to ſtand on till a quarter paſt ten, at which time I tacked
the Britiſh fleet together by ſignal, and ſoon after we were about,
the wind came ſome points in our favour to the weſtward, which
enabled us to lye up for a part of them; but in a dark ſquall that

almoſt

expected, not wondered at, confidering the extraordinary fchifm which his cafe and conduct had created, added to the

almoſt immediately came on, I loſt fight of them for above half an hour. When it cleared away at eleven o'clock, I difcovered that the French fleet had changed their pofition, and were endeavouring to form the line on the larboard tack; but finding they could not effect it without coming within gun-fhot of the van of the Britiſh fleet, they edged down and fired on my headmoſt ſhips as they approached them on the contrary tack, at a quarter after eleven, which was inſtantly returned; then, and not till then, I made the fignal for battle. All this happened in about half an hour, and muſt have been owing to the enemy's falling to leeward in performing their evolutions during the fquall; thefe we could not fee, and it produced this fudden and unexpected opportunity of engaging them, as the enemy were near three leagues ahead of me when the fquall came on.

" If, therefore, by making the fignal for the line of battle when the van of my fleet was thus fuddenly getting within reach of the enemy, and well connected with the center, as my accufer himfelf has admitted, I had called back the vice-admiral of the red, the French fleet might either have formed their line compleat, and have come down upon my fleet while in the confufion of getting into order of battle, or (what I had ſtill greater reafon to apprehend) might have gone off to windward out of my reach altogether; for even as it was, the enemy's van, inſtead of coming clofe to action, kept their wind, and paffed hardly within random ſhot.

" My accufer next afferts, as an aggravation of his former charge,

" That the French fleet was in a regular line on the tack which approached the Britifh fleet, all their motions plainly indicating a defign to give battle.

" Both which facts have already been contradicted by the teſtimony of even his own witneffes. That the enemy's fleet was not in a regular line of battle, appeared by the French admiral being out of his ſtation far from the centre of his line, and next, or very near to a fhip carrying a vice-admiral's flag; fome of their ſhips were abreaſt of each other, and in one, as they paffed the Englifh fleet together with other apparent marks of irregularity. Indeed, every motion of the French fleet, from about nine, when it went on the ſtarboard tack, till the moment of the action, and even during the action itſelf, I apprehend to be decifive againſt the alledged indication of defigning battle; for, if the French admiral had really intended to come to action, I apprehend he never would have put his fleet on the contrary tack to that on which the Britifh fleet was coming up to him, but would have fhortened fail and waited for it, formed in the line on the fame tack; and even when he did tack towards the Britifh fleet the alledged indication is again directly refuted, by the van of the French fleet hauling their wind again inſtead of bearing down into action, and by their hoiſting no colours when they began to engage.

Vol. V.   Y   " Not-

the very severe animadversions made by his friends on the behaviour of ministers towards him. He continued, however,

"Notwithstanding these incontrovertible truths, my accuser imputes it to me that a general engagement was not brought on; but it is evident, from the testimony of every witness he has called, that a general action was never in my choice; and that so far from its being prevented by my not having formed the line of battle, no engagement, either general or partial, could have been brought on if I had formed it: indeed, it is a contradiction in terms, to speak of a general engagement, where the fleet that has the wind tacks to pass the fleet to leeward on the contrary tack.

"Such was the manner in which, after four days pursuit, I was at last enabled, by a favourable shift of wind, to close with the fleet of rance.

"If I am justifiable on principle in the exerise of that discretion, which I have been submitting to your judgment, of bringing at all events an unwilling enemy to battle, I am certainly not called upon to descend to all the minutiæ of consequences resulting from such enterprize, even if such had ensued as my accuser has asserted, but which his own witnesses have not only failed to establish, but absolutely refuted. It would be an insult on the understanding of the court, were I to offer any arguments to shew, that ships which engage without a line of battle, cannot so closely, uniformly, and mutually support each other, as when circumstances admit of a line being formed, because it is self-evident, and is the basis of all the discipline and practice of lines of battle. In the present case, notwithstanding I had no choice in making any disposition for an attack, nor any possibility of getting to battle otherwise than I did, which would be alone sufficient to repel any charge of consequent irregularity or even confusion; yet it is not necessary for me to claim the protection of the circumstances under which I acted, because no irregularity or confusion either existed or has been proved, all the chacing ships, and the whole fleet, except a ship or two, got into battle, and into as close battle as the French fleet, which had the option by being to windward, chose to give them.

"The vice-admiral of the blue himself, though in the rear, was out of action in a short time after the Victory; and so far from being left to engage singly, and unsupported, was passed during the action, by three ships of his own division, and was obliged to back his mizen top-sail to keep out of the fire of one of the largest ships in the fleet, which must have continued near him all the rest of the time he was passing the French line, as I shall prove she was within three cables length of the Formidable when the firing ceased."

Answer to the second article.

"The moment the Victory had passed the enemy's rear, my first object was to look round the position of the fleet, which the smoke had

however, conſtantly to attend in parliament, where his mere preſence on ſome occaſions, and particular remarks which had till then obſcured from obſervation, in order to determine how a general engagement might beſt be brought on after the fleets ſhould have paſſed each other.

"I found that the vice-admiral of the red, with part of his diviſion, had tacked, and was ſtanding towards the enemy with top-gallant ſails ſet, the very thing I am charged with not having directed him to do; but all the reſt of the ſhips that had got out of action were ſtill on the ſtarboard tack, ſome of them dropping to leeward, and ſeemingly employed in repairing their damages: the Victory herſelf was in no condition to tack; and I could not immediately wear and ſtand back on the ſhips coming up aſtern of me out of the action (had it been otherwiſe expedient) without throwing them into the utmoſt confuſion. Sir John Roſs, who very gallantly tried the experiment, having informed the court of the momentary neceſſity he was under of wearing back again to prevent the conſequences I have mentioned, makes it unneceſſary to enlarge on the probable effect of ſuch a generel manœuvre with all the ſhips ahead. Indeed, I only remark it as a ſtrong relative circumſtance appearing by the evidence of a very able and experienced officer, and by no means as a juſtification for having ſtood away beyond the enemy to a great diſtance before I wore, becauſe the charge itſelf is groſsly falſe in fact.

"The Victory had very little way while her head was to the ſouthward, and although her damages were conſiderable, was the firſt ſhip of the center diviſion that got round towards the enemy again, and ſometime before the reſt were able to follow her. Even as it was, not above three or four were able to cloſe up with her on the larboard tack, ſo that had it even been practicable to have veered ſooner than I did, no good purpoſe could have been anſwered by it, as I muſt only have wore the ſooner back again, to have collected the diſabled ſhips, which would have been thereby left ſtill farther aſtern.

"The Formidable was no otherwiſe left engaged with the enemy during this ſhort interval than as being in the rear, a circumſtance which muſt always neceſſarily happen to ſhips in that ſituation, when fleets engage each other on contrary tacks, and no one witneſs has attempted to ſpeak to the danger my accuſer complains of, except his own captain, who, on being called upon to fix the time when ſuch danger was apprehended, ſtated it to be the time the Formidable opened her fire. This renders this application of it as a conſequence of the ſecond charge, too abſurd to demand a refutation."

Anſwer to the third article.

"As ſoon as I had wore to ſtand towards the enemy, I hauled down the ſignal for battle, which I judged improper to be kept abroad till the ſhips could recover their ſtations, or at leaſt get near enough to ſupport each other in action; and in order to call them together

which on others fell from him in debate, ferved to fan the fmothering embers of diffention and rancour, till at length time

"for that purpofe, I immediately made the fignal to form the line of battle ahead of all the center and red divifion. I embraced that opportunity of unbending her main-top fail, which was totally unferviceable, and in doing which the utmoft expedition was ufed, the fhips aftern of me exerting themfelves far as they could in the mean time to get into their ftations, fo that no time was loft by this neceffary operation.

" The Formidable was ahead of the Victory during this period. It was her ftation in the line on that tack; yet at the very moment my accufer dares to charge me with not calling the fhips together to renew the attack, he himfelf, though his fhip was in a manageable condition, as has appeared by the evidence of his own captain; and though he had wore, expecting, as he fays, the battle to be renewed, quitted his ftation in the front of the line of battle, the fignal for which was flying, paffed to leeward of me on the ftarboard tack while I was advancing to the enemy, and never came into the line during the reft of the day.

" In this fituation I judged it neceffary, that the vice-admiral of the red, who was to windward, and pufhed forward on my weather bow with fix or feven fhips of his divifion, fhould lead on the larboard tack, in order to give time to the fhips which had come laft out of action to repair their damages and get collected together. The fignal appointed by the thirty-firft article of the fighting inftructions not being applicable, as the French fleet was fo nearly ahead of us, that only by keeping clofe to the wind we could have fetched them, I made the Proferpine's fignal, in order to have difpatched captain Sutton with a meffage to vice-admiral fir Robert Harland to lead the fleet on the larboard tack, but before he had left the Victory with the orders he had received, the French fleet wore and ftood to the fouthward forming their line on the ftarboard tack. Their fhips advanced regularly out of a collected body, which they had got into from the operation of wearing, and not from any diforder or confufion, though, had fuch diforder or confufion really exifted, I could have derived no immediate advantage from it, not having a fufficient force collected to prevent their forming by an attempt to renew the attack. The Victory was at this time the neareft fhip to the enemy, with no more than three or four of the centre divifion in any fituation to have fupported her, or each other in action: the vice-admiral of the blue was on the ftarboard tack, ftanding away from his ftation totally regardlefs of the fignal that was flying to form the line; and moft of the other fhips, except the red divifion, whofe pofition I have already ftated, were far aftern, and five difabled fhips at a great diftance on the lee quarter.

" Moft of thefe facts are already eftablifhed by my accufer's own evidence, and I fhall prove and confirm them all, by the teftimony of that part of the fleet whofe fituations will enable them to fpeak to them with certainty.

" I truft

time extinguished their existence. The complete overthrow of the then ministry, in the month of March, 1782,

"I trust they will convince the court that I had it not in my power to collect the fleet together to renew the fight at that time, and that from their not being able to follow me, I consequently could not advance with them; that I did not shorten sail, but only shifted an unserviceable one, when I was far ahead and the ships unable to follow; that I did not hawl down the signal for battle till it ceased to be capable of producing any good effect; that during the whole time I stood towards the enemy I endeavoured, by the most forcible of all signals, the signal for the line of battle, to call the ships together in order to renew the attack; that I did avail myself of the ships that were with the vice-admiral of the red, as far as circumstances admitted; and that I therefore did do the utmost in my power to take, sink, burn, or destroy the French fleet, which had attacked the British fleet."

Answer to the fourth article.

"The French fleet having wore and began to form their line on the starboard tack by the wind, which if they had kept would have brought them close up with the center division, soon afterwards edged away, pointing towards four or five of the disabled ships which were at a distance to leeward, and with evident intention to have separated them from the rest of the fleet. To prevent this I made the signal to wear, and stood athwart their van in a diagonal course to give protection to these crippled ships, keeping the signal for the line flying to form and collect the fleet on the starboard tack. As I had thus been obliged to alter my disposition before captain Sutton left the Victory with my former message, I dispatched him with orders to the vice-admiral of the red, to form with his division at a distance astern of the Victory, to cover the rear and to keep the enemy in check till the vice-admiral of the blue should come into his station with his division, in obedience to the signal. These orders the vice-admiral of the red instantly obeyed, and was formed in my wake before four o'clock. Finding then that while, by the course I steered to protect the crippled ships, I was nearing the enemy, and that the vice-admiral of the blue still continued to lie to windward, by which he kept his division from joining me, I made the signal for ships to windward to bear down into my wake, and that it might be the better distinguished (both being signals at the mizen peak) I hawled down the signal for the line for about ten minutes and then hoisted it again. This signal for ships to windward to bear down he repeated, though he had not repeated that for the line of battle; but by not bearing down himself, he led the ships of his division to interpret his repeating it as requiring them to come into his wake instead of mine.

"Having now accomplished the protection of the disabled ships, and the French fleet continuing to form their line ranging up to lee-

1782, served to introduce Mr. Keppel again to the country as a public character. On the 30th of March, as one of the

---

ward parallel to the center division, my only object was to form mine in order to bear down upon them to renew the battle. Therefore at a quarter before five, after having repeated the signal for ships to windward to bear down into my wake, with no better effect than before, I sent the Milford with orders to the vice-admiral of the red, to stretch ahead and take his station in the line, which he instantly obeyed; and the vice-admiral of the blue being still to windward with his fore-top-sail unbent, making no visible effort to obey the signal which had been flying the whole afternoon, I sent the Fox at five o'clock with orders to him to bear down into my wake, and to tell him I only waited for him and his division to renew the battle. While I was dispatching these frigates, having before hawled down the signal to come into my wake, I put abroad the signal for all ships to come into their stations, always keeping the signal for the line flying. All this produced no effect on the vice-admiral of the blue; and, wearied out with fruitless expectation, at seven o'clock I made the signal for each particular ship of the vice-admiral of the blue's division to come into her station, but before they had accomplished, it night put an end to all further operations.

"It may be observed, that amongst these signals I did not make the Formidable's. If the vice-admiral chuses to consider this as a culpable neglect, I can only say that it occurred to me, to treat him with a delicacy due to his rank. This had some time before induced me to send him the message by captain Windsor, the particulars of which he has already faithfully related to the court.

"I trust I have little reason to apprehend that you will be inclined to consider my conduct, as I stated it in answer to this fourth article of the charge, as disgraceful to the British flag. After I had wore upon the same tack with the enemy, to protect the disabled part of my fleet and collect the rest together, there would have been little to do to renew the battle, but bearing right down upon the enemy, if my accuser had led down his division in obedience to the repeated signals and orders which I have stated. The Victory never went more than two knots, was under her double reefed top-sails and fore-sails, much shattered, which kept the ships that were near her under their top-sails, and suffered the French fleet, which might always have brought me to action if they had inclined to do it, to range up parallel with the center under very little sail. It was to protect the five disabled ships above-mentioned, and to give the rest time to form into some order, that I judged it more expedient to stand as I did, under that easy sail, than to bring to with my head to the southward. The court will judge whether it was possible for any officer in the service really to believe that these operations could give the appearance of a flight, or furnish a rational pretence to the French admiral to claim the victory, or publish to the world that the British fleet had run away."

Answer

the most powerful of the leading party, he was constituted first commissioner of the admiralty, and sworn in one

---

Answer to the fifth article.

" On the morning of the 28th of July the French fleet (except three sail which were seen on the lee quarter) was only visible from the mast heads of some of the ships of the British fleet, at a great distance from me. This afforded me not the smallest prospect of coming up with them, more especially as their ships, though certainly much damaged in their hulls, had not apparently suffered much in their masts and sails; whereas the fleet under my command was generally and greatly shattered in their masts, yards and rigging, and many of them unable to carry sail. As to the three French ships, I made the signal at five o'clock in the morning for the Duke, Bienfaisant, Prince George, and Elizabeth, to give them chace, judging them to be the properest ships for that purpose; but the two last were not able to carry sufficient sail to give countenance to the pursuit: and looking round to the general condition of my fleet, I saw it was in vain to attempt either a general or a partial chace. Indeed, my accuser does not venture to alledge, that there was any probability, or even possibility of doing it with effect, which destroys the whole imputation of his charge.

" Under these circumstances I trust I could not mistake my duty; and I was resolved, as I have already before observed in the introduction to my defence, not to sacrifice it to an empty show and appearance, which is beneath the dignity of an officer, unconscious of any failure or neglect. To have urged a fruitless pursuit, with a fleet so greatly crippled in its masts and sails, after a distant and flying enemy within reach of their own ports, and with a fresh wind blowing fair for their port, with a large swell, would have been only wantonly exposing the British fleet under my command without end or object. 'Twould have been misleading and defeating its operations, by delaying the refitment necessary for carrying on the future service with vigour and effect.

" My accuser asserts, by a general conclusion to the five articles exhibited against me, that from what he states as instances of misconduct and neglect in me, a glorious opportunity was lost of doing a most essential service to the state, and that the honour of the British navy was tarnished.

" The truth of the assertion, that an opportunity was lost, I am not called upon either to combat or deny; it is sufficient for me if I shall be successful in proving, that that opportunity was seized by me, and followed up to the full extent of my power; if the court shall be of that opinion, I am satisfied, and it will then rest with the vice-admiral of the blue to explain to what cause it is to be referred, that the glorious opportunity he speaks of was lost, and to whom it is to be imputed (if the fact be true) that the honour of the British navy has been tarnished."

one of the members of the privy council, an advancement attended immediately afterwards by profeſſional promo-

Mr. Keppel then pioceeded to the examinations of the witneſſes in ſupport of his caſe; and the court martial, which continued to ſit till the 11th of February, came on that day to the following reſolution,

"That it is their opinion the charge againſt admiral Keppel is malicious and ill founded, it having appeared that the ſaid admiral, ſo far from having, by miſconduct and neglect of duty, on the days therein alluded to, loſt an opportunity of rendering eſſential ſervice to the ſtate, and thereby tarniſhed the honour of the Britiſh navy, behaved as became a judicious, brave, and experienced officer."

The preſident then delivered him his ſword, and in a ſhort ſpeech congratulated him on its being reſtored with ſo much honour, and hoping ere long he would be called forth, by his ſovereign, to draw it again in the ſervice of his country.

A few days after his acquittal both houſes of parliament agreed unanimouſly in a vote of thanks for his gallant behaviour on the 27th of July: that of the lords was ſent by the lord chancellor; and that of the commons delivered to the admiral, in his place, by the ſpeaker. The city of London, and Weſt India merchants followed this example.

The author of the Continuation of Campbell, who appears rather more active as a partizan of Mr. Keppel than is conſiſtent with the ſtrictneſs of an impartial hiſtorian, concludes his account of this remarkable event in the following terms:—

"Thus ended this celebrated trial, from which the public were led to form a very different opinion of the action, of the 27th of July, from that which naturally preſented itſelf on reading the admiral's public letter to the commiſſioners of the marine department. This letter, though it contained nothing directly in oppoſition to truth, (unleſs the general panegyric beſtowed on the ſpirited conduct of ſir Robert Harland, ſir Hugh Palliſer, and the captains of the fleet, be ſuppoſed to imply an acquittal of every individual from the crime of diſobedience) yet by concealing part of the truth, tended to miſlead the judgment of the public, and to give them both an inadequate and erroneous idea of the action. It ſeemed from the letter that the admiral could have attacked the French fleet a ſecond time that afternoon while they were forming the line of battle; but it appeared from the evidence that this could not have been done, nor the engagement renewed at any time that day, without giving an evident advantage to the enemy, as ſir Hugh Palliſer's not coming into the admiral's wake, agreeable to the ſignal, left the Britiſh fleet, throughout the whole afternoon, greatly inferior to that of France. To this he is as it were compelled to add,

"When the voice of party ſpirit ſhall be heard no more, the impartial voice of hiſtory will aſk admiral Keppel, Why he did not make the particular ſignal for each ſhip in the blue diviſion ſeparately to come into his wake, when he ſaw ſir Hugh Palliſer refuſing to obey his ſignal? By this means the engagement might have been renewed, though

promotion, and his exaltation to the rank of viscount. On the 8th of April he was made admiral of the white, and on the 29th of the same month was created viscount Keppel, of Elvedon, in the county of Suffolk.

His station of first commissioner of the admiralty he quitted for a few weeks, on the 28th of January, 1783, but resumed it again on the 8th of April ensuing, the celebrated coalition then taking place between a select number of his lordship's party and several of the leading persons of the former ex-ministry, who had, in the preceding year, been ranked among the most violent of his enemies. He retained his high station only till the 30th of December following, when a political convulsion, equal in extent to that which first introduced him to it, caused him finally to quit this public character of first minister of marine. He survived but a very few years, dying on the 2d of October, 1786, having been long afflicted with the gout, and other grievous bodily infirmities, in the sixty-third year of his age.

It will be almost impossible to attempt any delineation of his lordship's character without incurring censure, either from his admirers, or those of a different description. This will ever be the case with a man who, by unfortunately having merits and qualities attributed to him superior to those he really possessed, has induced a denial from his opponents of such virtues as they would without opposition have unanimously allowed him the possession of, had not his friends, by their imprudent attempt to raise him into something more than an hero, caused the former to counterbalance extravagant panegyric by ill-founded censure. Prior to that ill-fated event, which all men must admit was injurious to the country, the service, and his own fame, he was the idol of all parties and ranks, whether in or out of service: his bravery, his prudence, his activity, his diligence, he

---

though the Formidable had continued in disobedience. However delicate a point it might be to criminate an officer who had behaved bravely, yet it will be allowed that every degree of delicacy ought to have given place to the duty Mr. Keppel owed his country. The letter written after the action, inserted in the London Gazette, will be a sufficient warning to future commanders not to bestow praise if they think censure is due."

had

had happily afforded reiterated proofs of: a franknefs of difpofition, an affability, that trait of character ufually diftinguifhed by the appellation of good humour, had acquired him, among the feamen, a degree of love bordering almoft on adoration. To a character anonymoufly given of him at the time of his deceafe it is fubjoined, "That on every occafion he proved himfelf the friend of the meritorious, and the feaman's protector; and that no officer in the fervice poffeffed the love of the navy equal to himfelf."

There was, however, a manifeft alteration, both in his difpofition and carriage, after his acceffion to the high rank he held in the miniftry, an alteration painfully obferved by his warmeft admirers; his former apparent opennefs and freedom of behaviour became, probably through neceffity, converted into referve; and his good nature funk into an habit of promifing thofe things which neither his power allowed, and, perhaps, on many occafions his inclination did not induce him to fulfil. This change caufed him, by infenfible degrees, to lofe much of that popularity he had before acquired; and it is by no means certain, if chance, or the political current of affairs had permitted him to continue much longer moving in the public fphere, he would have experienced the fame mortifying reverfe which has, ever fince the exiftence of governments, occafionally attended the brighteft meteors of popularity. As it was, he lived not to acquire the dignity of being publicly hated, but paffed through the latter end of life unmolefted, unfatyrifed, and nearly unnoticed.

With many excellent qualities poffeffed by this gentleman were certainly mingled fome failings, a confequence naturally attendant on the imperfection of human nature; and thofe who wifh to imprefs on pofterity confummate perfection of character, are certainly guilty of premeditated flattery and falfehood.

LESLIE, Lachlin,—was a gentleman of very honourable Scottifh extraction. The firft notice we find taken of him, as a naval officer, is in the year 1739, when he was appointed commander of the Hawke floop of war. He ferved after the commencement of the war in the fame ftation, till he was, on the 8th of September, 1744, promoted to be captain of the Sandwich, a fecond rate, at that time the flag fhip of Mr. Medley, but in which he remained a few days only. We have no information of any

any subsequent command held by this gentleman, or, indeed, after its conclusion, till the year 1758, when he commanded the Briftol, of fifty guns, one of the ships on the Weft India ftation under commodore Moore. He rendered himfelf remarkable by his very fpirited conduct, on the 17th of January, in the attack of Fort Negro on the ifland of Martinico. When the guns of the enemy were filenced by the Briftol, fupported by the Rippon, which had anchored aftern, the marines of both fhips were landed and took poffeffion of the fortrefs, which they found entirely abandoned. Captain Leflie being informed the fort was tenable againft any attempt that might be made by the enemy, confequently gave orders that it fhould be defended to the laft extremity; but when all farther attempts againft the ifland were given up, the powder and guns were deftroyed or rendered unferviceable by the detachment. He had it in his power to return the fupport and fuccour rendered him on this occafion by captain Jekyl[*], at the attack of Guadaloupe on the 23d of January, 1759, having difengaged the Rippon, which lay in a diftreffed fituation expofed to the fire of a formidable battery belonging to the enemy, from which danger fhe was not extricated but with confiderable lofs. Captain Leflie was immediately afterwards promoted to the Buckingham, but did not long continue in that fituation, being fent home, in the month of May, with intelligence of the furrender of the ifland juft mentioned.

On his arrival in England he was appointed to the Monarch, of feventy-four guns; in this fhip he was not equally fuccefsful, finding no particular opportunity of diftinguifhing himfelf. In 1761 he was appointed commodore commander-in-chief at the Nore; he accordingly hoifted his broad pendant on board the Princefs Royal, of eighty guns; but had not long the happinefs of retaining fo honourable a poft, dying on the 31ft of March, 1762.

LOFTING, Samuel.—We find this gentleman, in 1742, commander of the Wolf floop of war, and employed as a cruifer, a fervice in which he had confiderable fuccefs, having, about Chriftmafs, captured a ftout privateer, and re-poffeffed himfelf of two prizes taken by the

---

Of the Rippon.

the fame manner during the whole of the enfuing year, and in the month of December diftinguifhed himfelf extremely on the following occafion. He was cruifing off Oporto, when he received information that a ftout privateer, together with two prizes captured by her were lying within the river, and that the fort which defended the entrance had only a few guns mounted; he proceeded thither, and on the 16th cannonaded the fortrefs, which, in the official account, is called a caftle, from half paft eight o'clock in the morning till eleven. During this time he difpatched his boats manned and armed into the river, with orders to cut out whatever fhip they found there; they were accordingly fuccefsful enough to bring off the two prizes, but could not meet with the privateer, which had ran farther up out of their reach.

His gallantry on this occafion was rewarded by promotion, on the 22d of June, 1744, to be captain of the Wager, of twenty-four guns, in which he was employed in convoying the trade to Hamburgh. From this veffel he was, in the beginning of the year enfuing, promoted to the Kinfale, of forty guns, and fent to Holland, with fome other veffels, for the purpofe of convoying thither the yacht, having on board the duke of Cumberland, who was at that time commander-in-chief of the Britifh army in Germany. He was immediately afterwards ordered to the Weft Indies, where, behaving improperly, though in what immediate or particular inftance we do not know, he was, on the 16th of July, 1745, fentenced to be difmiffed the fervice. This is the laft occafion on which we find any mention made of him.

MOGG, Thomas.—This gentleman was promoted, in 1741, from the rank of lieutenant to be commander of the Spence floop of war, a veffel employed at that time on the Mediterranean ftation. He continued there till his advancement, in the year 1744, to be captain of the Rochefter; but is not otherwife mentioned than as having been the perfon who conveyed to Nice the intelligence of the encounter between admiral Mathews and the united fleets of France and Spain. He was not prefent at the action, but procured his information from two or three veffels he enemy a fhort time before. He continued occupied in cafually

casually met with at sea. We do not find any mention *
made of him in the service after his appointment to the
Rochester, and believe him not to have held any command
for some years previous to his decease. In the latter part
of his life he was much distinguished as a very active and
upright magistrate, he having, most probably on his retirement from the navy, been put into the commission of the
peace, not merely, we believe, as is the common compliment paid to private gentlemen of fortune, but from an
high opinion of the service he was capable of rendering
the community in a civic department. He died on the
22d of October, 1756.

NORBURY, Conningsby, — nephew to captain Con.
Norbury, whom we have already noticed, vol. iv. p. 12.
He was appointed captain of the Gibraltar frigate on the
17th of November, 1744. In 1748 he was captain of the
Loo, a fifth rate of forty-four guns, on the Virginia station,
which, we are sorry to say, is all the information we have
been able to collect concerning him, till, in 1757, when we
find him commander of the Hampshire, of fifty guns. He
retained this command some years, and in 1760 was on the
Jamaica station, under the orders of rear-admiral Holmes.
He distinguished himself very much in the month of October, in the attack of the French frigates † off Cape Francois,
two of them, the Prince Edward and the Fleur-de-lys, of
thirty-two guns each, being destroyed by captain Norbury.
This gentleman appears to have closed his naval career
with this action, not being mentioned as holding any
command after his return to England before the close of
the last-mentioned year.

He retired about the year 1763 totally from the service,
and was consequently not even put on the superannuated
list as a rear-admiral, having declined making any application for that purpose. We believe him to have died in
the year 1786.

O'HARA, Patrick.—We are almost in the same predicament with regard to this gentleman as we were respecting the former. He was promoted on the 16th of
November, 1744, from the rank of lieutenant to be cap-

---

* In the course of the month he is particularly mentioned as having captured eighteen small vessels, laden with provisions and other
necessaries for the use of the enemy's Italian army.

† See page 202.

tain of the Gosport. This, notwithstanding we entertain not the smallest doubt of his having held many intervening commands*, is the only information we have been able to collect concerning him, till the month of October 1759, when he was made captain of the Loo, a forty-gun ship. At the latter end of the year 1762 he was put on the superannuated list with the rank and half-pay of a rear-admiral. He died at his house in Park-street, on September 18, 1774, having been many years extremely infirm.

OSBORNE, James,—was, in the very beginning of the year 1744, promoted from the rank of lieutenant to be commander of the Merlin sloop. On the 28th of September following he was advanced to be captain of the Shoreham frigate. He continued a long time in this vessel, which was principally, if not wholly employed during that period as a cruiser, a service in which he met with no inconsiderable success, having captured several small privateers belonging to the enemy, which, though of inconsiderable force, were nevertheless capable of effecting great mischief against the British commerce. He is not again mentioned till the year 1749, when he was captain of the Bristol, and one of the members of the court-martial which was held on board the Invincible, for the trial of lieutenant Couchman and others, the mutineers on board the Chesterfield. Captain Osborne quitted the Bristol at the end of the year 1751, and was appointed not long afterwards, as it is said, † to a guardship, a second rate. He died, not improbably in this very command, on the 14th of December, 1754.

PARRY, William,—was the descendant of a very ancient and noble Welch family. In 1732 and the following year he served as midshipman on board the Torrington, a fifth rate, on the Mediterranean station. We find him to have been, in 1739, second lieutenant of the Ruby, a 50-gun ship, then commanded by the unhappy capt. Gooderе. The unfortunate conduct of his commander, contrasted, as we have already shewn in our account of him, with those good qualities, and, indeed, virtues, which, till his last

---

* Particularly one in the Mediterranean, but we do not know the ship's name.

† Some accounts say the Duke, but these are erroneous, there being no ship of that name then in commission.

melan-

melancholy and wicked act, had uniformly marked his behaviour and manners on all occasions, raised in Mr. Parry so poignant a grief at his fate, that he could not, even many years afterwards, bear the recollection of the tragic story without the greatest agitation, and shedding tears. It must, indeed, be particularly distressing to him, to have the disagreeable task of seizing a man, as a felon and murderer, whom he had on every former occasion perfect reason to respect, to love, and to revere. Of his intermediate appointments we are ignorant, otherwise than that we find him to have been commander of a bomb-ketch, and on the 2d of October, 1744, to have been appointed captain of the Sandwich, a second rate. In the month of June 1745, he was removed into the Prince George, a ship of the same force and rate. In 1747 he was captain of the Intrepid, one of the home squadron, but not among the ships engaged in the defeat of Jonquiere under lord Anson, or L'Étendiere under sir Edward Hawke. We find no other particulars of his service during the continuance of the war, for the next mention that occurs concerning him is, that in the month of December 1749, he was one of the members of the court-martial held at Deptford, for the trial of rear-admiral Knowles.

How long he continued in command after this time we know not, nor what commissions, if any, which he afterwards held, till early in the year 1755, when he was appointed to the Kingston, of sixty guns, one of the ships ordered to be equipped at Chatham in consequence of an apprehended rupture with France. In the ensuing year the Kingston was one of the fleet ordered to the Mediterranean under the unfortunate Mr. Byng. He continued in the same ship, with some short intervals, several years; and, in 1757, was employed on the unsuccessful expedition undertaken against Louisburg, under the command of Mr. Holburne; as he again was, in 1758, in that more fortunate one conducted by Mr. Boscawen. During a part of the year 1759 he did not command the Kingston, most probably on account of some temporary illness; and that ship being then employed in the Channel under sir Edward Hawke, he was not present at the defeat of the marquis de Conflans's armament. He resumed his command early in 1760, and was ordered to Quebec, from whence he returned in the month of November,

having

having on board a number of French prisoners captured at the relief of that fortress. Soon after his return to England he quitted the Kingston, and continued for some time unemployed. Before the conclusion of the war he was appointed, although a very old captain, to go out a passenger to the Montague, a fourth rate of sixty guns, then in the Mediterranean. The commander-in-chief there thinking it improper that the oldest captain of that squadron should serve in a sixty-gun ship, moved captain Edward Hughes from the Somerset, a third rate of sixty-four guns, into the Blenheim, the flag ship, a second rate of ninety guns, and appointed captain Parry to the Somerset, with orders to hoist a broad pendant and command a division. Notwithstanding this, when a promotion of flag-officers was made, captain Parry, though at that time in actual service, was left out. This was said to be done in consequence of a list left by lord Anson of the promotion he intended, had he lived. As captain Parry could then no longer serve, his juniors being promoted, he returned to England, and with some difficulty obtained his rank *.

On the 21st of October, 1762, he was advanced to be rear-admiral of the blue. In 1766, having hoisted his flag on board the Preston, of fifty guns, he was sent out commander-in-chief on the Jamaica and Windward Island station, where he remained three years, the time usually allotted for the duration of such appointments in time of peace, and, as might naturally be expected, without meeting with any occurrence interesting enough to demand our particular notice. He was, while absent, advanced, on the 18th of October, to be rear-admiral of the red, and in six days afterwards, to be vice-admiral of the blue. Not long after his return he was sent out in the same capacity to the Leeward Islands, where nothing remarkable happened, except a trivial dispute with the governor of Porto Rico relative to a claim made by the English on Crabb Island, which was amicably and honourably adjusted. On the 31st of March, 1775, he was advanced to be vice-admiral of the white; as he was, on the 3d of February, 1776, to be vice-admiral of the red; and, lastly, on the 29th of January, 1778, to be admiral of the

---

* We mention this circumstance as a proof of that injurious partiality so frequently displayed by his lordship, but which was never more strongly manifested than in the case of captain Parry.

blue.

blue. He never held any command after his second return from the West Indies, passing the remainder of his life in honourable and happy retirement, having very justly acquired the universal reputation of a good commander, as well as a truly honourable and worthy man. He died at his house at Addington-brook, in the county of Kent, on the 29th day of April, 1779.

PHILLIPSON, John,—was a young gentleman on the quarter-deck of the Torrington, a fifth rate of forty guns, so early as the years 1735 and 1736; he was one of the lieutenants of the Namur under admiral Mathews in 1743, and by that gentleman appointed to the command of the Salamander bomb-ketch, in which vessel he returned to England. On the 17th of February, 1744, he was promoted to be captain of the Dolphin, as successor to Mr. Geary. He was in a very short time afterwards advanced to the Deptford, of sixty guns, as captain to Mr. Barnet, who was appointed commodore and commander-in-chief on the East India station. He died there on the 30th of March, 1745.

ROBINSON, Robert,—was, in the year 1743, lieutenant of the Namur, at that time the flag-ship of admiral Mathews, and was, after the encounter with the French and Spanish fleets off Toulon, promoted, on the 22d of February, 1744, to be captain of the Marlborough, as successor to captain Cornwall, who was unhappily slain in the preceding engagement. He very soon removed into the Diamond frigate on the same station; but no other mention whatever, far as we have been able to discover, is made of him, either during the continuance of the war, the ensuing peace, or the succeeding period of hostilities; so that on whatever services he might be employed on, they must, unhappily for him, have been extremely unconsequential. At the end of the year 1762; he was put on the superannuated list with the rank and half-pay of a rear-admiral. He lived ever afterwards in retirement at Eltham, in the county of Kent, where his son was, on the 4th of June, 1766, married to Miss Kerby of that place. The admiral died at Eltham on the 10th of September, 1785.

SOMERS, Thomas,—was, on the 4th of September, 1744, appointed captain of the Superbe. He was not long afterwards removed into the Deal Castle; and from thence, in the month of June 1747, appointed to the

Expedition. Having been guilty of some misconduct, and particularly in ill-treating divers of the officers under his command, he was brought to a court-martial, and sentenced to be dismissed the service some time in the year 1748. The time of his death is unknown to us.

SPRAGGE, Edward, — a descendant of the brave and gallant sir Edward Spragge, who served as an admiral and lost his life in the third Dutch war, temp. Car. II, was promoted, from the rank of lieutenant, to be commander of the Saltash sloop; and being advanced to the rank of captain, was appointed to the Princess Amelia on the 11th of June, 1744. He did not long retain that command; but though he was immediately commissioned to some other on quitting the first ship he was appointed to, we have not been able to investigate its name, or the service in which it was employed, farther than that we know it to have been one of those on the home or Channel station, as we find him, in the month of January 1745, one of the members of the court-martial, held at Portsmouth, for the trial of captains Griffin, Mostyn, and others; and, in the month of September, engaged in the same disagreeable duty at Chatham, on the charge preferred against captains Burrish, and others, for misbehaviour in the action off Toulon.

He continued to be one of the members of the same court, in the month of May 1746, when it was removed to Deptford for the trials of the admirals Mathews and Lestock. No other mention is made of him far as we have been able to discover, except that he died on the 24th of January, 1757.

SWANTON, Robert. — The first information we have of this gentleman is, that in the month of January 1743-4, he commanded the Astrea, an armed ship in the service of government, and employed on the American station. This vessel was, at the time above stated, burnt at Piscataway, of which melancholy accident captain Swanton gave the following account.

" On Tuesday the 17th instant, about two in the morning, a fire broke out in the fore hold, and instantly the beams under the forecastle were in a blaze. We laboured hard, and once thought we had got the better of it; but the water alongside was no sooner in the buckets but it became ice, so that they scarce delivered a quart. By these means the fire broke out again with great violence, and rendered all our endeavours to extinguish it vain, for in a few hours she was burnt down to the water edge. Most of the officers stores were ashore, the powder in the public magazines; and as all the guns fell into the wreck I shall have no difficulty in recovering them."

On the 27th of August following he was promoted to be captain of the Mary Galley, but in what manner employed we know not. In the month of September 1745, he was one of the members of the court-martial, held at Chatham, for the trials of captain Burrish, and others, which is the only material mention we find made of him during the continuance of the war, or the peace which succeeded it. At the latter end of the year 1756, not long after the renewal of hostilities with France, he was appointed to the Prince, of ninety guns, and without doubt held many intermediate commands, of which we are unfortunately uninformed. He not long afterwards removed into the Vanguard, of sixty-eight guns, a ship employed on the home or Channel station*, till the year 1758,

---

* The following letter is said to have been written by a person on board at the time of the transaction alluded to took place. We have been the more induced to insert it, because historians, and even the gazettes have been silent on a business which certainly reflects too much honour on captain Swanton to be forgotten.

" This acquaints you that we sailed from Plymouth on the 7th of November to join sir Edward Hawke's squadron, but could not meet with it. Hard gales of wind with squalls from the westward were our constant companions for the first month. On the 17th, at night, we lost our main-top-mast and half the main-top. Next morning the remaining part of the top was brought down to be repaired, and by the 19th, in the evening, we had it over the mast-head again. Sunday the 20th, in the morning, we saw several ships steering E S E. at eight we wore and bore down to them. As it was squally and hazy, we ran very near before we could discover who they were; but as the weather cleared up found it was the French fleet, consisting of seventeen ships of war, returning from North America, commanded by a vice and rear admiral, with a commodore. This was in the latitude of Brest, 67 leagues from the Lizard. It being too great a force for us, we hoisted a French jack and hauled close upon the wind. The French are certainly the most polite people to strangers (at first sight) I have met with, for we were obliged to pass by the rear of their fleet within musket-shot, and not one of them offered to fire, though it was in their power to sink us. At nine their admiral made the signal for a general chace,

1758, when he was ordered to Louisburg with Mr. Boscawen. He continued in the Vanguard during the whole of the war, but no farther mention is made of the manner or service in which he was occupied till the beginning of the year 1760, when he was ordered to Quebec with a small force, of which he was senior or commanding officer.

chace, five of them soon got into our wake, and putting about, in less than an hour their whole fleet was in full cry after us. The loss of our main-top-mast (three days before) deprived us of several sails which would have been of great service at this juncture; and it blew so hard in squalls, that the cross jack-yard broke, the mizen-top sail split, and we were in danger of losing our fore-top-mast. Their rear-admiral with his division led large to intercept us if we had bore away; and the commodore kept to windward in order to weather us. A quarter before one in the afternoon their headmost ship came up with us, ran under our lee quarter, and gave us a broadside. Captain Swanton, our commander, whose behaviour (during the chace and in the engagement) was one continued scene of prudence and true courage, would not permit us to return the compliment till monsieur was within musket-shot, when all the guns we could run out were brought to bear upon him. He discharged three broadsides at us before we began to fire: the captain then ordered our colours to be hoisted; the officers and crew (who were all determined to defend the ship to the last extremity) gave three cheers, and poured a broadside into the centre of the French ship. Our people behaved extremely well, took good aim, and fought for more than two hours.

" Our antagonist, after having dropped astern several times, and in vain endeavoured to rake us fore and aft, at last bore away and fired several guns as signals of distress. She mounted seventy-four guns; and being to leeward of us ran them all out, while we could open no more than two of our lower deck ports, for it blew hard, and we were obliged to engage under all the sails we could set; consequently our adversary had the advantage of firing thirty-seven guns to our twenty-three. As most of our guns were directed to her hull, she must have received great damage between wind and water.

" We had several men wounded, and one killed by a grape shot, which came through one of the lower deck ports. The enemy tried to dismast us, and elevated his guns so high that many of the shot went over us. Our sails and rigging were cut to pieces.

" When the French admiral saw our adversary had been so roughly treated he made the signal to leave off chace. By this time the commodore, in a ship of eighty-four guns, was on our weather quarter, and in less than an hour would have been alongside of us: on seeing the signal he gave us two broadsides, but none of his shot reached us.

" They all bore away for Brest, and night coming on we lost sight of them."

He arrived on the 11th of May off the isle of Bec, in the river St. Lawrence, with his own ship and the Diana frigate only. He intended to have waited there for the rest of the squadron which had separated from him in the passage from England; but having, on the 14th, received advice from brigadier-general Murray, that Quebec was besieged and much pressed, he got under sail with all possible dispatch, and anchored above Point Levi on the 15th, in the evening. He there found the Lowestoffe frigate, one of his squadron, which had arrived a few days before him. Captain Deane, who commanded that ship, immediately came off with a message from general Murray, who earnestly recommended the attack of the French naval force, which then lay above the town, and consisted of two frigates, as many armed ships, together with several vessels of inferior consequence. The commodore in consequence, ordered captain Deane, together with captain Schomberg in the Diana, who was there also, to slip their cables early the next morning and attack the enemy. No sooner did they perceive the British ships approaching than they made off in the greatest confusion. One of them, called the Pomona, was driven on shore above Cape Diamond; the Atalante, which was the name of the other, ran ashore and was burnt at Point-au-Tremble, about ten leagues above the town; the greater part of the smaller vessels were either driven on shore, or otherwise effectually destroyed. The consequence produced by this success was of the most happy kind; the enemy, struck as it were by a thunderbolt, on viewing the demolition of their naval force, went off the same evening, and abandoned the siege with so much precipitation as to leave behind them their whole battering train, amounting to thirty-four pieces of heavy cannon, together with six mortars, all their camp equipage, provisions, and stores, collected with labour almost incredible, at an immense expence, as a last effort for the recovery of their conquered capital.

The commodore sailed from Quebec in the Vanguard, on his return to England, towards the end of October, and arrived at Spithead, with the Trident, after a very prosperous passage, on the 22d of November. In 1761 we find no other material mention made of the services on which he was employed, than his having been sent, towards the latter end of March, in conjunction with captain Rowley, of the Superbe, to convoy to a certain latitude the outward-bound East India ships. In 1762 he was employed in the West Indies under sir Geo. Rodney, and was ordered, with a small land force, against the Grenades, which, together with all their dependencies, surrendered to him on the 5th of March. This success having finally completed the capture of all the French possessions in that part of the world, we do not find any mention made of any farther enterprize in which he was concerned during the war. On the 21st of October, 1762, he was promoted to be rear-admiral of the blue, but never held any command as a flag officer. He died at Brighthelmstone on the 1st of August, 1765.

TOLL, Edmund,—in the early part of the year 1744, commanded the Grampus sloop. He is mentioned as having been in company with Mr. Boscawen, the captain of the Dreadnought, at the time he captured the Medea frigate. He was, on the 14th of June in the same year, promoted to be captain of the Phœnix; but we have not been able to collect any other particulars of his subsequent commands, or information in any degree relative to him, except that, in 1762, he was put on the superannuated list, with the rank and half-pay of a rear-admiral. He died on the 1st of August, 1767.

THOMSON, Ormond,—commanded a sloop of war, on the Jamaica station, in 1741, and had the good fortune in that year to capture two valuable Spanish merchant-ships. He returned to England in the month of July 1742, being then commander of the Vesuvius fireship, from which he removed, towards the close of the year, into the Peregrine sloop. In 1744 he commanded the Fly sloop; and on the 29th of January, being then on a cruise at the entrance of the Channel, about forty leagues from the Lizard, he fell in with a Spanish privateer, having an equal number of guns, but greatly superior in men *. Captain Thomson began to engage her about eight o'clock in the morning, and, after a very close and spirited encounter of two hours continuance, compelled her to surrender. The prize, which was carried into Plymouth, was called the Nostra

---

* Twelve guns, one hundred and thirty-three men.

Senora del Rofario, new from the ftocks, and only four days out of Bilboa. On the 26th of July enfuing he was promoted to be captain of the Rye, a twenty-gun fhip. This veffel was unhappily loft at the latter end of November in the fame year; the circumftances attending which misfortune were rather fingular. Captain Thomfon was chaced by a large Englifh fhip under French colours; in endeavouring to efcape from which he ran afhore. This affair was afterwards inveftigated by a court-martial, and the captain was very fairly acquitted. We have no account however of his holding any fubfequent command. He died in England·on the 17th of November, 1753.

VANBURGH, Giles Richard.—This gentleman was, in 1743, lieutenant of one of the fhips on the Mediterranean ftation, and was there promoted, on the 13th of January, 1744, to be captain of the Feverfham, of forty guns, an appointment given him merely to eftablifh his rank as a poft captain. He was appointed to fome other fhip, we believe the Durfley Galley, a few days afterwards. We have no farther account we can implicitly rely on concerning him, till the beginning of the year 1746, when he was captain of the Antelope, of fifty guns, on the fame ftation. He was left by commodore George Townfhend, who was driven off the coaft of Corfica in a violent gale of wind, and compelled to bear away for Mahon in order to repair the damages fuftained by the fhips of his fquadron, to watch that coaft during his abfence; but the fame kind of accident befalling captain Vanburgh himfelf, he was compelled to put into Leghorn with the reft of the fhips under his orders: and the Genoefe found means, during his abfence, to difpatch three large barks to Baftia, from whence they brought off all the principal leaders of the malcontent inhabitants, the prevention of which was the principal object of the Britifh force ftationed. Captain Vanburgh did not long furvive this misfortune, having accidentally loft his life in the following manner. He had vifited on board fome other fhip of the fquadron when at fea; he continued on board until it was dark, and put off in his boat from that fhip, to go to the Antelope; but, unfortunately, neither himfelf, boat's crew, or boat, were ever heard of. This unhappy accident happened in the courfe of the year 1746, but the particular month is not fpecified.

WILLIAMS, Thomas.—In 1740 he was promoted from the rank of lieutenant to be commander of the Charlotte, one of the fmall yachts then employed on fervices not confequential enough to require, as a captain, an officer of higher rank. On the 23d of April, 1744, he was promoted to be captain of the Deal Caftle; and afterwards, in the month of June 1745, advanced to the command of the Royal Sovereign, then lying at the Nore as a guardfhip, as captain to commodore Tho. Smith. No other particulars have come to our knowledge relative to this gentleman, except that he died in England on the 11th of May, 1754.

WILSON, John,—was, on the 13th of Auguft, 1744, promoted, from the Firedrake bomb-ketch, to be captain of the Seaford; and in the month of March 1746, was removed into a fhip of twenty guns, called the Hare. He died in England on the 3d of September, 1749, but we have not been able to collect any other information concerning him.

1745.

ADAMS, Roger,—was appointed captain of the Port Mahon frigate on the 12th of July, 1745; but no other mention is made of him in the fervice. He died on the 17th of October, 1749.

ANDREWS, Thomas,—was, on the 15th of July, 1745, promoted to be captain of the Worcefter; but is not otherwife noticed during the continuance of the war. In January 1753, he was appointed captain of the Cumberland, which was commiffioned as one of the guardfhips at Chatham. In 1755 he removed into the Defiance, a fourth rate of fixty guns, ordered to be equipped at Plymouth, in confequence of an apprehended rupture with France. In this fhip he was ordered to the Mediterranean, in the enfuing year, with Mr. Byng. On the morning of the well-known encounter off Mahon with the French fquadron, under Gallifoniere, captain Andrews being

being detached in chace, captured a French tartan, having on board four officers together with one hundred and two privates, part of a reinforcement of six hundred sent, as musketry-men, from the army under the duc de Richlieu, to the fleet. In the encounter which presently followed, captain Andrews, while living, behaved with the greatest gallantry; nor was the ship conducted with less spirit after he fell. Exposed to the enemy's hottest fire the Defiance bore the brunt of the action, having had no less than fifty-nine men killed and wounded, amounting to nearly one-third of the whole loss sustained by the fleet on that occasion. As we already said, captain Andrews himself fell in the action, universally beloved, honoured and lamented. He was killed on the 20th of May, 1756.

BARKER, John,—was lieutenant of the Solebay fireship in the years 1737 and 1738; as he afterwards was of the Lancaster, a third rate of eighty guns. He was, on September 19, 1745, appointed captain of the Gibraltar, and employed very early in the ensuing spring to convoy, to Scotland, the Hessian troops ordered thither in consequence of the rebellion which had broken out in that kingdom. He executed this service with the greatest attention and dispatch, the latter becoming doubly necessary in consequence of a vehement frost which set in at that time, and threatened to retard the whole embarkation. The subsequent commands he obtained, and services on which he was employed, were so little consequential, that the only farther account given of him during the continuance of the war is, that in the month of June 1747, he was appointed captain of the Thetis, of forty guns. We are unacquainted as to the time when, and in what manner was again employed during a long interval, the next mention we again find made of him being in the year 1759, when he commanded the Jersey, of sixty guns, one of the fleet under Mr. Boscawen on the Mediterranean station. His gallantry and good conduct were much noticed in the attack made, though unsuccessfully, by the captains Smith Callis, Harland, and himself, on the batteries at the mouth of Toulon harbour, and the attempt on two vessels which lay under their protection*

---

* See vol. iv. p. 333. and vol. v. p. 138.

Captain Barker was almost immediately after, on the promotion of captain Smith Callis to be a flag-officer, appointed to succeed him in the Culloden. He sailed in this ship, for Guadaloupe, on the 7th of September, 1760, and continued in that quarter we believe during the whole remainder of the war, or nearly so, during which period no farther mention, far as we have been able to discover, is made of him. On the 18th of October, 1770, he was advanced to be rear-admiral of the white; and again, on the 30th of March, 1775, to be rear of the red. His last promotion he did not long survive, dying on the 26th of January, 1776.

BATEMAN, The Honourable William, — was the second son of William, first lord viscount Bateman, and the lady Ann Spencer, only daughter of Charles, earl of Sunderland, by his second wife the lady Ann Churchill, second daughter and coheir to John, duke of Marlborough. This gentleman was, on the 27th of December, 1745, appointed captain of the Lys. He was captain of the Romney, a fifth rate of forty guns, a vessel reduced, in the year 1746, from a fourth rate of fifty guns; and he afterwards succeeded captain Thomas Hanway in the Windsor, a fourth rate of sixty guns. On the conclusion of the war, in 1748, he resigned is rank as captain in the navy. He was chosen representative in parliament for the borough of Gatton, in Surry, on the 10th of April, 1752; but, we believe, sat only during that session. On the 17th of April, 1755, he married Miss Hedges, of Finchley in Middlesex, and in the ensuing year was appointed extra-commissioner of the navy. This post he held till 1761, when he was advanced to be comptroller of the store-keeper's accounts, an office he continued to retain till the time of his death, which happened on the 19th of June, 1783.

BERMINGHAM, Honourable John,—was the second son of Francis, lord of Athunry, in the kingdom of Ireland, being the twenty-first who held the rank of baron, in descent from Pierce de Bermingham, summoned to parliament, by the title already stated, in the reign of Henry the Second. His mother was the lady Mary Nugent, eldest daughter to Thomas, earl of Westmeath. Being bred to the sea-service, he was appointed lieutenant of the Romney; from which he was afterwards removed to
the

the fame ftation on board the Phœnix. In the beginning of the year 1745 he commanded the Falcon floop of war, in which he captured, in the month of February, clofe in with Dunkirk, a French privateer, of eight guns, called the Union; as he did a fecond, of the fame force, in the month of March. On the 14th of May following he was promoted to be captain of the Glafgow frigate. He died, according to Mr. Hardy's account, on the 8th of May, 1746; but, in Archdale's Irifh Peerage, he is faid to have been killed fomewhat earlier, in an engagement with a French privateer. This affertion is in fome degree explained by the following extract of a letter from Newcaftle, dated May the 18th, 1745.

" His majefty's fhip the Faulcon, the Honourable John Bermingham commander, of fourteen fix-pounders, and about feventy men, fell in laft Tuefday, off Flamborough Head, with a French privateer of eighteen nine-pounders, fix fix-pounders, and about two hundred men. The Faulcon fought her feveral glaffes, but night coming on they both lay to, and in the morning renewed the engagement; when the privateer, having loft a great many men, thought proper to fheer off. The Fox man of war, of twenty guns, foon after falling in with the Faulcon, immediately gave chace to the privateer, who had not got out of fight, fo that we expect fhortly to have a good account of her. The captain of the Faulcon had his leg fhot off above the knee in the engagement; but none of the crew were killed, and only two hurt."

The fact probably is, that he was promoted to the Glafgow immediately on his arrival in port, as a reward for his gallantry on the preceding occafion; but did not long furvive the wounds he fuftained on the event which caufed his well-deferved advancement.

BLADWELL, William,—was, in 1743, commander of the Swift floop of war; but no farther mention is made of him till his promotion, on the 17th of September, 1745, to be captain of the Mercury frigate. He continued in the fame fhip during the following year, and was employed in the autumn to convoy the outward-bound Hamburg trade, which is the only account on which we find any notice taken of him during the war. Immediately after its conclufion he was appointed captain of the Rose, a twenty-gun ship, one of the small squadron ordered to the West Indies, under commodore Holburne, for the purpose of conveying thither, and causing to be carried into execution the orders of the king of France, for the evacuation of the islands of St. Lucia, Dominica, St. Vincent, and Tobago. The leading events of this expedition having been already given * we need only to refer the reader back, for the only mention we find made of captain Bladwell while occupied in that line of service. We find no mention made of his having held any naval command after his return, so that if any, they must, unfortunately for him, have been of an unconsequential nature. In 1770 he retired on the rank and half-pay of a rear-admiral, being put on the superannuated list. This honourable proof of the estimation in which the earlier part of his services had been held, he continued to enjoy till his death, which happened about the year 1789.

BONFOY, Hugh,—was a midshipman on board the Somerset in 1739, and made a lieutenant by Mr. Haddock. He was afterwards promoted in England to the command of the Ferret sloop, previous to his being, on April 12, 1745, appointed captain of the Greyhound frigate. The next subsequent account we have of him is, that in the very beginning of the year 1748, he commanded the Augusta, of sixty guns, one of the fleet ordered out on a cruise under rear-admiral sir Edward Hawke. In the month of July 1749, he was captain of the Berwick, a guardship of sixty-four guns, one of those put into commission immediately after the peace in 1748; and was one of the members composing the court-martial held, on board the Invincible, for the trial of the piratical mutineers who had attempted to carry off the Chesterfield, of forty guns, from the coast of Guinea. After his quitting this ship he went a voyage to Newfoundland captain of the Pensance, a fifth rate of forty-four guns, and on his return was appointed to be captain of the Dorset, the yacht stationed to attend on the lord lieutenant of Ireland. He died in Ireland, holding this commission, on the 12th of March, 1762 †.

---

* See vol. v. p. 35.
† He left a daughter, who married on the 14th of September 1775, the earl of Ely, of the kingdom of Ireland.

BUCKLE,

BUCKLE, Matthew,—was, in the month of March 1744, firſt lieutenant of the Namur, under admiral Mathews, then commander-in-chief on the Mediterranean ſtation. By him he was, not long afterwards, advanced to the command of the Spence ſloop of war: he was from thence promoted, on the 29th of May, 1745, to be captain of the Ruſſel, of eighty guns, one of the fleet employed in the ſame quarter. He continued in this ſhip a conſiderable length of time; and in the month of September, 1747, rendered himſelf remarkable by the capture of the Glorioſo, a Spaniſh ſhip of war, carrying ſeventy-four guns and upwards of ſeven hundred men, which had been unſucceſsfully engaged, at different preceding periods, by the captains Callis, Crookſhanks, Erſkine*, and, laſt, by captain Hamilton, who periſhed in the ſhort encounter, as will be ſeen hereafter. The diſpute laſted a conſiderable time, the Spaniard not having ſurrendered till after a conteſt of nearly ſix hours, in which he had twenty-five men killed, and a much greater number wounded, an obſtinacy of reſiſtance which tends much to lighten any ſuppoſed neglect or impropriety of behaviour in thoſe gentlemen, who had with leſs ſucceſs previouſly encountered ſo formidable an opponent. The number of the Spaniards ſtill ſurviving after their ſurrender was ſo great, that captain Buckle was obliged to put a conſiderable part of the priſoners on board the King George, and Prince Frederic, two ſtout privateers which were in ſight during the action, and had themſelves juſt before engaged the Glorioſo for a ſhort time: even this aſſiſtance was not ſufficient, for he was compelled, ſo inferior were the numbers of his own crew, to take ſixty men from each of thoſe veſſels to aſſiſt in guarding the remainder of the priſoners, and in navigating his own ſhip together with the prize to Liſbon, where he arrived in ſafety with her, though much ſhattered.

We have no other intelligence relative to this gentleman during the continuance of the war. In the month of December 1749, we find him to have been in commiſſion, though we are unacquainted with the name of the ſhip he commanded. He was at the time juſt men-

---

* See pages 138. 150. and 170.

tioned, one of the members compoſing the court-martial held, on board the Charlotte yacht, at Deptford, for the trial of rear-admiral Knowles. In 1751 he was appointed commodore of a ſmall ſquadron ordered out to the coaſt of Africa: it confiſted of no more than the Affiſtance, his own ſhip; the St. Albans, captain Byron; and Sphynx frigate, captain Wheeler. He found at Anamaboe three French ſhips of war, carrying from twenty-four to fixty-four guns, tampering with the natives, by prefents and large promifes, for leave to erect a fort there, in defiance of the treaty of peace concluded a ſhort time before. Mr. Buckle remonſtrated very warmly againſt the impropriety of their proceedings, informing them, that if they continued to perfevere he ſhould confider it a breach, and repel them by force. The French, intimidated at a conduct ſo firm, and at the ſame time ſo ſpirited, thought proper to withdraw, not, however, as ſome hiſtorians aſſert, till they had promiſed the natives to reviſit them at a ſubſequent period in greater force.

In the month of April 1755, we find captain Buckle on the Mediterranean ſtation, as captain of the Unicorn, he having at that time tranſmitted to the admiralty-board, an account of ſome preparations for war making by the French at Toulon, who were then actually occupied in equipping their ſhips in that harbour; and had, by beat of drum, publiſhed an order at Genoa, as well as other neighbouring neutral ports, for all their ſailors to repair thither under the uſual penalties. We have no farther particular intelligence concerning him till the year 1757, when he commanded the Royal George, of one hundred guns, one of the ſhips employed on the unſucceſsful expedition againſt Rochfort. He was one of the captains ordered, under admiral Broderick, to reconnoitre and make the neceſſary ſoundings along the coaſt, which is the only notice taken of him on this occaſion. Soon after his return, he removed into the Namur, of ninety guns, and ſerved on board that ſhip, in 1758, as captain to Mr. Boſcawen, at the ſiege of Louiſburg. He continued in the Namur till after the death of Mr. Boſcawen in 1761, ſerving under him, as his captain, during ſuch periods as his flag was flying on board that ſhip. In 1759 he was preſent, under ſir Edward Hawke, at the memorable defeat of the marquis de Conflans. Except

cept on such occasions which do not frequently occur, he could not, holding such, though at the same time so high and honourable a command, expect any opportunity of distinguishing himself. During a considerable part of the ensuing peace he does not appear to have had any connexion with the public service; but a rupture with Spain appearing towards the end of the year 1770 more than probable, and a consequent promotion of flag-officers becoming necessary, he was, on the 18th of October, promoted to be rear-admiral of the white, as also, on the 24th of the same month, to the same rank in the red squadron.

He immediately afterwards hoisted his flag at Portsmouth, being stationed to command there under admiral Geary, whom he accordingly assisted in superintending the armament which was then equipping for sea with the utmost expedition. The prospect of hostilities fading soon afterwards, Mr. Buckle again returned to his former quietude of private life. The next particular mention we find made of this gentleman is his promotion, on the 31st of March, 1775, to be vice-admiral of the blue. On the 3d of February, 1776, he was moreover advanced to be vice-admiral of the white. On the 29th of January, 1780, he was made vice-admiral of the red; and, on the 19th of March, 1779, admiral of the blue, which was the highest rank he ever lived to attain to. Highly respected and revered, whether considered as a naval commander or a private gentleman, he died on the 9th day of July, 1784, at his seat at Banstead, in Surry.

BULLY, William,—was, in the month of November 1744, appointed commander of the Vulture sloop of war, and, in the month of May following, was reduced to the very disagreeable necessity of bringing captain Green, of the Lizard, who was then under his orders, to a courtmartial for disobedience, in not properly engaging a French privateer they fell in with. The charge was fully proved: captain Green was sentenced to be dismissed the service, and imprisoned one year in the Marshalsea; and Mr. Bully was, on account of the great propriety of his own conduct, promoted, on the 12th of July ensuing, to be captain of the Sheerness*. He was employed during

---

* Some accounts say he was first appointed to the Bridgewater, in which ship, however, he continued only a few days.

the remainder of the year as a cruiſer off Dunkirk, and that contiguous part of the coaſt of France, for the purpoſe of preventing the paſſage of any ſupplies, or reinforcements from thence, for the pretender's party in Scotland. He was extremely active in this ſervice, and effected no inconſiderable blow to the rebel cauſe by the capture of the Soleil, a large French private ſhip of war, on the 22d of November. This veſſel had ſailed from Dunkirk on the preceding day, bound for Montroſe, having on board the titular earl of Derwentwater, with twenty choſen officers and about ſixty private men. Immediately after his return into port he was promoted to the Ludlow Caſtle, of forty-four guns, and ordered for the coaſt of Africa, where he died on the 7th of October, 1746.

COSBY, Henry.—This gentleman was, in the month of March, ſixth lieutenant of the Namur, at that time the flag ſhip of admiral Mathews. After this time we have no account of him till his promotion, on the 26th of Auguſt, 1745, to be captain of the Shoreham frigate. He quickly afterwards removed into the Amazon; and during the time he held that command, was unhappy enough, if the term be on ſuch an occaſion allowable, to incur the cenſure of a captain Webb, then under his command. He preferred a charge againſt him; in conſequence of which he was brought to a court-martial, the reſult of which, as well as the nature of the charge ſo inconſiſtently made, will be well explained by the following extract of a letter from Goſport, dated April the 2d, 1746.

" This day ended, at Goſport, the court-martial, held on board his majeſty's ſhip the St. George, commodore Griffin preſident, for the trial of captain Coſby, commander of his majeſty's ſhip Amazon, on a charge exhibited againſt him by captain Webb, commander of his majeſty's ſloop Jamaica, for loſing two opportunities of looking into Breſt harbour, and for cowardice in not endeavouring to take the South-Sea man, lately put into Breſt. The trial laſted two days, when not the leaſt part of the charge being proved, captain Webb received a ſevere reprimand and was mulcted four months pay."

No other material mention is made of this gentleman during the continuance of the war. The only occaſion on whic his name occurs is, that in 1747 he was captain of the Diamond frigate. Early in the year 1751 he was appointed to the Centaur, of twenty guns; in which ſhip, being not long afterwards ordered to New York, he died there on the 16th of October, 1753.

DANIEL. Lionel,—was, on the 28th of May, 1744, appointed captain of the Hampſhire; but is not again noticed till the year 1749, when he was commiſſioned to the Aſſurance. He was ſoon afterwards ordered to Jamaica in that ſhip, and died there in the ſame command on the 13th of November, 1752.

DENIS, Sir Peter,—was a gentleman of French extraction, being the ſon of the Rev. Mr. Jacob Denis, a Lutheran miniſter, born at Rochefoucault in France, from which kingdom he was compelled to fly on account of the general and grievous perſecution exerciſed againſt all perſons of his perſuaſion. The maiden name of ſir Peter s mother was Martha Leach; and he was the youngeſt, one excepted, of twelve children, the iſſue of the marriage above alluded to. Having betaken himſelf at a very early age to a naval life, we find him, in the year 1739, on board the Centurion, under Mr. afterwards lord Anſon, who promoted him to be the third lieutenant of that ſhip in the month of November 1740, on the advancement of lieutenant Cheap to be commander of the Trial ſloop. His lordſhip, who, during the many perilous adventures and difficulties which occurred on his long arduous undertaking and expedition, muſt have had the fulleſt opportunity of obſerving the conduct of Mr. Denis on almoſt every poſſible occaſion which could occur, as well in relation to public ſervice as life and manners of a private gentleman, conceived for him the higheſt affection and eſteem; an impreſſion, which the ſubſequent conduct and ſpirited generous demeanour of his pupil never cauſed in the ſmalleſt degree to diminiſh.

Mr. Denis, being only third lieutenant of the Centurion, held a ſtation too ſubordinate to enable him to diſtinguiſh himſelf ſo publicly, as to be very particularly noticed in a relation of the general events which took place during that period. The only occaſion on which his name appears is, as having been, on November 5, 1741 diſpatched, by the commodore, as commander of one of the cutters, with sixteen men well armed, in pursuit of a Spanish vessel, which a calm would otherwise have preserved from capture. This trivial event took place off the high land of Baranca, in the South Seas. After a very short pursuit Mr. Denis boarded and carried his prize without resistance, which proved to be a vessel bound from Guiaquil to Callao, with a cargo of considerable value in that country, though of little importance to the captors. The intelligence, however, derived from the foregoing success caused the attack of the town of Paita in a few days afterwards the most consequential hostile event which happened during the voyage, the capture of the Manilla galleon excepted.

On February 9, 1745, which was not long after the return of the Centurion to England, Mr. Denis was promoted to the rank of post captain, and appointed to the Greyhound frigate. He very soon afterwards, for a short time, commanded the Windsor, of sixty guns, by order. In this ship we find him employed, towards the end of the year 1746, as a cruiser, an occupation in which he was by no means unsuccessful. On Oct. 26, he recaptured, after a chace of some hours continuance, an English merchant-ship, called the Frere, laden with sugar from Barbadoes, which had been taken by a French privateer, of eighteen guns and two hundred men, called the Basques, belonging to Bayonne.

The very next day, at nine o'clock A. M. he saw two sail to the northward, to which he immediately gave chace; and in the ensuing morning fell in with the Leopard privateer, of twenty-two guns (nine-pounders) and twenty-four swivels, fitted out first with three hundred and sixty-seven men, belonging to Bayonne. The enemy had an English merchant-ship, her prize, in company. He soon came up with the merchant ship, which he found to be the Chester, from St. Kitts, and took possession of her: he then chased the Leopard, which he captured about four o'clock in the afternoon, and carried with him into Kinsale. Early in 1747 he commanded the Kinsale; but not long after this removed into his old ship the Centurion, which had undergone a sufficient repair, but was reduced down to a fifty-gun ship. In this command he served under admiral Anson at the

memor-

memorable defeat of the French fquadron under De la Jonquiere.

He diftinguifhed himfelf exceedingly on this occafion, and contributed in a very eminent degree to the fuccefs which crowned the encounter, having been the firft who got up with the enemy's rear and brought their fternmoft fhip to action, though two of the moft formidable of her companions bore down to her fupport, and the Centurion was for fome little time obliged to maintain, fingly, this unequal encounter till the arrival of the Namur, Defiance, and Windfor, to her fuccour, brought on a general action. Captain Denis was chofen by the admiral to be the bearer of his difpatches, a compliment we cannot think undeferved, though contrary to what was then the ufual cuftom f the fervice.

At the conclufion of the year he joined the fquadron under rear-admiral Hawke, but not till after the defeat of L'Etendiere. In the month of December, he was one of the members of the court-martial, held at Portfmouth for the trial of captain Fox, of the Kent. Captain Denis failed from Plymouth, with fir Edward Hawke and his fquadron, on the 16th of January enfuing, but met with no farther particular opportunity of diftinguifhing himfelf during the fhort remainder of the then exifting war.

Not long after the fettlement of the peace, that is to fay, on the 2d of September, 1750, he married Mifs Pappet, of St. James's, a lady nearly related to the very celebrated Swifs Heidigger, who affumed to himfelf the title of furintendant de plaifir d'Angleterre. He acquired by this marriage, in part of the lady's fortune, an houfe at the north-weft corner of Queen's-fquare, leading into Ormand-ftreet, which he afterwards fold to the late Dr. Campbell, and purchafed in 1753, of William Turner, efq. a feat in Kent, called Valence, pleafantly fituated near Wefterham. In 1766 he difpofed of that to William Gwinn, efq. who again fold it to the earl of Hillfborough, from whom alfo it has fince been alienated by fale.

In the parliament which met at Weftminfter for the difpatch of bufinefs, on the 31ft of May, 1754, captain Denis was, through the intereft of his firm patron and friend, lord Anfon, chofen one of the reprefentatives for the borough of Heydon, in Yorkshire. In the month of March, 1755, great preparations being then making for a rupture almost daily apprehended with France, he was appointed to the Medway, of sixty guns; but does not appear during the remainder of the year to have been engaged in any very memorable service. He retained the same command during the ensuing year, but was not otherwise employed than in occasional cruises. In the months of December and January succeeding, he was one of the members of the court-martial, held at Portsmouth for the trial of the unfortunate Mr. Byng. He was not long afterwards promoted to the Namur, of ninety guns, one of the fleet employed in the month of September, under sir Edward Hawke, on the unsuccessful expedition against Rochfort; and was one of the officers mentioned as ordered under Mr. Broderick, to reconnoitere and sound the adjacent coast.

Early in 1758 he was appointed to the Dorsetshire, a new ship of seventy guns, and was ordered out on a cruise as one of a small squadron put under the orders of captain Pratten. On April 29, he gained to himself the greatest honour in the attack and capture of the Raisonable, a French ship of sixty-four guns; the particulars of which very spirited encounter are inserted beneath*. During the year 1759, still retaining the same command, he served under sir Edward Hawke in the Channel fleet, and was

---

* About three o'clock in the afternoon, captain Pratten seeing a sail to the S. W. made a signal for the Dorsetshire, of seventy guns, and five hundred and twenty men, commanded by captain Denis, to give chase; but soon after, observing the chase to be a large one, he also dispatched the Achilles, of sixty guns, commanded by the Hon. captain Barrington, after her; and then followed them with the rest of the squadron. About seven o'clock the Dorsetshire came up with the chase, which proved to be the Raisonable, a French ship of war, of sixty-four guns and six hundred and thirty men. Captain Denis began to engage her very closely; the action continued till about nine o'clock, when the enemy's ship, commanded by the prince de Mombazon, chevalier de Rohan, struck, having suffered greatly in her hull; sixty-one men were killed, and one hundred wounded. She was going from L'Orient to Brest, a new ship not above four or five months off the stocks. The Dorsetshire's masts, yard, and sails were greatly shattered: she had fifteen men killed and twenty-one wounded in the action.

one of those captains who particularly distinguished themselves in the memorable discomfiture of the marquis de Conflans. He is stated in a private account, given by a person of intelligence and veracity then on board one of the ships, to have had the highest encomiums bestowed on him personally by the commander-in-chief, who, in the warmth of his gratitude, is said to have told him, in conjunction with captain Speke of the Resolution, that they had behaved like angels.

The storm which immediately succeeded the encounter was so violent as to compel the Dorsetshire, and some other ships, to put to sea: they were, however, fortunate enough to effect their return on the ensuing day without having received any damage. In the month of March 1760, he removed into the Thunderer; but having quitted that ship in the ensuing year, had no farther opportunity of particularly distinguishing himself during the remainder of the war. In the new parliament which met on the 3d of November, 1761, he was, under the same interest as on the preceding occasion, re-elected representative for Heydon. In the month of August he was appointed to the Charlotte yacht, then new named, on board which vessel his friend, lord Anson, hoisted his flag, for the purpose of conveying to England her highness, the princess Charlotte of Mecklenburg, now queen of Great Britain. He received her majesty at Stade on the 28th of August, and landed her at Harwich, after a very tempestuous and disagreeable passage, on the 7th of September.

At the end of the year 1763 he was again sent to Germany in the Charlotte yacht, on an errand almost similar, that of bringing to England the prince of Brunswick, betrothed to her highness the princess Augusta. On the 29th of December, 1765, he had the misfortune to lose his lady; and the next particular mention we find made of him is, his advancement to the rank of baronet on the 19th of September, 1767. On the 3d of November following he bore the train of the duke of Grafton, his grace then walking as chief mourner at the funeral of his royal highness the duke of York. Sir Peter continued to retain the command of the Charlotte yacht till the 18th of October, 1770, when, on a promotion of flag-officers, he was advanced to be rear-admiral of the blue; as he moreover was, on the 24th of the fame month, to be rear-admiral of the white. Not long afterwards he was farther advanced to be rear-admiral of the red ; and, for a fhort time, at the commencement of the year 1771, held the command in the Medway.

In the month of June he was appointed commander-in-chief in the Mediterranean as fucceffor to commodore Proby, who was made comptroller of the navy victualling accounts: and about the middle of Auguft, being then at Portfmouth, received the duke of Gloucefter, on board the Venus, his royal highnefs being then about to proceed to Lifbon and the Mediterranean for the recovery of his health.

During the time fir Peter held the Mediterranean command he had his flag on board the Trident: but his life during this period being totally undiverfified by any event out of the common routine of a peaceable command, we have not any thing farther to add. After his return to England he never re-hoifted his flag, fo that we have no particulars concerning him worth communicating, except that, on 31ft of March, 1775, he was advanced to be vice-admiral of the blue ; on the 3d of February, 1776, to be vice of the white ; and, on the 28th of April, 1777, to be vice-admiral of the red. Sir Peter died on the 12th of June, 1778, not having lived to attain any fuperior rank or command*. Leaving no children, his title became extinct.

As a private gentleman he was poffeffed of the trueft benevolence, having been ever ready to affift the diftreffed during his life. At his deceafe he bequeathed the fum of 23,000l. after the death of his fifter, to the corporation of the Sons of the Clergy, and for the relief of the neceffitous orphans and widows dependant on that charitable inftitution. Confidered merely as a naval commander, few have acquired greater honour, and, allowing for the opportunities he met with, none. Thus entitled to our praife, our love, and our vereration, we can only lament that Providence was not more munificent in affording

---

" * Mr. Charles Denis, author of fome ingenious poetical Fables, was his brother. The arms of the family are, Argent, a Chevron engrailed, between three Fleurs-de-lis Gules."—

Gents. Mag. An. 1778.

him more frequent occasions of displaying those qualities which have so justly excited them.

DURELL, George,—was advanced, by admiral Mathews, from the rank of lieutenant, in which station he had remained two years, to be commander of the Dragon's Prize zebeck: he moreover was, on the 3d of February, 1745, promoted to be captain of the Liverpool frigate, which is the next occasion on which his name occurs. We have some reason to believe he afterwards commanded the Eltham; but this is a point, though in itself extremely trivial, concerning which we have not been able to arrive at any degree of certainty, owing to the circumstance we have already had occasion to observe on, that there were at this time three gentlemen holding the same rank in the navy, and of the same name*. No other information concerning him has come to our knowledge, except that he died in England on the 15th of May, 1754, not at that time, as we imagine, holding any command.

DYVE, Henry,—was, on the 2d of September, 1745, appointed captain of the Winchelsea frigate. Few men have passed through the service less noticed, a circumstance imputable, in many instances as well as the present, to misfortune, and not the want of personal merit. No subsequent account relative to this gentleman has come to our knowledge till towards the latter end of the war which commenced in 1756, he was then employed as a regulating captain on the impress service. In 1771 he was put on the superannuated list with the rank and half-pay of a rear-admiral, and died about the year 1779.

FAWLER, John,—early in the year 1745 commanded the Deptford storeship; from which he was on December 2d, promoted to be captain of the Sterling Castle, and is in the same unnoticed predicament with the gentleman last-mentioned. We do not find any positive information of having held any subsequent command; during a considerable part of the time, indeed, we know him to have lived in retirement with respect to the service. He died at Maidstone, in Kent, on the 17th of August, 1766.

FERMOR, The Honourable William,— was the second son of Thomas, first earl of Pomfret, and Henri-

---

* Captains John, Philip, and the officer of whom we now speak.

etta Louisa, daughter and sole heir to John lord Jeffreys, baron of Wem, by lady Charlotte Herbert, daughter and heir of Philip, earl of Pembroke and Montgomery. Having passed progressively through the different inferior ranks of midshipman, lieutenant, and commander, he was, on the 12th of January, 1745, promoted to be captain of the Nightingale frigate: at the latter end of the year 1746 he was appointed to the Experiment, a vessel of the same description, stationed as a cruiser off the coast of Scotland. He afterwards returned to the Nightingale, and was ordered to the Mediterranean. He died, according to Collins, in the year 1749, but, by Mr. Hardy's account, not till 1758; and, to use the precise words of the latter, " at sea, coming from Lisbon, in a merchant-ship."

FINCHER, Thomas,—was, on the 6th of December, 1745, promoted from the rank of commander to be captain of the Pembroke, a sixty-gun ship. He continued to serve in the same station during the too short remainder of his life, a life which, as will be presently seen, ended tragically to himself and a considerable number of the unhappy persons under his command. The first particular notice we find taken of him is in the month of May 1747, the Pembroke being at that time one of the fleet under the orders of vice-admiral Anson which totally defeated and captured the French squadron under M. de la Jonquiere. In the month of November following he was ordered for the East Indies as one of the squadron sent thither under the orders of rear-admiral Boscawen. He appears to have been very actively employed in the different unsuccessful attacks on the island of Mauritius and the town of Pondicherry. The latter failure he did not long survive: the circumstances productive of his melancholy end are officially related in the following concise manner.

" His Majesty's ship Pembroke, of sixty guns, struck on Colderoon point and overset. Having parted her cable the 13th April, 1749, at six P. M. she made sail out of fort St. David road, but could not clear the point. Twelve men only were saved: captain Fincher and about three hundred and thirty men were drowned, and all the officers, except a captain of marines [*]."

FORBES,

---

[*] The following very particular account of this disaster, as related by Mr. Cambridge, the master, who was one of the fortunate survivors,

FORBES, Hugh,—is to be mentioned only as having been, on the 5th of July, 1745, appointed captain of the Phœnix

vors, will certainly be deemed not uninterefting, at leaft by all naval people.

" About ten o'clock in the morning it blew frefh, the wind at N. E. by E. and a great fea began to come in: we then having a cable out, the captain ordered half a cable more to be veered away. At one in the afternoon it blew very hard, the wind at N. E. His majefty's fhip Namur lying about a cable's length within us, and abaft our beam, I went to the captain, as did likewife the lieutenants, and defired him to go to fea. He replied, " He could not anfwer to go to fea, unlefs the Namur did" (on board which rear-admiral Bofcawen's flag was flying) but ordered all our ports to be barred in and well fecured.

" At three o'clock I went to the captain, who was fick and in his cabin, and again defired him to go to fea. He feemed angry, and faid " He could not, giving the fame reafon as above;" nor would he fuffer any more cable to be veered away, at the fame time the fhip rode hard, ftrained much, and made water.

" At five, the fea increafing, our cable parted, and we caft our head off to the fea, otherwife we fhould have fallen on board the Namur. We immediately fet the fore-fail and mizen, got on board the main tack, and fet our main-fail, fore and mizen ftay-fails; at the fame time fome of our people were employed in heaving in the cable, for the captain would not have it cut. This took up fome time : it blew fo very hard that the fhip would not bear any more fail.

" At fix, there being a great head fea, we made very little way, and were obliged to fet both pumps to work. At half paft fix our main-fail fplit in pieces: we got down the yard in order to bend a new fail; but it blowing hard, the fhip laid down fo much we could not get the fail to the yard. At eight the carpenter fent word to the captain, that the fhip gained upon them much; four feet water being in her hold. At half paft eight our tiller broke fhort off at the rudder head; and we likewife found one of the rudder chains broke; the fails we had now fet were our fore-fail, mizen and fore ftay-fails. The fea made a free paffage over us; and the fhip being waterlogged we hawled up our fore-fail to eafe her, but expected to go down every minute In hawling down our fore ftay-fail it fplit; and as I looked aft from the forecaftle I faw the main and mizen-mafts gone, but never heard them go. By this time the fhip righted much, and in about feven minutes the fore-maft went by the board, but the bowfprit held faft; our pumps continually working. The third lieutenant, being on the quarter deck, fent forward to me to clear and let go the fmall bower anchor, which was immediately done. We found the fhip drive to fhore very faft. At half paft ten we had eight feet water in the fhips hold; and kept all the pumps working. About eleven o'clock we found the fhip fettle, the depth of water twelve or fourteen

fathoms;

Phœnix frigate, and as having, on the 18th of August, 1750, died at Mahon commander, on that station, of some

fathoms. The anchor then brought the ship up, but the cable parted in a few minutes; then we let the sheet anchor go, which was all we had. The sea now making a free passage over us again, broke and tore away our boats and booms. The sheet cable tore out with such violence that no man could venture near it, till the clench brought up the ship: but the sea came with such force, and so very high, that in the hollow of the sea the ship struck, and the cable immediately parted. It was now near twelve o'clock; the ship struck fore and aft, but abaft very hard. The third lieutenant was near me when the ship first struck, but I saw no more of him afterwards. I kept the forecastle, accompanied by the boatswain, cook, and about eight men more. I got myself lashed to the bitts before the ship took heel, but shifted myself over to windward when she began to heel, and lashed myself as before, the sea continually beating over us. About two I saw the captain's cabin washed away, and the ship almost on her broadside. When day-light came we were sixteen men on the forecastle, and four hanging abaft to the timber heads; but three of the last got on a piece of the wreck which was loose, and drove away; the other was drowned: all this time the sea came over us in a dreadful manner, so that we could scarce take breath. About eight o'clock nine men were washed off the forecastle. We could now see the trees ashore between the seas. About nine o'clock the boatswain and cook were washed away from each side of me; then I removed to the cat-head, as did another man also. About ten o'clock all our men were washed away, except those who were lashed to the cat-head. We judged we were near two miles off the shore: we continued there all the day, the sea beating over us continually, so that we had little time to fetch breath, or speak to one another. At noon we found the sea to come every way upon us, and could perceive the wind was shifted, which was the cause thereof. This part of the wreck kept fast, but night coming on we had a dismal prospect before us, having no hopes of relief. About midnight the sea abated, so that we could speak to one another for the space of two or three minutes together; but I found myself so weak, having been sick ever since we arrived in the country, that when the sea washed me on one side in my lashing, I was not able to help myself up, but was obliged to get my companion to assist me. At day-light I found myself much weaker and very thirsty. The sea at this time came over us once in a quarter of an hour. We found the wreck much nearer the shore than yesterday. About noon we found the sea much abated, so that it seldom came over us, and the weather began to be fine; but I found myself very faint. About two or three o'clock we saw two paddy-boats coming along shore about a mile without us; we spread abroad a handkerchief, which I had about my neck, that the boats might see us. One of them seemed to edge towards us for some minutes, but hawled off again: we then saw several catamarans near the shore, which we

judged

some ship, the name of which is not mentioned. A fall from his horse is given as the immediate cause of his decease.

FORREST,

judged to be fishing. We spread abroad the handkerchief again, but none of them approached us. Soon after, we saw several people gather together ashore: the sun began to grow low, so that we judged it to be about five o'clock. At last we saw two of the catamarans above-mentioned coming towards us, with three black men on each. They took us off the wreck and carried us on shore. As soon as we were landed we found ourselves surrounded by about three hundred armed men. My companion told me we were fallen into the hands of the Mahrattas, who were at this time in arms against the English. They ordered us to come off the catamarans. I strove to rise, but found myself so weak, and my legs so terribly bruised, that I could not get up; upon which some of them came and lifted me off, and laid me upon the sand, for I could not stand. I made a signal to them that I wanted some water to drink; but they gave me none and only laughed at our condition. Their commander ordered some of them to strip us, which they did quite naked. As I was not able to walk they led us part of the way to Davecotta (a fort belonging to them) and there put us into a canoe, and carried us up a river to the fort walls. About ten this night they put us within the walls and laid us on the ground, where we had nothing to cover us but the heavens: and about eleven brought us a little rice with some water. Great numbers of people gathered round us, laughing at us, and expressing great contempt and derision.

"The country people flocked daily to the fort to see us, but none of them shewed us the least pity; but, on the contrary, laughed at and threatened us with death. Our lodging place was between the gate-ways, and when we had been there fourteen or fifteen days they carried us into the country. Though my legs were much better, yet still I could not walk; and my companion was extremely weak, which I believe was owing to our want of more victuals: so they put us into dooleys, or cradles, fastened together with ropes, which they got from the wreck. About four o'clock, on the 15th day, they carried us about twelve miles to their king, who was encamped against our company's troops. The king was desirous we should enter into their service, but we told him (by the interpreters, who were three Dutchmen) that we could not consent to it: with that they travelled us till we came to a fort, and were immediately put into a dungeon. There were two more prisoners, one of them our ship mate, the other a deserter from the India company's troops.

"In about three week's time my legs were almost well, so that I was able to walk. We now began to entertain some hopes of making our escape, and taking an opportunity, I with some difficulty got high enough upon the wall to look over it, and found it was very high surrounded with a wide mote, or ditch; but there was a path between the wall and the ditch, so that we might choose our place to swim

over,

FORREST, Arthur.—This gentleman was, in the year 1741, lieutenant of one of the ships composing the armament, under Mr. Vernon, sent on the unsuccessful expedition against Carthagena. He very eminently distinguished himself under the captains Boscawen, Watson, and Cotes, at the attack of the Barradera battery, having been among the foremost who entered the enemy's work at the head of a party of seamen. He does not, however, appear to have received that reward his intrepidity may seem to have justly merited, for he was not promoted to the rank of post-captain till the 9th of March, 1745, at which time he was appointed to the Wager. In 1746 he was employed in this ship on the Jamaica station, where he had the good fortune to capture a very large Spanish privateer, carrying thirty-six guns and upwards of two hundred men, which had done considerable mischief,

---

over, if it proved deep. We got, at several times, some strands of rope off the dooleys which they had carried us in, as they happened to be left within the bounds of our liberty: and in a few days got so many pieces, as, when knotted together, made seven fathom and an half. After some consultation we resolved to undermine the foundation of the dungeon, at the farthest part from the guards, and on the 27th of May began to work. On the 1st of June we came to the foundation, being six feet deep, and the wall thirty inches through. In two days time we had worked upwards, on the other side, so far, that the light began to appear through the surface, so that we let every thing remain till night. At seven, it beginning to grow dark, they put us into the dungeon as usual, and soon after we worked ourselves quite out. Without being discovered we got over the wall by the help of our rope, and in less than half an hour had crossed the mote, though very deep and wide. We travelled all night, we judged about sixteen miles, and in the day time hid ourselves among the bushes. The second night we travelled, as before, to the S. E. and day coming on we concealed ourselves among some rushes. About three in the afternoon we were discovered, which obliged us to go on, but we were not molested. We proceeded till about midnight; and next day, about ten o'clock met a cooley, who told us he would shew us to Carakal. About noon we arrived there, and were received with great humanity; but my fever was not at all abated. The next morning the governor sent to Mr. Boscawen to let him know we were there; and, by the return of the messenger, the admiral desired we might be furnished with what money we wanted. In twelve days we found ourselves well recovered, and went to Trincabar, a place belonging to the Danes, where we stayed three days, and then got a passage to Fort St. David's."

in the Windward Paſſage, to the Britiſh commerce, and had alſo a very ſhort time before captured the Blaſt bomb-ketch. We find no mention made of him after this time till the beginning of the year 1755, when he was appointed to the Rye. He was, in a ſhort time, promoted to the Auguſta and ordered to the Weſt Indies, where, in the month of October, 1757, he had a very memorable opportunity of diſtinguiſhing himſelf. This he very laudably ſeized, and, by exertions hardly to be exceeded, acquired, in conjunction with the captains who ſerved under him, the higheſt renown. The particulars of this encounter are thus officially related by rear-admiral Cotes, in his public letter, written in Port Royal harbour on the 9th of November following, and which is nearly an exact copy of captain Forreſt's own report to Mr. Cotes.

" On the 25th of laſt month captain Forreſt, in the Auguſta, with the Dreadnought and Edinburgh under his command, returned from the cruize off Cape Francois; on the 21ſt, they fell in with ſeven French ſhips of war. At ſeven in the morning the Dreadnought made the ſignal for ſeeing the enemy's fleet coming out of Cape Francois, and at noon diſcovered with certainty they were four ſhips of the line and three large frigates. Captain Forreſt then made the ſignal for the captains, Suckling and Langdon, who agreed with him to engage them; accordingly they all bore down; and about twenty minutes after three the action began with great briſkneſs on both ſides. It continued for two hours and an half, when the French commodore making a ſignal, one of the frigates immediately came to tow him out of the line, and the reſt of the French ſhips followed him. Our ſhips had ſuffered ſo much in their maſts, ſails and rigging, that they were in no condition to purſue them. Both officers and ſeamen behaved with the greateſt reſolution the whole time of the action, and were unhappy at the concluſion of it, that the ſhips were not in a condition to follow the French, who had frigates to tow them off. The French on this occaſion had put on board the Sceptre her full complement of guns, either from the ſhore or out of the India-ſhip, and had alſo mounted the Outarde ſtoreſhip with her full proportion of guns, and had taken not only the men out of the merchant-ſhips but ſoldiers from the garriſon, in hopes their appearance would frighten our small squadron, and oblige them to leave the coast clear for them to carry out their large convoy of merchant-ships: but our captains were too gallant to be terrified at their formidable appearance. So far from avoiding them, they bore down and engaged them with the greatest resolution and good conduct; and I have the pleasure to acquaint their lordships, that the captains, officers, seamen and marines, have done their duty on this occasion much to their honour. I hope their good behaviour will be approved by their lordships*."

It is added, though not officially, " that captain Forrest perceiving the shattered condition of all his ships (the masts, sails, boats and rigging, being mostly useless) thought proper to withdraw, lest the loss of a lower mast should leave any of them at the mercy of the frigates. Never was a battle more furious than the beginning; in two minutes there was not a rope or sail whole in either ship. The French use a shot which the English neglect, called Langridge, which is very destructive in cutting the rigging. The Augusta had nine men killed and thirty wounded."

A private letter from Jamaica takes notice, " that when a council of war was held, the question was not, What superior force the enemy had; or how unequal the combat? The commanding officer saying to the other two, " Gentlemen, you see the force of the enemy, Is it your resolution to fight them, or not? upon which they both resolutely answered, " It is." Here the council of war ended, having lasted about half a minute."

This highly distinguishable display of gallantry and intrepidity was quickly afterwards † followed by a success no less brilliant and remarkable, equally honourable to the service and his country, but happily much more advantageous to himself:—this was the capture of the Mars, a French frigate of thirty-two guns, twelve, nine, and six-pounders, with her whole convoy; Le Theodore, of

---

* The enemy's ships were, the Intrepide and Sceptre, of seventy-four guns each; Opineatre, of sixty-four; L'Outarde, of forty-four; the Greenwich, of fifty; and the Savage and Unicorn, of thirty-guns each. To encrease the disparity, the Edinburgh and the Augusta were both extremely foul at the time of the engagement.

† On the 24th of December, 1759.

twenty-

twenty-two guns; La Margaretta, of sixteen guns; Le St. Pierre, of sixteen guns; Le Solide, of fourteen guns; Le Flore, of fourteen guns; Le Morrice le Grand, of eighteen guns; Le Brilliant, of fourteen guns; and Le Monette, a brigantine of ten guns, bound from Port Prince to Old France, laden with sugar, indigo, coffee, cotton, &c. which cost 170,000l. The Mars struck upon receiving the first broadside, and all the rest followed her example. He returned to England not long afterwards; and, in 1760, being appointed to the Centaur, was sent out to Jamaica commodore and temporary commander-in-chief on that station. He sailed from England, with a convoy of thirty-four ships, on the 16th of January, and arrived at Port Royal on the 6th of March. He continued on the same station during the remainder of the war, but without meeting with any occurrence worthy particular notice. In 1769 he was re-appointed to the same command with the established rank of commodore; but he did not long survive his arrival there, dying on the 26th of May, 1770.

GARDINER, Arthur,—was, on the 27th of May, 1745, promoted to the Neptune, as captain to vice-admiral Rowley, who had his flag on board that ship. This circumstance of his appointment excepted, we find no mention whatever made of him during the continuance of the war. In 1752 he was appointed to the Amazon frigate, a vessel employed, as is not uncustomary even in time of peace, on the Irish station. The next situation in which we find him is, that of captain of the Colchester, of fifty guns; from which ship he removed, at the express request of the unfortunate admiral Byng, into the Ramillies. The ill success which attended the rencounter with Gallifoniere, is said to have lain so heavy on his mind, as to induce a species of melancholy which never was effaced during his life. He was undoubtedly a man formed with very nice feelings, and could not readily dispossess himself of an idea extremely ill-founded, that he, being so closely and materially connected in service with his unhappy commander-in-chief, must, in some degree, participate in that censure and clamour which was so loudly, industriously, and generally raised.

From the minutes of the court-martial, it appears that captain Gardiner, who was, as may be naturally supposed, ordered home to England as an evidence, depofed, that the fails were not all fet, nor did he know any impediment why the rear fhould not have got into as clofe action as the van. He added, that he advifed the admiral to bear down, but that he objected thereto, *foaring an inconvenience fimilar to that experienced fome time before by Mr. Mathews in the fame feas.* He concluded his day's examination by declaring, that he difcovered nothing in the fmalleft degree improper in the admiral's perfonal behaviour. On his fecond day's examination he made it appear, that the admiral took upon himfelf the entire command of the fhip, and that nothing was done that day except by his particular orders.

This circumftance certainly was one of thofe which bore hardeft upon the admiral; and the fubfequent grief felt by the captain might, in all probability, be as much encreafed by his being obliged, in honour, as well as in juftice to himfelf and his country, to bear any pointed teftimony * againft a man, with whom he had lived in habits

---

* In juftice, however, to Mr. Byng, be it remembered, that captain Gardiner alfo declared in the courfe of his examination, which lafted nearly two days, to the following effect:

" That the Trident, being abaft the larboard beam of the Ramillies, did fo impede the Ramillies in going down to the enemy, that the admiral muft have gone down without his force, which was not his intention: that the fignal was out for the line of battle ahead at that time, and the rear divifion went down very regular after the Trident and Princefs Louifa got into their ftations. Being afked, Whether it had not been a more fpeedy and regular method to clofe with the enemy, to have made the fignal for the line abreaft? The captain faid " No, becaufe it would be improper for fhips to go down in a line abreaft, to attack fhips that are laying in a line ahead, when they can go down with their bows to them; i. e. a flanting courfe to them; and therefore he was of opinion, that the rear did take the proper method to clofe with the enemy." Being further interrogated, Whether he meant as to the courfe fteered on the enemy, or the fail carried? He anfwered, " Both: but this (faid he) is matter of opinion, which I fhall hereafter avoid entering into, as there are many fuperior judges here-to me."

" He was alfo of opinion, that the rear would have engaged as near the enemy as the van did, had the French ftaid: that it was admiral Byng's intention to engage the chef efcadre, the third fhip from the enemy's rear, and not to throw away his fhot, as the enemy did, till he came near the enemy: that the admiral ftood on till it was imagined, on board the Ramillies, that every fhip, if fhe had gone properly

habits of intimacy and friendship, as we have already suggested him to have done Not long after the conclusion of the trial Mr. Gardiner was appointed to the Monmouth, of sixty-four guns, and ordered to the Mediterranean, where, on the last day of February, 1758, the British squadron, then under the command of Mr. Osborne, fell in with a small French armament, under the marquis du Quesne, bound from Toulon to Carthagena, for the purpose of reinforcing the French chef d'escadre de la Clue. The marquis himself was in the Foudroyant, the identical ship on board which Gallifoniere hoisted his flag at the time of his encounter with Mr. Byng. It was somewhat singular, though particularly grateful to captain Gardiner, that he was among those ordered to pursue the French commodore. It is related of him, whether correctly or no we cannot pretend to say, that, previous to this time, but after he was appointed to the Monmouth, he had been heard to declare, that if ever he was fortunate enough to fall in with the Foudroyant, he was determined to attack her though he should perish in the attempt. The Swiftsure, of seventy guns; the Hampton Court and Monmouth, of sixty four guns each, were dispatched after the Foudroyant, and other ships at the same time after the remainder of the squadron. Captain Gardiner far out-stripped his companions and brought the enemy warily to action, the other ships being nearly out of sight at the time. Captain Gardiner was unhappily shot through the arm with a musket ball at the very commencement of the action; but this disaster was not sufficient to prevent him from continuing his exertions. The rigging of the Foudroyant being fortunately much disabled in a short time, captain Gardiner seizing the opportunity given him by

---

properly steered a slanting course, could have gone down to the ship of the enemy, she should have engaged, with her broadside to her: that he recollected particularly to have heard the admiral say, when the Ramillies was abreast of the French, that such was his intention: that the admiral ordered the guns to be shotted with round and grape shot, two shot in the guns below, and proposed to set top-gallant sails on seeing the french going away; that he heard him express, at that time, his unhappiness at not having a sufficient force to make a general chase, as he thought he could materially have distressed the enemy in the situation they then were in, " if (said he) I had two or three ships more !"

that advantage, placed himfelf on his antagonift's quarter and maintained a very clofe action for upwards of two hours; when, about nine o'clock, while in the act of encouraging his people and enquiring what injury had been fuftained between decks, he received a fecond wound, by a mufket ball, in the forehead. He lived, indeed, till the next day, but the greater part of the time was totally infenfible.

The action was continued with the greateft fpirit by Mr. Carket, the firft lieutenant, who fucceeded to the command. The Foudroyant, having loft her main and mizen-mafts*, being completely difabled and the Swiftfure alfo getting up, the marquis, who, to do him juftice, made a good defence, furrendered about one o'clock in the morning. The Foudroyant mounted eighty guns, and had on board, at the commencement of the action, a chofen crew of nine hundred and eleven men: her lower battery confifted of thirty French forty-two pounders: on her upper deck fhe carried thirty-two twenty-four pounders; and on her quarter deck and forecaftle eighteen twelve pounders †. It was efteemed the fineft fhip at that time in the whole French navy: and the captain of a French privateer, taken a fhort time before by the Monmouth, is faid to have boafted, that fhe was a fhip capable of refifting any force by which fhe fhould be attacked. She would fight, he faid, to day, to-morrow, and the next day, but never could be taken ‡. Upon the whole, this

---

* Soon afterwards the captain fell. He is faid, immediately on receiving his fecond wound, to have fent for the lieutenant, and made it his laft requeft, that he would not give up the fhip or quit the enemy. The Monmouth's mizen-maft foon after came by the board, on which the enemy gave three cheers. The crew of the Monmouth returned the compliment in a few minutes, on the mizen-maft of the Foudroyant being alfo fhot away. This difafter was foon followed by the fall of her main-maft; which giving frefh fpirits to the Englifh, their fire became fo inceffant and intolerable, that the French failors could no longer be kept to their guns.

† The Monmouth on the other hand carried only twelve and twenty-four pounders, with a complement of four hundred and feventy men; and there was as much difference in fize and appearance as between a frigate and a fhip of the line.

‡ The French prifoners then in England, afferted in the laft war the fame thing of the Ville de Paris.

certainly was, as is remarked by many hiftorians, as gallant an action as ever was performed by a fingle fhip, but the death of Gardiner clouded the victory, and made both the conquerors and the whole nation almoft forget the joy they would otherwife have felt at fo glorious an event. Campbell adds to his account of this engagement the following remark. " This action, which is one of the moft glorious in the naval hiftory of Britain, muft ever remain an inconteftible proof of our naval fuperiority *." We have only to add, that fome fubfequent events feem ftrongly to corroborate this affertion.

GAYTON, Clark,—was, in the month of April 1744, promoted from the rank of lieutenant to command *pro tempore*, or, according to the term ufed in the fervice, by order, the Ludlow Caftle, of forty guns; but no other mention is made of him while retaining that ftation. He was not actually promoted to the rank of poft captain till the 6th of July, 1745, on which day his commiffion bore date for the Mermaid frigate. No other notice is taken of him during the continuance of the war, nor indeed after its conclufion, till the year 1755, when he was, about the month of April, appointed captain of the Antelope. He quitted that fhip in the following year, and was promoted to the Royal Anne, a firft rate; but we do not find any particular account given of him till the year 1758, when he commanded the St. George, a fecond rate of ninety guns, one of the fquadron ordered

---

* It is confidently given as an anecdote of captain Gardiner, that while in chafe, directing his difcourfe to a land officer who was on board, he faid, " Whatever becomes of you and me, this fhip muft go into Gibraltar." Harranguing his people juft before the commencement of the action, he faid, " This fhip *muft* be taken; fhe appears above our match, but Englifhmen are not to mind that, nor will I quit her while this fhip can fwim, or I have a foul left alive."

A private letter from Gibraltar gives us the following additional particulars relative to captain Gardiner and his private conduct.

" Two days before he left this port, being in company with lord Rob. Bertie and other perfons, he with great anguifh of foul told them, that my lord Anfon had reflected on him, and faid that he was one of the men who had brought difgrace upon the nation; that it touched him exceffively; but it ran ftrongly in his mind, that he fhould have an opportunity fhortly to convince his lordfhip, how much he had the honour of the nation at heart, and that he was not culpable."

to the West Indies, under commodore Robert Hughes, for the purpose of reinforcing Mr. Moore and enabling him to attack the French settlements in that quarter. The attack on the island of Martinico failed, as is well known: but the subsequent one against Guadaloupe was, as it may be equally well remembered, more successful. Conquest, however was not obtained without considerable and indeed formidable resistance.

The attack was, as it is said, productive of an anecdote too characteristic of this gentleman to be forgotten, or omitted. The citadel of Guadaloupe was a fortress of the first consequence, possessing great natural advantages of situation, improved and strengthened by the skill of the ablest engineers in the French service. So formidable did it appear to the British officers in that particular branch, that they were unanimous in declaring it impregnable to any attack by sea, unsupported by some collateral aid. The commodore thought otherwise; and, notwithstanding every remonstrance to the contrary, resolved on the assault; the event, indeed, justified his determination: but, nevertheless, it proved sufficiently arduous to exempt those, who were of a contrary opinion, from any imputation of coldness, or want of enterprize. Among those who thought so, and represented the service as difficult and dangerous, was Mr. Gayton, a man, whom certainly no one could with decency charge either with tameness of spirit, or deficiency in judgment, founded on experience. His difference of opinion is said to have excited some slight sensation of disgust and disapprobation in the commodore, so that when the latter had formed his disposition of attack, by which the citadel was allotted to the St. George, with two other ships, he thought proper to send a written order to Mr. Gayton, commanding him to proceed on that service.

This procedure was deemed by him a species of affront which, though improper to openly resent, he could bear strongly in his mind. Knowing his own attention to the rules and discipline of the service, his promptitude to obey the commands of his superior, even though they should be deemed by him bordering on impropriety, he considered the formality of a written order as an insult, he being perfectly disposed, in every refpect, to have obeyed a mere fignal indicative of the commodore's intention. After a cannonade of fome hours continuance, the profpect of fuccefs appeared, even to Mr. Moore himfelf, doubtful: the refiftance of the enemy, and the injury fuftained by the affailants, appeared to juftify the general opinion given in council, and evince that it was not the refult of timidity but prudence. The commodore wavered, and notwithftanding the fire of the affailants was violent and unremitted, he was, as has been reported to us, induced, after the attack had continued fome hours, to make a fignal for the St. George in particular, to defift and hawl off. Captain Gayton took no notice; a boat was fent to him with a verbal order from the commodore to the fame effect, but the captain, inftead of obeying, returned for anfwer, that as it had been thought necelfary to ufe the formality of a written order previous to the affault, fo fhould he on his part think it equally fo to infift on the fame punctilio authorifing him to defift. In the interim the afcendency of the Britifh fire became apparent, and the ceffation of that from the citadel * with all its dependencies clofed the difpute.

The St. George was in the preceding attack very confiderably damaged, and the † captain himfelf flightly wounded. The object of the armament, of which the St. George formed a part, being thus concluded, captain Gayton, with fuch others his companions as it was deemed unneceffary to retain on that ftation, returned to England in the courfe of the year. He remained in the St. George during the continuance of the war, employed in the Channel, under the admirals Hawke, Bofcawen, and others, but no poffibility of acquiring either fame or fortune prefented itfelf to the captain of any fhip of that clafs during that period.

---

* Which was taken poffeffion of the enfuing day.

† We muft not omit the following remarkable occurrence. A forty-two pound fhot from the citadel ftruck the centre of an iron hoop furrounding the main-maft, elongated, if the term be allowed, the hammered, which confequently is the moft elaftic ft te of the metal, and forming it into a cafe or focket, had penetrated into the centre of the maft. The quantity of powder expended by the St. George on the foregoing occafion, far exceeded that of any former fhip on any fervice whatever.

We do not believe captain Gayton to have held any fubfequent commiffion after the peace, till the year 1769, when he was appointed to the St. Anthonio, of fixty guns, a guardfhip at Portfmouth. This command he did not retain fo long as is cuftomary, being promoted, on the 18th of October, 1770, to be rear-admiral of the white. On the 31ft of March, 1775, he was advanced to be rear-admiral of the red: on the 3d of February, 1776, to be vice-admiral of the white; and immediately afterwards was appointed commander-in-chief on the Jamaica ftation. The difpute with America becoming daily more ferious, a reinforcement of feveral fhips of war was ordered out to join him early in the fummer*. By a judicious difpofition of his cruifers, aided by the activity of their refpective captains, two hundred and thirty five American veffels were captured by the fhips on the Jamaica ftation during the time Mr. Gayton held that command.

We muft not omit two anecdotes relative to this gentleman, ftrongly marked by that rough pleafantry natural to him, and of that high fpirit, with refpect to the fervice, which all perfons muft admit him to have poffeffed. The different fums allotted to him as commander-in-chief, refulting from the fale of the different American prizes,

---

* In confequence of an untrue affertion made in a pamphlet, written by T. Paine, Mr. Gayton publifhed the following declaration in the Jamaica Gazette, which we have been the rather induced to infert, as it contains fome particulars of his early life, which muft undoubtedly be genuine.

" I have feen a pamphlet, publifhed in Philadelphia, under the title of Common Senfe, wherein the author fays, that, forty years ago, there were feventy and eighty-gun fhips built in New England. In anfwer to which I do declare, that at that very time I was in New England a midfhipman, aboard his majefty's fhip Squirrel, with the late fir Peter Warren, and then there never had been a man of war built of any kind. In 1747, after the reduction of Louifbourg, there was a fhip of forty-four guns ordered to be built at Pifcataqua by one Mr. Meffervey: fhe was called the America, and failed for England the following year. When fhe came home fhe was found fo bad that fhe never was commiffioned again. There was afterwards another fhip of twenty guns, built at Bofton by Mr. Benjamin Hollwell, which was called the Bofton. She run but a fhort time before fhe was condemned; and thofe were the only two fhips of war ever built in America: therefore I thought it my duty to publifh this, to undeceive the public in general, to fhew that what the author has fet forth is an abfolute falfity.

" CLARK GAYTON."

were

were regularly invested in dollars, by the admiral, and packed in proper chests for the purpose of being conveyed to England. Some of his friends wishing to point out to him the trouble and inconvenience of transporting specie, recommended to him rather to remit his property to Europe in bills. The admiral, with an affected peevishness declared, he knew nothing so valuable as money itself; and that for his part he should not be fool enough to accept paper in exchange, when the latter might not be worth a farthing. His intimates having the safety of his and his descendant's property at heart, recommended to him to send his wealth to England in a frigate, for the Antelope, his flag ship, was so extremely old and crazy, that no inconsiderable fears were entertained she would founder on her passage. The admiral with much vivacity replied, "No, my money and myself will take our passage in the same bottom, and if we are lost there will be an end of two bad things at once."

The second is, that while on his passage home he fell in with a large ship, which, on its near approach, proved to be an English man of war. Every possible preparation was, however, prudentially made to receive the stranger as an enemy, though of force and magnitude infinitely superior, even supposing the Antelope in proper fighting condition, a circumstance by no means the case, she having had a considerable number of her lower-deck guns taken out for the purpose of easing her on her passage. The admiral himself, extremely infirm and almost unable to stand, came upon the quarter-deck, and after exhorting his people in few words to behave themselves like Englishmen, he told them for his part, "He could not stand by them, but he would sit and see them fight as long as they pleased."

Mr. Gayton never accepted any command after his return to England, where he arrived in safety on the 21st of April, and, that success might accompany him to the last, with a small American prize he captured on his passage. A short time previous to his arrival, that is to say, on the 29th of January, 1778, he was advanced to be vice-admiral of the red; as he was to be admiral of the blue on the 8th of April, 1782. His infirm state of health and advanced age, compelled him to live almost totally in retirement, a state rendered as comfortable as

bodily pains would permit it to be, by an handſome fortune, which he had acquired in ſervice, as honourably
as unremitted attention to his duty when employed, and
the moſt ſignal diſplay of perſonal gallantry and ſpirit on
all poſſible opportunities could render it. He died at
Fareham, where, when in England, he had for many years
reſided, about the year 1787.

GRIFFIN, Thomas,—can ſcarcely be ſaid to be entitled to a place here, on account of his rank, though
highly in reſpect to character, whether conſidered as an
officer or a gentleman.—In 1736, he was a petty officer on
board the Oxford, a ſhip of 50 guns, at that time commanded by captain Swale; and on the death of that gentleman, his ſucceſſor promoted Mr. Griffin to be third
lieutenant of that ſhip. He continued in the ſame veſſel
till the year 1741, by which time he was advanced to be
firſt lieutenant, and was ſoon afterwards removed into the
Marlborough of 90 guns, at that time the flag ſhip of rear-
admiral Haddock, the commander in chief on the Mediteranean ſtation. He was appointed, in the Eaſt Indies,
captain of the Medway Prize on the 25th of February,
1745; and afterwards was promoted, by Mr. Griffin,
the commander-in-chief on that ſtation; but who notwithſtanding the ſimilitude of names was in no degree
related to him, to the Princeſs Mary, in which ſhip he
died on the 17th of December, 1748. He is, however,
ſaid never to have had his commiſſion, as poſt captain, in
either inſtance confirmed by the admiralty board.

HILL, John,—was, on the 26th of Auguſt, 1745,
promoted to be captain of the Triton frigate; from thence
he is ſaid to have been promoted, in 1747, to the Gloire,
of forty-four guns, a prize taken from the French a ſhort
time before, by the ſquadron under vice-admiral Anſon.
He was re-appointed to the ſame ſhip in 1751, and is ſaid,
in ſome accounts which we dare not implicitly rely on,
to have afterwards commanded a ſhip, of twenty guns.
No other particulars relative to this gentleman have
come to our knowledge, except that he was, in 1770, put
on the ſuperannuated liſt, with the rank and half-pay of a
rear-admiral, and died on the 8th of March, 1773.

HORNE, Edmund,—is known to us only as having
been, on the 22d of February, 1745, promoted to be captain

tain of the Hector, a forty-gun ship, and as having died in England without having, to our knowledge, held any subsequent command*, on the 23d of May, 1764.

HUGHES, Robert, — was commander of the Shark sloop in 1744, and, on the 2d of April, 1745, was promoted to the command of the Kingston, a fifty-gun ship, to which he was re-commissioned two years afterwards. In 1748 he was appointed to the Tilbury, and we believe, in 1751, to the Deptford, of sixty guns. The next subsequent information we have concerning him is, that immediately previous the commencement of the war in 1756, he commanded the Port Mahon frigate; from whence he was, in the month of April, promoted to the Augusta; from this ship he removed, about the month of June following, into the Berwick, of seventy guns. He continued in that ship till the year 1758, at the beginning of which he was employed on the Mediterranean station under the command of admiral Osborne. On the last day of February he had the good fortune to assist in the defeat and capture of the small French squadron under the marquis de Quesne. Returning to England towards the conclusion of the year, he was appointed commodore of a squadron, consisting of eight ships of the line, ordered to the West Indies for the purpose of reinforcing commodore Moore, and enabling him to attack the different French islands and colonies in that quarter. Having hoisted his broad pendant on board the Norfolk, of seventy-four guns, he sailed from Spithead on the 10th of November, having under his convoy a fleet of store-ships and transports, on board which were embarked six regiments of infantry. He arrived at Barbadoes, without having been unfortunate enough to encounter any sinister accident, on the 3d of January.

The leading particulars of this expedition have been already given in the life of sir John Moore†, and to those it is not necessary to add any thing on the present occasion. Soon after his return to England, whither he was order-

---

* Except that of the Rupert, a fourth rate of 60 guns, to which he was appointed by the Admiralty, and ordered out to the Mediterranean for the purpose of superceding captain Ambrose, who was ordered home for trial, on account of his conduct in the encounter off Toulon.

† See p. 251.

ed back in the month of June to convoy the troops, which the object of the expedition being completed, it became unneceſſary to keep any longer in the Weſt Indies, he was appointed to the Kingſton, in which ſhip he continued but a very ſhort time, during a part of the abſence of captain Parry. We believe him to have held no command after this during the war. At the latter end of the year 1763, he was appointed to the Dorſetſhire, of ſeventy guns, one of the guardſhips ſtationed at Portſmouth, and on board which vice-admiral Holburne afterwards hoiſted his flag. He quitted this command after having retained it three years, the term cuſtomarily allotted to it, and is not known to have ever received a ſubſequent commiſſion. On the 18th of October, 1770, he was advanced to the rank of rear-admiral of the red, and died at Bath, ere he experienced any farther promotion, on the 19th of January, 1774.

HUME, John.—This gentleman we believe to have been appointed, early in 1742, commander of the Serpent bomb: he afterwards removed into the Mortar, a veſſel of the ſame deſcription: but nothing farther is known of him till his promotion, on the 20th of July, 1745, to be captain of the Sandwich. No farther account has been collected concerning him, except that he died in England on the 16th of November, 1759.

JASPER, Richard.—This gentleman was ſecond lieutenant of the Namur, under Mr. Mathews, at the time of the indeciſive engagement with the French and Spaniſh fleets off Toulon; and was the perſon ſent, by the commander-in-chief, to Mr. Leſtock, with a meſſage, intimating that he would lay to till the vice-admiral could get up with his diviſion to cloſe the line of battle. He was appointed captain of the Phœnix frigate on the 13th of February, 1745, and ordered not long afterwards to the Mediterranean, from whence after ſome continuance he returned to England in the Berwick.

The next account we have of him is, that in the year 1747 he was made captain of the Prince Henry, and was re-appointed to the ſame ſhip in the month of July in the year enſuing. He retained this command many years, but is not again particularly noticed till 1751, when he ſerved on the coaſt of Africa, as appears from the following minute, dated July the 31ſt.

"This day was read before the board of admiralty, a letter sent by captain Jasper, from the prince of Annamaboe, in which he expresses his gratitude for the civilities shewn his son while he was at our court, and offers the assistance of 20,000 men to build a fort on the coast of Africa in case of obstructions from the French. At the same time was read a long letter from captain Jasper, giving a very accurate account of the state of affairs on that coast, at which their lordships expressed great satisfaction."

He afterwards repaired to Jamaica, and from thence to England, where he arrived in the month of August 1752, having on board a considerable quantity of specie. He almost immediately returned back to the West India station; but on account of some misbehaviour at the Havannah*, was brought to a court-martial in the following year, and sentenced to be dismissed the service. He appears to have been a man possessing a very irritable irascible temper. This, unfortunately for him, caused his untimely death, he being killed in a duel, † by Mr. Brice, at the Cardigan-head tavern, on the 11th of May, 1761. The survivor was afterwards tried and honourably

---

* The following official mention is made of captain Jasper; and the misbehaviour alluded to, took place at the same time.

"Gazette, No. 9135. Havannah, Nov. 2, 1752.

"The 17th of October an English man of war, called the Prince Henry, Captain Richard Jasper, came to an anchor in this harbour, having lost all her masts, and suffered other considerable damages from the hurricanes which we have had in these seas during the month of September. She was received here with that humanity which is requisite upon such an occasion; and all possible assistance will be given her till she can be put in a condition to pursue her voyage. This ship, which was bound for London, sailed from Jamaica on the 3d of September: on the 4th the first hurricane happened, which would not suffer her to put in between Cayques and Mariguana. On the 23d she met with the second, off Cape St. Antonio, which carried away all her masts. Several Englishmen belonging to three merchant's ships, that have been wrecked, are likewise arrived in this port: they have all been collected together, and are incorporated amongst the crews of his majesty's ships. The captain of the Prince Henry has since demanded these men, and they will be delivered to him upon his paying the money that they have cost during their stay here; but this point is not as yet settled."

† The rencontre took place on the 10th: captain Jasper died on the following day.

acquitted

acquitted of the murder, it being very clearly and fatisfactorily proved, that the deceafed was entirely the aggreffor.

JEFFREYS, Robert.—We have been able to collect very few particulars relative to this gentleman: he was, on May 1, 1745, appointed captain of the Scarborough*; and we have no doubt but that he held fome fubfequent commands; thefe, however, we are forry to fay, are unknown to us. During a confiderable part of the war, which commenced in 1756, we find him to have been unemployed, not improbably through the whole of it. We may, however, fairly prefume he was, notwithstanding this, a man much refpected and efteemed; for though fortune appears to have denied him any opportunity of handing his name down to pofterity with that celebrity which is the reward of gallantry, particularly if fuccefsful, he was not, as has been fometimes the cafe, fet afide and continued on the lift of captains, when, according to his feniority, he became entitled to the rank of a flag officer, but was then put on the fuperannuated lift of rear-admirals. This has ever been confidered as an honourable proof of meritorious fervice, though age, infirmities, or wounds received while in command, may poffibly render the brave, though unfortunate man, incapable of encountering the fatigues and difficulties neceffarily attendant on a more active ftation. He died about the year 1780.

LLOYD, John, — was, on May 30, 1745, appointed captain of the Glafgow, a new fhip of twenty-four guns, launched a fhort time before at Liverpool. He continued in this fhip during the whole remainder of the war, without being fortunate enough to meet with any opportunity of particularly diftinguifhing himfelf. Soon as the preliminary articles of peace were figned, he was ordered, in the month of May 1748, to North America with the intelligence, for the purpofe of preventing any farther hoftilities from being committed. He furvived his arrival a very fhort time, dying at South Carolina on the 14th of September, 1748.

MAISTERSON, Samuel,—was, on the 26th of Auguft, 1745, promoted to be captain of the Squirrel; from

---

* He was employed during the enfuing fummer in crnifing off the coaft of Scotland.

which

which he is said to have been removed, early in the following year, to the Duke William, an hired armed ship mounting fifty guns. No mention is made of his having held any subsequent commission, nor have we been able to collect any farther particulars concerning him, except that he died in England on the 10th of September, 1762.

MAN, Robert,—from being lieutenant of one of the ships employed under commodore Warren, on the expedition against Louisburg, was, on the 22d of June, promoted, by that gentleman, to be captain of the Launceston, of forty-four guns; and was not long afterwards sent to France, as convoy to a fleet of cartel ships dispatched thither with the prisoners taken in arms *, and the principal inhabitants who chose to remove thither. In 1746 he was appointed to the Lynn, and ordered to the Mediterranean, where we believe him to have continued till the cessation of hostilities took place. No farther mention is made of him till the year

---

* A particular account of the ill treatment he received from the enemy while employed on this service, is circumstantially related in the following terms by Mr. Gibson, in his appendix to a journal of the siege.

" July 4, 1745, Fourteen cartel ships, with the Launceston man of war, set sail from Louisbourg, in Cape Breton, for France, with the French inhabitants. No sooner were we arrived in the road of Rochfort, but commodore Mac Namara, in a ship of seventy-four guns, obliged us to come to under his stern. We obeyed and shewed our passports, which, when he had read, he insisted that every master should deliver into his hands his particular journal. Some looking on it as an unreasonable demand, with resolution opposed it, but were confined in irons in his ship for their refusal. Soon after, he sent for me: being admitted into the cabin, he ordered me to sit down at his green table, and give an account of my own proceedings in writing; which orders I readily complied with, and delivered into his hands. Upon the receipt of it he told me, that the cartels could expect no favour at Rochfort: and since, he was informed by several passengers, that I had been a very busy active fellow against the interest of his most christian majesty at Louisbourg, if he could find out any article whatever that was in the least contradictory to the declaration I had delivered he would send me to the tower. He immediately sent on board for my trunk, and insisted on my giving him the key. I did; and he took out all my papers, and read them over in the first place. After that, he broke open the letters directed for London: those, indeed, he sealed up again, and, having put them into the trunk, dismissed me. His next orders were, that the cartels should not go on board the
Launceston

year 1755, when he was appointed captain of the Anson, a ship of sixty-four guns, one of those put into commission at Portsmouth in consequence of the apprehended rupture with France. In this ship he sailed soon afterwards for North America, as one of the fleet sent thither under the orders of admiral Boscawen. No other notice is taken of him till the year 1758, when he commanded the Prince Frederic, a ship of the same rate and force as the former, being one of the fleet commanded by the same admiral (Mr. Boscawen) which proceeded against Louisburg, and proved succesful. He afterwards was promoted to the Cornwall, of seventy-four guns; in which we believe he continued during the remainder of the war; after which we are uncertain whether he held any commission while he continued a private captain. On the 18th of October, 1770, he was promoted to be rear-admiral of the blue; as he also was, in six days afterwards, to be rear-admiral of the red. He was immediately sent to command on the Antigua station, where he continued the time usually allotted for the duration of such appointments.

On the night of the 27th of December, 1771, a most dreadful fire broke out in the town of St. George, Antigua. It raged with such violence that, before daylight, the

---

Launceston on any pretence. He charged us likewise not to go on shore: and gave strict orders to the garrison to watch us night and day; and in case any of us attempted to set foot on shore, the guard were directed to shoot us. He would not permit a boat to bring us the least supply of any kind; insomuch that we were obliged to live wholly on salt provisions, and drink water that was ropy and very offensive to the smell, for above six weeks succeffively. When this cruel commodore set sail with his fleet, confisting of about two hundred sail of merchantmen, and seven men of war, for Hispaniola, another as cruel supplied his place. On Sunday eve he sent out a yawl with orders for all the cartels to unbend their fails. We did as directed; and on Monday morning his men came in their long boats and carried all our sails on shore, into the garrison, which surprized us to the last degree, as we had been detained so long and lived in expectation of our passports every day. At this unhappy juncture captain Robert Man, who was commander of the Launceston, was taken violently ill of a fever; and, notwithstanding intercession was made that he might be removed on shore, as the noise on board affected his head too much: yet the favour was inhumanly denied him, and to every officer in the ship besides."

whole town was reduced to aſhes, except a few buildings in the carenage, near the court and cuſtom-houſe, which were fortunately preſerved merely by the great exertions of the officers and men, ſent from the ſhip under Mr. Man's command. This dreadful conflagration took place notwithſtanding every poſſible effort was made by the rear-admiral to put a ſtop to it. Every humane attention was paid by him to the diſtreſſes of the unfortunate ſufferers, whoſe wants he endeavoured to alleviate and provide for by every poſſible means in his power. Nevertheleſs there were ſome perſons unjuſt enough to prefer a formal complaint againſt him to the admiralty-board charging him with miſconduct, and in particular with having ſhewn great inattention to the diſtreſſes of the people. His defence, however, inſtantly quieted ſuch ſhallow ill-founded murmurs, it appearing there was not the ſmalleſt ſhadow of reaſon that could in any degree give colour to ſuch a report.

On the 31ſt of March, 1775, Mr. Man was advanced to be vice-admiral of the blue; as he was, on the 3d of February, 1776, to be vice-admiral of the white. Some time previous to this, however, he was appointed to command on the Mediterranean ſtation, on which occaſion he had his flag on board the Medway, of ſixty guns. Though the force under his command was, as is cuſtomary, in time of peace, very inſignificant, he had addreſs enough to render himſelf highly reſpected, as well by the Spaniards, as by the different Barbary ſtates, notwithſtanding two or three trivial diſputes occurred, which required no inconſiderable ſhare of firmneſs and management ſo as to enable him to maintain his own proper conſequence. He returned to England in the beginning of the year 1778, and did not afterwards accept of any command*, ſo that we have nothing farther to relate with regard to him, except his promotions, which were on the 19th of March, 1779, to be vice-admiral of the red; and, on the 26th of September, 1780, to be admiral of the blue. He died in the year 1783, revered and loved both as a gentleman and a commander.

---

* In the month of April, 1779, he was nominated one of the commiſſioners for executing the office of lord high admiral, but quitted the board in the beginning of the month of September 1780.

MONTAGUE,

MONTAGUE, The Honourable William,—was the second and youngest son of Edward Richard, viscount Hinchinbroke*, and his lady, Elizabeth Popham, only daughter to Alexander Popham, of Littlecote, in the county of Wilts, esq. Having betaken himself to the sea-service, he was appointed a lieutenant in the navy, we believe under captain Robert Long†. This gentleman entertained an high opinion for him; but observing in him a too gallant spirit, which at times rose to an appearance rather romantic for a moderate and prudent man to display, distinguished him, on all occasions, by the familiar appellation of his Dragon. He was promoted by commodore Warren, at that time commander-in-chief of the expedition against Louisburg, to be captain of the Mermaid, his commission to that ship bearing date May the 23d, 1745‡. He was the person afterwards chosen to be the herald of the success to England, where he arrived, after an expeditious passage, on the 29th of July, and was immediately appointed to the Prince Edward; as he was, in the month of July, 1746, to the Bristol. Hitherto he does not appear to have had any opportunity of manifesting that natural intrepidity all who knew him admit him to have possessed: but in the following year, he then commanding the Bristol, as indeed he continued to do during the remainder of the war, was present with Mr. Anson at the defeat and capture of De la Jonquiere's squadron, and contributed all that was possible for him towards the glorious success then obtained. He afterwards, on the 27th of February, 1747, had the good fortune to capture a very valuable French register ship, called the Union, bound from the Havannah to Cadiz, having on board 360,000 dollars, besides a valuable cargo of cochineal, cocoa, and other commodities. In 1748 the Bristol was taken into dock to be refitted, and when completed captain Monta-

---

* Eldest son to Edward, third earl of Sandwich.
† See Biog. Nav. vol. iv. p. 182.
‡ In the month of November following he was returned to parliament as one of the representatives for the county of Huntingdon, in the room of W. Mitchell, esq. deceased; and at the ensuing election was chosen for the borough of Bossiney, in Cornwall.

gue was re-appointed to her*. He remained however in that ſhip a very ſhort time, and was ſucceeded by captain John Montague. Some indeed doubt whether he ever was reappointed, and infiſt it is a miſtake, ariſing merely from the ſimilitude of names. About the year 1755 he commanded the Cumberland, a third rate, at firſt employed as a guard-ſhip at Chatham.

No public mention, after the time laſt ſtated, is made of him in the ſervice, from which he was ſnatched at a very early period of his life, on the 10th † of February, 1757. He married Charlotte, daughter of Francis Nailour, of Offord Darcy, in the county of Huntingdon, eſq. but died without iſſue. The whimſical eccentricities which pervaded the general conduct of this gentleman, procured him, both in and out of the ſervice, the familiar appellation of Mad Montague, an addition more frequently uſed than it otherwiſe, perhaps, would have been, in order to diſtinguiſh him from capt. J. Montague, of whom we have hereafter to give ſome account. Some of theſe anecdotes

---

* When in the Weſt Indies, in the early part of his life, an affair, very diſagreeable to captain Montague, unfortunately occurred;—a boat paſſing his ſhip in the night, was fired at, by his order, to compel it to bring to, ſome ſuſpicion being entertained that there were French people on board. Through inattention or careleſſneſs, one of the ſhot ſo fired, wounded a negro in the leg ſo terribly that he died the next morning. Mr. Knowles thought proper to ſuſpend him from his command on this account; and, as it is ſaid, not only refuſed to allow him a court-martial, but alſo the privilege, which the captain earneſtly requeſted, of being tried by the laws of the iſland of Antigua, where the unfortunate accident happened.

This unjuſt treatment afterwards underwent a legal inveſtigation; and Mr. Montague, with that honourable and generous eccentricity which ſo ſtrongly marked his character, was contented with vindicating his own honour, and proving, to the ſatisfaction of the court, the ill uſage he had experienced; for though it was ſuppoſed very conſiderable damages would have been recovered againſt the admiral, the trial was prevented from regularly proceeding to an end, the counſel for Mr. Montague being inſtructed by him, to declare, he would be ſatisfied with a verdict of ten guineas, and the coſts of ſuit. The ſum recovered we believe to have been afterwards diſtributed among the priſoners in the marſhalſea.

Mr. Montague's ſuit was long in agitation, and not finally ſettled till the month of June 1752.

† Some accounts ſay the 5th; Mr. Hardy the 11th

are almoſt too extravagant for belief; but we ſhall venture to relate two or three, which we have received as authentic from perſons of too much veracity to have them queſtioned for a moment. — In coming up the Channel during the time he commanded the Briſtol, he fell in with a very numerous fleet of outward-bound Dutch merchant-men. He fired at ſeveral in order to compel them to bring to, a meaſure authoriſed by cuſtom and his general inſtructions. The Dutch, aided by a fair wind, hoped by its aſſiſtance to eſcape the diſagreeable delay of being ſearched or overhauled, and held on their way: captain Montague purſued, but, on overtaking them, took no other ſatisfaction than that of manning and ſending out his two cutters, with a carpenter's mate in each, ordering them to cut off twelve of the uglieſt heads they could find in the whole fleet, from among thoſe with which, as it is well known, thoſe people are accuſtomed to ornament the extremity of their rudders. When theſe were brought on board he cauſed them to be diſpoſed on brackets round his cabin, contraſting them in the moſt ludicrous manner his vein of humour could invent, and writing under them the names of the twelve Cæſars.

Another anecdote is, that being once at Liſbon, and having got into a night affray with the people on ſhore, he received in the ſcuffle what is uſually termed a black eye. On the ſucceeding day, previous to his going on ſhore, he compelled each of his boats crew to black with cork one of their eyes, ſo as to reſemble a natural injury; the ſtarboard rowers the right eye, the larboard rowers the left, and the cockſwain both: the whimſical effect may be eaſily conceived.

When under the orders of ſir Edward Hawke, in 1755, he ſolicited permiſſion to repair to town. The admiral, aware of the impropriety of ſuch a requeſt, and at the ſame time wiſhing to palliate refuſal by impoſing, on his permiſſion, a condition he conceived impoſſible to be undertaken, even by a man of Mr. Montague's harmleſs, tho' extravagant turn of mind, jeſtingly ſaid, "The complexion of affairs was ſo ſerious that he could not grant him leave to go farther from his ſhip than where his barge could carry him." Mr. Montague, not to be foiled or abaſhed, is ſaid to have immediately repaired to Portſmouth, where he gave

orders

orders for the conſtruction of a carriage on trucks, to be drawn with horſes, on which he meant to row his barge; and having previouſly ſtored it with proviſions and neceſſaries requiſite for three days, to proceed to London. Having laſhed it to the carriage, the crew was inſtructed to imitate the action of rowing with the ſame ſolemnity as if they had been actually coming into the harbour from Spithead. Sir Edward, as it is ſaid, received intelligence of his intention ſoon after the boat and its contents were landed, and immediately ſent him his permiſſion to proceed to London in whatever manner he thought proper.

A variety of anecdotes equally ludicrous might be adduced, but the foregoing ſpecimen may, not improbably, be deemed ſufficient.

NOEL, Thomas,—is no way mentioned till his promotion, on the 12th of November, 1745, to be captain of the Greyhound frigate. In this ſhip he was in the enſuing year employed as a cruiſer off the coaſt of Scotland, an occupation in which he ſignaliſed himſelf as deſcribed beneath *. In 1748 he commanded the Severn, of fifty guns. No farther mention is made of him till we find him, in 1756, captain of the Princeſs Louiſa, of ſixty guns, one of the ſhips compoſing the ſquadron ordered to

---

* " Greyhound, in Alrofs Bay, May the 4th, 1746.

" Upon my arrival here from Ireland, I was informed of lord Loudoun's being at Sky, whither I went to offer him my aſſiſtance. I attempted getting to the northward, but wind and weather would not permit. Upon the 1ſt inſtant I had an account of two large ſhips being at Loch Nova. The next morning at daylight I weighed, in company with the Baltimore, and kept plying, the wind being contrary. In the evening the Terror joined me. Next morning at daybreak we ſtood in for the Loch, and a little after four I croſſed pretty cloſe to the commodore, gave him a broadſide, and then ſtood on to the other. The ſloops followed my example, and we were engaged till nine o'clock, when our maſts and rigging were ſo ſhattered that the ſloops were not capable of keeping under ſail, which was the only means by which we could propoſe to annoy them by, as we were inferior to them in ſtrength. One of the French ſhips carried thirty four guns, twenty-four of which were nine-pounders. The other carried thirty-two, twenty-two of which were nine-pounders. Wherefore, after lying at anchor ſome time, and having repaired our damages as well as we could, we made ſail and left them, and are now refitting. I have ſent to the Furnace and Raven to join me as ſoon as poſſible, and hope we ſhall ſtill have it in our power to give a better account of them."

the Mediterranean under the unfortunate Mr. Byng. In this ſhip he unhappily loſt his life, being deſperately wounded in the encounter with monſ. De Galliſoniere on the 19th of May. He died on the 5th of June following.

NUCELLA, Timothy,— was lieutenant of the Port Mahon in 1740, and of the Marlborough at the time of Mr. Mathews's encounter with the French and Spaniſh fleets off Toulon; he was conſequently one of the perſons ordered home as a witneſs on the trials which took place in conſequence of that event. Previous, however, to this, he was made commander of the Wolf ſloop; and on the 12th of April, 1745, promoted to be captain of the Chicheſter. He afterwards, in 1746, was appointed to the York, a fourth rate of ſixty guns, one of the ſquadron employed in the Eaſt Indies under Mr. Griffin; and on the trial of that gentleman gave teſtimony rather unfavourable to him, declaring in preciſe terms, "that if the ſquadron had been under his command he ſhould certainly have put to ſea and endeavoured to engage the enemy." In the month of July 1752, he was appointed captain of the Hind; and after having ſerved ſométime in Europe in that ſtation, was, at the end of the year 1755, ordered to the coaſt of Guinea, where he died on the 4th of April, 1756.

NUTT, Juſtinian, — ſerved as maſter of the Centurion, under Mr. Anſon, during the early part of his voyage round the world. In the courſe of it he was advanced to the rank of lieutenant, and was promoted, in the month of March 1745, to be commander of the Taviſtock ſloop. He was removed from this veſſel, on the 12th of Auguſt following, to be captain of a ſmall frigate, called the Grand Turk, a French prize purchaſed into the ſervice. In the beginning of the year 1748 he commanded a ſhip of fifty guns, ſaid to have been, as the ſloop juſt mentioned, called the Taviſtock. This was one of the ſquadron ſent into the bay under the orders of rear admiral Hawke: but no other particular mention is made of him during the current year. At the very commencement of the enſuing he was commiſſioned to the Anſon, a guard-ſhip, of ſixty-four guns, ſtationed at Portſmouth; where, in the month of June following, he was one of the members compoſing the court-martial held on captain Obrien Dudley, captain

of

of the Chesterfield, and on those subsequently held on Couchman the lieutenant, and others, who had piratically taken possession of that ship when the captain was on shore.

No farther mention is made of him as an officer in active service. In the month of August 1749 he married Miss Cook, a young lady of Winchester, with whom he is said to have acquired a fortune of 10,000l. In the year 1754 he quitted the service altogether on being appointed one of the captains of Greenwich-hospital. This honourable retirement he did not long live to enjoy, dying on the 11th of December, 1758.

OBRIEN, Lucius,—was the son of captain Christopher Obrien, of whom some account has been already given, vol. iv. p. 48. Having, after the example of his father, betaken himself to a maritime life, he was, about the month of September 1740, promoted to be commander of a sloop of war: he was, however, only commander acting by order, for almost immediately afterwards he returned to the rank of lieutenant, and served on board the Shrewsbury during the expedition against Carthagena in 1741. He signalised himself very much in the assault of the Boca Chica castle; and afterwards in the attack of the Spanish admiral's ship, the Gallicia, he being, as is confidently reported, the first person who boarded her. After this we find him, in 1744, commander of the Portsmouth storeship. He was from this vessel promoted, on the 3d of December, 1745, to be captain of the Sheerness frigate; in which vessel he was immediately afterwards ordered to the coast of Scotland. In the beginning of the month of April following he had the happiness of effecting a very signal piece of service by the re-capture of the Hazard sloop of war, which had been made prize of by the rebels, and was then called the Prince Charles. This vessel, after repairing to France, was on its return from thence with a sum of money for the payment of the rebel forces and a considerable number of veteran officers from the French service to head and direct them, both which the pretender's party stood much in need of.

Captain Obrien, after a long chace of nearly sixty leagues, drove this vessel on shore upon a loyal part of the coast, where the officers and crew landing with the treasure in hopes of forming a junction with their friends, were all of them captured, together with the wealth, the very sinews of war, which they wished to protect. Nor was this the whole of Mr. Obrien's success, for a few days before, he had taken possession of a ship from Boston, in New England, which having some arms and ammunition on board, was, by the captain, treacherously put into possession of the rebel adherents in that part of the country. No farther mention is made of this gentleman during the continuance of the war, nor have we been able to discover the services on which he was employed, or the names of the ships he commanded, except that, in 1746, he was appointed to the Colchester. We remain in the same state of ignorance concerning him during the whole of the peace which ensued, nor have we any just reason to suppose that, in that period, he held any command. At the recommencement of the war with France, in 1756, he was again appointed to the Colchester, of fifty guns, in which ship, having the Lyme, a twenty-gun ship, commanded by captain Edward Vernon in company, he fell in with, on the 17th of May, two French ships of war, one called the Aquilon, of fifty-eight guns, commanded by monsieur De Maurville; and the Fidelle, of thirty-two guns, by monsieur De Litarduis. Notwithstanding the superiority of the French, the English captains did not decline the contest; a long and spirited encounter took place, which, though highly honourable to the latter, did not end so successfully as their gallantry merited, owing to the disabled state of their masts and rigging at the conclusion of the action*, a circumstance by no means uncommon in encounters of this nature.

Notwith-

---

* No particular account of this transaction ever having been officially published, we have thought fit to add the following letter, written on board the Colchester soon after the action, inasmuch as, though it has been already printed, few persons probably may have seen it, and it contains a complete refutation of many infamous aspersions attempted to be raised against the character of Mr. Obrien.

" Colchester, at sea, June 20, 1756.

" The Lyme, captain Vernon; and the Colchester, captain Obrien, were ordered, by admiral Boscawen, from the fleet, to cruize together on the coast of Brittany, and scarce a day past but we either burnt or sunk some French vessel. On the 17th of May, in the morning, we took a French snow laden with deals and resin. An officer was sent on board

to

Notwithstanding the affair just mentioned was highly honourable to the commanders concerned, there were not wanting

to burn her: while he was doing it, the man at the mast-head called down, that he saw a sail in the offing; upon which captain Obrien hailed captain Vernon and desired him to make sail, and that he would follow, which he did with all the sail he could make. So soon as the officer was returned from burning the vessel, and our boat hoisted in, a second sail was espied by the man at the mast-head, and at half past eleven A.M. we discovered they were enemies, as they also did at the same time with respect to us, making all the sail they possibly could set to get from us, with top-gallant royals, lower, top-mast, and top gallant steering sails, keeping all full. Seeing they could not weather us on the other tack, sometimes they bore away two or three points, then hauled their wind; but finding we gained on them fast, and that it was impossible to escape us, they shortened sail by degrees, till they were under their three topsails, when they hoisted their colours and kept close together. We did the same; and as we neared them saw plainly the name of each ship wrote on their stern; the first called La Fidelle, of thirty-two guns; the other L'Aquillon, of fifty-eight, which we counted very distinctly: the latter having eleven guns below on a side, twelve on her upper deck, four on her quarter deck, and two on her forecastle, with a great number of men at small arms in her tops, poop, quarter-deck, and forecastle. We had a clear ship fore and aft, and every thing ready for action, with colours flying, our people in great spirits gave three cheers, as did the Lyme's people also. The French indeed answered us, but it was very faintly. Our captain's intention was to have gone between the two enemy's ships, and to have given them each a broadside: but they kept too close for us to put that scheme in execution; we therefore took the first of the Fidelle, reserving ours for the Aquillon, which was the headmost ship: and at half an hour past five in the evening, being close upon her weather quarter, she gave us her whole broadside below and aloft, as did the Fidelle also at the same time. We immediately returned it with our whole fire at the Aquillon, as did the Lyme at the other. The third broadside we received, most unluckily cut our tiller rope, great part of the steering wheel and lead trumpet, so that our ship directly came round too: upon which the Aquillon put her helm hard a weather, and raked us fore and aft.

Perceiving something extraordinary had happened on board us they let down their fore-sail and bore away, with design, as we supposed, to assist their comrade, then warmly engaged with the Lyme at some distance: but we soon got tackles upon our tiller below, shivered our after sails, put our helm aport, and following her, got between the two enemy's ships, and on the Aquillon's lee bow. Steering from bow to bow, we gave her five smart broadsides, most of which raked her fore and aft, and so near as to be almost on board each other; our yard arms very near touching hers. We then exchanged hand granadoes for some time from our tops; and one of hers falling on our forecastle blew up a great number of musket cartridges, but happily did no great mischief

wanting thofe who infidioufly and wickedly endeavoured to traduce their conduct, more particularly that of Mr. Obrien.

mifchief. When we raked her fhe was filent, and for fome time did not fire a gun; her enfign being foul, our people gave three cheers thinking fhe had ftruck; upon which the Aquillon put her helm alee, hawled up her forefail (for we were then going large) and began to fire again. At this time our braces, bowlings, &c. being moft of them fhot away, we got down our fleering fail tacks for braces, and hawled upon a wind; but fhe got upon the weather gage of us, which we could never after recover. We now reeved a new tiller rope, but it proved too fhort, fo that we were obliged to reeve the mizen-fheet for a tiller rope, and put a luff tackle in lieu; we continued engaging about point blank mufket fhot (the Lyme and Fidelle alfo ftill engaged, but at a confiderable diftance from us). The great quantity of bar fhot, pieces of old iron bars, &c. which the French fired in upon us, tore our fails and rigging all to fhatters, our mizzen top-fail was down, the fheets, floppers and flings entirely fhot away, and the mizzen all in rags. In fhort, every thing was fo torn and cut to pieces, that we had not the fhip under the leaft command; luckily for us, it was fine weather and fmooth water, or we muft have loft all our mafts, they being very much wounded, and fcarce a whole fhroud left to fecure them. We faw, before dark, two of the Aquillon's ports beat into one, and about ten o'clock feveral great explofions on board her. We were fo near that the wads from each fhip fell on the deck on fire; and one from her guns came into an upper deck port of ours, beat a cartridge of powder out of the man's hand that was going to put it into the gun; it fet fire to fome others, and blew up all the people near that gun in a terrible manner. Other wads fet fire to our hammocks on the poop, but it was happily foon extinguifhed. Thus we continued to engage till half paft twelve at night, when the Aquillon hawled on board her fore tack, fet all the fail fhe could, kept clofe upon a wind, and left us in fuch a fituation that it was impoffible for us to follow her. The Lyme and Fidelle had left off engaging about an hour and half before us. Befides the fhattered condition of our fails, mafts and rigging, we received feveral fhot between wind and water; and were obliged to turn our people from the guns to pump fhip, for we made four feet water an hour, and heeled fhip to ftop our leaks with plugs and tallow. All the remaining part of the night and next day we were employed in knotting, fplicing, and reeving new rigging, and bending other fails. Our officers and men behaved well and in high fpirits during the whole engagement; but our guns were very weakly manned, our people being obliged to help each other to run them out when loaded, and were all very much fatigued, having been up thirty-five hours. We had no more than four men killed on the fpot, and thirty-five wounded, feveral of whom are fince dead of their wounds, and others not expected to recover. The Aquillon (by the account we have of a Danifh fhip from France) had upwards of fixty killed and a great number wounded, and went into Rochfort with great difficulty,

being

Obrien. They strove to inculcate an opinion that, terrified by the superiority of the enemy, he strove to avoid the contest, which, had it been vigorously and ably conducted, would undoubtedly have ended in the capture of both the enemy's ships. Nothing can be farther from the truth; he is known to have expressed, from the first moment of discovering the supposed superiority of the antagonists, the highest satisfaction at the prospect of gaining honour from that circumstance; and was so bent on having the action continued even to the last extremity, that he told the first lieutenant, " You, sir, as next to me in command, must take charge of the ship in case I should be killed in the action, or so wounded as to be obliged to quit the deck. My positive orders are, that you never suffer the colours to be struck, while there remains a possibility of keeping the ship above water." In 1757 he accompanied commodore Stevens, in his way to India, as far as St. Helena; from whence he returned back to England, we believe with a convoy.

This gentleman was afterwards promoted to the Essex, of sixty-four guns; in which ship we find him, in 1759, serving in the main or Channel fleet under the orders of sir Edw. Hawke. After having borne a share in the memorable defeat of the marquis de Conflans, in the month of November, being on the following day ordered, by signal from the admiral, to pursue the Soliel Royal, which,

---

being much shattered in her hull. The disproportion of the killed and wounded between us and the French may be easily accounted for, by considering, that it is their continual practice to fire at our masts and rigging, in order to disable our ships that way, and that they have generally almost double the number of men. In this action we fired upwards of forty broadsides, all well expended: not a single gun fired, but so near as to do execution on the enemy wherever it took place, and every thing conducted with as little noise and confusion as possible during the whole engagement, which was full six hours and half. After this it might be expected we should immediately have steered for some port, (as we find the Lyme did) but our captain judged it more the duty of an officer to do his utmost to rejoin his admiral, which we did, and had the carpenters from every ship in the fleet to fix our masts, yards, &c. and repair our hull; when we have received a fresh supply of stores and ammunition, I do suppose we shall make our the time first intended for our cruize."

under

under cover of the night, had anchored in the midst of the British fleet, in attempting to execute these orders the Essex unfortunately ran on a shoal, called the Four, where, notwithstanding every possible assistance was given, she was totally lost; a part of the stores, and the whole of the crew were, however, taken on board different ships of the squadron, except one boat, with a lieutenant and as many of the crew as it could contain, which was driven on the French coast, where they were made prisoners.

Captain Obrien was early in the ensuing year appointed to the Temple, of seventy guns. He was ordered almost immediately to the West Indies, where, in the month of August, having the Griffin, of twenty-eight guns, under his orders, he distinguished himself very particularly in the attack and capture of a considerable number of French privateers, which he cut out from under the guns of Martinico. The following are the leading circumstances of the event: having received information that the Virgin, formerly a British sloop of war, and three privateers carrying twelve guns and upwards of one hundred and fifty men each, were in Petit Havre bay, he proceeded thither, in company with the Griffin, of twenty-eight guns, captain Taylor, and after a brisk attack, which continued several hours, succeeded in cutting them out, notwithstanding they were protected by three forts, one mounting eight twenty-four and thirty-two pounders; a second having six twelve and eighteen pounders; and a third, which flanked the entrance of the bay, with two batteries mounting two guns each. The forts themselves were totally demolished, their defences being beaten down into the sea. Not content with this success, they afterwards attacked another fort on the same island, mounting six twenty-four pounders, without much difficulty they completely destroyed it, and carried off three more stout ships which depended on it for protection. To crown the whole, on their return they fell in with a fleet of thirteen victuallers, which they captured and carried into Antigua with them, having had only two men killed and eight wounded during this very successful though short expedition.

Wishing to return to Europe towards the conclusion of the war, he removed into the Woolwich, of forty-four guns; and arrived at Spithead in the month of September 1762,

1762, with commodore fir James Douglas and a convoy*.
He does not appear to have held any farther command
till the year 1768, when he was commiffioned to the
Solebay, a cruifing frigate of twenty-eight guns. Previous,
however, to this he had, in 1766, a penfion of 150l. a
year fettled on him, in addition to his half-pay, he having
loft the ufe of his right arm. On the 18th of October,
1770, he was advanced to be rear-admiral of the white;
but did not long furvive his promotion, dying on the 17th
of December following, though Mr. Hardy afferts on
the 13th of July in the enfuing year.

ORME, Richard.—We know nothing of this gentleman previous to his advancement, on the 20th of Auguft, 1745, to be captain of the Royal Sovereign, at that time the Guardfhip at the Nore. In the month enfuing we find him to have been one of the members of the courtmartial held on board the London, at Chatham, for the trial of the captains charged with mifbehaviour in the battle fought off Toulon; as he alfo was, in 1746, of that held for the trials of the admirals. No farther mention being made of him, we are unacquainted not only with the fubfequent fervices on which he was employed, but even of the fhips he commanded. We only know him not to have been in commiffion at the latter end of the war, and to have died on the 23d of Auguft, 1764.

RICH, Edward.—We find this gentleman, in the latter part of the year 1743, commander of the Baltimore floop of war. He was ordered out in the month of December on a cruife off Oporto; and when on his paffage to the appointed ftation, fell in with and captured a Spanifh privateer, mounting fix carriage and fourteen fwivel guns.

---

* To the fafety and prefervation of which he paid particular attention, an attention, it fhould feem, ill requited, as appears by the following letter to the fecretary to the admiralty.

" I am forry I have occafion to fay it, but fince I have been in the fervice, and this is the thirteenth convoy I have been with this war, I never faw mafters of merchant-fhips behave fo ill, and with fuch difregard to fignals and his majefty's colours; fo that, with the affiftance of the Crefcent and Falkland, we could not keep them in order; nor did they ever obey a fignal that was not repeated more than once. The gunner's expence will fhow how great has been the confumption of powder."

He remained on the fame ftation feveral months, and in the month of July diftinguifhed himfelf highly in an encounter with a French privateer of equal force*. He was foon after his return to England, that is to fay, on the 28th of January, 1745, promoted from the Baltimore to be captain of the Bridgewater, of twenty guns. We have no farther intelligence concerning this gentleman, except what we derive from a memorandum affixed to his name in Mr. Hardy's lift of naval captains. By that we are informed that he quitted the Bridgewater in a manner by no means correct, or, as Mr. Hardy expreffes himfelf, ran away from that fhip; but afterwards was appointed captain of the Milford. He died in England on the 26th of July, 1753.

ROSEWELL, Henry,—was, on the 21ft of July, 1745, promoted to be captain of the Lively. This gentleman is in the fame predicament with many others already mentioned, in refpect to our total want of information relative to him. We know him only to have been employed during a confiderable part of the fucceeding war, and not to have attained to the rank of a flag-officer even on the fuperannuated lift. He died on the 9th of May, 1771, ftill continuing on the lift of captains, though fenior to many who had been advanced to the rank of admirals.

ROUS, John. — This gentleman was by birth an American; and having rifen to the rank of lieutenant in the navy, quitted for a time his majefty's fervice and took the command of a private fhip of war fitted out from New England. We have not been able to collect any

---

* Of which the following particulars are given officially.

" Being on a cruife off Oporto on the 8th of July, he was chafed by a fnow, but coming almoft within gun-fhot, and perceiving the Baltimore not to be a merchant-fhip, fhe hawled her wind. Capt. Rich however outfailed her fo much, that in an hour he came within piftol-fhot of her and fired a fhot to bring her to, which fhe anfwered with a broadfide. Captain Rich then ran alongfide of her, and after an engagement of two hours, yard-arm and yard-arm, fhe ftruck her colours. She proved a French fnow privateer of ten carriage guns, four-pounders, and ninety-fix men. She is called the Nymph, fitted out from Bourdeaux, Abraham Vernueil commander. The Baltimore had one man killed and one wounded, and the prize had fifteen killed and wounded."

subsequent information concerning him, except that having distinguished himself in this occupation so highly, as to attract the notice of sir Peter Warren, who, in 1745, was commodore of the armament sent against Louisburg; he was by him promoted to be a commander in the navy, and, on the 24th of September, 1745, advanced to be captain of the Shirley galley. This vessel was the same he had before commanded as a privateer; it was afterwards hired into the service as an armed ship on the sloop establishment; and, lastly, put on the higher footing of a post-ship, or frigate.

Immediately after peace had taken place we find a gentleman of the same name appointed captain of the Albany sloop. It is by no means improbable he was the same person, for many instances occur of a post captain having, in time of peace, accepted of such inferior commissions. In 1755, on the prospect of a rupture with France, and being then captain of the Success, a ship of twenty-two guns, he was ordered to North America, and distinguished himself very highly in the naval department of an expedition, made against the French settlement of Beausejour, under the command of colonel Monkton.

In the month of July he was equally fortunate in a second enterprize, conducted by himself only, against the French settlements on St. John's river*. We believe him to have continued on the American station a considerable time, as we find him, in 1757, employed in the

---

* Extract of a letter from Halifax, in Nova Scotia, dated July the 18th, 1755.

"The French have abandoned their fort at St. John's River, and as far as in their power demolished it. As soon as the forts upon the Isthmus were taken, captain Rous sailed from thence, with three twenty-gun ships and a sloop to look into St. John's River, where it was reported there were two French ships of thirty-six guns each. He anchored off the mouth of the river and sent his boats to reconnoitre: they found no ships there; but on their appearance the French burst their cannon, blew up their magazine, burned every thing they could belonging to the fort, and marched off. The next morning the Indians invited captain Rous on shore, gave him the strongest assurances of their desire to make peace with the English; and pleaded, in their behalf, that they had refused to assist the French upon this occasion, though earnestly pressed by them. Some of their chiefs are expected at Halifax in a few days."

fame ſhip under Mr. Holburne; who, immediately after his arrival on that ſtation, ſent him out for the purpoſe of collecting intelligence * relative to the ſituation and force of the French fleet at Louiſburg. Immediately after his return into port he removed into the Winchelſea, of twenty-four guns. He returned to England at the concluſion of the year, and was promoted to the Sutherland, of fifty guns, one of that more ſucceſsful armament ſent in the year following, againſt Louiſburg, under the ſame commander; and is mentioned as having been ordered out from Halifax, previous to the ſailing of the fleet, with inſtructions to reconnoitre Louiſburg harbour. He behaved on this as well as all former occaſions with the higheſt credit to himſelf, ſo that, although the ſervices on which he was employed were far from the moſt enviable, no man acquired a fairer reputation both for gallantry and general conduct. No particular mention is made as to the manner in which he was employed during the year 1759; nor, indeed, have we been able to collect any other intelligence concerning him, except that he died at Portſmouth on the 3d of April, 1760, having continued captain of the Sutherland till that time.

SPRY, Sir Richard,— was, in the year 1744, commander of the Comet bomb-ketch. He was advanced from that veſſel, on the 23d of September, 1745, to be captain of the Cheſter, of fifty guns. He continued in the ſame command till the year 1750, or, perhaps, a ſtill later period; and, in 1747, was ordered to the Eaſt Indies with Mr. Boſcawen, who then proceeded on the expedition againſt Pondicherry.

---

* Of which circumſtance we have the following particulars in an account publiſhed of the expedition.

"On the 15th of July the following ſhips were ſent out; the Succeſs, of twenty-two guns, captain Rous; the Elphingham, of twenty; and the Speedwell, of twelve, with one of the beſt ſailing tranſports. It is ſaid their orders were to ſend the tranſport veſſel as near the mouth of the harbour as poſſible, who might feign herſelf to be a prize and decoy a pilot, with whom ſhe ſhould immediately return to the general and admiral; or, if ſhe ſhould be diſcovered and chaced, the ſhips of war in the offing might get between the enemy and the land, and probably make a prize in order to obtain intelligence."

Sometime after his return to England, that is to say, in the year 1754, he was appointed to the Gibraltar, of twenty guns. Before the conclusion of the year he sailed for America, with commodore Keppel; and was sent home, in the month of March following, with intelligence of the safe arrival of the convoy, and the general state of affairs in that country. He was immediately promoted to the Fougeux, of sixty-four guns, and ordered again for America with the squadron commanded by Mr. Boscawen. He remained there during the winter, being left commanding officer of a small squadron at Halifax, stationed there for the purpose of watching Louisburg, and the movements of the French in that quarter. By a prudent disposition of his force, that port was much streightened, and a number of important prizes were taken, in particular three valuable transports, with stores, provisions and ammunition, and the Arc-en-ciel, a ship of fifty guns,

He was afterwards appointed to the Orford, and in 1757 served on the same station under Mr. Holburne; as he also did in the following year with Mr. Boscawen, who was more successful than his predecessors had been, having effected the complete reduction of the important fortress of Louisburg. He continued in the Orford during the remainder of the war, but was, unhappily for him, employed on services and stations so unconsequential, that very little material mention is made of him. In 1760 he commanded one of the small squadrons stationed in rotation, off the coast of France, to watch the motions of those ships which had escaped at the defeat of Conflans.

His conduct and activity on this occasion was highly noticed; and on the 16th of March, 1761, he was in consequence introduced, at St. James's, to his majesty, by whom he was most graciously received. His occupation during the years 1761 and 2 was exactly similar; it was marked also by the same attention to his duty, and distinguished by the same honourable applause from his sovereign and his countrymen. After the conclusion of the war, in 1763, he was made captain of the Fubbs yacht. In the month of June 1766, he was appointed commodore and commander-in-chief of the small squadron stationed in the Mediterranean, having his broad pendant on board the
Jersey.

Jerfey. He continued on that ftation employed in the fame uninterefting manner as fquadrons in that quarter generally are, till the end of the year 1769; when, having held it for the term ufually allotted, he returned to England, and arrived at Portfmouth on the 8th of November, having a confiderable quantity of fpecie on board, as remittances from the merchants in that quarter.

On the 18th of October, 1770, he was advanced to be rear-admiral of the blue; and, on the 24th of the fame month, to be rear of the white. In 1772 he was appointed to command a fmall fquadron, confifting of feven fhips of the line and two frigates*, ordered to be equipped for fervice in confequence of the encreafed armaments on the parts of France and Spain, but which, as it may be well remembered, produced no confequences in the fmalleft degree ferious. In the enfuing year he held a command in the fleet affembled at Portfmouth, and reviewed there by his majefty in the month of June. On this occafion he, on the 24th of that month, received the honour of knighthood; and afterwards, though in common with the reft of the flag officers and captains employed on that occafion, received his majefty's moft gracious thanks for his affiduity and attention. On the 31ft of March, 1775, he was advanced to be rear-admiral of the red. This promotion he unhappily did not long furvive, dying at his feat, in Cornwall, on the 1ft of December following.

This gentleman poffeffed, in a very remarkable degree, a fingular, though, on fome occafions, rather difagreeable turn of humour, he was extremely fond of perfuading thofe, who were credulous enough to confide in him, to the belief of ftories fo romantic as to excite univerfal laughter at the recital of them; and to encreafe the ridicule againft thofe whom he fo ftrangely impofed upon, he always, when called upon to juftify his account, was accuftomed to deny, not only that he never had related

---

* The fquadron under his immediate command confifted of the Ocean, Terrible, Royal Oak, Centaur, Albion, Raifonable, Worcefter, Thames and Cerberus.

" fuch circumftances, but that he had never even heard of them; and that the perfon who quoted him muft be miftaken. The ridiculous temporary effect produced by this conduct, which certainly was never intended as any other than an innocent jeft, though probably of rather too ferious a kind, can better be conceived than defcribed.

STANHOPE, Sir Thomas —was a defcendant from the very ancient and noble family of Stanhope, of which we have already had occafion to make fome mention †. He was, on the 12th of July, 1745, promoted to be captain of the Bridgewater; fome accounts ftate, though we believe erroneoufly, the Sheernefs; and others, among which is that of Mr. Hardy, equally deficient in correct ftatement, affert the Hector. No other mention is made of him during the continuance of the war, except that, about the month of February, 1748, he was appointed to the Fougeux, of fixty-four guns, a fhip taken, in the month of October preceding, by the fquadron under rear-admiral Hawke. This veffel was retained in commiffion as a guardfhip after the conclufion of the war: and, in 1749, we find him one of the members compofing the court-martial held at Portfmouth, on board the Invincible, for the trial of capt. Obrien Dudley, lieut. Couchman, and others. Captain Stanhope continued in the Fougeux during the ufually allotted period of three years; and, after he had for fome time quitted that command, was appointed to the Edinburgh, of feventy guns, one of the fhips put into commiffion at Plymouth, in February, 1755, in confequence of an apprehended rupture with France.

He afterwards accompanied Mr. Holburne to Louifburg when that officer was ordered thither, in the month of May enfuing, with a reinforcement to Mr. Bofcawen;

---

* A fingular inftance of this has been related to us. He perfuaded a lady, who is ftill living, and is, according to the public opinion, very juftly ranked in the firft clafs, as a woman of high judgement, fenfe, and underftanding, that he had feen a feaman hold the end of a large ball of packthread in one hand, and with the other throw the ball itfelf perpendicularly into the air with fo much force, that the whole of it fhould unroll. The conclufion of the ftory was confonant to that trait in his character which we have above defcribed.

† See vol. iii. p. 302.

and was, not long after his return, appointed to the Swiftsure, of seventy guns. In this ship he was employed, in the beginning of the year 1758, on the Mediterranean station, under the orders of Mr. Osborne; and was one of the commanders dispatched in pursuit of the Foudroyant; a particular account of which encounter has been already given in the life of captain Gardiner. The Swiftsure not being so fast a sailing ship as the Monmouth, the former was not fortunate enough to get up in time to put a speedier conclusion to the action. The Foudroyant being completely disabled by her first antagonist, deferred her surrender, through what the French commander called a point of honour, till the arrival of the Swiftsure rendered all farther resistance hopeless. Captain Stanhope remained in the Swiftsure during the continuance of the war, and on the same station till the month of August 1759, when he distinguished himself exceedingly, under Mr. Boscawen, in the attack and defeat of Monf. De la Clue's squadron.

He returned to England with the admiral immediately afterwards, and arrived at Spithead on the 15th of September; soon after which he received from his majesty the honour of knighthood. Having resumed the command of his ship, he was put under the orders of sir Edward Hawke, and was again fortunate enough to acquire the highest honour, in the encounter with the French fleet under Conflans. The Swiftsure was among the first ships who, in spite of the hurricane which then raged, got into action with the flying enemy; and was also among those who, after its glorious conclusion, was driven to sea by the violence of the tempest. No particular mention is made of the services in which this gentleman was employed during the year 1760, otherwise than in the occasional blockade of that part of the French naval force which survived their late defeat; but in the ensuing spring he was appointed to command, with the rank of commodore, one of the divisions in the armament sent, under Mr. Keppel, on the expedition against Belleisle. When the debarkation of the troops was first and unsuccessfully attempted, sir Thomas was sent, with his division of four ships of the line and some transports, to Sauzon, for the purpose of making a feigned attack on that quarter, and thereby distracting and

drawing

drawing the attention of the enemy from its real and intended point. In the second and more fortunate attempt made, on the 22d of April, sir Thomas was appointed to cover the landing with the ships under his command, and is spoken of by Mr. Keppel in the highest terms*. He continued, after the reduction of the island, to command one of the divisions, or squadrons, stationed off the coast of France, as well for the protection of the new conquest, as for the purpose of watching and counteracting any motions that might be made by the few ships still remaining at Brest, and the ports adjacent.

Several trivial rencounters took place between the ships under his orders and some prames, constructed by the enemy for the purpose of attacking him. In all these sir Thomas was successful, notwithstanding the many advantages possessed by the enemy, in particular that of being able, in consequence of their light draught of water, to retire among shoals, where the ships of war could not follow them: and, secondly, that from their low construction, it was a matter of uncommon difficulty to hit or cannonade them with any certain effect. Thus did he continue to be employed during the remainder of the war; before the conclusion of which he was, in 1762, appointed colonel of the Portsmouth division of marines, as successor to sir Piercy Brett, who was promoted to be a flag-officer. This appointment he held till his death, an event which took place on the 7th of March, 1770, being before he was entitled, in point of seniority, to the rank of a rear-admiral.

STRINGER, John,—is known in the service in no other respect than as having been promoted to be captain of the Syren, a ship of twenty-four guns, on the 16th of September, 1745, and as having been, on the 12th of January, 1747, dismissed from that ship, and from the service altogether, by the sentence of a court-martial, for behaving, as is stated, by Mr. Beatson, unlike an officer. The particular circumstances of his misbehaviour, as well as the time of his death, we have been unable to investigate.

STUART, The Honourable Archibald, — was the fourth son of Francis, eighth earl of Murray, in the

---

* See p. 320.

kingdom of Scotland, and Jane, daughter of John, fourth lord Balmerino. Having betaken himself to the naval service, and passed through the subordinate ranks of midshipman and lieutenant, he was promoted, in 1744, to be commander of the Scipio fireship. He was soon advanced to that of captain; his first commission, dated February 20, 1745, appointing him to the Squirrel, a twenty-gun ship. In the month of September following he was one of the members of the court-martial, held on board the London, for the trials of captain Burrish and others, charged with misbehaviour in the encounter off Toulon. We do not find him particularly mentioned as holding any command whatever after that time, and believe him to have remained nearly, if not altogether unemployed. In 1770 he retired totally from the service, as a captain, senior to several who were then created flag-officers, and consequently incapable of serving in the rank he then held. In pursuance of an act of parliament, passed in the year 1786, creating a distinct establishment for officers situated like himself, he was put on the list of retired captains, and is consequently no farther noticed. He died either in the month of February or March, 1795.

TIDDEMAN, Richard,—was, on the 9th of March, 1745, promoted to be captain of the Superbe. Early in 1747 he sailed for the East Indies as captain of the Eltham, a fifth rate of forty guns, one of three ships ordered thither, under the command of captain H. Powlet, afterwards duke of Bolton, to convoy the outward-bound company's ships and reinforce the squadron in those seas. He returned to England early in the year 1750, with rear-admiral Boscawen, as captain of the Harwich, a fourth rate of fifty guns. We do not find any farther mention whatever made of him, till after the recommencement of the war in 1756; when, in 1758, we find him captain of the Grafton, of sixty-eight guns, and to have been, in the month of February, ordered again to the East Indies, in company with the Sunderland, as a reinforcement to the squadron already employed in that quarter, under the orders of Mr. Pocock. On his arrival there he removed into the Elizabeth, the Grafton having been chosen, by rear-admiral Stevens, the second in command, for his flag ship. The different occurrences in which Mr.
Tiddeman

Tiddeman was concerned, that took place during the war, having been already related at no inconfiderable length in our account of fir George Pocock, Mr. Stevens, and Mr. Cornifh*, to which, for the fake of avoiding all needlefs repetition, we beg leave to refer. By the return of the former to Europe, and the death of Mr. Stevens, he became next in command to Mr. Cornifh, whom, as we have already fhewn, he accompanied on the very fuccefsful expedition undertaken by him, againft the important Spanifh fettlement of Manilla†. He acquired there the higheft honour, as he had uniformly done on every preceding occafion, where the fmalleft opportunity occurred, of difplaying his natural gallantry, or exhibiting thofe qualities which had defervedly acquired him the general efteem of all under whom he had ferved. He fcarcely lived to furvive the fuccefs, having, as is related in the difpatches of the commander-in-chief, been overfet in his barge when attempting to enter the river the morning after the furrender of the place, and drowned, together with five of his crew. This event took place on the 7th of October, 1762.

WELLER, John,—was, on the 29th of November, 1745, promoted to be captain of the Roebuck; after which time no material mention is made of him till the year 1748, when he was, in confequence of the refignation of his father, of whom we have already given a fhort account ‡, appointed to command the Dublin yacht. After a continuance of fome years in this ftation, we believe him, about the year 1759, to have been appointed to the Affiftance, and ordered to the Weft Indies §, where

---

* See vol. iv. p. 398, et feq.——Vol. v. p. 143, et feq.
† Having his broad pendant on board the Elizabeth, of fixty-four guns, he commanded a feparate divifion, confifting of five fhips of the line, which, as is related by Mr. Cornifh, was confiderably retarded by calms in proceeding to the appointed place of rendezvous.
‡ See vol. iv. p. 95.
§ Extract of a letter from admiral Cotes, dated Jamaica,
Dec. 5, 1757.
"On the 20th of November the Affiftance chafed a French privateer of eighteen guns and a fchooner privateer, with a prize, into Tiberoon bay, on the ifland of Hifpaniola, where the French had a battery of five guns. The veffels hauled clofe to the fhore, under cover of the battery; but it falling calm, captain Weller was obliged to tow in with his boats. On the 21ft he burnt the fnow, funk the prize, and difmounted all the guns on fhore. He had two men killed in the action, and his mafts and rigging much damaged."

he appears to have had some opportunity of distinguishing himself, which he improved to his best advantage. No other mention is made of him in the service; nor do we know him to have obtained any subsequent command. In 1770 he was put on the superannuated list, with the rank and half-pay of a rear-admiral, an honourable kind of pension, which he did not long enjoy, dying at Rolvenden on the 7th of September, 1772.

1746.

ALLISON, Thomas,—was, on the 9th of February, 1746, appointed captain of the Boyne: unhappily for him, of such trivial consequence were the commands and services on which this gentleman was employed, that we do not find the smallest mention made of him, either by Campbell or any other author; and our private information is equally deficient. We know no other circumstances concerning him, except that for a considerable part of the war, which commenced in 1756, he remained unemployed. His character, however, and conduct, were perfectly unimpeachable; for though the time of his service had been so short, he was, in 1770, raised to the rank of a rear-admiral and put on the superannuated list. This honourable testimony of his worth he consequently enjoyed till the time of his death, which happened on the 22d of March, 1776.

BLOSS, Thomas,—was a gentleman still less known than the former. He was, on the 2d of January, 1746, promoted to be captain of the Richmond, which is the only mention made of him. The time of his death has not been clearly ascertained by us, but is supposed to have happened soon after the year 1750.

BYRON,

BYRON, Honourable John,—was the second son of William, fourth lord Byron*, and Frances his third wife, second daughter of William, lord Berkeley of Stratton. He was born on the 8th of November, 1723; and having betaken himself to a naval life, was appointed a midshipman about the year 1731; he afterwards served on board the Wager storeship. In this vessel he sailed, in the month of September 1740, for the South Seas, with the squadron under the orders of commodore Anson. The distresses he experienced after the loss of that ill-fated ship have been but faintly recounted in our account of captain Cheap†; but a farther and more particular relation were we to attempt entering at all into the minute or even most striking hardships, experienced by this gentleman and his distressed companions, would lead us far beyond our limits, narrowed as they are through necessity. We cannot however refrain from lamenting, that Mr. Byron should, on many occasions, have rather harshly

---

* Collins informs us, "That this family had large possessions in the reign of William the Conqueror, is evident from Doomsday book, where it is recorded, that Gospatrick held, of Erneis de Buron, four bovates of land in Bengeley, in the county of York: and, in Borgesire, he held in Dunthorpe four bovates of land, &c. He also had in the same shire Drantune and Grattune, with three carrucates of land in Cathal; as also Hulsingore, the Soke of Chenatesburge, Ripestane, and Hamptone; Hatesbi, the Soke of Burg, Argendune, and Lotes; Copegrave, Bernekeham, Wipelei Berneslei, Burle, Dacre, Littlebran, Menson Wederbi, Bergki, Distone, Holstingoure Soke, Crane, Merdelei, Cotinglai, Colingaward, Denardium, Hageneword, East Reding, Cave, Hundret, Cotewood, and Stetlingetlet. In Lincolnshire he held Medelton, Ulvesby, Brochelesbi, Haburne, Newhuse, Waragebi, Hatune, Caldecote, Pavetone, Hardie, Barworde, Ternilo, Langestone, Fulnebi, Raude, Gusebi, Burg, Chinthorpe, Colebi, Wege, Baret, Walcote, Wintertune, and Graingeham.

"The wapentake of the west riding of Lincolnshire witness, that Erneis de Buron ought to have land which Wege held in Wintringeham, viz. Six bovates and one toft in the Soke of Gilbert de Gand, and one other toft with Soke and Sake.

"Likewise in the chapter of claims, in the south riding of the said county, the wapentake say, that Erneis de Buron, of right, ought to have the soc of four brovates of land in Sagesbi, about which there was a dispute between him and William de Perci.

"What relation this Erneis de Buron was to Ralph de Buron cannot certainly be made out; but the said Ralph held divers manors in Nottinghamshire and Derbyshire, and is the direct ancestor of the present lord Byron."

† See p. 78 et seq.

reflected on captain Cheap, particularly as he did not think proper to publish his account during his commander's life, when he was capable of refuting any semblance of a charge that might be objected against him.

Pursuing the generally received account, we have stated in our memoirs of captain Cheap*, that the barge was, after the secession of Mr. Byron and Mr. Campbell, left behind for their convenience by the people, who had embarked in the long boat. The story, as related by Mr. Byron, is widely different: these gentlemen, according to his narrative, had joined the majority in their opinion of proceeding to the southward, only because they conceived that captain Cheap, and all the persons saved from the wreck, were to be carried with them; but when they found that gentleman, the surgeon, and lieutenant Hamilton of the marines, with some deserters, were intended to be left behind, he seized the favourable opportunity of returning the next day to captain Cheap, with all that had embarked in the barge, ten in number, being sent back by the people in the long boat for some canvas which had been imprudently left behind. Captain Cheap, on this new accession of force, resolved to resume his original project of proceeding to the northward to the island of Chiloe, where it was hoped they might, by boarding and cutting her out, possess themselves of a Spanish vessel, in which they could, with the greater probability of success, attempt their return to Europe, or, what was still uppermost in captain Cheap's thoughts, proceed to the northward in quest of the commodore.

On this expedition they proceeded about the middle of December, and in about three weeks afterwards had the misfortune to lose the yawl, which was overset and sunk. By this lamentable accident one of their companions was drowned; and they were compelled to leave four others behind, the barge being incapable of containing their whole number. This misfortune, added to the other distresses they experienced, compelled them to abandon their original design, and return, with much reluctance, to Wager Island, where they arrived in the greatest extremity of distress, after an absence of two months.

---

* See page 81.

The detail of the subsequent miseries and adventures which Mr. Byron and his wretched companions underwent on their passage to Chiloe, in company with the Indian chief, who, as we have already related, was prevailed on to accompany them thither, would be affecting in the extreme. The characters of the relators remove every idea of their having embellished the account given by them of their distresses with any extravagant fiction, so that we can only admire the wonderful Providence which protected and preserved them through such a series of unprecedented (indeed almost incredible) distress, and point out their preservation as an useful, an almost preternatural lesson to mankind, never to despair even in the most abject state *.

On

---

* The two following anecdotes are pleasantly enough related by Mr. Byron in his narrative, as having befallen them while at Chaco and Castro.

"Some time after we had been here, a snow arrived in the harbour from Lima, which occasioned great joy amongst the inhabitants, as they had no ship the year before on account of the alarm lord Anson had given upon the coast. This was not the annual vessel, but one of those, that I mentioned before, which come unexpectedly. The captain of her was an old man, well known upon the island, who had traded here, once in two or three years, for more than thirty years past. He had a remarkable large head, and therefore was commonly known by a nick name they had given him, of " Cabuco de Toro, or Bull's Head." He had not been here a week before he came to the governor, and told him, with a most melancholy countenance, that he had not slept a wink since he came into the harbour, as the governor was pleased to allow three English prisoners liberty to walk about, instead of confining them, and that he expected every moment they would board his vessel and carry her away: this he said when he had above thirty hands aboard. The governor assured him he would be answerable for us, and that he might sleep in quiet; though at the same time he could not help laughing at the man, as all the people in the town did. These assurances did not satisfy the captain; he used the utmost dispatch in disposing of his cargo, and to put to sea again, not thinking himself safe till he had lost sight of the island "

" Amongst the houses we visited at Castro there was one belonging to an old priest, who was esteemed one of the richest persons upon the island. He had a niece, of whom he was extremely fond, and who was to inherit all he possessed. He had taken a great deal of pains with her education: and she was reckoned one of the most accomplished young ladies of Chiloe. Her person was good, though she could not be called a regular beauty. This young lady did me

the

On the arrival of their reduced party at Valparaiſo, which they did not reach till the month of January 1742, they were, through the miſerable timidity of, added to the inordinate deſire of diſplaying his power, poſſeſſed by the Spaniſh governor, confined in the common dungeon of the fort, from which captain Cheap and lieutenant Hamilton were taken and ſent up to St. Jago, as their commiſſions, which they had fortunately preſerved, proved them to be officers. Mr. Byron, and his companion Campbell, were left behind in priſon; but not long afterwards, in conſequence of the repreſentation of captain Cheap, were alſo ſent for to St. Jago, which is the capital of the province. Mr. Byron relates with ſome pleaſantry, a piece of ſerious advice given him by the muleteer, with whom he travelled to St. Jago, not to think of remaining in that city where there was nothing but extravagance, vice and folly. Inſtead of this he propoſed to Mr. Byron, that he ſhould proceed on with him as a mule-driver, a buſineſs which, he complimented him ſo far as to ſay, he would ſoon be very expert, and happy in, for that thoſe following his buſineſs led a very innocent pleaſant life, far preferable to any enjoyment ſuch a place as St. Jago could afford. Mr. Byron thanked him, aſſured him he was much obliged to him, but that he would try the city firſt, and if he did not like it he would accept his offer.

At St. Jago they continued two years treated with the utmoſt hoſpitality and tenderneſs. One anecdote, related

---

the honour to take more notice of me than I deſerved, ſhe propoſed to her uncle to convert me, and afterwards begged his conſent to marry me. As the old man doated upon her he readily agreed to it; and accordingly, on the next viſit I made him, acquainted me with the young lady's propoſal, and his approbation of it; taking me at the ſame time into a room, where there were ſeveral cheſts and boxes, which he unlocked, firſt ſhewing me what a number of fine cloaths his niece had, and then his own wardrobe, which he ſaid ſhould be mine at his death. Amongſt other things he produced a piece of linen, which he ſaid ſhould immediately be made up into ſhirts for me. I own this laſt article was a great temptation to me; however I had reſolution to withſtand it, and made the beſt excuſes I could for not accepting of the honour they intended for me, for by this time I could ſpeak Spaniſh well enough to make myſelf underſtood."

by

by Mr. Byron himself, is too honourable to the general character of the Spanish nation to be suppressed.

" Two or three days after our arrival, the president sent Mr. Campbell and me an invitation to dine with him, where we were to meet admiral Pizarro and all his officers. This was a cruel stroke upon us, as we had not any cloaths fit to appear in, and dared not refuse the invitation. The next day a Spanish officer, belonging to admiral Pizarro's squadron*, whose name was don Manuel de Guiror, came and made us an offer of two thousand dollars. This generous Spaniard made the offer without any view of ever being repaid, but purely out of a compassionate motive of relieving us in our present distress. We returned him all the acknowledgments his uncommon generous behaviour merited, and accepted of six hundred dollars only, upon his receiving our draught for that sum upon the English consul at Lisbon. We now got ourselves decently cloathed after the Spanish fashion; and, as we were upon our parole, went out where we pleased to divert ourselves."

After having continued thus comfortably situated for two years, a French ship, bound from Lima to Spain, put into Valparaiso, in consequence of which they were sent thither, and embarked for Europe about the end of December 1744. This vessel was called the Lys, and belonged to St. Maloes. There were, exclusive of Mr. Byron and his fellow-sufferers, several passengers of consequence on board; among whom was the well-known ingenious don Juan D'Ulloa, who had been in Peru many years, employed in making astronomical and other useful observations. The Lys was bound in the first instance to the Bay of Conception, where she was to be joined by three other French ships, belonging, as well as herself, to France. But though Talcaguana, the place of their destination, was only sixty leagues distant from Valparaiso, owing to the lee current and southerly wind, they did not arrive there till the 6th of January. They sailed from thence in three weeks afterwards, in company with the Louis Erasme, the marquis D'Antin, and the Deliverance, all which were taken by the English; two by a squadron of

---

* He was the first lieutenant of admiral Pizarro's ship.

private

private ships of war, called the Royal Family Privateers; and the third by commodore Warren, off Louisburg. In eight or nine days after they sailed the Lys sprung a leak, and was compelled to put back to Valparaiso, a circumstance, which, in all probability, preserved her from sharing the same fate.

The injury was however repaired, and they again put to sea on the 1st of March, 1745. After a tedious, and in some respects disagreable passage round Cape Horn, and along the coast of America, which was, however, happily unaccompanied by any misfortune, they were compelled to bear away for the West Indies, their stock of water not being considered sufficient to last them to Europe. They arrived at Cape François, on the 8th of July, having, in the first instance, narrowly escaped destruction, being hurried through the Granadillos, in the night, without the knowledge of any person on board; and being afterwards almost as singularly, according to Mr. Byron's account, preserved from being captured by two English ships of war, who gave up the chace in the night.

Mr. Byron takes occasion, and with much reason, to animadvert on the neglect and incivility with which captain Cheap, Mr. Hamilton, and himself were treated, as well by the French governor as by Mr. L'Etendiere*, who commanded the squadron which convoyed them to Europe. Their distresses were now, however, nearly drawn to a period, for on the 29th of October they made Cape Ortugal, and on the 31st came to an anchor in Brest road. After their arrival at that port they were all confined on board the ship, and treated with much asperity, not the smallest civility or attention being paid them by way of alleviating their situation. Our travellers were not, however, long in this disagreeable state, for about eight days afterwards they were conveyed to a town called Landernaw, situated about four leagues up the river. Here they continued on their parole for three months, at the end of which time an order came from the court of Spain, permitting them to return to England by the first ship that offered. They accordingly repaired to Morlaix, having

---

* The same man who was afterwards defeated by rear-admiral Hawke.

received intelligence that a Dutch veffel lay there, on board which it was probable they might procure a paffage. After a detention of fix weeks, in confequence of the veffel not being ready, they at laft embarked, having ftipulated for a certain price, which was paid beforehand, to be landed at Dover: but, as if Providence had ordained that this wretched and perfecuted triumvirate fhould be attended by vexation to the lateft moment, they were in the moft tyrannical and arbitrary manner prevented from failing for three days by a French privateer, who threatened to fink them if they attempted it, before he himfelf was ready for fea.

When they at laft got out, their paffage was long, tedious, and uncomfortable. The mafter of the veffel betrayed, as we obferved in our account of captain Cheap, a ftrong inclination to reland them in France, in breach of his pofitive agreement. But the Squirrel, an Englifh fhip of war coming up with the Dutchman, took out Mr. Byron, with his companions, and landed them the fame afternoon at Dover. Mr. Byron concludes his narrative with the following whimfical anecdote, defcriptive of his arrival in London.

" Captain Cheap was fo tired by the time he reached Canterbury, that he could proceed no farther that night. The next morning he ftill found himfelf fo much fatigued that he could ride no longer, therefore it was agreed that he and Mr. Hamilton fhould take a poft chaife, and that I fhould ride. But here an unlucky difficulty was ftarted, for upon fharing the little money we had, it was found to be not fufficient to pay the charges to London; and my proportion fell fo fhort, that it was, by calculation, barely enough to pay for horfes, without a farthing for eating a bit upon the road, or even for the very turnpikes. Thofe I was obliged to defraud by riding as hard as I could through them all, not paying the leaft regard to the men who called out to ftop me. The want of refrefhment I bore as well as I could. When I got to the Borough I took a coach and drove to Marlborough-ftreet, where my friends had lived when I left England; but when I came there I found the houfe fhut up. Having been abfent fo many years, and in all that time never having heard a word from home I knew not who was dead or who was living,

where

where to go next, or even how to pay the coachman. I recollected a linen draper's fhop, not far from thence, which our family had ufed, I therefore drove there, and, making myfelf known, they paid the coachman. I then enquired after our family, and was told my fifter, having married lord Carlifle, was at that time in Soho-fquare. I immediately walked to the houfe and knocked at the door; but the porter not liking my figure, which was half French, half Spanifh, with the addition of a large pair of boots, covered with dirt, he was going to fhut the door in my face; but I prevailed with him at laft to let me come in."

Immediately on his arrival, after undergoing this feries of difficulties, five years in continuance, he was promoted to be commander of a floop of war; and from thence advanced, on the 30th of December following (1746) to be captain of the Syren frigate. After this no mention is made of him during the war: not long after its conclufion he was appointed to the St. Alban's, and ordered for the coaft of Guinea with commodore Buckle. A trivial altercation took place there with a French fquadron, as we have already related in our account of the gentleman laft-mentioned, and which we believe to have been the only material circumftance which occurred during the voyage. On his return to England, that is to fay, in the month of January, 1753, he was appointed to the Augufta, of fixty guns, then ordered to be equipped for a guardfhip at Plymouth. From this fhip he was, before the expiration of the time ufually allotted to fuch commands, promoted to the Vanguard, of feventy guns, a fhip ordered to be fitted for fea at Plymouth, in the beginning of the year 1755, a rupture being then daily apprehended with France. He did not long continue in this command, nor while he did retain it was he ordered on any fervice memorable enough to merit a particular account of. In 1757 he was captain of the America, a fixty-gun fhip, one of the armament employed on the fuccefslefs expedition againft Rochfort, under fir Edward Hawke. At the clofe of this year he was fent out fenior officer of a very fmall fquadron, confifting of his own fhip (the America), with the Brilliant and Coventry frigates, ordered to cruife off the coaft of France. While abfent on this fervice he fell in with a very valuable fhip, laden

laden with furs from Quebec, called the Diamond, which endeavouring to get away, and firing her stern chace in the hope of facilitating her escape, her afterpart blew up, and the vessel itself also, after burning with great fury for half an hour. Twenty-four only of her crew, out of seventy, were saved, and many of these so miserably scorched that they died soon afterwards. The frigates had greater success, the Coventry having captured, after a short action, the Dragon, a large privateer belonging to Bayonne, a new ship, on her first cruise, carrying twenty-four nine-pounders, and two hundred and eighty-four men. The Brilliant about the same time sunk, by the discharge of her first broadside, the Intrepide, a French privateer belonging to the same port as the former, carrying fourteen guns and one hundred and thirty men, ten of whom were killed, but the whole of the remainder taken up by the Brilliant's boats.

No other material mention is made of Mr. Byron till the early part of the year 1760, when he commanded the Fame, of seventy-four guns, and was ordered to Louisburg with some transports, having on board a proper number of artificers and engineers, who were sent thither for the purpose of demolishing the fortifications of that once important place. While absent there he had, in the month of July, the good fortune to effect a very meritorious piece of service. Having received information from the governor of Louisburg, that some French ships of war, with storeships, were in Chaleur bay, he proceeded thither in quest of them, with his own ship, the Repulse and Scarborough. He succeeded in destroying the whole, consisting of three frigates, the Marchault, of 32 guns; the Bienfaisant, of twenty-two; and the Marquis Marlose, of eighteen, with twenty schooners, sloops, and small privateers, having on board some troops, with a considerable quantity of provisions and stores. This convoy had been dispatched from France for the relief of the garrison of Montreal; but finding the British squadron, under lord Colville, had reached the river St. Laurence before them, they put into the bay of Chaleur, hoping that, by landing the troops, the provisions and stores, they might still be conveyed to the place of their destination by land. In this the enemy found themselves fatally disappointed.

Captain

Captain Byron returned from Louifburg, and arrived in fafety at Plymouth, towards the end of November. We believe him, though no farther particular mention is made of him, to have continued in the Fame nearly, if not entirely, till the end of the war. Soon after peace had taken place it was refolved to fend out a fmall force on a voyage of difcovery; and Mr. Byron, in confequence of his univerfally acknowledged judgement and fkill in the art of navigation, was pitched upon to command it. He was accordingly appointed to the Dolphin, a fixth rate of twenty guns, which was purpofely fitted in the moft complete manner, and fheathed with copper, which was at that time an invention almoft new, and, indeed, never before this occafion ufed in fo great an extent; the rudder pins and other faftnings being all made of the fame metal. Orders were not iffued to equip this fhip till the 18th of April; but fuch expedition was ufed, that fhe went out of dock on the 14th of May, and having completed the rigging, taken on board her guns, provifions, ftores, and all neceffaries requifite for fo long a voyage, was ready to fail for the Downs on the 14th of the following month. On her paffage thither the fhip got aground on the fand, but happily floated on the rifing tide without having fuftained the fmalleft injury. Captain Byron repaired on board on the 17th; and after having put into Plymouth for a few days, in order to fully afcertain whether any injury had been fuftained by the Dolphin in confequence of the accident juft mentioned, took his final departure in the beginning of July, having in company the Tamar floop of war, commanded by captain Patrick Mouatt. Immediately on quitting port, Mr. Byron, in purfuance of his inftructions, hoifted a broad pendant, being appointed commander-inchier of all his majefty's fhips and veffels in the Eaft Indies. He got into the bay of Fonchiale on the 14th of July. and having recruited his water as well as taken on board fome neceffaries, departed on the 20th. On the 30th he reached the ifland of St. Jago; from whence he proceeded, after a very fhort ftay, for the coaft of Brazil, off which he arrived, having had a profperous paffage, on the 11th of September, and in three days afterwards anchored abreaft of the town of Rio de Janeiro.

The

The commodore quitted that place on the 20th of October; but, instead of steering towards the Cape of Good Hope, whither, as both his own officers and people, together with those on board the Tamar, imagined he was bound, he kept far to the southward, till, having arrived in the latitude where he was ordered to make his instructions known, he made a signal for the captain of the Tamar to repair on board the Dolphin. He then publicly communicated to him, and his own company, that they were bound on a voyage of discovery, during which they were to receive double pay for their better encouragement. On the 27th of November, after having encountered many severe gales of wind, they made Cape Blanco, on the coast of Patagonia, and in a day or two afterwards Pengwin island, situated three or four leagues only from Port Desire, where the commodore intended to put in. On the 1st of December they entered that harbour, and narrowly escaped destruction almost immediately afterwards. The weather being extremely temperate, the boats were all of them hoisted out, and attended the ship up the harbour; but a very violent and sudden storm of wind arising from the N. N. E. directly ahead of their course, all possible expedition was used to furl the sails; both anchors were let go, but before the ship could bring up she took the ground. A cold, tempestuous night succeeded; the boats were unable to get on board again, and, in the apprehension of their companions, were driven to sea. These gloomy thoughts were happily, however, of short duration, the barge providentially reached the ship, and by her assistance, a stern anchor was carried out just before the tide turned. The ship floated and soon warped into the middle of the harbour, where it was moored with both bowers; and the gale still continuing, the yards as well as top-masts were struck down.

As for the boats, the cutter and yawl were forced on shore, where the people suffered extremely from the inclemency of the weather, but returned in safety, as did the long boat, though driven two leagues to sea with only two men in it. They sailed from Port Desire on the 14th, sooner perhaps than they otherwise would have done, owing to the water found there being all so strongly tinged with mineral as to be unserviceable. On the 22d they came to an anchor off the coast of Patagonia, where a very friendly intercourse took place between the English and the gigantic inhabitants. After a continuance of a few hours only on this dreary coast, the commodore again departed. On the 29th he anchored in Port Famine; from whence having sailed on the 4th of January, on the 13th he made port Egmont, the possession of which, in a few years afterwards, had well nigh caused a rupture with the court of Spain. This harbour was taken formal possession of, by the commodore, on the 23d of January, with all the ceremony usual on such occasions; and the ships departed on the 27th. The commodore returned back to Port Desire for the purpose of meeting the Florida storeship, which he expected from England with a quantity of fresh cured provisions, in order to enable him to prosecute his discoveries, according to the plan laid down for him in England. This junction was effected, at the port just mentioned, on the 5th of February; and the rapidity with which the tide ran in that harbour rendering the necessary communication with the storeship not only difficult but nearly impracticable, the ships all sailed together, on the 8th, for Port Famine, where the Dolphin, and the Tamar, having taken on board as much provisions and stores, of different kinds, as they could stow, they parted company with the Florida on the 26th, in prosecution of their own voyage, leaving the storeship to return to England.

The commodore bent his course through the streights of Magellan, which intricate and dangerous passage he was six weeks and five days in making, though the distance was no more than one hundred and sixteen leagues. Contrary winds, repeated storms, and a variety of dangerous causes, united to oppose his progress: but at length all these difficulties appeared to be overcome by the entrance of the ships into the Pacific Ocean on the 9th of April. On the 26th they made the island of Masa Fuero, where, on account of its privacy, which accorded with his instructions and the nature of the expedition on which he was sent, the commodore thought it more prudent to put in, than at Juan Fernandez, from whence the Spaniards might have been able to discover, and consequently, perhaps, frustrate the object of the voyage. Two days after his arrival, Mr. Byron, having been duly authorised by his

his inſtructions, appointed captain Mouat to command the Dolphin under him, with the rank of poſt captain, and promoted his own firſt lieutenant to be commander of the Tamar. The ſhips having completed their water, ſailed from Maſa Fuero on the 1ſt of May, ſteering to the weſtward.

After a paſſage of thirty-ſix days, the Tamar, on the 6th of June, made a ſignal, at one in the morning, of ſeeing land, which, on the approach of day, proved two ſmall iſlands, affording no proper place of anchorage. On this account, added to his being unable to procure any vegetables or other relief for the uſe of the ſick, the commodore named them the Iſlands of Diſappointment. On the eleventh of the ſame month the Tamar again diſcovered land. Here, after a trifling ſkirmiſh with the inhabitants, ſeveral of whom were unfortunately killed or wounded, a large number of cocoa nuts, and a conſiderable quantity of ſcurvy-graſs, was collected for the uſe of the ſick: but no proper place of anchorage being found for the ſhips, they departed, compelled to be content with this temporary refreſhment. At the iſland next diſcovered, a circumſtance which took place very ſoon after having quitted the iſland laſt-mentioned, a very friendly, though ſhort intercourſe was eſtabliſhed with the natives, who behaved in the moſt hoſpitable and inoffenſive manner. This iſland was named, by the commodore, King George's Iſland, as was a ſecond Prince of Wales's Iſland. On the 21ſt of June land was again diſcovered, but, being ſurrounded with ſhoals and breakers, was named the Iſland of Danger: two others were afterwards ſeen, the firſt of which was named the Duke of York's Iſland, and the ſecond Byron's Iſland. The commodore had now ſkirted that cluſter of ſmall iſlands, which has been ſince ſo frequently viſited as to be completely explored by ſubſequent navigators, and now univerſally known by the name of the Society Iſlands. The commodore, by keeping to the northward after he left the Prince of Wales's Iſland, miſſed the opportunity of effecting thoſe diſcoveries which have ſince made ſo conſpicuous a figure in the annals of navigation. On the 8th of July, three days only after he quitted the iſland which bears his name, he fell in with the

the Ladrones, and came to an anchor the next morning in the road of Tinian, having effected his paſſage, from the ſtreights of Magellan, in four months and twenty days, without having buried one of the crew in the whole of that long run.

The Dolphin and Tamar continued at this iſland, which is repreſented by Mr. Byron, in conformity with the account given in Mr. Anſon's voyage, to have been a terreſtrial paradiſe, nearly three months, principally to effect the recovery of thoſe who were tainted with the ſcurvy, and of whom one perſon only, belonging to each ſhip, are ſaid to have died. The object of the expedition, which was merely to aſcertain whether there were not ſeveral iſlands lying in the track croſſing the Pacific Ocean, between the Southern Tropic and the Equator, being now completed, the commodore ſailed from Tinian on the 2d of October, intending to proceed to Batavia on his way to England. On the 22d of the ſame month he paſſed the Baſhee Iſlands; on the 16th of November he entered the Streights of Banca; and on the 27-8th of the ſame month came to an anchor in the road of Batavia. Here it became neceſſary to caulk the Dolphin; which ſervice being completed, as well as a ſufficient quantity of wood, water, and proviſions taken on board, the two ſhips ſailed on the 9th of December, and, after a paſſage undiverſified by any pleaſant or unpleaſant occurrence of moment, came to an anchor in Table Bay on the 14th of February. The ſhips ſailed from hence on the 2d of March, and, after a ſhort and proſperous paſſage, anchored in the Downs on the 9th of May, 1766. The Dolphin being immediately paid off, Mr. Byron held no command after this time till the year 1769, when he was, on the 3d of June, appointed governor of Newfoundland: he ſailed thither two days afterwards. He held this appointment during the length of time uſually allotted to it, returning to Europe at the accuſtomed periods. During the latter part of the time he had his broad pendant on board the Panther, of ſixty guns, but in what ſhip, in the earlier part of his command, we are ignorant.

In 1773 he derived a conſiderable addition to his private fortune, from a bequeſt of landed property, in the counties of York and Hants, worth 20,000l. made him by the lord Berkley, of Stratton, who alfo left 5000l. to his daughters, and 2000l. to each fon. After the expiration of the time of his appointment at Newfoundland he had no appointment, while he continued a private captain. On March 31, 1775, he was advanced to be rear-admiral of the blue; as he moreover was, on the 28th of April, 1777, to be rear-admiral of the white; on the 23d of January, 1778, to be rear-admiral of the red; and, in two days afterwards, to be vice-admiral of the blue. The hoftile intentions of France becoming at this time extremely apparent, and it being difcovered by adminiftration that a ftrong fquadron of twelve fhips of the line, commanded by the well-known count d'Eftaign, was actually equipped and under orders to fail, as it was fuppofed, to America, Mr. Byron was chofen to command a fquadron of nearly the fame force, which was ordered thither for the purpofe of counteracting their interference. Mr. Byron failed on the 9th of June, and the fquadron being attacked by a violent gale of wind, on the 3d of July, was almoft completely difperfed. Mr. Byron, who had his flag on board the Princefs Royal, of ninety guns, arrived alone off Sandy Hook on the 18th of Auguft, and found M. d'Eftaign at anchor there before him*, in fuch a ftation as to prevent all poffibility of his getting either into New York or Rhode Ifland: he confequently bore away for Halifax, which he reached in fafety on the 26th.

Having repaired the trivial injuries the fhip received on its paffage, he failed from Halifax to New York, in order to join lord Howe, with all the force he had been able to collect. This confifted of no more than his own fhip, the Culloden, of feventy-four guns; the Diamond frigate, with the Difpatch and Hope floops of war. But the enemy, after a trivial fkirmifh with fome of the Englifh fhips, put into Bofton, in New England, as well for the purpofe of repairing the damages they had fuftained on that occafion, as to prepare, in other refpects, for a voyage to the Weft Indies, whither they were bound. Mr. Byron having collected his whole force, followed thither in pur-

---

* Two line of battle-fhips from the enemy's fquadron chaced Mr. Byron for a fhort time, but ineffectually.

fuit, and arrived in time, at the beginning of the year 1779, to prevent any farther attack from being made on Mr. Barrington, who had with a force, comparatively speaking, contemptible, not only withstood the utmost efforts of the French admiral, but had made himself master of the island of St. Lucia even in his fight. Some succeeding months were spent in watching each other, during which time both sides received reinforcements; but the enemy still retained a manifest superiority, both in numbers and the size of their ships. Such was the situation of affairs, when, in the beginning of July, the vice-admiral having received intelligence that the French fleet, in very great force, had been discovered from St. Vincent's, immediately put to sea in pursuit of them; when on his passage to Grenada, he received advice that the island was attacked by a force not exceeding nineteen ships of the line. He hastened thither with all possible speed, and arrived off St. George's bay, where the enemy lay at anchor, soon after day-light. On the 6th of July, immediate measures were taken to bring them to a close and decisive action: but the enemy's fleet, when completely formed, was found to consist of twenty-seven ships of the line, instead of nineteen, which had been before stated as their highest force. Notwithstanding this great superiority, the whole of Mr. Byron's force amounting to twenty-one sail only, seven or eight of which were of sixty-four guns, while very few in M. D'Estaign's fleet carried less than seventy-four, the latter most industriously avoided a close action, a point he was enabled, from the great superiority his ships possessed in point of sailing, to carry into effect. The encounter * of course produced nothing decisive: encumbered as Mr. Byron was with a numerous fleet of transports, he was unable to effect any thing farther, and Grenada of course fell into their hands. Mr. Byron himself, in his dispatches, makes the following remark on the enemy's conduct.

"Although it was evident, throughout the whole day, that they resolved to avoid a close engagement, I could

---

* One hundred and eighty-three men were killed, and three hundred and forty-six were wounded.

not allow myself to think, that, with a force so greatly superior, the French admiral would allow us to carry off the transports unmolested."

Mr. Byron soon after this event returned to England in a frigate, leaving the command with rear-admiral Parker, and never accepted of any subsequent command. On the 19th of March, 1779, while absent in the West Indies, he was advanced to be vice-admiral of the white, which was the highest rank he lived to attain.

He died on the 10th of April, 1786, with the universal and justly acquired reputation of a brave and excellent officer, but, of a man, extremely unfortunate. He married, in August 1748, Sophia, daughter of John Trevanion, esq. of Carhays, in the county of Cornwall, who died in May 1786. By her he had issue two sons; John, born Feb. 7, 1756; and George Anson, afterwards a captain in the navy, born Nov. 30, 1758, died June 10, 1793: as also seven daughters, three of whom died infants. Of the remaining four, Frances was married to Charles Leigh, esq. lieutenant-colonel of the third regiment of foot guards; Juliana-Elizabeth, to her cousin William, son of the present lord Byron; secondly, Sept. 23, 1783, to sir Robert Wilmot, bart. of Derbyshire, and died March 15, 1788. Sophia-Maria, and Charlotte-Augusta.

COKBURNE, John,—was, on the 19th of July, 1746, promoted to be captain of the Princessa, on board which ship Mr. Lestock hoisted his flag as commander-in-chief of the expedition fitted out against the coast of Britanny, and in our account of whom, the events of that unsuccessful attempt have been already given. In the following year he removed into the Crown, a ship of forty-four guns, which is the only subsequent mention we find made of him, except that he died in England on the 8th of May, 1753.

CRAVEN, Thomas, — was the fourth son of John Craven, esq. and Maria Rebecca his wife, daughter of Henry Green, of Wykin, in the county and city of Coventry, Warwickshire, esq. In the beginning of the year 1746, he commanded the Weazle sloop, one of the vessels then employed to watch and reconnoitre the coast of France, a service in which he displayed great activity,

activity. He was, on the 8th of February, 1746, promoted to be captain of the Rye frigate, which is the only notice taken of him during the then current war; and, indeed, after its conclusion, till a recommencement of hostilities was daily expected. He was, about the month of July 1755, appointed captain of the Princess Mary, which is the only notice we find again taken of him during the continuance of the war, which broke out presently afterwards. During the latter part of the war, indeed, we know him to have been unemployed. He was chosen, by a very great majority, one of the representatives in parliament for the county of Berks, at the general election in 1768: and, on the 18th of October, 1770, was advanced to be rear-admiral of the blue. We have not, after the closest investigation, been able to collect any particulars, except those above given, relative to this gentleman. We find him however unnoticed, as he may appear to have been, from the concurrent testimony of all who had the pleasure of knowing him, to have been a person possessing the highest character, whether considered merely as a private gentleman or as an officer. He died on the 14th of December, 1772, being then representative for Berkshire, but having experienced no advancement, as a flag officer, from his original rank.

DENT, Cotton.—We find this gentleman, in 1744, to have been commander of a sloop of war on the Jamaica station; from whence he was dispatched to England, towards the close of the year, with an account of a very violent hurricane, which had done considerable damage in that quarter. The advice or packet boat, in which he embarked, was a small vessel, having on board a valuable cargo of gold dust, elephant's teeth, rhubarb, and other commodities to a considerable amount. It was unfortunately captured, about two hundred leagues west of the Lizard, by a large French privateer, the crew of which used the passengers extremely ill, plundering them without mercy, and stripping them even to their shirts. We do not know whether he was appointed to any other sloop of war after his return to England, but on the 23d of January, 1745, we find him promoted to be captain of the Kennington, a twenty-gun ship. No other mention is made of him during the war; soon after the close of which,

which, that is to fay, in the month of May 1750, he commanded the Culloden, of feventy guns, a guardfhip ftationed at Chatham. In 1753 he retired altogether from the fervice, being appointed one of the captains in Greenwich-hofpital. This ftation he held till the time of his death, which happened on the 28th of January, 1761.

DOUGLASS, John.—We labour under a confiderable degree of difficulty with refpect to this gentleman, being fcarcely able, for reafons already given in numberlefs preceding inftances, to diftinguifh between him and admiral fir James Douglafs, whom we have already given fome account of*. We find a captain Douglafs, in the early part of the year 1745, acting captain of the Mermaid, a twenty-gun fhip, and believe it to have been this gentleman, and not his predeceffor †. However that fact may be, we have no farther information concerning him during the war. The fucceeding peace, throughout the whole of its period, furnifhes us with nothing more interefting. On the approaching recommencement of hoftilities, in 1755, he was appointed to command the Fougeux, of fixty-four guns, one of the fquadron fent in that year to North America, under Mr. Bofcawen. In 1761 he appears to have been captain of the Unicorn, a twenty-gun fhip; but is in no other way noticed, while he held this ftation, than as having, in the beginning of the month of March, captured, in company with the Tweed frigate, a fmall privateer belonging to Breft, called the Marfhall Broglio, carrying eight guns and eighty men.

---

* See page 290 et feq.
† The following official account is given, of a very fpirited and fortunate tranfaction, in the Gazette, No. 8447.

"Admiralty-office, July the 8th, 1745.

"Captain Douglafs, commander of his majefty's fhip the Greyhound, of twenty guns, on his paffage from Cork to Lifbon, on the 15th of April laft, at fun-rifing, faw two fail in the latitude of 45. 58. N. to which he gave chace, and about nine got up with the fternmoft; after exchanging a few fhot, fhe ftruck. He then made fail after the other, and came up with her at two, when fhe ftruck without firing a gun. One proved to be the Benjamin, captain Daniel Suire, a fhip of twenty guns and fifty-feven men; the other the Neptune, captain Larroque Furgeau, a fhip of eighteen guns and forty-feven men, both from St. Domingo, but laft from Havannah. Their lading is indigo, fugar, and about fifteen hundred dollars."

After

After this time we have no account of him during the latter part of the war: we know him to have been unemployed, and have no reafon to believe him to have received any commiffion fubfequent to the ceffation of hoftilities. He was not, when in point of feniority he became entitled to fuch an advancement, promoted to be a flag-officer even on the fuperannuated lift, but remained on that of captains as retired from fervice. The time of his death is not precifely known, but is fuppofed to have happened in the year 1787.

DUDLEY, Obrien,—was, on Auguft 11, 1746, advanced from the rank of commander of a floop of war to be captain of the Rofe frigate. He was, not long afterwards, promoted to the Chefterfield and ordered to the coaft of Guinea. In the month of October 1748, the fhip being then off Cape Coaft Caftle, and the captain, with fome of the other officers on fhore, Couchman the firft lieutenant, together with the lieutenant of marines, the carpenter, and the greater part of the crew then remaining on board, forcibly poffeffed themfelves of the fhip, with an intention of turning pirates. Their infamous fcheme was, however, fruftrated by the intrepidity and excellent conduct of Mr. Gaftril the boatfwain, affifted by fuch of the inferior officers and crew as had not joined the mutineers, who retook the fhip after it had been in poffeffion of the infatuated infurgents about thirty hours*. Captain Dudley

---

* The following narrative of this tranfaction will probably not be thought uninterefting.

" On the 15th of October, 1748, captain Dudley, who was then on fhore at Cape Coaft Caftle, fent off his barge to Mr. Couchman, ordering him to fend the cutter on fhore, with the boatfwain of the fhip, to fee the tents ftruck on fhore, and to bring every thing belonging to the fhip on board that night: but Couchman directly ordered the barge to be hoifted in, and the boatfwain to turn all the hands to the quarter deck, where Mr. Couchman, coming from his cabbin with a drawn fword, faid, " Here I am, G-d d mn me, I will ftand by you while I have a drop of blood in my body." He was accompanied by John Morgan, the lieutenant of marines; Thomas Knight, the carpenter; his mate John Place a principal actor; and about thirty feamen with cutlaffes. They then gave three huzzas, and threw their hats over board, d-mning old hats, they would foon get new. Couchman then fent for the boatfwain, to know if he would ftand by him,

Dudley was, in confequence of the foregoing tranfaction, tried before a court-martial, of which fir Edward Hawke
was

---

him, and go with him. He replied " No;" and faid, " For God's fake, fir, be ruled by reafon, and confider what you are about." Couchman then threatened to put him in irons, if he did not join with him; but the boatfwain boldly told him he never would, in fuch piratical defigns. He was then ordered into cuftody, and two centinels put over him. Couchman foon after fent for Gilham, the mate of the fhip, and made the fame fpeech to him; who defired to know where he was bound, and upon what account? He replied, " To take, burn, and fink, and fettle a colony in the Eaft Indies." There were five or fix more put into cuftody with the boatfwain in the fame place, but they were confined only five or fix hours, for in the middle of the night after their confinement, Couchman fent for them, into the great cabbin, and defired them to fit and drink punch, after which he difmiffed them. The next day the boatfwain was invited to dinner by the new commander, who began to rail againft captain Dudley, and afked him, and one of the mates, what they thought of the affair? The boatfwain replied, " He thought it rank piracy." On which Couchman faid, " What I have done I cannot now go from; I was forced to it by the fhip's company." The boatfwain then told him, " That would be no fanction for his running away with the king's fhip." The carpenter and lieutenant then propofed their figning a paper, to which the boatfwain replied, " He never would, and would fooner fuffer death." The mate faid the fame. When the boatfwain came out of the great cabbin he went to the gunner's cabbin, who was then fick and unable to come out of it, but was of great ufe by his prudent advice and affiftance; for, after the boatfwain had told him that Couchman's party had taken poffeffion of all the arms, he faid, he could furnifh him with twenty piftols. By this time Mr. Frafier and Mr. Gilh·m, mates of the fhip; the gunner's mate and yeoman, with the cockfwain of the barge, were come to them, and the boatfwain communicated his defign of recovering the fhip that very night. To this they all agreed with the greateft refolution. It began then to be very dark, being ten P. M. when the boatfwain went to found the fhip's company. On the forecaftle there were about thirty men: he then in a plain, but prudent manner difclofed the fecret, and foon convinced them, both of the facility and neceffity of putting his fcheme immediately in practice. Accordingly, the firft ftep was to get up all the irons, or bilboes, on the forecaftle: he then fent for the twenty piftols, which were all loaded. He next ftationed three men upon the grand magazine, and two to that abaft; the remainder, who had no piftols, were to ftay by the bilboes and fecure as many prifoners as he fhould fend. This difpofition being made, he went directly down on the deck, where he divided his fmall company into two parties; and one going down the main, the other the fore hatchway, they foon fecured eleven or twelve of the ringleaders, and fent them up to the forecaftle without the leaft noife. The two parties then joined, and
went

was prefident, held on board the Invincible on the 26th of June, 1749. His cafe being very plain he was honourably acquitted after a very fhort enquiry, but we do not believe him ever to have held any fubfequent command. He died in England on the 26th of Auguft, 1759.

DUFF, Robert,— was, in the early part of the year 1746, commander of the Terror bomb-ketch on the coaft of Scotland, where he was extremely active, as appears, among many other proofs, by the following extract of a letter from him, dated off Coll, one of the Weftern Iflands, May the 19th.

"The day after our engagement with the two French men of war, off Loch Nouay, the Raven floop joined us; and having in the beft manner we could, repaired the damage done us in our mafts and rigging, upon the 6th, at four in the morning, we failed from Arras. About noon we were in Loch Nouay, but not finding the French fhips there, we proceeded to Cannay to endeavour to get intelligence of them. At Cannay we were informed they palfed by that ifland upon the fourth, in the afternoon. We fteered onward and fearched the harbours on that coaft; but not finding them there, went out to Stornway. Upon the 13th inftant, near Cape Wriath, we were joined by the Scarborough and Glafgow men of war, each of twenty guns; with the Tryal and Happy Jennet floops. Having intelligence of a French floop of eight guns being upon that coaft, I was ordered to fearch the Loch on the Main, from Loch Brim to Ardnamurchan, which I have accordingly done; but can get no other account of her, than that fuch a veffel was feen off the mouth of the Loch Brim on the 9th. Upon the 17th inftant I joined the Furnace off Glenaley; yefterday we went into Loch Nouay, and fent a party of men on fhore to fearch for arms and ammunition landed from the French men of war. We found twenty barrels of powder and about eighty mufkets, which we brought off."

He was, on the 23d of October, 1746, promoted to the rank of poft captain, and appointed to the Anglefea. Pre-

---

went directly to the great cabbin, where they fecured Couchman, the lieutenant of marines, and the carpenter, whom they immediately confined in different parts of the fhip."

vious to that time we have no information concerning him. He retained the fame command during the enfuing year, and not improbably as long as the war continued, employed, at leaſt during a part of it, as a cruiſer on the Iriſh ſtation, where he appears to have unfortunately experienced but little fuccefs; the only capture we find particularly mentioned, as made by him, being the Extravagant, a ſmall privateer belonging to St. Sebaſtians, carrying twelve guns and one hundred and twenty men.

During the greater part of the enfuing peace he is not known to have held any commiffion, his next fubfequent command being that of the Rocheſter, a fifty-gun ſhip, to which he was appointed in 1755, when the Britiſh government firſt became apprehenſive of an approaching rupture with France. He retained it till the year 1760. During the year 1756 he was principally employed in cruifing off the coaſt of France, a fervice in which he appears to have had good fuccefs, particularly in the capture of neutral ſhips, which, under the fuppofed protection of their flag, carried on a trade extremely lucrative to themfelves, and injurious to Britain, by fupplying the enemy with naval ſtores and ammunition. Five large Dutch ſhips, laden with commodities of this kind, were captured by the Rocheſter and Ambufcade about the end of Auguſt. He was employed in a fimilar manner during the fucceeding year; and in the month of April captured, in company with captain Geary, of the Somerfet, two large prizes, of the utmoſt confequence to the enemy, bound from Bourdeaux to Quebec, the particulars of which fuccefs have been already related at length in our account of the gentleman laſt mentioned, who was the fenior, or commanding officer*. Captain Duff was difpatched in purfuit of three ſhips which fled at the firſt fight of the Britiſh, and, notwithſtanding his diligence and activity, were fortunate enough to effect their efcape. When, however, on his return to Portfmouth, he fell in with a French privateer, called the Poſtillion, belonging to St. Jean de Luz, which he captured and afterwards burnt. No farther mention is made of him during the remainder of the year than as having, in the month of June, cap-

---

* See page 178.

tured a small privateer belonging to St. Maloes, called the Jean Baptiste.

In 1758 he served under lord Howe in the small squadron which covered the various desultory expeditions against different parts of the coast of France; and, at the unfortunate and perilous affair in St. Cas bay, commanded the flat-bottomed boats which took off the troops. This service, which acquired the utmost activity and presence of mind in the midst of the most imminent danger, he executed with all the adroitness and attention possible; so that to his exertions, aided by those of the gallant officers employed under him, we may fairly attribute, that the loss, sustained by the army on that melancholy occasion, great as it proved, was not far more extensive and lamentable. In 1759 he was employed as senior captain with the nominal rank of commodore of a small squadron, stationed off the coast of France, for the double purpose of protecting the British commerce from privateers, and watching the motions of the armament which lay ready for sea in the port of Brest. In the first mentioned part of his occupation his success was confined to the capture of one or two inconsiderable vessels; but in the second and more consequential object of his employment he was far more fortunate towards the close of the year. He took his station in Quiberon Bay, where he effectually blocked a numerous fleet of transports, which were to have taken on board the troops intended to be convoyed, by the marquis de Conflan's fleet, for the invasion of Ireland. This judicious measure adopted by the British government, and the great diligence used by Mr. Duff in the execution of his orders, contributed very much to impede the projected expedition, and at length to render it abortive.

The first object of the French admiral, when he put to sea in the month of November, in consequence of sir Edward Hawke and his fleet having been blown off the coast, was the destruction of Mr. Duff and his little squadron, consisting of four fifty-gun ships, the Minerva, Vengeance, Venus, and Saphire frigates. M. de Conflans was actually in chace of those ships when sir Edward came up with him; and it is not impossible but that glorious victory might be in some degree owing to his having too eagerly pursued, what he deemed a certain prize, and

by

by that means thrown himself so near the British fleet, that his escape back into Brest became impracticable. Mr. Duff was, not long after this time, promoted to the Foudroyant, of eighty guns, a prize taken from the enemy sometime before, by the Monmouth. He is not otherwise mentioned during the remainder of the war. We know of no subsequent command held by this gentleman during the time he continued a private captain, though it is by no means improbable, that, at some period during the peace, he was appointed to a guard-ship. On the 31st of March, 1775, he was promoted to the rank of rear-admiral of the blue; and, on the 24th of the ensuing month, was appointed to command on the Newfoundland station. Having hoisted his flag on board the Romney he sailed thither soon afterwards, with the Surprize, of 28 guns; the Aldborough, of 20, and the Egmont schooner, under his command. On the 3d of February, 1776, he was farther advanced to be rear-admiral of the red; but, during his continuance in command at Newfoundland, met with no occurrence in any degree worthy our notice. In the month of September, 1777, he was appointed to the Gibraltar station, whither he immediately afterwards repaired, having his flag on board the Panther, of sixty guns. Here he displayed his usual activity and diligence in the distribution of his cruisers, and met with no inconsiderable success among the American, the French, and Spanish ships, but more particularly the latter, after the commencement of hostilities in that quarter, in 1779. The blockade of Gibraltar being completely formed at the conclusion of the year just mentioned, and a Spanish force, far superior to what the British court deemed it expedient to leave there, being constantly stationed at Algeziras, Mr. Duff returned to England with Mr. Digby and the fleet which, under the chief command of sir George Bridges Rodney, in the month of January 1780, had defeated the Spanish fleet under the command of Don Juan de Langara, and for a time effectually relieved both Minorca and Gibraltar.

During his absence, that is to say, on the 29th of January, 1778, Mr. Duff was advanced to be vice-admiral of the blue; and, on the 19th of March, 1779, to be vice-admiral of the white; but never accepted of any command after his return to England at the time above-stated. On the

the 26th of September he was, moreover, promoted to be vice-admiral of the red. This was the higheſt rank he lived to attain, for, having been long grievouſly afflicted with the gout, he repaired to Bath, in the hope of meeting with ſome relief from the ſalutary effects of thoſe waters in ſuch caſes: but not experiencing the benefit he expected, was on his return to his native country, Scotland; when he died at Queen's-Ferry, in conſequence of a violent attack of the gout in his ſtomach, on the 6th of June, 1787 *.

FALKINGHAM, Edward,—the ſon of commiſſioner Edward Falkingham, whom we have already noticed, was, in 1744, commander of the Baſiliſk bomb-ketch. Afterwards he † was, on the 26th of March, 1746, appointed captain of the Succeſs frigate. We do not meet with any ſubſequent account or mention made of this gentleman till ſome time after the re-commencement of the war with France in 1756. In the ſucceeding year we find him captain of the Sutherland, of fifty guns, one of the fleet ſent on the unſucceſsful expedition, under the command of Mr. Holburne. About the month of October 1758, he was promoted to the Princeſs Caroline, of eighty guns; which ſhip was, not long afterwards, put out of commiſſion and converted into an hoſpital ſhip, as being unfit for any other kind of ſervice. We do not believe him to have ever held any command afterwards; but no particular circumſtances relative to him have come to our knowledge, except that he retired from the ſervice in 1770, being then put on the ſuperannuated liſt with the rank and half-pay of a rear-admiral. He died ſometime in the courſe of the year 1783.

FAULKNOR, Samuel,—in the beginning of the year

---

* This gentleman was of a very ancient Scottiſh family, nearly related to the earl of Fife, who is deſcended from Macduff, eighth thane and afterwards earl of Fife, well known in hiſtory as the deſtroyer of the tyrant Macbeth. Admiral Duff became ſtill more nearly allied to the family of the earl of Fife, by his marriage with the lady Helen Duff, fourth daughter of William, firſt earl of Fife; by her he had three ſons, and one daughter, afterwards married, at Edinburgh, on the 2d of January, 1791, to Mr. Clarke, ſon of Dr. Clarke.

† See vol. iv. p. 41 et ſeq.

1746,

1746, was commander of the Vulture sloop*; from which he was, on April 21st, of the same year, promoted from the rank of commander of a sloop of war, to be captain of the Amazon frigate. From this vessel he was removed into the Fox, a vessel of the same rate as the former, and ordered to Jamaica, where that ship was unhappily lost in an hurricane, which took place on the 11th of September, 1751, and did incredible damage to the shipping in that quarter. Capt. Faulknor and the greater part of his people were fortunately saved, and being afterwards tried he was most honourably acquitted of all blame. He was, after his return to England, about the month of June 1752, appointed captain of the Hind, which, as well as the two former ships he had commanded, carried twenty guns. Early in 1755 he commanded the Lyme, also a twenty-gun ship; but about the month of April, or May, was promoted to the Windsor, of sixty guns, in which command he continued during his life. He is mentioned in some accounts as one of the witnesses examined on the trial of admiral Byng; but we believe this to be a mistake, the Windsor certainly not having been in the action. The Windsor appears to have been principally, if not entirely, employed as a cruising ship, her name not occurring in any of the lines of battle, or lists of armaments sent on

---

* While in this command he is officially mentioned as having performed the following notable piece of service.

"Captain Faulknor, in the Vulture sloop, being arrived at Inverkeithen road, sent the cutter and boats before, who, upon their arrival in Kincardin road, saw a brig come out of Airth, which the rebels had seized in order to transport their cannon from Allowa up the Firth, to batter Sirling castle. The next morning captain Faulkner arrived in the road likewise; and upon the lieutenant of the Pearl's informing him of this, as well as of there being two more vessels in Airth that were liable to be seized by the rebels for the same purpose, he sent the boats manned and armed to burn them, which they effectually performed without the loss of a man, though the rebels fired some platoons from the town. While this was doing the tide fell so low that he could not return to the road that night; upon which the rebels in Airth opened a battery of three pieces of cannon, and in the morning began to play upon him very unexpectedly, but did him no damage. The fire from the sloop dismounted two of their cannon, killed their principal engineer (as they heard by a man of the town) with some others, and drove the rebels not only all out of the town but from their battery also."

Vol. V.   F f   different

different fervices, and in the line of his particular employment capt. Faulknor appears to have been remarkably fuccefsful. Early in 1758 he captured a French Eaft India fhip, bound to Port L'Orient, called the Pacifique; and in the month of April, having been difpatched, in company with the Efcorte frigate, to intercept two French frigates and three ftorefhips, which, according to information received by the admiralty-board, had failed from Dunkirk a few days before, he had the good fortune to fall in with them on the 27th of that month, about fixteen leagues diftant from the Ram Head.

The enemy's two fhips of war brought-to in a line as if they intended to engage the Windfor, while the ftorefhips crouded all the fail they could to the weftward, in the hope of effecting their efcape. When the Windfor had fetched within about two gun-fhot of the frigates they alfo made all the fail they could, ftanding towards their own coaft. Captain Faulknor obferving this, difpatched the Efcorte after the ftore-fhips, while he himfelf gave chace to the frigates. He continued the purfuit fome hours, till, finding that the enemy's fhips greatly outfailed him, he abandoned that part of the chace and ftood after the convoy, which was now barely difcernible from his poop. After continuing the chace with the greateft eagernefs during the night, one fhip only was vifible at day-light; this captain Faulknor foon afterwards came up with and captured. She was called the St. Peter, was a large fhip, and had on board nearly four hundred tons of provifions and ftores, with a thoufand ftands of arms, intended for Quebec.

In the fpring of the enfuing year captain Faulknor continued to be employed in the fame line of fervice we have already feen him occupied; and, on April 27th, fell in with four large fhips, which, on being chaced, formed a line to receive him. Captain Faulknor brought the fternmoft to action; upon which her companions broke the line, endeavoured to fave themfelves by flight, and the fhip engaged furrendered. It proved to be the Duc de Chartres, a fhip belonging to the French Eaft India company, and bound to Pondicherry, having on board a cargo, confifting of fixty tons of gunpowder, with one hundred and fifty tons of cordage, provifions, fail-cloth, and other ftores. It was

was pierced for sixty guns, but, being armé en flute, had only twenty-four twelve pounders mounted, with a crew of two hundred and ninety-four men, twenty-eight of whom were killed and eighteen wounded; while the injury sustained by the Windsor amounted to only one man killed and six wounded. The three ships which escaped were armed and laden in the same manner the prize was, but were of different rates, one being pierced for seventy, a second for fifty-four, and the third for twenty-four guns. Captain Faulknor survived this event but a very short time, dying on the 28th of May following.

FERGUSON, John.—This gentleman, in the early part of the year 1746, was commander of the Furnace bomb, then employed as a cruiser off the coast of Scotland*. He rendered himself so conspicuous on that station by his activity, diligence, and general conduct, that he was, on the sixth of October in the same year, promoted, as it is said, in consequence of the express interference and recommendation of the duke of Cumberland, to be captain of the Nightingale, a new frigate then just launched. During the ensuing year we believe him to have been principally employed as a cruiser; and in the month, either of September or October, he again very much distinguished himself by the capture of a French ship of somewhat superior force, called the Dauphin Royal, carrying twenty-two guns and one hundred and fifty men. The enemy made a very obstinate though running fight, and was not overpowered till after a contest of ten hours continuance. No farther mention is made of him till the year 1753, when we find him commanding the Porcupine sloop, on the coast of Scotland, and very actively employed in scouring that quarter, and preventing the return of the rebel chiefs, many of whom, after having escaped to France, it was then rumoured, were on the point of attempting to repair again to their native country, in the hope of exciting some fresh insurrection †.

We have no account of him after this time till the year 1758, when he was captain of the Prince of Orange, a fourth rate of sixty guns, one of the ships sent on the

---

* " Captain Fergufon, of the Furnace, has seized eight hundred stands of arms at M'Donald, of Barrasdale's-house, in the isle of Rafay."—Gaz. N̰,o. 8540.

† He was not long afterwards appointed regulating officer on the same station.

expedition againſt Louiſburg*, under the command of Mr. Boſcawen. He remained in the fame ſtation during a conſiderable ſpace of time, but neither himſelf nor his ſhip are again noticed till the year 1762, when the Prince of Orange was one of the Channel fleet under the orders of ſir Edward Hawke, and his royal highneſs the late duke of York. In both the ſervices laſt-mentioned, as well as every other in which he was employed during the war, he appears to have unfortunately had no opportunity of encreaſing either his fame or fortune. After the concluſion of the war he was, about the month of June 1763, appointed to the Romney, of fifty guns, but quitted that command ſoon afterwards, and was appointed to the Firme, a fourth rate of ſixty guns; as he afterwards was to the Prince of Orange, a ſhip of the ſame force. He died on the 13th of June, 1767.

FERRERS, Waſhington Shirley†, Earl of, — was the ſecond ſon of Lawrence, third earl of Ferrers, and Anne, fourth

---

* An anecdote is related of this gentleman in Entick's Hiſtory, which we think it would be an act of injuſtice to him to ſuppreſs. The coaſt in the neighbourhood of Louiſburg was ſo extremely well fortified, both by art and nature, that it was generally deemed almoſt an impracticability to effect a landing: the admiral took the advice of each commander ſeparately, and, to uſe the hiſtorian's own words, " It coming to the turn of captain Ferguſone, an old, brave and experienced officer, whom Mr. Boſcawen had requeſted from the lords of the admiralty to attend him in this ſervice, and in whoſe opinion and conduct on the moſt trying occaſions he could place great confidence. This captain having delivered himſelf in the moſt reſpectful terms in regard to the opinions of his brethren, whoſe reaſons the admiral ingenuouſly related to him, and deſpiſing the arguments drawn from the danger of the ſervice, for proving an impracticability without an actual attempt to land, and to force the enemy's poſts with all the art and ſtrength in their power, he adviſed the admiral, for his own honour and the glory of his country, to exert that power with which he was inveſted, and not to leave it to the uncertain reſolutions of a council of war, which had been ſo fatal at Minorca, at Rochfort, and even at Hallifax, to the diſgrace of all concerned, and to the extreme loſs of the nation."

The admiral acquieſced in the juſtneſs of the captain's obſervation on councils of war; thanked him for his open and honeſt advice; reſolved to call no council, but ſtrictly to adhere to his inſtructions, which were to land the troops on the iſland of Cape Breton.

† The ancient family of Shirley derive their deſcent from Saſuallo, or Sewallus de Etingdon, whoſe name (ſays Dugdale in his Antiquities of Warwickſhire) argues him to be of the old Engliſh ſtock:
which

fourth daughter to fir Walter Clarges, of Afton, in the county of Hertford, bart. Having betaken himfelf to a maritime life, and undergone the neceffary years of probation, as well as paffed through the feveral more fubordinate ranks of midfhipman, lieutenant, and commander, with the higheft credit and reputation, he was, on the 19th of April, 1746, appointed captain of the Fox frigate. He remained but a very fhort time in this fhip, having been, early in the enfuing year, promoted to the Dover, of forty-four guns. From this fhip he removed into the Renown, a frigate captured by him a fhort time before, while captain of the Dover. At the latter end of the year 1753 he was appointed to the Mermaid frigate, in which he probably continued till the commencement of the war with France, in 1756. In 1758 he was captain of the Duc D'Aquitain, of fixty guns, and the only fubfequent command in which we find him mentioned, is that of the Temple, a fhip of the line, carrying feventy guns, one of the Channel fleet under the orders of fir Edward Hawke, which totally defeated that of France, on the 20th of November, 1759, in Quiberon Bay. Captain Shirley on this occafion diftinguifhed in a very confpicuous manner, but fucceeding to the title of earl Ferrers, on the death of his unfortunate brother, Lawrence, the fourth earl, on the 5th of May, 1760, he from that time quitted the naval fervice. On the 14th of December, 1761, he was elected fellow of the royal fociety, in compliment to him for a feries of very accurate obfervations he made on the tranfit of Venus over the fun, on the fixth of June preceding, and which he had communicated to that learned body, together with many other useful and interefting difcoveries, tending to the improvement of mathematical and nautical knowledge. His lordfhip having for many years, as we have already ftated, declined the fervice, continued a long time at the head of the lift as the fenior captain capable of ferving; but after-

---

which Sewallus refided at nether Etingdon in com. Warwick about the reign of king Edward the Confeffor; which place had been the feat of his anceftors, as there is reafon to believe, for many generations before.

wards, as a very proper and honourable testimony of the abilities he had displayed when actually engaged in service, was, on the 31st of March, 1775, advanced to be rear-admiral of the white, which was his first appointment in the rank of a flag-officer. On the 3d of February, 1776, he was moreover promoted to be vice-admiral of the blue. This was the highest rank his lordship lived to attain to, he dying at Stanton Harold, in Leicestershire, on the 1st of October, 1778, was buried there. He married Anne, daughter of —— Elliot, of Plymouth, esq. but had no issue.

HARLAND, Sir Robert,—was appointed a lieutenant in the navy on the 25th of February, 1742, and served under Mr. Mathews, at the time of the encounter with the French and Spanish fleets off Toulon, as fourth lieutenant of the Namur. In the month of January 1745, he was advanced to be commander of the Scipio fireship. From this time we have no account of him till his promotion, on the 19th of March, 1746, to be captain of the Tilbury. He retained this command till the end of the year 1747, when he was made captain of the Nottingham, of sixty guns, one of the squadron stationed to cruise in soundings, under the orders of sir Edward Hawke. He had served under that gallant officer, during the latter part of his service as captain of the Tilbury. In this ship he distinguished himself, in the most conspicuous manner, at the attack and defeat of L'Etendiere's squadron, so that rear-admiral Hawke, in his account of the action, makes particular mention of him in the following terms. " Capt. Harland, in the Tilbury, observing that she (one of the enemy's ships) fired single guns at us, in order to dismast us, stood on the other tack between her and the Devonshire, and gave her a very smart fire." Soon after his appointment to the Nottingham, in consequence of the death of captain Saumarez, who was killed in the action just-mentioned, he had a fresh opportunity of distinguishing himself in the attack of the Magnanime, a French ship of war, carrying seventy-four guns and six hundred and eighty-six men, commanded by the marquis D'Albert, chef d'escadre. This ship was discovered by the squadron on the last day of January, 1747-8. The Nottingham, with the Portland, captain Stevens, being ordered to chase, captain

Harland

Harland got up with the enemy about ten o'clock, and immediately began to engage, as did the Portland, which ship was a confiderable diftance aftern at the commencement of the action, in about an hour afterwards. The fea ran fo high as to prevent both the affailants and the enemy from opening their lower ports, and ferved to prolong the action till four in the afternoon, owing to the uncertainty of firing with effect in fuch a fwell. In this encounter the Nottingham had fixteen men killed and eighteen wounded *; but the injury fuftained by the prize amounted to forty-five men killed and one hundred and five wounded.

After the conclufion of the war, an event which took place not long after this time, Mr. Harland was appointed captain of the Monarch guardfhip, at Portfmouth, where we find him, in the month of June 1749, one of the members of the court-martial, affembled on board the Invincible, for the trial of captain Dudley, of the Chefterfield, and the mutineers who had attempted to run away with that fhip. He was next appointed to the Effex, a third rate of fixty-four guns, in 1755, and afterwards removed into the Conqueror, a third rate of feventy-four guns, one of the fquadron fent into the Mediterranean, in the year 1759, under the orders of Mr. Bofcawen. He was one of the commanders detached by the admiral, as already related in the account of admiral Callis, and Mr. Bofcawen himfelf†, to burn two fhips which lay at the entrance of Toulon harbour. On this perilous, though unfuccefsful occafion, being cannonaded by two heavy mafked batteries, he behaved with the greateft firmnefs, intrepidity, and fpirit. This fhip having returned to England not long afterwards, captain Harland quitted her, and we do not find him mentioned as holding any command during the remainder of the war, or, indeed, as long as he continued a private captain, a ftation from which he was advanced, to be rear-admiral of the blue, on the 18th of October, 1770. Almoft immediately afterwards he was appointed to command-in-chief in the

---

* The lofs of the Portland, and the fhare that fhip held in this action, have been already related, page 231.
† See vol. iv. p. 331. and vol. v. p. 138.

East Indies*, and sent thither with a small squadron, consisting of four ships, the Northumberland, of seventy guns, his own ship; the Orford and Buckingham, of the same force; and the Warwick of fifty guns, which were ordered thither to counteract any attempt that might be made by the French against our settlements in that quarter, that nation having caused jealousy in the British, by sending thither a force more than usually formidable for a time of profound peace. No occurrence, however, in the least degree worthy our remembrance took place during the time he was absent on this station, from whence he returned in 1775, and arrived at Portsmouth on the 8th of May.

On the 31st of March preceding this, he was advanced to be rear-admiral of the red; as he was, on the 3d of February, in the year ensuing, to be vice-admiral of the blue; in 1777, of the white; and, in 1778, of the red. He had, however, no command till the appearances of approaching hostilities with France, in 1778, became serious: he was then appointed second flag officer of the main or Channel fleet, under the orders of Mr. Keppel. He hoisted his flag first on board the Hector, in the month of March, and removed it quickly afterwards into the Queen, of ninety guns; in which ship he continued to serve during the remainder of the year, and was fortunate enough, amidst the tremendous distraction and violence of parties, which then so strangely convulsed the service, to incur the censure of none, and merit the respect of all. The circumstances of the action are too recent, too generally known, and in other places too fully descanted on, to render any recapitulation of them necessary. He continued in service only during the remainder of the year, in which period no occurrence took place memorable enough to merit our particular attention. The retirement of Mr. Keppel we believe to have had considerable influence in causing that of sir Robert also: but whatever might be the cause he never accepted of any subsequent command.

On the 8th of April, 1782, he was advanced to be admiral of the blue, having, on the 30th of March pre-

---

* On the 19th of March, 1771, he was created a baronet.

ceding,

ceding, been appointed one of the commiffioners for executing the office of lord high admiral, a ftation he continued to hold till the 28th of January, 1783, within a very fhort time of his death. He died at Sproughton, not having attained any higher rank as a flag-officer, on the 28th of February, 1783.

HARMON, William,—after having been a fubordinate officer* in the royal navy, is, by fome accounts, ftated to have been many years employed in the fervice, firft of the Weft India merchants, and afterwards of the poft-office, in which he is faid to have commanded a packet boat. In 1741 he was lieutenant of the Folkftone, a fifth rate of 44 guns, and, in 1745, of the Pembroke, a fourth rate of 60. On the 26th of January, 1746, he was appointed captain of the Richmond frigate, and is not otherwife particularly mentioned during the war, or the fucceeding peace. Sometime after the commencement of the war, he was, about the year 1762, appointed to the St. Anne, of fixty-four guns. He quickly afterwards removed into the Berwick, a fhip of the fame force. He is faid in fome accounts to have incurred cenfure during the time he held the latter command, but of this we have no information that we dare rely on, nor have we any farther particulars relative to this gentleman, except that he died on the January 19, 1766.

HOWE, Richard, Earl. — This noble perfon, who is ftill living, is the third fon of fir Emanuel Scrope, the fecond lord vifcount Howe, and Mary-Sophia-Charlotte, eldeft daughter to the baron Kielmanfegge. Having betaken himfelf to a maritime life, he was, after paffing through the different fubordinate ftations†, on the 10th of April, 1746, promoted to be captain of the Triton

---

* A midfhipman or mafter's mate.
† At the time of the Scottifh rebellion, in 1745, we find him commanding the Baltimore on that ftation; and is particularly mentioned, in the journal of the fiege of Fort William, in the following terms.

"Tuefday, March the 1ft, 1746, the Baltimore, captain Richard Howe, went up towards Killarndy Barns in order to protect the landing of our men. He fired feveral fhot, and threw fome cohorn fhells, and let one hovel on fire; but could not attempt landing, for the rebels were intrenched by a hollow road, or rill, and in great numbers. The Baltimore's guns, being only four-pounders, had no effect on the ftone walls of thefe barns, which the rebels had loopholed. We brought our people back without any damage."

frigate; but no farther particular mention is made of him during the continuance of the war, except that he commanded the Rippon, a fourth rate of sixty guns, on the coast of Guinea; and the Cornwall, a third rate of eighty guns, under admiral Knowles. In the early part of the year 1751 he was made captain of the Glory, of forty guns: at the conclusion of the same year he was appointed to the Mary yacht, as successor to captain Allen, then deceased; but quitted this station in the month of May 1752, on being then commissioned to the Dolphin frigate. He was immediately afterwards ordered to the Streights, where he was employed in many delicate services, which he executed with the greatest adroitness*. He returned to England in the course of the year 1754; and, in the beginning of the ensuing, we find him commanding the Dunkirk, of sixty guns, one of the ships put into commission in consequence of the apprehended rupture with France; and which, in consequence of that expectation, was one of the fleet ordered to America under the orders of Mr. Boscawen. In their passage thither a very consequential event took place, in which captain Howe, much to his honour, bore a very distinguished share.

The particulars of this transaction have been variously related; but, from several corroborating circumstances, the following appears to be nearly the true state of the fact. The British fleet on its passage fell in with some ships separated from the French squadron under M. Bois de la Mothe. The Dunkirk, the Defiance, and some other ships were ordered to chace. The Dunkirk coming up with the Alcide, captain Howe hailed the captain, and civilly requested him to attend him down to the admiral. The French captain refused, and quaintly asked if it was peace or war? Captain Howe replied, he knew nothing of that, but was ordered to bring his ship down. The French captain again renewed his question, and in the same terms. He received the same answer, with an

---

* " Madrid, August 26th, 1753.
" We learn from Gibraltar, that the honourable captain Howe, commander of his majesty's ship the Dolphin, now in that bay, having been ordered to go to the port of Sallee, to inform himself of the intention of the Moors, with regard to Great Britain, was answered, that their design was, to observe their treaties with his Britannic majesty."

additional

additional requeſt, that he would prepare for the worſt, as he (captain Howe) ſaid he expected every moment a ſignal from the admiral to fire into him, in conſequence of his not bringing to.

To this account is added, that captain Howe obſerving a number of land-officers and their ladies, with many ſoldiers, ſtanding thick upon deck, he admoniſhed them to go below, which being ſoon afterwards complied with, the French ſhip, as it is confidently ſaid, fired into the Dunkirk; and the action, after ſome continuance, ended in the ſurrender of the Alcide*. No other memorable occurrence appears to have taken place during the abſence of the fleet on this expedition. During the enſuing year captain Howe retained the ſame command, but is not particularly mentioned, except as having poſſeſſed himſelf of a ſmall iſland on the French coaſt, in the neighbourhood of Guernſey, and having made the garriſon of the ſmall fort which defended it, amounting to about one hundred men, priſoners. He not long after this was promoted to the Magnanime, of 74 guns; in which ſhip he ſerved during the year 1757, as one of the fleet under the orders

---

* The following extract of a letter appeared in many of the periodical publications and newſpapers of the time, ſaid to have been received from on board the Monarque.

"On the 6th of June, being to the ſouthward of Cape Race, and the fog clearing up at break of day, we eſpied four ſail of French men of war four miles to the windward: the ſignal was given to chace and clear ſhip, which we obeyed; but the fog returning we loſt ſight of them. All the 7th foggy. On the 8th clear weather.

At ſun riſe we ſaw three ſail, which we obſerved perceived us at the ſame time, and prepared for an engagement, their hencoops, tables, cabins, hogs, &c. being floating. The Dunkirk ſtole away from us, and at twelve o'clock was alongſide the ſternmoſt ſhip of the French. The admiral ſeeing this, and we not being three miles off, the red flag was hoiſted at the fore-top-gallant-maſt head; upon which captain Howe diſcharged his guns below and aloft, and the French commodore did the ſame. By the time they had exchanged two broadſides we came up, both flags flying. He ſeeing that, brought the ſhip by the lee, with all ſails aback, and fired his lower and upper tier, but killed not a man: the enemy's ſhot tore our fore-ſail, killed two men in the Torbay, and ſeven in the Dunkirk. We fired two lower deckers and then ſhe ſtruck. She mounted ſixty-four guns, and had on board nine hundred men, moſt forces; the general being killed in the fight, the governor of Louiſburg and four officers of note were taken priſoners, and 30,000 l. ſterling."

of fir Edward Hawke, on the honourable, though unsuccessful, expedition againſt Rochfort. He was on this occaſion ordered, as may be well remembered, by all in any degree converſant in the hiſtory of his time, to attack the fort on the Iſle of Aix, an aſſault which he conducted with the greateſt vigour; and a conqueſt he happily atchieved, after an hour's cannonade, without either difficulty or injury. This was the moſt material and ſubſtantial ſucceſs which graced the expedition. In the following year * he removed into the Eſſex, of ſixty-four guns, and was appointed commodore of the light ſquadron † immediately deſtined to cover the landing of the ſmall army commanded by the duke of Marlborough, who was ſent to attempt the reduction of St. Maloes, while a fleet, under the orders of lord Anſon, proceeded off Breſt to prevent any interruption from the naval force in that quarter. Mr. Howe ſailed from St. Helen's on the 1ſt of June; and the troops, after being landed, completed the buſineſs on which they were ſent, as far as they were competent, without undertaking a regular ſiege. Having deſtroyed all the magazines, together with the ſhipping in the port, to the amount of one hundred and twenty ſail, they were reimbarked, without loſs or even interruption, on the 16.' of the ſame month. The ſquadron and the tranſports next procceded to Cherburg, an attempt which the unfavourable weather compelled the commander-in-chief to abandon for that time: ſcarcity of proviſions and other neceſſaries compelled him to return; and the troops being diſembarked, were ordered to encamp, for the purpoſe of refreſhment, on the Iſle of Wight.

---

* On the 10th of March, 1758, he married Mary, daughter of Chiverton Hartopp, of Welby, in the county of Leiceſter, eſq.

† Its force conſiſted of the Eſſex, of ſixty-four guns; the Rocheſter, Portland, and Deptford, of fifty guns each; the Pallas and Brilliant, of thirty-ſix; the Richmond and Active of thirty-two; the Maidſtone, of twenty-eight; the Flamborough and Roſe, of twenty; the Succeſs, Saltaſh, Swallow, Speedwell, and Diligence ſloops, of ſixteen; the Cormorant, of fourteen; the Pluto and Salamander fireſhips; two bomb-ketches, the Infernal and Granada; ten cutters; one hundred tranſports with the troops; twenty tenders and two ſtoreſhips. Theſe were a few days afterwards joined by the Iſis, of fifty guns, and four tranſports with troops.

The duke of Marlborough and a part of his army were ordered immediately afterwards to Germany. Lieutenant-general Bligh was appointed to command the remainder, which again being embarked, were ordered to return to the coaſt of France, as well for the purpoſe of alarming the enemy, as, by a diverſion, compelling them to make large detachments from their army in Germany, as in the hope of effecting ſome material injury, wherever it was found poſſible to make any ſerious impreſſion. His lord-ſhip, who had a ſhort time before this ſucceeded to the title by the death of his brother, who was unfortunately killed in America, before Ticonderago, ſailed from St. Helen's on the 1ſt of Auguſt, and came to an anchor in the bay of Cherburg on the 6th of the ſame month. No other attempt or attack was made that night, except by throwing a few ſhells into the town.

At ſeven o'clock the next morning the fleet got under weigh and brought up in the bay of Maris, about two leagues to the weſtward of the town. The troops were landed the ſame afternoon. The fortifications, which were intended for the defence of the place, were in a very unfiniſhed ſtate, ſo that poſſeſſion was taken of them without oppoſition. The braſs cannon mounted on them were tranſported to England. Nearly two hundred pieces of iron cannon and mortars were rendered unſer-viceable: the celebrated baſon was ruined, and twenty-ſeven ſail of ſhips and veſſels found in the harbour were deſtroyed. All this being accompliſhed without the ſmalleſt loſs, the troops were taken on board the tranſ-ports, without the ſmalleſt oppoſition, on the 16th.

Happy had it been if the Britiſh government, unintoxi-cated with theſe unalloyed ſucceſſes, which had incontro-vertibly proved to all the world, how vulnerable France was even in her vitals, had been content with what had been already atchieved, without making any farther at-tempt, at leaſt with ſo inconſiderable a force. General Bligh was inſtructed to proceed, after the deſtruction of the forts and baſon of Cherburg, to keep the coaſt of France in a perpetual ſtate of alarm, as long as the wea-ther and other circumſtances would permit. A ſecond attack on St. Maloes was reſolved; but the fleet was, by contrary winds, compelled to run over to its own coaſt.

After

After having continued two days in Weymouth roads it returned to its original object, and anchored in the bay of St. Lunaire, two leagues to the westward of St. Maloes, on the 4th of September. The destruction of the shipping in the harbour of Briac, near the town first-mentioned, was the first object. According to common report these amounted to one hundred and fifty sail. The orders were completely and successfully executed, but the number of ships and vessels was found not to exceed fifteen. After some days spent in deliberating with the land-officers, as to the practicability of any farther attack on St. Maloes itself, it was finally determined that success was hopeless, and that the idea should be totally abandoned.

Nothing now remained but to reimbark the troops, an operation which, being impracticable in the place where they landed, it was determined to march over land to the bay of St. Cas, which, on being reconnoitered, was found to be the nearest spot convenient and proper for the purpose. His lordship accordingly proceeded thither with his squadron, and immediately made all the necessary dispositions that lay within his department. The length of the march, and many other causes, contributed to retard the progress of the army on shore so long, that the French were enabled to collect and push forward a far superior force to harrass them in their retreat, and render their re-embarkation extremely hazardous, if not impracticable. No interruption, however, was attempted till the whole of the army, the rear-guard excepted, were actually on board the transports. The duc D'Aguillon, the French general-in-chief, then pushed forward, in the hope of capturing or destroying this devoted remnant, amounting to about fourteen hundred men.

Lord Howe, who was perfectly aware that the enemy might possibly meditate some stroke of this kind, had taken every precaution in his power to counteract them: he had stationed six frigates, four bomb-ketches, and two sloops, as close to the shore as possible. Their fire made considerable havock in the French army, and much impeded their attack, till an oversight, unfortunately committed by general Drury, who commanded on shore, in marching forward to meet the enemy instead of waiting behind a parapet of sand, which had been thrown up by the enemy on the beach, for other purposes some time before, rendered it impossible for the frigates and vessels to continue the cannonade, without probably doing more injury to the British troops than the French themselves. Nothing now remained but to dispatch all the boats, with the utmost expedition, to bring off as many as they could pick up. This was a service attended with the utmost peril and personal risk, insomuch that, in several of the boats, ten or twelve men, out of twenty, who were employed to row them, were killed; and in one of them sixteen, with the lieutenant. His lordship finding that this tremendous havock considerably intimidated the seamen, and that without some exertions the greater part of those who still remained on shore must be sacrificed, went in his own barge into the centre of the enemy's fire, and, standing up, began to encourage the men, by his voice and example, to despise the danger which appeared to threaten them, and exert themselves to the utmost for the preservation of their unfortunate fellow countrymen.

His lordship's heroism counteracted the fear which appeared to pervade the seamen: every body was alert; each man seemed animated almost beyond precedent; and many lives, which would certainly have been otherwise lost, were preserved by this singular and highly intrepid exertion[*]. After this check his lordship returned to Spithead with his squadron and the transports. The troops were instantly disembarked, and all farther attempts of a similar nature abandoned, at least for the current year. Immediately on his return into port his lordship removed back into his former ship, the Magnanime, in which he was employed, during the ensuing year, in the Channel, but had not any particular opportunity of distinguishing himself, till the month of November, at the memorable defeat of the marquis de Conflans, in which he engaged and captured the Hero, of seventy-four guns; but being prevented by the inclemency of the weather from taking possession of the prize, it unfortunately ran on shore and was irrecoverably lost. On the 22d of March, 1760, he

---

[*] His royal highness the late duke of York attended his lordship, on board the Essex, in this expedition, as a midshipman.

was appointed colonel of the Chatham divifion of marines, and the only enterprize in which he appears, owing to the extreme inaction of the French fleet, to have been concerned, was the attack of a fmall French fort on the Ifle Dumet, againft which he was ordered by fir Edward Hawke, in company with the Bedford and Prince Frederic. It furrendered after a flight refiftance, without effecting any injury to the affailants.

During the year 1761, in confequence of the palfied manner in which naval war was conducted on the part of the French, no particular mention is made of his lordfhip out of the ordinary routine of fervice. In 1762 he commanded, in turn with fir Thomas Stanhope, the fquadron ftationed in Bafque road, and off the coaft of France; on which fervice nothing occurred fufficiently confequential to require any particular detail. Towards the middle of the fummer he removed into the Princefs Amelia, of eighty guns, having accepted the command of that fhip as captain to his royal highnefs the duke of York, who had obtained the rank of rear-admiral of the blue, and ferved as fecond in command, under fir Edward Hawke, of the fquadron ftationed in the Channel to watch the motions of the remnants of the French naval force. For the reafons already given, it is not neceffary to enter into farther or more circumftantial account. During the fucceeding peace his lordfhip does not appear in any command*. In 1765 he was appointed treafurer of the navy, an office he continued to hold, as well as that of colonel of marines, till his promotion, on the 18th of October, 1770, to be rear-admiral of the blue. He experienced no farther advancement till the 31ft of March, 1775, when he was appointed rear-admiral of the white †; as he was, on the 3d of February, 1776‡, to be vice-admiral of the blue. In a very fhort time afterwards he was nominated commander-in-chief of the fleet employed, or to be em-

---

* We muft not, however, forget to record, that he was, on the 23d of April, 1763, nominated one of the commiffioners for executing the office of lord high admiral, a ftation which he continued to hold, through two commiffions, till the 30th of Auguft, 1765.

† At the general election which took place in this year, he was chofen reprefentative in parliament for the borough of Dartmouth.

‡ The admiralty lift fays on the 7th of December, 1775.

ployed

ployed on the American ſtation. Having hoiſted his flag on board the Eagle, of ſixty-four guns, which ſhip was equipped purpoſely for him, he arrived off Halifax, without having experienced any ſiniſter accident, on the 1ſt of July. The various events which took place during the American conteſt, are not only too recent, but alſo bear too little relation to his lordſhip to cauſe any very particular account of them neceſſary. Suffice it to ſay, every enterprize in which the fleet was concerned was uniformly ſucceſsful; every undertaking that was propoſed by the general on ſhore was warmly ſupported by the fleet; and, without affection to party, we may truly ſay, the unſucceſsful termination of the American conteſt is certainly attributable to cauſes which his lordſhip was not, in the ſmalleſt degree, concerned in the prevention of.

The conqueſt of New York, of Rhode Iſland, of Philadelphia, of every ſettlement within the power or reach of a naval force, are irrefragable proofs of his abilities and attention, and are ſufficient to ſilence the breath of calumny.

The year 1778 opens to us a new ſcene; France became a party in the conteſt, and ſent to America a fleet, under the count D'Eſtaing, far ſuperior to any force then poſſeſſed by Britain in that quarter. That under his lordſhip's command conſiſted only of ſix ſmall ſhips of the line, three of fifty guns, and ſome ſmaller veſſels and frigates, the greater part out of condition, and nearly unfit for ſervice; while Mr. D'Eſtaing's amounted to twelve large ſhips of the line beſides frigates and ſmaller veſſels. Mr. Byron, indeed, had been diſpatched from England with a formidable ſquadron, but it was ſo completely diſperſed and damaged by continued ſtorms, that ſcarcely two together reached the American coaſt: ſome put back, and thoſe which were enabled to proceed to their place of deſtination arrived there in a very diſabled ſtate.

Such was the ſituation of affairs when the French ſquadron, amounting to fifteen ſail, anchored off Sandy Hook. His lordſhip had uſed the utmoſt diligence in putting his ſhips in condition to meet the enemy: he was fortunately joined by the Cornwall, of ſeventy-four; the Raiſonable, of ſixty-four; the Centurion, and Renown, of fifty guns each; with ſome frigates and ſmaller veſſels; but ſtill there was

was a very manifest disproportion between his force and that of the enemy. The French admiral weighed anchor and put to sea on the 22d of July, and, after some movements, proceeded to Rhode Island for the professed purpose of co-operating with the American army, under general Sullivan, in attempting the reduction of that important post. His lordship, having made every possible exertion in his power, put to sea on the 9th of August, and arrived off Rhode Island the same evening. On the morning of the 10th the French admiral put to sea with his whole force, but such was his superiority that his lordship prudently considering the safety, not only of himself, and his whole fleet, but that of all the British possessions in America depended on the event, wisely determined to act merely on the defensive, unless some extraordinary and unforeseen occurrence should afford him an opportunity of attacking the enemy with manifest advantage on his own part.

The remainder of that day, as well as the whole of the succeeding, were spent in manœuvres productive of no remarkable occurrence. Towards the close of the second evening his lordship shifted his flag from the Eagle to the Apollo frigate, that he might be the better enabled to direct the subsequent operations of the squadron. A violent gale of wind arose immediately afterwards, dispersed both the squadrons, and separated his lordship, who still continued on board the Apollo, with the Ardent, Centurion, two forty-fours, and some frigates, from all the rest of his force. The Apollo itself sustained so much damage in the gale that his lordship was obliged to remove into the Phœnix, as, in a very few hours afterwards, he did into the Centurion. The storm just mentioned prevented the general engagement which was on the brink of taking place when it arose; but distinct encounters happened between three ships of his lordship's squadron, and as many of the French, superior in force, all which uniformly ended with the highest credit, though not attended with particular advantage to the British arms.

His lordship, immediately on his return into port, resigned his command to Mr. Byron, who had reached America with his scattered squadron, and repaired to England with the Eagle. He arrived at St. Helen's without having experienced any disaster, or memorable
occur-

occurrence, on the 25th of October. He immediately afterwards ſtruck his flag; and, though we believe frequently ſolicited for that purpoſe, did not accept of any ſubſequent command till the year 1782. In this interval we conſequently have nothing in our line to record, concerning him, except his promotion, on the 29th of January, 1778, to be vice-admiral of the white; and, on the 19th of March in the following year, to the ſame rank in the red ſquadron. When the complete and memorable change of miniſtry took place in the ſpring of the year 1782, he was advanced to the dignity of a peer of Great Britain, by the title of Viſcount Howe, of Langar, in the county of Nottingham, by patent bearing date April the 20th*, and immediately afterwards accepted the command of the fleet then equipping for the purpoſe of attempting the relief of Gibraltar. Its force was, as the conſequence of the expedition required, extremely formidable, though far inferior to that of the combined fleets of France and Spain which lay ready in Gibraltar bay to diſpute its entrance. It conſiſted of thirty-four ſhips of the line in ſix diviſions, under his lordſhip, as commander-in-chief, vice-admirals Barrington and Milbank, rear-admirals Hood and Hughes, and commodore Hotham. That of the enemy amounted to forty-ſix ſhips of the line, under eight admirals, or chefs d'eſcadres. The Britiſh fleet, with its convoy, entered the Streights on the morning of the 11th of October, and about five o'clock in the afternoon arrived off the bay of Gibraltar. Previous to this, the neceſſary diſpoſitions had been made, and inſtructions given to the Panther and Buffalo, under whoſe immediate protection the ſtoreſhips and victuallers were placed, to paſs with them under the guns of the fortreſs. The Panther and four only of her charge were able to effect it; the Buffalo with the remainder, and all the ſhips of war, were ſwept, by the rapidity of the current, into the Mediterranean.

On the 13th of October the combined fleet of the enemy put to ſea with an apparent determination of deciding the conteſt by a ſerious action, or, at leaſt, preventing the

---

* On the 8th of the ſame month he had been previouſly advanced to the rank of admiral of the blue.

introduction of any farther fupplies into the befieged garrifon. A favourable change of wind to the eaftward on the enfuing day enabled his lordfhip to pafs fuch of the ftorefhips, as were then with the fleet, into the bay, and without interruption, as from the circumftance of the enemy having been carried farther into the Mediterranean than the Britifh fleet, and by the fame caufe, his lordfhip was enabled to keep between the convoy and the enemy. Fortune, affifted by judgement, enabled all the reft of the tranfports, which had been ordered away to a fpecial rendezvous when the enemy's fleet appeared in fight on the 14th, in company with the Buffalo, to pafs to their place of deftination on the 18th. This fervice, together with the debarkation of the troops, intended as a reinforcement to the garrifon, the introduction of a proper fupply of ammunition and rum from fome of the fhips of war, was fcarcely effected before the enemy's fleet, having had the fame advantage from the eafterly wind which had fo happily enabled his lordfhip to execute the different objects of his expedition, appeared in fight on the 19th of October, at break of day.

The Britifh fleet was at that time between Europa and Ceuta Point, and confequently fo confined that there was not fufficient room for it to form in a line of battle on either tack: as an additional inducement that his lordfhip fhould avoid an action to the eaftward of the Streights, fuch fhips, if any, that might be difabled in the encounter would have had no port of refuge for refitment; he confequently ftood through the narrow channel which feparates Africa from Europe, in clofe order, followed by the enemy at the diftance of about three leagues. The Britifh fleet, as foon as it had cleared the Streights, brought to, as did that of the enemy, preferving its former diftance to windward. At daylight both parties began to form the line, a manœuvre which took up confiderable time, both on account of the formidable numbers of which each fleet was compofed, and of there being little or no wind to expedite the operation. Towards the evening, having arranged their whole force, the enemy manifefted fome difpofition of engaging, but with the greateft caution, as will appear very evident from his lordfhip's own account of this fkirmifh.

" The

" The British fleet being formed to leeward to receive them, they were left uninterruptedly to take the diftance at which they fhould think fit to engage. They began their cannonade, at funfet, on the van and rear, feeming to point their chief attack on the latter, and continued their fire along their whole line at a confiderable diftance, and with little effect, until ten at night. It was returned occafionally from different fhips of the fleet, as their nearer approach at times afforded a more favourable opportunity for making any impreffion upon them."

Thus ended this fkirmifh, for it fcarcely deferves the name of a more ferious encounter, and with it every attempt at retaliation made by the enemy for an enterprize, carried into effect in fpite of their utmoft efforts to the contrary, and by a force in the beginning, one-third, at leaft, inferior to their own*; an enterprize which they had exerted every nerve to prevent, by incurring an expence almoft incredible, and collecting a force which they arrogantly and prefumptuoufly boafted, defied oppofition. We having nothing left to add to this account, except that the whole lofs fuftained by the Britifh amounted only to fixty-eight men killed, two hundred and eight wounded, and the Minerva, a naval tranfport†, laden with the baggage of the regiments intended to reinforce the garrifon, captured by the enemy. This great object being atchieved, farther conteft was fruitlefs had the enemy even permitted it. They did not, but, fatisfied with the parade of announcing to the world that they had fought the Britifh fleet, retired into their own ports.

After having made the detachment ordered in his inftructions, his lordfhip returned to England, and arrived at Portfmouth on the 10th of November, not having met with any finifter occurrence whatever during his paffage. Peace being concluded immediately afterwards, he

---

* Their combined fleet originally confifted of fifty fhips of the line: a gale of wind, which arofe on the 10th, as it were awfully to precede the arrival of the Britifh fleet, had blown fix from their anchors, two of which had been driven into the Mediterranean, three put on fhore, one of them under the walls of the garrifon, where it was captured, and the fixth nearly difmafted.

† Which had feparated from the fleet on the night of the 13th.

of courſe quitted his commands, but on the 28th of January, 1783, was nominated firſt commiſſioner for executing the office of lord high admiral. His lordſhip retained this ſtation only till the 8th of April following, when he was ſucceeded by lord viſcount Keppel, whom he again diſplaced on the 30th of December in the ſame year. On the 24th of September, 1787, he was advanced to be admiral of the white, and retained that of firſt commiſſioner of the admiralty till the 16th of July, 1788, when he finally quitted it, and was created an earl of Great Britain on the 19th of Auguſt following, by the title of earl Howe. In 1790, a rupture being apprehended with Spain, his lordſhip took upon him the command of a formidable fleet which was equipped on that occaſion, and hoiſted his flag accordingly on board the Queen Charlotte; but the diſpute being quickly compromiſed, the ſhips were diſmantled and laid up at the cloſe of the year.

On the commencement of the war with France, in 1793, his lordſhip took upon him the command of the main or Channel fleet. During the firſt year in which he filled this high ſtation no very remarkable occurrence took place, except that, in the month of November, a ſlight ſkirmiſh happened with the enemy, which was productive of no material conſequence. In the following ſummer that very memorable encounter took place which will, to the lateſt time, make ſo conſpicuous a figure in the naval annals of Great Britain—the victory obtained on the 1ſt of June. His lordſhip ſailed from St. Helen's on the 2d of May, and on the 28th of the ſame month got ſight of the enemy's fleet. A partial action took place the ſame evening, as alſo on the following day. Theſe ſkirmiſhes were the forerunners of the general and deciſive engagement *. His lordſhip continued to command the fleet

---

* The account of which, as well as of events immediately preceding, we ſhall give in his lordſhip's own words.

" Admiralty-office, June 10, 1794.

" Sir Roger Curtis, firſt captain to admiral earl Howe, arrived this evening with a diſpatch from his lordſhip to Mr. Stephens, of which the following is a copy.

" Queen

fleet some time afterwards; but the enemy, smarting under their severe chastisement, gave him no second opportunity of

"Queen Charlotte at sea, June 2, 1794, Ushant E. half N. 140 leagues.

"Sir,

"Thinking it may not be necessary to make a more particular report of my proceedings with the fleet, for the present information of the lords commissioners of the admiralty, I confine my communications chiefly, in this dispatch, to the occurrences when in presence of the enemy yesterday.

"Finding, on my return off Brest on the 19th past, that the French fleet had, a few days before, put to sea; and receiving, on the same evening, advices from rear-admiral Montagu, I deemed it requisite to endeavour to form a junction with the rear-admiral as soon as possible, and proceeded immediately for the station on which he meant to wait for the return of the Venus.

"But, having gained very credible intelligence, on the 21st of the same month, by which I had reason to suppose the French fleet was then but a few leagues farther to the westward, the course before steered, was altered accordingly.

"On the morning of the 28th the enemy were discovered far to windward, and partial actions took place with them on that evening and the next day.

"The weather gage having been obtained, in the progress of the last mentioned day, and the fleet being in a situation for bringing the enemy to close action the 1st instant, the ships bore up together for that purpose, between seven and eight o'clock in the morning.

"The French, their force consisting of twenty-six ships of the line, opposed to his majesty's fleet of twenty-five (the Audacious having parted company with the sternmost ship of the enemy's line, captured in the night of the 28th) waited for the action, and sustained the attack with their customary resolution.

"In less than an hour after the close action commenced in the centre, the French admiral, engaged by the Queen Charlotte, crowded off, and was followed by most of the ships of his van in condition to carry sail after him, leaving with us about ten or twelve of his crippled or totally dismasted ships, exclusive of one sunk in the engagement. The Queen Charlotte had then lost her fore top-mast, and the main-top-mast fell over the side very soon after.

"The greater number of the other ships of the British fleet were, at this time, so much disabled or widely separated, and under such circumstances with respect to those ships of the enemy in a state for action, and with which the firing was still continued, that two or three, even of their dismantled ships, attempting to get away under a spritsail singly, or smaller sail raised on the stump of the fore-mast, could not be detained.

"Seven

of repeating it. At the death of admiral Forbes, on the 10th of March, 1796, his lordſhip ſucceeded to the high ſtation

> "Seven remained in our poſſeſſion, one of which, however, ſunk before the adequate aſſiſtance could be given to her crew; but many were ſaved.
>
> "The Brunſwick, having loſt her mizen-maſt in the action, and drifted to leeward of the French retreating ſhips, was obliged to put away large to the northward from them. Not ſeeing her chaſed by the enemy, in that predicament, I flatter myſelf ſhe may arrive in ſafety at Plymouth. All the other twenty-four ſhips of his majeſty's fleet re-aſſembled later in the day; and I am preparing to return with them, as ſoon as the captured ſhips of the enemy are ſecured, for Spithead.
>
> "The material injury to his majeſty's ſhips, I underſtand, is confined principally to their maſts and yards, which I conclude will be ſpeedily replaced.
>
> "I have not been yet able to collect regular accounts of the killed and wounded in the different ſhips. Captain Montagu is the only officer of his rank who fell in the action. The numbers of both deſcriptions I hope will prove ſmall, the nature of the ſervice conſidered; but I have the concern of being obliged to add, on the ſame ſubject, that admiral Graves has received a wound in the arm, and that rear-admirals Bowyer and Paſley, as well as captain Hutt of the Queen, have each had a leg taken off; they are, however, (I have the ſatisfaction to hear) in a favourable ſtate under thoſe misfortunes. In the captured ſhips the numbers of killed and wounded appear to be very conſiderable.
>
> "Though I ſhall have, on the ſubject of theſe different actions with the enemy, diſtinguiſhed examples hereafter to report, I preſume the determined bravery of the ſeveral ranks of officers and the ſhips companies employed under my authority, will have been already ſufficiently denoted by the effect of their ſpirited exertions; and, I truſt, I ſhall be excuſed for poſtponing the more detailed narrative of the other tranſactions of the fleet thereon, to be communicated at a future opportunity; more eſpecially as my firſt captain ſir Roger Curtis, who is charged with this diſpatch, will be able to give the farther information the lords commiſſioners of the admiralty may at this time require. It is incumbent on me, neverthelefs, now to add, that I am greatly indebted to him for his councils as well as conduct in every branch of my official duties: and I have ſimilar aſſiſtance, in the late occurrences, to acknowledge from my ſecond captain, ſir Andrew Douglas.
>
> "I am, with great conſideration,
> Sir,
> "Your moſt obedient ſervant,
> "HOWE."
>
> "P.S. The names and force of the captured French ſhips with the fleet is tranſmitted herewith."

"Liſt

ſtation of admiral of the fleet, as being the ſenior naval officer on the liſt of admirals.

HUISH, Henry,—is ſcarcely known to us but as having been appointed captain of the Experiment frigate on the 12th of July, 1746; and of the Deptford, a fifty-gun ſhip, about the month of Auguſt, 1751. He died in England on the 26th of February, 1763, having been, at leaſt during the latter part of his life, unemployed.

HYDE, Frederick,—was lieutenant of the Marlboro' at the time of the well-known encounter with the French and Spaniſh fleets off Toulon, and was one of the witneſſes examined on the ſubſequent trials, particularly that of captain Ambroſe. He was promoted, on the 11th of November, 1746, to be captain of the Gibraltar; but we have not been able to collect any other particulars concerning him, except that he died, on the 21ſt of March, 1764, having been, like the gentleman laſt-mentioned, during the latter part of his life unemployed.

JELFE, Andrews,—was the ſon of Mr. Jelfe, maſon to king George the Second, and, we believe, one of the contractors for erecting Weſtminſter bridge. We find him, at the end of the year 1743, lieutenant of the Victory, having been, as we ſuppoſe, many years previous to that time an officer in the royal navy; from this ſtation he was ſoon removed, and happily for him, the Victory being loſt not long afterwards. He was promoted, about the month of February 1744, to be commander of the Swallow ſloop, and advanced, on the 14th of April, 1746, to be captain of the Port Mahon frigate. He continued in commiſſion during the remainder of the war, and

---

" Liſt of French ſhips captured on the 1ſt day of June, 1794.

La Juſte - -	80 guns.
Sans Pareille - -	80
L'America - -	74
L'Achille - -	74
Northumberland - -	74
L'Impetueux - -	74
Vengeur - -	74 ſunk almoſt immediately upon being taken poſſeſſion of."

" N. B. The ſhip ſtated to have been captured on the evening of the 28th of laſt month, is ſaid by the priſoners to be the Revolutionaire of 120 guns."

was

was employed on the home station as captain of the Assurance, a fifth rate of forty-four guns: nothing farther being mentioned concerning him, except his having been, in the month of December 1747, one of the members of the court-martial assembled at Portsmouth for the trial of captain Fox.

The only subsequent account we have relative to him is, that, in the year 1758, he commanded a seventy-gun ship on the West India station, from whence he returned with a convoy in the month of October. We have no proof of his having held any subsequent command, and know him to have been, during the latter part of the war, unemployed. He died on the 14th of March, 1765.

INNES, Thomas, — was, on the 3d of April, 1746, appointed captain of the Aldborough frigate. In this ship he was soon afterwards ordered to the West Indies, where, on his arrival, he was promoted to the Warwick, as successor to captain Erskine, who was taken by Mr. Knowles, then commodore on that station, to be his captain in the Canterbury. Early in the year 1748 captain Innes was one of the commanders who, under the orders of Mr. Knowles, was engaged in making the successful attack on Port Louis in the month of March, as he was immediately afterwards in that less fortunate one on St. Jago, and the engagement with the Spanish squadron, under Reggio, in the month of September. The Warwick and the Canterbury, commanded by captain Clark, were so far astern at the time the van began to engage, that they could not get into action till after it had continued upwards of two hours. This event is not so remote but that, it may be well remembered, as having created a series of disputes productive of much injury to the service: the admiral censured some of those whom he commanded; and they in their turn were equally free in their animadversions on their superior.

A series of court-martials took place which tended to encrease the ferment, by keeping up the encounter between accusation and recrimination. Repeated duels succeeded to these; and one, in which captain Innes was a principal, with captain Clark, unhappily proved fatal to the former. The cause which immediately gave rise to it was, from the best investigation we have been enabled to make, an unhappy and violent declaration, made by captain Innes,

Innes, that captain Clark had endeavoured to take away his life, by giving falfe evidence againft him. This was a provocation which, it muft certainly be admitted, could not be endured by a gentleman, particularly one in a military capacity. Capt. Clark verbally challenged captain Innes, and the meeting took place, which produced the confequences already hinted at*. This melancholy difafter took place on the 12th of March 1750: the parties met at feven o'clock in the morning, and captain Innes furvived only till twelve o'clock the fame night.

KERLEY, Anthony.—We find this gentleman, early in the year 1746, commander of the Weazle floop of war, and ftated as the captor of a fmall French privateer fent into Falmouth. This circumftance, infignificant as it is, comprifes all we have been able to collect relative to this gentleman's naval fervice, except that he was, on the 2d of July in the year juft mentioned, promoted to be captain of the Grand Turk, a frigate, which we believe had been a captured privateer. He afterwards commanded the Ranger, which had alfo been a veffel of the fame defcription taken from the enemy. We do not find him mentioned in any fubfequent command, or noticed in any other way, than as having died, at Plymouth, on the 21ft of April, 1764.

KNIGHT, Sir Jofeph,—was, on the 31ft of July, 1746, promoted from the rank of commander of a floop of war, to be captain of the Ruby, a fifty-gun fhip, in which he continued during the remainder of the war, being, in the year enfuing his promotion, ordered to the Eaft Indies with admiral Bofcawen. He continued in India after the return of the admiral, ferving under commodore Lifle; and on the death of that gentleman, at the Cape of Good Hope, fucceeded to the chief command of the fquadron as fenior captain, in which ftation he returned to England. No farther mention occurs concerning him after this time till the end of the year 1758, when we find him commanding the Fougeux, of feventy guns, one of the fquadron fent, under Mr. Keppel, on the expedition againft Goree. In the fpirited attack of the citadel, which, as we have already related in our account of Mr. Keppel, took place on the 28th of December, Mr. Knight bore a very confpicuous

---

* The circumftances attending the duel itfelf will be found given, we hope with more propriety, in our account of captain Clark.

and diftinguifhed fhare, notwithftanding he was confiderably impeded from getting into his ftation by the Furnace bomb-ketch, which fell on board him when in the act of bearing down. We find no other mention made of him during the continuance of the war, except that he afterwards commanded the Belleifle, a fhip of the fame rate as the Fougeux. After the peace was concluded we do not meet with him as holding any commiffion till the year 1770, when he was captain of the Ramillies, of feventy-four guns, a guardfhip at Chatham. In this fhip he afterwards hoifted a broad pendant, and proceeded to Gibraltar with a fquadron carrying troops. He was afterwards promoted to the Ocean, of ninety guns, at Portfmouth, and had, on the 24th of June, 1773, the honour of knighthood conferred on him by his majefty, under the royal ftandard, on board the Barfleur, that being the time when the grand naval review took place at Portfmouth. On the 31ft of March, 1775, he was promoted to be rear-admiral of the white, which was his firft appointment in the rank of a flag officer. He was not invefted with any command, nor indeed did he live a fufficient length of time to receive fuch an appointment, dying on the 8th of September enfuing his promotion, as above ftated, after having been in the fervice fifty-two years.

KNOWLER, Charles,—was, on the 23d of January, 1746, promoted to be captain of the Bridgewater. No other mention is made of him during the war, nor indeed at any fubfequent period, for, notwithftanding it may be fairly concluded he held many fubfequent commands, we find no farther notice taken of him, except that, in 1770, he was put on the fuperannuated lift with the rank and half-pay of a rear-admiral. He died about the year 1789.

KNOWLER, Thomas,—brother to the gentleman laft-mentioned, was third lieutenant of the Namur, under Mr. Mathews, at the time of the encounter with the French and Spanifh fleets off Toulon, and was one of the witneffes ordered to England on the trials which afterwards took place in-confequence of it. On Auguft 11, 1746, he was promoted to be captain of the Lys, a French prize, which, as well as in the preceding inftance of his brother, is the only mention we find made of him during the then exifting ftate of hoftilities. Some time after the conclufion

sion of peace; that is to say, in the beginning of the year 1753, he was appointed to the Salisbury, of fifty guns, one of the ships ordered to be equipped at that time for a guardship at Plymouth. In the summer of the year 1755, not long before the actual commencement of hostilities with France, he was appointed to the Princess Louisa, of sixty guns, in which ship he could have continued only a very short time, it being sent in the ensuing year to the Mediterranean, with Mr. Byng, being then commanded by captain Noel. No other particulars relative to his services or commands have come to our knowledge after the closest investigation; nor, indeed, have we been able to collect any farther information concerning him, except that he was put on the superannuated list, as a rear-admiral, in the month of March 1775, and died about the year 1784.

LEGGE, Julian, — was, on the 6th of May, 1746, promoted to be captain of the Inverness frigate, at that time employed on the Scottish or northern station. He afterwards removed into the Fox, which he commanded in 1747, and which is the only particular mention we find made of him during the war; after the close of which he was, in 1751, promoted to the Bristol, of fifty guns. In this command he did not continue long, being, in 1753, appointed to the Shoreham frigate, and ordered to the West Indies, where he distinguished himself exceedingly by cutting down a number of crosses ornamented with the French king's arms, and copper-plate inscriptions put up by the people of that nation, asserting a claim to all islands which were not absolutely and decidedly possessed by settlers from other European countries.

A number of persons from Bermuda were in the habit of perpetually resorting to the islands in question, principally for the purpose of catching turtle; and, to prevent insult or ill-usage to them as the authors of this very spirited measure, captain Legge left the following written declaration at each place.

" To prevent any violence being used to any of the people who live on Grand Key, Salt Key, or Seal Key, it is thought proper to leave this declaration, that we cut down the arms of his most christian majesty, and the crosses which were set up as marks of possession upon the said islands, and carried away the same, pursuant to instruc-

tions

tions for fo doing: and further, that his Britannic majefty will not fuffer any marks of poffeffion to be put upon any of the keys or iflands, known by the name of Turks Iflands."

He continued in the Weft Indies for fome time afterwards; and, on his return to England, was brought to a court-martial, on a charge, the nature of which, as well as the foundation of it, cannot be better or more fully defcribed than by the following minute of its decifion.

" Portfmouth, July 1, 1756.—This day a court-martial was held on board the St. George, on captain Julian Legge, late of his majefty's fhip Shoreham. The charge againft him was for a very extraordinary expence made by him in purchafing more ftores than were neceffary, and for making an alteration in his fhip by removing the fireplace, contrary to the 20th article of the general printed inftructions; when, after a trial of eight hours, his accounts appeared to the court to be a neceffary charge, and he was acquitted of any fraudulent or unofficer-like act; but the alterations in his fhip being contrary to the general inftructions, the court did think proper to adjudge the fum of fifty pounds to be ftopped from his pay."

This adjudication bringing not the fmalleft impeachment on his character, either as a gentleman or an officer, he was ordered, in the month of September following, with many other diftinguifhed naval characters, as paffengers on board the Ambufcade, to proceed to the Mediterranean, there to take upon them the command of thofe fhips, whofe captains were ordered home to give evidence on the approaching trial of the unfortunate admiral Byng; that allotted to captain Legge we believe to have been the Princefs Louifa. No farther mention, far as we can find, is made of him till the year 1761, when he commanded the Sutherland on the Weft India ftation. He was afterwards promoted to the Temple, of feventy guns, a fhip employed in the fame quarter; and being ordered, with the greater part of the naval force ftationed there, to proceed againft the Havannah, under fir George Pocock, in the year 1762, died on the 29th of June, fome time before the conqueft was effected.

LLOYD, John,—was, on the 4th of September, 1746, appointed commander of the Deal Caftle. He was in the enfuing ensuing year one of the captains ordered to the East Indies under rear-admiral Boscawen; but on this occasion removed into the Eltham*. He is said to have afterwards commanded the Sphinx; but this we have many reasons to believe is an erroneous report. He is said, in 1753, to have commanded the Arundel; but even this we dare not assert as a fact, thinking it not improbable that he may be confounded with his name-sake William Lloyd, of whom hereafter. The same reason operates against us with respect to his having, in 1755, been appointed to the Chesterfield, of forty guns. If we are fortunately correct in these two instances, and which for the present we shall presume on as true, captain Lloyd continued in the Arundel till his removal into the Chesterfield. In this ship he afterwards proceeded to the Mediterranean to join commodore Edgecumbe, and continuing there, afterwards served under the unfortunate Mr. Byng. He was one of the officers ordered to England as an evidence on the subsequent trial. In 1759 he was senior captain, or commanding officer of a small flying squadron stationed in Quiberon Bay, where he displayed great activity and much address in watching and streightening the enemy. But no farther mention is made of him during the war, except that, towards the conclusion of it, he is said to have commanded a third rate, the name of which we have been unable to discover. About the end of the year 1770 he was appointed to the Cornwall, of seventy-four guns, one of the ships ordered to be fitted for sea at Plymouth, in consequence of the rupture which it was then daily apprehended would take place with Spain. How long he continued in this ship is not precisely known, but we do not believe him to have held any command after he quitted it.

On the 31st of March, 1775, he was advanced to the rank of rear-admiral of the blue, as he was, moreover, to the same station in the red squadron, on the 3d of February in the ensuing year; and, on the 29th of January,

---

* The particulars of his service, while employed on this expedition, will be found by referring to the life of Mr. Boscawen. See vol. iv. p. 317 et seq. He in particular commanded the corps of seamen which joined the army at the siege of Pondicherry.

1778,

1778, to be vice-admiral of the blue, but never appears to have accepted any command as a flag-officer. His laſt promotion he did not long ſurvive, dying on the 8th of March enſuing (1778).

MONTAGUE, John. — The firſt information we have of this gentleman is, that in the year 1745 he was commander of the Hinchinbroke ſloop of war; from which he was, on the 15th of January, 1745, promoted to be captain of the Ambuſcade, of forty guns: other accounts, we believe erroneouſly, ſay the Roſe: but if he really ever was appointed to the ſhip laſt-mentioned, he certainly continued in that command a very ſhort time only. In 1747 we find him ſtill captain of the Ambuſcade, and attached to the ſquadron employed in the Channel under vice-admiral Anſon. No other mention is made of him while he continued in that ſhip. He was about this time choſen repreſentative in parliament for the borough of Huntingdon, and in the beginning of the year 1748, was promoted to the Greenwich, of fifty guns; from which he was, almoſt immediately afterwards, advanced to be captain of the Kent. On the 2d of December he married Miſs Sophia Wroughton, by whom he left ſeveral children, two of whom we ſhall hereafter have occaſion to give ſome account of*. He continued in commiſſion during the two enſuing years, having been one of the members of the court-martial held on board the Invincible, in the month of June 1749, for the trial of the mutineers on board the Cheſterfield; and of that convened, in the month of December 1750, for the trial of admiral Griffin.

No particulars have come to our knowledge relative to this gentleman, ſubſequent to the above time, till the year 1755, when, on the apprehenſion of a rupture taking place with France, he was appointed captain of the Elizabeth, of ſeventy guns, one of the ſhips ordered to be got ready for ſea at Portſmouth, but no direct mention is made of the ſervices in which it was afterwards employed during that ſeaſon. In 1757 we find him captain of the Monarch,

---

* Captain James Montague, who was unfortunately killed in the action with the French fleet on the 1ſt of June, 1794, and the preſent vice-admiral, George Montague.

a third rate carrying feventy-four guns*, and employed on the Gibraltar and Mediterranean ftation, under Mr. Ofborne. In this fhip he had the good fortune to affift in the deftruction of the fmall French fquadron which endeavoured to get out of Toulon, in order to effect a junction with M. De la Clue at Carthagena. The Oria flamme, of fifty guns, was driven on fhore under the caftle of Aiglos, off the coaft of Spain, by captains Montague and Rowley, who; to form a whimfical coincidence of names, then commanded the Montague. In addition to the flender particulars juft given we have nothing to add relative to this gentleman, during the war, except that, in the year 1760, he was appointed to the Norfolk, of eighty guns; and, for a fhort time in the fucceeding year, commanded the Princefs Amelia, of the fame force, both of them employed in the Channel†, where, as we have already had frequent occafion to remark, no naval event in any degree interefting took place, after the memorable defeat of Conflans in 1759.

During the fucceeding period of peace we find him, in 1766, commanding the Dragon, of feventy-four guns, one of the guardfhips ftationed at Chatham, in which he continued, according to the general cuftom of the fervice, three years. A rupture with Spain being apprehended in 1770, and a promotion of flag-officers taking place in confequence, Mr. Montague was, on the 18th of October, advanced to be rear-admiral of the blue, and fent out

---

* The unfortunate admiral Byng was fhot on board this fhip, in Portfmouth harbour, on the 14th of March, 1757, captain Montague at that time commanding her.

† At the end of the year 1761 he narrowly efcaped being burnt in this fhip in Bafque road, as appears by the following account.

"Three fire boats, of fifty tons each, were fet a float under the command of the captain of the port's fon, affifted by four men of war's boats; but, through precipitation, miftake, or accident, two of them blew up and every foul perifhed. The explofion was terrible; they continued burning with great fury from one, till daylight. As the wind blew when they took fire they were in the ftream of the Princefs Amelia, captain Montague, an eighty-gun fhip; but providentially the wind fhifted from W to N. W. and drove them clear off the whole fquadron. They were chained together; and if they had been managed with that coolnefs and intrepidity which fuch an enterprize requires, they might have done fatal execution."

commander-in-chief to Halifax. Early in 1771, the appearance of hostilities vanishing, of course nothing material occurred during the time he was absent on that station. On the 31st of March, 1775, he was farther advanced to be rear-admiral of the red; as he was, on the 3d of February, 1776, to be vice-admiral of the blue. In the same month he was appointed governor of Newfoundland, and commander-in-chief on that station: he accordingly sailed at the usual period, having his flag on board the Romney. By a judicious distribution of the cruisers under his command he effected very material injury, not only to their American privateers but also to the commerce of that country*. In 1778, on the first intelligence of the rupture between Great Britain and France, having his flag on board the Europe, of sixty-four guns, he dispatched commodore Evans, with a sufficient force, for the purpose of reducing the islands of St. Pierre and Miquelon, an enterprize which was effected without difficulty or even bloodshed. He returned to England at the conclusion of the year, and never afterwards accepted of any more active command than that of port admiral at Portsmouth, which he was appointed to after the conclusion of the war: he held it during the usually-allotted period of three years, having his flag on board the Queen, of ninety guns.

Almost immediately on his return he was one of the members of the court-martial, held at Portsmouth, for the trial of admiral Keppel; on which occasion he appeared so strenuous an assertor of what he thought the honour of the court, that many violent altercations took place between himself, the prosecutor, and some of the witnesses who would not answer his interrogatories in the manner he wished. On the 8th of April, 1782, a complete change of ministers having taken place, he was advanced to be admiral of the blue, as he was farther, on the 24th of September, 1787, to be admiral of the white. Having never accepted of any appointment as a flag-officer, except that which we have already stated, nothing farther occurs

---

* On the 18th of April, 1777, he was advanced to be vice-admiral of the white; and, on the 29th of January, 1778, to be vice of the red.

for

for our observation, except that he died at his house near Fareham, Hants, towards the end of August 1795, with the universal reputation of a man possessing the strictest integrity, and a most benevolent heart, unhappily alloyed by some intemperance.

PALLISER, Sir Hugh, Bart.—This brave man, and judicious officer, was descended from an ancient and respectable family possessed of a considerable estate at Newby-wisk, in Yorkshire. His father, the younger son of a numerous family, was a captain of foot. He married the daughter of Humphrey Robinson, esq. of Thickethall, in the county of York, and was severely wounded in the battle of Almanza. His two elder brothers were also wounded, and died lieutenant-colonels in the army: but the eldest of them having nearly ruined the Yorkshire estate, sold it and settled in Ireland, where he improved his fortune, lived to the age of one hundred, and entailed six hundred pounds a year on the subject of this article. Another of the family was tutor and friend of the celebrated Locke; died archbishop of Cashel, and made considerable endowments on the college of Dublin. Sir Hugh Pallifer was born at Kirk Deighton, in the county of York, on the 26th of February, 1722. He was sent early to sea under the protection of his relation, a captain in the navy. He was attached to his profession, so that he soon gained the character of a skilful seaman and an able officer, together with the friendship as well as good opinion of his superiors, amongst whom were to be reckoned lord Anson, admiral Boscawen, and sir Charles Saunders. Under their auspices, without the aid of high birth, powerful connexions, or party interest, he gradually rose to eminent stations in both the military and civil branches of the naval service. He also received honourable marks of approbation from his sovereign, though experiencing what officers of the most eminent merit had encountered before him, the jealousy and ill-will of the envious, which attach to the nature of all popular governments like that of Britain. These in the end instigated the attack of a powerful party upon sir Hugh, who declared himself equally zealous for the public service under all administrations, without courting or professing to be of any party.

He was made lieutenant in 1742; in that ſtation he became firſt of the Eſſex, commanded by captain Richard Norris, in the engagement off Toulon, on the 11th of February, 1744. Captain Norris being backward and behaving ill, was ordered to be tried by a court-martial; but the court conſtruing the order to be only for a court of enquiry, the captain was permitted to quit at Mahon, and never appearing again, he was ſtruck off the liſt. The behaviour of the lieutenants of the Eſſex was much approved of, and the houſe of commons voted the court-martial proceedings arbitrary, partial, and illegal. The great trials ſhortly enſued, when ſeveral officers, and amongſt them, admiral Leſtock, paid many compliments to the abilities and judgement of lieutenant Palliſer, notwithſtanding a material part of his evidence tended to operate againſt that admiral.

In July 1746 lieutenant Palliſer was promoted to be commander of the Weazle ſloop; and, on his ſtation off Beachy Head in a very ſhort time he captured four French privateers*, which acquired him, on the 25th of November following, the rank of poſt captain in the Captain, of ſeventy guns, under commodore Legge, juſt appointed commander-in-chief at the Leeward Iſlands, on whoſe death captain Palliſer moved into the Sutherland, of fifty guns, that he might accommodate the ſenior captain (afterwards ſir George Pococke) with the large ſhip. The Sutherland

---

* The capture of two of them is officially related in the following manner, which is ſo extremely honourable to captain Palliſer, whoſe force was not more than equal to one of his opponents, that we have inſerted it at full length.

" Admiralty-office, October 14th.

" Captain Palliſer, in his majeſty's ſloop the Weazle, being on a cruiſe off the Iſle of Wight, on the 8th inſtant, at ten in the morning, ſaw a ſhallop, which he gave cꝏce to, and at one came up with her and took her. She was called the Jeantie, a French privateer belonging to Boulong, mounting ſix carriage and ſix ſwivel guns, and had forty-eight men on board, and was commanded by Antoine Colloit.

" When captain Palliſer had ſhifted the priſoners he gave chace to another veſſel, and at dark came up with and took her. She was called the Fortune, a French privateer, of Honfleur, mounting ten carriage and ten ſwivel guns, and had ninety-five men on board, commanded by John Gilliere. Both the prizes are brought into port."

having

having been difmafted in an hurricane, captain Pallifer loft the opportunity of fharing with the reft of the fleet in the capture of a very large French convoy, which had been difperfed by fir Edward Hawke. An additional misfortune afterwards befel him in the fame fhip when cruifing to the leeward of Martinico: being in want of water he procceded to Prince Rupert's bay, Dominica, at that time inhabited by only a few ftraggling French, and favages. Having ordered a party of marines to land for the protection of the waterers, the armourer, in taking the arms out of the cheft on the quarter-deck, by fome careleffnefs, ftruck fire: this communicated to the cartouch boxes therein, and occafioned all the arms to go off. The captain, who was then fitting on the other arm-cheft on the oppofite fide of the deck, was immediately wounded and difabled from moving, by a ball, which entered on the left fide of his back, and was taken out at his right groin; another ftruck his right hip, and a third his left fhoulder. The armourer and his mate were both killed, but the captain, having youth and health on his fide, with able affiftance, recovered contrary to the expectations of the furgeons themfelves. He remained ever after lame in the left leg, having a perpetual and fometimes very excruciating pain, which at length occafioned his death. Notwithftanding this accident he perfevered in following the fervice, being in commiffion for the Sheernefs frigate, on the peace with France and Spain in 1748, and was fent exprefs to admiral Bofcawen, in the Eaft Indies, with news of that event. In 1750 he was appointed to the Yarmouth guard-fhip at Chatham; and fhortly afterwards moving into the Seahorfe, a twenty-gun fhip, was ordered to the coaft of Scotland, to endeavour the interception of the diffaffected who had projected fchemes with the court of France, for returning fecretly to Scotland in order to raife new difturbances there. His diligence in this fervice gained him the ill-will of a numerous party in that country, who concerted together how to interrupt and diftrefs him. Many plans were unfuccefsfully laid to entrap him; and the captain having orders to enter all fuch volunteers as offered, they forged an indenture for one of that defcription, alledging that he was an apprentice to the mafter of a fhip, and engaged the judge of the vice-admiralty court of Scotland to proceed againſt captain Palliſer for entering him; but the captain refuſing to let the man be taken out of the king's ſhip, the next time captain Palliſer went on ſhore he was arreſted by warrant from the judge of the vice-admiralty court, and impriſoned for ſome days in the Tolbooth priſon at Edinburgh, until the lords of ſeſſions interpoſed their authority, ſuperceded the warrant and releaſed the captain. The maſter of the veſſel who countenanced the forged indenture fled the country.

In the beginning of the year 1753 he was appointed captain of the Briſtol, a ſhip of fifty guns, ordered to be fitted at Plymouth for a guard-ſhip. He did not, however, long continue to hold this command, for government having determined to ſend general Braddock with an army to Virginia, to drive the French from their encroachments on the back ſettlements of that province, commodore Keppel was ordered with two fifty-gun ſhips and ſome frigates to Virginia, and captain Palliſer, with the Seahorſe and Nightingale, was directed to convoy the tranſports, having on board two regiments from Ireland, to Hampton in Virginia. He ſailed in January 1755, but, inſtead of going the uſual tract, he ran to the ſouthward as far as the Tropic, thus avoiding the bad weather at that ſeaſon of the year, and found commodore Keppel, general Braddock, and the ſhips with them, had arrived a very ſhort time before at Hampton very much damaged by the heavy gales they met within the uſual tract. The ſhip's companies were extremely ſickly, and the commodore had provided hoſpitals for the troops under captain Palliſer's convoy, expecting they would arrive in the ſame condition. On the contrary, they all appeared in very good health, and proceeded immediately up the river Potomack to Alexandria, where no king's ſhips, or any ſhips ſo large as the tranſports, had ever been ſeen before. Here was held the firſt congreſs, conſiſting of the commanding general, commodore, and all his majeſty's governors of the colonies; and here the provincial troops of Virginia, under captain (ſince preſident Waſhington) joined the king's troops. After general Braddock's death and defeat, commodore Keppel returned a paſſenger to England, in the Seahorſe, with captain Palliſer.

Hoſtilities

Hostilities having commenced with France in September 1755, captain Pallifer was commissioned to the Eagle, of sixty guns. On the 30th May, 1757, being on a cruize off Ushant, in company with the Medway, of sixty guns, they in the night fell in with and gave chace to a French East India ship, named the Duc D'Aquitain, mounting fifty guns, all French eighteen pounders, on two decks, and four hundred and ninety-five men. She had landed her cargo at Lisbon, and was on her way to Port L'Orient. At day-light she appeared with her lower tier run out. The Medway shortened sail to clear ship; this gave the Eagle, she being clear for action, the opportunity to pass her and begin the attack at two ship's lengths, so that almost every shot took place. After a short but very sharp action she struck as the Medway came up, having fifty-one men killed, and the number of wounded not ascertained, with ninety-seven shot-holes through both sides. Her main and mizen-masts fell just as she struck. The Eagle had ten men killed and thirty-two wounded, with twenty-one shot through her sides. The commander of the Medway was very unjustly reflected on, for it is certain that nothing but his ship not being clear prevented his beginning the action, for he afterwards gave repeated proofs of his bravery in several actions during that war.

In July 1758, captain Pallifer being then commander of the Shrewsbury, of seventy-four guns, to which ship he had been appointed in the early part of the year, lord Anson detached him with a squadron to cruize as near the entrance of Brest as he could with safety, in order to watch the French fleet in the road. Whilst on that service he fell in with a fleet of coasters, under convoy of two frigates, which he drove on shore at the entrance of the bay D'Hodiernes, and captured some of the trading vessels.

In the year 1759 he was, with admiral Saunders, on the successful expedition against Quebec; on which occasion he commanded the body of seamen which landed and took possession of the Lower Town. In 1760 he served under the same admiral in the Mediterranean, who detached him with an equal force after a small French squadron which had slipped out of Toulon, and were gone up the Levant to parade and persuade the Turks that the French

French fleets were not blocked up by the English. Captain Palliser chaced them into the Turkish ports, under protection of the grand signor's batteries, in the harbours of Zudia, in Candia, and Napol di Malvazca, in Morea. Nothing but respect to the neutrality of the grand signor's ports prevented their destruction; and the English ambassador at the port made a proper use of the event, to the disgrace of the French and the high honour of the British name at Constantinople.

In 1762 he was dispatched with three ships of the line and a frigate to retake St. John's in Newfoundland; but on his arrival he found that lord Colville and colonel Amherst had anticipated that service: and, after the peace in 1764, he was sent out thither again as governor and commodore for the protection of that Fishery, against the encroachments of the French, having under him a fifty-gun ship, the Guernsey, which bore his broad pendant, and several frigates. He then met with a French commodore with a similar force pretending to regulate their own fisheries and settle disputes with ours, but, in reality, encreasing them; wherefore commodore Palliser warned the French commodore to quit the coast, informing him that the sovereignty of the island belonged to Great Britain, and that he would not suffer any foreign authority to interfere with his government. On account of this and other spirited exertions, the French ambassador, in London, presented many memorials against governor Palliser; but the latter was well supported by the ministry. Amongst other things the French pretended that Cape Ray was Point Rich, thereby introducing a claim to the fishery all along the west coast of Newfoundland. In support thereof they alledged that the English chart misnamed those places, and that the names therein had been transposed for the purpose of curtailing their bounds. Their ambassador produced a French chart sent to him, in which those places were named agreeable to the claim they contended for. But this commodore Palliser soon confuted, by showing, that all the English charts were extant before Point Rich was made a boundary point. He happened to have in his possession a French chart, being an impression from the same plate as that which the French ambassador produced. Point Rich and Cape Ray were there placed the same as

in

in the English charts. He clearly fixed the fraud of altering the plate and transposing those names with the French government, for the purpose of supporting the encroachments. Of this transaction the French ambassador himself seemed to be ashamed.

In 1770 commodore Pallifer was appointed comptroller of the navy, and elected an elder brother of the Trinity House. In 1773 he was created a baronet; in 1774 chosen representative in parliament for Scarborough; in 1775 promoted to be a flag-officer; and, as at that time it was a rule that a comptroller of the navy should not hold his feat at the board with his flag, he was appointed one of the lords of the admiralty, as successor to the earl of Bristol. In the same year his great friend, sir Charles Saunders, died, leaving him a legacy of 5000l. and sir Hugh Pallifer succeeded him as lieutenant-general of marines. On the 29th of January, 1778, he was advanced to the rank of vice-admiral of the blue.

Towards the end of 1777, and in the beginning of 1778, the warlike preparations made by the French manifested their intentions to support the revolted English colonies against the mother country. The American war at this time was very unpopular, and all possible means were made use of, according to a well-known phrase, both within and without doors, to retard the operations of government. There were notwithstanding many well-intentioned persons of rank in the opposition, who, though they disapproved the American war, could not silently behold the armaments of a natural enemy going forward; they therefore gave early intimation of the danger: of this number was admiral Keppel, who at that time resided on the Continent, and was in the habit of corresponding with sir Hugh Pallifer. When the opposing fleet of England was preparing, the latter laboured much, and at length succeeded in bringing about the appointment of the former to the chief command, being himself selected to serve under him in the third station: with this admiral Keppel expressed himself well pleased, and informed sir Hugh, by letter, that he was one of the very few he could depend on. The indecisive action which took place with the enemy on the 27th of July following, is not only too well known to be now described,

scribed, but has been already sufficiently enlarged on in our account of the commander-in-chief. The subsequent disagreement between those officers seemed converted into mischievous consequences, as we have already very forcibly remarked, by the rancour of party and the wickedness of interested persons. Doubtless both the admirals were unitedly zealous in doing their duty to the utmost against the infidious designs of France, the ambitious and hereditary enemy of their country; but as the event of the 27th of July, was unsatisfactory to the nation in general, the opposition took advantage of the discontents to inflame the country against the ministry, first by suggesting that admiral Keppel had orders not to act with vigour against the enemy; and, when the falsity of that assertion was exposed, by attributing, as a second charge, the ill success of the fleet to the difference between admiral Keppel and sir Hugh Pallifer, in political principles on the American war, they coloured the aspersion by referring to the situation of the latter as an active lord of the admiralty; they of course represented him as the supporter of the existing administration, and by implication subservient to certain pretended views of debasing their friend the commander-in-chief. Thus the whole weight of popular opposition was employed to transfer the cause of disappointment to the junior officer: this was done while both parties were again absent at sea, and apparently on the same confidential and friendly footing as before.

The fleet returned to Spithead on the 26th of October, and sir Hugh Pallifer finding that many envious insinuations and gross falsehoods had made strong impressions to his prejudice, he traced and discovered them, as he supposed, industriously circulated from dangerous quarters, on which he demanded, but could not obtain what he demanded, a fair discussion. Sir Hugh then took such decisive steps as brought on him the disagreeable but absolute necessity of calling for courts-martial on admiral Keppel and himself, that each might have an opportunity of vindicating his own conduct, and the nation be satisfied where the blame lay. The trials accordingly commenced: that of Mr. Keppel ended in the manner well-remembered and already stated: and, in conclusion, sir Hugh Pallifer was acquitted, and the sentence declared,

that

that his behaviour, on the 27th and 28th of July, was *highly meritorious and exemplary,* than which nothing could be more honourable *.

During

---

* As we have already given the material fubflance of the defence made by Mr. Keppel, we fhall, in equity and juftice to fir Hugh, fubjoin the following extract, from a fpeech delivered by him in the houfe of commons, on the 4th of December, 1780, in which he publicly affigns the reafons which actuated his conduct, both immediately after the action, while the two fleets were in fight of each other, as well as the meafures taken by him on fhore, previous to the commencement of the court-martial.

" The event of my trial confirmed me in the expectation with which I had before confoled myfelf. My judges proved fuperior to the influence of party and the dread of unmerited unpopularity, difcharged their office with a determined impartiality, and the refult was a fentence, which I fhall ever think moft honourable to me. In the introductory part of it my judges declared, that my conduct and behaviour were, in many refpects, highly exemplary and meritorious. Though too the court had fcrutinized into every part of my conduct with an almoft unexampled ftrictnefs, the only omiffion which could be fuggefled was, that I did not inform the commander-in-chief of the difabled ftate of the Formidable: but fo far was the court from imputing this to a blameable caufe, or from attributing the leaft ill confequence to it, that they ftated it in dubious and reluctant terms, fimply pointing it out as a matter of opinion; and having fo done, they concluded with an abfolute acquittal. Indeed, had I conceived that there was a probability of imputing fuch an omiffion to me, I fhould have been more full in my explanatios on this head. I did take notice that the fignal of diftrefs, in the fighting inftructions, was not applicable, and that the condition of the Formidable was fo apparent, as to make any information from me unneceffary. I alfo notcied that I had no frigate by which I could fend information; the Milford, which was the only frigate in my divifion, having been taken from me, by Mr. Keppel, early in the afternoon. But I might have advanced feveral fleps further to obviate the idea of omiffion. Till the Fox reached me between feven and eight at night, Mr. Keppel's own conduct did not leave me the leaft room to fuppofe him ignorant of the Formidable's inability to reach the length of my ftation in the line, for he not only did not make any enforcing fignal to fignify his expectation of feeing my divifion in the line, till thirteen minutes after fix, when the fignal for coming into his wake was hoifted a fecond time; but alfo, on putting out the pendants of feveral fhips of my divifion at half an hour after fix, he did not think fit to to make my pendant one of the number; whence I concluded that he knew my condition, and therefore did not expect me. In refpect to afterwards fending information by the Fox, if I had thought it neceffary I had not the opportunity, the Fox having feparated from me before I could finifh what I had begun to fay to her captain. What other means I could have devifed to fend an explanation to Mr.

Keppel,

During these commotions, sir Hugh Palliser having resigned the lieutenant-generalship of marines, and his seat

Keppel, time enough to answer any purpose, I am still to learn: but all this is not of importance to me; the terms in which the omission is stated, with the acquittal which follows, sufficiently protect my character, being repugnant to the most remote idea of criminal imputation.

"Since my trial I have patiently waited for the subsiding of the public prejudices, and, so far as regards my exculpation from the charges for my conduct on the day of engagement, I have reason to believe, that the proceedings on my own trial have opened the eyes of many, who, before they knew what was my defence, had been seduced into an injurious opinion of me; and, I trust, that the more thoroughly the grounds on which my judges acted are examined and understood, the more convincing the proofs of my innocence will appear.

"But still some unfavourable impressions continue to operate against me on account of my accusation of Mr. Keppel, and for this I have been blamed even by some persons of great respect, who were far from being indisposed to form an impartial judgment if they were furnished with the necessary materials.

"In this part of the case my ill fortune exposes me to the most embarrassing disadvantages. On the one hand there is a sentence acquitting admiral Keppel and declaring my charges malicious and ill founded: but, on the other hand, the manner in which I was urged and driven to become an accuser, and the grounds on which I could have sustained my charges, are not only ill understood, but, in truth, have never yet been explained by myself. The proper time for discussing this matter was when Mr. Keppel was on his trial, but then the opportunity was denied me. The trial being closed, and a judgment of acquittal irrevocably pronounced, it might seem invidious and unbecoming on my part to publish to the world what I should have offered in support of my charges: such a measure I have therefore declined hitherto, nor will I be ever induced to adopt it by any thing less than its being authoritatively called for, or the most apparent impossibility of otherwise resisting the attempts to compleat my ruin: but then the difficulty is how to avoid such an extremity without surrendering myself a quiet victim to the persecuting spirit of my enemies. The leaders of them have continually been loading my name with reproaches; and though some of them on many accounts have a title to much respect, yet even those so far forget all manliness of character, as to assail me with the most embittered eloquence in this house, when it was known that I could not be present to defend myself: now too that I am present they know the advantage they derive from my being unendowed with qualifications for a popular assembly, and thence they are encouraged to recommence their attacks, though surely they cannot imagine that I shall sit still without at least endeavouring to give a check to any aspersion aimed at me personally; under these circumstances, should I continue acquiescing in these public attacks of my character without any attempt to
repel

seat in parliament, to accommodate a timid ministry who stood in awe of a powerful opposition, his majesty, on his honour-

repel them; more especially at this time when I am threatened with new efforts to keep me out of the service of my country, I should establish the credit of the misrepresentations by which I deem myself so highly injured; some explanation on my part is, therefore, immediately requisite, to disappoint my enemies of the final accomplishment of their designs.

" It is not, however, my intention to revive the consideration of the past transactions relative to admiral Keppel and myself, further than he and his friends shall compel me by their hostilities. I am well convinced not only that very ill consequences have already arisen to the public service from the contest between that gentleman and me, but that new mischiefs will be generated if the subject is resumed; under this impression I think it incumbent on me to make great sacrifices of my own private feelings, rather than administer the least pretence for any further discussion of the grievances of which the honourable admiral and I respectively complain : therefore on the present occasion I shall avoid speaking to many points in which my character is interested, and I shall keep within much narrower limits than I should prescribe to myself, if I aimed at the full defence of my conduct towards the honourable admiral who is opposed to me.

" The friends of the honourable admiral, in their invectives against me, seem to place their chief reliance on the sentence pronounced by his court-martial, I mean that part of the sentence which declares my charges malicious and ill founded. This is the bitter spring from which my enemies draw poison to impregnate their licentious declamations.

" If the admiral's friends were content with appealing to this sentence as a testimony of his innocence, I, on my part, for the sake of public tranquillity, would forbear all complaint and objections : but when the admiral or his friends, aiming at a further persecution of me, apply that sentence to fix upon me the stigma of being a false and malicious accuser, I cannot acquiesce : the injury is too gross to be patiently submitted to; as such I feel and will resist it.

" It has been urged against me that I was too late in my accusation, and that, if I had thought the honourable admiral guilty of misconduct, I ought to have avowed my sentiments, immediately and without waiting till he accused me. I answer thus: from the beginning the conduct of the admiral was not adequate to my expectations; I thought that the engagement of the 27th July was injudiciously conducted; that the manner of carrying us into action was disorderly; that there was too much neglect of manœuvres, too much contempt of the enemy, too much confidence at first, and too much awe of the enemy, too much distance from them, too much diffidence of ourselves afterwards. But my friendship and esteem for the admiral, his previous services to his country, his high name in the world, these moved me to a favourable construction, and thus influenced, I imputed the miscarriage.

honourable acquittal, was graciously pleased soon afterwards to appoint him governor of Greenwich-hospital, on the

carriage of the day to error of judgment, to ill health, to ill advice, to ill fortune, to every thing devoid of that evident and positive criminality which might force me to undertake the painful office of accusing one whom I then deemed my friend. As there was not room for praise I did not bestow it; and as I then conceived that the admiral's failures might not be wilful, I both avoided public accusation and most rigidly abstained from se 'ret detraction : but new lights and new occurrences presented to my mind a very different view of the admiral's conduct. When the discontents encreased through the nation in consequence of the reflection that a superior fleet of England had for a time declined continuing to engage an inferior one of France, and permitted it to return into port, in the middle of summer, unpursued, the officers, relations, friends, and dependants of the honourable admiral, thought fit to account for this new phænomenon at the expence of my reputation, and, for that purpose, some of them published to the world, that my defaults had prevented a second engagement. Being thus injuriously attacked, I both personally and by letter solicited the honourable admiral to give a check to such aspersions; but he refused to do this justice to my character: and on conversing with him and his first captain, I found that they not only countenanced the slanders against me, but added to their number by refusing to acknowledge, either that on coming out of the action I instantly wore to return to the enemy, or that they had even once seen me on the proper tack for that purpose. This explanation from the honourable admiral and his first captain excited both astonishment and suspicion; I was amazed at their denial of such uncontrovertible facts, and at the admirals adopting a language so inconsistent with the high commendation of me in his public letter; and I then saw that there was a plot concerted to destroy my character without a trial, and so to make me chargeable for the admiral's failures. My feelings on the occasion were the stronger because I was conscious that the chief part of the battle had fallen to the share of me and my division; that I had set an example of forwardness to pursue our blow, by instantly returning upon the enemy, and continuing to stand towards them again; that though the last out of the engagement, I was advancing to be the first in the renewal of it; and that I should have had that honour if the admiral had not declined renewing the action and taken his fleet in a direction from the enemy. Under these circumstances it was natural that I should scrutinize the admiral's conduct more rigidly, and no longer see it with the partial eyes of a friend; and on such a view of the unhappy miscarriage, I at length imputed to real neglect what I before had ascribed to causes which might be pardoned, more especially in consideration of former services, and such as at first did not seem to me to preclude the hopes of better management in case of again meeting the enemy. Indeed, if in Mr. Keppel's place there had been a man indifferent to me, one of whom I had not before formed

the death of fir Charles Hardy. He was again chofen reprefentative in parliament for the borough of Huntingdon; but at the enfuing general election, his old connexions and friends having coalefced with the oppofition, his and their own enemies, he declined appearing any longer in fo public a character, and retreated to the comforts of retirement with the moft valuable bleffings that heaven can beftow in this life, contentment, peace, and purity of mind.

He died admiral of the white, governor of Scarborough-caftle, one of the elder brethren of the Trinity-houfe, and governor of Greenwich-hofpital, at his country feat, the Vache, in Buckinghamfhire, on the 19th of March, 1796, aged feventy-four, in confequence of a diforder induced by the wounds received on board the Sutherland, in 1747, as mentioned in the former part of this narrative. The title defcends to his great nephew, Hugh Pallifer Walters, efq. and he left confiderable fums for charitable purpofes, with many legacies; but the bulk of his fortune, real and perfonal, he willed to his natural fon, George Pallifer, efq. A fuitable monument is erected to his memory in the parifh church of Chalfont St. Giles's, in the county of Bucks, where his remains are interred*.

---

formed a very high opinion, it is probable that my mind would have fhaped a different courfe : probably my firft judgement of the matter might have been the fame harfh one as is conveyed by the charges againft the admiral. But what apology can he make for the latenefs of his accufation; he who had the charge of the fleet and the command-in-chief; he in whom the nation repofed its confidence, not only for the difcharge of his own duty, but to fee that thofe under him completely performed what they owed to the ftate? What apology can he make for firft praifing me by a public letter, and in equal degree with fir Robert Harland, and afterwards accufing me for the fame affair? Shall he be at liberty to retract his applaufe and to fubftitute accufation for it? Shall he be allowed to fay that his heart dictated cenfure whilft his pen wrote praife? And fhall mere filence reftrain me from accufation, or be imputed to me as infincerity and inconfiftency?

" As to the ftate of the proofs on the two trials I purpofely avoid all comparifon, becaufe that would be entering into the merits of them, which I think would at this time be improper."

* The funeral, in obedience to his ow requifition, was very private: the chief mourners were, admiral Bazely, captain Hartwell, George Hartwell, efq. and another gentleman.

An

An anonymous writer, who certainly was no relative or interested person, from his having much mistated the manner in which he received his fatal hurt, gives the following character of him.

" As a professional man, he was found superior to most of his cotemporaries in maritime skill, judicious in his dispositions and decisive in their consequent operations; in private life, conciliating in his manners and unshaken in his friendships; the wise and salutary laws which he caused to be enacted for the benefit of his country, and the comfort and happiness of the poor fishermen in Newfoundland, during his government of that island, are proofs of a sound mind, of a humane and benevolent disposition."

To this character we have briefly to add from ourselves, that however his friends may wish he had in some few points acted differently from what he did, his most violent enemies cannot but confess their own malignity, in having endeavoured to attach, as crimes to him, things which never existed even in his thought, and in having reprobated those very errors which their own conduct fatally gave birth to.

It is no difficult matter to draw a conclusion from facts after they have taken place; and we believe no moderate man will, at the present day, deny, that if the popular voice had been less clamorous, neither party would have proceeded to the lengths they did; the service would not have been rent into contending factions and parties, and the public cause of the country would have been materially benefited. No one can dispute on the one hand that the vice-admiral possessed a warm temper, and in too great a degree for a cautious or designing man; so on the other can no one disbelieve him to have possessed honour, judgement, and intrepidity.

For more than the last fifteen or sixteen years of his life he seldom or ever lay down on a bed from the constant pain in his leg, which he bore with the most manly fortitude. He was under the necessity of composing himself in an easy chair, sleeping at intervals; and when awake he placed the wounded limb on the contrary knee, in which position he employed himself in rubbing the bone (for it was literally no more) to assuage the pain till sleep again insensibly overtook him.

PIGOT,

PIGOT, Hugh,—was the brother of fir George, created baron Pigot, of Patſhull, in the county of Dublin, and, in 1775, appointed, for the ſecond time, governor of Madraſs, where he was treacherouſly ſeized by an infamous junto of people, who had been appointed to act under him in a ſubordinate ſtation, and by whom he was, not long afterwards, moſt vilely murdered. Mr. Pigot we find to have been lieutenant of the Romney, a fourth rate, of fifty guns, in 1743; and advanced, in 1745, to be commander of a fireſhip. He was afterwards, on the 22d of April, 1746, promoted to be captain of the Centaur. But after this time no mention is made of him till the year 1755, when he was captain of the York, of ſixty guns, one of the ſhips put into commiſſion in conſequence of the then juſtly-apprehended rupture with France. He continued in the ſame ſhip ſeveral years, and, in 1758, was employed, under the orders of Mr. Boſcawen, on the ſucceſsful expedition againſt Louiſburg. Early in 1760 he was promoted to the Royal William, of eighty-four guns, a ſhip employed, during the remainder of the war, in the Channel: but the moſt material notice we find taken of him is, his having, in the month of May 1760, chaced into the Groyne the Diadem, a French third rate, carrying ſeventy-four guns, which was bound to Martinico with ſtores, and ſpecie for the payment of the ſoldiery.

After the concluſion of the war nothing conſequential is ſaid of him till the year 1769, when he was appointed colonel of the ſecond or Portſmouth diviſion of marines; a ſhort time before which he had been choſen repreſentative in parliament for the borough of Penryn. In 1771 he was appointed to the Triumph, of ſeventy-four guns, one of the ſhips ordered to be equipped in conſequence of the diſpute with the court of Spain, relative to the Falkland iſlands. Matters being, however, amicably accommodated, thoſe which were not retained as guard-ſhips were put out of commiſſion and diſmantled ſoon afterwards. Mr. Pigot, after quitting the Triumph, held no ſubſequent commiſſion as a private captain. On the 31ſt of March, 1775, he was advanced to the rank of rear-admiral of the white; as he was moreover, on the 3d of February in the year enſuing, to be vice-admiral of the blue: on the 29th of January, 1778, to the fame rank in the white fquadron; and, on the 19th of March, 1779, to be vice of the red. In the new parliament, chofen at the end of the year 1780, he was returned member for Bridgenorth. During all this time he never accepted of any command, nor did he afterwards, till the æra of that extraordinary civil revolution which took place in the year 1782, and effected the downfall of the then reigning miniftry. On this occafion he was, on the 30th of March, appointed one of the commiffioners for executing the office of lord high admiral; on the 8th of April he was advanced to be admiral of the blue, and immediately afterwards invefted with the chief command in the Weft Indies, as fucceffor to the late lord Rodney.

He hoifted his flag on board the Jupiter, of fifty guns, that fhip being ordered to carry him out to his command. He failed from Plymouth towards the end of May, a day or two only previous to the arrival of the frigate bringing the important intelligence, that the count de Graffe had been totally defeated on the 12th of April preceding. This victory reflected fo fudden and dazzling a brilliancy on fir George Rodney, who, before, was neither in favour with the new miniftry, nor by any means popular as a commander, that to continue him on the fame ftation was thought a compliment due to him as an officer, under whofe aufpices fo brilliant a tranfaction had taken place. An exprefs of recal was accordingly difpatched after Mr. Pigot, but too late; he had failed too long to be overtaken, and the appointment was fuffered to proceed, modified, as it is faid, by a conciliating apology to fir George, who, at the fame time, was advanced to the dignity of a peer of Great Britain. Mr. Pigot proceeding to Jamaica, took upon him the command; and, having hoifted his flag on board the Formidable, of ninety-eight guns, proceeded, as was cuftomary at that time, to America, during the hurricane months.

The fhattered fleet of France, even though it had been poffible for it to have formed a junction with the naval force in that quarter belonging to Spain, which was of confiderable ftrength, not chufing, after the late chaftifement, to hazard a fecond conteft, the feafon paffed over, and, indeed, the
fhort

short remainder of the war also, without any remarkable occurrence taking place, or any enterprize being executed by the very powerful armament under his orders. When the treaty of peace was concluded, as may be remembered to have been the case early in the year 1783, Mr. Pigot, of course, returned to England, and never took upon him any farther command. He continued in the commission for executing the office of lord high admiral no longer than the 30th of December, 1783, and then quitted it on a well-known political convulsion, equally violent and extensive with that which first introduced him to it. He retired soon afterwards totally from public life, not having even been returned to the new parliament, as representative either for Bridgenorth, where he had considerable influence, or any other place. He was, however, on the 24th of September, 1787, advanced, as his right, according to the rules of the service, to be admiral of the white squadron, and died at Bristol, having attained the justly earned reputation of an able commander, as well as of an honest and gallant man, on the 15th of December, 1792.

PORTER, Jervis Henry,—entered into the navy about the year 1732; and, soon after the commencement of the war with Spain, was promoted to be commander of the Speedwell sloop of war: from thence he was, on April 3, 1746, advanced to be captain of the Flamborough, a twenty-gun ship. In 1748 he was appointed from this vessel to the Pensance, a fifth rate of forty-four guns; in which ship he proceeded to Louisburg with a squadron, commanded by rear-admiral Watson, and returned with him to England at the close of the year*. In the year 1755, he was made captain of the Prince Frederic of seventy guns. He was afterwards removed into the Hercules, of seventy-four guns, in which ship he had the fortune to fall in with a French ship of war, carrying seventy-four guns, called the Florissant†. The same which
had

---

* In the month of July ensuing, he was employed in convoying the homeward bound Baltic trade from the Sound.

† Of this encounter captain Porter gave the following account, which we have been induced to insert at length in justice to him, and that it may be seen, though unfortunate and unsuccessful, he behaved
with

had some time before been engaged in the West Indies, by captain Tyrrel, in the Buckingham. The wounds he

---

with a degree of gallantry and spirit highly meriting victory and conquest.

"On the 10th instant, at eight in the morning, being in the latitude of about 46 degrees 40 minutes, steering S. E. with the wind at S. W. we saw a sail to windward, which we chased and soon after discovered her top gallant studding-sails set, and that she came down lasking upon us. About noon the chace hoisted a blue flag at her main-top-gallant-mast head, which we answered by an English ensign at the mizen-top-mast head (a signal which is sometimes made between two French ships of war upon meeting, after parting company). She neared us very fast, and we plainly discovered her to be a large ship of war. At two in the afternoon, a Dutch galliot passing near us, we hoisted a French jack at our ensign staff, and fired a gun to leeward. At half past five, being about one mile to windward of us, and abaft our beam, coming down as before, seemingly with an intention of coming to action, as her guns were run out below, she hauled her jack down and hoisted her ensign and pendant. We shortened sail, hauled down the French jack, hoisted our colours, hauled our ports up (which were until this time down) and run our weather guns out; upon which she immediately hauled her wind and set her main-sail and stay-sails. We then discovered her to be a seventy-four-gun ship, having fourteen ports below. We made sail and stretched ahead of her and tacked, passing her to leeward. At six tacked again and stood after her: found she kept away large. We bore after her keeping her a little upon the lee-bow to prevent her choice of engaging at a distance. About three quarters after nine, being pretty near up with her, though not near enough to engage, she put her helm hard a starboard and gave us her larboard broadside, and then keeping on as before gave us her starboard broadside. We then immediately starboarded our helm ran right down upon her whilst she was loading her guns, and getting close to her ported our helm and began to engage, as the guns bore upon her. At half past ten we were so unlucky as to have our main-top-mast shot away, which she took the advantage of, and made all the sail she could from us; we did the same after her, and continued to chace until eight the next morning, when we saw the north end of Oleron about five leagues distance. The chase was about four or five miles from us: finding it impossible to come up with her in so short a run, and fearing to engage ourselves with a lee-shore, having our fore-yard shot through in two places, our fore-top-sail-yard so badly wounded that when we came afterwards to reef the sail it broke, and all our sails and rigging very much shattered (at which the enemy only aimed) we left off chace and wore ship, having one man killed and two wounded, including myself, being wounded in the head by a grape shot, and having lost the use of my right leg. The officers and men behaved with the greatest spirits and alertness without the least confusion."

received

received in the encounter, as ſtated beneath, compelled him to reſign his command on coming into port*, but he reſumed it again on his recovery, and afterwards ſerved, under the command of vice-admiral ſir C. Saunders, in the Mediterranean. We have no farther account of him, except that he died on the 31ſt of March, 1763.

PROBY, Charles†. — This gentleman, who is ſtill living, is the fourth ſon of John Proby, eſq. ſometime repreſentative for the county of Huntingdon; and afterwards, in two ſucceſſive parliaments, for the borough of Stamford. His mother, who died June the 10th, 1726, was Jane Leviſon, daughter to John, firſt lord Gower. Having betaken himſelf to a naval life, and ſerved with the greateſt credit to himſelf in the different ſubordinate ſtations, he was, on the 17th of September, 1746, promoted to be captain of the Lyme. In the month of Auguſt 1756, immediately after the recommencement of hoſtilities with France, he was appointed to the Syren frigate, and before the end of the ſame year was promoted to the Medway, of ſixty guns. Soon after this appointment a complaint was preferred againſt him, by ſome of the people under his command, of having exerciſed undue ſeverity towards them; a charge which, after proper

---

* In 1758 he commanded the Magnanime, a third rate, of seventy-four guns, in the Channel fleet, under the orders of lord Anſon, commodore Howe having removed from that ſhip into the Eſſex, for the purpoſe of commanding the various deſultory expeditions which then took place againſt the coaſt of France. His lordſhip reſumed his command on his return.

† The family of Proby came originally from Wales, and were there named Ap Probyn; but they have flouriſhed for many ages in the county of Huntingdon. Randolph Proby, of the city of Cheſter, ſettled at Brampton in that county at the latter end of the fifteenth century: and by his wife, the daughter of —— Bernard, had two ſons, Ralph Proby, of Brampton, eſq. who was living about the year 1580, and died in 1605 without iſſue; and ſir Peter Proby, knight, who ſucceeded his brother, at Brampton; and at Elton in the ſame county. He ſerved the high office of lord mayor of the city of London in 1622: in 1618 he was ſtyled of Rans, in the county of Bucks; and died in 1624, leaving, by Elizabeth, daughter of John Thoroughgood, of Chivers, in Eſſex, eſq. and relict of Edward Henſon, of London, gent. five ſons and one daughter. Charles, the third ſon of ſir Peter, was the great-grandfather of captain Proby and of the lord Caryſfort.

investigation, was found utterly void of foundation. In 1757 he was one of the commanders employed, under sir Edward Hawke, on the succefsless expedition against Rochfort *.

In 1760 he was appointed to the Thunderer, of seventy-four guns, and, not long afterwards, ordered out to the Mediterranean and Gibraltar. In the month of June, 1761, he was sent, by sir Charles Saunders, the admiral-in-chief on that station, to cruise off Cadiz with a small force of which he was senior or commanding officer, consisting of the Thunderer, his own ship; the Modeste, of 64 guns, the Thetis frigate, and Favourite sloop. The object of this little expedition was the interception of two French ships of war, the Achilles, of sixty-four guns, and the Buffon frigate, of thirty-two.

On reconnoitering the harbour of Cadiz, on the 14th of July, captain Proby found the enemy had so far escaped his vigilance as to have got out to sea. He immediately pursued, and with such success that on the 16th he discovered them. He came up singly with the Achilles about one in the morning on the 17th, and captured her after a very severe though short action of half an hour's continuance. The enemy made a most gallant defence, so that the Thunderer received very considerable damage in her masts and rigging, besides having seventeen men killed in the action, and one hundred and thirteen wounded, several of them so desperately that nearly twenty died. Captain Proby himself (though fortunately in a slight degree only, in the right arm) together with his second and third lieutenants, were among the wounded. He continued in the Mediterranean and in the same command during nearly the whole of the war. In 1766 he commanded the Yarmouth, of sixty-four guns, one of the guardships stationed at Chatham. Soon after quitting which, he was, in 1769, appointed commodore and commander-in-chief in the Mediterranean, as successor to commodore Spry. During a considerable part of the

---

* "In their passage captain Proby spoke with a Dutchman from Nantz to Dort, who told him that the French expected to be attacked at Rochelle, or St. Martin's, by the English; and that an embargo was laid on all the shipping in France."—Entick.

time he was abfent on this fervice he had his broad pendant on board the Pembroke, of fixty guns; and, in 1770, received a reinforcement of feveral fhips, in confequence of a fudden equipment which was faid to have taken place, on the part of France, at Toulon, which confequently raifed no inconfiderable grounds of jealoufy: but this cloud paffing away without creating any tempeft, Mr. Proby returned not long afterwards to England.

Soon after his arrival, that is to fay, in the month of June 1771, he was appointed comptroller of the victualling accounts, an office which he refigned before the conclufion of the year, on being made commiffioner of the navy refident at Chatham*. This office he has ever fince continued to fill with the higheft reputation for diligence, activity and integrity †.

REYNOLDS, John,—was, on the 30th of October, 1746, promoted to be captain of the Arundel. We believe him to have been immediately afterwards ordered to Georgia, where he continued many years. He is faid in fome accounts, particularly by Beatfon, to have been appointed governor of that colony as early as the year 1745, but we do not find any actual commiffion for that purpofe to have been figned till the year 1753 or 4, in one of which it is moft probable his actual inveftment with that office took place. Previous to the latter time, we conceive he was only commander of the fmall naval force kept on that ftation for its protection, a circumftance which, very poffibly, caufed the miftake. He retained the government till the year 1758, when he returned to England; but we do not find him mentioned during the remainder of the war except as having commanded the Firme, of fixty guns, on the Mediterranean ftation. No mention is made of him after this time till the year 1769 or 70, when he was appointed captain of the Burford, of feventy guns, one of the guardfhips ftationed at Plymouth. Early in 1771 he removed into the Defence,

---

* In the enfuing year he had the misfortune to lofe a fon, who unfortunately fell into the hold of the Victory then lying in ordinary at that port.

† He married Sarah, daughter of —— Pownall, efq. by whom he has had iffue two fons, Charles and Baptift Levifon.

of feventy-four guns, a fhip put into commiffion at the fame port in confequence of the apprehended rupture with Spain.

This appears to have been his laft command in the capacity of a private captain. On the 31ft of March, 1775, he was promoted to be rear-admiral of the blue, as he was, on the 3d of February, 1776, to be rear-admiral of the white; early in the month of January 1778, to be rear of the red; and, on the 29th of the fame month, to be vice-admiral of the blue. On the 26th of September, 1780, he was farther advanced to be vice-admiral of the white, a rank from which he experienced no farther promotion till the 24th of September, 1787, when he was made admiral of the blue. This advancement he did not long furvive, dying at the very beginning of the year enfuing.

SAYER, James,—was, on the 22d of March, 1745-6, promoted to be captain of the Richmond frigate, which is not only the earlieft information we have been able to collect concerning him, but alfo comprifes the whole of our intelligence relative to his fervices during the current war. We have no account of the ftations or fhips in which he was employed fubfequent to the above time, till the year 1758, when he commanded the Naffau, of feventy guns, one of the fquadron fent on the expedition againft Goree, under the orders of Mr. Keppel. The leading particulars of this attack and enterprize, even thofe in which Mr. Sayer bore a confpicuous fhare, have been already related at fome length in our account of the commander-in-chief*, and to which it is confequently, in the prefent inftance, needlefs to add.

He continued in the Naffau during the remainder of the war; but is not otherwife mentioned than as having, in 1762, been attached to the fquadron ftationed in the Channel, under the orders of fir Edward Hawke and his royal highnefs the duke of York. We have no account of his having, after he quitted this fhip at the conclufion of the war, held any fubfequent commiffion or appointment, during the time he continued a private captain. On the 18th of October, 1770, he was advanced

---

* See page 316 et feq.

to be rear-admiral of the blue, but does not appear to have been invested with any command. On the 31st of March, 1775, he was promoted to be rear-admiral of the red; and, on the 3d of February, 1776, to be vice of the blue: on the 28th of April, 1777, he was made vice-admiral of the white, which was the highest rank he lived to obtain, dying, in England, on the 15th of October following.

SHULDHAM, or SHOULDHAM, (as it is spelt by Archdale) Molineux, Lord, — is the second son of the reverend Samuel Shuldham, of the diocese of Ossory *, in the kingdom of Ireland. He went to sea at the very early age of ten years; and after passing through the different subordinate stations was, on the 12th of May, 1746, promoted to be captain of the Sheerness, a frigate at that time employed in cruising off the coast of Scotland. No farther mention is made of him in the service till towards the end of the year 1754, when he was appointed to the Seaford, of twenty guns. He was not long afterwards made captain of the Warwick, of sixty guns, and ordered to the West Indies, where, on the 11th of March, 1756, sometime before the actual declaration of war, he had the misfortune to fall in with three French ships of war, the Prudent, of seventy-four guns; the Atalante, of thirty-four; and the Zephyr, of thirty. According to the French accounts, their ships were mistaken for merchantmen, and captain Shuldham would not open his lower ports till a broadside from one of the frigates convinced him of his mistake. He then made all the sail he could set in the hope of making his escape, but in vain; the enemy's ships sailing and working much better than the Warwick, the latter was soon surrounded, and, after as good a defence as it was capable of making, compelled to surrender †.

Captain

---

* His lordship is descended from a family of Shuldham, in Germany; and his father, the reverend Samuel Shuldham, was beneficed in the diocese of Ossory. He married Elizabeth, daughter of Daniel Molyneux, of Ballymulvy, in the county of Longford, esq. (by his wife Catharine, daughter of Thomas Pooley, of Dublin, esq.) and sister to Pooley Molyneux, of Ballymulvey, who died, unmarried, in 1772; and bequeathed his estates, of about 1600 l. a year, to the eldest son of his sister, by Mr. Shuldham.

† We shall subjoin an account given of this transaction, in a letter from the West Indies, written soon after the time, and since that published

Captain Shuldham's conduct on this occasion was, immediately after his exchange, inveſtigated before a court-martial, by which he was moſt honourably acquitted, and, in conſequence, was appointed to the Panther, a ſhip of ſixty guns, launched a ſhort time before. In the month of November following he was ordered to the Weſt Indies under the orders of commodore Hughes, who was ſent thither with the ſquadron deſtined to join Mr. Moore, and proceed on the attack of the French iſlands. He particularly diſtinguiſhed himſelf at the attack of Baſſeterre, the capital of the iſland of Gaudaloupe, which ſurrendered after a very ſpirited defence, from which the aſſailants received very conſiderable damage.

In 1761 captain Shuldham was appointed to the Raiſonable, of ſixty-four guns, a ſhip taken from the enemy not long before. He was ordered at the cloſe of the year to the Weſt Indies, with admiral Rodney, who was ſent thither with a very formidable armament, to attack the iſland of Martinico. This ſhip was one of thoſe appointed, under ſir James Douglaſs, to ſilence ſome batteries on the coaſt; in endeavouring to perform which ſervice, when leading in, ſhe ran on a ſmall reef of rocks of which the pilot was ignorant. The ſhip was totally loſt, but all the people together with the ſtores, were ſaved. Captain Shuldham in a few days afterwards commanded the right diviſion of the boats which landed the army under general Monckton, but is not afterwards mentioned during the continuance of the war; and indeed after his laſt accident does not appear to have held any commiſſion. We have for ſome years no farther particulars to relate concerning this gentleman, except that, in March 1766, a ridiculous and ill-founded report of his death was circu-

---

liſhed verbatim, by ſome hiſtorians, as the moſt authentic that is to be met with.

"The Warwick, of ſixty guns, who had been cruiſing off the coaſt of Martinico, and had taken ſeveral French prizes, fell in with the Prudent man of war, of ſeventy-four guns, who had in company with her a ſixty gun ſhip, and a frigate of thirty-ſix guns. The Warwick perceiving herſelf thus over-matched endeavoured to get clear by making a running fight, and actually had got clear of the large ſhips, but the frigate, being ordered to chace, came up under her ſtern and raked her terribly, by which means ſhe was kept in play till the Prudent again came up, and the Warwick ſtruck."

lated,

lated, and with so much peremptoriness, as to gain no inconsiderable degree of credit.

The next mention we find made of him in the service is, that about the year 1768, he was appointed to the Cornwall, a third rate of seventy-four guns, lying at Plymouth; and afterwards, in the beginning of the year 1771, was commissioned to the Royal Oak of the same force, one of the ships ordered to be equipped, at Plymouth, in consequence of the apprehended rupture with Spain. In 1772 he was appointed governor of Newfoundland, and on his return at the close of that year to England, brought with him an Esquimaux chief, who was presented to his majesty. He continued in the same command during the three succeeding years without meeting with any remarkable occurrence. On the 31st of March, 1775, he was advanced to be rear admiral of the white, and, at the general election which took place in the ensuing autumn, was returned member for Fowey, in Cornwall. On the 3d of February, 1776, he was advanced to be vice-admiral of the blue; a short time before which he was appointed to command on the American station, and proceeded thither having his flag on board the Chatham, of fifty guns.

General Howe having evacuated Boston with his army early in the year 1776, proceeded to Halifax under the protection of Mr. Shuldham's small squadron, from whence he was, together with the troops and storeships, convoyed, in the month of June, to Staten Island by the vice-admiral, who, on the 31st of July, was, by writ of privy seal, bearing date the 24th of June preceding, raised to the dignity of a baron of the kingdom of Ireland. Numerous as was the fleet under his lordship's protection, consisting of an immense number of transports, victuallers, and storeships, it was convoyed in the greatest safety to its place of destination, having suffered not the smallest diminution or loss either by capture or accident. The troops were immediately afterwards landed on Staten Island without interruption, and every preparation made under his lordship's auspices for commencing offensive operations immediately on the arrival of lord Howe and the reinforcements which were daily expected from England.

Nothing

Nothing material, far as his lordship was particularly concerned, took place during the time of his continuance in America. He returned from thence early in the year 1777, and did not take upon him any active employment till after the commencement of hostilities with France in the ensuing year: he was then appointed to command the additional convoy sent with the outward-bound West Indian and American fleets, as is sometimes necessary in time of war in order to protect them to a safe latitude. This service he executed with success. After his return he received a commission, appointing him port admiral at Plymouth, a station he continued to hold, except at some intervals of absence; during which his place was supplied by vice-admiral Milbank, till after the conclusion of the war in 1783. Since that time he has not accepted any command, fo that we have nothing farther to give in addition to this relation, except the account of his several promotions: of these, we believe the following to be the dates: vice-admiral of the white, on the 19th of March, 1779; vice of the red, September the 26th, 1780; admiral of the blue, September the 24th, 1787; and admiral of the white, February the 1st, 1793.

SMITH, Abel.—The first information we have of this gentleman is, that he was promoted to be captain of the Surprize frigate on the 22d of January, 1745-6. In the month of July, in the ensuing year, he was, according to some accounts, appointed captain of the Crown, a ship then newly launched at Deptford: but we dare not assert this for a positive fact, being somewhat doubtful whether it was captain Abel, or captain Elliot Smith, of whom some account has been already given[*]. He is also said to have accepted, after the conclusion of the war in 1748, the command of the Hunter sloop; and, in the ensuing year, to have been promoted to the Centaur. The same cause, however, which raised our doubt as to his appointment to the Crown, is equally forcible with regard to his subsequent commands, and prevents our giving it as a certain fact, that he was the individual person who was, in 1753, appointed to the Royal Oak. This is the last account, even on presump-

---

[*] See page 228.

tion, that we have relative to this gentleman except that he died in England on the 12th of May, 1756.

STEPHENS, Nathaniel.—This gentleman is scarcely, to reckon with propriety, entitled to a place here. He was, on the 1st of February, 1746, promoted to be captain of the Lively frigate, and died in the East Indies holding the same station (but never having had his commission confirmed by the admiralty board) on the 23d of March, 1747.

VAUGHAN, John,—was, on the 11th of August, 1746, appointed captain of the Solebay frigate. He is one of those officers who have lived to reach, with the greatest credit to themselves, the highest rank in the service, without ever being fortunate enough to experience a single opportunity of acquiring that celebrity every gallant man is ambitious to obtain. So little mention is made of him while he continued on the list of private captains, that we have not been able to collect any account whatever even of his appointments, except that he at one time, not precisely to be ascertained, commanded the Subtile, a frigate of twenty-six guns, taken from the enemy by the Portland, at the end of the year 1746; and at another period the Juno, of thirty-two guns. Undistinguished as these are, so high was the opinion entertained of him, and from private information we have received it appears most justly so, that he was promoted, according to his seniority [*] on the list, through the several ranks and degrees of a flag-officer till he at length reached that of admiral of the blue. The following appear to be the dates of his different promotions: rear-admiral of the white, March the 31st, 1775; rear of the red, February 3, 1776; on the 29th of January, 1778, vice of the blue; on the 19th of March, 1779, vice of the white; and of the red, on the 26th of September, 1780: on the 24th of September, 1787, he was raised to be admiral of the blue; but never in any of these stations accepted of any command. He died at his seat at Trecon, near Haverfordwest, on the 7th of November, 1789.

---

[*] In 1771, on the prospect of a rupture with Spain, he was appointed regulating-officer for the port of Milford and the district of South Wales.

WEBB,

WEBB, James,—was, in 1745, commander of the Jamaica sloop, a vessel at that time employed as a cruiser in the Channel. At the close of the year we find him mentioned as having, in company with the Amazon, captured a stout French privateer, belonging to Granville, carrying sixteen carriage and swivel guns, with a crew of one hundred and five men. He afterwards made prize, in the month of April, of a second of the same force, called the Postillion, of Dieppe; as he also did a third, of inferior strength, on the 28th of May, at the back of the Isle of Wight, together with a prize taken by her immediately before. These repeated instances of his activity were rewarded by his promotion, on the 25th of June, 1746, to be captain of the Surprize frigate, in which he was equally assiduous and successful. In the month of November, being at anchor off Newhaven, he discovered two French privateers in chace of some merchant vessels. He immediately slipped, and giving chace came up with, and captured one of them after three hours pursuit; the other effected her escape. In the beginning of the ensuing month he was equally fortunate, having rescued an English West Indiaman, and captured the privateer * which was in pursuit of her.

At the commencement of the year 1747-8, he was ordered out on a cruise with the Rainbow, which was put under his command. On the 22d of January, being at the entrance of the bay of Biscay, he discovered two ships standing different courses. He immediately made a signal for the Rainbow to chace one, while he himself pursued the other, which he captured in the dusk of the evening, after firing a few shot at her. It proved a very consequential prize, being a packet, called the Palme, belonging to the French king, bound from Brest to the West Indies, and mounting twelve carriage guns. The Rainbow was equally successful, having taken the ship she was sent in pursuit of, a very large privateer belonging to Granville, called the Count de Noailles, carrying twenty-two carriage guns, and manned with a chosen crew of one hundred and fifty men.

---

* The Laurette, of Dieppe, carrying twelve carriage and swivel guns.

Still

Still in the current of fuccefs, captain Webb in three days afterwards re-captured a very valuable fnow from Antigua, bound to London, taken a few days before by the Dauphin Royal privateer of St. Maloes. From perfons on board this veffel the firft intelligence was received in England of the fuccefs which had attended the Britifh fquadron, in the capture of the greater part of the convoy which had efcaped from fir Edward Hawke, in the preceding autumn, when L'Etendiere's fquadron was fo completely difcomfited by him. We have no fubfequent account relative to him till after the recommencement of the war with France in 1756, when he was appointed to the Sunderland, of fixty guns. After quitting the fhip laft-mentioned he was made captain of the Antelope, in which he died on the 14th of May, 1761.

WELLARD, Robert,—was, on the 31ft of May, 1746, promoted to be captain of the Roebuck, from which fhip he was, not long afterwards, removed into the Haftings frigate. He was ordered early in the year 1747-8 to cruife in the North Seas, and off the coaft of Holland, principally for the purpofe of protecting the Britifh commerce in that quarter from the depredations of privateers. In this fervice he had no indifferent fuccefs, having, on the 26th of March, captured a veffel of that defcription, belonging to Calais, carrying twenty carriage and fwivel guns; and on the 23d of the enfuing month a fecond, belonging to Boulogne, called the Duke de Rambouillet, of fomewhat inferior force. We find no farther mention made of him in the fervice, from which we believe him to have retired many years previous to his death. He is faid by fome to have afterwards accepted the command of one of the Dover packets, and to have retained this ftation till his death, which happened, at Dover, on April 15, 1776.

WRAY, Charles,—was, on the 9th of December, 1746, promoted to be captain of the Rye frigate. He was not long after, ordered to America, on which ftation we find him mentioned, in the month of May, 1748, as the captor of two privateers, one Spanifh, the other French, which he carried into Charleftown. The next notice we find taken of him is in the year 1756, when he was one of the captains ordered to the Mediterranean, in the month of September, as paffengers on board the Ambufcade,

bufcade, for the purpofe of fupplying the place of thofe officers, who were ordered to England as evidences on the approaching trial of the unfortunate admiral Byng. We believe him, on this occafion, to have been appointed to the Captain, of feventy-four guns.

Soon after his return from thence he appears to have been appointed to the Augufta yacht. As we know him to have commanded that veffel in 1761; and do not find any intervening mention made of him in any more active ftation, we fuppofe him to have continued in that we have juft pointed out till the time of his death, which happened in the year 1773.

INDEX

TO THE

FIFTH VOLUME.

	Page		Page
ADAMS, Roger	360	Bully, William	367
Allen, Robert	3	Burnaby, Sir William	131
Allen, Edward	64	Bury, Thomas	134
Allifon, Thomas	422	Byron, Hon. John	423
Amherſt, John	275		
Andrews, Thomas	360	CALLIS, Smith	136
Aylmer, Henry, Lord	64	Calmady, Warwick	244
		Campbell, William	77
BALCHEN, George	4	Carteret, Phillip	139
Bamff, Alex. Ogilvie	66	Catford, Charles	245
Bargrave, Charles	67	Chadwick, Richard	284
Barker, John	361	Cheap, David	77
Barradall, or Borrowdell, Blumfield	279	Cockburne, George	83
		Cokburne, John	439
Bateman, Hon. William	362	Coleby, Charles	84
Beaver, Edmund	279	Collins, Richard	285
Bentley, Sir John	280	Colville, Alexander, Lord	286
Bermingham, Hon. John	362	Corniſh, Sir Samuel	139
Bertie, Lord Thomas	283	Cornwall, Frederic	288
Bertie, Lord Montague	4	Coſby, Henry	368
Bladwell, William	363	Cotes, Thomas	12
Bloſs, Thomas	422	Craven, Thomas	439
Bolton, Harry Powlet, Duke	5	Crookſhanks, John	149
Bonfoy, Hugh	364	DANDRIDGE, William	85
Bowdler, John	284	Daniel, Lionel	369
Boys, or Boyce, William	233	Dawney, Hon. George	160
Brett, John	67	De L'Angle, Merrick	161
Brett, Sir Piercey	239	Denis, Sir Peter	369
Broderick, Thomas	69	Dennis, Henry	86
Buckle, Matthew	365	Dent, Cotton	440

Vol. V.   K k   Dilke,

INDEX.

	Page
Dilke, William	87
Dodd, Edward	245
Douglafs, Sir James	290
Douglafs, John	441
Draper, John	88
Dudley, Obrien	442
Duff, Robert	444
Durell, Philip	167
Durell, George	375
Dyve, Henry	375
EDGCUMBE, Geo. Earl of Mount Edgcumbe	293
Edwards, Richard	16
Elliot, Elliot	298
Elliot, George	298
Ellis, William	88
Elton, Jacob	88
Erſkine, Robert	170
FALKINGHAM, Edw.	448
Faulknor, Samuel	448
Fawler, John	375
Fenwick, Benjamin	90
Fergufon, John	451
Fermor, Hon. William	375
Ferrers, Waſhington Shirley, Earl of	452
Fielding, William	246
Fincher, Thomas	376
Forbes, Hugh	377
Forreſt, Arthur	380
Forreſter, Right Hon. Geo. Lord	16
Fowke, Thorpe	173
Frankland, Sir Thomas	18
Frogmore, Rowland	21
GAGE, John	247
Gardiner, Arthur	383
Gayton, Clark	387
Geary, Sir Francis	175
Gideon, Solomon	21
Goddard, Samuel	247
Godſalve, Henry	90

	Page
Gordon, William	299
Graham, Right Hon. Lord George	22
Graves, Samuel	301
Gregory, Thomas	91
Grenville, Thomas	190
Griffin, Thomas	392
HADDOCK, Richard	304
Hamar, Joſeph	92
Hamilton, Hon. John	92
Hanway, Thomas	305
Hardy, Sir Charles	99
Hardy, John	307
Harland, Sir Robert	454
Harmon, William	457
Harriſon, Henry	24
Harriſon, Thomas	308
Herbert, Henry	104
Hewet, Sir William	32
Hill, John	392
Hodſell, James	192
Holburne, Francis	33
Holcombe, Eſſex	42
Holmes, Charles	193
Hore, Daniel	105
Horne, Edmond	392
Howe, Richard, Earl	457
Hughes, Sir Richard	43
Hughes, Robert	393
Huiſh, Henry	473
Hume, John	394
Hyde, Frederic	473
Jaſper, Richard	394
Jeffreys, Robert	396
Jelfe, Andrews	473
Innes, Thomas	474
Jolly, Thomas	44
KEPPEL, Lord Viſcount	308
Kerley, Anthony	475
Knight, Sir Joſeph	475
Knowler, Charles	476
Knowler, Thomas	476

4 LAKE,

INDEX.

Name	Page
LAKE, Thomas	107
Laton, Sheldrake	107
Legge, Julian	477
Leſlie, Lachlan	346
Limeburner, Thomas	44
Liſle, William	45
Lloyd, John	396
Lloyd, John	478
Lofting, Samuel	347
Long, Charles	107
Lovet, John	109
MAISTERSON, Samuel	397
Man, Robert	397
Marſh, William	247
Martin, Roger	47
Maynard, Robert	47
Mitchell, Matthew	48
Mogg, Thomas	348
Molloy, Sir Charles	203
Montague, Hon. William	400
Montague, John	480
Moore, Sir John	250
Murray, Hon. George	51
NOEL, Thomas	403
Norbury, Conningſby	349
Norris, Harry	53
Northeſk, Geo. Carnegie, Earl of	109
Nucella, Timothy	404
Nutt, Juſtinian	404
OBRIEN, Lucius	405
O'Hara, Patrick	349
Orme, Richard	411
Oſborne, Peter	54
Oſborne, James	350
PALLISER, Sir Hugh	483
Parry, Francis	204
Parry, William	350
Peers, James	111
Pett, Robert	54

Name	Page
Peyton, Edward	55
Phillipſon, John	353
Philpot, Thomas	112
Pigot, Hugh	497
Pitman, John	253
Porter, Jervis Henry	499
Powlet, Charles	254
Pratten, Edward	254
Pritchard, John	204
Proby, Charles	501
Purvis, Charles Wager	60
Pye, Sir Thomas	112
RENTONE, James	62
Reynolds, John	503
Rich, Edward	411
Robinſon, Robert	353
Rodney, Lord	204
Rogers, Sir Frederic	115
Roſewell, Henry	412
Rous, John	412
SAUNDERS, Sir Charles	116
Saumarez, Philip	256
Sayer, James	504
Scott, Arthur	258
Shuldham, Lord	505
Simcoe, John	259
Smith, Elliot	228
Smith, Abel	508
Somers, Thomas	353
Spragge, Edward	354
Spry, Sir Richard	414
Stanhope, Sir Thomas	417
Stephens, Nathaniel	509
Stepney, George	260
Stevens, Charles	229
Stewart, Henry	260
Stringer, John	419
Stuart, Hon. Archibald	419
Sturton, Thomas	261
Swanton, Thomas	127
Swanton, Robert	354
Swayſland, Henry	127

TAYLOR,

INDEX.

	Page		Page
TAYLOR, Polycarpus	261	Watkins, Richard -	270
Thompſon, Bradſhaw -	63	Watkins, John -	271
Thomſon, Ormond -	358	Watſon, Nathaniel -	129
Tiddeman, Richard -	420	Webb, James -	510
Toll, Edmund - -	358	Wellard, Robert -	511
Toms, Peter - - -	263	Weller, John - -	421
Tucker, Thomas -	127	Wickham, John -	233
Tyrrel, Richard - -	264	Williams, Thomas -	360
		Wilſon, John - -	360
VAUGHAN, John -	509	Wray, Charles -	511
Vanburgh, Giles Richard	359		
Utting, Aſhby -	128	YOUNG, Benjamin -	64
		Young, James -	272
WARD, Henry -	128	Young, Robert - -	130
Waring, Rupert - -	129		

END OF THE FIFTH VOLUME.

Lightning Source UK Ltd.
Milton Keynes UK
07 December 2010

164000UK00001BA/1/P